# Young Thomas Hardy

# Thomas Hardy's
# Later Years

## ROBERT GITTINGS

Book-of-the-Month Club   New York

# Young Thomas Hardy

Thomas Hardy aged 34 or 35.

# Contents

# Illustrations

*Frontispiece*

Thomas Hardy, aged 34 or 35
*from a photograph in the Dorset County Museum*

*Following Page 84*

1. (*a*) The Heath, near Hardy's birthplace, with a distant view of Dorchester. (*b*) The old West Gallery, Stinsford Church (*both from sketches by Hardy in the Dorset County Museum*)
2. (*a*) Hardy's maternal uncles, William, Henery, and Christopher Hand (*from a photograph in the possession of Gertrude S. Antell*). (*b*) Thomas Hardy senior (*from a sketch in the Dorset County Museum*). (*c*) Hardy's aunt's husband, John Brereton Sharpe (*from a silhouette in the possession of Lloyd Brereton Sharpe of Ottawa, Ontario*)
3. Young Thomas Hardy, (*a*) aged 16, (*b*) aged 19, (*c*) aged 21 (*from photographs in the Dorset County Museum*)
4. (*a*) 16 Westbourne Park Villas, Hardy's home in London, 1863–1867 (*from an original sketch in the Graphic, 5 September 1925*). (*b*) Young Thomas Hardy in London, 1863 (*from a photograph in the Lock Collection*)
5. The Moule family, Fordington, Dorchester (*from a photograph in the Dorset County Museum*)
6. Hardy's mother and his cousins, the Sparks girls, (*a*) Hardy's mother, (*b*) Tryphena, (*c*) Rebecca, (*d*) Martha (*from photographs in (a) the Dorset County Museum, (b–d) the Lock Collection*)
7. Three capitals in Turnworth Church, designed by Thomas Hardy, 1869 (*from photographs by Clare Gittings*)
8. Two views of Weymouth as Hardy knew it, (*a*) The Promenade, (*b*) Sandsfoot Castle (*from prints in the Weymouth Local History Museum*)

*Following Page 164*

9. (*a*) Emma as Hardy first knew her (*from a miniature in the Dorset County Museum*). (*b*) Emma in middle age (*from 'The Young Woman' (1894) in the possession of James Gibson*)
10. The Cornish coast near Boscastle (*from a print in the possession of the author*)
11. Emma and Hardy during their courtship, August 1870 (*from sketches by Hardy and Emma Gifford in the Dorset County Museum*)
12. Thomas Hardy's annotations to his favourite passage, I Kings, xix, 11 and 12, in his Bible, 1859–1870 (*from the original in the Dorset County Museum*)
13. Thomas Hardy in 1875, sketched by Emma in her "honeymoon" diary (*from the original in the Dorset County Museum, enlarged*)
14. (*a*) Death-bed sketch of Hardy's uncle by marriage, John Antell, by his son, John Antell junior. (*b*) Sketch by Hardy for John Antell's tombstone (*both from originals in the possession of Gertrude S. Antell*)
15. Hardy's relatives (foreground) in the High Street, Puddletown (*from a postcard in the possession of Gertrude S. Antell*)
16. Thomas Hardy in his old age (*from the original sketch by Augustus John in the possession of James Gibson*)

Acknowledgement is made to the Trustees of the Thomas Hardy Memorial Collection in the Dorset County Museum for permission to reproduce the following illustrations from the Collection: *Frontispiece*, 1a, 1b, 3a, b, and c, 5, 6a, 9a, 11, 12, 13.

# Acknowledgements

THOMAS HARDY'S secretive attitude towards biographers, set out
in the first chapter of this book, means that any authoritative study
must rely exceptionally on the gathering of materials from widely
differing sources. The help I have received in this task leaves me
greatly in debt to a vast number of people and institutions. All mentioned here have my deepest thanks. Any omitted by mistake have my
profound regrets.

Space prevents more than a brief listing in most instances, but
gratitude must make some exceptions. Chief among my personal helpers
and encouragers, I must single out the Hardy scholar, James Gibson.
This present book would have no real authority without his active and
invariably accurate assistance. With invaluable generosity, Mr. Gibson
placed at my complete disposal his unpublished Ms. variorum edition
of all Hardy's poems. The time, labour, and trouble this has saved me
are incalculable. He was the first to read and fruitfully criticize the
draft of this book, to which he has provided two most significant illustrations from his private collection. In numberless conversations and
discussions, he has given me the unique advantage of expert familiarity
and friendly, informed criticism.

As will be seen from the notes, this study depends for much of its
authenticity on the personal memories and knowledge of those related
to Hardy, and still living in Dorset. Chief among these is my friend
John Hardy Antell. His vivid family traditions, to which he always
applies his own sound critical commonsense, have given a body and
reality to Hardy's story that could not have come from any other
source. Once more, his generosity has extended to long and friendly discussions, from which I have learnt much that would otherwise have
remained obscure.

The three key institutions, whose staffs have helped me profoundly,
are likewise local to Dorchester: the Dorset County Museum, the County
of Dorset County Library, and the Dorset County Council County
Record Office. To the skilful Curator of the first-named, R. N. R.
Peers, M.A., F.S.A., F.M.A., I owe, like so many Hardy scholars, a
gratitude that goes well beyond formal acknowledgement. His care,
patience, and consideration for the exacting needs of scholarship have
been exceptional, as have been those of his staff. Formal acknowledgement to the Trustees of the Thomas Hardy Memorial Collection in the

Dorset County Museum will be found elsewhere, but I am additionally grateful to Mr. Peers for providing such an efficient link with the Trustees. Secondly, K. Carter, A.L.A., County Librarian, and his friendly staff at the Dorset County Library have provided an invaluable service in meeting my many demands with continual, thoughtful, and expert help; I am most grateful. Finally, the County Archivist, Miss M. E. Holmes, M.A., and her knowledgeable staff have given me help far beyond the mere production of documents. This has extended to suggestions for sources, and corrections of my ignorance, which have notably enlarged the body of firsthand documentation on which a work such as this must vitally depend.

The list of other helpful institutions is a large one. It includes, in the first instance, my local West Sussex County Reference Library, its reference librarian, H. R. H. Harmer, A.L.A., who, with his staff, has smoothed many of the paths of research so willingly and efficiently. Other bodies who have given much assistance are the Berkshire Record Office; the City and County of Bristol County Libraries; the Bristol City Art Gallery; the Bristol Record Office; the British and Foreign School Society; the British Museum; the Curator of Rare Books and Manuscripts, Colby College, Waterville, Maine; the Librarian and Deputy Librarian, King's College, London; the Greater London Record Office; the St. Marylebone Borough Library; the City of Plymouth Public Libraries; the Public Record Office; the Principal and staff of the College of Sarum St. Michael, Salisbury; the Diocesan Record Office, Salisbury; the Master and Fellows, Trinity College, Cambridge; and the Weymouth Local History Museum. I should like to thank personally Mrs. Christina M. Gee, Curator, Keats House, Hampstead, for examining census returns and ratebooks, and Mrs. Anna Winchcombe of Hardy's Cottage for help with the Sparks papers.

As I suggested, this book benefits greatly from the willingness of people in the most varied circumstances of life and experience to help me with knowledge or memory of matters otherwise unknown to me. Among these, I should like specially to thank Miss Gertrude S. Antell of Puddletown, for her reminiscences of the Antell family, her fascinating family records, and her kindness in providing me with family illustrations, which I have fully acknowledged elsewhere; Miss Mary A. Blyth of the Moule family; Mrs. June R. Boose of Windsor, Ontario, for much information about the Sharpe family; Henry Gifford for family records; Sister Kathleen Hawkins, of La Retraite, Clifton, for putting me on the track of Hawkins family information; H. E. F. Lock for permission to use photographs from the Lock Collection, on loan in the Dorset County Reference Library; Miss K. M. E. Murray for permission to use two unpublished letters from Hardy to Sir James Murray; Kenneth Phelps for the interesting points raised in his letters; Michael Rawcliffe, senior

lecturer in History, Stockwell College of Education, who has provided
me with valuable entries and material from the College archives;
the Misses Shepherd of Leigh-on-Sea, Essex, for their most delightful
and instructive conversation about Dorset, and their kindness in allowing me to use some unpublished letters of their grandmother, Catherine
Young Hawkins of Waddon; Miss Mary Stickland, also for her Dorset
reminiscences and dialect readings, and particularly for her valuable
memories of Hardy himself; J. C. Trewin for an authoritative note on
the nineteenth-century playing of Rosalind; Mrs. Troyte-Bullock,
present owner of Waddon; Dr. D. H. Twining, B.M., B.Sc., for medical
information; and the Warneford Hospital Secretary and Mrs. Brenda
Parry-Jones, Archivist, for making Hospital records available to me.
I should also like to thank my friend David Driscoll for identifying an
obscure reference in one of Hardy's early novels; Mrs. W. A. Dubben of
Sydling for lively conversation and local anecdote; the Vicars of
Hemington in Somerset, and Puddletown in Dorset, for allowing access
to their parish records; and Mr. Butterworth of Puddletown School for
access to the school logbooks.

The list of recognized writers and scholars on Hardy who have helped
me is a long one. It must include Professor J. O. Bailey; Professor
C. J. P. Beatty, with whom I have discussed details in his admirable
thesis and in his edition of Hardy's architectural notebook; Evelyn
Hardy, who first drew my attention to some errors and omissions in
certain areas of Hardy biography; Desmond Hawkins, for ideas of
great interest; Professor Michael Millgate; F. B. Pinion, for his splen-
didly meticulous comment on some biographical points; Professor
R. L. Purdy, to whom I am very greatly indebted for kind permission
to use his notes of conversations with Florence Hardy. There have also
been many informal discussions with these and other workers in the
Hardy field, from whom I have learnt much. It will be noticed that this
book is dedicated to my friends and students at the University of
Washington, Seattle. Among them, I wish to give special thanks to
Sister Victoria Seidel, as friend, student, and Hardy scholar. Her work
on Hardy's Literary Notebooks, in particular, filled many gaps in my
own research, and she will recognize in the present book many happy
parallels with our informal and always useful consultations.

My thanks must end with a few other personal ones: greatly, to my
wife, Jo Manton, for her clear and professional editing of my rough
typescript, and her knowledge of the Victorian scene; to our daughter,
Clare Gittings, for advice on Dorset memorial brasses, and for taking the
photographs of Hardy's work in Turnworth Church; and to my American publisher, Peter Davison, who first said I should write a book about
Hardy. I should add that the author acknowledges assistance from the
Arts Council of Great Britain.

To my friends
and students
at the University of Washington,
Seattle

# 1

# Young and Old

THOMAS HARDY determined to set up a barrier against biography. Angered by biographical speculations in books published in his own lifetime, and always abnormally sensitive about any reference to his private life, he devised a scheme by which he hoped to silence future writers. This was to produce an apparently authoritative biography, to be published shortly after his own death, which could discourage any later writers. This book was to seem to be the work of his second wife; the fact that she herself was an author of stories for children gave plausibility to Hardy's plot. For what he planned was a most deliberate deception. He wrote his own life, or what he cared to tell of it, in the third person, to be passed off as a biography written by her. No author can have taken more care that the future should know only what he wanted it to know, in the two volumes of his *Life* published in 1928 and 1930.

Unfortunately for the success of this scheme, he did not always guard his tongue. An old man when he started it, in the natural lapses of old age, he occasionally said too much in conversation, and this in spite of a lifetime of extreme secrecy and reticence. In 1925 a nephew of Mark Twain, Cyril Clemens, visited him. In a sudden expansive moment, he said to Clemens:

> I intend to write my autobiography through my good wife. Each day I slant my memoirs as though my wife were writing them herself. After she has copied the day's stint on the typewriter, we hold a discussion, and she makes invaluable suggestions which are almost always immediately incorporated in the text. Then my original manuscript is given to the flames. Thus is insured absolute accuracy. My idea, of course, is to have the work appear after my death as a biography of myself written by my wife.

Nothing could have been more explicit. Clemens perhaps did realize that Hardy had not meant to give the secret away. He did not publish his account of this interview[1] until 1943, when Mrs. Florence Hardy herself had been dead for five years; he also may have coloured it by plagiarizing from recent sources, such as Sir James Barrie's reminiscences.[2] In his wife's lifetime, the scheme worked just as Hardy had hoped. When anyone questioned Mrs. Hardy how she came to know certain facts in the Life, she replied with perfect truth, but with considerable disingenuousness, that she had had them from her late husband's own lips.

Of course, when the true story of this process began to emerge, some twenty years ago, the result was the opposite of Hardy's intention. Although the publishers keep up to this day the fiction of Florence Hardy's authorship, and though many recent critics still praise the work as a unique insight into the writer, the feeling that the Life is, in some sense, a fake has made biographical speculation, often of the most lurid kind, run riot. A host of amateur investigators has appeared, eager to invent a new story, and quite simple statements have been given fantastic meanings.[3] Moreover, the mere fact that Hardy chose this way of presenting himself has caused, even among reputable biographers, a certain suspicion of his motives. Yet the origins of his scheme, so far as they can be traced, seem to have been relatively innocent. At some time in 1917, Mrs. Florence Hardy began to type what she called some "Notes of Thomas Hardy's Life . . . (taken down in conversations etc.) ". These fragmentary typescript notes[4] break off during the first half of the 1860s, and it is clear this method of setting down information about Hardy's early life proved both haphazard and unsatisfactory. This can be seen by the large number of obvious typing errors,[5] which invade the notes; one of these, in fact, helps to date, for the first time, when this mirror image of ghosted autobiography must have begun. The notes are usually headed by an approximate date for the events described, and by page 14 the typescript has reached the middle of April 1862, when Hardy first went to London. The next note is, however, headed "Last week in April 1917".[6] Mrs. Hardy, in a moment of domestic distraction, had obviously substituted the year when she was typing for the correct year in Hardy's early life. This whole process was then abandoned, a few pages later, for a much more systematic one by which Hardy actually wrote his own life in the third person, to be copy-typed by Mrs. Hardy as if it were her own composition. Later Hardy himself made alterations and additions in a form of disguised hand.

The system therefore may have started simply as a more efficient way of dealing with Hardy's reminiscences than dictating scattered notes. What has caused suspicion is the way Hardy developed this process. First, not only did he destroy his manuscript as fast as Mrs. Hardy completed the typescript of each passage;[7] he and she also destroyed the greater part of the letters, and excerpts from diaries and notebooks used by him in preparing his manuscript. This destruction far outlasted the writing of the Life. Hardy left instructions to his wife, and to Sir Sydney Cockerell, one of his trustees, to destroy anything left over, particularly anything relating to his early days. Hardy's gardener has left a record of the thoroughness with which he saw Mrs. Hardy burning letters and papers after her husband's death.[8] The second cause for suspicion is the obvious one that, in the book as published, whole areas of Hardy's life and experience are clearly omitted. An almost ludicrous example of this, which has been noted by some biographers, while others try to explain it away,[9] is that, if one were to believe the Life, Hardy had no contact at all with young women from the time he was sixteen to the age of twenty-nine, when he met his first wife. A brief mention of a girl by her initials, in letters to his sister Mary in 1863 and 1865, and an equally brief and generalized reference to flirtations at Weymouth in 1869, are all he allows his readers. No wonder eager speculators have rushed in to fill the gaps with their fantasies. Moreover, it has emerged that in quoting a letter to his sister Mary, apparently in full, Hardy left out[10] a short paragraph mentioning the name of a girl; and this was a girl whom Hardy, according to the girl's brother, at one time wanted to marry.[11] Here again, though, it would be unwise to believe all Hardy's omissions have to do with sexual or deeply personal secrets of his life. Probably the most powerful motive was some sort of snobbery. Not only, as has been pointed out, does the Life tend to raise the social status of his mother and father. He omits almost totally all his other close relatives, uncles, aunts, and very numerous cousins. The touchstone throughout seems to have been social class. Labourers, cobblers, bricklayers, carpenters, farm servants, journeyman joiners, butlers have no place in Hardy's memoirs, though he was related to all of these; nor, among women, do cooks, house-servants, ladies' maids, or certificated teachers, regarded in the nineteenth century as little better than servants. Snobbery has usually been laid at the door of Hardy's first wife. Yet one finds that in the 1880s, she was a sympathetic friend to Hardy's sister Mary, herself a certificated teacher, who poured out to the first Mrs. Hardy her grievance that "nobody asks me to dinner or treats me like a lady".[12] In fact it was Hardy himself who did not want to record the lives of his lower-class relatives.

The most powerful witness to this is what he himself called "The Hardy Pedigree", a genealogical table which he also drew up in his old age, while he was writing the memoirs.[13] The most striking feature of this family tree is the differing fullness with which he sets out—how accurately it is difficult to say—the various branches of his family. He gives elaborate attention to a branch only very remotely related to his mother, called Childs. According to Hardy, this Childs family eventually came to contain a certain number of professional men, particularly surgeons, and, as a culminating triumph, an Assistant Commissioner of Metropolitan Police. All this, taking up practically one half of the "Pedigree", is meticulously noted by Hardy, with special attention to any learned qualifications, MA, MD, FRCS, and so on. The other half of the Pedigree, which should have contained Hardy's really close relatives, is left virtually blank. Hardy had about thirty first cousins; but not one was in the learned professions, and none appears here. Other small supplementary pedigrees, which do mention a cousin or two, only name relatives with distinction outside Dorset, such as his second cousin, Nathaniel Sparks junior, Associate of the Royal College of Art and Fellow of the Royal Society of Painter-Etchers.[14]

Yet snobbery is too sweeping and easy a dismissal for Hardy's purpose. In early life he had to fight the massive social stratification of the Victorian age. Finally he broke through from one class to another; but one can only guess what violence this did to his own nature. To shut the door on a social past from which he had escaped became a compulsion in his later life. Nor were his motives merely those of social and class distinction, though these were powerful in the years when he was struggling for recognition, and he still remembered and resented them deep into the twentieth century. This strange record also reveals Hardy's reverence for learning. The gulf between someone with whom he could talk freely in an educated way, and one of his own background, who, however full of simple wisdom, could literally not speak the language which Hardy had acquired, haunted his mind. In novels, he might extol the instinctive rightness of the peasant; in life, he always sought the company of the educated. Again, one can only guess the conflicts this caused. Certainly this secret life of the mind, almost too intense at times for him to bear, is hinted in his almost prophetic markings in his Bible.[15] Text and annotation, in Hardy's hand, suggest that he regarded himself as some latter-day seer, unregarded or misunderstood by those nearest to him. Hardy's isolation is shown in the difference between himself and his brother Henry. Henry to the end—he died in the same year as Hardy—retained a broad Dorset accent and even broader and more expansive country manners. He frequently refused to use a watch, preferring, he said, to tell the time by the sun, even in an age of trains and buses.[16]

So, to regard Hardy's autobiography—for such it is—as some kind of elaborate and devious mystification for posterity, is to ignore all the human elements. Hardy was in his late seventies, when he began, and probably well into his eighties when he finished. Although his memory for minute details could be exceptional, there are obvious moments when it plays him false. As he confessed to a friend, he suffered at times during these years from an "overclouding" of his mind.[17] Then again, his always thin-skinned nature must have winced at some of these reminders from the past, and it is no wonder that he showed reticence in recording them. On 7 May 1919, he wrote that he had been "mainly destroying papers of the last 30 or 40 years, and they raise ghosts"; later in the same year he wrote of "the dismal work" it entailed. Again, the round-about phrasing he often used, which has sometimes roused suspicion, was an effect of old age. It was twenty years since he had written his last novel, and his prose style, always uncertain, had deteriorated. This can be seen in the awkward and pedantic alterations he made in his first wife's manuscript, *Some Recollections*, often ruining the scatter-brained spontaneity of her style.[18] He had confessed a loss of grip in maintaining the interest of *Jude the Obscure* twenty years before; now his idea of narrative had degenerated into a set of clumsily-connected anecdotes, often, it seems, chosen for quaintness or oddity rather than for relevance to the main themes of his life. In fact, this heavy hand sometimes gives an extra impression of honesty; it must be true, one feels, because it is so baldly written. Hardy writes his auto-biography in the same style of commonplace naïvety as his letters. His style in both may be said, without much exaggeration, to be un-consciously that of the great comic book of the 1890s, George and Weedon Grossmith's *The Diary of a Nobody*. Hardy, in some of his unintentionally funny understatements, reminds one almost irresistibly of the Grossmith's lower-middle-class hero, Mr. Pooter; his references to his wife Emma, in particular, have an echo of Mr. Pooter's artless chronicle of the disasters of his dear wife Carrie. "E.'s shoulder, where the bicyclist ran into her, is practically well, though she occasionally feels twinges" is a typical passage from a letter.[19] It is matched by the autobiography's account of a visit to Guinness's Brewery: "On the miniature railway we all got splashed with porter, or possibly dirty water, spoiling Em's and Mrs. Henniker's clothes".[20]

The humourless and colourless pages of the autobiography almost always lack life, except where some flash of country anecdote or incident suddenly enlivens them, such as the brief dialogue between the street-preacher and the village girl, which ends by their going off into the woods together.[21] On the other hand, the lurid attempts of later writers to colour the story by fictitious means are even more misleading. Yet the life of the young Thomas Hardy meant even more than the early lives of most artists. "I have a faculty", he wrote, "for burying an emotion in my heart or brain for forty years, and exhuming it at the end of that time as fresh as when interred".[22] The most famous example of this process is one of his best-known poems, *In Time of " The Breaking of Nations"*, conceived during the Franco-Prussian War of 1870 and written during the First World War, about forty-five years later. The same is true of his later novels, and still more of the mass of personal poems of his old age. The death of his wife in November 1912 released a flood of memories, and the gates were opened still wider from 1917 or thereabouts by his attempted autobiography. His collections, *Moments of Vision* in 1917, *Late Lyrics and Earlier* in 1922, and *Human Shows* in 1925 are by far his largest publications of verse. Together they total 462 poems, one half of his published poetry. The greater part of this huge output of his old age deals with the remote past, either freshly written from the material and memories he was handling, or often quite specifically "from old notes" or "from an old draft". In these, the force of the far-off emotions he was re-experiencing broke through with startling effect. All his faults of style, sometimes painful and even on occasion faintly ridiculous, are transfigured or overcome by the deeply-felt personal urgency.

The true story of Hardy's early life is therefore essential to the understanding of some of his finest work. This cannot, however, be reached by treating his creative work as pure autobiography, and guessing at the early life by hints from the poems and novels. This is the way in which strange and far-fetched fictional accounts of the young Thomas Hardy have arisen. The only true method is to start from the facts of the life itself. Often these prove more strange and far more human than anything that has been invented. Only when we have these facts can we reverse the usual process, and explore some of the complexities and conflicts behind his mature work: to see this work, at least in part, in its relation to the life of the young Thomas Hardy.

# 2

# Bockhampton and Puddletown

IN HIS old age, Hardy was obsessed with "the decline and fall of the Hardys", as he called it, the idea that his family had once been far more important than in his own lifetime—"so we go down, down, down". In point of fact, this was a delusion which led him to do less than justice to his own father. Thomas Hardy the father, so his son said, was too easy-going to make a success of his career as master-mason, and "did not possess the art of enriching himself by business".[1] The truth was the complete opposite; Thomas Hardy senior rose from very humble beginnings to make a considerable amount. According to family tradition, his grandfather, John Hardy, walked one day into Puddletown with his bag of mason's tools and little else.[2] In the year of his own eldest son's birth, Thomas Hardy was simply, like most of the Hardys, a self-employed mason; although he had recently inherited the goodwill of his father's trade, the actual cash in hand was negligible.[3] Ten years later, he had become a bricklayer, employing two labourers. Another ten, and he was for the first time designated master-mason, employing six men; while in 1871, he employed eight men and a boy.[4] He seems to have prospered even more in the next twenty years, until at his death in 1892 he had a personal estate of £850—£10,000 in modern terms—and real estate at West Stafford and West Knighton.[5] He had done extremely well for himself, while far from being careless or improvident, the Hardys had a local reputation for being close-fisted.[6]

Local tradition, it is true, still puts down much of the elder Hardy's success to the driving force of his wife, Jemima, and credits him with carelessness in behaviour of quite another sort. According to this, Thomas Hardy senior, a handsome and well-formed man, had a reputation for getting village girls into trouble. He seems to have met his match, though, when early in December 1839, Jemima Hand, a woman who, like himself, was in her late twenties, was found to be three months pregnant by him. She had been a cook for the Reverend Charles Fox-Strangways at Maiden Newton, and had been a servant in other Dorset houses, including probably Kingston Maurward House in Thomas Hardy's own parish of Stinsford.[7] She had also worked in Weymouth, and for a few months in London. She was herself the daughter of a servant,[8] George Hand, who had died many years before in 1822; but her mother, Elizabeth Swetman of Melbury Osmond, seems to have come from quite another social class. A yeoman farmer's daughter, exceptionally well-read, she found herself, after her misalliance with Hand, a penniless widow, disowned by her father, with seven children, three sons and four daughters, and a bitterness against what she regarded as undeserved poverty, lasting deep into her old age.[9] She and her offspring had no intention of letting Thomas Hardy senior shirk his duty; and he and Jemima Hand were married on 22 December 1839 at her mother's family church of Melbury Osmond. The witnesses were the husband of Jemima's eldest sister, James Sparks of Puddletown, and one of her unmarried sisters, Mary Hand. There were no Hardy witnesses.

Whatever Thomas Hardy senior was doing in this marriage, he was most certainly not marrying for money. He was, in plain fact, marrying into a family who had been brought up as pauper children on parish relief. His famous son, who must have known this fact very well, could not actually bring himself to say that his mother had been a pauper child. In his old age, he made a cryptic account of this,[10] and its effect upon his own mother:

> By reason of her parent's bereavement and consequent poverty under the burden of a young family, Jemima saw during girlhood and young womanhood some very distressful experiences of which she could never speak in her maturer years without pain.

This veiled account has led imaginative biographers to invent all sorts of sensational adventures for Jemima, imagining her to be a prototype of Tess of the d'Urbervilles, and even to have been seduced and borne illegitimate children. The plain facts, though harsh, make such fantasies unnecessary. From her father's death in 1822 until the accounts end in 1836, her mother, Betsy Hand, is shown as receiving monthly sums of money for herself and her children from the Poor Law Overseers of her parish of Melbury Osmond.[11] As each child went out to work, probably at the age of about thirteen, the dole lessened. A drop of some shillings in autumn 1826, when Jemima was thirteen, probably shows when she and one of her sisters went into service. Her mother seems to have gone on drawing a small dole, perhaps unofficially, all her life.[12] This, then, a maid-servant and one of seven pauper children, was the wife of Hardy's father.

He took her to live with his own widowed mother, Mary Head Hardy, in a house in the hamlet of Higher Bockhampton, in his parish of Stinsford. This house, a little more substantial than most cottages, had been built by his grandfather, John Hardy, at the beginning of the century, on land leased from the Morton Pitt family.[13] There were only seven other houses in the hamlet, which lay along a lane leading to the heath, known as Cherry Alley or Veterans Valley. The former service officers, who had given it the latter name, had almost all disappeared by this time, apart from one retired naval lieutenant. Nearly opposite Thomas Hardy senior lived his elder brother James, also a mason, with his wife and three sons, George, Walter and Augustus, and a twelve-year-old apprentice.[14] Thomas Hardy's house was the last on the south side of the lane, next to the heath, and it was here on 2 June 1840 that his eldest son was born. The labour was a difficult one, and nearly cost Jemima her life; the child itself appeared to be dead, and was thrown aside into a basket by the surgeon trying to save the mother, until the midwife exclaimed, "Stop a minute: he's alive sure enough!" He was at first extremely fragile, and seemed unlikely to be a normal child. After the birth of a daughter, Mary, in the following year, 1841, Jemima Hardy took her unmarried sister Mary Hand into the house, to help to look after her delicate son.[15] Her own mother at Melbury Osmond was too poverty-stricken even to come and visit—"pretty little fellow I love him so well to[o] . . . poverty separates chieftest friends".[16]

As it began to appear that Thomas would live and develop, his parents' relieved affection was concentrated on him. Each had much to give him. They were a handsome and attractive pair. Jemima, like all the Hand girls, had great vitality, and looked much younger than she was. From her mother she had inherited a passion for reading and had obtained some of her library of books. It is astonishing to find that her own favourite reading was Dante's *Divine Comedy*,[17] and it may be suspected it was at her suggestion that Hardy's godfather gave the seven-year-old boy a book on the Jews.[18] Although his sister Mary became a lifelong companion and confidante, his mother was like an elder sister to him. She combined, to an unusual degree, vivid independence, a lively sense of humour, and a sombre view of fate, all of which could be seen transmuted in her son. His more obvious inheritance at first was his father's ruling passion for music. Thomas Hardy senior's father, yet another Thomas Hardy, had built up a choir of instrumentalists in the parish of Stinsford. It consisted of himself on the violincello, with two of his sons, Hardy's father and uncle James, and their brother-in-law James Dart[19] on their violins. Though smaller than the band in the larger parish of Puddletown, and that of Maiden Newton, where Hardy's mother had worked, the Stinsford choir was reckoned the finest in the district. Hardy's father also sang tenor and played and danced country tunes, and was in great demand at dances. Music was Hardy's earliest delight; his first recollection was of being given a small accordion by his father on his fourth birthday. At the same age he remembered dancing endlessly to his father's country tunes, many of which moved him to tears; he could tune a fiddle when still very young, and soon learnt to play hundreds of country dances from his father's and grandfather's old music books. Church services at Stinsford combined for him the two passions of words and music. Isaac Watts's hymns provided him with one of the verse-forms he used till the end of his life, and the western sun shining on the Venetian-red wall-paper at home found the child Hardy reciting every evening "And now another day is gone". In church, he stared with relishing horror deep into the jaws of the marble skull on the tomb of the Greys. On wet Sunday mornings he used to wrap himself in a tablecloth for vestments, stand on a chair and read the Morning Prayer, with one of his boy cousins from across the lane responding as clerk, while his grandmother formed the congregation. Not all occasions were as solemn as these tales suggest. When he could walk across the heath to the neighbouring Puddletown, he and his mother disguised themselves in weird clothes, with cabbage nets pulled over their faces, and surprised one of her two married sisters there.[20]

When he was nine, his mother took him to visit her other sister, Martha Sharpe; she had married at Puddletown in 1841 John Brereton Sharpe, who became a farm-manager on the Marquis of Salisbury's estate at Hatfield,[21] while his brother, George Brereton Sharpe, had a medical practice in nearby Welwyn.[22] John Brereton Sharpe was Hardy's favourite uncle, a dashing figure, who, Hardy believed, had been in the Lancers,[23] and who is said to have been the model for Sergeant Troy in *Far From the Madding Crowd*. A letter from him[24] has the jocular, man-to-man tone of Troy. This visit to Hertfordshire was Hardy's first great adventure, and served to knit him even closer to his mother. She made the small boy her companion, in her own words, "for protection"; for, unlike most countrywomen of that time, she was apparently still extremely attractive at the age of thirty-five. One of his most vivid memories was of their stay in London on the way back. This was at an old coaching-inn, the Cross Keys at Clerkenwell. From his small bed in the attic, he watched his mother search the huge old closets of the room, in case any man were hiding there, before she put out the light.[25] His other memory, the brutality of men to the beasts in Smithfield Market, was one which coloured his thought, and many of his poems, for the rest of his life. A year before he died, he noticed with horror the cattle-trucks on the railway near his home.[26]

On this stay, he also found minor brutality when he went briefly to a school kept by a Mr. Ray at Hatfield. This school and the whole journey may have been a scheme by Jemima Hardy to wile her impressionable son away from a rival emotional influence. In 1845, when Hardy was five years old, the estate of Kingston Maurward in Stinsford parish had been bought by Francis Pitney Brouncker Martin. His wife, Julia Augusta Martin, was only a few years older than Jemima Hardy, but she was childless. She became, for some reason, obsessively fond of the small Thomas,[27] and later claimed to have taught him to read,[28] though Hardy put his own reading at what appears an earlier time, "almost before he could walk".[29] His mother told his sister Mary that at the age of three Hardy read a book, which still exists,[30] containing verses of the Cries of London, and published by March's Library, with brightly-coloured pages of illustration. At all events, Mrs. Martin seems to have treated him as still a baby, "to take into her lap and kiss until he was quite a big child". An emotional attachment grew between them, which has been seen as the origin of a constant theme in most of Hardy's early novels, sexual attraction reaching across class barriers.[31]

The small boy also played his part in one of Mrs. Martin's dominant interests. She was a devout Churchwoman, and, shortly after coming into Stinsford parish, she decided to provide it with a school, newly-built and run under the auspices of the National Society for Promoting the Education of the Poor in the Principles of the Established Church. This was Thomas Hardy's first school, to which he went on the formal opening of its new buildings in the autumn of 1848, though it seems to have started in temporary quarters earlier in the year. Here, as he says, he worked at Walkingame's Arithmetic, and did well in mathematics and geography. His mother, however, had ideas for her son's reading far beyond anything even Mrs. Martin's model school could provide. Perhaps following the example of her own mother, and almost certainly from the latter's library, she gave Thomas, in this first year at school, Dryden's translation of Virgil's *Aeneid*, Dr. Johnson's *Rasselas*, and a translation of St. Pierre's popular *Paul and Virginia*.[32] In this situation there was bound to be some emotional tug-of-war for the child. Hardy's admiration for his mother was strong, and they shared their lives closely; Mary, one year younger, was an exceptionally self-effacing child, and— most unusually for a rural family—there were no further children for the first ten years of Hardy's life. On the other hand, his feeling for Mrs. Martin was, as he afterwards said, "almost that of a lover". He used to make special water-colour drawings of animals for her, and sing her his favourite songs.

It seems likely, then, that the expedition to Hertfordshire was an attempt by Hardy's mother to defeat her rival, first by removing him physically from Mrs. Martin, and sending him temporarily to another school, then, when they came back, taking him from Stinsford school, and entering him at a school in Dorchester.[33] Hardy's own account of this shows obvious embarrassment; he tries to justify his mother by saying that Mrs. Martin should have guessed he was only being sent to her school "till sturdy enough to go further". Hardy's mother apparently failed to foresee the offence Mrs. Martin took at the choice of school. This was the school in Greyhound Lane, Dorchester, run by the British and Foreign School Society, a Nonconformist group. Mrs. Hardy had been attracted by the academic reputation of its headmaster, Isaac Last; like most of the inhabitants of Stinsford and Puddletown, she did not see a great difference between their Church services and those of the Chapel. Mrs. Martin, however, was a keen Churchwoman. This, apart from emotional ties suddenly broken, made her resent a Nonconformist school for her favourite pupil. The row between the two women is said to have lost work for Hardy's father on the Kingston Maurward estate,[34] though there is no evidence that he actually did work on the estate; it certainly did not prevent him from being paid for work at Stinsford Church, of which Mr. Martin was a churchwarden.[35]

The emotional effect on Hardy was deep, and he goes out of his way to record it. Mr. Martin ran the Kingston estate farm through one of the many Scottish servants he and his wife employed, George Singer, an Aberdeenshire bailiff.[36] He lost money eventually on it—perhaps some foreshadowing of the relationship between Farfrae and Henchard in *The Mayor of Casterbridge*. In spite of the disastrously wet summer of 1850, Francis Martin decided to hold a harvest supper, and to insure its success by inviting some non-commissioned officers from Dorchester Barracks to dance with the local girls. One of the girls, a small farmer's daughter, offered to take the ten-year-old Hardy, and he jumped at the offer as a chance to see Mrs. Martin again. She and her house-party arrived late. When she saw him, she exclaimed, "O Tommy, how is this? I thought you had deserted me!" The exhausted small boy burst into tears, and promised he had not deserted her. She gave him her husband's small niece as a dancing-partner, and little Miss Campbell, the daughter of a Naval officer, duly danced with the strange peasant boy; but the house-party did not stay long. Thomas was left for hours before he could extract the girl who had brought him from the arms of the soldiers, and get home to the rebukes of his parents. This must have accentuated the quarrel between the two women, for Hardy, in an unpublished note,[37] remembered that his mother "openly defied" Mrs. Martin. The stress of these incidents impressed him so deeply that in old age he could still recall "the thrilling 'frou-frou' of her four grey silk flounces when she had used to bend over him, and when they brushed against the font as she entered church on Sundays",[38] a memory he reproduced in exact detail in the short story, *The Withered Arm*. Even more strangely, in his eighties Hardy still indulged in day-dreams about imaginary love-passages which he believed might have occurred between them, if he had taken up the relationship in later life.

This childhood vision of life as lived by the rich and fortunate—even though Mr. Martin seems to have got tired of being a farmer, and left the district in 1853—had a profound effect. There was a great deal more contrast between this life and his own than Hardy afterwards cared to admit, and his over-insistence on his own father's independence, and the leasehold for life on the Bockhampton house,[39] was meant to distract attention from the huge social gap. Although small craftsmen like his

father were, as Hardy rightly insisted, in a different class from the ordinary labourer, the distinction was often tenuous, and the slightest slip
could cause social degradation. None of Hardy's writings admits, and no
book on him points out, that his eldest uncle, John Hardy, was an
ordinary labourer. This uncle, whom Hardy never mentions, but who
was born in 1803, married a labourer's daughter, Sarah Dart, in 1825.[40]
They had four children, Albert, Rebecca, Rosina, and Frederick John,
but all completely disappear round about the birth of the last child in
1835. The renewal that year of the lease of the Bockhampton home on
10 October prolongs it for the lives of his father and of his brothers James
and Thomas, but John is not mentioned.[41] One probable explanation is
that, like so many Dorset labourers who found themselves in difficulties,
he was forced to emigrate.[42] Though Hardy cannot have met him, he
was an example, very near at hand, of poverty and perhaps despairing
emigration in Hardy's own immediate family. The Martins of Kingston
Maurward, with their two manor houses, one Elizabethan, one Georgian,
and their careless squandering on farming experiments, must have
seemed like creatures from another planet, compared with Hardy's
home.

Hardy's silence about his uncle John also covers his aunts, Martha,
Mary Anne, and Jane Hardy.[43] It is possible that these, though living
in the same parish, were not well known to him in his outlying hamlet.
At any rate, they were not as familiar as the household of his uncle and
neighbour James. This had just undergone an addition and a loss—the
birth of a girl Theresa in 1843, and the death in 1844 of the twelve-year-
old Walter. Still more surprising is his silence about his mother's vivid
and varied relatives, the Hand family of Puddletown. His grandmother,
Elizabeth Hand, only moved there shortly before her death in 1847, and
he probably knew little of her except through his own mother; but as
soon as he could walk the two and a half miles across the heath to
Puddletown, he was introduced to a teeming society, in which many of
his relatives were well-known characters. This small town, for it was
considerably more than a village, was still practically medieval in its
way of life, neglected by absentee landlords and untouched by
eighteenth-century enclosure. It remained so throughout Hardy's
youth, until a new reforming squire in the 1860s and 1870s literally
cleaned up and rebuilt the place.[44] Perhaps because its medieval and
manorial character had been retained so long, it was a busy and thriving
little town, whose population increased steadily all through the
eighteenth century. In the 1820s it shot up from just under the thousand
to 1200, where it remained for decades while most Dorset towns suffered
severe depopulation. Puddletown was always a town of artisans and
small craftsmen, serving the farming community, but skilled and
independent of the fluctuations of agriculture. About one-third of the

town worked in trade, manufacture and handicraft, a very high proportion for a rural place.[45] It was reckoned a thriving spot to live; when
James Sparks of Dorchester married Hardy's aunt, Maria Hand, in the
late 1820s, he left his much larger home-town to carry on his profession
of cabinet-maker in Puddletown among his wife's relatives.

These all belonged to the Puddletown Hardy knew and frequented in
his first twenty years. Most characteristic among them, as inhabitants
of the still-unreformed town, were his three uncles, Henery, William and
Christopher, bricklayers. Long-limbed, sardonic, rough-mannered,
quick-tempered, none of these three brothers, when Hardy first knew
them, owned or leased his own cottage, but lived in rented lodgings.[46]
Their fortunes varied, and sometimes rose, particularly Christopher's.
Like his brother-in-law, Hardy's father, he ultimately made a success of
the profession of mason, and his son and namesake afterwards went to
school with Hardy. Yet heavy drinking, for which Hardy himself said
Puddletown was then notorious,[47] prevented any of the Hands from
getting as far as the Hardys. Christopher's drinking and knocking his
wife about when she was with child distressed his own mother.[48] Two
Hand sisters, Maria and Mary, had married craftsmen who owned their
own homes by leasehold. Maria's husband, James Sparks, cabinet-
maker, lived at the bottom of Mill Street, on a curve opposite the river
that came to be known as Sparks Corner. He was well-connected, and
one of his relatives had been a freeman of Dorchester,[49] while an older
generation, leaving Dorchester, were country lawyers at Crewkerne in
Somerset, and had acquired a coat of arms. His double cob-and-thatch
faced the river Piddle, bounded on its other bank by one of the picturesque thatched walls typical of Dorset. The river, aptly named, was
swift-flowing but far from healthy, having received, at the next corner
higher up, the outgoings of the Old Cat, one of Puddletown's many
public houses. The traditional saying, describing a Puddletown Sunday,
still survives:

> Into Church,
> Out of Church,
> Into Cat,
> Out of Cat,
> Into Piddle.

The cottage itself was crammed to bursting with James Sparks's
numerous family, and it is no wonder that Maria Sparks, Hardy's aunt,
living in such surroundings, developed the slow consumption from which
she died.[50] The eldest daughter, Rebecca Maria, had served an apprenticeship, and carried on a dressmaking business to supplement the
family income, aided by her sisters Emma and Martha Mary as semps-
tresses. There was a son James, three years older than Hardy, and
another Nathaniel, three years younger, while in 1850 yet another child

was on the way.[51] The girls were lively, bustling, and attractive, though their mother kept a strict eye on them. Hardy was in and out of this household all his early life.

Another port of call was at his aunt Mary's in the High Street. She had married the cobbler John Antell, and though her children were much younger, she always had a welcome for the small Hardy, whom she had nursed through his delicate first years. Her husband was a wild and interesting character. Self-taught, he had dreamt of going to college, but poverty, hard work and drink had banished the dream. According to Hardy's second wife, he was partly—"but only partly"— the model for Jude Fawley in *Jude the Obscure*.[52] His self-taught Latin and his "great mass of black curly hair" certainly seem reproduced in Hardy's novel, and perhaps the manner of Jude's death; for his own, though at the age of 62,[53] is said to have been hastened by exposure through having spent the night in a ditch after a drunken bout. The savage alternations of Jude's life may well have been partly, though again "only partly", suggested by what Hardy came to know of the Antell household. On one drunken occasion, John Antell beat up his wife Mary, and blacked her eye. He had reckoned without her married sisters, Maria Sparks and Jemima Hardy. They in their turn beat him till he was forced to plead for mercy and swear he would not touch Mary again. Hardy had little need to go outside his own relatives for the brutal facts of rural life; yet, on the other hand, its dreams and ambitions, which he himself felt so early, were part of the same picture. John Antell's struggling genius descended through his family; a son John, who succeeded him in the business, wrote poetry of more than technical merit, had a talent for sketching and was a good musician.

Though the Sparks and the Antell familes were in the craftsman class, poverty was never far off; the former in particular, for all their family industry, never had a spare penny. Among real labouring families, the young Hardy saw worse than poverty; in the 1840s he actually knew a shepherd boy who died of starvation.[54] The Commons debates on the repeal of the Corn Laws in 1846 threw up a mass of information on the abject state of the Dorset peasantry. It was the subject of six special articles and much correspondence in *The Times*. Letters poured in, all confirming "the old story—7s. the average wages . . . the sexes of all ages inhabiting the same sleeping room" in the mud-floored, leaky and ruinous cottages,[55] and, as a labourer himself wrote, "young men and women living together like dogs".[56] Puddletown, not surveyed in *The Times* articles, was presumably better-off than most places; yet the average wage there of about 9s. a week—much less for single men— was too low for any decent life. There was a grumbling hopeless resentment against the gentry who opposed the repeal of the Corn Laws, and support, generally secret, for the Anti-Corn-Law movement. In 1846, the child Hardy heard enough to dip his toy wooden sword in the blood of a pig that had just been killed, and march about the garden shouting "Free Trade or Blood!"[57] His excitement had also been roused by seeing whoever killed the pig cut off a piece and eat it raw, in traditional propitiatory custom.[58]

Puddletown provided Hardy not only with a glimpse of the larger world, but, through his own relatives there, contact with broad and coarse social realities. As late as 1895, an indignant colonist, who had emigrated in the 1850s, wrote home to protest against the Victorian bowdlerization of the name of his native Piddletown.[59] If earthy humanity was to be found there, the walk home across the heath gave him the opposite extreme of mystery, poetry and fearful magic. Hurrying through the mists that came swirling up from the valleys of the Piddle and the Frome, along the bracken-covered heights, the fog itself seemed not so much an effect of the atmosphere, but an indefinable presence of sinister intent. Even in the ordinary winter dusk, he would suddenly run fast to escape his fears, roused by the movement of heath-pony or a deer or even an unfamiliar shape of bush.[60] Home was a re-assuring place of glowing rushlights and fireside; yet even the warm little house, with thick mud walls and long thatch-eaves, had attracted, by its isolation, strange history. Earlier in the century it had been a dumping place for smugglers, bringing their landings in from Ower-moigne or Lulworth; a whip-lash across the lower windows at nights would announce that some tubs had been temporarily stored. The lonely situation even encouraged them to come by day, in spite of the protests of Hardy's grandmother, which they countered by leaving her "a washing pan of pale brandy", to celebrate the birth of one of Hardy's uncles. They did not leave off until other houses began to be built, but the tradition lingered. When Hardy was a child, a gigantic woman known as Mother Rogers used to call at the door and ask if any of "it" was wanted cheap. Her hugeness was caused by bullocks' bladders slung round her hips, in which she carried the contraband spirits.[61] Another notorious visitor, though before Hardy's birth, was James Clase, otherwise Blue Jemmie the horse-thief, who stole the horse of a neighbour in the lane.[62]

The fascinating source of many of these traditions was, of course, Hardy's grandmother, Mary Head Hardy. Widowed in 1837, and in her seventies, she nevertheless managed the accounts of her son's business for the next dozen years,[63] and helped her daughter-in-law to keep a firm hand on the household. Born at Fawley, a village in Berkshire, in 1772, she never knew her father, who died in the same year. Her mother also died, perhaps in tragic circumstances, when she was only six and a half, and her memories of Fawley were so poignant that she never cared to return there.[64] How she got to Puddletown, where Hardy's grandfather seduced and then married her, is a complete mystery. Her stories and hints about her unhappy birthplace haunted her grandson so much that when his sister Mary had her first job at Denchworth in Berkshire, he urged her to visit Fawley and find out all she could about it.[65] Mary herself remembered their grandmother describing winters so snowy that she walked to church along the hedge-tops. Other traditions, folklore and legends clearly had their origin with this grandmother, who was thus the source of some of Hardy's most mysterious and moving poems and incidents in his novels. Tragedy seemed to follow her all her life; her husband was playing in the church choir one Sunday, and was buried on the next. Yet she remained, as Hardy remembered, gentle always.

On regular Sunday walks with his parents, they would take a more southerly track from the little wicket-gate across the heath to the silent pond, about a mile away, called Rushy Pond. According to legend it had been excavated by fairy shovels, and it was always a place of great significance for Hardy. Nearby, topping a further slope, was the tumulus group known as Rainbarrows, another favourite spot. Here Hardy's father would take a sweeping view with the telescope he always carried, and point out landmarks, including the houses where he was doing building work.[66] This habit, of taking a bird's-eye view of a whole area, stayed with Hardy all his life, like the mystical delight in high places which was most imaginatively expressed in his poem *Wessex Heights*. His father's easy-going enjoyment, contrasting with the more purposeful attitude of his mother, was something the small boy relished with a secret admiration. When his father died in 1892, Hardy wrote his name and date against the lines from *Hamlet*:[67]

> Thou hast been
> As one, in suffering all, that suffers nothing,
> A man that fortune's buffets and rewards
> Hast ta'en with equal thanks.

His father's enjoyment of nature was matched by his mother's extraordinary store of local legend and story. Together they filled Hardy's world with landscape and human dealing, the special blend that was to mark his poems and novels, so that emotion and place coalesce unforgettably.

The cottage home on the edge of the heath put Hardy into a companionship with all fellow creatures that never left him. Snakes and lizards flickered about the threshold, and even came into the house. When he was still a baby in his cradle, a large though harmless snake was found curled up with him as he slept. Heath-cropping ponies and deer looked in at the windows, and in the evening light the bats would fly in and out of the bedrooms. As he grew, he used to take a ladder and explore the thatch which was full of birds' nests; he went to sleep each night hearing small fluttering movements and subdued cheeping in the eaves. This characteristic close-up view of even the smallest living things, the sense of existing actually *with* them, never left him. As late as *The Dynasts*, written in his sixties, the field of Waterloo is seen as if by the tiny creatures that inhabit the battleground. With this went a sense of timelessness. He recalled distinctly an instance when, lying on his back in the sun, whose rays filtered through the straw of his hat, he decided that he did not want to grow up. His cousins George and Augustus were always talking of what they would do when they were men, but he "did not want to be a man, or to possess things, but to remain as he was, in the same spot", and only know his half-dozen friends and relations in the Higher Bockhampton hamlet. [68] As always, he felt more sense of identification with the dead than with the living, and used to pick up the flint arrowheads of stone age inhabitants of the heath, and ponder on these tokens of former life there.[69] He was perhaps over-quick to read horror into any situation. The two mysterious seated men, who terrified him once on Stinsford Hill, were probably merely smugglers, sitting on their contraband tubs to try and conceal them.

Stories of savage events were told him by his mother and father. These tales of their own childhood had a deep influence on the morbidly sensitive boy; it seems clear they had little idea how far these memories of a rougher and more brutal age, commonplace to them, would sink into the imagination of their small son. One story from each parent was re-called by Hardy long after, with a kind of amazed horror. His father's tale was of a hanging that had taken place when he himself was young.[70] He had witnessed the execution of four men, whose only crime was that they had been present when others had set fire to a rick. One of these was a lad of eighteen, so emaciated and half-starved that they had to put weights on his feet before they could break his neck. This story horrified Hardy more than any other; but his mother's tale, though again a country commonplace, must have seemed almost equally terrible, especially to an ultra-sensitive boy. She told him about a girl who had committed suicide, and whose burial she remembered as an event in her own childhood. The girl was buried on Hendford Hill, near Yeovil, at a cross-roads on a bleak hill-top. Few followed her to her unblessed grave. There was no coffin to carry her, and no wreaths, though one other girl threw flowers on the exposed body. When it was put into the grave, a stake was driven through it, before the earth was heaped over her, sloping up the sides of the stake like a prehistoric tumulus.[71] The parents left the thoughtful boy with impressions of human nature that darkened his youthful views of life, appalling and true.

Other stories of his own childhood at Bockhampton show him as a solitary introspective boy, much more in touch with the animals around him than with the small group of fellow human beings. He was with his father in the garden on a bitterly cold winter's day, when they noticed a fieldfare, half-frozen. His father idly took up a stone, threw it in the bird's direction, and hit it. The bird dropped dead, and the small boy picked it up. It was as light as a feather, practically skin and bone, starved. The memory haunted him to the end of his life. At another time, he was crossing the ewe-lease on the way to Puddletown, which was full of sheep; he decided to get on all fours himself and pretend to eat grass, in order to see what the sheep would do. When he looked up, they had gathered around him in a close ring, gazing at him with what seemed astonished faces.[72] Poems of imaginative entrance into the minds of dogs, cats, and even other animals, which he wrote later, all have this in common, that they are not sentimental, though full of feeling. They seem to be describing actual states of being and ways of life. This solitary identification stayed with him, even though the next move he made was away from Bockhampton, in the opposite direction from Puddletown, to the larger and urban world of school in Dorchester.

# 3

# Dorchester

DORCHESTER, in which Thomas Hardy went to school sometime in 1850,[1] was a town in a state of transition. The coming of the railway in 1847 is generally taken as a symbol of change. This change, however, was not so abrupt as Hardy himself afterwards made out. Stage coaches still raced into Dorchester along the main Puddletown road, half a mile from Hardy's home,[2] and local travel was still largely on foot or by carrier's wagon. Hardy's dramatic statement that the orally-transmitted folk-ballads were "slain at a stroke" by London comic songs on the arrival of the railway is to be doubted. The singing of "The Outlandish Knight" by the local girls at Mr. Martin's harvest supper was not such a last landmark as Hardy himself implied.[3] Much later, he still heard sung the cheerful bawdy ballad of King Arthur and his three sons, "three sons of whores", a favourite for a long time in the ale-houses of Puddletown frequented by his Hand uncles.[4] What killed the rough local ballads Hardy knew was Victorian respectability in the person of John Brymer, Squire of Puddletown. His mark can still be seen in the fearsome (though sanitary) Victorian Gothic terraces, designed by a firm of land surveyors from Shepton Mallett, which he put up in the 1860s and 1870s with pride of place for a new school, under a cricket-playing headmaster, and the Men's Reading Room of 1870.[5] Not only did this house London newspapers and magazines, but it became the centre for penny-readings of an improving kind. These were decorous entertainments, sponsored by Brymer and his ladies, and it was here that the inhabitants of Puddletown first heard the drawing-room ballads and the comic songs of London that Hardy deplored.

The same process in the county town of Dorchester a little earlier, in the 1850s, showed itself in the same two aspects, roughly building and books. The first affected Hardy's father, the builder, and the second Hardy himself, the boy and scholar. Benjamin Ferrey, pupil of the elder Pugin and fellow-student with the more famous younger Pugin, had already designed many churches, vicarages, and manor-houses in and around Dorchester. It was by coincidence that his new Town Hall appeared at the same time as the railway; yet his prolific output indicates a quickened tempo in building. Squires, farmers, and parsons, the latter often "squarsons", or landowning clergy, prospered on low wages and the high price of wheat, and were tempted to express themselves in bricks and mortar. It was a profitable time to be a builder; Hardy's father, in spite of his energetic wife's protests, had no need to seek work. Lying in the sun, and watching the grasshoppers from the thymy bank leaping over him,[6] he was confident that plenty of those needing his services would seek him out, as indeed they did. He worked on at least one of Ferrey's mansions near Stinsford, either Clyffe House to the north-east, or, more likely, Stafford House to the south-east.[7]

Dorchester's prosperity brought building orders to Hardy's father; to his son it brought newspapers, magazines, books, bookshops, and a variety of opportunities in education. The Dorchester directory for 1851 shows a remarkable number of schools, one of which Hardy's sister Mary also attended, two circulating libraries, and several bookshops. It was now possible to get London papers and periodicals, and the flood of Victorian books of popular education. Hardy as a small child had the habit of self-education. His fascination with the Napoleonic Wars had as much to do with a magazine, *The History of the Wars*, which he found in a cupboard at home, as it had with the handsome soldiers whom he had seen partnering the girls at Kingston Maurward.[8] On Christmas Eve 1849, he became the possessor of *The Boys' Book of Science* by John M. Moffatt,[9] and in the same year Walkingame's Arithmetic or *The Tutor's Assistant*.[10] His passion for solitary reading was noted by other pupils at both his schools. He was seen by neighbours at Stinsford, on his three-mile walk into Dorchester, as a solemn small boy, odd-looking and with a big head, carrying a full satchel of books.[11] His appearance and habits invited teasing, though not of a very severe kind. In South Street, Dorchester, was a shop, one step down from the street, kept by an old woman called Sally Warren. A country lad from Broadmayne used to throw Hardy's cap down the step, and watch Sally chase him with a broom when he went to fetch it.[12]

Dorchester itself provided a number of contrasts for a thoughtful boy. On the face of it, there was the busy and thriving atmosphere common to all county towns. The steep long High Street divided, at the point where Cornhill joined it from the south, into High East and High West Street. There were fairs in Cornhill itself, and the bustle of a weekly market. Handsome tree-planted Walks bounded the town still, and the fields came right up to what had been the old walls. Public buildings, many of them newly-constructed, like Ferrey's Town Hall, with its Corn Exchange on the ground floor below, gave an air of importance. The streets were full of farm-carts, in for the Saturday market, carriers' wagons, the neat dog-carts of the local residents, the carriages-and-pair of country gentry, each with coachman and footman. Dorchester was a garrison as well as a county town, its dash and colour enhanced by the brightly-uniformed artillery and cavalrymen. Military bands played in the Walks; military funerals, frequent in the crowded barracks, were accompanied by solemn music on the way to church, and brisk marches on the way back. Hardy's youthful confusion of the Dead March in *Saul* and "See the conquering hero comes" probably arose on one such occasion. Gun-carriages rattled out along the south-west roads, for exercises on the prehistoric slopes of Maiden Castle, and troopers would stand in their stirrups to slash with sabres at overhanging tree-branches as they went.[13]

The excitement and display of a military barracks stirred the civilian inhabitants; some of Hardy's most successful ballad poems, such as "The Dance at the Phoenix", are about the effect of dashing uniforms on the women. Rivalry affected the men too; demonstrations and riots were often spectacular. Until the late 1870s, the toughs of the town used to celebrate Guy Fawkes Night by rolling barrels of blazing tar down the steep High West Street, until a peaceful vicar managed to substitute a torchlight procession for this hair-raising tradition.[14] Anti-Catholic feeling was genuinely strong in a town that had suffered for Monmouth's Rebellion. In November 1850,[15] Cardinal Wiseman returned from Rome as Archbishop of Westminster, to effect, as he announced, the restoration of Catholic England. Feeling ran high in Dorchester, and a monster demonstration took place in Maumbury Rings, the Roman amphitheatre on the south edge of the town. Effigies of the Pope and the Cardinal were burnt, among insulting anti-Catholic tableaux. The ten-year-old Hardy was taken by his father to see this violent display; he was bewildered when, in the lurid flame-lit procession of men dressed as monks following the figure of Wiseman, the hood of one blew aside, and he recognized the face of one of the two workmen his father now employed.[16]

There were other still more violent elements in a county town that was also an Assize town with a hanging gaol, and where the hangman's cottage, with a loft where the rope was kept, was a mecca for prying boys. The sinister atmosphere when the Judge was sitting in Shire Hall, and High West Street was muffled with straw to deaden the clatter of horse-traffic, was not a matter of imagination. Although it was now over 150 years since Judge Jeffreys at his Bloody Assize had ordered wholesale massacre after Monmouth's Rebellion, the memory stayed; fascinated horror at cruelty lingered on in this little town. Stories of Jack Ketch, the brutal hangman who had actually executed Monmouth, were still told: how he used to march through the streets holding aloft the whipcord cat o' nine tails, with which he had lacerated his victims at the Dorchester Town Pump.[17] The horrible story of the burning of an alleged murderess in Maumbury Rings was also part of Hardy's folklore.[18] Very close to his own time were the savage sentences of transportation passed on the Tolpuddle labourers at Dorchester in 1834, only half a dozen years before he was born. Numerous whippings, "severe and private", were imposed for quite small offences during his own lifetime.

Transportation and unspeakable happenings in Tasmania and Australia were also part of Hardy's childhood. Dorset peasants were starving and despairing, Dorset magistrates punitive. A John Hardy of Wareham, probably no relation, has left a searing account of his experiences.[19] When this degrading punishment ended, it is an irony that the Dorchester district was brought face to face with its substitute. After protests by the colonies themselves, transportation to New South Wales and South Australia was ended in 1850 and to Tasmania in 1852,[20] while an attempt to ship convicts to Cape Colony nearly caused a revolt and had to be abandoned. Meanwhile the authorities, realizing that this country would now have to live with its own criminals, had already begun to build fortress-like single-cell prisons. Portland, begun in 1848, was one of the earliest purpose-built penal servitude prisons. Here, the convicts were to labour, after a term of solitary confinement, on the huge new breakwater enclosing Portland Harbour. The foundation stone of these works was laid by Prince Albert in July 1849, a visit to Dorchester remembered by Hardy and recorded in *The Mayor of Casterbridge*. The convict gangs hacked out rubble near the summit of the promontory, and lowered it to sea-level by wire-rope incline, a process later sketched by Hardy.[21] As the railway was extended to Weymouth in 1857, and a few years after to Portland itself, the faces of these men, dazed and brutalized by their previous solitary confinement, their grey uniforms marked with the Government broad arrow, became a familiar local sight. Warders in charge of gangs working on the road would make their men turn their faces to the wall when anyone drove by. This grim area aroused a morbid curiosity; sightseers made wagonette trips from Dorchester to Portland, and stood at certain points to watch the convicts in the stone quarries, creatures from another world.[22]

Hardy shared this ugly fascination. Many of his stories and poems deal with hangings, convicts, murders, and prisons. While these reflect his early environment and the history of the place where he was brought up, in adolescence, as will be seen, they took a more sinister turn. He also, of course, joined in the normal pleasures of schoolboys, watching with excitement when Mr. Curtis's fighting-cocks were let into the street from a cellar next to the Corn Exchange,[23] untroubled by reflections on the cruelty of the sport which came to him later. Isaac Last in the little school in Greyhound Yard was a strict disciplinarian, but was always pleased with Hardy; so were the other boys, since he was ready to help with their lessons. The habits of reading learnt from his mother carried him on at a tremendous pace; when he was twelve, and the family business flourishing, his parents arranged that he should be taught Latin as an extra. He was started on the old Eton Grammar with readings from Eutropius and Caesar, devised for himself a visual system for remembering the genders, and shot ahead. Earlier in the year 1852, he read a book of exploration, Bruce's *Travels in Abyssinia*.[24] At home he read the romances of the elder Dumas in translation, historical novels such as Harrison Ainsworth's *Old St. Paul's*, James Grant's *The Scottish Cavalier*, with G. P. R. James's works, and the plays of Shakespeare, though at that stage for the plots rather than for the poetry. *The Pilgrim's Progress* alarmed him so much that once, reading it on his way home from school, he felt convinced Apollyon would spring out from the dark trees overhanging the road.[25]

It was in the next year, 1853, that Hardy felt the benefit of Dorchester as a growing centre of education. Isaac Last's school belonged to a Nonconformist body, the British and Foreign School Society; he was a Congregationalist, and owed his appointment to the fact that the actual founder of the school, William Manfield, a local solicitor and landowner, was a Congregationalist too. Last was an ambitious teacher, whom ill-health had kept from going farther afield; but he determined to widen his scope in Dorchester. In 1853, therefore, he set up his own private fee-paying and partly boarding school. He was undoubtedly encouraged to do this by the very powerful Congregationalist colony in the Dorchester area. They nearly all, like Manfield himself, lived west of Dorchester, though one family, that of Wood, bought Athelhampton Hall, near Puddletown, founded their own Nonconformist school, and became rivals of Squire Brymer of Puddletown. This group of Congregationalist landowners, Manfields, Woods, Samsons and Homers, provided a body of backing for Last's further plans, and, incidentally, a lucky addition to Hardy's further education. At an ordinary British school, this would have ended at twelve or thirteen, unless he decided to go in for teaching himself, and stayed for another five years' apprenticeship as pupil-teacher. Now, with parental help, he could follow his master to the new school, continue his Latin, and prolong his school life.[26] In later life he was determined to regard the higher education afforded by Last's new "Academy" as some sort of equivalent of going to College. In an angry annotation to a book, which had described him as self-taught, he wrote that this was an "impertinent personality & untrue, as he was taught Latin & French at School and College".[27]

The driving force behind this continued self-improvement was, of course, Hardy's determined mother. She appears to have been as watchful over his moral development as she was over his intellectual growth. He and Mary felt the full weight of their mother's influence. Henry, born in 1851, and Kate, in 1856, seem to have been allowed to be easygoing; indeed, they were so different in later life as to appear, quite apart from the big gap in age, almost another generation. Two anecdotes show the values to which Hardy was expected to conform. Both also

show him as the precocious one in a gathering of adults. At one of the
local cottages, a live hen was put up as a prize, to be won by "raffling"
—that is, throwing dice—at an entrance fee of twopence a head.
Hardy, not much more than ten, joined the raffle. As he was almost a
child, and the only one there, he was made to throw first, the superstition
being that the first thrower was the least likely to win. To everybody's
consternation, including his own, the three dice all came down the same
number, in gambling terms "a pair royal" and the highest possible
throw. Even worse than having ruined the sport was his reception at
home when he arrived with the unwanted bird. As he remembered it,
"The event was considered such a direct attempt by the devil to lead
one of tender years to ruin that I was forbidden to gamble any more—&
as a matter of fact, never did".[28] The incident, which helped him with
the dicing scene in *The Return of the Native*, resembles one a year or so
later, connected with his fiddle-playing. He was beginning to play outside the family circle at village weddings and dances. His mother strictly
told him that he must never accept any payment, but on one occasion
his hosts insisted, and a hatful of four or five shillings was given. Hardy
had been longing for a book in a Dorchester shop-window, and bought it
with the forbidden money.[29] The mother refused to see any good in the
volume, a book of sports and pastimes, *The Boys' Own Book*. Hardy,
however, stored it in his long memory, and later extracted from it
Sergeant Troy's method of treading water and Farmer Shiner's technique for catching bullfinches for two of his early novels.[30]

Last and his Academy gave Hardy a full curriculum of mathematics
and Latin, and the master rewarded his progress and good behaviour by
giving him a prize at Christmas 1854, *Scenes and Adventures at Home
and Abroad*, and at midsummer 1855 Beza's Latin Testament. Mrs.
Hardy supplemented his school education by subscribing to Cassell's
*The Popular Educator*, and, the habit once formed, persuaded him to
continue spending his pocket-money on these improving issues.[31] He had
already acquired several Cassell's publications, such as *Lessons in
Latin*, and *The Illustrated Magazine of Art*.[32] Perhaps luckily, her
second boy, Henry, claimed attention, and she seems to have begun to
relax her exclusive affection; for though Hardy did not make schoolboy
friendships, and always hurried home, avoiding other boys, he began at
fourteen to have an interest in girls. Seeing a pretty girl riding in the
South Walk, near school, he showed the susceptibility that was always
to mark him, and fell for her for a whole week, until the sight of her
riding again with a young man ended his fantasy.[33] The incident was
recorded forty years later in exact detail in his novel *The Well-Beloved*.

It was from about this time, in fact, that Hardy later recalled a whole
bevy of Stinsford village beauties, each one with her special charm, and
all a few years older than himself. The leading lady in his memory was a

beautiful creature with bay-red hair, Elizabeth Bishop. She was the daughter of the Stinsford gamekeeper, Joseph Bishop.[34] She fascinated Hardy sufficiently for him to immortalize her after many years in a delightful ballad-like lyric *To Lizbie Browne*: the difficulties of rhyme and rhythm in the name Bishop had naturally been too much for him. Next on the list[35] was Emily Dart, whom Hardy remembered for what he called "her mere prettiness". He might also have recollected, though he does not say so, that she was an illegitimate relative of his. She was the bastard daughter of Rebecca Dart, younger sister of Sarah Dart who had married Hardy's uncle, John Hardy.[36] Next came Rachel Hurst; Hardy noted "her rich colour and vanity, and frailty, and artificial dimple-making", which he copied into the character of Arabella in *Jude the Obscure*. Finally, there was a girl with blonde curls, Alice Paul.[37]

Nothing seems to have come of these temporary attractions. At the age of fifteen there was a typically negative but more long-lasting event. The largest farmer in Stinsford parish, as distinct from landowning gentry, was Stephen Toghill Harding, of Stinsford Farm, a holding of over 400 acres.[38] Hardy's father had done building work for him. As a churchwarden, Stephen Harding had allowed the strange learned boy to join the vicar's two sons as a Sunday School teacher to the slow-witted though often very pretty rustic girls of the parish. It was another matter when the young Hardy began to be smitten by one of Harding's own six daughters. This was Louisa, a cheerful, lively round-faced girl, just over a year younger than Hardy. There is no knowing if she felt anything for him, but to her family he was, for all his precocious learn-ing, just another village boy; Louisa was forbidden to respond to his obvious glances, and his murmured "Good evening". He seems to have hung about her for years, gazing at her in church, at Stinsford and when she went to finishing school at Weymouth, and even trying to meet her when he came home during his first year in London. This totally negative encounter caused him to write several poems on her death in 1913, to seek out her grave anxiously in his own old age, and in his youth to moon about singing the air "How oft, Louisa" from Sheridan's *The Duenna*.[39] It was part of the curious psychological tendency in Hardy always to prefer a remote relationship to a close one. It may be allied to his dislike, from boyhood, of anyone touching him. He mentioned that his school-friends first found this out, and thought that no one else had. In fact, in a gossiping small town like Dorchester, where every hint of eccentricity was noticed, everyone observed how Hardy, to the end of his life, always walked in the road, regardless of traffic, to avoid brush-ing against passers by on the pavement, and how servants were instruc-ted never to help him on with his coat.[40] In his old age, outdoors, friends were careful to drop a shawl lightly over his shoulders, avoid-ing contact.[41]

The picture of Hardy's adolescence, so far as it emerges from these scattered anecdotes, suggests a strangely divided personality. He seems to have been very susceptible emotionally, yet at the same time fearful and nervous of physical contact. Mental precocity forced him into the company of his elders, with what often must have been bewildering results. Some of this bewilderment shows in his account of one of the dominant passions of his boyhood, his fiddle-playing. His reminiscences in old age[42] take on the oddly evasive tone which he almost always adopts over topics of deep significance to him. The Stinsford church choir of instrumentalists had closed down when Hardy was only two, and he never knew his father as a church musician; but Thomas Hardy senior was still in great demand for weddings, dances, and festivals, and from an early age Hardy himself went with him as a player. His own account shows curious overtones. He says it is strange that his mother, so ambitious for his purely intellectual development, allowed these performances, then adds "Possibly it was from a feeling that they would help to teach him what life was", an odd motive for a woman who had objected to innocent dice-throwing. On the other hand, he says his father, whom he always portrays as so easy-going, objected strongly to Hardy coming to such gatherings, though he failed to carry his point with his wife, "as he himself had not been averse to them when young". Perhaps this set of non-sequiturs about his parents, in which mother and father seem to reverse their usual roles, conceals some adult use of the boy for their own purposes. With an infant son, Henry, Jemima Hardy was house-bound again for the first time in ten years. She no longer had the help of her sister Mary Antell, now coping herself with a violently temperamental husband and four young children, John, George, Francis, and Mary (known, like her mother, as Polly). On the other hand, Mr. Hardy was still attractive and youthful-looking, blue-eyed, dark-bearded, and handsome. Moreover, his reputation among the girls was not forgotten, and even the county ladies, for whom he worked, found him charming. Was Mrs. Hardy's real motive in letting her son accompany his father to insure the latter's good behaviour and not-too-late return home? No doubt many of these dances were innocent lively fun as Hardy always makes out, especially when local gentry attended them. He and his father were remembered playing at the West Stafford house of Mr. Floyer, when the squire joined the dance, "up the sides and down the middle".[43] Yet village gatherings were not always under such control. If squire and parson were not present, or had left, and particularly at "Club" meetings got up by the villagers themselves, dancing could develop into the one relief in their hard-pressed lives, drunken and animal love-making. As *The Times*'s correspondent on the life of the Dorset labourer confessed, "scenes are enacted which can at least rival, if not exceed, the disgusting orgies of antiquity".[44] Hardy himself found suitably explicit classical allusion when he wrote in *Tess of the d'Urbervilles* of "Lotis attempting to elude Priapus, and always failing"

The boy was highly emotional where music was concerned, and these occasions excited him beyond measure. At one party his hostess had to seize his bowing-arm to make him stop, in case three-quarters of an hour of playing a favourite dance, "The New-Rigged Ship", should actually harm his health. The late journeys home had their incidents too; on one he was terrified by what appeared to be a white human figure without a head. His father, more used to such late-night sights, found it to be a drunk man in a long white smock-frock, leaning against the bank with his head on his chest. The boy had to help his father guide and push this apparition to its own cottage-door, where the man's wife pounced on her husband and knocked him down.[45] These were introductions to life that his mother can hardly have bargained for. The unconcealed love-making after the dance must have been tumultuous for the reserved adolescent boy. One incident in his puberty has come down to suggest this. Many of these dances and entertainments were at the homes of friends and relatives, and, in any case, the young Hardy was always in and out of the cottages of his Puddletown cousins. Mary Antell, in spite of her demanding family, welcomed the boy she had nursed, but his chief port of call was the home of his other aunt, Maria, at Sparks Corner. This busy but improvident family was reorganizing itself to deal with continued lack of money. The birth of yet another daughter, Tryphena, on 17 March 1851, had meant a fresh mouth to feed. It was uneconomic for the two middle daughters, Emma and Martha Mary, to continue helping their eldest sister Rebecca in her dressmaking business, when they could both be out and earning. Accordingly, sometime in the 1850s, both left home to go into domestic service, Martha Mary, the smarter of the two, to London, and Emma somewhere in Somerset; but the boys, Jim and Nat, were still around as companions for Hardy. Rebecca, with her own business and her mother's bouts of ill-health, was virtually head of the Sparks family. The Hand girls of all generations had strong family likeness, and with maturity Rebecca greatly resembled her aunt, Hardy's mother. This is perhaps part explanation of what happened. At the Christmas Mummers' rehearsal at Sparks Corner, while drink was flowing in the unofficial beer-barn next door, Thomas started making violent approaches to his older cousin Rebecca. He was caught and there was a family scene. The Sparkses, who had witnessed the enforced marriage of Hardy's parents, suspected that the boy might take after his father. All members of the Hand family were apt to flare into quick temper, women as much as men; Hardy's own mother had shared in the beating-up of her brother-in-law, John Antell. Maria Sparks, Rebecca's mother, is said to have shown the door to young Hardy and forbidden him the house. Though this did not last—his early twenties saw him visiting Nat Sparks at Christmas[46]—it was a severe shock to his adolescence.

What this shock, or perhaps something of the same nature, meant to him, is contained in another cluster of hints by Hardy himself:[47]

His immaturity [he wrote] . . . was greater than is common for his years, and it may be mentioned here that a clue to much of his character and action throughout his life is afforded by his lateness of development in virility, while mentally precocious.

Part of the difficulty in interpreting exactly this "clue" is the term "virility". Other usage by Hardy seems to confirm that he means the dictionary definition, "the capacity for sexual intercourse". In another part of his autobiography, he makes an amount of satisfied play with the fact that he was a founder member of the Rabelais Club, instituted in 1879 by Sir Walter Besant as "a declaration for virility in literature". It is clear that the Club equated "virility" with the portrayal of sex in literature, but Hardy, perhaps wishfully, seemed to associate it with sex in life. A subconscious envy of notoriously "virile" and sexually potent public men remained with him all his life. In his old age, he recorded a dream of his,[48] which could be the theme for endless psychoanalytical study. In this, he saw himself climbing a ladder, carrying a baby, which he was trying to put with great difficulty into a hay-loft. He wrote

My endeavour was to lift it over the edge of the loft to a place of safety. On the loft sat George Meredith in his shirt sleeves, smoking; though his manner was rather that of Augustus John. The child was his, but he seemed indifferent to its fate, whether I should drop it or not.

The association of Hardy's efforts with the indifferent onlooking of a spectator, who mingles in himself two of the most generally-known sexual symbols of their time, George Meredith in the nineteenth century, Augustus John in the twentieth, need not be stressed.

Hardy's own analysis of his sexual "virility", written at about the same time as this dream, does seem to indicate that he developed sexually very late, if indeed he developed at all. His voice was always considered to be very quiet, though not as noticeably as that of Sir Edward Marsh, a well-documented case of total lack of sexual development after mumps complicated by German measles.[49] The evidence with Hardy is too fragmentary for any final judgement; yet delayed or imperfect physical development is quite consistent with sexual curiosity, an attraction to the idea of love without the power to fulfil it. Hardy's continual speculation about almost every woman he meets, and his apparent habit of passing from one to another virtually without conscious volition, suggests such a pattern.

Whether the experience with Rebecca Sparks was really traumatic, or whether in fact there was some more general physical condition, the age of sixteen, up to which Hardy himself said he was "a child", was in many ways a turning-point. His own and his mother's ambition had added French to his intellectual attainments. At fifteen he had been given a text-book, *A Stepping Stone to the French Language*, and acquired a French dictionary and teacher, the French governess from the school in Dorchester attended by his sister Mary.[50] On the other hand, his father, though finding money for the extra fees, could see no exact profession for his bookish son, apart from a vague idea that he might enter the Church. Chance and the building boom provided the next move. Hardy's father was engaged to restore Woodsford Castle, a fortified fourteenth-century manor-house, a few miles across the Heath to the south-east of Bockhampton. While with his father, Hardy met the architect, John Hicks of Dorchester, who noticed the boy's all-round ability, and suggested he should help with a survey, as a test. According to Hardy,[51] Hicks then offered to take him in an apprenticeship. Hardy's mother, whom perhaps recent events made anxious her son should be settled away from Puddletown, struck a favourable bargain over the premium. She managed to knock down Hicks's original suggestion of £50 (he usually took £100) to £40 for ready money. So, a month after his sixteenth birthday, Hardy started as an architect's apprentice in John Hicks's office at 39 South Street, Dorchester.

# 4

# Apprenticeship

UNTIL his apprenticeship in 1856, there is no instance of Hardy writing either poetry or prose. In the previous December, he had copied in pencil, on the inside of the door of the grandfather clock at Bockhampton, the homely and sentimental verses by the Manchester poet, Charles Swain, *The Old Cottage Clock*;[1] but original composition seems to have been outside his thought. As for prose, his sole experiment had been the second-hand exercise of writing, for the village girls he taught in Sunday School, their love-letters to Army sweethearts in India. This may have brought him close to human emotions, since India was a dangerous place to be on the eve of the Mutiny; but, once again, it was hardly an original form of composition. Hicks's office in Dorchester, though, was an exceptionally literate place for a young man who already had a stock of reading in his head. The architect himself was very well-educated; the son of a country rector who had been a classical scholar, he was widely read, and allowed his apprentices plenty of time for their own reading outside their architectural studies. Hardy's fellow-apprentice, Henry Robert Bastow, was also well-educated. A handsome, cheerful-looking youth, a year or so older than Hardy, he had been to school near London, and had literary and scholarly interests, and religious ones too. Bred as a Baptist, he became convinced of the doctrinal necessity of adult baptism, and, in fact, was baptised during the time of their apprenticeship,[2] probably on 2 September 1858, when he joined the Baptist Church at Dorchester.[3] Lively intellectual and religious arguments and discussions took place between the two apprentices, in which their master Hicks himself joined. It is likely that Hardy found assistance for his part in these by buying two books, George Campbell's *Philosophy of Rhetoric* and Richard Whately's *Elements of Logic*, both of which he marked heavily.[4]

In the atmosphere of friendly rivalry in Hicks's office, and the light-hearted competition on points of learning and literature, Hardy came naturally from apt quotation and construing of classics to trying his own hand at writing. His first effort was as anonymous as the love-letters he was writing for the Stinsford girls, and has not survived. It was a skit for a Dorset paper in the form of an imaginary letter from the clock which had formerly stood over the Dorchester Alms Houses, and which had been taken down for repairs. The success of this adolescent piece of humour, which, Hardy claimed, caused the clock to be restored to its proper place,[5] indicates the lines along which his mind already worked. Letter-writing, thanks to his village practice, came easy to him; so did a clever boy's humorous misuse of quotation, and the adoption of a disguising persona. His effort was perhaps suggested by someone else's contribution earlier that year, in March 1856, another mock letter containing some of the excruciating puns fashionable at that period, and signed "The Wareham Town Pump".[6]

Another less imaginative form of prose-writing also occupied his apprenticeship time. He wrote for the *Dorset Chronicle* accounts of the numerous church restorations carried out by Hicks. These were all anonymous, but it is likely that Hardy wrote about St. Peter's, Dorchester, in both 1856 and 1857, the churches at Rampisham (10 March 1859) and Powerstock (3 November 1859), St. Mary's, Bridport (19 July 1860), the church at Combe Keynes (29 August 1861), and the newly-built churches at Athelhampton (2 January 1862) and at Bettiscombe (3 April 1862).[7] None of these contributions, if they are Hardy's, rises above the standard of competent prose. It is certainly likely that the two articles on St. Peter's, Dorchester, are his, since he definitely worked on the chancel east window and on the north vestry himself. The architectural plan signed by him still exists, and hangs in the church.[8]

His imagination, however, was strongly stirred in other directions which show the peculiar bent of his adolescent mind. Shortly after he started his apprenticeship with Hicks, Hardy attended a public hanging, and, as it appears, was very close to the gallows, which was put up high above the entrance to Dorchester Gaol.[9] It was, moreover, the hanging of a woman, who had killed her husband in a crime of jealousy, which had so many mitigating circumstances that they nearly brought a reprieve. Indeed, if she had not maintained almost to the last her husband had died from a kick from his horse, instead of, as she finally confessed, a blow from her hatchet, public sympathy might have persuaded the Home Secretary to leniency. The woman, Elizabeth Martha Brown, was nearly twenty years older than her husband, John Brown, who had been a fellow-servant with her. He had married her, according to gossip, for money, and the couple had lived at Birdsmoorgate, near Beaminster. She had caught him making love to a local woman, and had a violent quarrel late at night, during which he struck her with his tranter's whip. She retaliated with the wood-chopper, killed him, and then tried to conceal the crime.

This sensational story was well known, and a large crowd turned out in the early morning drizzle on 9 August 1856. Her handsome appearance, younger than her years, and her lovely hair, added to the morbid curiosity. So did her utterly calm behaviour, though her own vicar, a national authority on oriental languages but with a passion for capital punishment, chose to regard this as callousness. After shaking hands with the prison officials, she walked firmly to the scaffold, and seemed to show no fear. Even Calcraft the executioner showed nervousness. Since it was some time since he had executed a woman in public, he forgot to tie her dress so that she should not be exposed as she swung, and had actually to reascend the scaffold to do this. The execution was even the occasion of a leading article in the *Dorset County Chronicle* advocating the abolition of the death penalty.

It is clear that the sixteen-year-old Hardy, instead of going straight to Hicks's office that morning, got himself a good place to view this sight. In a crowd of three or four thousand, his favoured position close to the gallows can hardly have been an accident. He was so close that he could actually see her features through the rain-damp cloth over her face. It made an impression on him that lasted until old age.[10] The nature of that impression offers a somewhat disturbing insight into his mind as it then was. The well-remembered occasion had for him distinctly sexual overtones. He wrote in his eighties, in words whose unconscious tone is barely credible, "what a fine figure she showed against the sky as she hung in the misty rain, and how the tight black silk gown set off her shape as she wheeled half round and back", after Calcraft had tied her dress close to her body. For one ardent watcher at least, the hangman's would-be humanitarian action had created an additional excitement.

Even Hardy seems to have realized that these reminiscent delights were abnormal, for he added the excuse, whenever he wrote of this, that he was very young at the time.[11] The second Mrs. Hardy, assiduous to present her famous husband in a good light, wrote of the pity that he had been "permitted" to see such a sight—though he seems to have gone entirely at his own volition—and added "It may have given a tinge of bitterness and gloom to his life's work". This verdict hardly accounts for Hardy's obvious sense of enjoyment and anticipation, followed by a sensation of calm that seems to give the whole experience a sexual character. As for its effect on his life's work, or at least upon his most famous novel, another account, perhaps the most telling and circumstantial, certainly does suggest a deep impression with extraordinary personal overtones. On 2 November 1904, *The Sketch* printed the following paragraph.

Mr. Neil Munro tells a curious story of the origin of Mr. Hardy's "Tess". When Hardy was a boy he used to come into Dorchester to school, and he made the acquaintance of a woman there who, with her husband, kept an inn. She was beautiful, good and kind, but married to a dissipated scoundrel who was unfaithful to her. One day she discovered her husband under circumstances which so roused her passion that she stabbed him with a knife and killed him. She was tried, convicted, and condemned to execution. Young Hardy, with another boy, came into

Dorchester and witnessed the execution from a tree that overlooked the yard in which the gallows was placed. He never forgot the rustle of the thin black gown the woman was wearing as she was led forth by the warders. A penetrating rain was falling; the white cap was no sooner over the woman's head than it clung to her features, and the noose was put round the neck of what looked like a marble statue. Hardy looked at the scene with the strange illusion of its being unreal, and was brought to his complete senses when the drop fell with a thud and his companion on a lower branch of the tree fell fainting to the ground. The tragedy haunted Hardy, and, at last, provided the emotional inspiration and some of the matter for "Tess of the D'Urbervilles".

Hardy cut this out and pasted it into a scrapbook, which was marked "Personal".[12] He crossed out and altered the sentence suggesting he knew Martha Brown and also the erroneous account of the Browns' profession; but he then headed the cutting with the word "Corrected", and made no further alteration. This shows that the story, apart from slight details such as the exact murder-weapon, was accepted by him as generally a true picture. Years later, he himself repeated the story, almost exactly, to a young visitor "with a sort of gaiety".[13] He emphasized again the weird effect of the woman's features showing through the execution hood. "That was extraordinary", he commented in the later conversation. Yet the most significant detail is one found in this newspaper account only. Munro, a serious journalist and novelist, who would hardly invent at this point, records that Hardy "never forgot the rustle of the thin black gown the woman was wearing". The rustle of a woman's dress had enormous sexual meaning for Hardy. It will be remembered that when he recalled his feeling for Mrs. Julia Augusta Martin, which, he himself said, "was almost like that of a lover"[14] he paid special attention to "the thrilling 'frou-frou' of her four grey silk flounces when she used to bend over him", and even recollected the same sound having an effect on him when she came into Stinsford Church on Sundays. There can be hardly any doubt that hanging, and particularly the hanging of a woman, had some sort of sexual meaning for Hardy, which remained powerfully in his thoughts to the end of his life. This account hints that it supplied at least part of the emotional power of his best-known novel.

The sense of suspended animation at the moment of execution, and the feeling of anticipation, both virtually sexual in character, were again shown by Hardy quite soon after, at the next Dorchester execution. This was one which he clearly took great and extraordinary pains to witness. Almost exactly two years to the day after the execution of Martha Brown, another public hanging took place at Dorchester Gaol. The hanged person was a young man called James Seale, and his crime was a specially horrible one, the apparently motiveless murder of an

inoffensive and deformed young woman of twenty-three, Sarah Ann
Guppy. The murder and trial attracted a good deal of attention, and
a broadsheet was printed, giving full details.[15] The date fixed for the
execution was Tuesday, 10 August 1858. Hardy, far from being appalled
by the execution he had witnessed just two years before, noted the
coming event with interest and anticipation, as his own remarkable
memories show:

> One summer morning at Bockhampton, just before he sat down to break-
> fast, he remembered that a man was to be hanged at eight o'clock at
> Dorchester. He took up the big brass telescope that had been handed on
> in the family, and hastened to a hill on the heath a quarter of a mile from
> the house, whence he looked towards the town. The sun behind his back
> shone straight on the white stone facade of the goal, the gallows upon it,
> and the form of the murderer in white fustian, the executioner and
> officials in dark clothing and the crowd below being invisible at this
> distance of nearly three miles. At the moment of his placing the glass to
> his eye the white figure dropped downwards, and the faint note of the
> town clock struck eight.
>
> The whole thing had been so sudden that the glass nearly fell from
> Hardy's hands. He seemed alone on the heath with the hanged man, and
> crept homeward wishing he had not been so curious.[16]

What may well seem so strange about this narrative is the almost total
lack of horror at the hanging itself, and the fate of the hanged man.
Hardy is disturbed not by the event nor the moral and social ideas connected with it, but by his own sensations at the moment, and his own
isolation. "He seemed alone on the heath with the hanged man"
suggests almost a pleasant kind of horror, and he only half-heartedly
rebukes himself for having been so "curious"—itself a monumental
understatement for his eager early-morning dash out on the heath.
There is no doubt that he treasured the moment morbidly, since it is
surely the basis for one of the weirdest incidents in his first published
novel, *Desperate Remedies*. For plot purposes, Hardy had to make his
heroine suddenly lose her architect father. Almost any kind of death
would have done for her orphaning; but he chose to let her see, at a
distance, her father abruptly drop to his death from a scaffold round a
church tower. These two scaffold scenes, the execution and the accident,
are described in almost the same way. There is no doubt Hardy was
remembering the hanging when he wrote the novel.

This suggests an early thread of perverse morbidity in Hardy, something near abnormality. That he developed normally may be due to new
and powerful intellectual influences. When Martha Brown went to the
scaffold, the prison chaplain, Dacre Clemetson, was too overcome to go
with her. Instead, with firm steps, walked a tall, handsome clergyman,
known to Hardy through his mother as the preacher she had most

admired in Dorchester in the days of her youth. His name was Henry Moule.

The Reverend Henry Moule, Vicar of Fordington, had just won, in dramatic circumstances, his battle to be accepted by the parishioners of that teeming parish in southern Dorchester. The son of a Wiltshire banker, he had been in another Dorset parish before coming to Fordington in 1828, but his views and actions had brought him into head-on collision with the Dorchester locals. A strong preacher, he attacked the morality of places like the well-named Cuckold Row in the parish; his ear for music made him critical of the church choir. Finding the vicar interfering with both morals and music, his Dorchester flock conducted a long-drawn-out war with him. Each Maundy Thursday night, they marked Easter Festival by uprooting the vicarage railings and garden shrubs, and his children were jeered at in the streets.[17] Nor was he any better liked by the gentry, who decided, at a Hunt meeting, he must be a Methodist. This went on for the best part of twenty-five years, until the sensational year 1854 changed him from a villain into a kind of folk-hero. This was the year of the third great cholera epidemic, when another type of folk-hero, Dr. Snow of London, forcibly demonstrated his theory that the disease was water-borne by taking the handle off the pump in Broad Street, Soho. Henry Moule's action in the Dorchester outbreak was similarly dramatic. He moved single-handed among his dying and diseased parishioners, burning clothing, cleansing and comforting, absolutely without fear. Realizing that his church itself might be a focal point for infection, he held instead open-air prayers.[18] From that moment he could do no wrong for them, and both his sermons and his church singing were loyally supported.

Not only his physical bravery, but also his moral courage and social conscience won their hearts. Fordington, by an historical anomaly, was part of the Duchy of Cornwall, of whose Council Prince Albert was then President. At the height of the cholera outbreak in London, the Home Secretary found himself faced with the disease in the huge Millbank Prison. Since Dorchester lay remote from the public eye, 700 prisoners and their warders were evacuated to the Dorchester Cavalry Barracks, which was now vacant because the Crimean War had taken the troops. This was in West Fordington parish. The poverty-stricken homes there, long neglected by the Duchy, took in the prisoners' washing, and the clothes polluted the primitive water-supply. Moule was so moved by this administrative crime that he boldly wrote no less than eight letters direct to Prince Albert about the responsibility of the Duchy in this matter, and had them published in the following year. To see someone respectfully but firmly putting the plain fact of appalling housing and disease in their parish to the Prince, who had passed through cheering crowds in Dorchester five years before, was a revelation, never forgotten.

From being objects of derision, Henry Moule's children now shared their father's popularity, a dynasty of local heroes. They were themselves an impressive race. Seven sons[19] (one child had died in infancy) seemed to carry on their father's ideals of scholarship and service. Two became missionaries in China (one of them a Bishop there), one a country vicar. On the scholarly side, Handley Carr Glyn Moule was, first, Fellow of Trinity College, Cambridge, and then for nearly two decades Bishop of Durham. Charles W. Moule was Fellow and finally President of Corpus Christi College in the same university. Horatio Mosley Moule was a member of Queens' College, while Henry Joseph Moule, after a life of travel, found an ideal home for his strong archaeological interests in the curatorship of the Dorset County Museum in Dorchester.

It is not quite clear how Hardy got to know the family, nor which member he knew first. It was probably the last-named, Henry Joseph, since they were drawn together by water-colour painting, which the sixteen-year-old Hardy, after his childish efforts to please Mrs. Martin, was now taking up seriously. Henry Joseph Moule was an accomplished water-colourist, and Hardy first remembered him, in about 1856, standing by while Hardy sketched,[20] and criticizing freely, in a way common to the Moule family. Yet though they remained friends for nearly fifty years, it was one of his younger brothers, met in 1857, who had the greatest influence on Hardy.

This was Horatio Mosley Moule, usually known as Horace. Regarded by his brothers as the most brilliant of the family, his career suggests tragic inner tension and intellectual contradiction. He had first gone to Trinity College, Oxford, as a scholar in 1851, but had left in 1854 without a degree. In that year he matriculated at Queens' College, Cambridge, yet went down some years later with the Hulsean Prize (1858) but still no degree, and was not actually awarded his B.A. until 1867. According to what was virtually his obituary,[21] he was, however, a fine classical scholar. Whatever the reason for this curious record, it was a symptom of something deep-laid. Many large nineteenth-century families produced one member in each generation who was impaired physically, mentally, or merely temperamentally; the history of the Giffords, the family of Hardy's first wife, shows something of the same pattern. It is likely that there were some depressive elements in Horatio's make-up, quite apart from the disappointments of his academic career and even more disastrous personal events. At some undefined time, he started talking of suicide in fits of depression; he also tried to ward off these fits by drinking. It became an open secret with his relatives that he sometimes slept with a razor under his pillow, to be removed by them secretly.[22] He was the typical casualty of an outwardly successful and happy family.

There is no doubt, though. that whatever his temperamental handicaps, Horace Moule was a brilliant and inspiring teacher. This was officially recognized during a short spell (1865–68) as assistant master at Marlborough but unofficial, personal tributes are even more explicit. The chief of these came from his youngest brother, Handley Moule. He wrote[23]

> My dear brother Horace had a hundred charming ways of interesting and teaching me, alike in scholarship and in classical history. He would walk with me through the springing corn, translating Hesiod to me. He would draw a plan of ancient Rome with lines of pebbles on the lawn . . . Wonderful was his subtle faculty for imparting, along with all due care for grammatical precision, a living interest in the subject-matter, and for shedding an indefinable glamour over all we read.

This was the man who took virtual control of Thomas Hardy's life in the year 1857, not only as a teacher but as a friend. He gave Hardy, some time in this year, *Elements of Experimental and Natural Philosophy . . . for the use of Youth and Schools* by Jabez Hogg, and inscribed it "from his friend Horace".[24] This was intellectual food of a not much more elevated kind than the encyclopedic, self-improving volumes Hardy was still buying for himself, such as *Things Not Generally Known, Familiarly Explained* by John Timbs, and G. A. Mantell's *Wonders of Geology*, both purchased the following year.[25] Yet is was clearly in these friendly and intimate rambles in the fields round Dorchester[26] that Hardy breathed, just as described by Horace Moule's brother, a new world and atmosphere.

Many of Hardy's later references to Moule are laconic and formal; he is merely "a scholar and critic of perfect taste".[27] Such phrases carry little hint of the emotional inspiration Moule provided at these first meetings. There is, however, a later poem which seems to catch this moment with feeling and insight. It is called "An Experience" and addressed to "My friend", the term which Hardy always reserved, in other poems, for Moule.[28] This little-known poem has puzzled the few critics who have noticed it, one of whom[29] exclaimed in bewilderment that it suggests "an incident during a picnic". Hardy's totally exclusive use of the word "friend" for Moule, and the poem's likeness to the prose description by Moule's brother of Horace's effect on younger pupils, make it certain that here we have Horace Moule as he first appeared to the youthful Hardy.

> Wit, weight, or wealth there was not
>   In anything that was said,
>   In anything that was done;
> All was of scope to cause not
> A triumph, dazzle, or dread

To even the subtlest one,
        My friend,
To even the subtlest one.

But there was a new afflation—
        An aura zephyring round
        That care infected not:
It came as a salutation,
        And in my sweet astound,
        I scarcely witted what
                Might pend,
        I scarcely witted what.

The hills in samewise to me
        Spoke as they greyly gazed,
        —First hills to speak so yet!
The thin-edged breezes blew me
        What I, though cobwebbed, crazed
        Was never to forget,
                My friend,
        Was never to forget!

This fresh world of experience was given intellectual shape and back-bone by an altogether new type of reading. There is no instance, until now, of Hardy reading any weekly periodical other than the highly provincial and parochial *Dorset County Chronicle*, with its recital of farmers' meetings, rick fires and sale prices. In 1857, according to his own account, and certainly under Moule's influence, he began to read regularly a leading London weekly. This was *The Saturday Review*, and it had a determining effect on many of his basic attitudes and beliefs; he was still reading it seventy years later. Much of Hardy's peculiar mental approach can be found in its pages, and Horace Moule's intro-duction to this paper was deeply significant for Hardy's outlook on life. No dramatic fantasies are needed to explain Hardy's scepticism and criticism of human affairs, if one studies the files of this magazine, to which he was introduced at such a susceptible time of adolescence, and by such a winning personality.

*The Saturday Review*, founded in 1855, was one of the most brilliantly-written journals of its time. It was said, with something of an élite snobbism, that a writer for it who had not first-class honours at Oxford or Cambridge was a distinct rarity. Its chief task was to expose, in all fields, the hypocrisy and smug sentimentality of a large part of Victorian morals and manners, and to lash out at the smothering woolliness of most middle-class conventions. "There is no such thing," it announced, "as what is vaguely called absolute morality." It believed that social evils were, in the main, accentuated by social inequality. It declared that landlords were responsible for rural immorality, and that the two-roomed cottage was productive of incest to a degree that could hardly be conceived. In a leader called "Sweet Auburn" on 14 March 1857, just when Hardy began to read it, it took the lid off the sentimental middle-class view of village life in withering sentences.[30]

At the same time, the social criticism of *The Saturday Review*, though it bitterly exposed hypocrisy, was, in the main, intensely conservative. This was so much Hardy's attitude in most of his novels that it clearly corresponded with his early reading of this magazine; he accepted social inequality with little more than an ironic shrug. Alec d'Urberville has the power, and Tess Durbeyfield has not. When she usurps that power in despair, and kills him, society takes over and kills her. Hardy has his famous final comment, but he does not suggest any change in the nature of a society that can exact this ending. The same is true of the view of religion that he also imbibed, perhaps rather more slowly, from the *Saturday*. All forms of religious excess were criticized by the magazine, mainly for their intolerance of other forms; but no one religious position was ever defended. Equally, it attacked the vast revivalist meetings, the sensational tactics of popular preachers, and Anglo-Catholics and Roman Catholics alike. It was accused, naturally enough, of being an irreligious paper; but, it claimed, it only attacked those who made religion intellectually impossible for the modern man to accept. This reply was very much that which Hardy was later to make, in answer to criticisms of such novels as *Tess* and *Jude*. The Church, in all its aspects, he claimed, had not kept pace with modern life and modern intellectual developments; yet like the *Saturday*, he hardly gave any practical suggestion as to how the Church should perform this change.

What emerges from the pages of the *Saturday*, for all the verve and hard-hitting style of the writing, is an essentially negative attitude. The comment on the *Saturday*, made by Walter Bagehot in 1860, put this account of its purely negative nature in telling form:

> We may search . . . for a single truth which it has established, for a single high cause which it has advanced, for a single deep thought which is to sink into the mind of its readers. We have, indeed, a nearly perfect embodiment of the corrective scepticism of a sleepy intellect.

"Corrective scepticism" is exactly the phrase one can apply to an aspect of Hardy's own work, especially some of the early novels, when the reading of the *Saturday*, and its exposition by Horace Moule, was still fresh in his mind, to be introduced into the novels in pieces of some-what naïve digressive comment on life. In his first published novel, *Desperate Remedies*, what Hardy calls, rightly enough ,"a depressing picture of married life among the very poor of a city" is introduced by the quite unnecessary piece of cynicism, "Mrs. Higgins was the wife of a carpenter who from want of employment one winter had decided to marry". At the other end of the social scale, there are the paraders in

Rotten Row in *A Pair of Blue Eyes*, who "bear on their faces, as plainly as on a phylactery the inscription 'Do, pray, look at the coronet on my panels.'". Such destructive comment on human habits stayed with Hardy obsessively even among the far more sympathetic analyses of character in his later novels; in *Jude* one gets the absurd equation that all married people look miserable, so happy faces show no marriage has taken place. The *Saturday* habit of exposing pretension and sham often left him with nothing but a negative outlook to put in its stead.

It is clear, too, that Hardy soon absorbed Horace Moule's own habits of mind. One of the earliest prose studies by Moule appears in a little book of proceedings of a Dorchester intellectual society, which held its meetings at his father's vicarage.[31] An essay on Patriotism, just after the Crimean War, sets out to deflate the usual idea of patriotism as a military or militant virtue. There is a better way, not to die but to live for one's country, and to follow "the highest and best fulfilment of my duty to God and my neighbour". Hardy's own poems, both in the Boer and the First World War, explore this idea; it is those at home who have to go on living, who show what may be called true patriotism. Yet *how* they are to go on, he does not suggest.

These, and other such attitudes of mind, the young Hardy learned from this unofficial tutor, eight years older than himself, whose sensitive, almost feminine face shows him to be as attractive physically as he was mentally. Hardy was not the only pupil of Moule at this time. One of the many schools in Dorchester that took more advanced pupils was that of the Dorset poet, William Barnes, next door to Hicks's office in South Street. Knowing Barnes to be a philologist as well as a poet, Hardy, in some of his linguistic arguments with his fellow-apprentice Bastow, used to call on him to settle points of grammar, and triumph when the elderly schoolmaster-poet came down, as he generally did, on Hardy's side. Though Barnes was not one of Horace Moule's literary society, he had been an honoured guest there, and had contributed an original poem to its proceedings. Among the youths then at Barnes's school was one about a year younger than Hardy, Thomas William Hooper Tolbort. He possessed a passion and an ability for languages, which naturally found encouragement from Barnes; but there seemed no outlet for this gift in Dorchester, and he was apprenticed to his uncle, James Froud, a chemist in High East Street. At this point, Horace Moule took a hand in the making of his future, as he was doing with Hardy, but to an even more decisive effect. Impressed by Tolbort's gifts and hard work, he persuaded him to sit for the Oxford Local Examination. Tolbort took first place out of 900 candidates, and later went on to do as brilliantly in the entrance examinations for the Indian Civil Service.[32] Moule's walks in the fields with these two youths led him to see the more academic boy as a natural success for the new system of competitive entry, which was introduced by the Indian Civil Service Act of 1853. He did not, as yet, see as clearly what his other bright but not so narrowly-talented apprentice-pupil might eventually do with his passion for self-improvement. Besides, Hardy, rather healthily, also read popular thrillers such as Goldschmidt's *The Jew of Denmark*, which he purchased on 14 October 1857.[33]

In fact, Thomas Hardy's world was far more varied and broad-based than that of the usual bookish provincial boy. He recognized this when, looking back, he described it as "a life twisted of three strands—the professional life, the scholar's life, and the rustic life, combined in the twenty-four hours of one day".[34] He would read his copy of the *Iliad*, Greek text with Latin interleaved, from six to eight in the morning out at Bockhampton, then walk into Dorchester and work at Gothic architecture all day, and then rush off with his fiddle under his arm, often with his father and uncle James, to play at remote village festivals till dawn. Sometimes the bookish element was uppermost, as when he caught himself soliloquizing in Latin during his evening and morning walks to and from Bockhampton.[35] Yet his feet were kept on the earth by the human scene around him, the fund of human experience at home, among relations in Puddletown, and the events of the neighbouring villages.

One such experience was the death of his father's mother in the year 1857. She had meant much to him, and her stories were an enduring memory, deeply felt and demonstrated in a later poem to her, *One We Knew*. One hot thundery summer in his childhood, she had said casually, "It was like this in the French Revolution, I remember".[36] Now her death was almost certainly the seed of his first effort at original poetry. The form this took was also almost certainly determined by his new intellectual guide, Horace Moule. Moule, like nearly all vicarage children, wrote himself in a sort of sub-Wordsworthian style, lyric or blank verse. Hardy did not buy himself a Wordsworth until some years later, but he caught the style faithfully from his friend, and perhaps from actual reading with him, since his lines are much more exactly in the Wordsworthian manner than many imitators. However imitative and literary, their observation of the country scene gives them a reality that breaks through the conventional description and sentiment. Their ending, when he imagines his grandmother talking of her life when she first came to live in the newly-built house at Higher Bockhampton, has his own sympathetic identification with all forms of wild nature, and a foretaste, however immature and derivative, of what he might later achieve as a poet.

> Our house stood quite alone, and those tall firs
> And beeches were not planted. Snakes and efts
> Swarmed in the summer days, and nightly bats

Would fly about our bedrooms. Heathcroppers
Lived on the hills, and were our only friends;
So wild it was when first we settled here.

The voice from the past, and particularly one from a recently dead woman, always the most powerful inspiration for Hardy, is earliest heard in this, the very first of his numerous poems, and by no means the least successful among them.

# 5

# Religion

THOMAS HARDY described himself as being in his early twenties still "quite a pink-faced youth".[1] This is certainly borne out by photographs. Even more striking in their youthfulness are the two photographs taken in Dorchester at sixteen and nineteen, while he was still apprenticed to Hicks. For all his frock-coat, portfolio and knotted cravat, these show an almost boyish creature, like a child dressed in adult clothes.[2] The exceptionally slight figure and schoolboy face remind one of portraits of Swinburne. Nothing could be a greater contrast with the typical Dorset man, broad-shouldered and barrel-chested, rural·yet shrewd, walking town and village to the present day. Among these people in Dorchester, Puddletown or in his own parish, young Hardy must have appeared like some changeling, an innocent in a rough, practical world.

Hardy's is so much the traditional look of the fresh-faced Victorian curate that one can see why friends and relatives assumed the precocious boy would go into the Church. The times were certainly ripe for a youth of intelligence, even if self-taught, to think of ordination. Earlier, in the 1820s, one out of three beneficed clergy was an absentee from at least one of the livings which he held; but by the 1840s, reform had halved this number. A flood of money for church building had begun, and by 1858, over 3000 new churches had been built in fifty years, a process from which, as we have seen, Hardy's builder father had benefited. Church organization was reformed; in 1835 the Ecclesiastical Commission was set up by Sir Robert Peel, absenteeism became illegal, and there were other strenuous efforts for improvement, both public and private. In 1854, a leader of the Church commented that "It is a very rare thing to see a careless clergyman, a neglected parish, or a desecrated church".

Yet this good work, and the optimism it engendered, had received a devastating blow in the year 1851, when statistics about church attendance in England were gathered. In 1851, at the first thorough Census of Population,[3] a census of church attendance was also taken. It proved that on Sunday, 30 March 1851 only 7,261,032 out of a total population of 17,927,609 had gone to any form of religious service.[4] The general message was plain. In an outwardly worshipping Christian country, less than half the adult population went to church or chapel. The percentage of Church of England worshippers who actually went to church on this last Sunday in March, as compared with that of other denominations, was only fifty-two per cent to forty-eight per cent.[5] Not only was England merely half Christian, it was only one quarter orthodox and Anglican. This underlined a difference between church and chapel, which Hardy himself was to point out from his own observation, not many years later. "There are two sorts of church people," he wrote in his notebook, "those who go, and those who don't go: there is only one sort of chapel people; those who go."[6] This proverbial fact, numerically demonstrated in the 1850s, was the second blow to the pride of the Church of England, just when young Hardy might have thought of turning his talents to the ministry.

In one sense it might have seemed an ideal time for the Church to welcome a promising young recruit. There had been a huge leap in population. In the fifty years since 1801 the population in England and Wales had actually doubled; the growth in urban manufacturing areas had been phenomenal. A whole new race had grown up as heathens, hardly knowing the name of Christian belief. This was a challenge which the Church in the 1850s certainly tried to meet. Not only did it provide even more buildings; it set itself to man them. The 1861 Census, ten years later, showed nine clergy for every eight of the previous census; the reclamation of one's fellow-countrymen to Christ took on the nature of a crusade for many young men.

Yet there were limitations, imposed largely by the older and more conventional clergy. Bishops were on the look-out for any lowering of standards. Many required of ordination candidates not only a specialized training in a theological college, but also a university degree. The standard guide for any youth intending to enter the ministry was John James Blunt's *The Duties of a Parish Priest*; published posthumously in 1856, it went into four editions in five years.[7] Blunt, a Cambridge professor of divinity, assumed that all the men for whom he wrote had been well-educated at some university, and even that most of them were likely to be the sons of clergy. His typical parson is of the same social class as the squire, sharing many of his duties and attitudes. He is a learned man, who can read and study the Hebrew and Greek texts, and expound their meaning to his unlearned and simple congregation. An observant foreign visitor at this time noted[8] that "The clergyman . . . is a gentleman, often by birth and fortune, almost invariably by education."

This was far from Hardy's background; in fact, it is remarkable that until the age of twenty-five he still considered entering the Church.[9] Markings in his treasured copy of *The Popular Educator* seem to show that he took special interest in the regulations for entry into the University of London, which had provisions for "self-taught students".[10] Thomas Hardy senior, though, was already paying for his daughter Mary to attend Miss Harvey's School in South Street, and to prepare to enter Salisbury Training College for teachers. The expense of sending his elder son on a much longer course of education would have been far beyond his means, though Hardy himself liked to think his father could have afforded it,[11] and the project of his going to a university does seem to have been at least discussed.

Legend says that Hardy, about this time, actually applied for candidacy for the Christian ministry, and was rejected on the ground of his humble origins. There is no evidence at all for this unconfirmed oral tradition. Even if he had applied to the Bishop of Salisbury, any rejection would more likely have been for his technical lack of formal education rather than any matter of class. Walter Kerr Hamilton, Bishop of Salisbury, who established one of the new theological colleges there in 1861, was more likely to reject candidates on educational grounds than for any ungentlemanly qualities. A manuscript note from him can be taken, though conjecturally, as implying a certain disapproval of the number of non-graduates then, as he says, "pressing into H. orders".[12] The legend that Hardy suffered some sort of snobbish rejection is really derived from his own bitter and sarcastic remarks about the clergy in some of his novels, and particularly some short stories. A Bishop of Salisbury (Melchester) is pilloried and made a fool of in *Two on a Tower*. Perhaps the most unpleasant character in all Hardy's works is the egregious and cruel young snob who becomes a clergyman in *The Son's Veto*, which Hardy seems to have considered his best short story, and in which the horrible youth, Randolph, is probably drawn from his wife's nephew, Walter Randolph Gifford.[13] The passage most quoted to illustrate what are supposed to be his own experiences is from another very unpleasant story, *A Tragedy of Two Ambitions*.

> To succeed in the Church, people must believe in you, first of all, as a gentleman, secondly as a man of means, thirdly as a scholar, fourthly as a preacher, fifthly, perhaps, as a Christian—but always first as a gentleman.

It is perhaps significant that these two stories were produced when Hardy was conceiving and writing *Tess of the d'Urbervilles*, in which the gentlemanly Angel Clare and his clerical family—though allegedly based on Hardy's friends, the Moule family—behave so cold-heartedly to their social inferior, Tess herself. Yet these were not necessarily Hardy's feelings some thirty years before in the 1850s and early 1860s. He had experience, through the Moule family as they appeared to him then, of clergy who were far from setting themselves apart from the parishioners. His particular friend was not even a graduate, though he had been to two universities; this may have disqualified Horace Moule for the ministry, though he wrote a prize religious essay and an excellent text-book, *The Roman Republic*.

It is also untrue that Hardy suffered at this time the dramatic loss of faith which was such a feature of the lives of well-educated people in the mid-Victorian era. The two books generally taken to mark this revolution in the spiritual life of England are Darwin's *Origin of Species*, published in November 1859, and, perhaps even more immediately influential, the symposium entitled *Essays and Reviews*, which came out in the following year. Both, in their various ways, struck at the literal acceptance of Bible teaching and biblical infallibility. *Origin of Species* argued a process of evolution through natural selection instead of a divine creative act; *Essays and Reviews* largely subjected the Bible to the latest methods of textual and interpretive criticism. Out of its seven contributors, three, Baden Powell, Mark Pattison, and Benjamin Jowett, were the most powerful.[14] Powell, on the study of the evidence of Christianity, ruled out all ideas of miraculous intervention; Pattison, on the tendencies of religious thought in England, provided a brilliant analysis of the changing history of belief in the last 150 years; Jowett, with his slogan of "interpret the Bible like any other book", provided a standard of criticism which, for all its reverence, seemed to many a trenchant criticism of the Church itself.[15]

Hardy himself was impressed by these essays, and discussed them on his walks in the fields with Moule;[16] but there is no evidence that they changed in any way his own habits of worship or belief, at this very early stage. Though the evolution controversy was pushed into prominence by the famous clash between Thomas Huxley and Bishop Wilberforce at the British Association meeting at Oxford in June 1860, the idea that there was a definite conflict between science and religion took several years more to spread; it was not until May 1864 that *The Times* first had a leading article on the topic.[17] Similarly, the full agitation about *Essays and Reviews* was delayed until February of the same year, when a judicial committee of the Privy Council decided that what two of the contributors taught was not inconsistent with the formularies of the Church of England.[18] It was only in the mid-1860s that the struggle between new thought and old faith became acute; and this is the reason that up to the summer of 1865, Hardy could still think of a career in the Church for himself. It should also be noted that his virtual *vade mecum*, the *Saturday Review*, did not touch *Essays and Reviews* for a year after it was published, and then only did so to play down its revolutionary nature.[19]

Hardy's continuing orthodoxy at this time is best illustrated by the facts that at Easter 1861 he acquired and began to annotate copiously both a prayer book and a Bible of his own, and that on 27 September the same year, he got for similar purposes a copy of John Keble's popular pocket-book of Christian verse, *The Christian Year*, which consisted of poems specially designed for every Sunday and Holy Day throughout the Church calendar.[20] From these three books, it is evident Hardy was a punctilious church attender, not only at Sunday morning and evening service, but on most important Saints' days, sure evidence of his upbringing "in High Church principles".[21] Almost his first act after buying *The Christian Year* was to go, two days later, to the Feast of St. Michael and All Angels at Fordington Church, and to record the fact against Keble's verses for that festival. His pencilled annotations were, in fact, very seldom doctrinal or interpretive, and certainly not in any way questioning. Many in his prayer book and *Christian Year* form a kind of diary of the church services he attended, the actual church and the dates of attendance. We can therefore trace for at least the next two years, 1861–63, and often much later, just where Hardy was on any particular Sunday or church festival. His record for these years bears out his own statement that "he knew the Morning and Evening Services by heart including the rubrics, as well as large portions of the New Version of the Psalms".[22] What he meant by this new version was the metrical version by Brady and Tate, included at the back of the prayer book; this had a vital influence on him, both as an expression of religion in memorable form, for which it was designed, and also as a basis for his schooling in the twin arts of music and poetry.

In fact, though Hardy was an exceptional attender at church all through the 1860s, as these meticulous records show, the result was not any increase in belief—this could hardly have been greater—but a greater awareness of words and of the music associated with such words. Words, with Hardy, were never solely literary; they were almost always linked to a remembered and familiar tune, undivided. This is his real strength as a lyric poet; his poems are hardly ever formal exercises on the page, but contain the most subtle modulations, stresses, and changes, entirely reminiscent of musical composition. These variations, with their dramatic breaks in rhythm or emphasis, are used with almost infallible skill when they underline emotional states. This is what makes Hardy consistently our most moving lyric poet. His markings in his copy of the Brady and Tate "New Version" of the psalms[23] show again and again how a poem was identical in his mind with a tune. Often these tunes are named as those sung, as he notes, by the "Old Stinsford Choir", and appear in the music-books of his grandfather, father, and uncle. Psalm 16 was sung to the tune called "Frome", Psalm 23 to "Shirland", Psalm 78 to "Cambridge New", Psalm 106 to "Wilton", and Psalm 133 to "Lydia". Nor were words and music associated only with church-going; some were favourites for home singing by his mother. Psalm 16 and its tune are marked "M^r used to sing this", and the words do seem to express some of the stress of her upbringing and character:

> Protect me from my cruel foes,
>   And shield me, Lord, from harm,
> Because my trust I still repose
>   On thy Almighty arm.

The grim Psalm 53, denouncing God's enemies, was also a favourite with Mrs. Hardy, according to her son.

Although the emotional timbre given by the old psalter tunes must have been deeply stirring as they filled the rafters of the country church, the words themselves provided by Brady and Tate were little more than commonplace versification. Inspiration of a different and far more genuinely poetic sort came from John Keble's *The Christian Year*. From September 1861, Hardy followed these weekly poems for Sundays and Feast Days. They were the work of a considerable poet, whose best can stand comparison with the religious poems of Herbert and Vaughan, especially some of their openings:

> O for a sculptor's hand,
>   That thou might'st take thy stand,
> Thy wild hair floating on the eastern breeze,
>   Thy tranc'd yet open gaze
>   Fix'd on the desert haze,
> As one who deep in heaven some airy pageant sees.

Again, in the autumn poem for the twenty-third Sunday after Trinity:

> Red o'er the forest glows the setting sun,
>   The line of yellow light dies fast away
> That crown'd the eastern copse: and chill and dun
>   Falls on the moor the brief November day.

One critic compared the poems to the paintings of Gainsborough. Admittedly, few lived up to such beginnings. Many are from the start a kind of sub-Wordsworth. Wordsworth himself is said to have wished he had written them, though with characteristic reservations.[24] Yet the book was phenomenally popular. When Hardy purchased his copy in 1861, over eighty editions had been printed since its first appearance in 1827. Its main appeal was to people of all sorts who found its poetry easy and its sentiments orthodox; yet, in fact, both were based on the concealed power of Keble's scholarship, which had made him "the first man in Oxford".[25] It was just the book for someone like Hardy, with reverence for learning and a taste for literature, but with an unsophisticated background.

What held most fascination for Hardy was the variety of technique and form. Keble was no innovator; but he was a tireless experimenter with forms already tried and proved by the known masters of English verse, Spenser, Milton (especially his Nativity Ode), Wordsworth himself, and the seventeenth-century lyricists. His own lectures as Professor of Poetry at Oxford stressed the use of complicated metrical devices. Hardy's debt to Keble in his own later poems is not only in verbal half-memories, like the "bright hair flapping free" of his lyric to his first wife; it also lies in his ceaseless lyric invention. We may compare the two poem-openings by Keble just quoted with the last verse of Hardy's *Later Autumn*:

> Spinning leaves join the remains shrunk and brown
>         Of last year's display
>         That lie wasting away,
> On whose corpses they earlier as scorners gazed down
>         From their aery green height:
>         Now in the same plight
>         They huddle; while yon
>         A robin looks on.

The technique is virtually the same. What is different is the emotional charge generated in the Hardy poem. Although *The Christian Year* followed a much-loved young sister's sudden death, Keble's ingenious verses lack intensity of emotion.

Hardy's markings of favourite passages in his Bible seem to be of a different nature. These have the air of being chosen not for poetical or religious reasons, but because they had some personal application. Two passages are marked again and again, one in the Old Testament, one in the New. The first is among the verses in the First Book of Kings, chapter 19, which describes how Elijah came to hear the voice of God in the wilderness:

> And he said, Go forth and stand upon the mount before the Lord. And behold, the Lord passed by, and a great and strong wind rent the mountains, and brake in pieces the rocks before the Lord; but the Lord was not in the wind: and after the wind an earthquake; but the Lord was not in the earthquake:
> And after the earthquake a fire; but the Lord was not in the fire: and after the fire a still small voice.

Hardy marked this passage retrospectively for 1859 and 1860, and thereafter for every year up to 1864, and again in 1870.[26] It is, as he also noted, the first lesson at evensong on the ninth Sunday after Trinity, occurring in August. He made special mention of it during his first summer in London, in the year 1862.[27] His second favourite passage was the fifteenth chapter of the First Epistle to the Corinthians, which was the second lesson at evening service on the Tuesday in Easter Week,[28] and which he marked at various times and at various dates in April when he heard it. It is also, of course, the chapter on resurrection, read at the service for the burial of the dead.

Regular church attendance, the association of Biblical texts with himself and his personal life, the learning by heart of both the "Metrical Psalms" and *The Christian Year* poems, all suggest a young man of such high seriousness that the Church would be his natural home. On the other hand, Hardy had other interests and talents; his time in church was not entirely occupied in worship, as can again be seen in those little volumes, the Prayer Book and *The Christian Year*. On the fly-leaf of the first-named, during some service at Stinsford in 1861, Hardy occupied himself by making a sketch of a labourer friend of the family, William Bishop, dressed in his church-going Sunday best.[29] At a similar place at the back of his copy of *The Christian Year* are little sketches of a woman in a bonnet and a man, almost certainly his own mother and father, since the woman has the distinctive Roman nose Jemima Hardy inherited from her own mother.[30] Hardy was often reduced to impending giggles by the face of his vicar, which, he noted, had the clerical peculiarity of always seeming to be on the verge of a smile, even on the most solemn occasions.[31] Hardy's human interests and his sense of the ridiculous were saving graces in a young man whose intellectual growth might have made him a prig. These interests themselves were not, however, without their religious side. Robert Bastow, Hardy's companion in Hicks's office, following his own adult baptism, urged the doctrine strongly on Hardy, and advised him to be baptised too. He put the case for adult baptism as against the Anglican baptism of infants so strongly that Hardy actually came to discuss this with his own preternaturally smiling vicar.

The Vicar of Stinsford, the Reverend Arthur Shirley, was obviously bewildered by the weird and earnest young man. Nothing in his Oxford training had prepared him for such a question, nor had his own upbringing. He came from a well-known county family in Warwickshire, and his nearest brother had just commanded the Connaught Rangers in the Crimean War.[32] Grasping hopefully at the set reading he himself had done at Christ Church, some thirty years before, he produced for Hardy a copy of Richard Hooker's *The Laws of Ecclesiasticall Politie*. Somewhat mystified, Hardy ploughed through the eight books of this Anglican classic, but found nothing in it to his purpose. He had still less luck when he appealed to a curate of another parish; all that the latter was able to lend him was a handbook on the Sacraments of the most elementary kind.

Finding so little help from the clergy of the faith in which he himself had been so thoroughly brought up, Hardy characteristically struck out on his own, and got hold of as many notes and books about Infant Baptism as he could lay hands on. Though he found himself appalled by the feebleness of their arguments for infant christening, he decided to stick to those of "his own side". These, he still believed, were those of the Anglican Church, although, he later confessed, at some cost to his intellectual conscience. He and Bastow then went at it hammer and tongs, until Hicks's wife, in her drawing-room over their office, would send down imploring them not to make so much noise.[33] Bastow called to his aid the two Aberdeen University sons of the local Baptist minister, Frederick Perkins, who could quote in the original Greek from the required texts in the New Testament. Faced with this challenge, Hardy bought himself on 7 February 1860 the latest edition of Griesbach's text, which he had seen advertised as more accurate than his older one, and sat up at night studying this to confute his opponents.

Whatever the controversy did, it gave Hardy a scene in a later novel. The Scots father of the two young Perkinses appears in *A Laodicean*, where the arguments over infant baptism are faithfully rehearsed. Hardy was impressed by the character of these people, and their stubborn Scots virtues. His feeling that they were right on adult baptism was countered by a certain narrowness in their views, however much he grew to admire them as people. He even rejoiced when he caught them deserting their strict principles, and in his old age related with some malicious glee how, on one occasion, they had forgotten about a prayer-meeting when Cooke's popular Travelling Circus paid a visit to Dorchester.[34]

This friendly religious controversy also stimulated Hardy's further study of Greek. He had already learnt the rudiments from the companion volume to the old Latin Eton Grammar he had studied under Isaac Last. This second publication was Clement Moody's Greek Eton Grammar, first published in 1852. Hardy, in schoolboy fashion, showed his delight in the unfamiliar Greek characters by transcribing his name in them, Θωμὰς 'Αρδυ.[35] Now, far beyond such adolescent delights, he sat with Bastow on summer evenings on the gate of the enclosure of Kingston Maurward ewelease, comparing notes and readings of the Greek Testament, and even deserting Homer for the pleasure of more advanced scholarship.[36] This pursuit was broken late in 1860, when Bastow finished his term of apprenticeship, and hearing of the building boom in Australia, went to seek his fortunes as an architect there. Without the stimulus of controversy, Hardy went back to his more general classical studies, and a letter from Bastow, in May 1861, lamented enviously that while Hardy was reading Homer, his former companion, now in Tasmania, had not touched a Greek book since he emigrated. Hardy's *Iliad* once more became daily reading, and as at this time he started to lodge in Dorchester near the office, so as not to waste time on walks home, he got through a prodigious amount of study in his spare moments.

He had renewed his apprenticeship to Hicks for a longer term than the original three years, but what should be his next move? He was ob-

viously a promising architectural pupil, but his learned interests surely
indicated a larger sphere. Should it be the Church, fortified by his recent
study, and might that be preceded by a university career, to which his
basic grasp of the classics could be directed? It was natural in such
questions to consult his local link with these middle-class worlds, the
Moule family of Fordington. Early in June 1860, he heard the head of
that family, the Reverend Henry Moule, preach in his fluent extempore
way on the text from the Book of Job, "All the days of my appointed
time will I wait, until my change come".[37] Hardy's habit of applying
biblical texts to his own life made this an occasion he remembered for
the rest of that life, still recalling the vicar's intonation in his own
extreme old age. Was this a sign that he should passively wait for the
signal from God, whatever it might be? On the other hand, he had a
ready aid and adviser in his particular friend among the vicar's sons,
Horace, now living at home in Dorchester.[38] Notes dating from about
1860 show a close friendship between the two, in spite of their different
social background.[39] Moule addressed him as an equal, gave him books,
including a translation of Goethe's *Faust*, and even borrowed for him
from the Cambridge University Library.

Yet Moule's decision, when Hardy put the question to him was clearly
a surprise. Hardy had enquired, in his roundabout way, whether he
should not now read some Greek plays, Aeschylus or Sophocles, as a
preparation perhaps for a university career? Moule advised against this.
His opinion, which Hardy says was given reluctantly, was that Hardy
should press on with the architectural career, for which his parents had
provided the money. Since Hardy's father could probably not have
afforded university fees, this was sound worldly advice. Yet it also seems
to show that Hardy, in spite of early promise, was not an exceptional
scholar. Moule had backed young Hooper Tolbort's leap from his social
class into the Civil Service, seeing the boy had something special to
offer the larger world in his gift for languages. He did not see Hardy as a
pure scholar in the same light. It is difficult to know how he put this,
but something may be gathered from later advice to Hardy by another
member of the Moule family, Charles Walter. A dozen years later,
when Hardy was hesitating whether to go all out for a career as a
novelist, he consulted this brother. C. W. Moule quoted[40] from
Coleridge's *Biographia Literaria* to suggest "that literature will be most
efficiently pursued by those who are tied down to some regular employment, official or professional". Some dictum of this nature (which,
incidentally, poor Coleridge never managed to follow in his own life)
may have been the basis of Horace Moule's advice in 1861. Hardy,
he said, should not try to branch out into a life of scholarship or a career
in the Church, but stick to his trade, as architecture then was. Psycho-
logically, Hardy was young enough and hero-worshipping enough to

obey, just as he notably disobeyed the other Moule brother a dozen years later. At the latter time, he was urged and encouraged by his future wife. Now he had no one to give him courage in his own vocation. When his change should come, to use the words of the Vicar of Fordington's text, it would come from inner conviction alone.

# 6

# London

A FEW months before his death, Thomas Hardy declared that if he had his life over again, he would prefer to be a small architect in a country town.[1] Now, in 1861, at the age of twenty-one, he might well have had that prospect. Mr. Hicks was to die in eight years' time; Hardy could have succeeded him, and set up a profitable local combination of architect and builder with his own brother Henry, who seemed destined to follow their father. In actual fact, his mind was in a ferment. He was strangely learned, emotionally immature, pious and vaguely ambitious. His darker patches of sexual fantasy are perhaps hinted by a retrospective entry in his prayer-book. In spring 1860, he visited his sister Mary at her training college in Salisbury, and first saw Salisbury Cathedral. He noted the fact,[2] and then put a cross against verse 9 of Psalm 119; "Wherewithal shall a young man cleanse his way: even by ruling himself after thy word." He underlined the words "ruling himself"; but he also underlined, later in the psalm, "My soul breaketh out . . . My soul melteth away".

What move, if any, should he make? The examples among his own immediate friends and relations were not encouraging. His fellow apprentice, Bastow, seemed slightly disillusioned in Tasmania. Those of his family who had tried a move had little to show for it. His sister was pursuing her usual unobtrusive way at Salisbury, and was soon due to pass on to her life's role of certificated teacher, after a blameless college career. His cousins, James and Nathaniel Sparks, had gone to be carpenters, one to London, the other to Rode in Somerset; neither, in the event, ever made any money, though the latter eventually supplemented his wages by doing some violin repairs.[3] Of their elder sisters, Emma Sparks, in service at a house in Somerset, had married on 14 August 1860 Thomas Cary, the improvident carpenter son of a small Somerset farmer. It was possibly on a visit to them in March 1861 that Hardy made a sketch, which still exists, of Glastonbury Abbey.[4] They had settled in the hamlet of Faulkland, near the Mendips, and in August 1861 Emma produced the first of a brood of children, whose mouths eventually proved too many to feed. Failure, ruined health, emigration, and death a month or so after landing in Queensland were to be her lot.[5] Her smarter sister, Martha Mary, was away from home as an upper servant, and seemed likely to better herself, while the youngest Sparks girl, Tryphena, was doing well at the little Nonconformist school at Athelhampton, under its conscientious bachelor head-teacher, Mr. Holmes. Though only eleven, she showed enough intelligence to hope to follow her cousin Mary Hardy, and train as a teacher, the one legitimate way for a working-class girl to break through social and economic barriers. Apart from this, the rest of the Antells, Hands, and Hardys stayed where they were. Hardy's dashing aunt, Martha Sharpe, had also succumbed to frequent child-bearing and the hardships of emigration, dying at Paris, Ontario, on 28 August 1859 at the age of only forty-two. The Planet Ruler, an itinerant astrologer, had prophesied "she would have a large family, travel, and so on".[6] This had come tragically true.

Nothing suggested it would be to his own advantage to move; yet early in 1862, he determined to do so. It is impossible to say what made him feel that his "appointed time", in the words of the Vicar of Fordington's text, had come. Horace Moule may have relented so far as to advise him to seek a wider sphere in architecture, and perhaps combine it with literary interests. One of the books Hardy was reading under his influence was Walter Bagehot's literary studies, *Estimates of Some Englishmen*, and in January 1862[7] he gave Hardy a copy of the newly-published *Golden Treasury* anthology of lyric verse. Its editor, Francis Turner Palgrave, was the art critic of *The Saturday Review*, Hardy's weekly reading, for which Moule himself was beginning to write. The inscribed copy evidently had both literary and sentimental associations. Folded into it was a large skeleton leaf and, later, a printed cutting of Moule's own poem, *Ave Caesar*. A second and more dubious reason for Hardy to seek his fortune outside Dorchester is the story that he had just proposed marriage to a girl in the Mantle Showroom there, and had been rejected.[8] The girl, Mary Waight, was seven years older than him. The story of this proposal, and of a signed photograph of Hardy, was handed down in her family; but there is no confirmation of its truth, nor, if true, that it had anything to do with Hardy's move to London. More to the point, Hardy's father was in favour of the move, and his connection with house-owners and architects might help. He obtained from one of the former, described by Hardy as "a gushing lady", whom, presumably, the elder Hardy had charmed, a letter of introduction to Benjamin Ferrey. Hardy's other introduction, probably through his master, was to John Norton of 24 Old Bond Street, a friend of Hicks, who had been associated with him in Bristol before their ways parted, one to Dorchester, the other to London.[9]

On the Sunday before Easter, 13 April 1862, Hardy sang in Stinsford Church

> Lord, hear my prayer, and to my cry
> Thy wonted audience lend;
> In thy accustomed faith and truth
> A gracious answer send.

On Maundy Thursday, 17 April, he was in lodgings at 3 Clarence Place, Kilburn, where he spent his first Easter in London.[10] In his pocket was the return half of a ticket, from Paddington to Dorchester. He was ready to retreat if the adventure proved unsuccessful.[11] His landlords were a middle-aged couple called Allen, with three sons, the eldest, a GPO letter-carrier, being about Hardy's age.[12]

Hardy's unfledged appearance, his youthful and abnormally boyish expression, were evidently plain to see. "Wait till you have walked the streets a few weeks and your elbows begin to shine, and the hems of your trousers get frayed as if nibbled by rats," he was told. "Only practical men are wanted here." To his prospective employers he looked an innocent abroad as he ventured, the following week, into the West End. Benjamin Ferrey, at 1 Trinity Place, was polite about Hardy's father, whom he remembered, but had nothing to offer the son. Nor had John Norton; but rather than see such a mother's boy tramp the streets, he offered his office as a place to practise drawing, even though he had no actual vacancy. To this protective kindness, Hardy owed his first real job. When he presented himself on Monday, 28 April to Norton, he was told of a lucky encounter at the Royal Institute of British Architects. Norton had been asked by Arthur Blomfield if he knew of a young Gothic draughtsman who could restore and design churches and rectories; he packed Hardy off then and there to apply. On the following Monday, 5 May, Hardy found himself starting work in Blomfield's drawing-office at 8 St. Martin's Place.

For such a provincial adolescent as Hardy, this was a plunge into the very deep end of sophistication. The regular opening remark at the office, "Any spice in the papers?", recorded by Blomfield's own nephew twenty years later,[13] was already typical in 1862. The Thomas Hardy who punctiliously attended St. Mary's, Kilburn, and St. Stephen's, Paddington, was to find church architecture conducted in an atmosphere very far from "churchy", as he described himself. The two or three architectural assistants, of whom Hardy was one, and the half-a-dozen articled pupils, were left very much to their own devices, in a bustling office, whose Principal was usually away, supervising work on site. Blomfield had a fashionable practice, charged a stiff premium, and his pupils were public school men from the upper classes; Etonians were not unknown. Little or no formal instruction was given, either on the theory and history of architecture, or on applied construction. It was a kind of free-for-all plan-producing factory, full of distractions, high spirits, and horseplay.[14]

The character of the office in which Hardy found himself was that of its Principal. Arthur Blomfield was the son of one Bishop, and brother of another. He was now thirty-three years of age, brilliant, handsome, witty, a first-rate amateur actor, singer, and water-colour painter. He had unbounded energy and humour; at Trinity College, Cambridge, he and his older brother had been nicknamed Thunder and Lightning.[15] A famous oarsman and a well-travelled man, he was immensely sought-after, both professionally and in society. Ultimately, this was to his dis-advantage. He took on too many commissions, left too much to his assistants, and a great deal of his work became a matter of mechanical repetition, a stale hash of his early ideas. In the high Gothic revival of the 1860s his work does not stand the test, like that of Street, Butterfield, and others. Yet at this time his reputation was probably at its height. He was President of the Architectural Association, founded in 1847 to promote original ideas and to foster the training of young architects; at its meetings, papers were read and new designs freely criticized in healthy competition. Blomfield appreciated youth, and it is to his credit that he could recognize something in the diffident and uncertain West Country lad, so reserved and unsure of himself. It was the beginning of a mutual liking, and a friendship of many years. Hardy later paid tribute to his influence at this time, and to others who, in spite of their mistakes, "were really artists just awakening and feeling their way".[16]

The unguarded tone of the office, the racy talk and doings of the public school and university men there, were poles away from Hardy's previous experience. The strict upbringing of puritanical women, the doctrinal discussions with Bastow and the Perkinses, the homely provincial Church of England chat at Fordington Vicarage could hardly prepare him for this raffish company and their London ways of life. One of the pupils battened on to him to borrow money, which he could ill afford, and in later life even went so far as to forge Hardy's signature on a cheque.[17] All had a façade of worldly-wise experience. Hardy's sole hint of the sophisticated pleasures of Town had been gained from a fellow-apprentice during his first years at Hicks's Dorset office. This was a young man with the Dickensian name of Herbert Fippard, son of a Dorchester grocer and draper,[18] who had been on trips to London. Four years older than Hardy, he had demonstrated the delights of London society by whistling and dancing the latest quadrille in the office, while, in Hardy's words, "embracing an imaginary Cremorne or Argyle *danseuse*".[19] The memory of Fippard's action in Hardy's retentive mind now sent him off eagerly to the Argyle Rooms in Great Windmill Street and the Cremorne Gardens in Chelsea, where his childlike face must at once have attracted attention; for the girls there, disguised by Hardy's euphemism of *danseuse*, were all prostitutes, and their clients moneyed men of pleasure, prepared to spend, in modern terms, at least fifty pounds a night. A French visitor in this year described the Argyle Rooms as "a kind of lust-casino".[20] An English diarist wrote that in Cremorne Gardens on Sunday, 25 May 1862, "there was hardly an innocent face among the women, or a noble one among the men", while a mill-girl from Bolton, who visited the Gardens in June, roundly exclaimed "It's no fit for respectable lasses".[21] The respectable old age of Thomas Hardy caused him to muffle this experience: but it flickers in the ending of an otherwise decorous poem, *Reminiscences of a Dancing Man*, written in his restless fifties:

> Whither have danced those damsels now!
> Is Death the partner who doth moue
>     Their wormy chaps and bare?
> Do their spectres spin like sparks within
> The smoky halls of the Prince of Sin
>     To a thunderous Jullien air?

The office-talk was similarly startling; the morning cry of "Any spice in the papers?" can seldom have gone unanswered. Hardy himself said that the conversation was about notable courtesans, Cora Pearl, "Skittles", and Adah Isaacs Menken,[22] the powerful equestrienne of Astley's, who fascinated Swinburne, and performed her sensational ride as Mazeppa in a vest and shorts that made her appear naked.[23] His memory as an old man, however, somewhat telescoped the years. In 1862, the first two ladies had deserted London for more profitable conquests in Paris, while Menken, beloved by the literati as much for her quite professional poetry as for her apparent nudity, had not yet left her native America. Another lady he mentions, Agnes Willoughby, had in fact just hooked a rich husband and retired in triumph. What must have struck Hardy, though, was the class nature of the talk he heard. Many upper-class Englishmen, including clergy, kept a well-established lower-class mistress, and the fantasy-talk of the office made free with these names. An even greater shock for a provincial in London was to see the widespread and open street prostitution. At this exact time, it was estimated, there were no less than 80,000 prostitutes in London, many of them children.[24] One could be accosted twenty times in a short stroll along the Strand or Haymarket. A gentleman walking after dark in Pall Mall would be seized by a prostitute, and offered *fellatio* then and there.[25] Other women would promise to behave like dogs in every detail.[26] "The Social Evil", as it was popularly called, was the subject of a current show at a place Hardy also visited, the Cider Cellars in Leicester Square, where it packed the house. In a mock trial, the notorious "Lord Chief Baron" Renton Nicholson, having settled himself with a cigar and brandy-and-water, would "try" a case of prostitution, with girls and bawds represented by male actors; when the last ounce of indecent humour had been extracted, this was succeeded by more-or-less nude *poses plastiques* with real girls.[27]

The fact that Hardy, in spite of his architectural occupations, found time to be drawn into such places shows how much good sense there had been in John Norton's feelings that he should on no account be left idle in London. Even the innocent and outwardly respectable places he also frequented had their rough side. One of these was the popular Evans's Supper-Rooms, in an underground hall in Covent Garden. Here, it was possible to find two drunk and incapable clergymen waiting for a third who, when he arrived, proved even more drunk than they.[28] Observation of the clergy on the loose in London may have begun Hardy's gradual disillusion with the goings-on of Ministers of the Church. It was in this year that a West End bawd told Henry Mayhew, with rather charming diffidence, that "although we mustn't mention it, we hooks a white choker now and then, coming from Exeter Hall".[29] Yet perhaps more than drink or prostitution, it was sheer poverty that would impress a youth, who had already been trained to observe this in a county of huge differences between rich and poor. Here the contrast was even more apparent. The monogrammed carriages in the Park, which Hardy later satirized in *A Pair of Blue Eyes*, passed within a short distance of the human flotsam and jetsam, mere bundles of hopeless rags, sleeping out like beasts, men and women, in the dirt.[30] Quite apart from these workless down-and-outs, many working men and women were so scarred by hard labour that they had features more like animals than humans. Maids of all work and the dustwomen, who swept the mounds of refuse off the streets, had hands so calloused that the dead skin could be cut away as a blacksmith would pare the hooves of a horse.[31] Brawny milkwomen carried pails on a huge wooden yoke that bent their shoulders and rubbed them raw.

As always with Hardy, however, morbid curiosity into the seamy side, and horror at the hideous aspects of human life, were balanced by his insatiable intellectual pursuit of knowledge and self-improvement. The artistic and scientific side of a great metropolis drew him like a magnet. The chief draw, as always in his life, was music, and here the office had something positive to offer. Choral and church music was one of Blomfield's passions, and he had formed an office choir, into which Hardy was at once welcomed as an accurate though not strong tenor. Slack times in the office were used for practising glees and catches, aided by the Principal's own powerful bass, and Hardy records Blomfield's remark, "If you meet an alto anywhere in the Strand, ask him to come and join us".[32]

London also gave Hardy a chance for professional musical experience on an unlooked-for scale. It was the era of the great sopranos. Adelina Patti had just begun a career that was to stretch into the twentieth century, Therese Tietjens was at her best, and Christine Nilsson, the Swedish soprano, was also just beginning. Hardy heard all three, and others, in the operas of Rossini, Donizetti, Verdi, Meyerbeer, and Bellini. With a musical young man from his lodgings, he went to the newly-rebuilt Opera House, Covent Garden, and to the Queen's Theatre, Haymarket, Vanbrugh's original building, then known as the Royal Italian Opera House, two or three times a week. He was so enthusiastic about Italian opera, particularly the broad and beautiful melodies of *Il Trovatore*, that he bought himself a second-hand fiddle, and practised transcriptions of the famous arias with his lodging-companion, who luckily was an adequate pianist. English opera also offered a company performing at this time, where Hardy heard William Vincent Wallace's *Maritana* and Michael William Balfe's *The Bohemian Girl*. The work of these two Irishmen gave Hardy an opportunity to hear the failing voice of William Harrison, a moving and even painful experience.[33] By contrast, the drama was less of a passion for Hardy, though he saw Charles Kean and his wife Ellen Tree in Shakespeare at the Princess's Theatre, and was still able to enjoy, at the Haymarket, the actor-dramatist John Baldwin Buckstone, a comedian whose voice off-stage set audiences laughing[34] before he even made his entrance.

An even stronger passion was Hardy's obsession with the acquisition of knowledge and information of any kind. He afterwards said that one of his motives for going to London at this time may have been that the world fair or Exhibition was opening there early in the summer of 1862, and his movements in his first six months in London seem to support this. He went down to see it at the Cromwell Road for an hour every evening after work, two or three days regularly every week, and every now and then spent half a day there.[35] Shadowed by the death of its patron Prince Albert, the International Exhibition of 1862 seemed to many people only a pale reflection of the Great Exhibition of 1851. Unable to bear the contrast, the Queen herself had taken her widow's weeds to Balmoral on the very day it opened. Yet in the six months before it closed on 1 November, it drew almost exactly the same number of people as its famous predecessor, and showed the material progress of the past ten years. There was a comprehensive photographic exhibition, reflecting what was now the latest craze; William Morris exhibited furniture, and his firm was commended for its medieval design; the machinery section, mostly from the North of England, with cotton operatives from Lancashire and Yorkshire, was extremely popular. Exotic items included jewellery from an Egyptian tomb, astonishing in its modern appearance.[36]

Undoubtedly, one of the chief attractions of this Exhibition for Hardy was the excellent art galleries there. In Dorchester, he had practically never seen a painting, and his visual imagination had to rely on the black and white reproductions in Cassell's *Illustrated Magazine of Art*.[37] Now the Exhibition gave him not only the best from previous Royal Academy shows in the modern English section, but a particularly strong collection of French, German, Flemish, and Dutch paintings. It stimulated Hardy's new interest in art, already in full career from the permanent exhibitions in London, and reinforced by his methodical study. He and his room-mate at Kilburn, known to us only by the enigmatic initials P.S., were reading Ruskin's *Modern Painters* at this time, though it was not for another year, on 12 May 1863, that Hardy made a systematic précis in one of his earliest notebooks of all the European schools of painting, ancient and modern. He rounded off these regular visits by going to the reading room of the South Kensington Museum, only a short distance away, and at that time housed in iron sheds known to Londoners as the Brompton Boilers; here he could do an evening's reading before catching the horse omnibus back to Kilburn Gate.[38] It was pleasant, too, this summer to show his sister Mary round London, taking her to the Exhibition and to the theatre.

In these first few months of Hardy's new pursuits in London, he also promised himself to renew an old loyalty; he may even have hoped that his fresh veneer of sophistication might cause it to develop in surprising directions. He had often thought about Julia Augusta Martin, who had caused such an emotional upheaval in his childhood, before she left Stinsford in 1853. In the nine years since he last saw her, the Martins had established themselves in London intellectual society. Francis Pitney Brouncker Martin had not wasted his time as a landowner at Kingston Maurward, though Hardy hints he lost money on the home farm.[39] An M.A. of Wadham College, he was an amateur scientist and meteorologist. The disastrous wet and stormy year of 1850, when the Kingston harvest supper had been such a traumatic experience for young Hardy, had been the scene of a series of experiments by the Lord of the Manor. During the wild and windy April that had ushered in the season, Mr. Martin had observed the weather minutely from a spot "about 16 miles North of Portland Lighthouse, in the open air, on a high commanding situation".[40] This was almost certainly Hardy's own favourite vantage-point of Rainbarrows on the heath, where the whole circuit of the horizon could be viewed. Here he made exact calculations, which seemed to show a constant pattern of atmospheric currents. He had been instructed in meteorology by Major-General Sir William Reid, who had developed a circular theory of hurricanes and published a book on it.[41] Mr. Martin now extended his purely local observations in Dorset by collating numerous log-books of ocean-going ships in files of the Board of Admiralty. He had easy access to these, since his wife's father and grandfather had both been admirals, and indeed the former had suggested this study.[42] He emerged with, in his own words, "a settled conviction that . . . THE LAW OF STORMS is Universal, Semper, Ubique, et ab omnibus".[43] He demonstrated this theory in a book privately printed at Kingston House in 1852, which claimed to show a system by which the main storm tracks of the North Atlantic could be charted, their course forecast, and shipwrecks obviated; and though a companion volume, which he announced, on the Indian Ocean was apparently never printed, his original volume gained him scientific notice when he came to London in 1853. In 1857, he was elected a Fellow of the Royal Geographical Society, his proposer being none other than the President of the Royal Society.[44] As for his wife, she had a fashionable connection with literature of the day in her much-younger cousin, Hamilton Aidé, a most popular if now-forgotten novelist. It was on the doorstep of this distinguished pair that Hardy found himself standing one summer day in London. One does not know if he had done his homework, and read Mr. Martin's treatise. It is tempting to see the observations of the heavens by the young astronomer in *Two on a Tower* as some parallel to Mr. Martin's activities—he was at least five years younger than his wife. Again, though Hardy certainly did not need a rich amateur meteorologist for his knowledge of the Dorset weather, the strange fluctuations of the path of the storm in *The Hand of Ethelberta*, which the heroine watches as "typical of her own fortunes", have their likeness to some of Mr. Martin's exact descriptions. At all events, when the door of 14 Bruton Street opened, it was a pleasure for him to see William Henry Adams, the butler from Blandford whom he had known in the Kingston Maurward days.[45] He at least was unchanged. "But", as Hardy afterwards remarked in mock-comic dismay, "the lady of his dreams—alas!' Hardy's reminiscences here adopt the obliquity of reference that always afflicts him when any topic becomes acutely embarrassing. One can only guess that this reunion of the young man of twenty-two and the lady of fifty-two was somehow like the eventual meeting of Ellen Terry and Bernard Shaw, and even more disparate as to age. Hardy implies that she was very much "altered", being now in her early fifties, and that she was embarrassed by meeting "a young man of over twenty-one, who was very much of a handful in comparison with the rosy-cheeked, innocent little boy she had almost expected 'Tommy' to remain."[46] On the other hand, on his own evidence, he was still absurdly youthful-looking, and extremely innocent. He did not respond to her invitation to come again to her house, though he still had day-dreams of love-passages with her.[47] It is more than probable that much of the embarrassment was on his side, and had to do with her social status, even more obvious in London than it had been down in Dorset. His flight from her, cloaked by his off-hand remarks about his own "fickleness", may have been a panic action, and may indeed have lost him some of the professional advantages he needed as an architect. Her cousin, Hamilton Aidé, was not only a popular novelist; he was a lifelong friend and exact contemporary of Hardy's boss, Arthur Blomfield.[48] To be in Mrs. Martin's "set" would have given Hardy the social entrée that he afterwards said he lacked in his profession. At all events, any such opportunity was soon lost; for the Martins gave up their London house a year later.[49]

That it was some sort of flight is suggested by another incident later in the summer. One of Hardy's many girl cousins, Martha Mary Sparks, was now a ladies' maid in Paddington.[50] Early in August, Hardy sought her out, and took her for an evening to the International Exhibition.[51] The setting was not by any means a purely cultural one, in spite of Hardy's insistence on self-improvement. The fountains wafted a highly-scented spray all over the passers-by, the French Court was adorned with "two lifesize female figures, . . . in which bronze for the limbs & alabaster for the garments are combined in a manner quite unique".[52] Crowds gathered before the Tinted Venus, a piece of coloured sculpture by the veteran John Gibson, pupil of Canova and Thorwaldsen. Hardy had a romantic setting in which to entertain a young woman of his own class. According to her own brother,[53] he became attracted by her, just as he had been by her elder sister Rebecca, and more deeply. He even, at some unspecified time, wanted to marry her, but her mother barred the way. Martha herself was nearly six years older than Hardy; but this was perhaps part of the attraction. All the girls had the features of the Hand family, and therefore of Hardy's own mother. More than most mother-fixed youths, Hardy was falling in love with his own mother over and over again, in a physical and consistent way that was a typical part of his almost literal-minded nature. Besides, at this time Martha represented a welcome break in the alarming class-barriers of London.

We should know more about these aspects of Hardy if we could possibly find means to interpret the extraordinary "Diagrams shewing Human Passion, Mind, & Character—Designed by Tho⁸ Hardy. 1863". In these tree-like and snake-like pencilled constructions, often like designs by William Blake, it seems clear that the Passions are central, the pith of the whole growth. As the three elements come together, "Impossible Monster of the Will", "Impossible Monster of Intellect", and "Impossible Monster of the Passions", the last-named seems to gather itself into some kind of nuclear cluster. After an amalgamation of all three, there is a section marked "Moral Harmony", which then seems to produce various "Affectives Dominant", such as Friendship, Love, Ambition, and so on, of which only one, the Familial, appears to be adorned in any way, with curious-looking fruiting buds or flower-heads. Whether this really represents Hardy's intense familial sense, even to the exact interpretation of his apparently automatic reaction of falling in love with his cousins, is extremely difficult to say; but some such clue may very well lie in this strange exercise, which he evidently thought worth preserving among his notebooks,[54] though it may also be his attempt to reproduce pictorially "The Passional Tree" from a book known to him, The Passions of the Soul by Charles Fourier.[55]

We are on more certain ground in the events of his life that concern the "affectives" of friendship and of ambition. Both these received an addition in November 1862. In this month, his friend Horace Moule was admitted to the Middle Temple, and could be expected more in London.[56] Indeed, he had visited Hardy the previous August, and taken him out to dinner at the Old Hummums Hotel in Covent Garden, where he used to stay while in Town.[57] Also in November, Hardy himself was elected a member of the progressive Architectural Association, proposed by Blomfield, its president.[58] He had decided to enter for the silver medal of the Royal Institute of British Architects, and had chosen to write his essay "On the Application of Coloured Bricks and Terra Cotta to Modern Architecture", the title being picked from the four set by the Council of the R.I.B.A. for their annual competition.[59] It is possible that Blomfield, who had just built a church at Shoreditch of red, yellow, and blue bricks, guided his choice, and helped his work,[60] while he himself continued to gather material for it from his reading in the South Kensington Museum. Early in 1863, too, Blomfield's expanding practice made him move office; and by February, Hardy, the other assistants, the pupils, with masses of drawings and papers, were in 8 Adelphi Terrace. A few weeks later,[61] Hardy moved his own lodgings. The far side of Kilburn was proving too distant for his many activities. He went to 16 Westbourne Park Villas, in the parish of St. Stephen, a church where, from some of his earliest weeks in London, he had attended services.[62] Though it was still a fair way, he could now walk to the office. The exact reason for his choice of lodging is not known. One curious feature in this choice is that Westbourne Park Villas was, at that time, a fairly select social area, and not the row of Paddington lodging houses it later became. Only at the far end, a long distance away from No. 16, had the lodging houses just begun to sprout. Otherwise it was a street of middle-class professional people, civil servants and stockbrokers, or retired ladies and gentlemen living on investments.[63] There was a flourishing school for young gentlemen. No. 16 did not apparently normally take lodgers, and the owner seems to have been a gentleman of independent means. One possible clue is that the house next door, No. 18, contained an elderly architect, Richard Armstrong, and his son, who was an architect's pupil, though not one of Blomfield's. There is the curious fact that the father, and later the son, did architectural work for a brother of the new owner of Kingston Maurward House.[64] No. 16 was a pleasant, countrified semi-detached villa, with a small oak tree in the front garden.[65] Hardy must have found considerable comfort in his new digs; but he seems also to have found considerable loneliness, lacking the fellow-lodgers of a normal lodging-house: no more duet-playing and mutual reading.

# 7

# Self-help

THE new office was an instant success. Larger and south-facing, it also afforded exhilarating surroundings. Hardy drew and studied just inside the easternmost window on the first floor. When he felt idle, he went out on the iron balcony and looked along the river below. The natural shores of the Thames were not yet obscured by the new Embankment, though the works were due to start. Wharves and shipping still made the West End of London like some West Country sea-port. There was even one small dock, just below where he stood, an old quay by the side of it with some eighteenth-century buildings. These contained a little counting-house and a range of sheds with rough blackened timber and old dun-coloured tiles. Casks and kegs heaped the quay, and brightly-painted barges with reddish-brown sails lay at anchor.[1] With its sailor-like men coming and going, it could have been Weymouth. Hardy described it with enthusiasm to his sister Mary, now in her first teaching post at Denchworth village school, near Wantage in Berkshire.

The new quarters had their effect on the assistants and pupils in the office, now more light-hearted than ever. These cheerful iconoclasts scrawled caricatures on the white marble mantelpieces, with which the brothers Adam had provided the elegant rooms. An extreme splinter-group of the philosophical radical movement, the Reform League, had its offices on the ground floor below. Well-known left-wing characters could be seen coming and going. The architectural pupils, "Tory and Churchy" as Hardy said, decided to torment these worthies. They resorted to one of the oldest schoolboy ploys, letting down, on a string, little bits of paper inscribed with ironical and ribald satire to dangle on the heads of the reformers. The joke went so far that they eventually had to apologize to the secretary, though the matter was kept from Blomfield's ears. Hardy, a reader of the right-wing *Saturday Review*, and himself never keen on doctrinaire reform, seems to have enjoyed this upper-class activity.[2] His closer companions, though, were two young men from Benjamin Ferrey's office nearby, named Molsey and Paris. They were perhaps more of his own social class, and he lunched and dined with them frequently at Bertolini's Restaurant in St. Martin's Street, a picturesque old house with sanded stone floors.

He was, of course, intensely busy. The result of the R.I.B.A. prize essay competition was due to be announced some time in March 1863.

In the meantime, he decided to put in, by the twenty-seventh of that month, a design for a prize offered by William Tite, the architect of the Royal Exchange, who was largely concerned with the plans for the coming Embankment. The set subject was a design for a country mansion. With memories of his father's work, and his own memories of Kingston Maurward revived by his encounter with the former Lady of the Manor, Hardy found this a congenial task. A grandiose scheme, which still exists, very neatly drawn on a page in his notebook, may represent his entry. It indicates his interests that a very large library leads off the spacious entrance-hall. Ironically, on the page opposite he drew plans for "Labourers Cottages—4 under one roof at £80 each".[3]

As usual he was reading intensely, and enjoying discussions with Horace Moule, when the latter came up from Dorchester to eat dinners at the Middle Temple. Moule was suffering from one of his periodic attacks of nervous depression, which he put down to overwork and wrong hours, though the causes may have been deeper. He was now contributing regularly to *The Saturday Review*, and was also preparing a topical lecture to deliver in Dorchester, based on former Princes of Wales and marriages with Danish princesses.[4] Hardy's entry of Princess Alexandra's name in his copy of *The Christian Year* shows that the forthcoming royal wedding was much in his mind too.[5] A tremendous procession through the streets of London was planned for the actual day of the wedding, 10 March. The public, kept short of such occasions for over a year by the Queen's determined and prolonged mourning, responded hysterically. The crowds got out of hand, and Hardy had a lucky escape. He left the Mansion House area before the greatest crush there began. Spectators saw a woman carried out above the heads of the mass, and at first assumed she was drunk;[6] but she, and five others with her, proved to be dead. Hardy's friends, Paris and Molsey, were trapped here, and scarcely expected to get out alive. Hardy by that time had got back to the West End, having planned his walk in the reverse direction from most people. Even so, he was caught at the bottom of Bond Street, his waistcoat buttons torn off his small frame, and his ribs bruised before he managed to slip into a doorway out of the mob.[7]

By April he had received a boost to his self-esteem. Both of his current "*Ventures*", as Horace Moule called them, had succeeded. His design for the country mansion received the small Tite prize, and the R.I.B.A. awarded him their silver medal for his essay. He received this at the Institute's headquarters in Conduit Street from the hands of George Gilbert Scott. Hardy had studied Scott's own work on a visit in 1861 to Cattistock church,[8] where the London architect had added a south aisle with a polygonal apse in early thirteenth-century style, having found traces of an unusual medieval apse there already.[9] This presentation, on 18 May, was not without its ironic side. According to one authority, the judges' approval of this essay as "a very fair one" was accompanied by some criticism.

> The author of this essay has scarcely gone sufficiently into the subject proposed, and that portion referring to moulded and shaped bricks has scarcely been noticed.

They therefore could not recommend that the money prize of £10, which should have accompanied the medal, should be awarded. Hardy does, however, seem to have received some sort of consolation prize, in the shape of books on Gothic Architecture by Norman Shaw and William Nesfield.[10]

One does not quite know how this somewhat condescending verdict may have affected Hardy; in the reminiscences of his old age he takes care not to mention it. He does, however, say that at this point he began to be disillusioned with the type of architectural training he was getting, mere mechanical drawing: and, perhaps more significantly, that he had no ability for "pushing his way into influential sets", which might lead to a profitable practice. After a year in London, he was finding himself up against the class barrier that forms such a part of his earlier novels. Such was the snobbery in the professions at this time that he might have received the money prize without question if he had belonged to the right public school and university background; the judges felt free to teach a lesson to the unconnected young man from the country. At all events, Hardy dates from this time his return to literature and reading, which was in full swing by the end of the year. He had paid what was always for him a reviving visit to his sister Mary at Denchworth, and on 26 April had sketched her school there, nestling against the village church and graveyard.[11] Her simple admiration for a genius brother with his knowledge of Greek and Latin, a wonder she maintained till her old age, gave him the confidence his diffident nature always needed. According to his second wife, Hardy spent the smaller money prize which he was allowed to receive, the William Tite award of £3, on buying a set of Buckley's translations of the Greek dramatists in the Bohn Library series.[12] His annotations to these books belong to a much later date, but it does seem likely that here was the turning-point when Hardy took up again his systematic self-improving reading in all subjects. He bought the complete works of Shakespeare in a ten-volume edition, and by the autumn he was helping himself to take notes by teaching himself shorthand from Harding's *Universal Stenography*.[13]

Hardy, of course, turned in any matter of intellect to Horace Moule down in Dorchester, and the two kept up a regular exchange of ideas by letter. Moule was now writing steadily for the *Saturday Review*, and his application and conscientious reading made him a useful reviewer of all types of books. He did not adopt, except in minor details, the slashing

and destructive style of the rest of the paper. His notices are always
kindly and considered, if firm. In this, he is most unlike the character
Hardy is sometimes said to have based on him, Knight, the literary
critic in *A Pair of Blue Eyes*. For instance, Moule actually directed
Hardy's attention to his review, on 21 February 1863, of the posthumous
stories by Hugh Miller. Miller, like Hardy, was a working-class man,
and a stone-mason who had literally carved out a reputation for himself
with his geological essays, the classic *Old Red Sandstone*. Moule perhaps
asked Hardy to look at the review because it contained a message for
himself. "Self-education", wrote Moule sympathetically of Miller, "is
probably, at the best of times, a great deal harder than most of us are
disposed to imagine", though he goes on to chide Miller gently for having
written too much. Another review by Moule, a fortnight later, which he
also recommended to Hardy, was of a book on the claims of canal or
railway to cross Panama; here the detailed background reading Moule
had obviously put in was itself a lesson to Hardy.[14]

By June, therefore, Hardy was fully absorbed in the passion of self-
education. His view of intellectual matters, which in some ways he
retained to the end of his life, was that anything and everything could
be learnt, if one used the right books and took enough trouble. Even
style and technique in English literature was something which could be
got up from a text book, as a schoolchild gets up set homework. One
only needed to find the correct text books. He therefore applied himself
to the popular books and anthologies of English literary extracts.
Following the recommendations in these, he proceeded systematically
to analyse the style of the leader-writers in *The Times*, and to send his
conclusions to Horace Moule in Dorchester. Moule, perhaps a little
alarmed by such sorcerer's apprentice activity, sent a reply,[15] striking
a warning note which is of great interest when applied to Hardy's later
work. While admiring these analyses, he did not feel they led to much
real appreciation of style; such formulae only led to a superficial view.
Real style lay in the thoughts of a writer, and a real appreciation of his
style lay in a full understanding of his thoughts. One's own style likewise
emerged from one's essential thought. He advised Hardy to take a subject, and then jot down every thought on it that occurred to him, "just
*as* they occur", without any reference to logical order. Next day or
next time, Hardy could arrange the thoughts into headings, and then
have the basis for a piece of writing in which the prime motive had been
thought, and not merely external style. His warning against inserting
from others "some felicitous methods or phrases" was one which Hardy
might have remembered more often when he began to write novels, in
which odd bits of learned comparison or imagery are so often tacked on
with ludicrous effect, destroying instead of completing the point he is
trying to make.

Hardy was still very much Moule's pupil. The letters, with all their affectionate endings, are those of a university tutor to an undergraduate, and this correspondence was, as it turned out, Hardy's university. Early in the next year, 1864, the book that Hardy buys, though still in a sense another text book, is significantly titled *Thoughts from Latin Authors*.[16] Moule's advice on the importance of thought in literature was so well assimilated that, exactly two years after Moule's letter, on 2 July 1865, Hardy was applying its precepts to one of Moule's own heroes:

> Worked at J. H. Newman's *Apologia*, which we have all been talking about lately. A great desire to be convinced by him, because Moule likes him so much. Style charming, and his logic really human, being based not on syllogisms but on converging probabilities. Only—and here comes the fatal catastrophe—there is no first link to his excellent chain of reasoning, and down you come headlong . . .[17]

Hardy's notes on Newman's *Apologia*, which still exist,[18] bear out how well he has mastered this method of reading and criticism. They almost entirely concentrate on the stages of Newman's thought, hardly quoting and extracting from any of his brilliance of style or phrase.

What was Hardy to do with this new burst of intellectual activity? It clearly made him less and less able to think of himself as an architect; although he went on at the office, he began to consider this only a nominal activity, "an awful imposter at that, really", he said later.[19] Moule began to suggest that Hardy might follow his own footsteps, and go in for some sort of mild journalism. It indicates his tutorial estimate of Hardy's mind that he never thought of Hardy as a fellow-contributor to the *Saturday Review*, that province of those with university privileges and attainments. An architectural critic, using his specialized knowledge, was one suggestion. Another, in a letter early in 1864,[20] was the rather mundane one that Hardy could turn a useful guinea by being the local correspondent for London affairs to some provincial paper, like the *Dorset County Chronicle*—"Yr. chatty description of the Law Courts & their denizens is just in the style that wd. go down". One may wonder how much Moule's informal tutorship both helped and hampered Hardy's development. On the one hand, there were certainly appreciation and encouragement: "I cannot say enough in praise of yr. analyses. They *must* do your head good". Yet, so often, there is the almost embarrassed tone of a mind adapting itself to a less able one. The letter which suggests the job of provincial journalistic correspondent for Hardy is mainly concerned with a text book exposition of how to use the subjunctive properly. Though it is clearly a reply to an enquiry by Hardy on this topic, the fact that Hardy could not decide without applying to his mentor shows lack of confidence. When Hardy himself plays the instructor to his sister Mary by commenting on Thackeray's novels, he writes[21]

> He is considered to be the greatest novelist of the day—looking at novel writing of the highest kind as a perfect and truthful representation of actual life—which is no doubt the proper view to take . . . People say it is beyond Mr. Thackeray to paint a perfect man or woman—a great fault if novels are intended to instruct, but just the opposite if they are to be considered merely as Pictures. Vanity Fair is considered one of his best.

The interest of these opinions lies in their diffident expression. Hardy was not writing for publication, nor in a letter that might be handed round. Yet the tone is as though someone were looking over his shoulder, and the frequent qualifications sound as if he were expressing not his individual views, but what he had been told was correct by someone else. "He is considered"—"if they are to be considered"—"is considered"—all these phrases seem to shift the burden of judgement into more experienced hands. Hardy's natural uncertainty was increased by the unseen censorship of habitually submitting his opinions to Moule.

Another very curious indication of the same diffidence is that, as far as can be found, Hardy in the 1860s never visited either Oxford or Cambridge. In the same letter to his sister, he notes that she herself has visited Oxford twice already from her Berkshire village of Denchworth, and remarks, with what sounds like affected casualness, "It must be a jolly place. I shall try to get down there some time or other". There is, indeed, a persistent legend that Hardy had a hand in the building of the Radcliffe Chapel at Oxford by Blomfield in 1864;[22] but on examination, there seems to be no evidence for this, and much to the contrary. Apart from people who say that he "must have" done so, because of the Oxford scenes in *Jude the Obscure*, the idea relies on a misreading of Hardy's introduction to this novel. He wrote, "The scenes were revisited in October 1892", with exact precision as to the month. In October 1892, he revisited the village of Fawley and its neighbourhood in Berkshire, where, in fact, many of the major scenes in the novel do take place. He did not visit Oxford, apparently for the first time, until June 1893.[23]

Nor did he visit Cambridge in the 1860s. He may not have liked to ask Horace Moule to take him to the scene of the latter's academic failure; but from 1865, he had an opportunity through another member of the Moule family. In that year, Horace Moule took over the post of classical master at Marlborough.[24] He did so in succession to his brother Charles Walter Moule, who left for Cambridge to take up a Fellowship at Corpus Christi College there. Charles Walter Moule was well enough known to Hardy to warrant a visit to that university too; but again Hardy did not go. For a young assistant in Gothic architecture to avoid either place suggests some feeling of social or intellectual inadequacy in Hardy. It may be that he was even now, in some sense, his own Jude, and that this feeling of mental inferiority was an unconscious legacy from Moule. Then, too, there was Moule's own position. In spite of his connections with both places, he still had no degree from either university. There was some element of Jude there too; and Hardy must have pondered on the strange anomaly of his friend's unsatisfactory career. Moule's own family loyally supported the idea that he was prevented from taking a degree for so long "by stiff mathematical requirements that were shortly to be modified".[25] Yet in actual fact, these requirements, similar to those that had prevented the poet Wordsworth from obtaining a fellowship, had already been abolished at Cambridge by the time Moule should have taken his degree.[26] There are already hints of a greater mystery in the life of this man, who had such a dominant influence on Hardy at this time, though their contact lessened with Moule's job at Marlborough. Busy at schoolmastering from 1865, Moule had time only for occasional visits to London, to stay at the New Hummums Hotel in Covent Garden, and to go to the neighbouring Opera House with Hardy.[27] His bouts of depression, drink, and suicidal thoughts were by now established;[28] but it seems possible that in 1865–66 a new and alarming fact also entered his life. This was probably not fully revealed to Hardy till much later, though the enigmatic early sonnet "A Confession to a Friend in Trouble" may refer to it. The shadowed life of the man who meant so much to him was an added cause for disillusion in Hardy.

The stress and uncertainty for Hardy of these years, 1863 and 1864, should not, however, be exaggerated, though it is significant that on 31 July 1863 he underlined the text, "The spirit truly is ready but the flesh is weak".[29] Dissatisfied and feeling his way, he still had much to satisfy him and keep him in a more healthy mood. One factor was the reinforcement of his home and his family. Hardy renewed his country roots by going home regularly every Christmas, as did many of his relatives, including his sister Mary. At Christmas 1863, he anticipated having "a bit of a lark" down in Dorset with her.[30] The lark included a great deal of visiting and gossip and drinking all around Stinsford and Puddletown. At Christmas 1864, Hardy spent the afternoon and evening of Boxing Day with his cousin Nathaniel Sparks, back from his carpenter's job in Somerset. The Sparks home was much as it had been before, and Hardy was clearly welcomed there, in spite of his earlier contretemps with Rebecca. The youngest daughter, Tryphena, was continuing to show promise at the Athelhampton school, where she had been a monitor, helping to teach the younger children, since summer 1862. A sampler which she had lately worked, showing all the counties of England and Wales, demonstrated that like her eldest sister Rebecca she was becoming a good needlewoman. Hardy also saw his other cousins, the Antells, and spent some time in the company of a young schoolmaster, Arthur Brett, who like himself and Mary was spending Christmas holidays in his native Dorset.[31] The restraining hand of Squire Brymer was as yet not too heavy on Puddletown, and public-house drinking and family parties were in full swing all over Christmas.

These family contacts were clearly more real to Hardy than the varied but somehow unsatisfactory life in London, what he himself called "the fitful yet mechanical and monotonous existence that befalls many a young man in London lodgings".[32] His life was always coloured not only by the living personal presence of relatives and friends, but by the mysteries and obscure, often horrifying hints from the past and the dead. It was only seven years since his paternal grandmother, Mary Head Hardy, had died in the Bockhampton house, with her strange and hardly spoken childhood history at Fawley in Berkshire. Now Mary Hardy, her namesake, was teaching at Denchworth, a few miles north of Wantage. The hamlet of Fawley lay due south of Wantage, tucked among the fine escarpments of the Ridgeway and the Berkshire downs. Early in May 1864, Mary Hardy, obviously prompted by her brother, set off to spend a sketching week-end there, and wrote him a full account.[33] She found it a pretty place, "up among the finest hills I ever saw. The people seem quite cut off from the rest of us . . . They are among the most original & hearty set ever could be I think". She questioned them, but could find no memories of her grandmother, though the name Head brought from the parish clerk a strange story of a farmer of that name in a nearby hamlet. He had left his bride on the day after their wedding, and was never heard of till he came back quite an old man and died at Fawley. This addition to the family mystery, and Mary's news that the old church was being pulled down and re-placed, sent Hardy himself there in the autumn. He made a small pencil sketch of Fawley old church,[34] similar to the drawing of Denchworth schoolhouse and church which he had made the previous year. Whether he had more success than his sister in finding their Head ancestors is uncertain. If he had, he would have found suggestions of a tragedy and an unexplained illegitimacy there, a hint of his grandmother's horror.

Family and personal history loomed far larger in his life than the general history of the world around him, even when this touched on essentially working-class issues, which might have seemed relevant to his own life. The only external event that seems to have excited him was, characteristically, the public hanging in 1864 of five men for piracy and murder.[35] The American Civil War of 1861 to 1865 finds not one single mention in all Hardy's writings; it is as if it had never occurred. Yet it was the subject on everybody's lips in all classes of society during these years. When the Lancashire mills were deprived, through the war, of raw cotton, over a million pounds relief was raised for the out-of-work cotton operatives, thought to be the largest sum ever contributed up to that time by voluntary effort. Yet none of this seems to have interested Hardy, nor even the whole question of slavery, although Horace Moule sent him in 1864 a pamphlet by the liberal reformer, Goldwin Smith,[36] a Christian Socialist document[37] of considerable power and rhetoric, condemning "that supreme tyranny of capital which makes its victims slaves".

Again in 1864, Garibaldi, the hero of revolutionary Italy, made his remarkable triumphal progress through London. According to one diarist,[38] this was "The greatest demonstration so far that I have beheld", and it has been said that up to the present time, there has never been another like it.[39] One great feature of this was that, as *The Times* said, it was "a working-men's reception from first to last".[40] Another was that it was almost incredibly orderly, and the police had nothing to do. The contrast with the murderous hysteria of the Royal wedding crowds a year before was amazing. There was neither drunkenness, theft, nor a single serious accident. It was perhaps the most successful and peaceful working-class demonstration in the whole of the century. Yet again Hardy ignores it totally.

It is possible that he was so absorbed in his own affairs that he was not there to see it. On the day that Garibaldi's ship entered the Solent, 3 April 1864, Hardy was at St. Peter's Church, Brighton.[41] In spite of quite unsupported conjectures that he was there to take the sea-breezes for his health,[42] his obvious architectural goal was this remarkable church itself, which Sir Charles Barry had designed—winning an open competition—when he was still under thirty. This was a natural source of inspiration for a young Gothic architect.[43] At this time, it still had the polygonal apse, similar to that which Hardy had seen in George Gilbert Scott's work at Cattistock. For all the deprecating tone of his reminiscences, it is clear that at this time Hardy was still taking his work as an architect seriously, even though it may have been becoming irksome. His notebook shows a full awareness of all the exciting new developments in the world of building, some of which were taking place only a short distance from the offices in Adelphi Terrace. The new Charing Cross Station which opened on 11 January 1864, obliterating the old Hungerford Market, was generally reckoned to be a disaster, and a gloomy forerunner of utilitarian buildings without any sense of beauty.[44] Yet the Strand Music Hall, afterwards the Gaiety Theatre, which opened further along the Strand nine months later, was quite another matter, and of great interest to Hardy. Its much-criticized design by E. Bassett Keeling had individuality, and a novel use of modern materials, influencing later building, and fascinating Hardy. Its roof was constructed of wrought iron and zinc, and its cast iron columns had copper foliations to their capitals. Hardy, who often passed it, copied a part of a description of it from *The Building News*, and noted minute details, in which comparatively new materials were used to cope with some of the stresses of traffic, dirt, and other hazards of modern life.[45] He paid special attention to the bedding of the coloured glass sheets, in their zinc frames, on to india rubber, "thus facilitating the removal of the glass for cleaning, overcoming the difficulty of expansion & contraction, & obviating by the india r. beds liability to breakage or vibration", while in another place,[46] he noted from *The Builder* the durable qualities of the zinc, "abt. 35 years". Here was utility and use of manufactured materials that did not have to be brutal or unaesthetic, an architecture that kept pace with both modern life and older values. This idea runs through all Hardy's novels to *Jude*, and is exemplified in *A Laodicean* (1880). In this novel, Hardy said, he put more of his past life than he had done in any other up to that time, and for his architect-hero he coins the term "technicist" to express his ideal, the union of the technologist and the artist.[47]

At the end of 1864, Hardy seemed to be at some sort of spiritual cross-roads. Still technically absorbed by architect's work, revived in self-improving literature; still "churchy"—he seems to record attending Communion in Westminster Abbey in summer 1863 and other churches in 1864—and perhaps slower to adopt advanced ideas than has generally been thought; still waiting for his "appointed time" and the "still small voice" of his favourite passages in the Bible; beginning, as he had written a year before to his friend Bastow, to consider "the pen as one of his weapons" in his "*struggle for life*".

# 8

# Poetry

ON 21 SEPTEMBER 1864, Thomas Hardy had his head examined by a phrenologist. The "science" of phrenology, having had its heyday in the first half of the century, was now in decline, although it still had many advocates, notably George Eliot, Charles Dickens, and Harriet Martineau. It was categorized by Leslie Stephen as "popular with the half-educated", and indeed occupied much space in the type of self-educating journals read by Hardy. By the 1860s it was beginning to be rejected by scientists, and to fall into the hands of unqualified self-styled "professors". To one of these, Professor C. Donovan, M.A., 111 The Strand, Hardy submitted his bumps. He received a detailed report, long afterwards rescued by his mother from an old coat pocket. The three dozen "Faculties", into which the report is divided, animal, moral, and intellectual, often appear contradictory. It seems strange that those of Destructiveness and Constructiveness should both be "large". Among Hardy's intellectual faculties, it is interesting to note, Tune and Language are similarly labelled "large".[1] Although presumably the Professor did not know it, Hardy was on the brink of becoming an author.

On 18 March 1865, he contributed to *Chambers's Journal* a short humorous article, originally written to amuse Blomfield's pupils, entitled "How I Built Myself a House", for which he received £3. 15s. This little work, which has been heavily handled by some critics,[2] has great charm and is worth noticing. Parts of it are obviously imitative of his favourite writers of the day; the style of some of the opening sentences remind one of Thackeray, whose work Hardy had been recommending to his own sister:

> The new residence was to be right and proper in every respect. It was to be of some mysterious size and proportion, which would make us both peculiarly happy ever afterwards—that had always been a settled thing. It was neither to cost too much nor too little, but just enough to fitly inaugurate the new happiness. Its situation was to be in a healthy spot, on a stratum of dry gravel, about ninety feet above the springs. There were to be trees to the north, and a pretty view to the south . . .
> After a considerable time had been spent in these studies, I began to see that some of our intentions in the matter of site must be given up. The trees to the north went first. After a short struggle, they were

followed by the ninety feet above the springs. Sophia, with all wifely tenacity, stuck to the pretty view long after I was beaten about the gravel subsoil. In the end, we decided upon a place imagined to be rather convenient, and rather healthy, but possessing no other advantage worth mentioning . . .

This is very much in the manner of Thackeray's *The Book of Snobs*.

We were reading the passage lately at the house of my friend, Raymond Gray, Esquire, Barrister-at-Law, an ingenuous youth without the least practice, but who has luckily a great share of good spirits, which enables him to bide his time, and bear laughingly his humble position in the world. Meanwhile, until it is altered, the stern laws of necessity and the expenses of the Northern Circuit oblige Mr. Gray to live in a very tiny mansion in a very queer small square in the airy neighbourhood of Gray's Inn Lane.

As Hardy's effort proceeds to dialogue and character, the model is unashamedly Dickens. The client is taken by the builder's foreman up on the scaffolding to look at the chimneys:

Then a workman, with a load of bricks, stamped along the boards, and overturned them at my feet, causing me to shake up and down like the little servant-men behind private cabs. I asked, in trepidation, if the bricks were not dangerously heavy, thinking of a newspaper paragraph headed "Frightful Accident from an Overloaded Scaffold."
"Just what I was going to say. Dan has certainly too many there," answered the man. "But it won't break down if we walk without springing, and don't sneeze, though the mortar-boy's hooping-cough was strong enough in my poor brother Jim's case," he continued abstractly, as if he himself possessed several necks, and could afford to break one or two.

Yet there are individual touches of human observation which are quite Hardy's own. The swift financial calculations of the architect and his clerk, and his grasp of the lay-out of the building, so that "His professional opinions, propelled by his facts, seemed to float into my mind whether I wished to receive them or not" are all delicately and amusingly sketched. Over one human detail, Hardy was even more observant than he can have known. The plan of the house, when first marked out on the ground, looks so small, that although the clients "were told that houses always looked so", the wife insists the drawing-room must be lengthened. When Hardy architected his own house, Max Gate, just twenty years later, the rooms were found to be too small and dark, and extensions had to be built shortly after.[3] Even in miniature, Hardy already shows a grasp of human failings, including his own.

Hardy afterwards dismissed this small but successful exercise in comedy as "a trifle" and "unrepresentative".[4] The second description was not false modesty; for his mind was now set not on prose but on poetry. He was now evidently a kind of licensed literary feature of the office, a local pundit: a characteristic way for a shy youth to establish an individual position for himself. In this allowed character, he delivered half-hour orations on poets and poetry, whose burden was the superiority of poetry to prose; he even criticized Dickens, though at about this time, he was going to the great novelist's public readings. It is a mark of this new phase that in 1865 he began his own systematic self-education in poetry too. His markings in the *Golden Treasury* that Horace Moule had given him showed that what he mainly enjoyed were ballads and songs,[5] especially when they reminded him of his musical days in Dorset; Herrick's *Gather Ye Rosebuds* is annotated "My grandf<sup>rs</sup> song". There is also a habit, which was to become almost obsessive in his novels, that of comparison with well-known paintings. Against the lines from Gray's *The Progress of Poetry*,

> O'er her warm cheek and rising bosom move
> The bloom of young desire and purple light of Love

he made a note that they reminded him of an Etty nude, seen in the South Kensington Museum in 1863. He often was to quote the "purple light" in much this sense.

Such markings and stray preferences, however, were far too haphazard for someone consciously fitting himself to be a poet. In 1865, Hardy began what may be called his grand assault course on poetry. Like everything he did, it was thoroughly methodical; its concentration and detail remind one of another great self-educator of an earlier generation, John Keats. First, there were the basic tools of the trade. In quick succession, he bought *English Literature from Chaucer to Tennyson* by Henry Reed, P. A. Nuttall's *Standard Pronouncing Dictionary*, and, perhaps most practical of all, the *Rhyming Dictionary* by John Walker, edited and revised by J. Longmuir.[6] He is also said[7] to have possessed the recent *Manual of English Literature* by Matthew Arnold's brother Thomas. These were to be the guides to his new systematic ambition of reading and writing poetry. That he felt he needed such guides is shown by one of his markings in Reed's book. On page 11 of this work, there is the observation "It is a bewildering thing to stand in the presence of a vast concourse of books". Hardy put a marginal line alongside these words; they express the dilemma he faced.

Part of the trouble was the cost of this vast planned exploration of the poets. For Shakespeare, luckily, there were the cheap, popular seasons at Drury Lane. With one of Blomfield's more bookish pupils, Hardy managed always to be among the first in the crowded pit, leaning on the front barrier with only the theatre orchestra between him and the actors.[8] Here he saw *King John* and *Henry IV*, bringing to each play a good edition of the text, which he propped sideways in front of him to follow the speeches. In this way, he enjoyed the fine performances of Samuel Phelps, no longer actor-manager but still a great player, as Falstaff. If Hardy did not quite, like the architect-hero of his first published novel, "know Shakespeare to the very dregs of the footnotes", he certainly acquired a working familiarity with the text by this direct method. His later novels show a large number of references to both parts of *Henry IV*.[9]

Non-dramatic poetry was provided for him mainly by one of the many cheap editions of the time, Moxon's Popular Poets series. He had the works of Spenser, Milton, Herbert, and Thomson, with Butler's *Hudibras* and Percy's *Reliques*, in this handy form.[10] Of the Romantics, he bought and dated in this year an edition of Coleridge,[11] and he clearly already had an acquaintance with Wordsworth and Shelley through the *Golden Treasury*. Odd as it may seem, his annotations to these two are not matters of appreciation, but attempts to make their meaning clearer, a literal-minded way of treating poetry, which he retained to the end of his life.

There is no doubt, of course, that Hardy read Shelley at this time far more widely than in the limited selection of the *Golden Treasury*, though it was the lyric he annotated there, "O World! O Life! O Time!" that he later named as being one of the finest passages in all English poetry.[12] Hardy's first published novel is so packed with quotations from Shelley[13] that this poet must have been among his staple reading in the 1860s, just as a further burst of enthusiasm for his works in the 1890s left its mark everywhere in *Jude the Obscure* and in *The Well-Beloved*. J. M. Barrie, who saw and later owned the copy Hardy had used in his youth, said, "There are a hundred, a thousand, pencil marks on those two volumes that look now like love messages from the young poet of one age to the young poet of a past age".[14] Although Barrie may have been wrong in thinking all marks he saw were Hardy's youthful notes, since some passionate markings were probably inspired by Hardy's middle-aged fervour for Mrs. Florence Henniker, whom he called "the child of the Shelleyean tradition",[15] there is no doubt that Hardy read Shelley fervently in the 1860s too. He seems to have used two odd volumes.[16]

Luckily, one volume of Shelley that Hardy was reading in the 1860s still exists. It is a small one-volume edition, *Queen Mab and Other Poems*, bought and inscribed by Hardy in 1866.[17] His markings are numerous. Though many are linked with poetic appreciation, it is clear he is applying much of Shelley personally to himself and to his own life in London. Round the title of *The Revolt of Islam*, for example, he wrote the words "Hyde Park—morning", though one can only guess at the occasion prompting him. This poem, which remained an obsessive favourite all his life, clearly influenced his own work at this time. His

marking of the heroine's resolution to share an "undivided tomb" with
the hero is echoed in Hardy's poem "1967", written in the year 1867,
although Hardy's imagery—"That thy worm should be my worm,
Love!"—is that of Donne rather than of Shelley. His marking of
*Prometheus Unbound* was specially extensive. In this, he paid detailed
attention to passages of natural description, the exact effect of the
interplay of natural forces, with which more modern appreciators of
Shelley have been so concerned, the effects of wind upon water, of
shadow upon light. These, continuously marked by him here, were
afterwards used by him with the most complete mastery in poems such
as *Beeny Cliff*. His final marking

> To love, and bear; to Hope till Hope creates
> From its own wreck the thing it contemplates

has much of the style and stoic philosophy of Hardy's own early poems.

As for Wordsworth, Hardy certainly bought a copy of his works
during this time at Westbourne Park Villas;[18] but his reading of the
famous preface to *Lyrical Ballads* seems to have come later. It does not
seem that he was influenced yet by Wordsworth's theories of poetic
diction, although in his middle age he wrote poems of an obviously
Wordsworthian character, such as *The Widow Betrothed* and *A Sunday
Morning Tragedy*. Although these later poems also remind one of
Crabbe, whose works Hardy was reading in London, none of his own
poems bears much resemblance, except perhaps in the "realism",
which he himself said he learnt first from Crabbe.[19] On the other hand,
his addiction to Scott as a poet dates from this time. He probably read
him in another cheap edition, the one published by Routledge, and he
set very high store by Scott's poems.[20] *Marmion*, in particular, became
for him almost a touchstone for poetry, and it is somewhat surprising
to find him afterwards using as a term of praise the astonishing statement that Homer "was very kin to *Marmion*".[21] His sympathy for
Scott was probably heightened by the way the Scottish poet had
retrieved the old Border ballads.

Among poets living and publishing in the 1860s, Browning is always
cited as having the greatest influence on the early poems of Hardy;[22]
but, on examination, this hardly seems to be so. Hardy's convolutions
of style and syntax in these beginnings are peculiarly his own, and
seem to owe nothing to Browning's daring effects of rhyme and
grammatical order. Apart from two quotations from *The Statue and the
Bust* in his first published novel, all Hardy's references to Browning
come from much later in his life. So do those narrative poems which
echo Browning in their abrupt and colloquial way of story-telling, and
often in their choice of subject. Such are some of the historical poems
that form a large part of Hardy's *Wessex Poems*, printed in 1898. The

earliest date to any one of this group, all clearly associated in style, is
1878. The only poem of the 1860s to show any marked influence by
Browning is the curious and unsatisfactory set of verses entitled *The
Two Men*. Here one has a typical Browning subject, the ironic contrast
between the careers of two schoolmates, and a typical Browning
opening stanza:

> There were two youths of equal age,
> Wit, station, strength, and parentage;
> They studied at the selfsame schools,
> And shaped their thoughts by common rules.

Its original title, *The World's Verdict: a morality rime*, also suggests
Browning; but apart from this, and perhaps the equally curious verses
written for Blomfield, *Heiress and Architect*, the influence of Browning
on Hardy's early poems seems negligible.

If Browning, among contemporaries, had little effect on him at this
time, still less had Tennyson. Yet poets for whom Hardy did have an
enthusiasm equally failed to affect his own style. In this year, 1865,
Swinburne's *Atalanta in Calydon* was published, and Hardy was one of
its earliest admirers. When this was followed in 1866 by *Poems and
Ballads*, Hardy used to walk from Westbourne Park Villas to the office
with a copy in his pocket, even reading it, as he said, "walking along
the crowded London streets to my imminent risk of being knocked
down".[23] In spite of this enthusiasm, and his indignation at the attacks
on Swinburne, which, as he also said, made his blood boil, there is not a
touch of Swinburne's style in his own work. He seems to have let the
liquid lyric gift wash over him in a tide of pure pleasure, without once
considering it as a model.

In actual fact, the one book of contemporary verse from which Hardy
seems to have learnt anything was George Meredith's *Modern Love*,
published in 1862. Hardy was unaffected in his admiration for this work
even when his own favourite *Saturday Review* launched its notorious
and violent attack on Meredith for writing it:[24]

> With the great literary error of *Don Juan* before his eyes, it was
> scarcely worth his while to commit the sickly little peccadillo of
> *Modern Love*.

It was probably the unfair abuse of this work, pilloried elsewhere as
"modern lust", that made Hardy give it special attention. It is certainly the major influence on Hardy's sonnets, which form at least half
of the poems he allowed to remain from these years in London. Yet even
here, there must be one reservation. Hardy's sonnets and the *Modern
Love* sequence have in common that both derive from Shakespeare.
Meredith disguised his debt by adding to his own "sonnets" two extra
lines, giving a breadth and rhetorical emphasis; he also—and here he

was followed by Hardy—used a variety of extended and non-Shakes-
pearian images, the type of language that, in its own day, could truly
be called "modern". It is sometimes the language of new, contemporary
thought—

> What are we first? First, animals; and next
> Intelligences at a leap;

More often it consists of similes which introduce a romantic and non-
Elizabethan touch into what seems a Shakespearian opening:

> Thus piteously Love closed what he begat;
> The union of this ever-diverse pair!
> These two were rapid falcons in a snare,
> Condemned to do the flitting of the bat.

Hardy, in his own sonnets, is not so skilful in escaping the purely
Shakespearian echo. These lines, written in the summer of 1866, could
have come straight from a Shakespeare sonnet:

> As common chests encasing wares of price
> Are borne with tenderness through halls of state,
> Their core their warrant,

One is instantly reminded of Sonnet 52:

> So is the time that keeps you as my chest,
> Or as the wardrobe which the robe doth hide,
> To make some special instant special blest,

Yet at other times he achieves, within the Shakespearian form, a
Meredithian freedom of imagery.

> Amid the happy people of my time
> Who work their love's fulfilment, I appear
> Numb as a vane that cankers on its point,
> True to the wind that kissed ere canker came:

or again, writing of an untoward thought,

> It goes, like murky bird or buccaneer
> That shapes its lawless figure on the main,

and, in some better-known lines in their earliest known version,

> Remembering that with me lies not the blame,
> That Sportsman Time but rears his brood to kill,

He also expresses the "modern" scepticism, common in Meredith:

> —Crass Casualty obstructs the sun and rain,
> And dicing Time for gladness casts a moan . . .

What certainly emerges, even from these smoother and more imitative
examples of Hardy's early poetry, is his intense and original treatment
of words. It is true that in what has been considered his most auto-
biographical novel, *A Laodicean*, he has a clumsy and jocular satire on

himself as a poet in his mid-twenties, when he describes his architect-
hero's efforts at verse:

> For two whole years he did nothing but write verse in every con-
> ceivable metre, and on every conceivable subject, from Wordsworthian
> sonnets on the singing of his tea-kettle to epic fragments on the Fall of
> Empires.

Although the literal truth of the epic fragments on the Fall of Empires
may be doubted, there is no doubt that, as he confesses elsewhere,[25]
Hardy tried at this time to turn the Book of Ecclesiastes into Spenserian
stanzas, an extraordinary task that fortunately defeated him before he
had gone too far with it. In fact, the main tone of the surviving poems
of these two years, 1865–67, is one of a fierce and determined individual
concern with words. In this, they are unlike the early verses of any
other writer. To be fascinated by words themselves is common with
young poets; but to try and manipulate and vary them, until they form
what is virtually a new language, is unique. Even Hardy's contemporary
Hopkins, in poems written at this exact time, is not nearly as original,
although drastic later revision to such poems as *Heaven-Haven* and *The
Habit of Perfection* may make it appear that he was.[26]

Part of this determined originality can be seen in Hardy's copy of
Walker's *Rhyming Dictionary*, which still exists.[27] Hardy not only took
attractive rhyming words from the dictionary itself—"buccaneer", in
the sonnet just quoted is probably one; he also set about enlarging the
dictionary's list of rhymes with his own individual collection. These
additions are interesting, first of all, in showing how he plundered for
literary purposes the vocabulary of his own profession. A number of
these are both architectural and "churchy". They include the words
ogee, epistyle, peristyle, introit, and terce, the last further glossed by
Hardy with the word "service" in brackets. The fact that he added some
new words to existing lists of rhymes also gives an illuminating clue to
his own pronunciation, which was not always in the standard English
he afterwards claimed to use. "Groat" in his added annotation is given
as a rhyme for "ought" and "bought". It is clear that he pronounced it
"grought", as he had perhaps heard people do in Dorset.

In fact, the largest number of additional rhymes, recorded by Hardy
as acceptable, are country or sometimes specifically Dorset words. It is
clear that these were natural to him, and that he added them not as
curiosities but for legitimate usage in his poetry. This is fully borne out
in the paragraph, with which he prefaced, many years later, his first
published book of verse:[28]

> Whenever an ancient and legitimate word of the district, for which
> there was no equivalent in received English, suggested itself as the most
> natural, nearest, and often only expression of a thought, it has been
> made use of, on what seemed good grounds.

This is the great difference between Hardy's poetic vocabulary and that of Barnes. Barnes is writing in a calculated dialect, observed by him as a philologist; this is why his Dorset poems, even at their best, have something of the air of an academic exercise. With Hardy, the use of a local word was, as he says, natural, and this is seen by the way he recorded such terms in his copy of the *Rhyming Dictionary*. Not all these terms, of course, were actually used in the poems of this date which have survived, attractive though some of them seem to us. One can only regret that he did not find use for "fellowfeel", meaning sympathize, or "palampore" for counterpane. On the other hand, the delightful "wanze" for grow pale, or decay, was effectively used by him in a much later poem, *The Beauty*.

It is true that sometimes, when he had used one of these words for a particular, and, as he would say, legitimate effect, he seems to have grown self-conscious and removed it in a later draft. An example of this is the first line of *The Temporary the All*, which begins *Wessex Poems*. This poem, although undated, seems obviously to come from the 1860s which it describes. For one thing, it is an essay in writing English Sapphics, a task almost as difficult as trying to turn Ecclesiastes into Spenserians, and typical of what Hardy tells us of his experiments at that period. It also uses a large number of local words, and, in fact, originally started with the line

> Change and chancefulness in my bloothing youthtime

The bold oddity of "bloothing youthtime" appealed to Hardy in his early experimental stage, and in his *Rhyming Dictionary* he had added the word "Blooth", meaning bloom, to the rhymes there for "youth". When he came to print the poem thirty years later, however, Hardy seems to have felt he had gone too far in his first dashing enthusiasm, and substituted the innocuous but feeble "flowering".

What is perhaps most interesting of all, in the light it throws on one distinctive habit of Hardy's first poems, is the large number of words he added to the dictionary with what are, to us, unusual prefixes. Some are usages found in country places still. "Eachwhere", "everywhen" and especially "anywhen" can be heard today in south-west England. Less usual, possibly even in Hardy's own time, is his use of "fore" (with a hyphen) for "former". He added to the dictionary the words "fore-wife" and "fore-strife". Most significant for their use in the poems are the number of words he added with the prefixes "un" and "out", particularly the former. It seems clear from this that he did not regard the prefix "un" as implying a negative modification of the original word, but as the complete negation of it, and therefore an entirely separate word. In this sense, it is used freely throughout all his early poems. It appears again and again in the sonnets. "Unblooms" in the

1  (*a*) The Heath, near Hardy's birthplace, with a distant view of Dorchester

(*b*) The old West Gallery, Stinsford Church

Old West Gallery, Stinsford

2  (a)  Hardy's maternal uncles, William, Henery, and Christopher Hand

(b) (*left*) Thomas Hardy senior

(c) (*right*) Hardy's aunt's husband, John Brereton Sharpe (possibly the original of Sergeant Troy)

(a) Aged 16

(b) Aged 19

(c) Aged 21

3 Young Thomas Hardy

(b) Young Thomas Hardy in London, 1863

4 (a) 16 Westbourne Park Villas, Hardy's home in
London, 1863–1867

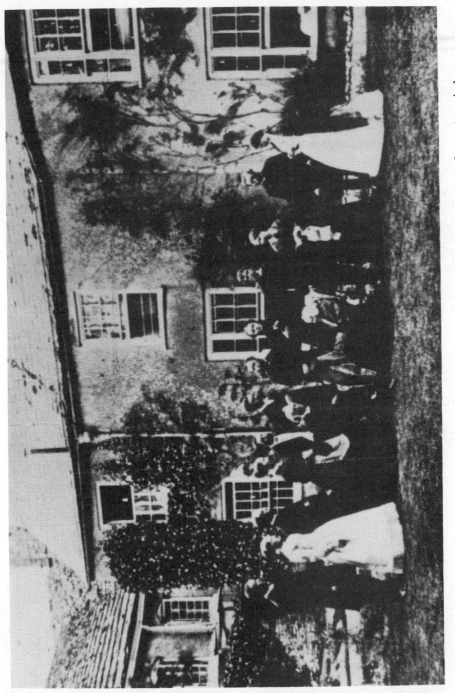

5　The Moule family, Fordington, Dorchester; Hardy's friend Horace Moule against the centre window

(a) Hardy's mother (née Jemima Hand)

(b) Tryphena Sparks

6 Hardy's mother and his cousins, the Sparks girls

(c) Rebecca Sparks

(d) Martha Sparks

7   Three capitals in Turnworth Church, designed by Thomas Hardy, 1869

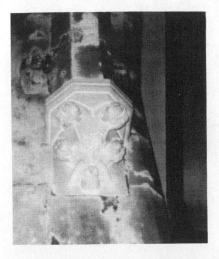

(*a*) The Promenade

8   Two views of Weymouth as Hardy knew it

(*b*) Sandsfoot Castle

sonnet *Hap* is used in the sense of "never blooms" (not of having bloomed and then having ceased to bloom). "Unknows" in the sonnet *At a Bridal* is used in the sense of "never knows": and there are many others. This most characteristic, and incidentally most parodied, aspect of Hardy's poetry is shown by his dictionary markings to be a totally natural form of expression in his own habitual mind.

It is true, of course, that he probably used this and similar forms to achieve an effect of terseness and brevity in his verse, and to avoid a Tennysonian lushness so popular at that time. Once again, this can be deduced from other books that Hardy was conscientiously reading and marking, in his poetic self-education. In his copy of the collected poems of Coleridge, bought in 1865, Hardy underlined in the preface a passage[29] where Coleridge attacks "the sleek favourites of fortune", and this probably includes in his mind those whose verse can also be regarded as sleek: for in his copy of Reed's *English Literature*, he took a passage quoted from one of those favourites of fortune of his own time, Elizabeth Barrett Browning, and wrote in the margin the critical comment "not terse enough".[30] Hardy, then, was drawn to uncompromising brevity and compression. It is the style in which nearly all his early poems are written; yet it is, as now seems, a style that was not self-consciously adopted, but derived from a language and usage natural to him. The only exceptions to this rule are the two surviving narrative poems of 1866. These tell a story in a much looser metre and style, and they are both, quite openly, in Dorset dialect. They are also both extremely funny. The humour and observation of his *Chambers's Journal* article have found their way into these riotous excursions into rustic satire, *The Ruined Maid* and *The Bride-Night Fire*. Both deal with familiar village-ballad figures, the seduced village-maiden, who has done very well out of the experience,[31] and the young girl who manages, by luck, to escape going to bed with an old husband.

It is as well to remember that Hardy's early verses contain these two delightful, successful and light-hearted story poems, since practically all the rest of his poems at this time are in some way flawed, and their tone almost universally sombre. Though there are fine moments in nearly every poem, each one has lines that show Hardy's inexperience at this stage. The line already quoted from the sonnet *Hap*,

> And dicing Time for gladness casts a moan,

is not only clumsy but obscure—one has to substitute "in place of" for the word "for" to make any sense of it.[32] Another powerful sonnet, *Discouragement*, has an odd cliché in the seventh line,

> Over her purposed genial hour a chill,

which has often been criticized.[33] The modernisms of Hardy's time do not always succeed. It is a little absurd that the creator of the universe, in the sonnet *To an Impersonator of Rosalind*, is credited with having had "telescopic sight". The pomposity of "junctive law", meaning marriage or love, spoils the close of another moving sonnet, *Revulsion*. In the lyric *Amabel*, which is itself something of an exercise in rhyming on the name of the title, one of Hardy's attempts is

> All find in dorp or dell
> An Amabel.

The obvious dragged-in rhyme of "dell" is accentuated by the odd archaic "dorp", a word probably got by Hardy from his newly-bought copy of Dryden.[34]

Yet out of these two years of trial and error, there emerged one almost totally perfect poem, one of the finest and most moving in the language. It often happens that in a cluster of early work, a poet will suddenly anticipate his more mature and assured style in a completely unforeseen way. One thinks of Keats's sonnet, *On First Looking into Chapman's Homer*, a swan among the ducklings of his first book of verse. In exactly the same way, Hardy's poem *Neutral Tones* stands out from the thirty-odd poems of 1865–67. It was written in his lodgings at Westbourne Park Villas in the later part of his two-year stint of verse, some time in the first half of 1867;[35] it therefore may be thought to have gained from the cumulative efforts of the previous two years. Yet, on any account, it is a startling achievement, in what, as far as can be gathered, is its first version.[36]

> We stood by a pond that winter day,
> And the sun was white, as though chidden of God,
> And a few leaves lay on the withered sod;
> 　—They had fallen from an ash, and were grey.
>
> Your eyes on me were as eyes that rove
> Over tedious riddles solved years ago;
> And some words played between us to and fro
> 　On which was more wrecked by our love.
>
> The smile on your mouth was the deadest thing
> Alive enough to have strength to die;
> And a grin of bitterness swept thereby
> 　Like an ominous bird a-wing. . . .
>
> Since then, keen lessons that love deceives,
> And wrings with wrong, have shaped to me
> Your face, and the God-curst sun, and a tree,
> 　And a pond edged with greyish leaves.

This poem is uniquely Hardy's own. It is true, though not previously noticed, that there are superficial resemblances with Meredith's *Modern*

*Love* poems. Hardy's poem, like these, is a sixteen-liner and has the identical rhyme-scheme. It also has the exact touches of observation that mark the poems of *Modern Love*. Its withered leaves

—They had fallen from an ash, and were grey.

have some counterpart in Meredith's

Her tears fall still as oak-leaves after frost.

The situation of the two lovers by the pond "edged with greyish leaves" has something of the same precision as the description of Meredith's lovers by the sea-shore.

In hearing of the ocean, and in sight
Of those ribbed wind-streaks running into white.

Yet one has only to read a few lines further in any of the Meredith poems to find such exactitudes dissolving into rhetoric and gesture, while Hardy remains true to the terse and moving sincerity that owes nothing to any model. Again, although the rhyme-scheme is the same, the shorter and more varied lines, which seem to flicker and play over the scene like the emotions of the unhappy pair, have the effect of speech, and the air of an actual happening—the eighth line, one of Hardy's early clumsinesses, was revised for publication. It is the first poem of a type Hardy made uniquely his own, the catching of a momentary incident in such a way that its emotional truth long outlasts the occasion. The influence of Meredith is certainly seen in Hardy's dialect poems, partly derived from similar ballad-poems printed by Meredith in his *Modern Love* volume; but the emotional charge of *Neutral Tones*, though recalling the *Modern Love* sequence, is essentially and typically Hardy's own.

# 9

# Loss of Faith

THE singular difference between *Neutral Tones* and any other poem by Hardy in this period can best be seen by comparing it with a poem written within a few months, *The Musing Maiden*. This is not a bad poem; but beside the other, it appears a neat exercise in conventional poetic ideas. Though pleasant and well-turned, every part is predictable, and lacks that distinction which has made even the most selective critics rank *Neutral Tones* with the finest of Hardy's lifelong poetic output. Its title originally was *The Imaginative Maiden*, and the form given here is, so far as can be judged, its earliest version, before revision by Hardy for his publication in the posthumous *Winter Words*.

> "Why so often, silent one,
> Do you steal away alone?"
> Starting, half she turned her head,
>    And guiltily she said:—
>
> "When the vane points to his far town
> I go upon the hog-backed down,
> And think the breeze that stroked his lip
>    Over my own may slip.
>
> "When he walks at close of day
> I ramble on the white highway,
> And think it reaches to his feet:
>    A meditation sweet!
>
> "When barges hence to London sail
> I watch their outlines waning pale;
> His window opens near the quay;
>    Their coming he can see.
>
> "I look upon the moon at night;
> To mark the moon was our delight;
> Up there our eyesights touch at will
>    If such he practise still."

This, written at Westbourne Park Villas in October 1866, has many of the attributes of the greater poem. It is exact and factually descriptive. The "He" of the poem is Hardy in his office at Adelphi Terrace. He sees the "barges" and the "quay", just as Hardy did, looking down on the Thames from his office window. "The hog-backed down" is an

accurate description of the Ridgeway, running along the hills above
Weymouth, from which, as Hardy himself showed in one of his imaginative illustrations to *Wessex Poems*, the coastal vessels leaving Weymouth
Harbour can be seen. These pictures are effectively organized, and so
are the ideas associated with them. The idea that the same breeze may
blow over the girl's lips that had stroked Hardy's lip in London was
repeated, long after, in *Jude the Obscure*, where the boy Jude imagines
that the breeze he is breathing, coming from the north-east, may have
touched the face of his old schoolmaster in the streets of Oxford. The
final stanza has a poetic conceit that reminds us how early Hardy, quite
unusually for his time, was reading John Donne; the geometrical image
of the lines drawn along the track of their two eyesights meeting in the
same moon seems to echo *The Extasie*.[1] Yet the whole effect of this
otherwise charming poem, perhaps likely to be associated with his own
sister Mary rather than Louisa Harding, or some other village maiden,
is one of a poetic exercise; nothing could be less like the deeply-felt and
agonized *Neutral Tones*.

At all other stages of Hardy's career, emotional shock or personal upheaval heralds a new outburst of creative energy, and a new peak of
achievement. It is worth, then, looking for some such happening in the
years 1865 to 1867, to account for the depth and maturity of his 1867
production, *Neutral Tones*. The pointers are few, for of all the holocaust
of his private papers in his old age, he seems to have been most active
over those of this period; hardly a note survives. This in itself is no
proof of intense emotion, but it may incline us to look in that direction.
It would also be interesting to know in what exact year Hardy decided
to disguise his preternaturally innocent and youthful face with the
heavy dark beard he is found sporting by 1870. We may not be wrong
to guess it was in these years, for the small evidence we have suggests
that they were a time of intense searching and doubt about his whole
personality.

One of the few personal notes from these years occurs on his twenty-
fifth birthday. On 2 June 1865, he wrote:[2]

> My 25th. birthday. Not very cheerful. Feel as if I had lived a long time
> and done very little.
> Walked about by moonlight in the evening. Wondered what woman, if
> any, I should be thinking about in five years' time.

His two concerns, career and women, significantly in that order, can be
examined through the scattered traces he has left, mainly in those
virtual diaries of his days, Bible, prayer book, and, to a lesser but
important extent, Keble's *The Christian Year*. The external events of
his life, few in 1865, apparently non-existent in 1866, appear in some
more random brief notes, letters and later memories. In the middle of

July, there were two occasions he felt worth chronicling. He saw John Stuart Mill, who had been persuaded to stand as Liberal candidate for Westminster in the general election, speak in front of St. Paul's, Covent Garden. The political philosopher spoke somewhat above the heads of the crowd, which, Hardy says, was not "unimpressed by his words; it felt they were weighty, though it did not quite know why".[3] At about the same time, at the end of a walk from his lodgings to Harrow, he came across signs of another national event. Knots of people in doorways were discussing the disaster of the Matterhorn, when three men, two of them from Harrow, Lord Francis Douglas, Mr. Hudson, and Mr. Hadow, had been killed, only Edward Whymper surviving.[4] A third public event he recorded was the state funeral of Lord Palmerston on 27 October 1865. Blomfield obtained tickets for Hardy and a friend from the office named Lee, to have a complete view of the service from the triforium in Westminster Abbey. "I wd. not have missed it for anything", Hardy wrote to his sister Mary, sending her a map to show where the grave was, and where he himself stood.[5]

The two aspects of his birthday note on his life, his ambitions for himself and his relation with women, are charted even more sparsely, though in old age he attempted to put into words a curious episode connected with the first. His poems, sent hopefully to numerous magazines, had all come back. Not a single one was accepted. In some curious way, as he afterwards himself admitted, he rationalized these rejections by deciding that his architecture, of which he was swiftly tiring, could not be combined happily with poetry. A hint of his disappointment, and the attempt to shift the blame on to the circumstances of his life, runs through his notes at this time. He came up with the idea that poetry could be combined with a career in the Church. He plunged into theological study, and even wrote to a friend at Cambridge— possibly Horace Moule's brother Charles at Corpus—to ask for details of university matriculation.[6] This was a strange volte-face, since all the signs are that he was at this time falling away from the regular pious church-going of his earlier years in London. His favourite prophetic passage from the First Book of Kings remained totally unmarked for this year, 1865, and did not reappear in his Bible markings until a new love-situation brought it back in the year 1870. Indeed, in the throes of this idea, he actually attended Communion in Westminster Abbey on 5 July 1865—"a very odd experience, amid a crowd of strangers"—and went to church as late as 1 September;[7] yet it can be more than suspected that the collapse of this revived scheme to enter the Ministry had something to do with his love-life at this time late in 1865. The two aspects of his life, on which he had pondered, were thus connected.

The evidence for this connection between love of some woman and final loss of faith may seem tenuous, since it is derived from a single entry in one of his religious books. Yet one must remember how much these cryptic and abbreviated jottings always meant to Hardy, with his vision of himself as something of a nineteenth-century biblical prophet. Anything that occurs in the context of his annotations in any of his religious books has an importance beyond its laconic appearance. With Bible and prayer book now virtually abandoned, Hardy still went on marking his copy of Keble's *The Christian Year*. On the twenty-fourth Sunday after Trinity, which in 1865 was 26 November, Hardy carefully put the year and a heavy line down the margin of this stanza of Keble's verses:

> For if one heart in perfect sympathy
>     Beat with another, answering love for love,
> Weak mortals, all entranced, on earth would lie,
>     Nor listen for those purer strains above.

The moral of the poem is that since, Keble says, such earthly enchantments are so strong, one should avoid them to have true faith; but Hardy by marking so emphatically this particular stanza, seems to announce that he has found more satisfying the "one heart in perfect sympathy" with his own, and turned from the "purer strains above"; for he made no mark against the remaining stanzas of the poem, in which these "purer" pleasures are detailed.[8] Not many weeks later, Hardy marked with great emphasis this stanza from Shelley's *The Revolt of Islam*, describing the girl Cynthna's effect on the hero Laon:

> She moved upon this earth a shape of brightness,
> A power, that from its objects scarcely drew
> One impulse of her being—in her lightness
> Most like some radiant cloud of morning dew,
> Which wanders through the waste air's pathless blue,
> To nourish some far desert: she did seem
> Beside me, gathering beauty as she grew,
> Like the bright shade of some immortal dream
> Which walks, when tempest sleeps, the wave of life's dark stream.

Laon and Cythna, at the end of many cantos and stanzas of Shelley's poem, leave behind them triumphantly

>                          the long array
> Of guards in golden arms, and Priests beside,
> Singing their bloody hymns, whose garbs betray
> The blackness of the faith it seems to hide.

It seems clear that Hardy was passing through some such extreme emotional experience just at this time, in which love for a kindred spirit, some woman in whom he felt complete sympathy, was associated with an abandonment of the faith of his upbringing, still more of his recent plans to become some kind of poetic clergyman.

It is likely the exact name of the girl will never be determined, so thoroughly did Hardy expunge this episode from nearly all his records. The one named girl he is known to have seen in London is his cousin the ladies' maid Martha Sparks; but she cannot possibly be the girl of his loss of faith. Quite apart from her strict religious upbringing in her own family at Puddletown, she appears as a devout believer at her mother's death there in 1868, three years later. Though very well-educated for her social class, there is no evidence that Martha had the intellectual sophistication any woman would need at that time to renounce conventional Christianity. Although Hardy certainly wanted at one time to marry her, until prevented by her watchful mother, the total absence of dates for this event makes any exact speculation impossible. It may even be that the affair of Martha Sparks, like the much earlier one of Hardy and her elder sister Rebecca, was over by this time, or at any rate fading away. Nearly all Hardy's impulses toward women were, on the evidence, extremely short-lived.

There was, however, one association with a girl in London which seems to have survived for some years, and to have been quite close, though here again the evidence is fragmentary. In two letters to his sister Mary, one on 19 February 1863 and the other on 28 October 1865 itself, Hardy mentions a girl, only referred to by her initials, H.A.[9] A survey of his markings in his Bible at this period shows only one mention of someone associated with London. This is his cryptic entry at the end of the first chapter of the first Epistle to the Thessalonians. It ends a page, at the foot of which Hardy has written "H. Lond$^{n}$". This cannot possibly be his friend Horatio Mosley Moule, to whose name Hardy's notes always give the full initials, H.M.M.

It is therefore reasonable to connect the "H. Lond$^{n}$" of Hardy's Bible with the H.A. of his letters to Mary Hardy. What emerges from these letters, though not much, does place her as someone well known to Hardy's sister, as well as to him. In the first letter, he mentions that she has been recently ill, and asks if she has written to Mary yet. In the second letter, when her relationship with Hardy had apparently lasted for over two and a half years, Hardy wrote to his sister at her cottage in the Berkshire village at Denchworth, where she was still teaching,

> Will it be a good thing or will it be awkward for you if H.A. and I come down for Xmas day and the next?

The girl was evidently well known to Mary Hardy, as indeed were most of Hardy's friends whom Mary had met on her fairly frequent visits to London. What is remarkable is both that Hardy's association with the girl has lasted for so long, and has reached a stage when he is proposing to come away alone with her, even if they are to be chaperoned at the end of the journey by Mary. Unaccompanied journeys by two young people of opposite sexes were sufficiently remarkable then, as indeed Hardy's own early novels stress, to suggest that the relationship between Hardy and this girl was by now very close.

There are other suggestions of a close relationship, in Hardy's care that this visit should not be "awkward" for his sister. Mary Hardy adored her brother, and would never have complained at anything he did, even if she secretly disliked it. Hardy applied to her peculiarly reserved nature the verse he marked in his own prayer book, from Psalm 39, "I kept silence, yea, even from good words".[10] Knowing she would not complain even if the situation were awkward for her, through local gossip perhaps, he gives her every opportunity to make some excuse. The fact that H.A. was proposed at all for Mary's small cottage lodgings—her own sketch[11] shows how small they were—seems to show that she was of the same class as Mary. It is probable she was also a schoolmistress, the only type of girl of Mary's and Hardy's class at all likely to hold advanced or freethinking opinions at that date. Other professions for poor but educated girls were only just getting under way, if at all. The Working Women's College at 29 Queen's Square, Bloomsbury, had been open barely a year.[12] If this visit took place, and Mary, with her passive nature, was not likely to have prevented it, it was in the middle of a bitter winter. It is just possible that the bleak scene described in *Neutral Tones* may have happened at Denchworth, or more likely Fawley, the nearby home of Hardy's mysterious ancestors. The frozen pond at Fawley plays its part in *Jude the Obscure*. It may be the actual setting for the much earlier poem.

It does seem certain, though, that Hardy's loss of faith, connected with the influence of a woman, during these years in London, had a strong bearing on his hero and heroine when he came, in the 1890s, to write *Jude the Obscure*. Writing to Edmund Gosse in 1895, Hardy said, of his spiritual heroine, Sue Bridehead, that

> Sue is a type of woman which has always had an attraction for me, but the difficulty of drawing the type has kept me from attempting it till now.[13]

"Always" is a vague word; but it indicates an early experience of such a woman. None of Hardy's known early loves—for example, two and eventually three Sparks girls—resembles in the slightest way the intellectual Sue. Hardy, of course, combined many elements in his drawing of Sue, as he did, even more, in his portrayal of Jude; but one striking element in the early character of Sue is her rationalism and anti-Church bias. Hardy, in fact, ironically contrasts this with her money-earning employment, which is designing illuminated texts for churches, an idea left over from a minor theme he had used in *The Poor Man and the Lady*. Sue herself, however, is wedded to the new historical criticism of the Bible, which Hardy had found expounded by Jowett in *Essays and Reviews*. In pursuit of this, she makes herself what she calls "a *new* New Testament" on historical lines. She achieves this by chopping up the Epistles and Gospels, as she explains, "into separate *brochures*", and rearranging them into their probable order of composition, thus beginning the new book with the Epistle to the Thessalonians. It was against this Epistle that Hardy wrote, in his own Bible, "H. Lond$^n$"; it seems then more than likely that the London girl of the initials was responsible for this action by Sue Bridehead.

The character of Sue Bridehead was seized on by critics in the 1890s as representing "the New Woman" of that era, restless, intellectual and in some ways unfeminine. In reality, she is very much more what was called "The Girl of the Period" in the 1860s. The genuine New Woman of the 1890s was likely to have political affiliations with socialism, to play some part in opening the professions to women, and probably to have received some sort of university training. Sue is still back in a period some thirty years before that, when a band of enthusiasts in London ran *The Englishwoman's Journal*, and aired, for practically the first time, the independent views of women. The works of John Stuart Mill, whom Hardy had just seen on his way to be elected for Parliament, were their standard reading, and the editor of *The Englishwoman's Journal*, Bessie Rayner Parkes, wrote two long articles expounding his principles. By the 1890s, Mill was out of date, superseded by the new socialism; but Sue reads and quotes Mill even obsessively. "What do I care about J. S. Mill!" moans her poor husband, "I only want to lead a quiet life!" Sue's intellectualism is very much that of the 1860s; she is not attached to party politics, nor is she striving for male professional qualifications, nor economic independence. She accepts the very minor jobs then allotted to women.

Still more typical of the 1860s is Sue's own loss of faith, and the idea she finds as a substitute for it. She is never quite explicit about this; but, in fact, the terms she uses show her to be a follower of the Positive Philosophy of Auguste Comte, made fashionable in the 1860s among English intellectuals by Mill's exposition of it in the 1840s, and Harriet Martineau's two-volume abridged translation of it in the 1850s. In her religious arguments with Jude, Sue mocks him by using terms that would be familiar to any reader of Comte. When Jude is in his phase of studying to be a clergyman, as Hardy was in 1865, she ridicules the theology of Oxford which, she says, is anti-intellectual. She condemns Oxford and its orthodox religious beliefs as "a place full of fetichists". Here she is using the language of Comte, or rather of the Harriet Martineau translation. For Comte believed that mankind passed through religion in its early history, to arrive, via metaphysics, at scientific or "positive" philosophy, which was the "religion" of the future. He analysed, at great length, the history of religion itself, and found its origins in the "fetichist" superstitions of primitive tribes: hence Sue's expression. Sue then mocks Jude as merely himself being in a later era of Comte's tracing of religious history—"You are in the Tractarian stage just now . . . Let me see—when was I there?—In the year eighteen hundred and—". She thus shocks Jude, by assuming that, even in slow process, he will grow out of religion itself, as she has already done. Finally, like Comte, she believes in a secular "pantheon" of intellectuals, rather than one of saints.

In all this, Hardy is clearly modelling Sue, in her anti-religious, rationalist, and scientific "positive" phase, on a girl of the 1860s, and not on one of the 1890s when he was writing. By 1890, Positivism in England was virtually dead, except for small groups in London and in Liverpool. Although its handful of believers were constant to its general principles, it had been disastrously split in the 1870s into two groups, represented in London by those who congregated at Newton Hall, off Fetter Lane, and those who worshipped at the hall in Chapel Street, off Lamb's Conduit Street. For Comte, feeling the need for a spiritual element in his rationalist philosophy, had come in later stages of it to construct a system very like the Catholic Church, in which he had originally been brought up, with a hierarchy of scientists, philosophers, and humanists instead of saints—Sue's "pantheon"—and an actual worship of what was vaguely called "Humanity", with some sort of service resembling a Catholic Mass without Christ. This split the already tiny number of English positivists, never more than a few hundred, into two even smaller groups, those who stuck to the original "positive" philosophic principles, and those whose need for a substitute Christianity made them welcome the later more "religious" form of Positivism. No new intellectual woman in the 1890s would have been a positivist. Sue is, once more, a girl of the 1860s, and so perhaps, once more, the girl through whom Hardy, like Jude, lost his faith then.

The immediate result of this shadowy episode seems to have been for Hardy one of the utmost gloom, both personally and poetically. Poems of 1866, such as *At A Bridal, Postponement, Revulsion,* speak of obscure but bitter and disillusioning situations. A marriage takes place from which Hardy is excluded, so that the children he dreamed of for his own marriage will never be. Nature, he says, is indifferent,

If all such aimed ideals have such a close.[14]

It is also hinted that lack of money has been a stumbling-block to any marriage for himself. He was not

Born to an evergreen nesting-tree,

which, in his old age, he interpreted as meaning enough money to

marry on.[15] The sonnet *Revulsion* seems to mirror a mood in which all
love-endeavour is so doomed that it is better not to love at all. How
far these all apply to one love-affair, and whether all or any are associated with the girl of the enigmatic initials can perhaps never be finally
settled, though the probability is that they are.

More certain is the concentrated gloom that seems to gather over all
Hardy's doings in the year 1866. There are, of course, signs that he
pursued many of his usual activities, and among these the passion for
self-education and self-improvement intellectually was still dominant.
On 10 October 1865, he entered himself to study French from seven to
nine each Tuesday and Friday evening at King's College.[16] In this
pursuit he spent two terms, lasting until March 1866. The head of these
courses was Professor Alphonse Mariette, whose *Half-Hours of French
Translation* was the set text. Hardy was actually taught by his assistant,
M. Stièvenard, whose *Lectures Françaises* was also used. He liked
Stièvenard, and remembered him well in old age,[17] though he recollected
that "being also engrossed in English poetry, I did not do much in
class". The fly-leaf of his copy of Mariette's book may show that his
mind wandered both to architectural and personal matters. There is a
shorthand note on an architectural problem, and both a map and a
sketch of Weymouth, with the bulk of Portland Bill in the background.[18]
The view of Weymouth, with ships in the bay, resembles the scene of
one stanza of his 1866 poem, *The Imaginative Maiden*, and perhaps
formed a basis for his later illustration in *Wessex Poems*.

As this suggests, his attention was taken up by his own emotional
problems rather than any progress in education or career. The small
number of notes that he allowed to survive all show a brooding introspection. Early in 1866 he wrote "A certain man: He creeps away to a
meeting with his own sensations", and the "certain man" was presumably his ultra-diffident self. What these difficult "sensations" were
may be indicated by the note which almost immediately follows:

> There is no more painful lesson to be learnt by a man of capacious mind
> than that of excluding general knowledge for particular.

This seems to hint at something more painfully personal than the
experience of studying the minutiae of French grammar under M.
Stièvenard. On 14 May, his despair had crystallized into a kind of
Byronic world-weary resignation. On that day, he wrote the date against
a stanza in Canto Three of *Childe Harold*:[19]

> Secure in guarded coldness, he had mix'd
> Again in fancied safety with his kind,
> And deem'd his spirit now so firmly fix'd
> And sheath'd with an invulnerable mind,
> That, if no joy, no sorrow lurk'd behind;

And he, as one, might 'mongst the many stand
Unheeded, searching through the crowd to find
Fit speculation; such as in strange land
He found in wonder-works of God and Nature's hand.

Within a week, he tried what the wonder-works of Man's hand and
Nature's would do for him, and made an expedition, on 20 May, to the
little village of Findon, underneath the Sussex Downs.[20] Here he made
a charming sketch of the Gothic church, nestling in trees, and seen from
the hills above, the spire backed by the deep leafage of early summer:
but another country visit on 6 June was not so happy. For some reason
he chose to revisit Hatfield,[21] which he had not seen since his three
weeks' stay there at the age of nine. In retrospect, all its associations
seemed sad. Whether this was because of his dead aunt, or whether,
more deeply, he now realized his mother had taken him there to break
him from Mrs. Martin, he now felt that he

regretted that the beautiful sunset did not occur in a place of no
reminiscences, that I might have enjoyed it without their tinge.

Hardy's Byronic attitude of a determined and lofty gloom finds typical
expression in an entry of 13 July—"A man's grief has a touch of the
ludicrous unless it is so keen as to be awful".

In actual fact, and perhaps healthily, his own grief took a slightly
ludicrous direction round about the turn of the year. He conceived the
ambition to write plays in blank verse; and as, unknown to him, Ibsen
had just been doing, he tried to get himself a job in the theatre. He
planned first to try a walk-on part in one of the big London manage-
ments, and obtained an interview with Coe, Buckstone's stage-manager
at the Haymarket. This does not seem to have been successful—Hardy
had scarcely the physique or extrovert personality for the stage—and
his one job came through a quite different source. The man who executed Blomfield's designs for church metalwork also did trick-scenery,
such as stage trap-doors, for pantomimes. Through him, Hardy found
himself in a walk-on part in *The Forty Thieves* at Covent Garden. The
result was far from giving him the desired education in dramatic verse.
Perhaps as might be expected, it led to a set of would-be serious though
definitely pantomime-type couplets describing a rehearsal, which he
later marked as not fit for publication. The frowsty atmosphere of the
empty theatre and the yawning actors in shabby clothes under a dim
works-light is quite well caught, though it breaks down as poetry when
Hardy tries to moralize about their private lives.

Hardy tended, in spite of his Byronic pose, to be innocently and
youthfully stage-struck. Contact with actors, and particularly actresses,
even from the level of one among (presumably) forty thieves, seems to
have had an effect on his always susceptible nature. There is a note of

this in his couplet on the leading lady, at the rehearsal, whose private life is, predictably, said to be "shady". This, and perhaps a reaction from the romantic majesty of his Byronic persona—"Remember", he noted on 18 February 1867, "that Evil dies as well as Good"—brought about something in April which reminds one how very young Hardy still was emotionally, in spite of experiences which may have been genuinely searing in themselves. He performed the typically youthful action of falling in love briefly with a very pretty though not very good actress. On 8 April, a great-granddaughter of the legendary Mrs. Siddons made her debut on the London stage. This was Mrs. Mary Frances Scott-Siddons, performing Rosalind in *As You Like It* at the Haymarket, adding as an after-piece some extracts from *Romeo and Juliet*. The reviews tended to concentrate, in the slightly suggestive way of much Victorian journalism, on her physique. *The Daily News* praised her "neat figure, pretty face", the *Daily Telegraph* noted she had "the advantages of a neat symmetrical figure" and "the external requisites" for the part, while the *London Review* said she "has a figure admirably suited to the part".[22] Her acting ability was discreetly soft-pedalled, and indeed seems to have been negligible.

What was obviously not negligible was her appearance in tights, in a part beloved for that reason by all right-thinking Victorian gentlemen. Hardy was no exception to the general taste, though, with his reading, he might well have reminded himself that her famous great-grandmother disdained such a costume. He saw her at a repeat performance on Saturday, 20 April, and the next day wrote a sonnet to her, which he followed with another. The sonnets revert to an earlier, immature technique and a much more youthful style and feeling. The second is full of romantic sentiment in such lines as

When now the knowing you is all of me,

and in its idea that Hardy's world has been entirely changed by seeing this one performance of an actress who, apart from her figure, had little to recommend her except a certain "saucy" and "arch" delivery of her lines, and a number of free gestures and movements, which showed off her natural advantages. Perhaps he himself may have felt he had gone a little far, though physically he does not seem to have got even as far as the stage-door. Only a week later, his journal shows the solemn reflection that

Had the teachings of experience grown cumulatively with the age of the world we should have been ere now as great as God.

The teachings of experience had certainly not advanced Hardy beyond an almost pathological habit of falling in love with each woman he encountered, particularly if there was something striking about the surrounding circumstance. His later encounter with the woman he was to marry showed how unusual and dramatic settings could work upon him, so that he literally did not see what he was doing. Stage glamour provided that factor in the affair of Mrs. Scott-Siddons, which was nevertheless so real to him that he was still writing about it twenty years later.

Nor, for all its obvious touch of absurdity, as the Byronic and, by now, surely bearded Hardy behaves like a lovesick teenager, should the whole matter be treated without sympathy. It may even be an indication of actual malaise in Hardy, an illness, part physical, part psychological, induced by the emotional and mental tempests that had clearly assailed him over the past few years. His five years in London were ending almost in breakdown. For one should never underestimate the part played by the loss of faith. Few of the Victorians were in the relatively happy position of Leslie Stephen, who said that he had never lost his faith, but simply found he had never had one. The majority would have endorsed Mark Pattison's poignant view. "Agnosticism", he wrote, "has taken away Providence as death takes away the mother from the child and leaves us forlorn of protection and love".[23] In such a state, for one reason or another, Thomas Hardy now found himself.

# 10

# First Novel

WHATEVER the cause, by 1867 Hardy's health seemed to be seriously affected. This decline probably dated from sometime in the year 1865. In that year, he bought for himself a recent edition of *Modern Domestic Medicine* by Thomas J. Graham.[1] This was a standard home medical guide, "intended", as the title-page announced, "for the use of clergymen, heads of families, emigrants, etc.". In an earlier edition, it had been the stand-by of the Reverend Patrick Brontë, who relied on it for his own cures, though it had notably failed to check disease in his doomed family. Hardy marked heavily the hundred or more pages devoted to materia medica, containing notes of the chief ingredients of prescriptions; but nothing did him any good, and he grew shockingly pale and debilitated. The exceptionally wet and cloudy weather of the year 1867 did nothing to help, and the climax came in the dreadful month of July. The rainfall in that month was twice the average, and it must have been practically impossible to go out of doors. The first of Dr. Graham's general principles in Hardy's medical handbook read

> Remember that the restorative powers of nature are great, very great; and consequently many disorders will be cured by time, mild diet, cheerful conversation, rest, and pure air.

Arthur Blomfield seconded this advice by saying that Hardy should go into the country for a time; and at the crucial moment, Hicks of Dorchester, also suffering from ill-health, wrote asking for a good assistant. Hardy replied that he himself would come. A further draw was that his beloved sister Mary had just returned from Berkshire to teach at a Dorset school,[2] Minterne Magna, just north of Cerne Abbas, whose patron was the local landowner, Lord Digby. So, at the end of July, Hardy returned to Bockhampton. Admittedly, the weather in Dorset was no better than it had been in London. August and September were more than usually cloudy and wet, to be succeeded by one of the worst Octobers on record.[3] However, Hardy's country routine of walking each day in all weathers from Bockhampton to Dorchester soon had its effect. Health began to return. Dr. Graham's book had recommended, as well as fresh air, "the bitter ales of Bass and Allsopp", and according to local tradition, Hardy had been prescribed a bottle of milk stout a day.[4] As these simple remedies brought the colour back to his cheeks, his energy increased too. He began to think how he might impress the literary world as he had so singularly failed to do in the past two years. He decided to use the experiences he had accumulated. In Walter Bagehot's essays, he had read the description of Shakespeare as "a first-rate imagination working on a first-rate experience". This was to be his model; as he wrote,[5]

> He considered that he knew fairly well both West-country life in its less explored recesses and the life of an isolated student cast upon the billows of London with no protection but his brains—the young man of whom it may be said more truly than perhaps of any, that 'save his own soul he hath no star'. The two contrasting experiences seemed to afford him abundant materials out of which to evolve a striking socialist novel—not that he mentally defined it as such, for the word had probably never, or scarcely ever, been heard of at that date.[6]

Hardy entitled this *The Poor Man and the Lady*, and at first sub-titled it "A Story with no plot, Containing some original verses". He evidently hoped to include some of the poems rejected by journals during the past two years. This subtitle was abandoned, but when it came into the hands of publishers' readers, their main complaint was that it still had indeed "no plot".[7] As far as can be gathered,[8] the "plot" seems not so much non-existent as very naïve. The story was told in the first person by the Poor Man, the son of a Dorset labourer, named Strong, an obvious synonym for Hardy. Strong shows such promise at the village school that the squire and his lady, the Hon. and Mrs. Guy Allancourt, pay for him to be further educated as an architect's draughtsman. However, he and the squire's lovely daughter fall in love, and the squire banishes him to London. There he assists a leading architect, and makes such progress that he wins a prize, which, however, is withdrawn—a clear echo of the withdrawal of the money award to Hardy by the R.I.B.A. In spite of her father's disapproval, Strong and the squire's daughter consider themselves engaged, and write each other letters, until the squire forbids this also.

Strong, in his resentment, then adopts radical politics. The squire and his family come to London, and the daughter hears Strong make a socialist speech in Trafalgar Square. Offended by his sentiments, she breaks off their understanding; but shortly afterwards, the two find themselves at a public concert, Strong in the front row of the cheap seats, she in the back row of the expensive ones. They hold hands, and she invites him to call at the squire's London house. Through one of those accidents so common in Hardy's later novels, she is out when he calls. There is an angry scene with her mother, who faints. Strong pours water on her face, her rouge runs, and she is doubly angry. The squire has Strong thrown out, the family returns to Dorset, and the lovers cannot correspond. Strong hears, however, that the girl is about to marry, hurries to Dorset, and, the night before her wedding, has a meeting with her in the church. She confesses that he is the only man she has ever loved. She falls ill, and her father sends for Strong, but she dies. Strong designs her memorial, free of charge. There are other isolated incidents, whose position in the story is impossible to determine. There was a scene in Rotten Row, and one where a gentleman pursued his wife at midnight, and struck her. There was also the episode of an architect's mistress, who was a ballet dancer, but who also designed church furniture, a typical Hardy adaptation from his acquaintance with Blomfield's metal-smith who also made stage machinery.[9]

It is extremely difficult to say which of these incidents is auto-biographical. Hardy already handled raw materials professionally, as in his later work, transposing sexes, names, relationships, and professions from people and incidents actually experienced into their artistic and fictional form. One example of this method seems actually to have occurred in this novel. Early in his work for Blomfield, Hardy assisted in the latter's commission for All Saint's Church at New Windsor; his sketch of Windsor Castle, dated 24 August 1862, may indicate a visit to the site.[10] On 21 November 1863, Hardy was present at the laying of the commemorative stone for this new church. The English Princess Royal, who in 1858 had married Prince Frederick William of Prussia, was there with her husband to perform the ceremony, and was handed a trowel by Blomfield, from which she got her glove daubed with mortar. She thrust the trowel back to Blomfield with a distressed whisper of "Take it, take it!"[11] This seems almost certainly to have been preserved in a scene between the architect hero and the heroine in Hardy's novel.[12]

Hardy had also evidently learnt the novelist's method of asking professional advice when he wanted a piece of specialized, technical information. At one time—though this may not have occurred in the completed novel—he wished his hero to become temporarily blind through overwork. More important, he wanted his heroine's midnight escapade in the church to result in an illness, which would be fatal, but which would leave her in command of speech and faculties to the last, presumably so that she could die still expressing her love for Strong. His copy of Graham's *Modern Domestic Medicine* gave him no sure guide on these points; but he remembered that on his boyhood visit to Hertfordshire with his mother, he had met his aunt's doctor brother-in-law, George Brereton Sharpe. Dr. Sharpe had made a switch in middle life from medicine to the church, and was now a vicar in Wales; but Hardy wrote off hopefully for information and advice, and in January 1868 he received a long and detailed reply.[13] His idea that the hero might go temporarily blind "from *continued* study late at night of small print or Greek characters" was confirmed. Dr. Sharpe then set himself to solve plausibly the problem of a naturalistic cause for the heroine's fatal yet conversible illness.

> For the young lady I think Haemorrage on the lungs beginning with a slight spitting of blood would be most suitable—it is less prosaically common than inflammation would be for your purpose.
>
> Haemorrage would very naturally follow the hurry and exertion—and if you like—external chill that the enterprise you name would entail.
>
> It also admits your object of perfect self-possession & consciousness till a sudden late flow of blood stops utterance and produces suffocation with the mind perfectly clear. . . .

Dr. Sharpe also added the warning, with which Hardy was to become familiar in the next few years, that it would be unwise to build any hopes of financial success on the work—"that is the lot of but few". However, he made the kindly remark, "I don't say it may not be yours", and enquired in a friendly way about Hardy's present whereabouts and doings. This letter, which Hardy kept for reference, is a reminder how even in this unfledged attempt, Hardy showed a serious concern to teach himself about every aspect of life, a continuation into his new life as a novelist of his deliberate self-tuition since boyhood, and his retentive memory for every useful source of information. The hero's temporary blindness "from *continued* study" formed a vital part of *The Return of the Native*, a decade later.

This one glimpse of his methods certainly suggests that much of the book, where it was not autobiographical, was carefully worked out from authentic sources now lost to us.

For instance, it would be fascinating to know more of the hero's radical politics, which Hardy saw as the unifying feature of the novel. He may well have got a hint for these from his cousin the carpenter, James Sparks of Windsor, described by his own brother Nathaniel Sparks as "a real loyal Rad".[14] If so, the accent should probably be on the word loyal. As has been said, politics is almost entirely absent from Hardy's own autobiography and notebooks; socialism, in the sense of economic and political socialism, hardly, if at all, appears. Although J. S. Mill had examined theoretical socialism twenty years before in his *Principles of Political Economy*, Hardy's early reading in Mill's works has probably been exaggerated; though he claimed himself to know the reformer's *On Liberty* "almost by heart" in the year 1865,[15] he did not apparently buy, read, and annotate his own copy until at least 1867.[16] From the plot, it would seem that the main emphasis was not on political socialism, but on what we should now call class-consciousness, expressed in crude satire of the ruling classes. It is clear that he overreached himself in some of this; the first publisher who read it mildly rebuked Hardy for the impossibility of the final idea in the novel, that the Hon. Guy Allancourt should be mean enough to rejoice at getting the hero's design for his daughter's tomb free of charge.

The main targets of satire were predictably those he saw attacked every week in his reading of the *Saturday Review*, namely "London society, the vulgarity of the middle class, modern Christianity, . . . and political and domestic morals in general".[17] In addition, there was probably some commonplace moralizing on the theme of countryman versus townsman. In the spring of 1869, when he still hoped the novel had a chance of being published, Hardy, down in Dorset, wrote in his notebook,[18] "One of those evenings in the country which make the townsman feel: 'I will stay here till I die—I would, that is, if it were not for that thousand pounds I want to make, & that friend I want to envy me.'". Similar touches of peasant cynicism appear in all Hardy's early novels and, no doubt, did in this one.

The story of the writing and the reception by publishers of *The Poor Man and the Lady* seems to have been more dramatic and interesting than the plot of the novel itself. Hardy noted with pride the distinguished *dramatis personae* of those who, in one way or another, had to do with his first immature attempt.[19] Once started, in the middle of August 1867, he wrote with great concentration, in the intervals of his architectural work for Hicks, only pausing for a flying visit to London in October to pick up the books and papers he had left there. In five months, by the middle of January 1868, he had finished the first draft. The fair copy took him just a week under another five months, and was finished on 9 June 1868. In all, with draft and fair copy, he must have completed nearly a thousand handwritten pages in under ten months, a steady rate which left him little time for anything else, though he records reading Browning and Thackeray in April, when he also took down the exact sound of the nightingale's song in the thickets outside the Bockhampton house.[20]

There then followed a pause of six or seven weeks, while he sent the completed novel to his mentor, Horace Moule at Marlborough. Moule's opinion has not survived, but he evidently liked it well enough to write Hardy a letter of introduction to the publisher Alexander Macmillan, which Hardy enclosed with one of his own. Moule's letter did not tell Macmillan about Hardy himself, and did not mention his age; but the publisher must have guessed he was dealing with a young man from Hardy's own letter.[21] It is typically youthful in its slightly hectoring tone, as Hardy tabulates, as if in some youth club debate, those considerations that had led him to write the novel: among them,

That the upper classes of society have been induced to read, before any, books in which *they themselves* are painted by a comparative outsider. . . .

That, nowadays, discussions on the questions of manners, rising in the world, etc. (the main incidents of the novel), have grown to be particularly absorbing.

Alexander Macmillan, who had succeeded his brother Daniel, the founder of the firm, on the latter's death in 1857, was well known for his good relationship with authors. For many years the firm ran a weekly social meeting with its contributors, and showed an understanding sympathy with their problems. Macmillan himself had come from a poor croft in Scotland, and a novel dealing with "rising in the world, etc." was likely to be of special interest to him. He showed this interest not only by reading it very carefully himself, but by sending it to a brilliant young man who had just become, while still under thirty, the editor of the *Fortnightly Review*. This was John Morley, whose own youth and radical views would bring him in sympathy with Hardy's novel. On 12 August, Macmillan wrote Hardy a long letter enclosing these extracts from Morley's opinions.

A very curious and original performance: the opening pictures of the Christmas Eve in the tranter's house are really of good quality; much of the writing is strong and fresh. But there crops up in parts a certain rawness of absurdity that is very displeasing, and makes it read like some clever lad's dream: the thing hangs too loosely together. There is real feeling in the writing, though now and then it is commonplace in form as all feeling turning on the insolence and folly of the rich in face of the poor is apt to sound: (e.g. p. 338). If the man is young, there is stuff and promise in him: but he must study form and composition, in such writers as Balzac and Thackeray, who would I think come as natural masters to him.

For queer cleverness and hard sarcasm—e.g. p. 280—a little before and after: p. 333–p. 352. For cynical description, half worthy of Balzac, pp. 358–9.

This last episode, "half worthy of Balzac" was probably the scene of the rouge on Mrs. Allancourt's face, both from its evident position in the manuscript, and from the fact that Macmillan himself in his own detailed criticism, did not mention it. In several other scenes he picked up Morley's suggestion of "a certain rawness of absurdity", and gently and kindly reasoned with the author about their unlikely nature. He also made a more general criticism, again in some detail, about the wholesale blackening of the upper classes, which, as he said, "falls harmless from very excess . . . It is inconceivable," he added, "that any considerable number of human beings—God's creatures—should be so bad without going to utter wreck within a week." He also very acutely noticed the *Saturday Review* style, natural to a young man who read it every week, and took up Morley's suggestion of the likeness to Thackeray. Yet he pointed the difference that while Thackeray only meant fun, "you mean mischief". He gave Hardy credit for great sincerity and for some excellent writing, and certainly showed no political prejudice; he singled out the Trafalgar Square speech for praise, "full of wisdom". He ended

> You see I am writing to you as a writer who seems to me, at least potentially, of considerable mark, of power and purpose. If this is your first book I think you ought to go on.

He had, in fact, been so impressed that he had decided to send the manuscript to another reader, "who knows more of the upper class than either" Morley or himself.[22]

This was almost as good as Hardy could have hoped, apart from instant acceptance; but after another month of waiting for the opinion of the other reader, whose name was never divulged, his natural impatience got the better of him. He wrote on 10 September, showing great respect for Macmillan's judgement. Taking the criticism of his scenes from fashionable life to heart, he wrote that he had been "hunting up matter for another tale, which would consist entirely of rural scenes and humble life". Yet he confessed he had not the courage to go on with it until he knew what was happening to *The Poor Man and the Lady*. His inner anxiety may be reflected in an entry in his notebook, "How people will laugh in the midst of a misery! Some would soon get to whistle in Hell!"[23] In the first week in December, he had a personal interview with Macmillan, who said that though he could not publish it, Hardy should have no difficulty in placing it with a firm such as Chapman and Hall; he gave Hardy an introduction to Frederick Chapman, to whom Hardy delivered the manuscript, slightly revised, in person on 8 December. There was the usual publishers' delay over the Christmas season, and on 17 January 1869, the agitated author once more left for London. The visit brought a friendly gesture from the book's first reader, John Morley, who offered to try and get him reviewing work with the *Saturday Review*—more than Hardy's friend Moule had ever done—but on 8 February Chapman's reader gave a report, which was less favourable than Morley's had been, though he put his finger on the same main weakness, the lack of plot; "you have not got an interesting story to work upon and thus some of your episodic scenes are fatally injured".[24] There was, however, a suggestion that Chapman and Hall would risk the book if Hardy paid the relatively small sum of £20 as guarantee against loss. Hardy agreed, and returned home with this partial success, and the experience of having seen the aged Carlyle in Chapman's Piccadilly shop. Yet still neither contract nor proofs arrived; and early in March he received a note asking him to meet "the gentleman who read your manuscript".

At this summons, enough to make any author nervous, Hardy went to London once more, and in a dusty back room at Chapman's office, was confronted with a tall, impressive, handsome and dramatic-looking person, who turned out to be none other than George Meredith. The novelist and poet, whose *Modern Love* sequence had influenced Hardy's own early poems, gave the young man an eloquent lecture, waving the manuscript in his hand. The gist was that while the firm was still willing to publish, he thought the book might be so heavily attacked by reviewers that it would handicap Hardy's future. He advised Hardy either to rewrite considerably, or, better, write a new novel with less social purpose and more art, taking care this time to give it plenty of plot.[25]

So Hardy returned once more to Dorset with the novel. He did not, however, at once take Meredith's advice. These two near misses had made him feel, as any author would, that it was worth trying one more publisher. His choice was a curious one for an author who had just been warned that his book might not be to the popular taste. William Tinsley of Tinsley Brothers was at that time the publisher of best-selling authors, including the vastly-popular Miss Braddon and the prolific journalist, George Augustus Henry Sala; his list was frankly on the lighter and more sensational side. However, Hardy sent him the novel, and once more suffered the pangs of waiting for a decision. By 8 June 1869, he was again writing for news of his manuscript, and offering to obtain another letter of introduction if necessary. Tinsley scrawled "Return" across this letter, but he did not mean an outright rejection. He put terms to Hardy for publication, through the negotiation of a friend of Hardy's, who may possibly have been either Moule or Morley. These evidently involved a much greater payment by the author than the £20 Chapman had suggested; and finally, on 14 September, Hardy wrote to say the terms were beyond him.[26] Two years in pursuit of success for this prose work had brought him the same result as the previous two years of poetry.

This recital of hope and rejection shows there was in Hardy, for all his basic timidity, a strong strain of obstinacy, and a determination to succeed against all odds. It was something he inherited from his mother, and shared with other members of her family, many of whom had ambitions to strike out for themselves. Maria Sparks, Jemima Hardy's sister, was like her, ambitious for her children, and resentful of anyone who seemed to stand in their way. She supported the idea that her clever youngest daughter, Tryphena, should, like the child's cousin, Mary Hardy, become a teacher. Tryphena had already taken the first step on this career by becoming, at the age of eleven in 1862, a monitor in the Nonconformist school at Athelhampton.[27] The next step was to become a pupil-teacher, but here the plan ran into difficulty owing to the small size of the school. It already had one pupil-teacher, and was too small to need another. In the late 1860s its average attendance was only sixty-one.[28] Squire Brymer was now well in control of Puddletown, and his "National" or Church of England school there had recently expanded into two large sections, one girls' and one boys'.[29] Although an earlier education at a Nonconformist school cannot altogether have recommended her to the squire, Tryphena was accepted late in 1866 as a pupil-teacher in the girls' section under Mrs. Sarah Ann Collins, Mr. Collins taking the boys. The job was arduous. Mrs. Collins's bad health, and unruly mothers—one called Tryphena a fool—saddled her with responsibility.[30]

Schools at this time were still organized under the somewhat unsatisfactory Revised Code of 1862, attacked by Matthew Arnold, among other things, for weakening the status and tenure of pupil-teachers. Under the Code, they were now employed and paid by the school managers, without indenture, instead of being apprenticed. Lacking the safeguard of an apprenticeship for a stated period, they were at risk of being arbitrarily dismissed, and could lose their jobs and have their careers ruined for trivial causes.[31] Tryphena, however, satisfied her employers all through 1867, apart from a weakness in geography; this was a topic on which heads of local schools were sensitive, since the Inspector's report for that year in Dorset had commented that the subject was either not taught in schools or taught very poorly.[32] She did much better anyway than the pupil-teacher of the boys' section, Frances Dunman. Early in 1868, though, she ran into trouble. Mrs. Collins entered in the school log-book that she had "reproved pupil-teacher for neglect of duty" and added "parents very angry in consequence, & determine to withdraw her a month hence". One does not know what the "neglect of duty" was. One possible cause was that her mother's increasing illness gave Tryphena more work at home; Mrs. Collins herself, too, was heading for a breakdown that disabled her for the next three months. What is certain is that it cannot have been any moral cause.[33] H.M. Inspector of Schools, who examined the log-book, and must have enquired into the cause, specially named Puddletown School in this year as having a healthy moral tone.[34] Since the scene with Mrs. Collins, and Mr. and Mrs. Sparks's annoyance, would make further work under Mrs. Collins difficult, Tryphena was transferred to the boys' section of the school almost immediately, in exchange with Frances Dunman.

The quarrel with the school, however, was not made up—Tryphena's mother, though ill, had the quick temper for which all the Hand family were noted—and Tryphena then appears helping to teach at another school. This was the little school at Coryates, a hamlet under Blackdown Hill, east of Dorchester. The family of the local landowner, Catherine Hawkins, had a tradition that a relative of Thomas Hardy had taught there.[35] This cannot have been either Mary or Kate Hardy;[36] and, moreover, Tryphena, in a later letter,[37] showed an intimate knowledge of the people and places in this district, remote from her own home. She got the job, by a coincidence, through the same group of people who had backed Isaac Last's Academy, which Hardy had attended in his youth. This was the powerful group of Dorset Congregationalists. Coryates School, like the Athelhampton School Tryphena had first attended, was a "British" or Nonconformist school. It had been founded by Thomas Samson, whose friend and relative, George Wood, founded the Athelhampton school. Samson died soon after but Coryates school was now run by his elder unmarried daughter, Miss Elizabeth Samson of Upwey. Miss Samson was a frequent visitor of the Woods at Athelhampton.[38] After Tryphena's good record at Athelhampton, Miss Samson would willingly appoint her pupil-teacher at Coryates. The connection was lasting; Miss Samson was one of Tryphena's earliest visitors at the school where she had her first job after passing through college.[39] She also stayed with Miss Samson at Upwey during a later school holiday, an extraordinary privilege for a girl of her class; "don't you seem to see me with a servant behind my chair at meals?", she joked to her brother.[40]

One cannot tell how much Hardy saw or knew of his cousin while they were both battling out their careers in their various ways; but the most interesting link between Tryphena's story at this time and Hardy's later work is her connection with the landowner, Mrs. Catherine Hawkins. Tryphena shows a close and longstanding friendship with Mrs. Hawkins's farm bailiff, Robert Spiller, and his wife.[41] It is probable that she lodged in the Spillers' house while teaching at Coryates. Mrs. Hawkins was an enterprising young widow who, with Spiller's assistance, ran her own large farm of 525 acres.[42] The story of the farm managed by a young woman became a local legend; and it would even seem, from chapters 8 and 10 of *Far From the Madding Crowd*, that Bathsheba Everdene in the novel employed the same number of men and boys Catherine Hawkins did in real life at Waddon House. Hardy, when he came to write the novel, transferred the setting from Waddon to Puddletown.

This work, his first fully popular novel, was still some years in the future. At present all he had for his pains of 1867–69 was a novel which he had been advised not to print. Perhaps worse, the labour and anxiety of novel-writing seems virtually to have dried up his poetry. On 17 July 1868, he noted "Perhaps I can do a volume of poems consisting of the *other side* of common emotions", but nothing remains of this project. A month earlier, while Moule was reading the fair copy of *The Poor Man and the Lady*, Hardy sketched the plan of a narrative poem on the Battle of the Nile. This was not finished and has not survived. Nor has a lyric entitled *A Departure by Train*, written earlier in the year.[43] The only poem that has survived, from the middle of 1867 to the middle of 1869, is a draft *Song* dated 22 June 1868.[44] This is only interesting in showing how Hardy used to compose poems at this time. He later wrote to Edmund Gosse: "Many of the poems were temporarily jotted down to the extent of a stanza or two when ideas occurred, and put aside till time should serve for finishing them—often not till years after".[45] This *Song* demonstrates the process, though the draft shows more than "a stanza or two". The poem is in stanzas of eight lines each. Stanza 1 has only one and a half lines, and then "&c" and dots. Stanzas 2, 3, 5, and 7 are written in full, and then worked over with corrections, the last heavily altered. Stanza 4 is represented by the first two lines, and then dots, stanza 6 by dots only. The system seems to show that Hardy, at least at this time, "architected" a poem rather as he would a building, sketching the whole of the main outline, and filling in embellishments and details later. However, this is the only poem of his in any way associated with the date 1868; apart from the few instances mentioned, he does not speak of any others. This is not to say that his poetic observation failed him. In a poem obviously written much later, entitled *Life and Death At Sunrise* (*Near Dogbury Gate*, 1867), he recalls in chilling and exact detail one of the many thick foggy mornings of the grey October of 1867. All the evidence, though, is that his grapple with full-length prose narrative had temporarily silenced his poems. What it had not silenced was the inner voice which told him of his destiny as a prophetic creative writer.

# 11

# Tryphena and the Sparkses

HARDY'S secret mind in these years, including this inner confidence in his own destiny as a writer, is shown in a very curious and typical piece of personal evidence. This evidence is contained in the markings he made during the years 1868 to 1872 in his Bible and his prayer book. Compared with the prolific annotations of the years 1861 to 1864, these marks are very few. If the complete lack of annotation in the years between 1865 and 1867 does indeed show his loss of faith in this period,[1] it does not seem that there was any fervent renewal from 1868 onward. Rather, it seems likely that the return home to the familiar habits of childhood and youth had caused a revival of church-going and Bible-reading, but with none of the previous intensity of belief. One must, of course, guard against reading too much autobiography into all of these. Often, even when they seem most specific, the dates he added in the margin of the text simply indicate that this was part of the lesson or psalm for that day in the Church calendar, noted by him after some service, or reading of the appropriate passage. For example, he annotated verse 17 of chapter 4 of the Epistle of St. James, with what appears great exactitude, "Dec. 11 –70: 10.40 p.m." Yet this was simply part of the second lesson at evening service that day, and probably indicates no more than a late night reading or recall of that passage. Similarly, in his prayer book, the date "8.9.72" written above Psalm 41 indicates that this was one of the psalms for evening service on the eighth day of the month.

On the other hand, a few of Hardy's datings from 1868 onward do suggest an intensely personal application, quite unconnected with the Church calendar. The most striking of these is his dating of Job, chapter 12, verse 4, "I am as one mocked of his neighbour". Against this underlined passage, Hardy wrote "1868–71". What this meant in his personal life is expanded in a poem written much later, and called *In the Seventies*. He headed this poem with the Latin version of exactly the same passage from Job, and wrote

> In the seventies I was bearing in my breast,
> > Penned tight,
> Certain starry thoughts that threw a magic light
> On the worktimes and the soundless hours of rest
> In the seventies; aye, I bore them in my breast
> > Penned tight.

In the seventies when my neighbours—even my friend—
     Saw me pass,
Heads were shaken, and I heard the words, "Alas,
For his onward years and name unless he mend!"
In the seventies, when my neighbours and my friend
     Saw me pass.

In the seventies those who met me did not know
     Of the vision
That immuned me from the chillings of misprision
And the damps that choked my goings to and fro
In the seventies; yea, those nodders did not know
     Of the vision. . . .

Hardy, even in the poem, does not specify exactly what "the vision" was; but the dates in the Bible against precisely the same passage from Job which heads the poem show it was the inner consciousness of his own power as a writer through all his battles to become published during these years, starting with 1868, when he first sent a novel to a publisher, working through to 1871, when his first published novel, *Desperate Remedies*, finally appeared.

Other marked passages suggest a feeling of destiny in his work at this time; there seems no doubt that he had found encouragement in Morley's judgement that there was power in his writing, even though *The Poor Man and the Lady* had eventually proved unpublishable. Yet there are other notes which suggest that during his two-year struggle to get that novel accepted, there was also a struggle in his emotional and personal life. The exact nature of this conflict will probably never become completely clear; certainly, the exact order of events will always remain in doubt. At the same time, the general course of the emotional difficulties, in which Hardy now found himself, can be fairly well traced, in spite of the fact that it has become wildly confused by later guesswork, conjecture, and controversy.[2]

The situation involved his close relatives, the Sparks family of Puddletown, and, in the first instance, his mother's sister, Maria Sparks, born Maria Hand. Strong and strict, like all the Hand women, it was she who had held her family together and kept them to what she hoped would be profitable careers. Her last effort seems to have been her defiance of the Puddletown school over Tryphena, and her success in seeing her daughter settled as teacher in the British school at Coryates, early in 1868. During that year, her own health, never good, deteriorated alarmingly. Her husband, James, wrote on 29 August that she was "like a person in a decline",[3] and on 2 November she died. Through failing health, her driving force on her family had already lessened. Her easy-going husband had failed in his cabinet-making business, and was obliged to seek employment as a travelling journeyman.[4] His own health, in his late sixties, was unable to stand this, and in the next few years he complained of feeling so ill that he could hardly walk long distances to seek work[5] as a joiner. In fact, before many years, in 1874, he himself was to die sadly from an injury contracted at work, a poisoned wound in the hand resulting in erysipelas.[6]

With even less money coming in than usual, it was necessary for the Sparks children to have successful careers to help support their father. The two boys, James and Nathaniel, both like him struggling carpenters, and like him improvident, had nothing to send home from their respective jobs in London and Somerset. One daughter, Emma, also in Somerset, the hardest worker in the family,[7] was already submerged by numerous children and an unsuccessful husband, Thomas Cary. The eldest daughter, Rebecca, still managed her dress-making business in Puddletown; but with the decline in population there, and the drift to Dorchester at this time, she was not getting as much work as she had in the past.

There remained the family's two most promising members, Martha and Tryphena. Martha was now a ladies' maid in a good job in a new fashionable quarter of London, the freshly-built Prince of Wales's Terrace, Kensington, where she worked for a Mrs. Molineux at No. 16.[8] Petite, well-dressed and smart, she had profited by her employment, during which she had visited Paris and learnt French. Upper servants like herself, though not well-paid, could command better salaries than in the country, and with good references could expect steady employment. Even more promising was the future that lay before Tryphena. If she could complete her three years' of pupil-teaching, which had started in November 1866, pass an examination, and receive a testimonial of good conduct, she could qualify for a two year course at a training college. If she passed through this successfully, she could at once receive a salary as a teacher which might be as much as £100 a year or more.[9] This would lift her into a different social bracket from all the rest of her family, and she could find herself, in her twenties, earning far more than her own father in his sixties.

The question was, now that the tight rein of the mother was removed, whether Martha and Tryphena would stick to their promising careers, and particularly whether Tryphena would complete her next qualifying year from November 1868 to November 1869. In a later and grimly humorous poem, Hardy pictured the breaking-out of just such a family after their strict mother's funeral, when "Mother won't know".[10] He himself was now specially involved in the situation caused by his aunt's death. It was she who, when he was only a youth, had disapproved of his adolescent advances to Rebecca and shown him the door. It was she who when, according to her son Nathaniel, Hardy seriously wished to marry Martha, refused to allow the match and claimed that it was "against the law of the church" for cousins to marry.[11] What would be his action now that this uncompromising relative was removed? He could have taken up his hopes with Martha again; but it is impossible to tell what had passed between them by now, and whether either or both would have considered it. There is no evidence, and conjecture is useless.

What is certain is that Hardy became involved in some way with Tryphena. He was attracted again and again by the same type of woman, a replica of his own mother, with the striking features shared by all women of the Hand family. Tryphena, with her dark hair and eyebrows, fine eyes and strong, intelligent face, was a younger version of both Rebecca and Martha. From photographs, she seems to have had one quality not so apparent in their likenesses, a lurking sense of fun about her full wide mouth. In fact, her own letters show a lively, not to say broad type of humour. Writing to her brother Nathaniel in 1869, she added a mocking postscript, "How's your sweetheart old blow porridge Bibican?"[12] This rough term, obviously indicating some tendency in Nathaniel to blow hot and cold in his love affairs, also shows a certain shrewdness by Tryphena about human nature. In the event, Nathaniel Sparks did not marry his sweetheart, a girl called Annie Lanham, who had been a near contemporary at training college with Mary Hardy,[13] until almost the last possible moment, when she was already seven months pregnant.[14] Since her home was at Trowbridge,[15] only a few miles from where he worked at Rode, he had only his own dilatory nature to blame.

How deep was the attraction that Hardy felt towards this sequence of cousins? His almost passive preoccupation with the type rather than the individual suggests something less normal than any ordinary love-attraction. This involuntary pattern indicates that none of these attachments showed real strength and depth. It is a pattern remarkably repeated in Hardy's curious novel of his fifties, *The Well-Beloved*, in which the hero, Pierston, falls in love, again almost without volition, with three generations of girls, all with strong physical resemblances. In the large Sparks family, his three girl-cousins were so widely separate in age as to suggest three generations. The eldest, Rebecca, was over twenty-one years older than the youngest, Tryphena. One of the few, puzzled reviews of *The Well-Beloved* remarked that it seemed to present "a man who all his life is in love with love rather than any particular woman".[16] This could well be the verdict on Hardy himself during these attachments, whose extraordinary sequence lay behind the basic scheme of the later novel.

On the other hand, his impulse toward each girl seems to have been strong enough at the time, however little it was to last, for Hardy to express his feelings in a more normal way. Martha's brother witnessed

that Hardy had wished to marry Martha; his own son reported this in a
description of Tryphena, during which he remarked, "Thomas Hardy
first wanted to marry Martha".[17] Then, so he writes, Hardy afterwards
wanted to marry Tryphena; but with his rebuffs over Rebecca and
Martha, Hardy is not likely to have expressed this wish until after the
mother's death early in November 1868. His attachment to the youngest
cousin, Tryphena, can probably be dated in 1869.[18]

It was helped by a change, during this year, in the circumstances of
Hardy's professional life as an architect, or rather an "architeck's
clerk", as he was described locally.[19] The prolonged negotiations over
*The Poor Man and the Lady* had made his work for Hicks in Dorchester,
as he admits, fairly desultory; but it entered into a new phase when, on
12 February 1869, Hicks himself died at the early age of fifty-three.
Hicks's firm was taken over by G. R. Crickmay, A.R.I.B.A., who already had a flourishing architectural practice at Weymouth, with a
contract for what was virtually a large middle-class housing estate in
the Green Hill area of that town. Crickmay found that Hicks had a
number of unfinished contracts for church restoration and re-designing
still outstanding. In April, just after Hardy had received Meredith's
advice not to publish *The Poor Man and the Lady*, Crickmay approached
him for help over these commissions. The most urgent was for the large-
scale conversion and expansion of an Early English church at Turnworth. Hardy took this on as Crickmay's assistant, and was left
effectively in charge of many details of design. The rebuilding was
financed by the Parry Okeden family, as a memorial to the late squire,
the major part of the backing coming from his widow, Julia Parry
Okeden. Hicks had drawn up a plan on 3 December 1868, which was not
so much a restoration as an almost complete rebuilding. The whole of
the old and ruinous church, except the tower, was to be demolished, and
a new church built with the addition of a north aisle. The faculty for
this was published on 7 May 1869, and on 13 May work started under
Hardy's supervision, the specification having already been drawn up by
Crickmay,[20] with what appear to be Hardy's revisions. Demolition
finished, the new foundation stone was laid on 19 June.[21] The interior
building was to be of Corsham Down stone, and considerable freedom
was left for the embellishment of the capitals and corbels. Hardy's
designs for the capitals are delicate traceries of birds, fruits, and flowers
in the French Early Gothic style, which he had probably learnt from the
work of William Burges. Even more striking, though less successful, are
the bearded heads serving as corbels. Furthest west, there is a particularly pert and lifelike owl, which is almost certainly Hardy's
individual design. It resembles the small, witty animal drawings, also
based on the work of Burges, which appear in Hardy's own architectural
notebook, and in which an owl is actually included.[22] This delightful

interior shows that Hardy, in church architecture at least, had brought considerable skill from his experiences in Blomfield's office. This commission also added to his knowledge of the great houses of the district; he later took Turnworth House as the model for Hintock House in *The Woodlanders*.[23]

This work, and other church architectural designs prepared by Hardy for Crickmay in Hicks's old Dorchester office, proved so satisfactory that, later in June, Crickmay came forward with a further proposal. This was that Hardy should come and work in his main office at Weymouth, for a three months' summer spell in the first instance, with possible longer extension.[24] Hardy, on 8 June, had just written an anxious letter from his home at Bockhampton to Tinsley the publisher about the fate of *The Poor Man*. It seemed likely to repeat its failure with Macmillan and Chapman. In the circumstances—and especially if he were contemplating marriage in any practical way—Crickmay's offer seemed providential. Sometime in June, Hardy took lodgings at 3 Wooperton Street, Weymouth, which gave him rooms with an open view to the Ridgeway and the downs to the north.[25] His first stroll along the seafront, coming away from his interview with Crickmay, delighted him. Bands were playing, the sun was shining, little pleasure steamers were leaving for Lulworth Cove and other excursions. June, July, and August were beautifully fine that year, and in a holiday town everything seemed set fair for pleasure over the next three months at least. He bathed at seven every morning, rowed a boat on the bay every evening, and felt better in health than he had done for nearly ten years.

Also to the point was that Weymouth, not Dorchester, was the central town for Tryphena Sparks, working at Coryates in the Waddon Vale; Coryates news, in fact, when it occurred, was reported in Weymouth papers rather than in Dorchester.[26] The place was easy of access, with the more energetic walking habits of that age, within a short distance of Weymouth through the village of Chickerell. This raised the question whether the small but intense revival of poetry in Hardy at Weymouth was connected with this new attachment. He had apparently written hardly any poems for a year or more; and poetry, with the young Hardy, always reflected a new emotional phase in his life. The few poems definitely written at Weymouth,[27] *Her Father*, *The Singing Lovers*, *The Dawn after the Dance*, and *At Waking*, three of them specifically dated 1869, are of very uneven quality. They range from a somewhat formal exercise in a conventional idea, in the first-named, to a poem of great emotional charge, reflected in its shifts and explosions of rhythm, *At Waking*, which is the Weymouth counterpart of his London *Neutral Tones*. This poem, like *Neutral Tones*, is a revelation of the power as a poet that was to come to the mature Hardy. Its vision of disillusion with

the beloved one is most dramatically conveyed in the sudden broken
beat of the last verse:

> O vision appalling
> When the one believed-in thing
> Is seen falling, falling,
> With all to which hope can cling.
> Off: it is not true;
> For it cannot be
> That the prize I drew
> Is a blank to me!

Just over a year later, Hardy made a notebook entry about "lying just
after waking", and the sad but accurate disillusion that it can bring.[28]
In the poem, incidentally, it is a vision, and not the actual appearance
of his love in bed that he is seeing. It is something, as the poem says,
that he "seemed to behold", an "insight" and a "thought". A cancelled line—"Those words she had written awry"—even suggests that
the vision was of a disillusioning letter. Yet it also suggests the doubts
that always came to his nature in human relationships, the mood of
earlier works such as *Revulsion* among his London poems. The difference
here is that he does not now accept as easily the idea that failure in love
may be better than success and its attendant risk of later loss. Here the
tone is anxious, possessive, and even hysterical. It is the note of Shakespeare's Troilus—"For it *cannot* be".

What passed between Tryphena and Hardy during this summer at
Weymouth is difficult to say. His obvious enjoyment of life at this time,
the delights of the sunlit promenade, the changing colours of the distant
cliffs, the bands playing the Morgenblätter waltz, all suggest that
pleasure was heightened by a lively, attractive companion. Yet their
meetings must have been circumscribed by her work alone, and by her
concern for the future. Only an absolutely unblemished moral character
could insure her entry into a Nonconformist college, or, indeed, any
teaching employment afterwards. As late as the 1880s, a Nonconformist
teacher was dismissed for having once been seen entering a public
house, and although she tried hard to get a teaching post in another
part of the country, the stigma followed her everywhere.[29] Tryphena
had her school-manager and patron, Miss Samson, living at Upwey,
halfway between Waddon and Weymouth. Very little would escape her,
and she would judge Tryphena as she would a servant. Indeed, when
Tryphena, as a head-teacher, stayed with her half-a-dozen years later,
Miss Samson, taking her to Weymouth by train, paid for her fare
second-class, while she herself travelled first, an arrangement most
employers made with servants.[30]

At the same time, the cousins' attachment deepened to such an
extent that Hardy bought her a ring. Again, any sequence of dates is

hard to establish, but the fact is clear; the story that Hardy at this time bought a ring for a Dorset girl was handed down through most reliable channels.[31] Tryphena's own daughter later said that Hardy actually gave Tryphena the ring, a small inconspicuous one, and here again the fact should be accepted, though the witness is less reliable.[32] What the ring meant to both of them is again less easy to say, at a time when the lives and careers of both were in the melting pot. As cloudy autumn came after this idyllic summer, there may well have been elements of crisis for Hardy. In mid-September, his final resolve to abandon all hopes of publication for *The Poor Man* led him to re-engage himself to Crickmay, who accepted with alacrity, in spite of the fact that a new young assistant had just joined the office. With obstinate determination, Hardy reckoned this would give him time for a new novel. He did not go back to the rural tale he had sketched a year before, but, with Meredith's advice in mind, launched on an invention of melodramatic plot and arresting title, *Desperate Remedies*. He wrote fast; and as always when he was writing at such a pace, filled in many of the descriptive and incidental details from actual experiences and happenings. Most of these were near at hand, though, as has been said, the melodramatic incident of the heroine's father falling abruptly to his death off a scaffold, which begins the book, certainly harks back to his own youthful experience of seeing the sudden drop of the hanged man.[33] Otherwise, much of the background of the book was reproduced from sources close to him. The beautiful July weather, with which the main part of the story opens, shows almost photographically the bay at Weymouth, the deep and varied colours of the water, the rowing in small hired boats, the steamer excursions to Lulworth. One of the most successful descriptions in the book, a disastrous fire burning the inn and several cottages, caused by a smouldering heap of couch-grass, owes much to an actual happening at this time. On 28 October, the paper carried the story of a destructive fire in the property of Mrs. Wood of Athelhampton near Puddletown, where "some workmen had been engaged in drying a quantity of flax near" and it was conjectured that "the sparks were blown by the wind on to the roof of the barn, which, becoming ignited, led to the outbreak", just as Hardy makes it happen in the novel.[34] It is almost equally likely that Farmer Springrove's failure to insure the property, after having done so for many years, had its real-life parallel in the account of another extensive fire in Puddletown itself a year earlier. In this "Mr. William Brown, whose premises had been insured for the past 40 years, had unfortunately only a few months ago discontinued his policy".[35] Brown's loss amounted to between four and five hundred pounds; Springrove's, in the novel, to six hundred. The most fascinating use of actuality is perhaps where Hardy fills out his novel with a satirical description of the doctors attempting to treat the mysterious lameness of the heroine's brother. First diagnosing rheumatism, they use "hot bran, liniments . . . and also severe friction". This is followed by a treatment during which "they pricked the place with a long needle several times". In Hardy's heavily-annotated copy of *Modern Domestic Medicine* by Thomas J. Graham, heat (though not necessarily produced by bran), liniments, and severe friction are advised for rheumatism; but what makes the source certain is that Graham, unusually for the time, recommends "Acupuncturation", which "consists in making a small puncture in or near the part of the body affected, with a long needle".[36] After this treatment, specifically with "a long needle", the exact phrase used by Hardy, it is no surprise that when the doctors in the novel then diagnose erysipelas, they give the remedies also found in Graham's book, "Blisters, flour, and starch".

While Hardy was using local life and his own interests to colour and enlarge his melodramatic novel, real and dramatic events close at hand caught his own emotional life, coming to a head in November 1869. In that month, the mother of Martha and Tryphena Sparks, the two girls on whose careers their family fortunes now mainly depended, had been dead just a year. Her firm influence had waned; perhaps the freedom had been too much for Martha, who now found herself heading for disaster. In this month, she discovered herself to be pregnant by the butler at her place of work in Kensington, William Duffield, a handsome and virile-looking man. He was the son of a farm-bailiff, and he probably came from Yorkshire, where the name is a common one.

Marriage by licence took place at Kensington Parish Church on 30 November;[37] but Martha's career as a ladies' maid was ruined. Mrs. Molineux, her employer, dismissed them both. Duffield found a job as a coffee-house keeper in the Notting Hill district, at 61 Kensington Park Road.[38] He did not take kindly to the work. Nor did her family take kindly to him; Rebecca Sparks was full of lamentation for the fate of the brilliant and attractive Martha, "the flower of our flock".[39] Whether Hardy viewed the event in the same light, or indeed how he viewed it, one cannot tell; but Martha was a girl who, on good authority, he had once wanted to marry. The pregnancy of girls to other men had been a theme in his earlier poems. It may be that with his extremely volatile nature towards women, the attraction to Tryphena had driven out or lessened the feelings he had once had for Martha. Yet the date of 7 November 1869, which he put in the margin of his prayer book against verses 14–17 of the 35th Psalm,[40] is significant; the 15th verse reads

But in mine adversity they rejoiced, and gathered themselves together; yea, the very abjects came together against me unawares, making mouths at me, and ceased not.

Perhaps this refers to his working struggles; but it may not be accident that it coincides with news of Martha's ruin, perhaps hinted at in verse 17, "O deliver . . . my darling from the lions".

On the other hand, whether or not he was at all deeply affected by Martha's worldly failure, he must have been closely affected in this same month by Tryphena's success. In this month, she completed the three years as pupil-teacher that would qualify her for training college.[41] She could easily be recommended personally to any of the colleges of the British and Foreign School Society by the powerful local Congregationalist group. Miss Samson's friend, Mrs. George Wood, lady of the manor of Athelhampton, had the maiden name of Vaizey.[42] Her niece, Mrs. John R. Vaizey, was a Life Governor of the British and Foreign School Society,[43] and branch meetings of the British and Foreign Bible Society, attended by all of them, were held at Athelhampton Hall.[44] A reference from a minister of religion was generally needed, and this was probably provided by Mr. Miles of Athelhampton, since he, like Miss Samson, is found visiting Tryphena during her first job. The favour of this Athelhampton group insured Tryphena a place; entry was often by personal recommendation only, and an allowed ten per cent of the entry were not even pupil-teachers first. She seems to have been successful at Coryates, to judge by the happy tone of a letter written in the month's Harvest Holiday that summer. With the character she had retained, she could enter without even doing very well in the college examination. In point of fact, she passed in at second class, not first, but this was enough for her to be accepted by Stockwell Normal College in South London for the term beginning at the end of January 1870.[45]

The effect this was likely to have on her relationship with Hardy must be measured by the discipline of the colleges, and their attitude to these girls, largely escaping in this way from the only other employment open to them, domestic service, in which Tryphena's own sisters had been. Only a very few years later, the senior teacher at Stockwell College wrote these rules[46] on the first page of a student's autograph album:

1. Never go out alone.
2. Don't speak at dinner time.
3. Never speak after 10–10 p.m.
4. Always wear a bonnet on Sunday.
5. Never go upstairs without asking.
6. If you go for a walk with a young gentleman always leave at the corner.
7. Never leave a square inch of dinner on your plate.
8. Take a constitutional daily either between 12 and 1 o'clock or 6 and 7.

These, it must also be observed, were intended as friendly advice, rather than setting out the official regulations of the college, which were even more stringent.

So, while the improvident Sparks family were whipping round to

scrape together the money for her text books,[47] Hardy was faced with
the prospect of losing Tryphena for large portions of the year; for the
holidays, even in the summer, were particularly short at Stockwell, and
Tryphena, in her second year there, joined in signing a round robin
pleading for a longer break.[48] After the relative freedom of Weymouth,
a life where short walks with young gentlemen were barely coun-
tenanced was acute deprivation. Yet Tryphena's determination to do
well in her career, and rescue her family, was obviously strong, and
carried on after college into her first job. Reasonably, it was something
to encourage. Irrationally, it might be a total blow to their relationship.
What Hardy made of it, and what went on between them in this crisis,
is unknown, though poems now and later seem to speak of conflicts,
perhaps associated with this time, between duty and desire, and are
filled with a sense of sudden unforeseen, yet foreseeable deprivation. All
we know is that Hardy plunged this month into the winter dancing-
classes at Weymouth, to which, he says, he had been introduced by the
new recruit to Crickmay's office; he also wrote even more desperately at
*Desperate Remedies*.[49] There is, in fact, a slightly hysterical tone about
the half-dozen poems Hardy wrote at Weymouth. In the final verse of
*At Waking*, as we have seen, there is almost a note of panic—

> For it cannot be
> That the prize I drew
> Is a blank to me!

Other poems are artificial and strained. *The Dawn after the Dance*, with
its commonplace sentiments matched by its commonplace metre, is an
artificial "situation" poem, and seems to tell a contrived and fictional
story.

One poem, however, fused the authentic Hardy mixture of a place
and an emotion so that they stand for one another indissolubly. Originally
called *In the Crypted Way*, he ultimately printed it as *In the Vaulted
Way*, somewhat obscuring the picture of two lovers huddled under a low
archway, and making it sound as if their emotional parting took place
in some high-arched cathedral. With its original opening restored, it
catches, in simple, moving terms the feeling of an actual situation.

> In the crypted way, where the passage turned
> To the shadowy corner that none could see,
> You paused for our parting,—plaintively;
> Though overnight had come words that burned
> My fond frail happiness out of me.

> And then I kissed you,—despite my thought
> That our spell must end when reflection came
> On what you had deemed me, whose one long aim
> Had been to serve you; that what I sought
> Lay not in a heart that could breathe such blame.

> But yet I kissed you; whereon you again
> As of old kissed me. Why, why was it so?
> Do you cleave to me after that light-tongued blow?
> If you scorned me at eventide, how love then?
> The thing is dark, Dear. I do not know.

If the poem, written in 1870, was composed in the January of that year, it may represent, with its account of an ambiguous parting, with fluctuating emotions, something of the situation between Hardy and Tryphena; its scene may be Sandsfoot Castle, Weymouth, also used in *The Well-Beloved* as the setting for an assignation and lovers' separation.

The most likely guide is again Hardy's Bible.[50] Tryphena entered Stockwell College at the week-end of 28/29 January 1870. In his Bible, Hardy wrote the words "Sunday night Jan. 29–70" at the head of the book of Joel. An inch further down, in this unlikely prophet, he underlined verse 5 of chapter 1:

> That which the palmer-worm hath left hath the locust eaten; and that which the locust hath left hath the canker-worm eaten; and that which the canker-worm hath left hath the caterpillar eaten.

Associated with this date, which has no relevance in the Church calendar, this marking seems to show a triple deprivation such as Hardy had suffered in the strange repetitive history of his three cousins. Moreover, all his other underlinings in Joel speak of acute deprivation;[51] the fig-tree is stripped bare, the pasture has ceased, "the stars shall withdraw their shining". The full force of this history may have overwhelmed him at this week-end, and aroused his homing instinct; for within a few days of Tryphena's college incarceration, Hardy gave up his Weymouth lodgings and was back with his mother at Bockhampton.[52]

The long, low cottage-like house at Bockhampton, on the edge of the heath, was always his refuge in stress; and here, reassuringly, he found his family in full strength. His father, by now prospering, had set up a little office by the stairs, with a tiny window facing the heath, through which he paid his workmen, who filed past the outside of the house. One can see here Jemima Hardy's dislike of muddy boots in her neat rooms. With his father was now Hardy's brother Henry, aged eighteen, and officially known as "father's assistant",[53] especially in his family capacity as mason. He was a cheerful, outgoing youth, a complete contrast with his withdrawn elder brother. Identical with Hardy in quiet unassuming temperament was his sister Mary, now living permanently at home. She had left Minterne Magna and was now teaching in Piddlehinton,[54] the next village up the Piddle valley, and in easy distance of Bockhampton. The renewal of this brother–sister relationship meant much to Hardy, and was reinforced by its frequent appearance in his favourite poet, Shelley. Finally, there was Kate, aged thirteen and still at school, but starting on a course that would lead her to her sister's college, and a similar career as a school-teacher. Like Henry, she was cheerful, forthright, and amusing. In this family atmosphere of encouragement, Hardy pressed swiftly on with his novel, and by the beginning of March, he had finished it, all but the last three or four chapters.[55]

On 5 March, he sent the manuscript, as far as he had gone, to Macmillan, hoping that John Morley would find the same power he had noted in *The Poor Man*, together with the greater care over plot that he had demanded. The long friendly letter he had first received from Alexander Macmillan, and his subsequent kindness, added to his hope. There was one significant difference from his earlier application to Macmillans. Hardy did not, this time, consult Horace Moule, nor apparently get him to write a recommendation.[56] It is possible that Moule did not altogether approve of a novel of sensation, written so much with the advice of Morley and Meredith in mind, since Hardy in his poem, *In the Seventies*, suggests that "my friend" looked askance at the course he was taking. On the other hand, the main reason may simply be that Moule had enough troubles of his own. Just over a year before, at the end of 1868, he had gone into "unexpected retirement" from his teaching job at Marlborough.[57] There is nothing official to show that he left under a cloud, and in any case a fairly newly-fledged public school would need to be reticent; but this was one more in the series of mysterious failures that beset his career, and their cause was now becoming a more or less open secret. Horace Moule had for some years already devised his own way of dealing with the cycle of depression, which he tried to relieve by drink, which in its turn prevented his work. He had reached a stage in this cycle when the drinking was beginning to show itself in prolonged bouts. Unwilling to give pain to his father, and his family at Fordington, he would go off by himself to remote Dorset villages, and disappear into solitary drinking. When these absences became prolonged, his younger brother Frederick, who had for some years assisted their father as curate in Fordington, would search through the likely places until he could find Horace and bring him back.[58] Unfortunately, perhaps on the assumption that Horace was settled in his job, the sympathetic Frederick, who was married, had in 1868 got himself a living at Yaxley near Peterborough. It is therefore possible that Horace's troubles had become more obvious about now, with his return to live at Fordington Rectory, unemployed, and self-styled as a "classical scholar".[59] At all events, it is pretty clear that Hardy, who knew Moule as well as anyone, had a close idea. Some years afterwards, in his Literary Notebook, he broke off his philosophic quotations from George Eliot and Carlyle to enter the description from Trollope's *Orley Farm*:[60]

> But Mr. Moulder did not get drunk. His brandy-and-water went into his blood, & into his eyes, & into his feet, & into his hands—but not into his brain.

The irony of the similar name was part of a deeper irony. To see this collapse of his friend was enough to convince Hardy alone that the universe was ruled by a power indifferent to Man.

With his own manuscript off his hands, Hardy had to attend to a matter over which Crickmay had been pursuing him. This was one of Hicks's former commissions for church-restoration, which had come unexpectedly to light just when Hardy thought he had finished the whole batch.[61] It concerned the mouldering parish church of St. Juliot, near Boscastle, in North Cornwall, with its dropsical and dangerous tower, needing a massive restoration long-delayed by lack of money and an absentee patron who lived in Antigua. Hicks surveyed it and drew up a plan in April 1867;[62] but only two months later, the wife of the elderly rector, the Reverend Caddell Holder, died, and the plan was put into cold storage. However, the rector quickly married again, this time a woman half his age, who, like Hicks, came from a Bristol family, and she took up the cause of church restoration with energy. Then Hicks himself died, but his successor was pursued with summonses to St. Juliot, and wrote to Hardy on 11 February, asking him to go and make a fresh survey at this remote place, all expenses paid. Hardy, intent on getting the novel off to Macmillan, did not at once respond; but after another urgent appeal from Crickmay, he set off at four o'clock in the starlight from Bockhampton on Monday, 7 March. It took him twelve hours by various trains to reach Launceston, from which he had to hire a trap to go the final sixteen or seventeen miles. A poem he drafted shortly afterwards describes his thoughts of Tryphena Sparks in her college in London as he progressed toward a spot that seemed as far west from her as it could possibly be. Indeed, he was scribbling a poem on a piece of blue paper now. As the fine day darkened in the early March evening, his journey took on a weird strangeness, heightened by the approaching sound of the Atlantic breakers, and the swivelling flash of the coastal lighthouses. A small lane to the left led to the rectory, and he rang the bell in complete darkness, hastily thrusting the blue paper with the poem into his pocket. He was led into the drawing-room, and found there neither the rector, who had suddenly retired to bed with gout, nor his wife, who was nursing him. Instead, he was received by a young lady in a brown dress. She was a full-bosomed creature with a high colour, bright blue eyes and masses of blonde hair. Her open-air complexion and her energetic movements were dazzling to the tired traveller. In her extreme vitality, she seemed unlike any woman he had met before. She was the rector's sister-in-law, Emma Lavinia Gifford, Hardy's future wife.

# 12

# Emma and the Giffords

EMMA LAVINIA GIFFORD, named after her mother and an aunt who died in infancy, was the youngest daughter of John Attersoll Gifford and Emma Farman. Though her father's family had originally come from Staines in Middlesex, he and his bride were both Bristolians, and at one time had been brought up in the same street in that city, Norfolk Street in the parish of St. Paul's.[1] Mr. Gifford was the son of a schoolmaster, Richard Ireland Gifford, one of whose early eighteenth-century connections had kept a girls' school at Kingston. His own profession may have prompted his granddaughter's quaintly ingenuous remark that "the scholastic line was always taken at times of declining fortunes";[2] he himself kept a small private school, described as "French and Commercial", at his home in Norfolk Street. Emma Farman, whom John Attersoll Gifford married at Raglan, Monmouthshire, on 24 April 1832, came from an old-established Bristol family. Her ancestors had been traders and merchants, and her father, William Farman, was an apparently well-to-do accountant.[3] John Attersoll Gifford had qualified as a solicitor, and had practised in Plymouth for a short time before his marriage. He returned to his native Bristol and practised there for the first five years of his married life, before going back again to Plymouth, where his mother, a Devonshire woman, had moved after her husband's death. Emma Lavinia Gifford, the youngest but one of a family of five, was born there on 24 November 1840; she was therefore a few months younger than Hardy himself.

She herself described her childhood home as "a most intellectual one and not only so but one of exquisite home-training and refinement". In her recollections in old age, there are idyllic pictures of family music and singing, of readings and discussions of books.[4] Yet there was a darker side, which even memory could not altogether disguise. Part of this came from a peculiar money situation. John Attersoll Gifford was his widowed mother's favourite son. When he rejoined her in Plymouth, she decided to live in the same house with him, contributing her own considerable private income. She not only used this to bring up his children, but, in his youngest daughter's words, "she considered it best that he should give up his profession which he disliked, and live a life of quiet cultivated leisure".[5] One gets the impression, incidentally, that his own wife, a simple character who read nothing except the Bible and *East*

*Lynne*, did not count for much in this household dominated by the older woman. The awakening came when the latter died in 1860. She had set up a trust, from which her favourite son and his wife were to receive all the interest. Unfortunately, she had so depleted the capital that there was hardly any left, her estate being sworn at under £1000.[6] Though still appearing in the Law lists as a solicitor, John Attersoll Gifford had evidently taken his mother's advice, and failed to build up a practice. Money was desperately short; the house had to be sold, and the family moved to the remote district of Bodmin in North Cornwall, where living was cheaper. Even then, Emma and her elder sister had to go out to work as governesses. The sister, Helen Catherine, then became an unpaid companion to an old lady, in whose home she met her husband, the Reverend Caddell Holder. Emma joined her in 1868, and was helping with the duties of the rectory two years later when Thomas Hardy arrived on the scene.

As well as poverty, there was an even darker shadow on the Gifford household. In times of crisis, John Attersoll Gifford drank heavily. As his daughter artlessly but frankly put it, "never a wedding, removal or death occurred in the family but he broke out again".[7] The origin of this pattern of outbursts is more than a little puzzling. Its so-called explanation came from his mother, who "sympathised with him in the great sorrow of his life". Her own father, William Davie, had had the reputation of never going to bed sober,[8] so that she may well have felt sympathetic. Her son's alleged sorrow was that he had originally been engaged to his wife's elder sister, a girl of eighteen with beautiful golden hair. She had died of scarlet fever; his drinking habits started then, and continued through his subsequent marriage. Emma was his only child with fair hair like her dead aunt; he used, she said, to stroke it, sighing at the memory. This romantic story, which Emma obviously felt gave her a special place in her father's affections, is perhaps not true. Neither in the St. Paul's parish registers, nor in the Bristol newspapers is there any trace of the death of an elder Farman girl.[9] Though there may be some other explanation, it is at least possible that the story was partly invented by his doting mother to excuse her favourite son's alcoholic outbreaks. Its probable basis is that a younger Farman girl did die, aged fifteen, three weeks before John Attersoll Gifford's marriage.[10]

Emma Lavinia Gifford certainly appears, in the light of all this, as the spoilt child of a spoilt father. There is no doubt at all that wilfulness and lack of restraint gave her a dash and charm that captivated Hardy from the moment they met. He did not consider, any more than most men would have done, that a childish impulsiveness and inconsequential manner, charming at thirty, might grate on him when carried into middle age. It is likely, too, that her spontaneous gaiety and high spirits lightened the somewhat heavy mouth and powerful jaw, which were to become so sadly grotesque in her fifties. Yet as disillusion later set in, there was one more sinister trait which Hardy came to think he should have observed.

Briefly, Hardy came to convince himself that there was a strain of insanity in his wife's family; moreover, he led himself or was led to believe that he could have observed its signs in Emma herself in the early days of their courtship. This is most clearly indicated in poems such as *The Interloper*, *At the Piano*, and possibly though not quite so certainly, *The Man with a Past*. The image he uses for this threat of insanity—"that is a better word than 'madness'", he himself remarked —is that of a spectrelike figure, gaunt, grim and menacing, which intrudes on even the most happy occasions. *The Interloper* in Hardy's manuscript was first entitled *One Who Ought Not To Be There*,[11] and in that poem the warning is present even in these first light-hearted days in Cornwall. When questioned about the poem eight years after his wife's death Hardy would say nothing more definite than to remark, "I knew the family". It was the second Mrs. Hardy, however, who firmly pinned the label of insanity on Emma Hardy's family, saying: "She came of tainted stock. More than one of her relatives had been in a lunatic asylum". In various remarks, she picked out which members of the Gifford family she meant. She specified Walter Edwin Gifford, Emma's younger brother, as having "died in an asylum", and his daughter, Ethel Lilian Attersoll Gifford, as having been in and out of asylums too.[12] Later, she actually said that Emma's father was "in an asylum" when Hardy first met Emma.[13]

The question seems to be exactly on what evidence Hardy came to accept his second wife's judgement—for all the poems containing this belief appear to have been written in the years after his remarriage. His only personal statement was, as has been said, "I knew the family". In point of fact, he seems to have known very few of them, and characteristically only troubled to get in touch with many of Emma's relatives after her death. When he did, he seems to have gone into it fairly closely and compiled a tentative family-tree of the Giffords, to match that of his own family and of the family of his second wife.[14] How much he found during these researches is uncertain, for none of these genealogies is entirely accurate; but it is likely that his enquiries into the Giffords did reveal something that he might take for a strain of insanity. In fact, one Gifford in each generation, Emma's own and the generation before and after her, could be said to have had mental trouble. There is, however, no indication, and much to the contrary, that these showed any familial strain; and the most remarkable fact that emerges is that, in all three generations, the sufferer was not the one named by Hardy's second wife. She was doubtless speaking at random, and certainly on hearsay only; yet a curious pattern can be seen in her accusations of mental instability. In every instance, she makes the relationship closer than it was to Emma. Even when the victim was a brother, it proves to be a brother whom Emma hardly even knew, and not the one with whom Emma was in constant touch, named by Florence Hardy. Florence Hardy herself became obsessed with the idea that Emma Hardy was mad, and there is a clear reason for this obsession. She was determined to pluck out of Hardy's mind the things said in the derogatory diary that Emma had kept about her husband, and which he destroyed after her death. She was terrified that he would end by believing it.[15] She therefore tried to prove it the work of a madwoman. To prove the diary insane, she consistently shifted insanity nearer to Emma, without the slightest regard for the truth, as can be seen.

To begin with Emma's father: though the second Mrs. Hardy said he was in a lunatic asylum at the time of Hardy's courtship, he was not. In the early 1870s he is found living at home, at Kirland near Bodmin.[16] He visited Emma at her home soon after her honeymoon,[17] and he continued to visit other members of his family until late in his life.[18] There is, moreover, quite specific medical evidence that he was in good mental health at the age of eighty.[19] In 1890, his death was given, at the age of eighty-two, as due to senile decay and a long-established prostate condition;[20] but this, though showing his health had failed in old age, is hardly insanity. The truth was, he had a brother who had died *non compos mentis* long before Emma was born. Most of Emma's uncles and aunts show the pattern familiar in large Victorian families by either dying young or living to a ripe and tough old age. Her uncle, the Reverend Canon Edwin Hamilton Gifford who officiated at her marriage, lived to be eighty-five, and to complete his magnum opus, an edition of Eusebius, two years before his death.[21] An aunt, Charlotte Eliza, was sufficiently *compos mentis* to make a codicil to her will at the age of seventy, two years before her death.[22] On the other hand, several died young, including John Attersoll Gifford's elder brother, William Davie Gifford, who succumbed to tuberculosis in his twenty-fifth year, and his youngest brother, Nathaniel Richard, who died aged sixteen of typhus. Among these younger deaths, Philip Henry Gifford, the third Gifford boy, is recorded as having died at the age of twenty "of a deep decline",[23] but family papers explain this vague non-medical phrase by adding the words *non compos mentis*.[24] In actual fact, the two terms, together with his brother's tuberculosis, almost certainly indicate that he died of tubercular meningitis,[25] a non-familial condition, and one that can hardly be characterized as insanity.

Emma's father, then, was not "in an asylum" or insane at the time of her marriage or any other time; nor was he, as the second Mrs. Hardy also said, a bankrupt.[26] Of Emma's own generation it will be remembered that the second Mrs. Hardy picked on Emma's younger brother Walter as having died "in an asylum". Walter, however, died in his own London home at the age of fifty-eight of a prostate condition like his father.[27] He was certainly a lifelong hypochondriac and grumbler, characterized by Hardy himself as "a tiresome brother whose children Emma largely helped to educate".[28] In fact, Walter, who worked all his life in London at the Post Office Savings Bank, had the habit of dumping his two elder children, Gordon and Lilian, on any of his out-of-town relatives, his excuse apparently being that it was so damp and unhealthy in his own house in Maida Vale. Not only Emma but Hardy himself virtually adopted this niece and nephew, the latter being sent to school in Dorchester and trained as an architect with Hardy's help.[29] Walter, therefore, far from being insane, showed a self-protective shrewdness, which included, as Hardy said, never doing anything in return for his helpful relatives. He certainly did not die in an asylum. On the other hand, Emma's eldest brother, whom she hardly ever saw, Richard Ireland Gifford, certainly did. His death is recorded in the Warneford Asylum at Oxford in 1904 at the age of sixty-nine.[30] It is worth noting, though, that the dementia, from which he had suffered for several years, was apparently not at all familial, but proceeded from chronic Bright's disease.

In the next generation, the second Mrs. Hardy singled out the niece, Ethel Lilian Attersoll Gifford, Walter's daughter, whom the Hardys virtually brought up, as having been "in and out of asylums". There is no evidence of this, and although, like Emma, she had rather a childish manner, this could be quite charming. When she first stayed at Max Gate as a small girl, Hardy drew her a number of comic sketches. On the anniversary of her aunt's death, when she was helping to keep house for the widowed Hardy at Max Gate, she wrote him a pathetically sentimental little note,[31] in which she reminded him that "It is more than a year ago that I renamed you 'Daddy-Uncle' and that is what you are to me, and God bless you". In his will, drawn up in 1922, he left her a legacy, in addition to the annuity he and Emma had already provided for her, and there is no doubt she was treated as mentally capable in every legal sense. She died, like her brother Gordon, in her seventies, of a long-standing heart condition. There is no hint of mental trouble in the medical history of either. Far from providing any hint of mental instability in his first wife's family, Lilian Gifford was a supporting factor in Hardy's life after Emma's death. On the other hand, though he may not have known this, there was one member of the younger Gifford generation who had some form of mental trouble. This was Emma's much-loved second cousin, Leonie Gifford. She was the daughter of Emma's cousin, Charles Edwin Gifford, who held the post of Paymaster-in-Chief in the Royal Navy, and was part-editor of a handbook of Naval Law. His own father, Emma's uncle, George

Mitchell Gifford, was a bank manager in Launceston, a profession that does not suggest insanity. Leonie Gifford, however, had a series of "nervous breakdowns" from her forties onward,[32] which might lend colour to the idea that some mental instability was present in the generation after Emma.

From this family pattern, it is apparent that the story of Emma's relatives having been insane was slanted by the second Mrs. Hardy to bring it closer to Emma herself. As to Emma's own mental health, it is true that Hardy twice wrote of her suffering from delusions in later life. Immediately after her death, he wrote of "certain painful delusions she suffered from at times",[33] and two years later, on 23 November 1914, he wrote to her cousin Kate Gifford of "In later years an unfortunate mental aberration for which she was not responsible". It is not true, however, that any of her Gifford relatives noticed anything wrong with her.[34] It must be noted also that the hospital report on her brother Richard said that none of his siblings showed any signs of insanity.[35] Perhaps the best judgement was given by the person best placed to judge, the second Mrs. Hardy's trustee, Irene Cooper Willis. She examined a large collection of letters to Emma, some of which still exist. Her verdict was, "These letters seem to me to dispose of the idea that Mrs. Hardy No. 1 was 'mad'—as Mrs. Hardy No. 2 so often declared". It seems absolutely certain that Emma was never insane in any medical sense, and that there was no familial strain of insanity in the very large Gifford family. If Hardy came to think afterwards that there was an inherited abnormality he should have observed when they first met, it is mainly because his second wife persuaded him this was so.

Whether her over-protective action sprang from jealousy or irritation —and the second Mrs. Hardy had good reason for both—it is a paradox that she persuaded Hardy into a belief which produced some of his most poignant poems. It is an even greater paradox that there was, in fact, an inherited tendency in Emma to account for this "aberration" of which her husband spoke. This again was pinpointed by Irene Cooper Willis after her study of Emma's letters. She concluded that Emma had an obsession about "Romish practices in the Church of England".[36] This has been shown, from Gifford family papers, to be inherent in Emma's family, especially on the female side. A letter from her grandmother Gifford warns one of Emma's uncles against the wrong type of clergyman, "a double minded man—who will lead the people half-way to Rome".[37] Emma's mother, with her belief in the literal truth of the Bible, seems to have been some sort of fundamentalist. It was perhaps Emma's tragedy that her erratic fifties coincided with the foundation in 1890 of the notorious Protestant Truth Society, whose members disrupted ritualistic services. Though Emma herself subscribed later to the more tolerant National Protestant Church Union, she is said to have written religious letters to the local Dorchester paper, and she did not stop at letters. To a relative, Leonie Gifford, she announced[38]

> I have been scattering beautiful little booklets about—which may, I hope, help to make the clear atmosphere of pure Protestantism in the land to revive us again in the *truth*—as I believe it to be—so I send you some of them. Do read & *pass them* on.

There was also, it appears, a Gifford family tradition that, presumably in the war scares of the early 1890s, Emma Hardy kept a suitcase packed with supplies; her fear was that the French would invade England to enforce their Romish practices, and she was prepared for herself (and perhaps her husband) to take to the fields.[39] This, though highly eccentric, was no stranger than some actions of the Protestant Truth followers of the well-known John Kensit; but one can imagine the effect on Hardy, never very tolerant of extreme forms of belief. Her action in sending the typescript of her apocalyptic vision *Spaces* to Horace Moule's brother, President of Corpus Christi College, Cambridge, must also have shaken Hardy badly.[40]

The truth seems to be that in her impulses, her foibles, her frequent angers and jealousies, but also in her enthusiasms, ideals, and gaieties, Emma remained all her life a perpetual adolescent. This was her charm. Her recklessness and wilfulness, though sometimes alarming, were equally fascinating for Hardy. In her own words,[41] we see her as he must first have seen her

> scampering up and down the hills on my beloved mare alone, wanting no protection, the rain going down my back often and my hair floating in the wind . . . The Villagers stopped to gaze when I rushed down the hills. A butterman laid down his basket once to exclaim loudly for no one dared except myself to ride in such wild fearless fashion.

This, for all its ludicrous and pathetic contrast, is the same woman who, thirty years later, and grossly overweight, wearing a green velveteen dress, freewheeled on her matching green bicycle down the steep Dorchester High West Street to distribute Protestant tracts, while the stubborn locals tapped their foreheads significantly.[42]

What, even more than religion, seems to have convinced some of Dorchester that Emma was "half-cracked", as one of her neighbours put it,[43] was the fact that she wrote bad poetry. She was said to keep wooden boxes full of her poems in an attic at Max Gate.[44] We may be more tolerant, since the modern flood of "vanity" publishers has revealed how many people of little or no talent think they are poets, and are ready to get into print at all costs. Emma Hardy's "poems" are certainly no worse than those which are now printed, at a price, by presses which feed on such innocent and pathetic impulses. What seems obvious is that her husband's *Wessex Poems*, published in 1898, with its verses so explicitly about other women in his life, was a wounding shock to her. Although a kind friend[45] tried to reassure her over these poems by Hardy "that all his reminiscences are little fancies evoked from the days of his youth & absolutely without bearing on the real happiness of his life", the message in them of his extreme susceptibility to women was plain to see. Her own poems, prolific from this date, are some form of self-justification. Another form was her estimate of her own power of composing tales and novels. Up to *Tess of the d'Urbervilles*, she had helped him by suggesting incidents;[46] after, she began to claim she could actually have written such novels as well as he. This again sprang from simple sexual jealousy. In 1893, Hardy met and was deeply attracted by Florence Henniker, novelist and short-story writer. He helped her with her work, partly portrayed her in his next novel, *Jude the Obscure*,[47] and actually collaborated with her.[48] To Emma, with her own literary aspirations, and not inconsiderable, though unorganized, gifts of expression, this was, once again, deeply wounding. Finding that Hardy had introduced his new lady-friend's short stories to be handled by the well-known literary agent, his friend A. P. Watt, Emma appointed the embarrassed Watt,[49] a few months later, to be agent for the stories she herself had written. It does not seem that he was able to place any; but her action is fully understandable as a symbol of hurt sexual and intellectual pride, and carried with it no hint of abnormality.

Ironically, too, there were elements of real and shared poetry in Hardy's first acquaintance with her. There is no doubt at all that Hardy and Emma Gifford found themselves caught up in a love situation from the moment they met; though some modern writers have expressed doubts, all the evidence points to the truth that they were genuinely in love from the start. The second Mrs. Hardy, as well as telling Irene Cooper Willis that Emma was "mad", told her that Emma's sister, Mrs. Holder, trapped Hardy into marrying her;[50] but this seems to have been yet another of her jealous inventions. If Mrs. Holder had engineered the match, Hardy and Emma would surely have been married by Mr. Holder at his church, not by Emma's uncle in London. Nor was the interval of four years between their meeting and their marriage a long one by the standard of the age, but, in fact, a comparatively short time; the famous Pre-Raphaelite picture, "The Long Engagement", presents a situation that was meant to be self-explanatory to its mid-Victorian viewers, and the idea that the four-year gap indicated something wrong[51] is quite unhistorical.

Certainly there were elements of illusion, or "magic" as Hardy later called it, about this first meeting; there are about the meeting of most lovers, and there was much to heighten this one. The "lovely Monday evening in March", as Emma remembered their first encounter,[52] was

itself part of a weather-sequence that seemed to have something
unnatural or magical about it. Ever since 22 January, the climate all over
England had been fine and rainless,[53] and this abnormal drought was to
continue, with its charged and dreamlike atmosphere, through this first
year of Hardy's attraction to Emma, until the third week in August.
As for the setting, its startling and wild nature has to be seen, as Emma
said,[54] in the winter months to be truly appreciated—

> the wild Atlantic ocean rolling in with its magnificent waves and spray,
> its white gulls and black choughs and grey puffins, its cliffs and rocks and
> gorgeous sunsettings sparkling redness in a track widening from the
> horizon to the shore.

Nothing had prepared Hardy for the full force of this Atlantic seascape,
with its dark cliffs against which the rollers broke in huge pillars of
foam, shooting hundreds of feet up the perpendicular rock. Even the
bulk of Portland Bill, the grinding undertow of West Bay, or the
battery of windblown spume flying inland across the Chesil Bank, could
not compare with this gigantic and ghostly atmosphere, haunting his
mind for the rest of his life. The scene still held something unearthly
for him, even when the magic had dismally faded from their love. In
1895, in the lowest depths of married estrangement, he could write of it
as

> the region of dream and mystery. The ghostly birds, the pall-like sea, the
> eternal soliloquy of the waters, the bloom of dark purple cast, that seems
> to exhale from the shoreward precipices, in themselves lend to the scene
> an atmosphere like the twilight of a night vision.[55]

Quick to plunge into any new experience, Hardy absorbed in a few
days both the unfamiliar landscape and a fresh relationship. His work
of drawing and measuring for the church restoration seems to have kept
him there only a day; he noted how the bells, taken down for safety
from the cracked roof, were tolled for a funeral by a man lifting the
clapper and letting it fall against the side, as it stood inverted in the
transept. In the evening there was singing by the ladies at the rectory,
where he had returned for his meals. Next day, partly for work, partly
for pleasure, he drove with them in the family basket-carriage to the
Penpethy slate quarries, to select some for the new church roof, and to
Tintagel, where the castle ruins jutted into the ocean. The next day, still
prolonging his visit, he spent the morning on Beeny Cliff, looking down
its sheer drop to the seal-caves. He was alone with Emma; he walked
and she rode her mare recklessly to the edge. "The run down to the
edge. The coming home" are all he allowed to survive from his laconic
journal, but the emotional tension that was growing between them is

hinted by his quotation from the last lines of Tennyson's *Break, break, break*:

> Break, break, break,
>     At the foot of thy crags, O Sea!
> But the tender grace of a day that is dead
>     Will never come back to me.

By the afternoon, when Emma and her sister walked with him for three-quarters of the way down the Vallency valley to Boscastle, she had become "E". in his diary, after the more formal stages of "Miss Gifford" and "E.L.G.", and had begun to tease him flirtatiously—"E. provokingly reading as she walked". The fine March weather allowed them to stay late in the rectory garden that evening, and then again there was singing in the house. At dawn the next morning she saw him off on his journey home; a somewhat elliptical remark in his auto-biography suggests that he snatched a kiss in parting.[56]

Emma afterwards wrote,[57] "Scarcely any author and his wife could have had a much more romantic meeting with its unusual circumstances", and there is no doubt that this strange coast, with its booming artillery of waves, its edge-of-the-world atmosphere, and the great sweeping lighthouse eyes of Hartland Point and Trevose Head, themselves like legendary Cornish giants, caught them up in a mood of poetic romance. Yet there were real sympathies and common interests as well, and poetry itself was one. Hardy's quotation from Tennyson was not fortuitous, suggested as it was by the crash of waves on Beeny Cliff. He and Emma read the Poet Laureate, and there is interesting proof in the poem Hardy himself wrote after their meeting. Its first stanza is unlike anything he had written till then.

> Beneath a knap where flown
>     Nestlings play,
> Within walls of weathered stone,
>     Far away
> From the files of formal houses,
> By the bough the firstling browses,
> Lives a Sweet: no merchants meet,
> No man barters, no man sells
>     Where she dwells.

This, avoiding the Laureate's glutinous syllables, yet with its own effective double rhymes, is closely related to Tennyson's popular early poem, *Claribel*.

> At eve the beetle boometh
>     Athwart the thicket lone;
> At noon the wild bee hummeth
>     About the moss'd headstone:

> At midnight the moon cometh
> And looketh down alone.
> Her song the lintwhite swelleth,
> The clear-voiced mavis dwelleth,
> The callow throstle lispeth,
> The slumbrous wave outwelleth,
> The babbling runnel crispeth,
> The hollow grot replieth
> Where Claribel low-lieth.

There was another poet shared on this first meeting, even more appropriate to the wildness and grandeur of the surroundings. This was Coleridge. One of Emma's favourite poems was his *Youth and Age*, learnt by heart at school, and quoted by her more than once even in her own old age.[58] Hardy, too, associated his experience in Cornwall with Coleridge, to judge by his famous poem recalling it many years later. In this, he catches the tone of Coleridge's *Kubla Khan*—

> And all should cry, Beware! Beware!
> His flashing eyes, his floating hair!

almost exactly in his own poem's ending—

> All marked with mute surmise
> My radiance rare and fathomless,
> When I came back from Lyonnesse
> With magic in my eyes!

Yet, however much they were instantly drawn together by apparently shared interests, there were grave elements of self-deception in the sympathetic magic of their first association. Neither saw the other truly; both had illusions, which were liable to become dangerous. To Emma, isolated in remote provincialism, Hardy seemed part of a much larger world of sophistication, a London-trained and qualified architect. She did not see that he was, as he himself insisted,[59] simply an assistant, or rather, as he was described in the following year, an architect's clerk,[60] who had the good fortune to belong to a notable firm in London. She herself was collecting Cornish folklore to make into stories, and it was a romantic form of fellow-attraction that he had written many poems and two novels; yet at that time all the poems had been rejected. So had the first novel; the second was to suffer the same fate within a month. His life in London had not been at all what she must have imagined; she cannot have dreamt that he had walked out with a ladies' maid and actually wanted to marry her. Nor had she any conception of the side of his life associated with Puddletown, the cobblers, carpenters, labourers, and servants who were his relatives there. She cannot have known, or perhaps, flattered, may have concealed the thought from herself, of his extreme susceptibility to every fresh woman: she had no inkling of the three successive sisters, dressmaker, ladies' maid, and pupil-teacher, to whom he had become attracted. In her dull life, among people "slow of speech and ideas", he seemed far more of an exotic than he actually was. His intellect, self-developed and concealing his immaturity in emotions and experience, dazzled her.

The same falsity may be seen in his view of her. To him, conditioned by his fantasy of poor man and lady, she was better connected and more intellectual than she was to prove. To a man who, only five years before, had considered going to Cambridge and entering the Church, it counted for much that her uncle was a former Fellow of St. John's, an honorary Canon of Worcester Cathedral, and Examining Chaplain to the Bishop of London,[61] while her brother-in-law had been to Oxford. Her gift of quotation from Shakespeare, learnt from her father who recited particularly well during his bouts of drinking,[62] and a school acquaintance with other poets, concealed a basic lack of education. While her talented uncle and her two elder brothers had been taught at the admirable Queen Elizabeth Grammar School, Plymouth, Emma was sent to a local school run by "dear refined single ladies of perfect manners . . . two daughters of a Colonel in the Army". The actual teaching at such schools had just been exposed, by the Schools Enquiry Commission of 1864–66, as scrappy, lifeless, and superficial.[63] Even without Horace Moule's further coaching, Hardy had received from Isaac Last in Dorchester a far better education than Emma with the Plymouth ladies. Moreover, her family background, though respectable, was excessively provincial; both her mother and grandmother interlarded their conversation with local terms.[64]

These are the illusions they had about one another. What each really found in the other was the cure for a lack in their own lives. Emma supplied for the two of them all the physical vitality and energy in which Hardy was so obviously wanting. It was her quality of "living", as he afterwards realized, that attracted him, and had always attracted him in women, the violent bodily gusto for life, of which he always seemed such a wistful spectator. For Emma, Hardy seemed the answer to her ten barren and barbarous years in Cornwall, cut off from what she remembered as the "most intellectual" home she had enjoyed in her girlhood in Plymouth. He could not possibly foresee that her very energy would lead her to bully and domineer in later years, and even to insult and belittle his own mental powers; nor could she imagine the huge intellectual gulf that would widen between them. For the moment, buoyed up by their separate illusions, they seemed miraculously at one.

# 13

# Desperate Remedies

ON SATURDAY, 12 March, Thomas Hardy, returned from his Cornish trip, went to Crickmay's office in Weymouth for his expenses of £6 10s. 9d.[1] His mind was in a ferment, and although he took up again his Weymouth lodgings, and proceeded to elaborate the plans for St. Juliot in some detail,[2] his thought was elsewhere. He was caught in the type of ironic complex that he was to use so frequently in his own later stories and novels. He was swept off his feet by the energy, dash, and obvious attractions of Emma Gifford, all the more since it was the first time since his childhood that a woman of superior social class had shown interest in him. It was a boyhood fantasy come true. On the other hand, Tryphena Sparks in London had his ring. Though he might—and probably did—argue that in choosing a career first rather than him, and shutting herself away, she somehow justified his inconstancy, this would be impossible to explain to her, when, all too soon, she was in Puddletown to take her brief Easter break. In the background, but still present in his thought, there was her sister whom he had first wanted to marry, the small-bodied Martha, growing heavily pregnant by another more virile man. He hugged to himself the secret power he felt he possessed in his novel, *Desperate Remedies*: but on 5 April, he received a letter from Macmillans. They had refused to publish it.[3]

The novel was, in fact, a curious amalgam of composite elements, though that was not the reason for John Morley's horrified rejection. In his haste, Hardy had packed it with local incidents known to him, details from his surroundings, and even extracts, such as the medical information, from his daily reading.[4] On the other hand, to write a novel with a plot, which both Morley and Meredith demanded, he had delved into a former work which had held him fascinated since childhood. It is often said that the story is a mixture of the sensation-novel of the contemporary Wilkie Collins and the older form of Gothic romance; but the point is that they do not combine. Indeed, almost mathematically, the first half of the book is semi-Gothic romance, the second half is the realistic detective-type affair of clues and the unravelling of factual incidents that lead to the exposure of a murder. The murder itself takes place precisely halfway through the book, and dictates this change. This double plot necessitates a double ending to the book. The final chapter first clears up the circumstances of the murder, by the villainous steward's confession of how he killed and concealed his wife, and then reveals the original Gothic mystery, namely that his power over the Lady of the Manor derives from his being her illegitimate son. For this Gothic atmosphere, which dominates the first half of the book, Hardy borrowed a style and manner from an early favourite.

This was the fustian historical novel, *Old St. Paul's* by Harrison Ainsworth. Hardy himself said it "was the most powerful literary influence of his boyhood", and it was more than that. He immersed himself so deeply in this novel as a child that he never quite threw off its influence on his style. The first great romantic event of his life, his stay in London, at the age of nine, with his attractive mother on their way back from Hertfordshire, was linked with this romantic novel, which he had already read. The small boy got himself a map of the city of London, marked all the streets and alleys mentioned in *Old St. Paul's*, and then, imagining himself the hero, followed every one of them on foot.[5] His mother, looking in every closet of their lodging in case a man were hiding, was to him like the heroine, who is continually finding the villainous Earl of Rochester concealed in her father's city house, ready at any moment to carry her off. Not only plot, but the style of Ainsworth's novel made its lasting mark. This is the origin of both the grandiose and the flat prosaic that never ceased to haunt Hardy's writing. Ainsworth's characters "vociferate" rather than speak; they "traverse" rather than cross a street. On the prosaic side, nearly every paragraph begins with a resounding, dull cliché. These—"The foregoing description"—"Involuntarily drawing in his breath"—"Repeating his injunctions"—"At this juncture"—"thus ruminating" and thousands more, may make the book virtually unreadable today, but, deeply absorbed in childhood, they were the stuff of which Thomas Hardy's style was first made, when he tried to write what he thought would be an acceptable, readable novel. "Thus musing"—"Relieved from her apprehensions"—"At this announcement" invade the story from its beginnings, and the grandiose is equally pervasive. The love-affair of the heroine's father does not end: it "terminates"—and so on.

This stylistic habit never left Hardy. Even after his prose came to acquire the most subtle and often beautiful effects, this deep-laid influence perked out to disconcert the faithful readers of his major novels. So, too, did the Ainsworth villain. The features of the Earl of Rochester, "the almost feminine beauty by which they were characterized" which "gave place to a fierce and forbidding expression" are those of nearly all Hardy's villains; though he finally gave Alec d'Urberville a certain coarseness, he did so explicitly because Alec was not really an aristocrat. The smooth face hiding incredible evil-doing reached its height in the baby-faced and demonlike Dare in *A Laodicean*. In fact, Hardy himself, with his own childlike features, may have seen himself in fantasy as the Earl of Rochester, prototype of these ingenious miscreants. It is hard to see otherwise how he should have thought *A Laodicean* contained more of his own life than any other novel,[6] for the poetry, architecture, and arguments for infant baptism of the hero take up very small space in that book. If Dare-Rochester was his own fantasy self, Hardy's comment has some point.

The perverse ingenuity of a small boy in Hardy's plotting of the second half of the book, outdoing even Wilkie Collins in factual detail and attention to the smallest points of realism, drew from John Morley his reluctant praise, "the plot being complex and absolutely impossible, yet it is worked out with elaborate seriousness and consistency".[7] Literary influence is slighter here, though Collins and perhaps even more Dickens in his own later Wilkie Collins phase are present; both Hardy's detective and, particularly, his journalist have the touch of a Dickens sketch. Their laconic understatement is matched by a change in style. Nothing could be further from this quiet realism than the scenes in the first half when the villain fascinates the half-horrified heroine by playing the organ to her in an ancient building illuminated by flashes of lightning from a tremendous storm. Realism that owes nothing at all to literature is certainly dominant in the scenes of sordid London lodging-houses, in which the heroine's defenders seek for clues. Some of the social protest of lost passages in *The Poor Man and the Lady* had clearly been worked in here, notably in the *tour de force* "picture of married life among the very poor of a city".

A few chairs and a table were the chief article of furniture in the third-floor back room which they occupied. A roll of baby-linen lay on the floor; beside it a pap-clogged spoon and an overturned tin pap-cup. Against the wall a Dutch clock was fixed out of level, and ticked wildly in longs and shorts, its entrails hanging down beneath its white face and wiry hands, like the faeces of a Harpy ('foedissima ventris proluvies, uncaeque manus, et pallida semper ora').

The spoon "pap-*clogged*" and the clock "fixed out of level" remind one what a social realist the early Hardy could be. On the other hand there is the extraordinary out-of-place "faeces of a Harpy" and the obtrusive Virgilian quotation. This type of learned allusion has been thought to be borrowed from Ainsworth, but it was natural to Hardy's own self-taught mind, and runs through all his work to the last, loading his novels with untoward digressive references to literature, painting, and architecture. In *Desperate Remedies*, the heroine becomes sexually and personally attractive to the mysterious Lady of the Manor by a chance look which "Those who remember Greuze's 'Head of a Girl'" are asked to appreciate.

There is, in fact, a constant tension throughout the book, not only between the Gothic and the factual, but, cutting across these, between real life observation and laboriously acquired taste. For instance, there are no less than three other quotations from Virgil in the book, one in the original and two in Dryden's translation, and all appear forced. The final one, when epic terms are applied to the villain chasing the heroine round a table, topples over into absurdity. On the other hand, Hardy's quotations and half-absorbed echoes from Shelley are beautifully adapted to the feeling of the book. They fit with the brother and sister relationship, which is at the heart of the novel, and they heighten the natural description. Hardy had marked his own Shelley specially for its passages about nature.[8] Here, the idyllic sea-pictures, though taken from Weymouth, are completely Shelleyan, with their glassy surfaces, purple and blue shades, and strange shapes of weeds on the sea-floor. Most directly, and half-quoting, is his landscape without hope, viewed by the heroine in depression, taken from Shelley's *The Sensitive Plant*. Hardy's garden, "purposeless, valueless . . . overgrown and choked with mandrakes" is the "leafless wrack . . . the mandrakes" of Shelley's poem.[9]

Hardy's own gift for natural description is, in fact, so strong that elsewhere it clashes with the more artificial parts of the novel. His harbour lights "seeming to send long tap-roots of fire quivering down deep into the sea", his cottage hearth-fire "giving to every grain and tumour in the paving a long shadow", show such loving care in their observation, that there is a shock when they are then associated with some piece of Gothic fustian. The overdrawn Gothic thunderstorm, when the villain fascinates the heroine by playing the organ in a mouldering mansion, begins with beautifully simple natural observation:

He pointed to a round wet spot as large as a nasturtium leaf, which had suddenly appeared on the white surface of the step.

The heroine's Gothic nightmare, during which, with extraordinary masochism, she "dreamt that she was being whipped with dry bones suspended on strings" while being tied to a wall, gives way to a wonderful naturalistic explanation, in its picture of a heavy night-frost weighing down and cracking the boughs of trees.

The chief tension in the novel, though, comes not from style and description, but from the disparate characters. The sinister outsize literary people simply do not fit with those observed from real life. The mysterious middle-aged Lady of the Manor, her evil illegitimate son, who has the habit of quoting the Bible in the midst of his villainy, even his "American actress" wife and his mistress, "an improper woman" from the haunts of "Paphos" (a word much on the lips of Ainsworth's Restoration gallants) are in a different world from the simple heroine, her brother, her architect lover, and his countryman father. These are real because they are close to Hardy's experience. The passive, patient, and modest heroine, with her occasional panic moments of spirit, seems in almost every respect a close portrait of his own sister Mary, with whom he had taken up their always fruitful quiet association while writing the novel. Equally, the brother and the lover, both architects, seem to be two sides of himself. The brother Owen, ineffective, withdrawn, until reluctantly spurred to action on his sister's behalf, is the shy, socially-uncertain Hardy in youth. Small incidents are even autobiographical. Owen is asked to come into an architect's office, where there is no vacancy, to fill in time doing drawings, just as Hardy had been when he first went to London. His first big job on his own is the superintendence of a church "which was to be nearly rebuilt" fifteen or sixteen miles from Weymouth, which has been identified convincingly as Turnworth.[10] On the other hand, the architect lover, Edward, though physically drawn from the fellow-worker in Crickmay's office, is in every other way the more ambitious Hardy, the country boy made good, the man who knows Shakespeare "to the dregs of the footnotes", and has written, though given up, poetry. His relationship, too, with his easy-going father is Hardy's. This close identity is increased by Hardy paraphrasing into prose some of his own unpublished poems. The heroine's long meditation on how future generations will regard her[11] is prosed direct from Hardy's 1866 sonnet beginning

Perhaps, long hence, when I have passed away,

even more like in the original manuscript, where the "two small words" of the world's verdict were, as in the novel, "Poor girl!". Incidentally, since the meditation in the novel is addressed by the heroine to her brother, it increases the likelihood that the "She" of Hardy's "She to Him" sonnets is his own much-loved sister. Their whole relationship, their sympathies, and equally their irritations and differences, form perhaps the most convincing part of the novel, against the lurid backdrop of the more melodramatic characters.

It was not, however, these discrepancies that caused the novel to be rejected: but, in Morley's verdict,

> the story is ruined by the disgusting and absurd outrage which is the key to its mystery—The violation of a young lady at an evening party, and the subsequent birth of a child, is too abominable to be tolerated as a central incident from which the action of the story is to move.

"After reflection", he added ruefully, "I don't see how this could be modified in any way ... Don't touch this—but beg the writer to discipline himself to keep away from such incidents as violation—and let us see his next story."[12] It is worth noticing that Miss Aldclyffe's early lapse *was* modified, at the request of another publisher, and its only description in the novel we now have is simply the words "a young girl of seventeen was cruelly betrayed by her cousin, a wild officer of six-and-twenty". There is no "evening party" and no described "violation". Obviously, Hardy had treated this clumsily and with the "certain rawness of absurdity" that Morley had already found "very displeasing" in *The Poor Man and the Lady*.

Morley also noted that there were "some scenes (e.g. between Miss Aldclyffe and her new maid in bed) wh: are highly extravagant". This we still have; and it raises the question of Hardy's portrayal of sex. What has been called the "sexual comment" of the novel has perhaps been exaggerated;[13] much of it seems to be of the pasteboard *Old St. Paul's* type, especially that of the Rochester-like Manston. If Hardy did later find in this early work of his "a similar plainness to *Tess*"—which is doubtful[14]—it is probably because what he described naïvely and almost unconsciously in this first published novel had by then become explicit to him. In later life, he also said that *The Poor Man and the Lady* had shown "a wonderful insight into female character", and added with what was perhaps a false simplicity, "I don't know how that came about!".[15] How it came about in *Desperate Remedies* is probably that Hardy was copying literally something he had been told personally, without perhaps understanding its full implications. After all, his cousin Martha Sparks had been for many years a ladies' maid. There are plenty of instances where the master of the Victorian household gets into bed with the ladies' maid, and there is no reason to believe that the mistress of the house did not do so too. The highly sexual lesbian scene is most probably a straight retelling of one of Martha's experiences, and its realism is not so much evidence of Hardy's maturity as of his still youthful immaturity. Similarly, the comic naïvety of Cytherea's remark to the villain, "I am not at all used to an organ", simply echoes the words of Mary Hardy in her first village job at Denchworth.[16]

One does not know how much of Morley's criticism, if any, was passed on to Hardy in Macmillan's letter of rejection. Very little, it would seem; for Hardy at once sent the unaltered manuscript, with a précis of the four missing final chapters, to William Tinsley. He afterwards pretended to believe that this was a mistake, and that Meredith, at Chapman and Hall, would have taken more interest in the book. Almost certainly, such a work would have only earned him another Meredithian lecture, whereas Tinsley, with a list of sensation-novels, was a much likelier house. Even he took time to consider, and it was exactly four weeks before he sent Hardy his reader's report. This indicated that the novel could not be published without some alteration—probably including the dropping of the "violation" scene—and Hardy wrote by return promising to comply in every way. This brought an offer from Tinsley, on 5 May 1870, to publish the novel when revised, if Hardy would pay in advance £75 of the expense. Again Hardy at once agreed, and Tinsley confirmed for an edition of 500 copies.[17]

A week later, on 16 May, Hardy dropped Crickmay's work, and left Dorset for London again.[18] His own evasive phrase, "possibly as a result of the correspondence", fails really to explain. It is true that a section of chapter 16 takes place in London, but that had almost certainly been written, since there are four chapters after it; nor, as he confessed later, did he do anything much toward the novel when he got there. Tryphena's daughter afterwards claimed that he was "tagging after" Tryphena at college; but her regulations gave him little encouragement, and the signs are that he was avoiding rather than pursuing her, for much of his time was taken in writing letters and sending books to Emma Gifford in Cornwall. In another evasive phase, he admitted "it is not clear what he was waiting for there".[19] The exact time, the second half of May, may be more significant; it was now that Martha was due to give birth. The event proved to share the tragi-comedy that seems to haunt so many of the actual events of Hardy's personal life. On 30 May, she gave birth to twins, James Sparks Duffield and Martha Mary Duffield.[20] At one stroke, the Duffields were set on a path of poverty that was to send them to Australia in half-a-dozen years. It may not be without deep personal meaning that Hardy entered in his notebook this month "A sweet face is a page of sadness to a man over 30"—he was within two days of his thirtieth birthday—"the raw material of a corpse".[21] The almost grotesque metamorphosis of the smart Martha, whom he had once hoped to marry, may have had much to do with his mood, quite apart from all the other complications he had now brought on himself. It is no wonder he found himself desultory, doing a little work in Blomfield's office, a little more for an interesting older architect in Clement's Inn, Raphael Brandon, and seeing a good deal of Horace Moule, who had come out of his retirement in Dorchester to take up his literary-journalist work in London. He was able to confide in Moule his new attachment to Emma Gifford, the "vague understanding" he already felt it to be.[22] It is unlikely that he told Moule anything about Tryphena Sparks.[23] To judge by dates, Hardy was playing an extraordinary and evasive game of Box-and-Cox with Tryphena, which may mirror his emotional dilemma. Late in June, midsummer brought her summer holiday, and it is likely she went down to Dorset, to help her sister Rebecca with dressmaking assignments, and look after their widowed father, as she had certainly done on her holiday from school in summer 1869. Hardy, however, stayed in London, working in an on-and-off way for Brandon. On the other hand, directly Tryphena returned to college, at the beginning of the second week in August,[24] Hardy hastily threw up his job with Brandon, and set off on 8 August for Cornwall.

This was, he afterwards emphasized, not a professional visit;[25] the demolition and rebuilding of St. Juliot church did not start till the following year. He had been invited by Emma's brother-in-law, presumably at Emma's prompting, though he himself seems to have been on good personal terms with Holder, an easy-going tolerant cleric, with the actor's gift of counting the number of people in the pews in the first few moments of the service.[26] It was for him an occasion of supreme adventure: would the first lightning attraction, fuelled by letters, prove permanent? The whole journey afterwards seemed to him to have elements of destiny. Even climatically, it was a strange year. There had been persistent drought since the last week in January. He travelled through a countryside where the foliage was crisped and almost charred by lack of water, crops and vegetation stunted on every hand.[27] On a larger scale, it was the summer of the Franco-Prussian war. The French nation was falling, "heart-rending" as Moule observed to him, continuing to send Hardy his own articles and leaders to read with Emma in Cornwall.[28] He and Emma had the sense that their own drama was being played against this mighty background, and he remembered their domestic incidents by the dates of the great battles. They were left alone to do more or less what they liked with the fine days. The few clouds that there were, dazzling white, hung almost motionless in still air. Emma, in the brilliant weather, wore a light blue summer dress. They walked, picnicked, and sketched each other, Emma's sketches showing a good deal more dash and freedom than his designs, still reminiscent of the drawing-board. They forgot the time in Tintagel Castle, and were nearly locked in for the night. They went to church at the neighbouring Lesnewth on Sunday 14 August,[29] for Hardy, under Emma's influence, had regained the habit of church-going. On 18 August, after a walk up the hill in the morning, they read Tennyson in the garden during the afternoon, and talked about the war. The sight of an old horse harrowing the dry earth in the valley below, symbol of peaceful habit in a time of destruction, made an indelible impression on Hardy, and he returned to it forty-five years later in one of his most famous lyrics. The next day they took a picnic down the winding fern-green Vallency valley, whose shaded banks were fresh even in the drought. The little picnic tumbler they lost in the stream, wedged for ever between two boulders, became for both a symbol of undying love. On 22 August the long drought broke, but they faced the rain that swept in over the beak of Beeny Cliff, and Hardy sketched Emma in a scene that was to reappear in much of his writing.

Indeed, writing was never far away, and as the bad weather set in, they had plenty of time to discuss it. She was taking pains to copy his reading, and he must have been pleased to find her reading his mother's favourite, Dante.[30] Before leaving London, he had rescued the manuscript of *Desperate Remedies* from Tinsley's office. He began the alterations, and she offered to make a fair copy, so that the publisher should be favourably impressed when he had the revised version. They were full of shared hopes for the future. All the same, past experience had made him cautious, and the advice of friends that he might never make money from writing had sunk in. On 25 September, he dated in his Bible the proverb: "in all labour there is profit; but the talk of the lips tendeth only to penury".[31] In the middle of the next month, he made a deeply-felt note about how a "noble nature" might unfit one for earning a living—"a high soul may bring a man to the workhouse".[32]

Even more than economic problems, emotional ones continued to press on him. He seems to have returned to his safe home at Bockhampton, and reassuring contact with his mother. Yet his dating on 16 October of the text "So I returned and considered all the oppressions that are done under the sun" may well show personal unease. In the last week in October, he had a letter from Emma, who was copying the novel with the new chapters which he was now writing and sending to her. She wrote that all around her seemed a dream, their love the reality. More than that: she gave him confidence that his shy, withdrawn nature, his uncertainties about himself, which he had confided to her, would be no drawback to their love. "I take him (the reserved man)" she wrote,[33] "as I do the Bible: find out what I can, compare one text with another, & believe the rest in a simple lump of faith." The time was far distant when he would be irritated by such simple-minded Protestantism. He felt full of gratitude at her sympathy. Moved by this, and by memories of their halycon August days, he put her initials and the date—28 October—against the first two and a half verses of the fourth chapter of the Song of Solomon,[34] beginning "Behold, thou art fair, my love" and ending "Thy lips are like a thread of scarlet, and thy speech is comely". Perhaps it was also at this time that he put her initials to a stanza of Spenser's *Epithalamion*. Yet he still had the unresolved problem of Tryphena, who was in a different class and world, with a good many less than comely associations. A feeling of fate overcame him, the maladjusted timing of events, and the frustration of over-optimistic hope. Two days later, he entered in his notebook[35]

> Mother's notion, & also mine: that a figure stands in our van with arm uplifted, to knock us back from any pleasant prospect we indulge in as probable.

It was not so much that fate was malignant, but that one's own indulgence in any form of hope could lay one open to disaster. In such a dilemma, he felt he could do nothing; or at least, he did nothing, in this emotional double path that seemed inevitably to lead to some clash.

Earlier that summer, he had made an aphoristic note[36] on how to conduct one's public life,

> It is not by rushing straight towards fame that men come up with her, but by so adapting the direction of their path to hers that in some point ahead the two must inevitably intersect.

In his private life, the intersection seemed to be growing more and more dangerous, and he did not see how any adaptation could prevent it, or resolve it happily.

At all events, *Desperate Remedies*, revised, finished, and copied by Emma, was finally "packed off" to Tinsley early in December[37] and acknowledged by the publisher on 9 December. On 15 December, Tryphena finished her first year at Stockwell College triumphantly. By hard, concentrated work, she had improved the second class, with which she had entered, to a first class.[38] Yet the date, for Hardy, meant her return to Dorset where he was deeply involved in correspondence with quite another lady. He was also on tenterhooks about his novel; but it was almost certainly for emotional reasons that he wrote[39] this exact date, 15 December, in the margin of his copy of *Hamlet* against the words

> Thou wouldst not think how ill all's here about my heart: but it is no matter.

On the exact date of Tryphena's college entrance, he had noted his sense of complete deprivation in his Bible; now, with the advent of Emma in the meantime, he marked the exact date of Tryphena's breaking-up day with a far different sense.

On 20 December, his professional life at least took an upward lift. Tinsley had written that his reader now approved of *Desperate Remedies*, and thought that, with the alterations Hardy had made, the book ought to sell. He would publish it on the terms he had offered before, a down payment of £75 by Hardy. The only further suggestion was another small alteration "that the woman who is Mrs. Manston's *substitute* need not be put forward quite so prominently as his *mistress*".[40] Hardy willingly agreed. He also snatched at the chance of escaping from embarrassment during the holidays in Dorset by going to London on the pretext that he wanted to hand over the £75 personally in Bank notes, "rather, as it seemed, to Tinsley's astonishment", as he himself remarked.[41] No wonder, since the publisher could hardly know the complications of his author's private life. He then returned to Dorset, as Tryphena went up for her second year. What she made of all this is unknown; but she was a young woman with a good deal of shrewdness and knowledge of human nature, which emerges in her own letters. A few years later, as a respectable headmistress, she still made broad jokes about "baiting her hook" for young men.[42] She doubtless had her thoughts.

In fact, with Hardy in this position, there were plenty of occasions for embarrassment in his life. The next came on St. Valentine's Day, 1871. Hardy had very special feelings about home-made valentines. In his middle-age, he wrote[43] to a young woman that her valentine had made him feel young again,

> very young . . . for I can just remember the time when written Valentines were customary—before people became so idle as to get everything, even their love-making, done by machinery . . .

He was in the habit of sending them. Now he had to send to two young women. It is no wonder that he put the date, 14 February 1871, against a marked sentence in the Book of Isaiah, "They that see thee shall narrowly look upon thee".[44] What he was doing would hardly bear looking into. The fatal effects of a personal valentine were to be recalled in *Far From the Madding Crowd*. It was about now that he recorded the long note about lying at dawn just after waking—"The sad possibilities of the future are more vivid than at any other time".[45] He was marking time, doing little with it except copying down from old people the words of the country ballads[46] that the improvements of Squire Brymer were beginning to banish from Puddletown. Yet if he was at a standstill, his book was not. Advertised as ready by 11 March, it was in his hands on the 25th. Long after, he recalled[47] that no sensation could match the feelings of an author on first publication. "Never will I forget the thrill that ran through me from head to foot when I held my first copy of *Desperate Remedies* in my hand."

# 14

# Under the Greenwood Tree

HARDY went back to Weymouth, to work for Crickmay while he waited for the reviews. It was a necessary move. In all his years as assistant architect, he had managed to save £123. Now £75 of that was invested in the book. If the gamble failed, he would have to earn again, for marriage or for another book. He was not only unknown, but anonymous, and had nothing to recommend the book to the reading public. This public, for a three-volume novel on the usual pattern, was largely a family and circulating library readership. If the reviews approved of the book for general and family reading, he was started on his way financially. If they did not, however they might praise it as a book, he might never have written it for any money that it would bring.

He did not have long to wait. The *Athenaeum* had a regular section for novels of the week, which it kept admirably up to date. On 1 April, *Desperate Remedies* was one of the books reviewed. It was a mixed notice. The story was "unpleasant", dealing as it did with crime, but it was certainly powerful and well-told. The country scenes were praised, specially that of Farmer Springrove's cider-making, and Hardy must have smiled to be congratulated on his authentic west-country dialect. What partly bothered the reviewer was the exact sex of the anonymous author. A woman, he first thought, since the book showed such "close acquaintance with the mysteries of the female toilette", which, the reviewer permitted himself to say, seemed entirely accurate. On the other hand, it contained some expressions "so remarkably coarse" that he could not believe a lady could have written it. The mystery would have easily been solved if the reviewer had known anything of Hardy's private life. An author who had walked out with a ladies' maid, and heard from Martha Sparks about her work and her employers, could hardly fail to be accurate about the "toilette". As for the coarseness, he had heard plenty of that, and from women of his own class. Basically, what the reviewer did not realize was that here was a novel about middle-class people written by someone of working-class experience. He returned in a puzzled way, to this "occasional coarseness, startling as it once or twice is". Almost certainly, he was thinking of Miss Aldclyffe's sexual and explicit use of the word "had"; it was a use that the mature Hardy was to repeat with tremendous and dramatic effect in a later novel *The Woodlanders*. He concluded, in an encouraging way,

> if the author will purge himself of this, though even this is better than the prurient sentimentality with which we are too often nauseated, we see no reason why he[1] should not write novels only a little, if at all, inferior to the best of the present generation.

This, though encouraging and gratifying, was not wholly the selling review that the author wanted. An imputation of coarseness, however occasional, might frighten off the circulating libraries and the watchful paterfamilias. It was all the more welcome then that on 13 April, the *Morning Post* gave it a short but unreservedly favourable notice. Though it noticed passages that seemed to imitate Wilkie Collins, it judged the book "eminently a success" of its kind.

On 22 April, however, the *Spectator* reviewed *Desperate Remedies*. It was, he saw as he bought the copy in Dorchester, immensely long, and he carried the magazine with him to the stile into Kingston Maurward ewelease on his way home. As he read the first sentences, as he afterwards said, "The bitterness of that moment was never forgotten; at the time he wished he were dead".[2] It expressed the kind of horror that John Morley had anticipated, and fixed the blame firmly on the anonymous author, adding that it was hardly just that the publishers had to reveal their names in association with such a work, which contained "no display except of the brute kind", and was devoid of any hint of Christian virtue. As a parting shot in this introductory onslaught, the reviewer said he had set this down in the hope of stirring the author "to better things in the future than these 'desperate remedies' which he has adopted for ennui or an emaciated purse".

One wonders if Hardy read any further than this ill-timed joke, which, as has been pointed out,[3] he quoted in old age inaccurately, making it sound even more damning than it was. For the major part of the review, which then followed, was something that many authors would have welcomed. As if feeling he had perhaps gone too far, the reviewer proceeded to quote, at very great length, what he called the redeeming features of the book, as examples of "powers that might and ought to be extended largely in this direction". Like the *Athenaeum* critic, he enjoyed the cider-making scene, and reproduced several paragraphs. To these he added the dialogue between the bell-ringers at the wedding from the end of the book, also at length. Then he praised the passages of natural description, and chose, with some acuteness, two from early in the book, the scene in the cool of the Town Hall, where the heroine sees, framed in her view from the window, her father on the building-scaffold outside, and the detailed effects of a hot summer on the landscape, as the heroine journeys down to Weymouth, drawn closely from Hardy's real-life experience there. "We wish", he added, "we had space for the description of the village fire, and its silent and stealthy growth in the autumn night", a phrase which showed how much he appreciated the good things of the book, and Hardy's power to create authentic atmosphere.

Yet all this literary appreciation, which might have led a less one-track mind to accept the moral strictures, was useless comfort in face of Hardy's immediate obsession that the book must be a financial success. The verdict that the villain was moved throughout by "the merest sensuality", and that Miss Aldclyffe, his key-figure in the plot, was "uninteresting, unnatural, and nasty"—the reviewer could not bring himself actually to mention her scene in bed with the ladies' maid—would totally ban the book from family reading. No library and very few private purchasers would risk it. He had lost his money. He plunged into the depths; his habitual lack of confidence as always threatened to erode his compensating conviction, expressed in his prophetic Bible entries, that he was somehow destined for greatness. When he completed the book, in the middle of the previous November, he had dated the passage in Revelation, "Thou must prophesy again before many peoples, and nations, and tongues, and kings".[4] Now, utterly chastened, he wrote a note, "Strictly, we should resent wrongs, be placid at justice, and grateful for favours. But I know one who is placid at a wrong, and would be grateful for simple justice; while a favour, if he ever gained one, would turn his brain".[5] All his life, he remained quietly, bitterly sensitive. His friend, Horace Moule, now becoming even more horribly involved in his own depressions, realized the effect this review would have on Hardy. He wrote a brief note, telling him not to mind the article, and got the book, over which he had not been consulted, to review himself for the *Saturday Review*. Here again, there was an ironic turn to Hardy's fortune. If Moule had placed a notice quickly, some of the damage might have been repaired. Yet, one must suspect because of the increasing frequency of his own drinking bouts, this did not appear for another six months, far too late to do any good.

The one remedy, for pride and for purse, was Crickmay. Also, the St. Juliot commission provided an excuse for Hardy to take his hurt feelings to Emma. She, at least, copying the book in her admiration for Hardy, had seen nothing wrong with it. The St. Juliot restoration, having hung fire for a year, was set in motion, perhaps by Hardy's contriving, and in May he was off for a long visit to Cornwall, for professional reasons this time, as he carefully noted.[6] Crickmay's designs of the previous May were put into operation, under Hardy's supervision. One intention was frustrated by the local builder. Hardy had drawn a careful restoration of the medieval screen, using as much as possible the old framing.[7] Going into the church one day, he found his design executed throughout in glaring modern yellow pitch-pine, and heard the builder's well-meaning explanation: "Well, Mr. Hardy, I said to myself, I won't stand on a pound or two while I'm about it, and I'll give 'em a new screen instead of that patched-up old thing".[8] Possibly, for various reasons, he did not supervise the job as closely as he might have done. Emma, energetic, forceful, and anxious as he for their future, seems to have helped him to collect a number of favourable extracts from the three reviews, to use as publicity and offset the *Spectator* notice. It was too late, though he sent these to Tinsley on his return to Weymouth on 7 June. On his way back to Dorset on 3 June, he had seen the fatal sign of lack of sales. His three-volume book was already remaindered by W. H. Smith on Exeter station at 2s. 6d.

Yet Emma, it may be suspected, had restored his confidence, and given him the next move. Ever since, Morley's first report on *The Poor Man and the Lady* in the summer of 1868 he had played with the idea of a novel with an entirely rural setting. Now, the tone of the reviews, good and bad, the popularity of the cider-making scene, and Emma's faith in him spurred him on. His personal life was still in chaos, and Tryphena's return to Dorset at midsummer, as much as his failure as a novel-writer, may have prompted his marking of *Macbeth*.[9]

> Things at their worst will cease, or else climb upward
> To what they were before.

Yet for all ills, writing now seemed to be the obvious cure. This was not to say, though, that Hardy could ignore the immediate advantages of work for Crickmay; so he put himself this summer into double harness, to write a novel—necessarily a short one—and to carry out Crickmay's local designs. Two jobs to hand were the new schools at Radipole and Broadwey, both just north of Weymouth. This was part of the urgent drive by the voluntary school societies to provide adequate schools to fulfil the recent Education Act of 1870; if they did not, a secular school board would take over. The number of Church schools built in the six months after 1870 was enormous, and these two both opened in 1871. Drawings of details for both exist, in Hardy's hand,[10] and for a few months they were his main task. As general work, there was the Green Hill housing estate, which can be seen today. Green Hill, a gentle slope, starts just where Weymouth Bay begins to curve to the east. The spiky pale-grey Gothic of St. John's church, vicarage, and schools had already been built; but behind it there was a residential area to fill. Following Crickmay's plans, and under Hardy's direction, imposing stone-built villas of multiple bow-windows and slightly crazy turrets began to appear nearest the sea, and, behind them, more modest pairs of brick villas on a smaller scale. As to materials, yellow brick alternated with polychrome red and blue; Hardy was putting his R.I.B.A. prize essay into practice. Not that he was showing any originality; this was, by every neighbouring sign, the standard Crickmay style for domestic buildings. When Hardy later built his own house at Max Gate, he took up the Crickmay manner, and gave it the Crickmay trade-mark of a useless turret. Domestic building was something of a routine chore to him, and though he paid careful attention to detail,[11] there is no evidence that his heart was much in the houses, which were probably as uncomfortable as Max Gate proved to be.

The new book, of course, was a major concern. He wrote fast, helped by incorporating scenes that had been praised in *The Poor Man and the Lady*. The party at the tranter's, which Macmillan had liked, probably went in more or less wholesale. A bee-keeping scene took the place of the popular cider-making from *Desperate Remedies*. Its original title, *The Mellstock Quire*, embodies the theme, an evocation of the doings of Stinsford church choir in the days of his own father and grandfather, slightly updated to bring the choir into conflict with the new church music, approved by the new vicar, and played on the organ by the new-style college-trained school-mistress, Fancy Day. Music, as has been said,[12] runs throughout the slight story, dance, song, and church voices all playing their parts. Fancy's unsuitable suitor, the rich farmer, a character adapted from an innkeeper in *The Poor Man*,[13] bellows the unseemly pothouse ballad about "three sons of whores" that Hardy had heard from his Hand uncles. Not that there is an unsuitable word in the whole of the writing. The *Spectator* review had taught its lesson, and it was not until 1896 that Hardy, writing a new preface for the work, dared to mention "that ancient and broad humour which our grandfathers, and possibly grandmothers, took delight in, and is in these days unquotable"—the "possibly", even at that late date, a concession to the horror at the coarseness found in his first work by middle-class reviewers.

The book seems to have started, indeed, as a set of pictures, designed to carry out the *Spectator*'s approval of scenes in *Desperate Remedies* which reminded the reviewer of the genre paintings of Teniers and Wilkie. In fact, changing the main title to *Under the Greenwood Tree*, Hardy put as sub-title "A Rural Painting of the Dutch School". This might suggest his habit of dragged-out artistic analogy. Yet, refreshingly, there is hardly any of this in the book itself. A suggestion that the silhouetted choir look like figures on a Greek vase, and a reference to the paintings of Moroni, are all that obtrude. Even more welcome, the simple characters and plot, or lack of plot, absolved Hardy from feeling he must write in the grand Harrison Ainsworth manner. His style is miraculously, and for the only time in all his output, purged of these

pomposities. The lapses can be counted on the fingers of the hand—
"adhering thereto", "consequent upon", "subjoined words", "just
subsequent", and hardly any others. The purity and unity of the style
is miraculous. Partly, this is due to a very simple and unsensational plot.
It would have been even more simple; but Hardy, perhaps realizing
that it was too much like his very earliest "Story with no Plot", added
at a late stage a third rival for the hand of Fancy Day. As well as the
tranter's son, Dick, and the rich farmer, Shiner, he gave an interesting
sociological twist to the story by making the new young vicar fall in
love with the coquettish Fancy, incidentally but unconsciously also
giving him the Christian name of his own Stinsford vicar.

It seems likely that Fancy herself, the girl who has bettered herself
by becoming a certificated teacher, has a good deal to do with Tryphena
Sparks. Her brunette beauty certainly corresponds in general with
photographs of Tryphena, and her lively character is much the same as
Tryphena's letters, though purged, like the whole novel, of any coarseness. She has plenty of faults, and the last words of the book underline
both them and her native shrewdness, such a feature of Tryphena, when
she decides not to tell her newly-wedded Dick ever of the young vicar's
proposal to her. In later years, Hardy was asked the sort of stupid
question inflicted on novelists about their creations, "what kind of a
wife he imagined Fancy Day . . . would turn out in the future".[14]

> He replied, "I don't quite know. We had better draw a veil over her;
> and yet I have known women of her type turn out all right, some of those
> early examples of independent schoolmistresses included."

The personal tone of his reply suggests a personal application. The
other "early" schoolmistress he seems to have known was his own
mouse-like sister Mary. Triffy Sparks seems indicated—perhaps even
by her name—as Fancy Day.[15]

The speed of writing, and the brevity of the book, meant that by
7 August Hardy was able to send it, with carefully selected extracts
from the *Desperate Remedies* reviews, to Alexander Macmillan, who had,
of course, heard rumours of such a work for the past three years. The
publisher had just lost his wife, and on 17 September his son Malcolm
replied, enclosing John Morley's report.[16] Morley found the book
praiseworthy but slight. He made the curious criticism that it was not
as good as George Sand, and that Hardy should study that author.
Horace Moule's belated review of *Desperate Remedies* in the *Saturday
Review* of 30 September was evidently written after Hardy, in puzzlement, had sent him this comment, for in it he claims that Hardy is *like*
Sand. Moule liked the characters in a way neglected by earlier reviewers
—"the essence of the book is . . . the evolution of characters". He even

approved of the study of Miss Aldclyffe, and found her lesbian scene
showed "an effective and analytical power that recalls the manner of
George Sand". Following the *Spectator*, he developed the slow progress
of the fire as an example of Hardy's mastery of narrative. He criticized
Hardy acutely for seeming to delight too much in what he called
*sententiae*, or moral reflections and aphorisms. This ingrained habit
hardly ever left Hardy, though again fruitfully dormant in *Under the
Greenwood Tree*. It was not, as Moule seemed to suggest, a borrowing
from George Eliot. It was a legacy from his reading in eighteenth-
century authors. As early as his first days in London, he had read Henry
Fielding's *Joseph Andrews* and carefully marked the "Moral Reflections" on page 166 and the "Philosophical Reflections" on pages 219
to 220;[17] but the chief influence in this direction was his habitual
reading in the six-volume *Letters to Sir Horace Mann* by Horace
Walpole.[18] The Walpole type of aphorism in his work should be perhaps
distinguished from the less obtrusive type of observation which comes
from Hardy's own experience. One at least, in *Desperate Remedies*, seems
to point to his grandmother Elizabeth Swetman, her library of books,
and her marriage beneath her:

> In looking back upon our line of descent it is an instinct with us to feel
> all our vitality was drawn from the richer party to any unequal marriage
> in the chain.

Moule's review, anyhow, led to a new chain of activity by Hardy,
both about *Desperate Remedies* itself and about the new work. Though
in a gloomy poem, *The Moment Before Meeting*, he categorized any
meeting as only leading to further separation, he set off, as if unable to
help himself, on another architectural expedition, early in October, to
St. Juliot. There, probably at the urgings of Emma, Hardy wrote to
Tinsley that he had done "a little rural story"—which, of course, though
he did not say so, he had submitted to Macmillan—but "the representa-
tion of critic-friends"—in fact, one friend, Moule—had now made him
start on yet another novel with more plot, "*without crime*—but on the plan
of D.R.".[19] This letter on 20 October followed a disappointing letter he
had just received from Macmillan about *Under the Greenwood Tree*. He
liked the novel but found it slight, and wanted to postpone doing anything about it till the following spring, when he might publish it if it
were still free. Involved still with two women in his private life, Hardy
anticipated no difficulty in keeping two publishers in play; but the
publishers were less easy to hoodwink. Tinsley, who had already remarked that Moule's review had come too late for sales, wrote on 23
October to point out just how small these sales were, and how much
money Hardy was liable to lose on *Desperate Remedies*. He did not rise

to the bait of the new plot-novel without crime, which seems to be the first mention of *A Pair of Blue Eyes*, sketched with its Cornish setting at this time, and with a heroine based, at least physically, on Emma. Hardy now had two novels on hand, one more or less complete, one half-started, both unwanted at this stage. He also had two women on hand, each corresponding to the heroine of a novel.

In these dilemmas, he left St. Juliot, his work there finished, on 30 October, to plunge into the Green Hill work at Weymouth. He was disillusioned, tired of critics, about whom his covering note to Macmillan had contained some foolish remarks.[20] He wrote to Emma renouncing novel-writing, and was urged by her not to despair. All the same, in his own words, "he applied himself to architectural work . . . more steadily than he had ever done in his life before", and the polychrome brick of Green Hill continued to spread. Meanwhile, one of his heroines had reached a point of decision. On 15 December, Tryphena Sparks completed her course at Stockwell. She maintained the first class she had achieved in the first year, and added to it a certificate for drawing. Her next move was dramatic. She applied for and obtained the headship of the Plymouth Day (Girls) School. This was a startling achievement for a girl just out of college. Her own brother said that it was the second largest school in the provinces.[21] It shows how her record impressed the managers, in spite of her youth. What her feelings toward Hardy were by this time, it is impossible to say. She may well have grown tired already of his vacillating and wavering behaviour, his lack of decision, and his mysterious movements. It is not certain she still had his ring, though it seems likely she at least took it with her to Plymouth.[22] On the other hand, there is a family tradition that she applied for the Plymouth job partly because Plymouth was on the normal route from London, where Hardy was now intending to work again, and Cornwall, where he always seemed to be going.[23] Either by express from Paddington, or by coastal packet from the Port of London it would be the obvious way; Hardy used both these methods in the next year, both in real life and in the story of *A Pair of Blue Eyes*. What is absolutely certain is that with great strength of mind, Tryphena had done all she had set out to do. Her salary was just under £100, just over with private pupils. She was the only one of the Sparks family to earn anything like that, and the only one with the sense to save. In her half-dozen years as head teacher, she saved £400,[24] an unheard-of sum for a girl whose labouring relatives earned at most £25 a year. It is an ironic thought that financially she was far better off than Emma, with her small portion of her grandmother's depleted New River Company shares: but for her class, Tryphena was a better match. Whether by choosing her career so wholeheartedly, she sacrificed Thomas Hardy on the way may possibly never be known.

Hardy did not stay long in his new lodgings at 1 West Parade, Weymouth. By 19 March 1872, he was in his new London lodgings, situated, for cheapness, in a less fashionable area and above a tailor's shop, back in Paddington, but this time at 4 Celbridge Place, Westbourne Park. Here he received a cheque for just under £60 as the final account for *Desperate Remedies*—£15 less than he had invested in it. Tinsley sent with his statement a well-meant remark, "I hardly think you *should* be disheartened because the first book has not done well, but this you know best about".[25] What Hardy knew was that he must make some money soon. His method of doing this showed the same self-protective shrewdness that his cousin Tryphena had followed in choosing a career. He attached himself to Thomas Roger Smith, Professor at the R.I.B.A. and twice President of the Architectural Association. Hardy, incidentally, lost his membership of the latter body just at this time for not paying his fees, some indication of his poverty.[26] The connection with Smith was particularly valuable at this moment. He was concerned with designing schools for the London School Board. The Education Act of 1870 had just given wide powers to school boards to create schools where needed. The need was urgent; there were vast areas of London, where, with the increase in population, no school existed at all. It was a key job in the society of the day; like his cousin, Hardy was to benefit by the boom in education. Hardy's intense concentration on this essential work, though, led to yet another complication in his life, which threatened once more his peace of mind.

He had not seen Horace Moule for some time; Moule's habits, as depression and drink increased, seem to have been getting less and less accountable. Meeting him quite by chance in Trafalgar Square, Hardy told him of his concentration on architecture as a career. Moule warned him that the intense work might lead to eyestrain, and advised him, even if only on these grounds, not to give up writing as a career. Whether Moule had seen actual signs of strain, or Hardy, in his agitated state, was ultra-suggestible, within a few days floating spots began to appear before his eyes. Would the temporary blindness he designed for his hero in *The Poor Man and the Lady* afflict its author in real life? He wrote to Moule, who had gone back to Dorset. Moule consulted his mother, and, in London again, wrote to Hardy from his lodgings in Garrick Chambers to say that Mrs. Moule strongly recommended one of the leading ophthalmic surgeons of the day, William Bowman of 5 Clifford Street.[27] Whether or not Hardy took her advice, he may have noted the coincidence that the specialist's surname was already one which he had introduced, presumably at random, among those of his rural choir in *Under the Greenwood Tree*. For the fortunes of that novel had revived. Another chance meeting, this time in the Strand, brought Hardy face to face with Tinsley; that is, if we are to believe his own account in old age, which has many marks of fiction—Tinsley, for instance, is made to talk a kind of stage-cockney throughout their interview. Whatever the truth, Tinsley read the short novel, and on 22 April he offered Hardy £30 for the copyright.[28]

This was not specially generous, but Hardy was in no position to bargain. He agreed, and Tinsley, in fact, paid him £10 extra for the Continental copyright. Faith in himself as a novelist revived. Moule promised that he would review the book for the *Saturday Review*, "Before another member of the staff gets it". In point of fact, though the book came out early in June, Moule, who was more than usually occupied at this time with his own problems, did not get his review in until late that September. Luckily, however, the book did not need his help. *The Athenaeum*, in its books of the week for June 15, gave it generous attention. Hardy was praised for following up all the good qualities the reviewer had noted in *Desperate Remedies*, and developing them with great skill. The love story was thoroughly approved. The only criticism was that his villagers spoke rather too grandly. It was a good selling review and so was that of the *Pall Mall Gazette* on 5 July. Here again it was objected that "the humble heroes and heroines of the tale are much too shrewd, and say too many good things to be truthful representatives of their prototypes in real life"; but the freshness and originality of the book were soundly praised, though the reviewer did not like the late introduction of the vicar's romance into the story, and thought it spoiled the simplicity of the plot.

At all events, it was a good enough start to attract the publisher to further things, and three days later, on 8 July, Tinsley wrote to Hardy with an electrifying suggestion.[29] Tinsley ran a monthly popular publication, *Tinsley's Magazine*, which even contained scurrilous articles about the Queen and her gillie, John Brown. On the more serious side, he was looking for a serial story to start in the September number, which would appear in the middle of August, and asked if Hardy's "new story"—*A Pair of Blue Eyes*, known tentatively at this time as *A Winning Tongue Had He*—was far enough advanced to fill the bill. Hardy had put out feelers for his novel before, but he had not dreamt such an offer would come, or so soon. His account of the negotiations that then ensued, written up in his old age, is once more almost entirely fictional. For one thing, he represents his encounters with Tinsley as taking place in the street on his way to Roger Smith's office in Bedford Street, near the publisher's own office in the Strand, and purely by chance. In actual fact, the whole proposal, and the discussion over financial terms, seems to have been conducted quite normally through letters, which still exist.[30] Hardy's written-up account, in which Tinsley once more appears as a heavy-handed comic cockney,[31] is therefore very much to be doubted. For example, Hardy's copy of *The Law of*

*Copyright in Works of Literature and Art* by A. W. Copinger, which he said he bought to help him in negotiating with the wily publisher, was not, in fact, purchased until the following year.[32] There was no doubt, however, about the result. On 27 July, Hardy agreed for publication as a serial and in a three-volume edition for the sum of £200.

# 15

# A Pair of Blue Eyes

BY ONE of those coincidences whose truth Hardy was often to defend in his novels, the month of August 1872 marked a time of similar personal crisis both for Hardy and his friend Horace Moule. Moule had been unemployed for nearly three years. Though he continued his reviewing work, this was not well-paid. Now something made him seek work with a permanent salary. Though there is an absence of dates, the most likely reason is that this was the time of his engagement to that "highly cultivated governess of sterling character", which his family so well remembered,[1] and which, they hoped, would defeat the depression and the drinking that threatened to destroy his life. Yet even to think of marriage, he would need money. He had hardly any. Thirteen months later, after drawing a year's regular salary, his assets were under £200.[2] As an attempt to earn, he obtained this August a post as Assistant Inspector to the Local Government Board for the district of East Anglia. It was dull and routine work, involving the administration of workhouses and other local institutions, but there were certain advantages in the area chosen. He could make his centre Cambridge, where one of his brothers, Charles Walter Moule, was a Fellow of Corpus Christi College. He would also be within thirty miles of Yaxley Vicarage and the sympathetic Frederick Moule, who had so often before rescued him when stranded on his drinking bouts. Both would be able to keep an eye on him. As a further precaution, a local doctor, James Hough of Trumpington Street, was entrusted with his care. He was to inform Charles Moule of any onset of depression and, when necessary, provide a nurse, so that Horace Moule should not be alone in his lodgings.

Thomas Hardy's crisis this August was of a slightly different nature, but it also concerned work and marriage. Tinsley's advance of £200 for *A Pair of Blue Eyes* gave him for the first time a reasonable financial footing. This, with his architectural earnings over the last intensive year, put him at least in a better position than Moule to offer marriage. On the other hand, unlike Moule, it is doubtful whether he had the approval or even the knowledge of his own family, and he had not approached Emma's father. His absence from the dedication of the newly-restored St. Juliot church earlier that year[3] may have been a politic one. Mr. Gifford, attending a ceremony taken by his son-in-law, might not have been in a mood to meet another prospective one. His own outbursts were apt to coincide with the idea of marriage in his family.[4] It was therefore essential that Hardy should make a good impression and appear to have money in his pocket. It was perhaps to heighten such an impression, as well as for convenience, that Hardy instructed Tinsley to send the proofs of the September instalment (five opening chapters) to him, care of Mr. Gifford at Kirland House, near Bodmin. He himself left London for the west country on 7 August, taking the steam packet-boat from London Bridge to Plymouth. It is highly probable he saw Tryphena Sparks in her new job at Plymouth. One does not know exactly what state their relationship had now reached; but it is also possible that this marked the end of their relationship, and the return of his ring.

At all events, he went straight away to Mr. Gifford's house near Bodmin, for the proofs of *A Pair of Blue Eyes* had to be dealt with at once for publication on the 15th. At this point, Hardy's own reminiscences show all the irrelevance and evasion he reserves for something deeply personal and sometimes unpleasant. He dismisses the whole visit to Cornwall in a short paragraph.[5] He does not mention Mr. Gifford, nor even Emma. He does not say where he was staying, speaking vaguely of driving to St. Juliot, walking to Tintagel, and calling on some friends[6] of Emma at Lanivet, Captain and Mrs. Serjeant. A large part of the paragraph is taken up with a pointless anecdote about another elderly friend of Emma, Miss d'Arville, and her canary, which fainted whenever a cat came into the room, or even when it was shown a picture of a cat. There is absolutely no mention of Mr. Gifford nor Kirland House. Hardy's complete silence at this point has led some biographers to invent an exciting and dramatic scene, in which Mr. Gifford abused him for being of low origins. There may well have been some scene, since the unwelcome thought of a daughter's marriage inclined Mr. Gifford to drink, but it is not certain that it took this form. Admittedly, Irene Cooper Willis annotated her copy of Hardy's reminiscences with the remark that Mr. Gifford "was very contemptuous of Hardy's social position";[7] but she had the information from the second Mrs. Hardy, a suspect source, and even she did not speak of any angry confrontation. She described Mr. Gifford as "that amiable gentleman who wrote to him [Hardy] as a 'low-born churl who has presumed to marry into my family.'"[8] The imputation of low birth was, then, by letter, and even sounds as if it were made after marriage; for it is difficult to see how Mr. Gifford could have visited the Hardys, as he did, after their marriage, if he had made such a remark before.

On the other hand, some deep emotional conflict certainly happened. It is hinted by the curious companion poem Hardy wrote to balance his famous *When I set out for Lyonnesse*. This is the poem, almost identical in metre, *I Rose and Went to Rou'tor Town*. The place of the poem is

Bodmin, from the prominent height Rough Tor, just under ten miles away.[9] The poem mentions "The evil wrought at Rou'tor Town". When Hardy, in his old age, was asked point-blank what this "evil" was, he answered gruffly and cautiously, "Slander, or something of that sort".[10] This hardly sounds like an accusation of low birth only, but of something to do with his personal character.

Two other poems by Hardy, one almost certainly drafted at this time, may, when taken together, and their connection shown, indicate what this "slander" was. They sound as if Emma learnt that Hardy had been involved with other girls before her. Whether this was simply a lucky shot by Mr. Gifford, the natural and usual gambit of the Victorian father to point out his daughter knew little of Hardy's past, or whether he had heard something, is unsure; but the Giffords still had many friends and relatives in Plymouth, and it is conceivable that, with Tryphena now there, something about her and Hardy had leaked out. The two poems, which seem to indicate this kind of emotional crisis, are *Near Lanivet, 1872* and *The Chosen*. Curious and mysterious when apart, they may help to explain one another. The first at least was drafted early in Hardy's life, and probably, as its dated title shows, at about this time. Hardy referred to it frequently after he published its final version in 1917. He told Edmund Gosse it described a scene between him and Emma before their marriage; to Mrs. Henniker, he wrote that it was "literally true". He was disappointed that critics did not select it for comment, expecting them to do so, as he said, because it described "a strange incident, which . . . really happened". He took pains to identify the setting of the poem precisely as "Handpost on the St. Austell Road". This was Reperry Cross, under a mile from Lanivet, where there is an ancient monument consisting of a pillar two feet high, surmounted by an eighteen-inch circle with a cross carved on it, a typical Celtic, early Christian relic.[11] He describes how Emma, weary and depressed, leant against this, and laid her arms along the arms of the cross. He feels a touch of horror at her attitude; she too says "I wish I had not leant so!"

> And wordless we moved onward down from the hill
>     In the west cloud's murked obscure,
> And looking back we could see the handpost still
>     In the solitude of the moor.

Yet the poem does not end there, as a less deeply-felt poem might. Both he and Emma are haunted by the accidental vision of her crucifixion, if not bodily at least possibly "In spirit".

> And we dragged on and on, while we seemed to see
>     In the running of Time's far glass
> Her crucified, as she had wondered if she might be
>     Some day.—Alas, alas!

The poem is mysterious, as so many of Hardy's more personal poems are, because its terms are not completely stated; one is left in doubt about the exact nature of Emma's ultimate "crucifixion".[12]

It may have more meaning, though, if it is taken in association with another mysterious poem, *The Chosen*. One must be warned that there is much that is in doubt about this second poem. No one knows when Hardy composed it; he himself announced it in a sub-title as an allegory; and it has already been subjected to highly imaginative interpretation.[13] What strikes anyone reading it without preconception, however, is the likeness to the landscape and setting of *Near Lanivet, 1872*. In the same dark twilight, the woman breaks away from the man,

> And wanly she swerved, and went away.
> I followed sick: night numbed the air.
> And dark the mournful moorland lay . . .
>
> At length I came to a Christ-cross stone
> Which she had passed without discern;
> And I knelt upon the leaves there strown,
> And prayed aloud that she might turn.

The reason for the woman's horror and flight may help to explain both poems; for *The Chosen* begins,

> "A woman for whom great gods might strive"
> I said, and kissed her there:
> And then I thought of the other five,
> And of how charms outwear.

Hardy then recalls the features and ways of five women loved previously, and admits these to "the woman desired—at last!" She, on the other hand, greets the news with utter dismay:

> "—I feel a strange benumbing spell,
> As one ill-wished!" said she.
> And soon it seemed that something fell
> Was starving her love for me.
>
> "I feel some curse. O, *five* were there?" . . .

She turns back, however, to the "Christ-cross stone", though drooping and weary, as Emma had done in the other poem. Hardy then perceives, in allegory, that she has become in herself all the other five women. He takes her "composite form", and cares for it tenderly,

> Not passion-moved, but even because
> In one I could atone to all.

This highly-complex and curious poem, with its incantatory ballad-metre, its hardly-concealed sexual guilt, and its Christian echoes of the doctrine of atonement, is perhaps most interesting for the light it throws on the far more finished and profound poetry and meaning of *Near Lanivet*. It may give some hint of the stress of the occasion in Cornwall, if Hardy had admitted, or been forced to admit to Emma, that there had been a number of girls in his affections before her—and five seems roughly the number, though identification is perhaps misleading. However lightly he may have glossed this at the time, Emma's "crucifixion" may be said to have come in her fifties, when his *Wessex Poems* produced publicly his poems to all these loves; even the assurance of her own friends could not prevent her from feeling exposed and humiliated. Quite literally, at that time, she mourned to a friend, "alas . . . The *thorn* is in my side still",[14] actually using some sort of muddled crucifixion image of her own to express her wounded, martyred feelings.

This month of stress is perhaps reflected in Hardy's movements in Cornwall. He briefly visited St. Juliot, and made a long note about the look of Beeny Cliff, "green toward to the land, blue-black towards the sea. Every ledge has a little, starved, green grass upon it; all vertical parts bare."[15] This was to be expanded to startling effect later in the serial. Towards the end of the month, he was just over the Devon border, at Brent Tor, on the edge of Dartmoor, a few miles east of Launceston;[16] this was probably on some visit to Emma's favourite uncle, George Mitchell Gifford, bank manager at Launceston. Meanwhile, he had to provide another instalment of three chapters. He settled at St. Juliot once more, and on 30 August wrote to the publishers promising copy in a week's time, only to receive, on 4 September, a peremptory demand for it. He got it off, with apologies, on 7 September, assuring them that in future the instalments would arrive on the first of each month.[17] Whatever may have happened with Emma's father, he was well received by her brother-in-law, who on Sunday, 8 September, allowed Hardy to read the first lesson at evening service, Jeremiah chapter 36, in the new St. Juliot Church.[18] His attachment to Emma had survived whatever had passed between them; but the strain of an emotional crisis and the writing of a regular serial-story was considerable.

This is reflected in the first eight chapters of *A Pair of Blue Eyes*, though some of the uneasy construction of the early parts of the novel must come from the fact that this was Hardy's first commissioned serial, written to order. For the first instalment, corrected in proof when he was at Mr. Gifford's, he had frankly fallen back on previous experience and previous work. Once more, he cannibalized *The Poor Man and the Lady*. Even the heroine's family name, Swancourt, is only a few letters off Allancourt, the squire's name in *The Poor Man*, and her father's insistence on blue blood is very much the squire's too; biographers who see Mr. Gifford in this snobbery have failed to notice that these chapters were written before Hardy met him. The Swancourts' London address

9 (a) Emma as Hardy first knew her

(b) Emma in middle age

10 · The Cornish coast near Boscastle

11  Emma and Hardy during their courtship, August 1870

B. C.
cir. 906.

down, that the rain stop thee not.

45 And it came to pass in the mean while, that the heaven was black with clouds and wind, and there was a great rain. And Ahab rode, and went to Jezreel.

1 ‡ Kings 4. 29.
k 9. 1.
2 Heb. *till thou come to Jezreel.*

46 And the hand of the LORD was on Elijah; and he *k* girded up his loins, and ran before Ahab 2 to the entrance of Jezreel.

**CHAPTER XIX.**

1 *Elijah, threatened by Jezebel, fleeth to Beer-sheba.* 4 *In the wilderness, being weary of his life, he is comforted by an angel.* 9 *At Horeb God appeareth unto him, sending him to anoint Hazael, Jehu, and Elisha.* 19 *Elisha, taking leave of his friends, followeth Elijah.*

a ch. 18. 40.

A ND Ahab told Jezebel all that Elijah had done, and withal how he had *a* slain all the prophets with the sword.

b Ruth 1. 17.
ch. 20. 10.
2 Kin. 6. 31.

2 Then Jezebel sent a messenger unto Elijah, saying, *b* So let the gods do *so*, and more also, if I make not thy life as the life of one of them by to morrow about this time.

3 And when he saw *that*, he arose, and went for his life, and came to Beer-sheba, which *belongeth* to Judah, and left his servant there.

c Numb. 11. 15
Jonah 4. 3, 8.
3 Heb. *for his life.*

4 ¶ But he himself went a day's journey into the wilderness, and came and sat down under a juniper tree: and he *c* requested 3 for himself that he might die; and said, It is enough; now, O LORD, take away my life; for I *am* not better than my fathers.

5 And as he lay and slept under a juniper tree, behold, then an angel touched him, and said unto him, Arise *and* eat.

6 And he looked, and, behold, *there was* a cake baken on the coals, and a cruse of water at his 4 head. And he did eat and drink, and laid him down again.

4 Heb. *bolster.*

7 And the angel of the LORD came again the second time, and touched him, and said, Arise *and* eat; because the journey *is* too great for thee.

8 And he arose, and did eat and drink, and went in the strength of that meat *d* forty days and forty nights unto *e* Horeb the mount of God.

d So Ex. 34. 28.
Deut. 9. 9, 18.
Matt. 4. 2.
e Ex. 3. 1.

9 ¶ And he came thither unto a cave, and lodged there; and, behold, the word of the LORD *came* to him, and he said

unto him, What doest thou here, Elijah?

10 And he said, *f* I have been very *g* jealous for the LORD God of hosts: for the children of Israel have forsaken thy covenant, thrown down thine altars, and *h* slain thy prophets with the sword; and *i* I, *even* I only, am left; and they seek my life, to take it away.

f Rom. 11. 3.
g Numb. 25. 11, 13.
Ps. 69. 9.

h ch. 18. 4.
i ch. 18. 22.
Rom. 11. 3.

11 And he said, Go forth, and stand *k* upon the mount before the LORD. And, behold, the LORD passed by, and *l* a great and strong wind rent the mountains, and brake in pieces the rocks before the LORD; *but* the LORD *was* not in the wind: and after the wind an earthquake; *but* the LORD *was* not in the earthquake:

k Ex. 24. 12.

l Ezek. 1. 4. & 37. 7.

12 And after the earthquake a fire; *but* the LORD *was* not in the fire: and after the fire a still small voice.

13 And it was *so*, when Elijah heard *it*, that *m* he wrapped his face in his mantle, and went out, and stood in the entering in of the cave. *n* And, behold, *there came* a voice unto him, and said, What doest thou here, Elijah?

m So Ex. 3. 6.
Isai. 6. 2.

n ver. 9.

14 *o* And he said, I have been very jealous for the LORD God of hosts: because the children of Israel have forsaken thy covenant, thrown down thine altars, and slain thy prophets with the sword; and I, *even* I only, am left; and they seek my life, to take it away.

o ver. 10.

15 And the LORD said unto him, Go, return on thy way to the wilderness of Damascus: *p* and when thou comest, anoint Hazael *to be* king over Syria:

16 And *q* Jehu the son of Nimshi shalt thou anoint *to be* king over Israel: and *r* Elisha the son of Shaphat of Abel-meholah shalt thou anoint *to be* prophet in thy room.

p 2 Kings 8. 12, 13.

q 2 Kings 9. 1—3.

r Luke 4. 27, called Eliseus.

17 And *s* it shall come to pass, *that* him that escapeth the sword of Hazael shall Jehu slay: and him that escapeth from the sword of Jehu *t* shall Elisha slay.

s 2 Kings 8. 12.
& 9. 14, &c.
& 10. 6, &c.
& 13. 3.
t See Hos. 6. 5.

18 *u* Yet 2 I have left *me* seven thousand in Israel, all the knees which have not bowed unto Baal, *x* and every mouth which hath not kissed him.

u Rom. 11. 4.
2 Or, *I will leave.*
x See Hos. 13. 2.

19 ¶ So he departed thence, and found Elisha the son of

13  Thomas Hardy in 1875, sketched by Emma in her "honeymoon" diary

14  (a) Death-bed sketch by
John Antell junior of
Hardy's uncle by
marriage, John Antell,
partly the original of
Jude Fawley in *Jude
The Obscure*

IN·MEMORY·OF
JOHN ANTELL
Who was Born
............................... 18...
.. Died ... ...... -- 1878
HE WAS A MAN OF CONSIDERABLE
LOCAL REPUTATION AS A SELF-MADE
SCHOLAR, HAVING ACQUIRED A VARIED
KNOWLEDGE OF LANGUAGES, LITERATURE
AND SCIENCE BY UNAIDED STUDY, &
IN THE FACE OF MANY UNTOWARD
CIRCUMSTANCES·

(b) Sketch by Hardy for
John Antell's tombstone

15 Hardy's relatives (foreground) in the High Street, Puddletown (identified by Gertrude S. Antell)

16  Thomas Hardy in his old age, sketch by Augustus John

turns out to be the same as the Allancourts'. Even more strikingly, the style reverted in haste to old faults. The *sententiae* Horace Moule had criticized pervaded it from the first; the serial began with two paragraphs of sententious moralizings, though these were cut in the published book.[19] Still worse, the notebook-style references to painters and literature invaded the writing again; the second page of the final book introduces Rubens, Correggio, and the Madonna della Sedia, while it is not long before a Cornish servant has "a double chin and thick neck, like Queen Anne by Dahl"; Elfride, just as Cytherea had done, strikes a Greuze attitude.

Even more remarkable is Hardy's use of scenes from real life. The opening chapters are a word-for-word reconstruction of his own first experience of the St. Juliot Rectory, though the architect is made much younger, and Emma's elderly brother-in-law is made the heroine, Elfride's, clergyman father, as the real Mr. Holder was old enough to be. One wonders, in fact, what Hardy's host made of all this; for though his sense of humour is portrayed in quite a kindly way, he is, from the first, a terrible snob, as the plot, or that part of it borrowed from *The Poor Man*, compels him to be. He is also somewhat of a fool, not to have realized that the young architect, Smith, is, like Strong in the lost novel, the son of a local workman. Yet he is introduced with every sort of circumstantial detail, such as his attack of gout on the night the architect arrives, which pinpoints his resemblance to Mr. Holder. The latter must have needed all his sense of humour as he read his fictional likeness in the printed pages.

Elfride, the heroine, was as Hardy confessed, based in character and physical detail on Emma,[20] though not, he hastened to add, in the story of love-affairs and adventures that Elfride experienced. Yet it is clear that much of her actual dialogue is also based on things Emma had said or written; if more of Emma's letters and diaries survived, it is likely that the resemblance would be startling. For instance, one of the few fragments from an Emma letter to Hardy is her comforting comment on her attitude toward such a reserved and withdrawn character as Hardy was:

> I take him (the reserved man) as I do the Bible: find out what I can, compare one text with another, & believe the rest in a simple lump of faith.

In the middle of the novel, when Elfride is talking to the reserved and withdrawn literary man, Knight, who becomes unknowingly the younger architect's rival, she says,

> I suppose I must take you as I do the Bible—find out and understand all I can; and on the strength of that, swallow the rest in a lump, by simple faith.

Since this is copied into the novel with only minor transpositions of words, we probably have a great deal of Emma's actual sayings in Elfride's dialogue, if we could recover them; while Smith, visiting Emma's former home, Plymouth, echoes her letter, in which all going on around her seemed a dream.[21]

If the major characters all borrow from real life, so much more do the minor persons and incidents in the book. The satirical and elaborate description of the rings worn by the heroine's stepmother must come, possibly by way of *The Poor Man*, from one of Martha Sparks's accounts of her employer's dressing-table, another verbatim picture of "the female toilette" for reviewers to ponder. The long padding chapter when the chief characters, for no reason, decide to travel from London to Cornwall by boat, reproduces Hardy's own journey that August. As for minor figures, although Hardy once said that Voss, the chorister in *Under the Greenwood Tree*, was the only real person in the novels to be introduced under his own name, he had forgotten the pig-killer's anecdote in *A Pair of Blue Eyes* about the pig that was deaf:

> Ye could play tricks upon en behind his back, and a' wouldn't find it out no quicker than poor deaf Grammer Cates.

This was Rachel Keats, who lived next door to the Hardys at Higher Bockhampton, and who was stone deaf.[22] She had already appeared casually, in *Under the Greenwood Tree*, as "Grammer Kaytes", from whom candles are borrowed by the tranter's wife. Her son, who was a tranter or carrier, William Keats, lived exactly opposite the Hardys, and he and his family were the Dewys in that novel. Hardy's two spellings of her name were typically East Dorset, representing local pronunciation. In Cornwall, where she appears in the later novel, she would probably have been Keat or Keate.

Such resemblances, though some, like the last, have remained unobserved till now, tempt biographers and critics to see the two rivals in *A Pair of Blue Eyes* as Hardy and Horace Moule, the humble young architect and the man of letters who has befriended and tutored him.[23] Superficially, the relationship is certainly suggested. Knight writes for London reviews, and is very slightly patronizing to Smith, his former pupil. Hardy, however, maintained that Knight, aged thirty-two, his own age when writing the novel, had much more in common with himself; and a closer examination seems to bear this out. Not only does Knight write for a radical paper, while Moule wrote for the High Tory *Saturday Review*, but in every way Knight is intellectually most unlike Moule. All accounts of Moule stress his easy manners, his direct way of expressing himself, his simple methods of teaching, his personal charm;[24] his family, his sister-in-law,[25] his friends, all witness this. Knight is pedantic, comparatively charmless, and even something of a prig. Moreover, he uses in criticizing poor Elfride's romantic novel just those heavy-handed *sententiae* or moralizings that Moule had advised Hardy to avoid, and from which Moule's own reviews were refreshingly free. Knight is made to utter remarks that seem to come straight out of Hardy's own quotations in his Literary Notebook. When he produces a damning letter, signed with Elfride's name, he pontificates, incredibly at such a moment of emotional stress,

> In the time of the French Revolution, Pariseau, a ballet-master, was beheaded by mistake for Parisot, a captain of the King's Guard. I wish there was another "E. Swancourt" . . .

Quite apart from difficulties in making the distinction clear in pronunciation, this,[26] and similar oracular and literary utterances, are precisely what Moule avoided. His great gift was to simplify. It was the self-improving Hardy who could not resist the learned allusion. Some critics have seen Knight as a failed intellectual with morbid uncertainties, and drawn a parallel between these and the history of Horace Moule.[27] Yet the occasional references to *Hamlet*, a play which anyway pervades many scenes in the book, are hardly enough for that. Knight's weaknesses are nothing like the grim reality of Moule's dilemma, caught between constitutional cyclic depression and the drink that made him incapable. Above all, Knight is never humiliated academically; he achieves the college fellowship which poor Moule never attained.

What Hardy seems to have done, urged by the effort of serial-writing, was to repeat with more care and maturity a part of his technique in *Desperate Remedies*. In that novel he had represented two sides of his own nature by the two architects, one nervous and ineffective, the other intellectually accomplished even though self-taught. Now, merely taking the pupil and teacher pattern as a framework, he demonstrated in the two characters two deeper aspects of himself. There is the emotional immaturity, which is part of the boyish charm of Smith. There is the advanced intellectual stature, which nevertheless sits uneasily on Knight, because he too is emotionally unsure. "His lateness of development in virility, while mentally precocious",[28] Hardy's description of the key to himself, might apply exactly to Knight, like Hardy always uncertain when put to the test of a real human relationship. These two sides, underlined physically by the boyish Smith, spring from Hardy's inner self, and are the making of the two men in the novel. He himself was at pains to say[29] that he had made Smith look like a nephew of Hicks the architect, but he is essentially the young Hardy.

Yet when all this is said, and however much the novel in its haste became "a kind of rag-bag of information, ideas, descriptive vignettes, personal experiences, fragments of the author's brief literary past",[30] there is an impressive and professional side to the writing, which

explains why it was so much admired by readers as different as Tennyson, Coventry Patmore and Proust. The inconsistent, shifting, and even
stagey manner of the work in the early chapters gradually settles to be a
more controlled style and a study of character in far greater depth. This
was preceded and eventually helped by a change in the place and
circumstance of Hardy's own life. Back in London on 11 September,
he found he could not write there. Nor could he do his architectural work
for Roger Smith, whose surname and experiences in India he had given
to his young hero. Smith was anxious to give Hardy a better contract
and wider employment, since the Board School plans had been successful, and this was an expanding market. Hardy realized he must decide
once and for all to give his time to writing, and Smith let him go. He
was encouraged by the delayed but excellent review of *Under the
Greenwood Tree* by Horace Moule in the *Saturday Review* of 28 September, as "the best prose idyl we have seen for a long while past". Moule
had also the intelligence to praise the social aspects of the book, and to
see that, like all Hardy's early novels, it commented on society. Hardy's
countryfolk were not to be regarded as quaint literary characters,
recorded in patronizing pages, but

> It is a book that might well lie on the table of any well-ordered country-
> house, and that might also be borne in mind by the readers during kindly
> rounds undertaken among the cottages.

Pursuing this theme, and in a gentle vein of criticism that distinguishes
Moule once more from any likeness to Knight, he added that it was a
weakness in the author occasionally to make these genuine countryfolk
"express themselves in the language of the author's manner of thought
rather than in their own". His review came as timely and welcome
encouragement; on the same day that it appeared, Hardy left for
Bockhampton. He was to stay there, with no distractions, no other job
nor personal problem, until he had finished the serial, ahead of time as it
proved. The healing power of a settled and familiar background begins
to make itself felt in the greater assurance of touch, which he shows from
the middle of the book onward.

   The far more serious nature of the love-affair between Elfride and
Knight brings a more mature tone to the second half of the book. However much of a bookish figure Knight may seem, we accept that Elfride
preferred his "instructive and piquant snubbings" to the diffident
expressions of the youthful Smith, just as Emma, in spite of her different
class, was impressed by Hardy's own intellect. The rather tiresome and
often-pouting young lady of the first half, Miss Capricious as Hardy was
unfortunately led to call her, gives way to a real character of a woman,
with overtones that verge on tragedy, and excite our interest and
sympathy. This was once more acutely noticed by Horace Moule, when

he received the published book in the following May. He at once commented how much better Hardy drew the woman than the lady.[31] Elfride, the superficially described lady of the first half, becomes a woman in the second.

As so often in a Hardy novel, a striking natural event serves as a fulcrum in the middle part of the book, to tip the balance of the writing into a higher seriousness and maturity. Such had been the fire at the inn in *Desperate Remedies*, ushering in at least more reliance on real life and less on Gothic melodrama. In Hardy's coming novel, *Far From the Madding Crowd*, the enormous thunderstorm, during which Bathsheba helps Gabriel Oak to cover the ricks in her farm, draws together their characters into a deeper relationship that pervades the second half of that book. In *A Pair of Blue Eyes*, the point is reached in the chapters where Knight slips over the cliff, and is rescued, after his agonizing ordeal, by Elfride's improvised rope of underwear. For the first time, Hardy exploits in prose what he had already achieved in some of his poems, the union of a scene from nature and an emotional relationship of his people. The cliff, minutely described from Beeny and its coastline companions,[32] becomes a part of the emotional life of Knight and Elfride; their instinctive embrace when she pulls him back to safety is the beginning of their love and their tragedy. The end of their drama, though not so often noticed, shows the same power to make a natural scene draw out the living state of the people in it. When Knight, by relentless and jealous cross-examination, produces from Elfride the final confession of her former love-affair with Smith, the two of them restlessly wander in an autumn stubble field that surrounds them with half-seen decay, as their love itself disintegrates around them, until the scene itself is made explicitly a symbol of their tragic desolation.

> The scene was engraved for years on the retina of Knight's eye: the dead and brown stubble, the weeds among it, the distant belt of beeches shutting out the view of the house, the leaves of which were now red and sick to death.

This is the type of unity that Hardy had till then only effected in poems such as *Neutral Tones*, where the frozen pond and fallen leaves are totally at one with the lovers' disillusion and icy parting.

Not all this second half is equally realized, though Elfride's hasty, instinctive, even sometimes absurd, prevarications under Knight's obsessive harrying, have a reality that derives perhaps from Hardy's own manoeuvres in trying to keep a former and a later love, Tryphena and Emma, separate and secret from one another. It must also be said that the stagey conventions of the earlier chapters take over the final episodes of the novel. Elfride's tragedy suffers from Hardy's falling-back on the novelettish convention that a Victorian heroine should tell enough of the truth to make her seem guilty, and remain unnaturally silent on the final facts which would exonerate her. Elfride's confessions end with the admission that she had spent a night alone with Smith. Her author, anxious to leave the implication of sexual misconduct in Knight's mind, does not allow her to add *how* she had spent it; that is, in a journey by express train from Plymouth to Paddington, a mad rush, when doubts assail them, by the two young people from platform to platform at Paddington to catch the down train back, and a journey home via Bristol, during which it is carefully and explicitly planted that there were two or three other persons in their compartment. Theatrical convention, too, takes over in the final stages when, in yet another train journey—Hardy was not immune from the typically Victorian pride and wonder at the steam-engine—the two rivals, now self-confessed, find that the special compartment coupled on to their train contains the body of Elfride in her coffin, thus providing a curtain scene of frank melodrama.

Yet if the ultimate effect of *A Pair of Blue Eyes* is still one of confused abilities and uneven performance, it had enough mastery over its materials to add to Hardy's confidence. He had overcome the haunting demands of serial-writing, and even turned them to advantage; he had learnt not to let the standard of a novel drop, but increase in power as it progressed. Indeed, the falling-off at the very end, and the perfunctory finish, may not be so much that Hardy had run out of ideas, as that a new and dominant idea for further writing had already occupied his attention, and a chance to present it had been offered to him in a quarter more important than any which had so far come his way.

# 16

# Far From the Madding Crowd

HORACE MOULE'S belated review of *Under the Greenwood Tree* was too delayed, thought Tinsley the publisher, to rescue the sales of that book; for although the other reviews were also universally good, the public had not responded. Yet on 4 October Tinsley at least promised to try more advertisement, quoting Moule's praises from the *Saturday Review*.[1] The public, however, continued to find the story, just as Alexander Macmillan had prophesied they would, "very slight and rather unexciting".[2] Tinsley softened the blow by promising a massive advertising campaign for *A Pair of Blue Eyes*, and encouraging the author to press on with the next instalment. "I *shall* lose my reputation as a judge of good fiction if you don't do great things", he wrote, although he had so far seen only two rather scrappy instalments of Hardy's serial, and afterwards confessed that he thought it "by far the weakest of the three books I published of his".[3] Moule's review, though, even if useless for general publicity, probably, by its very isolation, brought the book more attention in intellectual circles. Then, at the beginning of November, it was seconded by an even more delayed notice in the dreaded *Spectator*, which, far from its previous satirical style, seemed to be almost a copy of Moule's own review, praising the same points, and having the same minor reservations about the unnaturally literate rustic conversation.

Yet though these reviews failed to make the public clamour for the book at the circulating libraries, they were perhaps the most important literary assistance in all Thomas Hardy's early writing life. For they drew the still-anonymous author to the attention of one of the country's leading literary figures. In November 1872, Leslie Stephen read *Under the Greenwood Tree*. Stephen was the dominant English man of letters of the second half of the nineteenth century. Just forty, he was at the very height of his powers, which included top-class athletics and mountaineering as well as literature, and a college tutorship, which he had resigned in 1862 when fashionably losing his faith although still in Holy Orders. In 1882, having started the "English Men of Letters" series, he went on to initiate the *Dictionary of National Biography*, and become the father of Virginia Woolf. In the present year, 1872, he had been for the past twelve months editor of the *Cornhill Magazine*, which had been started in 1860 under the editorship of Thackeray. It had acquired a reputation for serialized fiction and essays of the highest quality, and

Stephen was looking for new young talent. Reading *Under the Greenwood Tree*, he found it pleased him as much as Moule said it would. It was not, he saw, a magazine story in itself, and he had evidently not yet identified the current serial by the same author now appearing for Tinsley; but the style of the rural "prose idyl" made him read it with great pleasure. It was well known that Horace Moule had written the notice. Stephen obtained from him the author's name, and wrote to Hardy himself with a proposal that would have delighted any new author: "If you are, as I hope, writing anything more, I should be very glad to have the offer of it for our pages".[4] He hinted that if Hardy agreed, the financial terms would be generous.

Stephen's letter reached Hardy at Bockhampton early in December, just when he was despatching the instalment of *A Pair of Blue Eyes* for January, nearly halfway through the book. The inspiration of feeling wanted in such distinguished company may have helped to give Hardy the greater confidence of the later instalments. The problem was, how to reply promptly, and keep this glittering proposal in play. He must say something concrete and practical, knowing how soon editors and publishers cool off. Stephen's letter had already been delayed by the rural post, picked up from being dropped in the muddy lane.[5] Eventually Hardy answered, with a mixture of frankness and shrewdness. He could not start at once on a fresh work, since he was already committed to his present serial. If Stephen could wait, the next novel should be at his disposal. It was necessary not merely to leave it at that, but to say something about what this might be. It was to be, he said, a pastoral tale with a pastoral title—*Far From the Madding Crowd*; both were calculated to attract Stephen, who had already found Hardy's "descriptions of country life admirable". More than this was needed, though, and Hardy added that the chief characters would probably be a young woman-farmer, a shepherd, and a sergeant of cavalry.

Whether Hardy made this up on the spur of the moment, or whether he had genuinely planned such a book, may never be known; but all the signs are that the main idea came into his mind this December. They were the peaceful first-fruits of his return to the home surroundings that had first nourished him. Gradually, from October through the autumn and winter, calm and certainty returned to his life, the familiar healing of all he saw and met. In misty October, walking back from Dorchester, or travelling in Burden the carrier's one-horse van with village food, saltfish and sides of bacon, dangling around the passengers,[6] Hardy could look back on Dorchester from Stinsford Hill,[7] and see, in the gleaming wet dusk, the town encircled by a halo like an aurora, a place of fearful yet familiar mystery, as it had appeared to him as a child. Next month, out early in the tranced November dawn, everything he saw seemed as still and remote as if it were at the bottom of a pond.

When the first frost came in the middle of the month, he noticed the miniature ruin of the cottage vegetable gardens, scarlet runners and cucumber leaves collapsing at a blow. Frost and December drove the family indoors, to long evenings of talk and memory round the glowing kitchen hearth. Here, as always, Hardy was in the spell of the most powerful presence in his life, his mother. His summer manoeuvres with other women, the awkward break with an old love, and the perils and uncertainty of a new one, were nothing to the assured care and special understanding she gave him as a matter of course. Though Mary, his second self, might add to the calm and pleasure, coming home each day from school-teaching, even she was only a shadow to Jemima in Hardy's life; she could add to their mother's memory of old children's rhymes, the special local verses used by her own school-children at Piddlehinton,[8] but hers, as always, was the supplementary role in the firelit evening kingdom of which their mother was the centre.

The long strange history of his mother's own childhood was the chief theme of their nights of talk: how her own mother, the dispossessed daughter, had lived in a mean cottage at one end of Melbury Osmond, while her father, wealthy farmer, lived at the other: how, penniless for life through her improvident marriage, she had brought up seven children, after her husband's death, on parish relief; how even before his death, her husband, farm servant, out of work for the most part by family tradition, got occasional jobs as a shepherd. She talked of the superstitions and weird apparitions of an isolated childhood. In one long evening this December, she talked to Hardy about his aunt Martha, and the strange figure of the fortune teller, who used to pass through Melbury Osmond every month. Martha gave him the day and hour she was born, from which he prophesied her large family and her emigration[9] with her ex-cavalry husband, to die in Canada. Mother and son were reminded of their three weeks' visit to Martha in Hertfordshire, when Hardy was only nine. That journey in his mother's company, to break the spell of Mrs. Martin, held many memories for Hardy as the great emotional adventure of his childhood, touched with magic and tragedy. Did his dashing uncle, a riding master, Hardy thought, in crack regiments, dazzle the small nephew one evening in his scarlet regimentals? At any rate, he and the daring, impulsive aunt,[10] now unhappily dead, were brought as vividly back to Hardy as was his grandmother, the farmer's daughter, married beneath her to a poverty-stricken shepherd.

So, by some such process, and by the folk-ballad atmosphere always evoked by his mother, perhaps even by her singing of *On the Banks of Allan Water*—

> For his bride a soldier sought her,
> And a winning tongue had he—

he could well believe that he had in his head for Stephen a tale about a woman, a shepherd, and a sergeant of cavalry. How then did he arrive at the bold stroke of the woman-farmer? As we have already seen, this almost unheard-of fancy was, again, something he had literally heard, and from yet another member of his mother's family. Bathsheba came to Hardy through Tryphena, when she was teaching at Coryates, from her stories at Weymouth about the landowner of Waddon, half a mile from her school, Catherine Hawkins. Widowed early in her thirties, Mrs. Hawkins had disregarded the advice of her relative and trustee, Granvile Hill, to sell the 525-acre farm and another property, with all their stock, combine the proceeds with her marriage settlement, and live on the income.[11] She refused and, though with little experience, determined to run the farm for her seven-year-old son Charles, to keep it in the family until he came of age. The first test of her resolve had been the terrible winter of 1865–66. Thanks to a shepherd with thirty years' knowledge behind him, William Slade, she had lost only four ewes and a few lambs; but, a worse disaster than any other, she had lost the shepherd, who died suddenly, and left her looking for another, though she felt it would be "a long time before his place will be so well supplied".[12] The fruit of Hardy's attachment to Tryphena was her story of the lady at Waddon, who ran the farm and needed a shepherd; Catherine Hawkins's venture combined with the bold character of Hardy's aunt to make Bathsheba Everdene, whose farm, otherwise so well equipped, is unaccountably in need of a shepherd, among all the Puddletown rustics of *Far From the Madding Crowd*, just when the first snows of winter fall.

Indeed, Tryphena herself may have recalled this offshoot of their 1869 attachment by her presence in Puddletown this same December. She had come to visit her ailing father, and to be involved, as it proved, in an odd family affair. Her sister Rebecca had decided, at the age of over forty, to marry a man she had been keeping company with, Frederick Pain, a Puddletown saddler. Three months after their marriage on Christmas Day, with Tryphena and her father as witnesses, she left him, and went to live with Tryphena at Plymouth. None of the Sparks family knew why she did this,[13] though a sensational and totally undocumented theory has been evolved that she was not Tryphena's sister but her mother, something which, if true, would certainly have appeared in the family papers. The probable cause, as of most actions in the Sparks family, was money, or lack of it. It may be conjectured that Pain had none, since he almost immediately emigrated to America.[14] Rebecca, more than the rest, was obsessive about money; she made a bee-line for the only member of the family who had any, possibly on the rebound of disappointment with Pain, and settled down at Plymouth as her sister's housekeeper. This Christmas visit may have been the last time that Hardy ever saw Tryphena, if indeed his own mother let him.

For Hardy had returned, just like some man in a D. H. Lawrence story, to the world of his mother, a fortress against the vagaries of other women. Although he seemed in old age to remember a flying visit to Cornwall in the New Year of 1873, other evidence suggests his memory misplaced this, and that winter and spring were spent entirely in his mother's home.[15] From this time there began to appear in his books the sharp aphorisms about the wiles of marriageable women that have disturbed some critics, who rightly find them obsessive in their frequency,[16] and even surprising in a man working toward marriage. They are not so surprising when one hears in them the voice of Jemima Hardy, providing, from the depths of folk-wisdom, a sexual philosophy for her favourite son. "Well, mind what th'rt about. She can use the corners of her eyes as well as we can use the middle"—Hardy, noting this saying, merely added the words, "Heard in Dorset";[17] but if he did not actually hear it at his mother's fireside, he certainly heard many similar warnings. As winter deepened, the hearth grew increasingly a place for folklore, and the legends of Melbury Osmond flowered in full superstition. His mother told him of the haunted barn there, where a lady in a white riding habit could be seen riding a buck at midnight, only to vanish at the sound of a chance spectator's sneeze.[18] The rationalist Hardy, sceptic and anti-clerical, retained to his end a belief and a relish in the supernatural that surprised his contemporaries.

In these surroundings, protected, without even the need to lift a finger for meals or mending, Hardy raced ahead with the instalments of *A Pair of Blue Eyes*, so fast that Tinsley was able to bring out the revised and completed book at the end of May 1873, before the last instalment had actually appeared in magazine form. The postponed discussion with Stephen about the new novel was, of course, partly behind such speed, and the perfunctory ending of the Tinsley serial has been noticed. On 9 June, Hardy, in his first break from home since the previous September, left for London to pick up threads, including the most important one of his interview with Stephen. In actual fact, he avoided seeing Stephen, perhaps becoming nervous at the last minute that the great man might treat him as Meredith had done. On the wave of undisturbed writing, however, Hardy managed to send him instead a few loosely-sketched chapters of the new book, and a few others in outline. Stephen approved, though he did not officially accept the novel until the autumn. Meanwhile, the publication of *A Pair of Blue Eyes* had for the first time revealed Hardy's name to the public. The response in the June reviews was a good one. The *Spectator*, perhaps taking to itself some credit for the lesson taught over *Desperate Remedies*, was officiously complimentary about the author's "rapid strides". It praised the humour, the artistic observation, the analysis of character, as well as Hardy's usual power in narrative. It even commended him for having an unhappy ending instead of a more conventional one, and so maintaining truth and artistic integrity though the reviewer, John Hutton, wrote to Hardy personally regretting this as a member of the reading public. Hutton had been the reviewer of *Desperate Remedies*, and his correspondence[19] this spring and summer shows him in a better light than the still-touchy author. He did not apologize for his previous review,[20] though regretting that he had tactlessly brought it again to Hardy's notice; indeed, he exclaimed, "I should much like to know why you wrote that sensation novel",[21] since he now recognized Hardy had such high potential abilities. Also, in both letters and review, he sounded a warning note. In the review he hoped to "hear of Hardy soon but not too soon again".

For Hardy this was a brief break from home and writing, diversified for a few days by showing London to his country-bred brother Henry. The first personal tie to be renewed was his old friendship with Horace Moule, a theme of impending crisis. At the New Year, Moule had obtained rooms in his old College of Queens', Cambridge, a privilege possibly linked with taking his M.A. that year. He was at any rate to have the company of dining in Hall,[22] and was not in lonely lodgings, but the signs are that once more all was not well with him. He was not only finding his work for the Local Government Board increasingly arduous and exacting; but it was almost certainly now that something went wrong with his engagement to the governess which, his family hoped, might save him from himself. She broke it off, under circumstances which will never be known. A sensational story that she was alienated by an exhibition of drunkenness may probably be discounted,[23] for, as will be seen, there was another even more sensational factor in his story. His watchful physician, James Hough, kept an eye on his increasing depressions, and provided a nurse when necessary. Moule confided to him his fears that he would be unable to carry on his Local Government work, though the district inspector was so far satisfied with it. When it was term-time, and Cambridge was full of young people, he found relief in his habitual though unofficial care for them. Late in May, he wrote to Hardy[24] on office notepaper to ask advice for a young B.A. of Trinity, who wanted to be an architect. He also gently chided Hardy for getting his designation of Lord Luxellian wrong in the recently-published *A Pair of Blue Eyes*, a solecism which Hardy corrected in later editions. In the most affectionate terms he proposed a meeting. This took place on 15 June in London, and was followed on 20 June by Hardy's first visit to Cambridge, where he stayed in college with Moule. After dinner, they strolled about the Backs in a magnificent sunset. Next day, Moule took him on the classic site for a visitor, the roof of King's College Chapel, where in the morning sunshine they had an unforgettable view over the flat East Anglian levels, all the way to Ely Cathedral. He also opened the west door of the chapel, for Hardy to have a view of the rich, dramatic interior, with the fan-vaulting, on which they had walked, like a huge stone flower. He saw Hardy off for London, in an affectionate parting.[25]

The next journey was also a visit of affection. Emma Gifford was staying at Bath with her friend the old lady, Miss d'Arville, owner of the sensitive canary. Hardy travelled down there that same night, and spent a happy ten days with Emma, discreetly chaperoned, in expeditions about Bath and Bristol. On 1 July they got away on their own to Chepstow, the Wye Valley, and Tintern Abbey, where they repeated Wordsworth's lines to one another in the sky-roofed tracery by the river. Looking through the empty windows at the green steep hills around, Hardy characteristically compared the age of these to the stonework of ephemeral man which they guarded, a parallel to the reflections of Knight as he clings to the age-old cliff-face.[26] One does not know what was settled between them on the emotional side, but Emma, in old age, wrote of Hardy being at that time her "chosen",[27] and Hardy remembered their love in a tender poem.[28] Stephen's offer must have made the prospect of an early marriage more practical, and Hardy confidently pressed on with more specimen chapters for the editor.

For, having once found the background for successful work, he did not stay long away, even with Emma. By the next day, 2 July, he was back at Bockhampton, getting ahead with the new novel, *Far From the Madding Crowd*, in a setting that lived up to its title, based closely on the old, unreformed Puddletown, before it was improved by the Gothic building and public institution of a respectable façade by Squire Brymer. It was, as Hardy said in a later preface to the book, a place "notoriously prone" to "that love of fuddling", which he knew very well from his Hand uncles, with their drinking and wife-beating. In fact, he eventually made one of the key turns of the plot depend on an inhabitant getting drunk, the incident of Joseph Poorgrass, drawn from an actual Puddletown man, and his "multiplying eye" after drink. He brought everything into close contact with his own immediate surroundings. The woman-farmer, borrowed from the example of Mrs. Hawkins of Waddon, acquired a Puddletown setting, and the farmhouse he had chosen for his heroine, Waterston House on the way up the valley to Piddlehinton, took its fine Caroline gables on what Hardy afterwards called "a witch's ride of a mile or more" closer to Puddletown itself. The picture of an unreformed, partly unenclosed rural community of the old sort was deepened by the exact painting of an area only a very few miles in size, and known to Hardy all through his impressionable youth.

The foreground figures to this background were still the three he had promised Stephen, and probably remained so for the first dozen chapters, which, it has been plausibly conjectured, were what he had completed by the end of September.[29] These, the woman-farmer, the shepherd, and the cavalry sergeant, are already there, though the shepherd has been given a more respectable pedigree, being formerly a small independent farmer who has lost his stock by natural disaster, and the sergeant, though present, is still more or less waiting in the wings of the action. The fact that a fourth and deeply tragic figure was eventually added to this dancelike quadrille of folk-ballad characters may have been due partly to the stunning real-life tragedy which now invaded Hardy's peaceful and settled world of deep-laid affection. On 2 August, Horace Moule made what proved to be his last gesture for his former pupil's career in literature. Though he had sworn never again to review a friend's book, he broke the rule in the *Saturday Review* of that date. It was the best of all his reviews of Hardy's work. He found that though Hardy had produced rapidly, this was a work of mature thoroughness, and genuine depth. "Out of simple materials there has been evolved a work of really tragic power." Once more recognizing the social nature of Hardy's mind, he showed that this was a real portrayal of some of the more destructive social barriers of their time. He admitted that Hardy still had "much to learn and many faults still to avoid", and was uneasy at the priggishness of Knight. This criticism was, again, an additional sign that the portrait of the reviewer in the novel was not in any way meant for his own generous self, and that the relationship between Smith and Knight had very little to do with the friendship Moule enjoyed with Hardy. In details, he picked on the obvious and literal cliff-hanger of Knight's two chapters of peril on the rock-face: "worked out with extraordinary force . . . they recall the intense minuteness and vivid concentration of the most powerful among French writers of fiction." None of this friendly criticism could have prepared Hardy for the coming event, which caused him later to double-mark the two lines from *In Memoriam*,

> Diffused the shock thro' all my life,
> But in the present broke the blow.

# 17

# Moule

MOULE's words were the last message he was to direct towards Hardy. On Friday, 19 September, he came back from a summer holiday to his rooms in Queens'. Cambridge was empty, a fortnight before Michaelmas Term, and even his brother Charles was not yet in his rooms at Corpus. The onset of autumn is a melancholy time in Cambridge, with the mists rising from Coe Fen over the causeway, and the drenched Michaelmas daisies drooping their heads in the college gardens. A wave of melancholy and restless agony about life and work seized him in a way that at once alarmed his doctor. It was the worst bout he had seen, and he felt it urgent to provide a nurse, who came on the Saturday morning, and to send a telegram to Charles Moule that night. His brother arrived on the Sunday, and had a distressing and all-too-familiar talk with him. The drink he took to try and combat his depression seemed to him to threaten his work. The possibility of losing his position was very much on his mind, and he became at first excited and then deeply depressed. After a three-hour discussion, he said he felt so ill that he was going to bed. Charles remained writing in the outer room. After a few minutes he heard a sound, which at first he could not place, a kind of trickling. He went into the bedroom, and found Horace Moule lying on the bed covered in blood. Thinking at first he had broken a blood vessel, Charles Moule ran to the Porter's Lodge, and sent a messenger for Dr. Hough. Hastening back, he found his brother lying there, bleeding but still just able to speak. He said, "Easy to die" and "Love to my mother". Only then, perhaps, did Charles realize that Horace had done what he long ago threatened to do, and taken his own life. The surgeon, when he arrived, confirmed that he had cut his throat. The nurse, also summoned, found an open razor. Horace Moule never spoke again. At the inquest, held the next day, the jury returned a verdict of "suicide whilst in a state of temporary insanity".[1]

On the Sunday his friend died, Hardy had spent the day walking to and from the great autumn fair at Woodbury Hill, east of Bere Regis, which was to appear in *Far From the Madding Crowd*. On Wednesday, 24 September he heard the news. Next day, Horace Moule's body was brought to Fordington, for burial on the Friday in consecrated ground, which the form of words of the jury's verdict had allowed. On the previous evening, 25 September, Hardy, according to a later poem, went to Fordington churchyard, and contemplated the mound of chalk dug from the newly-prepared grave. It was this day, rather than the day of death, or that of the funeral, which he attended, that he always remembered.

Hardy reserves for this cataclysmic event in his life the almost total reticence he displays when anything has moved him most deeply. Any notations of it, when they occur, have therefore all the more meaning. In the poem, *Before My Friend Arrived*, he says he sketched the mound of chalk in the churchyard that Thursday evening. In his copy of *The Golden Treasury*, given to him by Moule, he sought out Shakespeare's Sonnet 32, ironically finding it under Palgrave's title of *Post Mortem*, and put the Thursday's date against these bracketed lines:[2]

> "Had my friend's Muse grown with this growing age,
> A dearer birth than this his love had brought,
> To march in ranks of better equipage:
>
> But since he died, and poets better prove,
> Theirs for their style I'll read, his for his love."

His journey to Cambridge that June now moved him so much that he added to his account of it, retrospectively, the words, "His last smile". Reading *In Memoriam* later in the 1870s, he came across the section where Tennyson revisits the university, with its memories of Arthur Hallam, and against the opening lines,[3]

> I past beside the reverend walls
> In which of old I wore the gown;

he noted "(Cambridge) H.M.M.", also pencilling the line

> Another name was on the door:

Otherwise, there is barely a mention of his tragic friend. Though it has been said[4] that Hardy left instructions to his second wife and executors to destroy anything about "M—", this is not in fact true. Quite apart from the Hardy notation for Moule always being, as we have seen, "H.M.M.",[5] which was Moule's own way of signing his letters to Hardy, the abbreviated instructions are to delete "M——ls",[6] that is Memorials, meaning useless memoranda.

We have little evidence, either, of what Hardy thought of the whole question of suicide, though his later notebooks deal extensively with quotations about this topic, as they tend to do about all morbid states of mind. It may be significant that in his Milton, which he had been reading since the middle 1860s, he heavily lined the margin of Eve's long plea for suicide in *Paradise Lost*, Book X, and that in *Samson Agonistes*, where Samson's death is described as "self-kill'd Not willingly", he underlined the words and put an exceptionally large question-mark against them, thus perhaps tacitly opposing the verdict of the Cambridge jury.

With so little direct evidence, and in the absence of some vital dates in Moule's life, much must necessarily be speculation. There is, though, one hitherto unknown factor, which is perhaps the most important of all. It may even be that it was first revealed to Hardy on that memorable last visit to Cambridge, for it remained vividly in his mind in his old age, when he confided it in detail to the second Mrs. Hardy.[7] On that evening of 20 June, as they talked in Moule's rooms in Queens', the conversation between the two men went on deep into the summer night. Moule stood by the mantelpiece of his keeping-room, with the candles guttering behind him. As he spoke on and on excitedly, he seemed to Hardy to be pointing unconsciously at the long trailing overflow of wax that was gathering on the candle. This, in country-superstition terms, was known as the "shroud", and it was held to foretell the death of the person to whom it applied. This is the factual basis for Hardy's later poem *Standing by the Mantelpiece*.[8] There was another fact, though, far more significant than a mere legend, that must have entered into the long discussion. This was the fatal secret of Moule's personal life; whether it caused or followed the open secret of his drunken bouts, will probably never be known, though the fact itself, concealed by his own family, is fully attested. At some unspecified time, Moule had had, or had been persuaded he had, a bastard child by a low girl in his father's parish at Fordington. This was, according to Florence Hardy, the "tragedy of his life". There were other even more lurid details. At all events, and whenever in fact Hardy first knew it, it certainly bears on the one poem by Hardy, to which he gave the date of composition in this year, 1873,[9] the brief verse Hardy called *She At his Funeral*.

> They bear him to his resting-place—
> In slow procession sweeping by;
> I follow at a stranger's space;
> His kindred they, his sweetheart I.
> Unchanged my gown of garish dye,
> Though sable-sad is their attire;
> But they stand round with griefless eye,
> While my regret consumes like fire.

There have been many guesses about the background to this poem (including the fantasy[10] that the girl is Tryphena Sparks, who on this very day[11] was nervously preparing her staff for a school inspection), but the "character of the girl", to quote Florence Hardy on Moule, gives sense for the first time to Hardy's words, "gown of garish dye". If this is indeed a literal picture, it is unjust to the Moule family, who were totally devastated by Horace's death, both at this time and for long after. Their grief was deep and genuine. Charles Moule himself wrote a poem in that year,[12] both depicting Horace's character, and trying to find acceptable terms for the suicide.

> O kindly heart, & tongue, & pen,
> To advise, to do unlooked-for good! . . .
> A strange disquiet wore his brain,
> Till restlessly he seized on rest.

Members of the Moule family regretted for years afterwards that they had been able to do so little for him. The heaviest burden of regret and horror at the event naturally fell on Charles, who had been a few yards from the suicide. The anniversary, mourned by the whole family, was always a time of particularly deep personal trial to him. Handley Moule, noting the day in his diaries[13] for the rest of his life, recorded five years after, "Our beloved H.'s day . . . Dear C. better than our fears", and, a few years later, "A fine day. Oh how solemn in its recollections of 1873. The Lord be with dearest Charlie". If Hardy shared in any way the feelings of the girl, and felt excluded from the grief of the Moule family, it was the exclusion of his own peculiar kind of grief. Modern thought is apt to deal heavy-handedly with the topic of Victorian male affection. Hardy has left the evidence we have seen that he felt for Moule in some way as Shakespeare did for his friend, and as Tennyson did for Hallam. There is no other point of definition.

What seems more sure, though not precisely definable, is the effect on his work. It does seem likely that, until this moment in time, *Far From the Madding Crowd*, for all its deeper assurance of style, was something of the mixture as before which Stephen had seemed to suggest he wanted. Bathsheba and Oak, in their early wooing scenes, are simply a more mature version of Fancy Day and Dick Dewy in *Under the Greenwood Tree* and even to some extent Elfride and Stephen Smith in *A Pair of Blue Eyes*. It is a conventional comedy treatment of the blunt and over-simple wooer and the capricious lady, who blows hot and cold in her moods. Even the figure of Sergeant Troy is so far only a worldly voice speaking through a barrack window, the sexually-accomplished male person whom Hardy never seemed to draw with much conviction or inside knowledge. Yet with Farmer Boldwood, at this point only a character who knocks at the door with an enquiry and goes away, an entirely new note of introspective tragedy is struck. It is probably right to regard Boldwood as a minor character developed into a major one, rather than a new character introduced,[14] but once developed, he takes on unforgettable stature. Not only does he play a decisive part in the chief action of the story; he is, as a man, more fully analysed than any Hardy character before him. It is a study in morbid psychology, which was very close to Hardy's inner life, but which, until this time, he had hardly allowed to be explicit in his work. Now he could write with frank power:

> The phases of Boldwood's life were ordinary enough, but his was not an ordinary nature. That stillness, which struck casual observers more than anything else in his character and habit, and seemed so precisely like the rest of inanition, may have been the perfect balance of enormous antagonistic forces—positives and negatives in fine adjustment. His equilibrium disturbed, he was in extremity at once. If an emotion possessed him at all, it ruled him; a feeling not mastering him was entirely latent. Stagnant or rapid, it was never slow. He was always hit mortally, or he was missed . . . Bathsheba was far from dreaming that the dark and silent shape upon which she had so carelessly thrown a seed was a hotbed of tropic intensity.

Such analysis of character in depth makes the conception in the previous novel of Knight, the man who cannot like a girl who has already been kissed, as trivial and superficial as it indeed is. This is not to say that Boldwood *is*, in any way, Horace Moule any more than Bathsheba owes anything more than the factual matter of farm-ownership to Mrs. Hawkins, though there are odd reminders. Hardy cannot bring himself to let Boldwood actually commit suicide after shooting Troy; he lets a servant knock the gun he turns on himself out of his hand; yet he brings him in, like Moule's jury, a verdict of insanity, even at the cost of denying himself the hanging he had meted out to the melodramatic Manston in *Desperate Remedies*. What Hardy is doing, almost for the first time, is to explore the morbid recesses he knew were concealed behind the appearances of human nature, and to face them unflinchingly. Moule's death taught his old pupil a more profound lesson than any they had shared in his lifetime.

For the influence of this personal disaster in Hardy's life went far beyond the novel he was writing at the time. Though it deepened the tragic sense of life in *Far From the Madding Crowd*, still that novel could end happily as its central hero, Gabriel Oak, overcomes the troubles and vicissitudes of his early wooing, and marries Bathsheba with some hope of their future stability. In the end, we are told of their love that

> the compounded feeling proves itself to be the only love which is strong as death—that love which many waters cannot quench, nor the floods drown, beside which the passion usually called by the name is evanescent as steam.

No Hardy hero from that time onward ever comes to such a settled and assured ending. From this moment, the tragic and defeated hero arrives for good in all Hardy's works. In the earlier novels, his heroes had indeed suffered, often quite severely, and often through their own faults, but the way had been made relatively clear for them at the end. Edward Springrove rescues and marries Cytherea, Dick weds Fancy Day, and never even knows of her love-passage with the parson. The joint heroes of *A Pair of Blue Eyes* are indeed cheated by death, but the tragedy is that of Elfride herself, and the novel ends with the two men recognizing the rightful grief of her mourning husband is greater than theirs. Even the most put-upon—and most Hardy-like—of all Hardy's heroes, Christopher in *The Hand of Ethelberta*, is eventually given the consolation prize of marriage with Ethelberta's younger sister Picotee.

Yet, from the time of Horace Moule's suicide, no hero of a Hardy novel ever receives anything like the optimistic comment which he even allows to Boldwood's reprieve in *Far From the Madding Crowd*, "Hurrah! . . . God's above the devil yet!" Such a remark would be unthinkable if applied to the tragic destinies of Clym Yeobright, Michael Henchard, Giles Winterborne, Angel Clare (even though the greater tragedy is that of Tess) or, most of all, Jude Fawley. Jude dies quoting the bitter reproaches of Job to God for bringing him into the world at all. The tragedy of these men is that not only do they suffer humiliation and various forms of defeat during life; nothing alleviates in any way that suffering at the end. Rather, turn after turn of ironic circumstance seems to conspire to make their agonies worse. Whether they have brought tragedy on themselves by fatal weakness, or whether it seems to attack them gratuitously, does not matter. Their plight is always accentuated and underlined by whole sequences of horrors that need not have been, and yet are. Life batters at them until they hardly think it worthwhile to live. Several of them, in fact, notably Henchard, Winterborne, and Jude, commit what is virtual suicide; though not of such an immediate and dramatic kind as Moule's own, in one way or another, their end is meant as self-destruction.

Even in the minor novels, where the deeper tragedy of self-slaughter would outweigh the lighter plot, arbitrary disaster is evoked to prevent a happy ending. Swithin is reunited with Viviette, in *Two on a Tower*, only to clasp her dead body, while in *The Trumpet Major*, John Loveday, in the last paragraph, is sent, by what seems a casual dismissal on the novelist's part, to a lonely grave in the Peninsular campaign. In all his later novels, Hardy never seems to tire of inventing twists of fate that will frustrate even the faintest hopes of his heroes. They no sooner have a respite than another damning circumstance is unravelled for their discomfiture. Hardy has been criticized for the coincidences by which he brings this about. The furmity-woman turns up at the critical moment to reveal the secret of Henchard's wife-selling twenty years before. In *Jude the Obscure*, the number of times that the ill-fated quartet of Jude, Arabella, Sue, and Phillotson accidentally cross each other's paths is almost beyond belief, and even totally minor characters such as Conjuror Vilbert reappear pat to the minute to add some further twist of irony.

Hardy rebuffed the idea that he was not playing fair in these coincidences, and always hinted darkly that real life could show instances even more strange, yet wholly true. This is borne out by yet another horror from Moule's tragic real-life story. Whether or not Hardy knew this at the time of Moule's suicide, he must certainly have known it by the time he came to write *Jude the Obscure* in the 1890s. For the bastard child of Horace Moule and the Dorchester girl was, according to Florence Hardy,[15] brought up in Australia, and, to add a final touch to the whole macabre story, was hanged there. When and why this happened is not specified; but the story obviously is closely connected with what has seemed to many critics the height of improbability in *Jude*, that part of the novel which has to do with Jude's son by Arabella. The child in the novel is brought up in Australia, and is then sent to Jude in England. In a sequence of events whose brutality seems out of key with even the worst of the rest of the novel, the boy eventually hangs himself, together with the two small children of Sue and Jude.

Once more, the timing of the real-life tragedy in Moule's life is uncertain. What is certain, because of all the circumstantial likeness, is that Hardy used this part of his friend's actual story to create the weird child, little Father Time, in *Jude*. Just as the real hanging of Martha Brown contributed to what seems the inevitable hanging of Tess, so the manner of life and death of Moule's bastard boy must have some bearing on the most terrible part of *Jude*. The alternations in Jude's character between the sensual—women and drink—and the spiritual—learning and religion—may not come entirely from the character of Moule. Hardy, in writing the novel, gave them some flavour of the other real-life character in his own class, who had started the idea of the novel, his own uncle by marriage, John Antell.[16] Yet the whole incident of the child, which gives such a gratuitous and fatal turning-point to the novel, by completely altering the former relationship between Jude and Sue, can only come from Horace Moule's disastrous history.

One wonders if it also throws light on one of the most debated symbols in all Hardy's poetry and prose. In *Jude*, the boy arrives by rail in a third-class carriage. He has the key of his box tied round his neck by a string, and his ticket is stuck in his hat. As everyone has pointed out, this is the same picture that Hardy paints in his poem, *Midnight on the Great Western*, the unforgettable appearance of the journeying boy.

> In the third-class seat sat the journeying boy,
>      And the roof-lamp's oily flame
> Played down on his listless form and face,
> Bewrapt past knowing to what he was going,
>      Or whence he came.

> In the band of his hat the journeying boy
> Had a ticket stuck; and a string
> Around his neck bore the key of his box,
> That twinkled gleams of the lamp's sad beams
> Like a living thing. . . .

The current of barely-suppressed emotion both in this poem and in its prose counterpart is so strong that all critics agree it must be based on personal experience; and this would seem to be confirmed by the exact details of description precisely repeated in both. This has led to speculation, of which the most extreme example is that the child might be a bastard son of Hardy himself.[17] Even the reference in another very personal poem, *Wessex Heights*, to "a ghost . . . in a railway train" has been thought[18] to refer to this suppositious bastard, although an early manuscript version of that poem distinctly names the figure as "her".[19] With Moule's actual bastard fully vouched for, sharing at least some of the circumstances of the child in *Jude the Obscure*, it does not seem necessary to saddle Hardy with the fatherhood of a child who never existed.[20] The picture, for all that, may be a real one; it is even possible Hardy saw it, or at the least had it described to him in conditions of emotion, such as his last meeting with Moule, which burnt it into his visual memory. No one knows if the son of Moule by the Dorchester girl came back at any time to England; but if he did, as described with so much circumstantial detail in *Jude the Obscure*, it is not impossible that he might be sent to his father, Moule, in such a way. The Great Western Railway served both Dorchester and Marlborough, the two places where Moule lived.

This, however, must be conjecture. The certainty is that, from the time of the death of Moule, Hardy never portrayed a man who was not, in some way, maimed by fate. He did not hesitate to load the dice at every point against his tragic heroes. Even if a case can be made that their own weakness or foolishness or rashness of choice caused their downfall, Hardy also made sure that the results would be as dire as possible by introducing other elements of coincidence, irony, and what seems like divine indifference or even malevolence. He does this with absolute conviction, because, he is now fully persuaded, such things do occur, in all their extremes, in real life. However much his naturally sombre mind inclined that way before, however much his own identification with Job and the prophets of destruction may have coloured his expression, we can date the emergence of Hardy as a fully tragic artist, an expounder of man's true miseries, from the suicide of his friend, and the appalling revealed ironies of that personal history.

# 18

# Success and Marriage

MANY other incidents in Hardy's personal life certainly seem to pre-figure his later conception, in *The Dynasts*, of an overworld where spirits, ironic, sinister or pitying, play cat and mouse with human fate. One of these moments had now arrived with the death of Moule. For, within a few days of the funeral of his friend, Hardy received another letter from the man whose philosophy was to influence his own more than any contemporary,[1] and who was to have more effect on his actual progress as a writer than any other person. This was Leslie Stephen. By an extraordinary mixture of luck and irony, Stephen was exactly the same age as Moule, and everything that Moule had attempted and failed to be. It was not only his sound mathematical degree at Cambridge, nor his college fellowship, which he had been obliged to resign on his marriage in 1867.[2] Stephen had at once become one of the senior *Saturday Review* writers, discoursing, it was said, on every topic from the University boat-race—he himself was a bad oarsman but a marvellous coach—to modern metaphysics. Everything he touched turned to success. He had had his pick of magazines before Smith, Elder had given him the *Cornhill*, and he was married to the elder daughter of the first editor, Thackeray himself. He was the acknowledged leader of advanced thought in London; beside his brilliant light, Moule was a flickering candle, and now snuffed out.

Hardy had not yet met Stephen, but he was already attracted by him and his thought. Since the *Saturday Review* was High Church and Tory, he did not find Stephen's agnostic articles there. Stephen kept these for another periodical, *Frazer's Magazine*, edited by J. A. Froude, to which he had contributed since 1867. It is pretty sure that some of the realistic detail, in which Hardy described Knight hanging on the cliff-face in *A Pair of Blue Eyes*, was based on Stephen's essay, "A Bad Five Minutes in the Alps". This first appeared in *Frazer's*, and in it Stephen imagines himself in just such a situation on one of his mountaineering expeditions. When Hardy wrote a later sonnet on Stephen, he compared his personality to that of one of the famous mountains he had climbed, gaunt, craggy, and outwardly unprepossessing, "In its quaint glooms, keen lights and rugged trim". Stephen's daughter, Virginia Woolf, wrote that this poem was incomparably the truest and most imaginative portrait of her father.

In all this many-sided, and often contradictory, person, it was Stephen as a literary editor who affected Hardy most. For Stephen had a different view of editorial duties than any Hardy had yet encountered. Tinsley, for instance, after voicing a few of his reader's opinions, had put Hardy on the market more or less as he stood, with hardly any alteration of manuscript. This was not all Stephen's way as an editor. Muttering to himself in the manner pilloried by his talented daughter in *To The Lighthouse*, he would go through the manuscript scribbling in its margins and sometimes all over it.[3] He was an adept in seeing where an expression should be changed, and particularly where the proportion of the whole book demanded that a passage should be shortened or cut out altogether. He was also prompt and businesslike in his dealing with authors, leaving them in no doubt of his intentions, unlike all the other publishers Hardy had known. When he received the first dozen chapters of *Far From the Madding Crowd* from Hardy on 1 October, he wrote straight back, confirming the contract for the whole serial. Hardy was therefore able to press on with confidence, and was not caught out when Stephen wrote to him, at the end of the month, suggesting that *Cornhill* might start printing it in January 1874. Such instant occupation, and the pressure of such an influential mind, probably did much to keep Hardy from brooding on Moule's suicide. He was at once in a relationship with a powerful intellect, beside which Moule's, though remembered with personal affection, must have seemed slight. Hardy had, in fact, the best conditions for successful work, a much stronger guide and mentor than he had had before, and the inspiration of his home and family and neighbourhood, on which to draw for the deepening of his original story and its people.

The effect of these surroundings is evident in almost every sentence in the novel, and can even be traced to special words and phrases. Hardy gives some hint of it, when he speaks himself of helping his father with the cider-making while writing the novel, and of wandering in the countryside, finding he had no notebook, and scribbling ideas and phrases on large dead leaves, white chips of wood, pieces of stone or slate, whatever came to hand.[4] Every personal experience was pressed into service. On 3 November, Hardy put in his notebook the peculiar effect of the late autumn sunset:[5] "a brazen sun, bristling with a thousand spines which struck into and tormented my eyes." This strange sunset description, pointed by the unusual word "bristling", is reproduced in the beginning of the famous chapter 28 of the novel, *The Hollow Amid the Ferns*, which paints the scene as "evening, whilst the bristling ball of gold in the west still swept the tips of the ferns". On the next day, 4 November, he recorded a note on a thunderstorm at the Bockhampton cottage: "The light is greenish and unnatural . . . A silver fringe hangs from the eaves of the house to the ground."[6] In the equally celebrated passage in the novel, when Oak covers Bathsheba's ricks from the thunderstorm, the lightning is described as "emerald", and the rain, when it comes, is "in liquid spines, unbroken in continuity".

One of the most remarkable features of this book is, in fact, the large number of scenes of natural observation, each one more striking than the last. In earlier books, as has been noticed, a spectacular event concerned with man and nature has almost always formed the fulcrum of the book's balance, tipping the human characters in one direction or another. Such was the insidious spread of fire in *Desperate Remedies*, and, even more sensationally, Knight's ordeal on the cliff in *A Pair of Blue Eyes*. Now, the decisive and highly suggestive scene where Troy, in the fern hollow, woos Bathsheba by the wizardry of his sword drill, —a scene from real life, as Hardy once told a friend[7]—is followed, not many chapters later, by the even greater scene where the shared peril of the terrible thunderstorm and the saving of the ricks brings Oak and Bathsheba closer together. Just as the characters are not only deeper, but more deeply related, so the scenes from nature that form symbols of their emotional development become infinitely more varied. There are no less than three major scenes which involve, in a highly dramatic way, the vicissitudes of a flock of sheep, expertly described, and each one forming a background to some stage in Gabriel Oak's character—his stoicism as his own flock plunges to ruin on the precipice, his independence in the saving of Bathsheba's sick flock, and the shearing scene where his faithful wooing of Bathsheba is symbolized by his tender care for the shorn ewes. There might even have been a fourth sheep-flock scene, relating Oak and Troy, had it not been for Leslie Stephen.

For the corollary to such richness as Hardy was now achieving, while the people and places familiar from childhood took life from his pen, was that a firm editorial hand should be laid on any sign of over-writing. This is what Stephen provided, He had a genius for seeing not only where but how compression should be applied, just how far pruning was healthy to the progress of a whole book, what parts, though attractive in themselves, were out of proportion. It is not quite sure that the fourth sheep-flock scene[8] was actually omitted at his insistence, but almost certainly his general attitude persuaded Hardy to cut it, and this forms a case in point of a passage, highly interesting in itself, which would have held up the book at a critical stage, Hardy clearly wished to show in it that Troy, after his marriage to Bathsheba, tried to run her farm by "trickster" means, a tactic successful in his dealings with Boldwood, but foiled on this occasion by Oak's knowledge and honesty. The passage, of at least nine pages, requires a long, technical explanation to the reader of the effects of the disease of sheep-rot. If sheep are infected by this deliberately, by letting them graze in damp pastures, they will apparently fatten early—a result of the first stages of the disease—and be sold profitably to unsuspecting buyers. Hardy has Troy attempt this trick by artificially flooding the pasture, and be caught out by Oak, who had conveniently been absent long enough for Troy's strategem. Oak, outraged both as a shepherd and as Bathsheba's secret admirer, confronts Troy with proof of his wrong-doing, and forces him by physical violence to give up the practice. This passage, though intriguing, makes such demands on the reader's time and understanding, is so digressive, and, above all, out of character, that Hardy, almost surely at Stephen's suggestion, removed it bodily.

Often too, Stephen made exact and precise suggestions to Hardy about how to improve the novel. Another heavily-cut extract[9] shows how Hardy followed Stephen's advice about the chapters of the sheep-shearing and the shearing supper. These two, chapters 22 and 23, were originally three. Stephen, in a letter of 17 February 1874,[10] pointed out that it was one chapter too long, and asked whether the story told by the dismissed bailiff was relevant to the progress of the whole book, as indeed it was not. Hardy obediently, and to the good, removed seven pages of heavy-handed rustic humour, including a long pointless story by a minor character, Coggan, and an endless discussion about eating salad. As a result, not only is the action swifter, but the relation of the main characters, Bathsheba, Boldwood, Oak, to be joined in the following chapter by Troy, is kept in the forefront of the reader's attention, undistracted by picturesque but long-winded local colour. Another later example of Stephen's creative editorial intervention was the curtailment, presumably at his request, of the rather artificial scene where Troy goes for a swim and is thought to be drowned, which involved a cut of three and a half pages.[11] Even near the beginning, Stephen had apparently made firm and practical suggestions that the scene of Bathsheba paying her workmen was too long.[12] The malthouse conversations in chapters 8 and 15 also show heavy and beneficial cutting and revision.[13]

It does seem, then, that some of the mature quality of the book, astonishing when compared with much that Hardy had written before, its firmness of construction, its steady and adult development of character, was due to Stephen as a critic, shaping the luxuriant and often poetic material that Hardy presented to him, without losing its fullness and strength. Edward Garnett was to adopt the same method with D. H. Lawrence over *Sons and Lovers*, persuading Lawrence to revise, rewrite, and compress the whole book, with artistic judgement that Lawrence would have done well to heed in his own later work. It is most noticeable too, whether Stephen was responsible or not, that many of the pedantic and "self-improving" digressions seem also to have gone from Hardy's style, though only to return in later novels which did not have the benefit of Stephen's quick ear and eye. There is little recourse to the minor painters, though Bathsheba blushes like the painting "Sunset at Sea after a Storm" by Francis Danby, and the more homely features of her maid, Liddy Smallbury, take on the Flemish character of pictures by Terburg and Gerard Douw: Ruysdael and Hobbema are also invoked for the watery sunrise that shines over Fanny Robin's storm-ruined grave, and a farm woman in a brown work-dress has the mellow hue of a sketch by Poussin. Yet such educational nudgings are mercifully infrequent. Nor is there anything to match in inappropriateness the historical information that Knight, in *A Pair of Blue Eyes*, had provided about Parisot and Pariseau, though there is one curiously dragged-in reference to the quack doctor, John St. John Long.

The writing of *Far From the Madding Crowd* seems to show that Hardy wrote at his best under the guidance of a trained but sympathetic mind. He had always needed this, in a pathetic and almost Coleridgean want to supplement his own self-taught judgement. In addition, he needed, as he said to Stephen in the later stages of the book,[14] to be living on or near the spot that he was writing about, in this case Puddletown with its rich, varied and, for him, highly personal history, the home of his cousins, the Sparks and the Antells, of his uncles, the Hands, and farther back of the somewhat mysterious origins of the Hardy family itself. Most of all, he needed, in the marrow of his being, the reassurance of the familiar, the scenes and the people of his boyhood home, mother, father, brother, sisters, and the Hardy cousins down the road. It is highly significant that after his deep and convincing analysis of the character of Boldwood,[15] he adds, as if instinctively, a warning that such a character might become unbalanced because of its lack of just these family ties. "No mother existed to absorb his devotion, no sister for his tenderness, no idle ties for sense".

Being so close to his originals in real life, Hardy had no need of literary models. There is an almost total absence of the second-hand, the novelistic, the Harrison Ainsworth clichés that disfigure earlier novels. In fact, an attempt by one critic[16] to suggest that Hardy drew his thunderstorm from one in Ainsworth's *Rookwood* disproves the case it sets out to make, and can hardly produce more than two words, "lurid" and "metallic", that these accounts have in common. The artificial thunderstorm in *Desperate Remedies* had indeed borrowed Ainsworth's stage-properties. The storm in *Far From the Madding Crowd* is real life. Unlike Ainsworth and his generalities, it is so close to nature that the smallest details convince us. Oak, quick to observe weather signs, stumbles over a toad that is trying to squeeze under his door, "soft, leathery and distended, like a boxing glove", the description aided by Hardy and his brother Henry recently practising the "manly exercise" of boxing.[17] On his kitchen table he finds a large slug, and two big black spiders drop from the ceiling. He realizes that these creeping creatures, seeking shelter indoors, presage abnormal rainfall. He then observes the flock of sheep, huddled in a tight knot, their tails to the storm quarter. This means some abnormal storm. One prophesies a heavy soaking, the other dangerous lightning; both kinds of weather threaten Bathsheba's unprotected ricks. These precise details add an invincible air of truth, so that we then seem to go as readers with Oak through every phase of the storm, to be singed by the lightning, drenched by the downpour, equally with him.

That is the virtue of Hardy's life-study method. On the other hand, it leads him, as intelligent critics were to see, sometimes to be too particular and quaint. One cannot help feeling that Oak's defective old watch, and his "constant comparisons with and observations of the sun and stars" to tell the time are copied too literally from that habit in his own brother Henry, with whom Hardy was now sharing a good deal of his life at home. It also seems that the rustics, some of whom, Hardy said, were actual men from Stinsford and Puddletown.[18] were allowed too many proverbial quirks of expression and oddities of personal habit, as reviewers again pointed out. Henery Fray's insistence that the central "e" in his name should be sounded is like Hardy's actual uncle, Henery Hand, who carved this spelling of his name in Puddletown church. Above all, there is the pervasive influence of Hardy's mother, in the acid remarks about women and marriage, which critics of our own time have found obsessive and odd; there are gratuitous remarks on women enjoying a sense of power at the end of the shearing feast, and cynical sentences about woman's ability to deceive herself after Troy has first kissed Bathsheba.

In fact, one of the most remarkable things about this deeply home-centred production is that Emma Gifford was not allowed to see any of it, in draft. It is one of the few among Hardy's novels that do not have any pages fair-copied in her hand. In his memoirs, he claimed that he did this to give her a "pleasant surprise" when she should eventually see the printed serial.[19] Such a schoolboy excuse seems incredible, in a grown man who had discussed all his previous novels with her, used her as an amanuensis for them, and been inspired by her not to give up writing. The much more plausible explanation is a double one. With such a watchful and possessive mother, Hardy, even though in his thirties, may well have felt awkward about a to-and-fro constant exchange of letters and packages with his fiancée. Mrs. Hardy's disapproval of designing mates for her children was powerful and it is notable that Hardy was the only one eventually to marry. Secondly, this was a novel entirely populated by the working-people from whom Hardy himself was sprung. How much of this he had by now revealed to Emma is doubtful; but it is even more doubtful that he had told her anything like the whole truth—that his mother, for instance, had been brought up by Poor Law charity, and that all his relatives in Puddle-town and Stinsford had been, at one time or another, servants and labourers. This was a book deeply entwined with Hardy's personal background. Emma's bewildered remark when she read it in serial form, was "Your novel sometimes seems like a child, all your own and none of me".[20] It seems likely that this secretive man did not want to give away too much too soon to his middle-class fiancée.

He may also by Christmas have become aware that her superficial young-lady attainments were not quite so striking as they had seemed in the provincial isolation of remote Cornwall, where the occasional visiting clergyman, school inspector, school lecturer, or the dentist from Camelford provided the only intellectual stimulus.[21] For some time in December, Hardy at last had his meeting with Leslie Stephen, and was introduced to an intellectual world, which, if sometimes daunting, was unlike anything he had met before. His introduction was, in fact, invested with all the eccentricity of a former University don. A few days before Christmas,[22] Hardy called at his newly-built house in South Kensington, to be greeted at the gate by Stephen hauling back a huge barking dog. The apparition, which startled many first acquaintances, of this tall gangling figure, with strange flat-topped head and bright red hair, was accentuated for Hardy when Stephen's shouts of command revealed the dog's name as Troy. To Hardy's surprised remark, "That is the name of my wicked soldier-hero", his host replied, "I don't think my Troy will feel hurt at the coincidence!" When Hardy, typically methodical, revealed that he had looked up the street directory for this new area, and found there was another Leslie Stephen nearby, Stephen retorted in his brusquest Cambridge manner, "Yes, he's the spurious one."[23]

Stephen, however, touched Hardy's human heart at this first encounter by confessing that he lived in a street so brashly new that the paving and the road were not yet made up, because he had played in the fields nearby when he was a child. Hardy does not seem to have responded with the confidence that he had himself wooed Martha Sparks in the basement of another new house close to Stephen's own. Yet a shared reticence was obviously one factor that drew the two men together. Stephen, who could withdraw into gloomy silence with anyone over-forthcoming, did not treat Hardy to this alarming experience when he came to lunch the next day, in a thick yellow fog, to meet Mrs. Stephen and her sister Anne Thackeray. The ordeal of two other young writers, Edmund Gosse and Robert Louis Stevenson, on a recent similar occasion was not repeated. Then Stephen and his wife had sat in frigid wordlessness all evening, while his voluble sister-in-law had chattered, provoking occasional groans from Stephen, and imminent giggles from his young guests. Stephen was comparatively genial with

Hardy, even going so far as to treat him to an imitation of the extraordinary antics that Carlyle went through to light his pipe. True, he returned to form in a discussion by the ladies about the story of David and Saul, in which Hardy naturally extolled the Bible version of his upbringing. Stephen sardonically recommended them all to read Voltaire's cynical account. Otherwise, he left Hardy with a friendly feeling that quite cancelled his first impression, and, added Hardy, "never changed".

This was the well-educated and distinguished intellectual atmosphere that Hardy enjoyed before going for a brief and parochial Christmas holiday to Emma at St. Juliot. He would not have been human if he had not felt the contrast. In one home, advanced women held an equal place with the men; though Stephen gave his deepest groans at his sister-in-law's extravagant housekeeping, he published her articles in the *Cornhill* and they were highly commended. This is not to support the theory, put forward by Siegfried Sassoon, that Hardy should have married Anne Thackeray.[24] A wild, amusing, creative, and muddle-headed creature of impulse, she shattered her freethinking but sexually puritanical brother-in-law by flirting with, and eventually marrying, her own godson and cousin, who was seventeen years younger than herself. Her inconsequent chatter would surely have irritated the reserved and studious Hardy as much as Emma's eventually did, and in Emma he at least had a frugal housekeeper, brought up to make the most of genteel middle-class poverty. Yet Hardy noticed in Anne with admiration "some of her father's humour", and his later memoirs show how attractive he found it to be only one remove, so to speak, from one of his great heroes of literature.[25] Emma's breathless attempts at scribbling, perhaps not unfairly portrayed in *A Pair of Blue Eyes*, were in a different world from those envied names of English letters. It was a circle into which he himself was to be fully accepted in the following spring.

Even at the present time, everything connected with the new book seemed a startling step forward into another world. Coming back from Cornwall on the last day of 1873, Hardy bought the *Cornhill* at Plymouth station, and there was the first instalment of *Far From the Madding Crowd* in the chief place at the beginning of the magazine. Even more, it was brilliantly illustrated. Hardy had written more than one letter to Stephen, hoping that the illustrator would not make his rustics boorish and quaint, and saying that he could send authentic details of peasant clothes and farm implements. He added, though, that perhaps the illustrator might be "a sensitive man and . . . would rather not be interfered with".[26] To Hardy, brought up in a rural background, where only lucky girls like his cousin Tryphena could escape from a life of brute drudgery, it was inconceivable that an artist for a London paper could be other than a man. It was one of the biggest surprises of his life to find a woman illustrating his serial, and in the most expert fashion, with authentic research and feeling for local colour. His own sister's naïve little water-colours, and even the slightly more skilled sketches of Emma had never prepared him for anything of the sort. A society where women were competing on equal terms was, indeed, a new thing. The first woman doctor had qualified in 1865, the first suffrage petition been presented by J. S. Mill in 1866, and the Cambridge College for Women, afterwards Girton, had opened in 1869. Hardy had seen the rigid *Saturday Review* mount virulent attacks on the Girl of the Period and her unpleasant manifestations. Yet here was one of them, Helen Paterson, chosen by a leading editor to illustrate his story, and doing it to perfection. Once again, his ideas of what constituted an educated woman received a jolt.

Only a few days later Hardy received a curious shock of the same nature, by having his own work mistaken for that of the most intellectual woman of the age. The *Spectator* of 3 January 1874, in its review of current magazines, came out firmly with the idea that *Far From the Madding Crowd*, which the *Cornhill* was printing without Hardy's name, must be by George Eliot. "There is a passage descriptive of the companionship of the stars, so learned and so poetical that it seems to be irrefutable evidence of authorship." This, to Hardy's ultra-sensitive mind, was both flattering and irritating. Shepherd Oak's vigil under the stars was such a personal part of Hardy's country-bred world that he could not admit it might have been the work of a woman, country-born, indeed, but for a quarter of a century town-based. He continued to grumble at this otherwise complimentary guess all his life, though Stephen at once wrote advising him to take the praise as praise, however wrong-headed.[27] It must also have given Hardy food for thought to find a critical article by Anne Thackeray highly praised in the same paragraph.

Yet even in this apparently brave new world, there were pitfalls for the unsophisticated author, of a most unexpected and contradictory kind. Stephen, though agnostic and progressive, was deeply imbued with his Evangelical upbringing in one direction. This was sex. He had a puritan obsession, which he attempted as an editor to disguise by blaming it on the prejudices of the reading public. In March, Hardy had an ominous little note suggesting that Troy's seduction of Fanny Robin would have to be treated "gingerly". Stephen added, "Excuse this wretched shred of concession to popular stupidity; but I am a slave." In fact, the very independent editor was a slave to his own complex emotions. On 13 April, he was deeply worried that Fanny had died in childbed and wondered "whether the baby is necessary at all". When Hardy dined with him on 24 April, Stephen tried to reinforce his own prejudices by saying that some lady subscribers had been shocked by the humorous story in the very first instalment, where Bathsheba's father only keeps faithful to his wife by taking the ring off her finger and pretending "he was doing wrong and committing the seventh" in adultery with her.[28] With the usual display of groaning, Stephen blamed himself for passing the passage, but the whole exhibition was clearly designed to warn Hardy against any dangerous frankness in the ticklish later stages of the book. Hardy countered by a similar display of hypocrisy on his own part. He wrote

> The truth is that I am willing, and indeed anxious, to give up any points which may be desirable in a story when read as a whole, for the sake of others which shall please those who read it in numbers. Perhaps I may have higher aims some day, and be a great stickler for the proper artistic balance of the completed work, but for the present circumstances lead me to wish merely to be considered a good hand at a serial.

Nothing in Hardy's life has been more misinterpreted than this last sentence. Book after book repeats this as a guiding principle in his writing life, and patronizes him for having such low and utilitarian aims. The fact is, it should simply be taken as a gambit in his temporary manoeuvres with Stephen, to allay the editor's alarms, and to insure a profitable sale for his novel elsewhere; for this was Hardy's first big success in America, carefully prepared by skilful advertising. He needed the money; for now he was taking the plunge and intended soon to marry.

It is once more an irony that he took this decision when all the evidences are that he was moving among women very different from Emma. Just as Emma herself had seemed educated and "a lady" beside Tryphena Sparks, so the women he met with Stephen and with George Smith, the publisher, were in another class, of both intellect and manners, from the provincial Emma. He had in May met his woman illustrator, Helen Paterson; she too was about to be married, to William Allingham, the poet. In old age, Hardy had extraordinary day-dreams about what would have happened if he had married her instead of Emma, and wrote one of his most inept poems on this fancy.[29]

When Emma came up to London that August to stay with her brother Walter Gifford at 54 Chippenham Road, Westbourne Park,[30] she was very much of a country cousin, bewildered by the size of Town, the distances between places, and, in her own words, "very much embarrassed at going in an omnibus".[31] Hardy, putting in his own residence qualification for marriage at his old lodgings in the nearby Celbridge Place, cannot have helped noticing the difference between this and women such as Anne Thackeray, Helen Paterson, and the almost legendary literary lady, Mrs. Procter, whom he had just met.

Yet on 17 September 1874, the marriage took place at St. Peter's Church, Paddington. Though it is always said it was against the wishes of Emma's family, the fact remains that two of her relatives were there, and none of Hardy's. Her brother, Walter, gave her away and signed the register, while the ceremony was performed by her uncle, Edwin Hamilton Gifford, Canon of Worcester. The most remarkable absences are those of Hardy's own family. His mother and father, though the latter was beginning to suffer from rheumatism, could have had an easier journey to Town than Mr. Gifford from remote Bodmin. Perhaps the strangest and yet most understandable absence is that of Hardy's virtual other self, his sister Mary. She had shared nearly every decisive move in his life, except this one. Their relationship had been something like that of Wordsworth and his sister Dorothy. Perhaps, like Dorothy Wordsworth, she felt she could not bring herself actually to witness the ceremony. Nor was it to her that Hardy wrote home announcing that the wedding had taken place, but to his brother Henry,[32] now adult enough to be more of a confidant on a man-to-man basis. At all events, and whatever the attitude of either family may have been, the marriage took place in a mellow September sunshine, almost fifty-five years to the day after Keats had written Hardy's favourite *To Autumn*. The couple spent their wedding night at the Palace Hotel, Queensway,[33] and travelled next day to begin their honeymoon at Brighton on the way to Rouen and to Paris.

# Ethelberta

By the time the newly-married couple reached Martin's Hotel in Queen's Road, Brighton, the Keatsian calm of their autumnal wedding-day had reverted to a stormy week-end, with rough seas and a gale. It was hardly a good augury for the channel-crossing they were to make early the next week, but Brighton provided plenty of bad weather distractions. Emma was fascinated by the aquarium, and noted closely the habits of the turtles, seals, and various fish. There were also concerts on both the Saturday and Sunday evenings, and a Brighton Sunday, she found, was like the type of Sunday she expected to see in Paris, "all enjoyment & gaiety & bands of music & excursionists". On Monday, Hardy braved the still-rough seas and bathed. Emma sketched in her tiny pocket-diary, and noticed with delight the exotic architecture of the Pavilion and the Dome. The night crossing to Dieppe, with the waves still white-capped, was an unmixed ordeal, with all the ladies, "low-lying", but she recovered enough on the train to Rouen to enjoy dinner at the Hotel D'Albion there,[1] in the Quai de la Bourse on the banks of the Seine.

Hardy himself left no account anywhere of this honeymoon. He had made to his brother the somewhat strange announcement, "I am going to Paris for materials for my next story". It may be conjectured that the stay at Rouen, on the way, was for him to see the French Gothic architecture he had so often studied in books. Like some of his later journeys with Emma, this was to be in one way or another a working trip. He says nothing of her. She would understand, however, a honeymoon on which one of the considerations was authorship, since she regarded herself as an author too, and her diary notes, often very vividly phrased, slowly develop into plans for stories. When the lively chambermaid at the hotel burst into their room unannounced, she found them both writing at the desk.[2]

Hardy's plans for future writing are obscured by various more or less vague statements he made much later in life. The idea that anyone writing about rustics might be mistaken for George Eliot seems to have weighed oddly heavily with him. So does a piece of newspaper gossip that he was a house-painter. He afterwards said it was events like these that made him give up a story also set in Dorset, and try one with an exotic background. The cancelled story was, he later said, one on the idea that became *The Woodlanders*. If so, it is a good thing he waited for that conception to mature, for he was clearly in no state for a considered work at this time. He felt a forced uprooting from the settled home atmosphere that had produced the unity and solidity of *Far From the Madding Crowd*, and did not apparently try to write another novel until the following March. A few days before marriage, he had posted off a pot-boiling short story to the *New York Times*. The main value of this feeble effort, called "Destiny in a Blue Cloak", was that it won him a contract for the American serializing of his next published novel. What, though, should the next novel be? In spite of his remark to his brother, Paris was not used as the setting of any subsequent story. Apparently the gossip about the house-painter, which otherwise he would hardly have remembered, made him feel that he must somehow conceal his own humble origins. Possibly he had not even yet revealed these fully to Emma, still less, in his abnormal reticence, to Leslie Stephen and his set. Already he foresaw problems raised by his own past. What would newspapers and column-writers make of an author whose mother had been a charity-child and a cook, and whose closest relatives, some of whom he had wished to marry, were in the servant class? What, for that matter, would provincial middle-class Emma make of the full story of his past life?

So Hardy seems temporarily to have given himself up to energetic sight-seeing, and shelved the future, while at home *Far From the Madding Crowd* ran through its final and much-praised instalments. With Emma he climbed the hundreds of steps of the central tower of Rouen Cathedral, up the incongruous iron spire surmounting it, the Fleche, and was rewarded with the view of the townscape breaking through dissolving September mists. After a few days, they moved to Paris on Thursday, 24 September, staying at the good, moderately-priced hotel recommended by Baedeker for English and American visitors. This was the Hotel St. Petersbourg in the Rue Caumartin, adjoining the Madeleine and the Opera, near all the sights.[3] These they did for a solid week, more or less in the order laid down by Baedeker, the Place de la Concorde by moonlight, the Louvre, the Tuileries, Versailles, Notre-Dame, the Hôtel Cluny, and the Morgue, which Emma found "*not offensive* but repulsive". Les Invalides and Napoleon's tomb were a point of pilgrimage for Hardy, with his family legends of the 1804 and 1805 invasion scares, in which his grandfather had been one of the local militia. Emma noted that, like many Englishwomen with a rather eccentric idea of fashion, she was subjected to a good deal of staring from men, women, and children. "Am I a strange-looking person—or merely picturesque in this hat?", she questioned herself, somewhat uneasily and a little pathetically, for she always tended to dress younger than she was, and she may have had secret doubts about the hat itself. She was, however, clearly reassured when Hardy, suffering from a cold since his bathe at Brighton, felt chilly and left her for twenty minutes alone, while he fetched his coat from the hotel. In that short space, there were attempts to pick her up by no less than "three hommes", as she confided to her diary in tiny writing.[4]

On the last day of September, the short honeymoon was over. "Adieu", wrote Emma, in the pigeon English-French of her Plymouth school. Everything had been "charmante", particularly the people, and even including the cats, which were "superbes" and "magnifiques".[5] It had been a schoolgirl dream come true, and though she hardly mentions her husband, clearly a time of great excitement for her. Some of Eustacia's obsessive longing for Paris in *The Return of the Native* may derive from this. London on the first day of October seemed "dirty London", and the week-end spent looking for houses in the Wimbledon and Surbiton area was a trial. Emma consoled herself by playing with an idea for a story derived from the conversation and appearance of ladies on the homebound cross-Channel steamer, while Hardy busied himself with his first task as a married man, rents and rooms. By Tuesday, 6 October, they were settled in St. David's Villa, Hook Road, Surbiton, and on that day they had a visitor for tea. This was Emma's father.[6] He brought with him the little daughter of Emma's eldest cousin, Robert Gifford Watson, whose father was abroad. One does not know how Mr. Gifford viewed his own daughter's beginnings of married life with her author husband; though the Surbiton district was a respectable enough address, no Victorian middle-class father would feel happy about furnished lodgings as a first home. It was possibly after this visit that he wrote the wounding letter about Hardy having "presumed" to marry into the Gifford family. At all events, it is the sole entry in Emma's diary for the Surbiton house, where they were to stay for the first five and a half months of their married life.

In the meantime, publication of *Far From the Madding Crowd* in two volumes took place on 23 November 1874. Hardy inscribed a copy to Canon Gifford, who had married them, and later signs show that he was far from being cut off from his wife's family. There is no mention, however, of his usual return to his own home this Christmas. He may have felt that it was not yet time for his family and Emma to be fully revealed to one another. Also, this December, Tryphena's poverty-stricken father, James Sparks, died at Puddletown, and the district was full of Hardy's Sparks cousins, dividing their father's few poor sticks of furniture, and making arrangements for a headstone in the church. It was not a time to bring home his new bride. So Hardy sat back at Surbiton, and read the reviews of his novel. By and large, they were very good, though by no means uncritical. The only bad one, which Hardy perhaps did not see, was a vicious attack by Henry James in the

New York *Nation*. James foreshadowed his later insufferably patronizing attitude towards Hardy's work by saying in this notice that "the only things we believe in are the sheep and the dogs", a remark which had the distinction of providing a model for a reviewer, nearly twenty years after, who could find nothing good in *Tess* except "the few hours spent with cows".[7] James, whose own novels seldom admitted any signs of his characters having to work for a living, was doubtless repelled by just what *The Times* of 25 January 1875 praised so discerningly.

There is not a lady or gentleman in the book in the ordinary sense of the words. They are all working people, and ever so much more interesting than the idle lords and ladies, with the story of whose loves and sorrows Mr. Mudie's shelves are always crammed.

This review saw for the first time that Hardy was an essentially working-class author, of exceptional talent, best employed with settings and people he understood at first hand. He would have agreed with those modern critics who find the ultimate union of Oak and Bathsheba so satisfactory because it is a genuine working one.[8]

All reviews agreed on the book's power. The chief complaint was centred on the likeness, real or imagined, to George Eliot, and the overwritten dialogues of the rustics, which even Stephen had questioned in the final instalments.[9] The *Examiner, Athenaeum, Spectator, Academy* (by Andrew Lang), *Westminster*, and *Saturday Review* all brought in George Eliot, some finding too much likeness, others finding that she excelled him in the same medium. It was an undertow of critical opinion which might well disturb the settled praise of the general verdict. Only the *Manchester Guardian* in February 1875 came out unequivocally for the "perfect, solid, and substantial" character-drawing, with no qualification. There were signs of individual prejudice too. The *Athenaeum*, which had long ago been bothered by the "coarseness" of *Desperate Remedies*, found it present again. More constructively, it advised Hardy to write more slowly and carefully. This was a note struck in a private letter[10] by John Hutton, who had not this time reviewed Hardy in the *Spectator*, his brother the editor, R. H. Hutton, having taken the book. R. H. Hutton had been among those who found the rustic dialogue far-flown. John Hutton's private letter recognized that Hardy knew more about rural talk and its semi-Biblical overtones than his brother did. Yet even he suggested that Hardy had "multiplied or rather drawn together into one society instances of this remarkable union of humour and satirical philosophy". He added a note that repeated the pointed warning of the *Athenaeum* in his own more tactful style.

Will you pardon me if I beg you not to be prodigal of your power but to make *every* book better than the last, with the thoughtful conscientiousness of *true* genius & greatness.

This was only to underline what the publisher Tinsley was to say bluntly a few weeks later. Annoyed, admittedly, that Hardy had, as he thought, broken faith, by giving the serial and book without warning to the *Cornhill* and Smith, Elder, Hardy's former publisher wrote,

> I hope you will not think me impertinent but how you could have made· such mistakes *in art* in a work so brim full of genius as "*The Madding Crowd*" is one of the things I cannot understand.

Prophesying all the same future greatness for Hardy, he naturally refused to part with the rights and stock of *Under the Greenwood Tree*, except for an exorbitant sum. Even with American publication of *Far From the Madding Crowd*, Hardy, with a wife now to support, could not throw money away.[11]

The winter of 1874–75, when she observed copies of the novel regularly carried by ladies in the trains between Surbiton and London, must have been one of triumph for Emma. She clearly had the Victorian, romantic view of the great man of letters as a popular hero. In this naïve but touching belief, she had brought back from Paris an ivy leaf from the grave of Balzac in Père-Lachaise.[12] It was glory that her husband was on a way to become one of that company, and perhaps a justification in the face of her own family. Sympathetic John Hutton divined this when he wrote,[13] "How your wife must glory and triumph in your genius—Tell her we sympathize in her glory". Yet bills had to be paid. Furnished lodgings in a middle-class suburb were a different matter from living at home with Mother, in a country cottage where meals came cheap and there was no responsibility. The hours writing in the little room with its view westward to Blackdown and the Hardy Monument, with no interruption except a call upstairs to say that supper was ready, must have seemed far away. Consulting Anne Thackeray, Hardy found her surprised that he should not like society, and positive that it was necessary for a novelist. He felt still that the settled life of his upbringing was the most productive, but he had got himself into an awkward position by marriage. One does not know the reaction at this point of the Hardy family to Emma, but to them as to all his cousins she was "a lady", just as Hardy's associates in London were those dubious things, ladies and gentlemen. One of these was even Jemima Hardy's old rival, Julia Augusta Martin, who, hearing of her former child-pupil's triumph, had written to him about it,[14] though, remembering the fiasco a dozen years before at Bruton Street, he did not try to see her.

Something of what the Hardy family felt about their relative moving in such incomprehensible worlds may be gathered by the attitude of the surviving members at his death. Even so many years later, when Thomas Hardy was a national and even international figure, his brother

Henry, his sister Kate, and his first cousin Theresa (his uncle James's surviving daughter) were bitterly and locally possessive. They felt that ladies such as Hardy's second wife, and gentlemen such as Sydney Cockerell and Sir James Barrie, had taken all the arrangements about their famous relative out of the hands of the people to whom he had belonged. To Kate, the official dispositions made by the society in which Hardy had moved were all "staggering blows" to what she felt was due to his nearest.[15] To find Florence Hardy and Cockerell had arranged the funeral in Westminster Abbey, cremation and not burial, and the removal of the heart only to the family grave in Stinsford churchyard, were virtual insults to those who shared blood-relationship.[16] His cousin Theresa, still living eccentric and witch-like in the lane in Higher Bockhampton, had a short way with enquiring ladies and gentlemen from London, since she always told them that Hardy should have led a useful life like his brother Henry the builder, and not bothered with writing.[17] If these were the reactions of Hardy's relatives after fifty years of his fame, one can understand how marriage to a "lady" and his mixing with London society must have seemed now, and his reluctance to risk confrontation yet.

The pressures of this situation were obviously great, and increased proportionately as the success of the book with the public aroused curiosity about its author. *Far From the Madding Crowd* had a sale whose speed and extent even surprised the publisher. By the third week in January 1875, after only two months, nearly the whole first edition of 1000 copies was gone, and Hardy was able to make some alterations for a second edition. These show, as usual, some influence of Stephen. Pompous or over-literary words, such as "circumambient" and "rotundity", had more simple substitutes in the passages of natural description they had previously disfigured, and a piece of abstract philosophy about Boldwood was removed bodily.[18] Another removal, this time bowing to Stephen's prudish side, was a cut in the description of Bathsheba's father as standing godfather to illegitimate children in the parish. In the early months of 1875, relations between Hardy and his editor deepened to a mutual sympathy and understanding. Both were abnormally reticent, and Stephen had no answer to Hardy's problems, even if he had been told them. It is all the more remarkable then that Hardy was witness to a phase of Stephen's own intimate life.

Reluctantly taking the advice of Stephen's sister-in-law, Hardy had moved with Emma on 19 March back to his familiar Westbourne Park area, a compromise that brought him nearer the fashionable West End, though not quite of it. Next day, Hardy went to the University Boat Race, presumably taken by the enthusiastic Stephen, though the latter must have groaned mightily at an Oxford win by nearly ten lengths. It was only a short step, for a country walker, across Hyde Park to

Stephen's home in South Kensington. Here, only a few days later, Hardy found himself urgently summoned, to call in the evening as late as he liked. Stephen was pacing his library in carpet slippers, his lean body encased in a heather-coloured dressing-gown. He briefly indicated that he could do with another serial for the *Cornhill*, but a more personal matter was occupying his mind. He produced a document, which Hardy at first took to be his will, but it was an even more intimate screed which he wished Hardy to witness. Stephen had never renounced Holy Orders. In 1870, the Clerical Disabilities Act debarred clergy from standing for Parliament. Stephen never entered politics, but thought it was time now to end a false position, which he had only partly removed by resigning from the college tutorship in 1862. It is notable that of all people in London, he thought Hardy the most appropriate to witness this symbolic act. The conversation that followed the witnessing is also revealing. Stephen, according to Hardy, spoke of having wasted his time on religion and metaphysics, and to be now fascinated by "the new theory of vortex rings".[19] This shows Stephen as a follower, at least at this time, of the Positive Philosophy of Auguste Comte. Comte, whom Hardy had also been reading for at least the past five years,[20] believed that mankind had passed through the stages of religion and metaphysics, and was now ripe for a more scientific or "positive" way of thought and worship. Though both Hardy and Stephen seem to have stopped short of Comte's ultimate Religion of Humanity, that curious hybrid with its pantheon of philosophers and scientists taking the place of saints, and a chapel of devotees off Lamb's Conduit Street, they evidently subscribed to Comte's idea of man's progress being in what Hardy called "a looped orbit".[21] This was a kind of evolution, it seemed to them, which allowed for apparent regression, but always curved round to a point of progress again, so that a temporary decay could be followed by an advance. Hardy even persuaded himself that similarity of ideas caused his writing to be mistaken for that of George Eliot, though she, in fact, was only marginally a Positivist;[22] he himself was sufficiently attracted by "the new religion" to believe that if Comte had retained Christ in its pantheon, it would have gained wide acceptance.[23]

At all events, here was an intellectual sympathy which made it all the more difficult for Hardy to deny Stephen's request for a new *Cornhill* serial. Stephen knew that Hardy had partly planned a new book; he did not yet know what form the book was to take, and Hardy himself had inklings that Stephen might be surprised. For Hardy had arrived at a decision, which was itself surprising, and must be suspected to be very personal indeed. It had to do, not perhaps at first consciously, with the situation in which he found his own life, as a writer of humble origins acclaimed by a society which might, if knowing, have found them contemptible. The general dilemma was perhaps made even more acute by his wife, still in half-ignorance of his true background. For Emma, like many middle-class housewives, regarded servants generally as "problems", and continued all her life to speak of them in those terms.[24] A family of servants was the last thing she would normally think of marrying into, or consider a fitting background for a famous author. As for their morals, she would have been horrified to learn that Hardy's cousin, Ellen Hand, had just had a bastard daughter.[25]

So, perhaps from an inborn necessity to write the teasing problem somehow out of his system, was evolved the most uneven and contradictory of all Hardy's novels, *The Hand of Ethelberta*. Its theme was to be that of a person moving in high, intellectual society, a writer, poet and story-teller, who, in fact, came from a family all of whom were servants and workmen. More than that: this family were to be shown sharing the principal character's life, a secret always to be kept and always on the verge of being discovered, to everyone's general shame and discomfort. The threat is made plain in one speech:

People will find you out as one of a family of servants, and their pride will be stung at having gone to hear your romancing . . .

It would be too near home, however, in all sorts of senses, to make this chief character a male author; so Hardy, in his typically devious way, chose, as he had done in poems and tales before, to project his own dilemma into that of a woman.

So, or by some such process, was born his new heroine, Ethelberta Chickerel, who, by a rather improbable marriage with a rich young man who almost immediately dies, appears in society as Ethelberta Petherwin, a mysterious widow. Almost the first thing we know of her is that, like Hardy, she has written a large number of sonnets putting woman's point of view, a natural echo of the mass of "She to Him" sonnets written by the young Hardy. Unlike Hardy, but like him in intention, she has these published in a book; it will be remembered that Hardy had intended to print his own sonnets in *The Poor Man and the Lady*, and had even "prosed" one of them in *Desperate Remedies*. In the *Cornhill* serialization, which started in July 1875, Hardy called this book of verse by the really childishly improbable title of "Metres by Me". If it seems strange that he should employ such a schoolboy device to indicate his own part in the character of his heroine, it may be considered even more strange that he should use the title at all. At all events, he altered it in the volume version to "Metres by E."—i.e. Ethelberta—even though this entailed the rewriting of an incredibly laboured pun about Me and U. The whole novel, in fact, seems like an exercise in what Morley had called "a clever lad's dream", full of such schoolboy and private asides. The word "Hand" in the title has a double meaning: both the heroine's hand in marriage and her playing of her "hand", as in a game of skill, are indicated. There is surely a third and private meaning, personal to the novelist himself. "Hand" was the maiden name of Hardy's own mother, and Ethelberta's family, when they emerge, are other related members of the Hand family of Puddletown.

For Ethelberta, after her book of poems, goes on like Hardy to be a story-writer. Here again, though this thin disguise for Hardy's own career may seem far-fetched, it was obviously suggested by certain aspects of his own recent success in this form of writing. Quite apart from the George Eliot fable of the reviewers, it was consistently thought that the author of *Far From the Madding Crowd* might be a woman. Though the *Spectator* had corrected its first mistaken guess as early as February 1874, the legend still persisted. The basic idea for the Hardy-into-Ethelberta sex-change may have been started by a remark of Anne Thackeray. Besieged by enquiries about the sex of the author of *Far From the Madding Crowd*, and pestered by requests for an introduction to him or her—a situation parallel to Ethelberta's—she would reply, "*It* lives in the country, and I could not very well introduce you to *it* in Town".[26] Ethelberta, of course, tells her stories publicly by word of mouth; but there is some corresponding idea to that of Hardy serializing his stories in the *Cornhill*. Serial and first edition were extensively revised for the edition of 1892, and we can see that the earliest version, in fact, gives most clues to Hardy's secret intention in the novel. In this, the likenesses to himself and to his own nearest relatives, significant through their omission in later versions, are most obvious. The hero, Christopher, the name of Hardy's uncle, passive and ineffective, is the diffident side of Hardy himself, mutely accompanied by his pallid sister Mary, in the novel named Faith. Their scenes are much extended in the serial and first edition, and Faith, noted there and there only as "the youngest of old maids", is a speaking or more often unspeaking likeness of Hardy's unobtrusive sister. Hardy's mother does not appear, but a hint of her survives in most significant form. One of Ethelberta's upper-class suitors is a person called Alfred Neigh, most improbably surnamed as the caustic *Saturday Review* was to point out, though missing yet another juvenile joke in that the man's father had been a horse-knacker. Neigh is portrayed as hating servant-class women, because of the "goings-on" of his own father. These are revealed, again in the serial and first edition only, as the fact that the elder Neigh had actually married his cook. Hardy, the son of a cook, had already discovered, in his short experience of intellectual middle-class society, that this was the unforgivable Victorian crime. Mark Pattison, the distinguished Oxford scholar, became almost insanely furious at the idea—quite false

—that his sister Dorothy was friendly with a man who was alleged to have performed this socially unspeakable action.[27]

When Ethelberta's socially unmentionable relatives appear, they turn out to be a fascinating amalgam of Hardy's own. Her father, Mr. Chickerel, named after the village between Weymouth and Coryates where Hardy had walked with Tryphena Sparks, is a butler, an older version of William Duffield, whom Martha Sparks had married. Ethelberta's brother Sol Chickerel is, like Martha's brother James Sparks, a carpenter of radical tendencies, and has a fine speech of independence in his disgust at his sister's eventual marriage to a viscount. The other workman brother's name, Daniel, suggests Nathaniel Sparks. The backstairs and below-stairs scenes in London houses are sketched with the accuracy of a man who had visited and indeed courted his Sparks cousin in such circumstances. Even the most improbable incident in the novel, the infatuation of the juvenile Joey Chickerel for a ladies' maid twice his age, may refer to Hardy's own teenage excitement over his much-older dressmaker cousin, Rebecca Sparks. The winding-up chapter, where two of Ethelberta's maidservant sisters marry and emigrate to Queensland, coincides exactly in time with the emigration in May 1876, the month this chapter appeared, of Martha Duffield to Queensland, her ex-butler husband having failed to make a living in England.[28] Hardy was so involved with secret family history that he even wrote into his novel this otherwise unnecessary detail of his former love, whom he himself had wanted to marry.

The theme of class concealment is indeed such an obsession that it throws the novel out of balance in a way which puzzled all reviewers. As the *Saturday*, trying to be fair, said "An author prepares many difficulties for himself when he invents such a character", not knowing of course, that the character was in the author's own situation. The reviewer indeed felt that Ethelberta as a woman was difficult of belief. He might have noticed, had he known Hardy's emotional history, that she starts physically as Emma, powerful with white columnar neck "firm as a fort", and "squirrel-coloured hair", and only in a much later rewriting of the book borrows the dark eyebrows, arched "like two slurs in music" of Tryphena Sparks, via the portrait of the latter in *Under the Greenwood Tree*, when Fancy Day has just these "two slurs" above her dark eyes. This synthetic character and her dilemmas were meant to express, in secret guise, Hardy's own. They were also useful for a hard-pressed serial-writer, since he could import chunks of his own and his family's experiences to fill up a chapter. Hardy's boyhood experiences as a musician at dances accounts for at least two early chapters. Later chapters utilize Rouen—though not Paris—and even phrases from Emma's honeymoon diary. The French servants "spin" about, just as she described, the houses seen from the Fleche look like "mosaic" and the Ile Lacroix is "gorgeous" in colour. It is a pity he did not import, with these, Emma's poetic description of the Cathedral bell, "deep-toned, like a spirit speaking".[29] Hardy has nothing similar to glean from his own notebooks, except for a rather perfunctory mention of the 1875 Boat Race, when the tideway proved too narrow for the numerous barges anchored to watch it.[30]

The most vivid chapters of this manufactured and cryptic book, in fact, mark a decisive move in Hardy's married life. In mid-July 1875, after some unsuccessful house-hunting in Dorset, Emma and Hardy on Monday, 12 July, left London, stayed three nights in Bournemouth, and then went by boat to Swanage, where they were to live for the next ten months while he completed the novel. In the pretty West End Cottage, they were near enough Bockhampton for Emma to be introduced cautiously to the family. The most notable occasion, though not perhaps the first, was on 13 September, when Emma, Hardy, and his sisters Mary and Kate all went on a picnic to Corfe Castle. It was an expedition recorded by Emma as "a splendid day",[31] and she clearly got on well with Hardy's two schoolmistress sisters—Kate, following Mary, was preparing to go to Salisbury, and may have already been helping her as pupil-teacher at Piddlehinton School. What they thought of Emma, as they took their separate ways home, is not recorded, but there were later expeditions and letters were exchanged. The whole event was expanded by Hardy to furnish Ethelberta with a long expedition to Corfe, where she takes part in a meeting of a Historical Society. Swanage itself, and their seafaring landlord, Captain Masters, supplied all the more convincing local colour for these chapters of the novel. Bockhampton and Hardy's mother did not appear in any way, either in the novel or in his wife's diary, but he can hardly have held off the meeting at this time.

Hardy, in fact, records a good deal of the Swanage atmosphere at this time. He relished the sea-tales of their landlord, especially the grim ones of the seas at West Bay stripping their drowned victims in the powerful undertow, and the amusing reminiscences of smuggling and the outwitting of revenue men. He and Emma, before the stormy autumn and winter gales set in, also had a perfect day's sea-outing by steamer, the "Heather Bell", round the Isle of Wight, though Emma's sketch of Hardy on the boat shows a withdrawn slightly gloomy figure, like one of his own apprehensive heroes. Indeed, whether through marriage or not, he seems to have reverted to the old pessimistic state of his lonely days in London. As he described his hero,

He looked sad when he felt almost serene, and only serene when he felt quite cheerful. It is a habit people acquire who have had repressing experiences.

The hero's sister Faith, herself so recognizable as Mary Hardy, also comments on her brother's temperament,

If I had to describe you I should say you were a child in your impulses and an old man in your reflections.

He himself later bursts out to her

The only feeling which has any dignity or permanence or worth is family affection between close blood-relations.

Was he already regretting that he had to abandon or conceal these close blood-relationships through the pressures of marriage and popular fame? A poem written about himself and Emma at Bournemouth, *We Sat at the Window*, suggests that marriage had already begun to pall. The original line,[32] later changed,

We were irked by the scene, by each other; yes,

sounds as if lack of sympathy was beginning to show, and that Emma's unthinking vitality was starting to grate on his thoughtful and surely often depressing melancholy. She came to irritate him, and he came to wear down her energy into self-defensive anger. Victorian reticence prevents any hint of their sexual compatibility; but Hardy's reversion to ineffective attitudes, and his dimly feeble portrait of his hero, might well show that he had failed himself in that aspect of marriage. At all events, there were no children; nor were there ever to be. The rough Hardys and the Hands of Puddletown, able to multiply their descendants at will, seemed to have produced, as he himself often so gloomily wrote and said, a final member who had no fortune or perhaps force in that direction.

It was perhaps at this point that Hardy decided to put all to the test with his one successful achievement, his writing and the position he had won by it in society. *The Hand of Ethelberta*, an enigma to critics, a puzzle to the reading public, a disappointment to its editor and publisher, and a stumbling-block to its talented illustrator, Du Maurier, was of great private importance to its author. In it, Hardy made his last gesture from the class to which he really belonged. He wrote out of his system the Hardy who was one of the people who toiled and suffered. From now onward, he surveyed such people as one who had escaped from their world. Their sufferings are no less intense, and he does not cease to portray them, but always now as one who has made his escape. The note of social protest, which had begun with *The Poor Man and the Lady*, is virtually dropped, its last flarings perhaps being Sol Chickerel's speeches to his sister. Hardy accepts the world in which he, as a novelist, must now move. Even as he accepts it, he satirizes it. In *The Hand of Ethelberta*, there is satire of the world of Leslie Stephen and the world of Emma, two aspects of Hardy's new official milieu. The curious tendency of almost every upper-class person in the novel to swear under his breath—even the mild hero whispers "an ancient exclamation", presumably of four letters—seems a direct satire on Stephen's behaviour. As for Emma, there is a significant early version of the expression in chapter 5, "fingers of a corpse". In the serial, it was "fingers of a woman who does nothing". Poor Emma's amateur novel, *The Maid on the Shore*, which she wrote at Swanage,[33] though it has moments of disorganized poetry, lacks the hard realities of a life that has been experienced at a basic level of human effort and suffering.

Hardy's farewell to the class in which he had been brought up, and his reluctant satire on the class he was now to enter, made this novel, as the critics found it, a "deliberate oddity".[34] It was, in fact, an oddity that was to pursue much of his subsequent life, the attempt to live in a world to which, like his self-portraying heroine, he did not really belong. In the world of letters and of society, he appeared strange and withdrawn, a man nursing an inner secret. In the world of his Dorset upbringing, he appeared, except to his close family, as one who had deserted them. From the second half of the 1870s, all mention of his cousins and relatives drops out of his notes and writings. A passing reference to his cousin James Sparks in 1879 seems to be the last mention of a near relative. He did not apparently communicate with Tryphena Sparks, even when in December 1877 she married "my old man",[35] Charles Frederick Gale of Topsham. He still kept in touch with her brother Nathaniel, who had also married hastily, earlier that year, Mary Hardy's student friend, Annie Lanham, just in time to legitimize her baby; but their correspondence was mainly on the subject of fiddles and cellos, of which Nathaniel, to supplement his meagre carpenter's wages, had become a repairer.[36]

Hardy found himself suppressing yet another part of his life. He had never ceased to think of himself as a poet, "anxious to get back to verse". Ethelberta had been, in part, a secret manifesto of his own poetry, and her "Metres by Me" a hope that his own verses, like hers, might gain popular success. Now that he was well known as a novelist, he would surely be able to get his poems, rejected ten years before, published at last. Hopefully, he took the idea to Leslie Stephen, and told him that he "planned some tragic poems".[37] To Hardy's chagrin, the editor seemed entirely indifferent and disinclined to encourage the idea. Stephen frankly did not want poems, but, after *Ethelberta*, another pastoral novel; in the event, he did not get one, for his prudish suspicions were aroused by the marital tangles that seemed to be developing in the early chapters of *The Return of the Native*. He declined to serialize it, and Hardy, though he continued as a friend, lost his only good literary adviser and editor. With Stephen's rejection of "tragic" poetry in mind, Hardy, asked for a "brief story", tried *The Gentleman's Maga-zine* with his comic poem, *The Bride-Night Fire*. It was printed in November 1875, Hardy's first published poem, but only after such cautious bowdlerization as made it hardly the same work. The heroine's "cold little buzzoms" become "her cold little figure", the hero, who "Made a back, horsed her up", is not allowed such an indecent way of rescuing her from the fire, and she is provided throughout with a chaperone, his old mother. Hardy had reason to feel cynical at his ruined handiwork; it was worse than no publication. So yet another prime passion of his life was driven underground.

Life for him now seemed to become full of concealments. Although Hardy introduced Emma to his sisters and brother, and eventually at last to his mother and father—they spent Christmas 1876 with his parents at Bockhampton—he seems to have taken pains that she should never know the personages of his Puddletown background. In March 1876 he moved her from Swanage to Yeovil, just over the Somerset border, to look for houses in North Dorset, where in May he saw cow-slips shining like "Chinese lanterns or glow-worms".[38] Then followed another holiday on the Continent, this time to Holland and the Rhine. The Hardys finally got their first home at Sturminster Newton, in Dorset certainly, but many miles distant from the area where many of his relatives still lived. Two of Emma's brothers visited them there;[39] but as far as can be made out, none of Hardy's relatives ever came. It is perhaps significant too that these eighteen months at Sturminster were remembered by Hardy as "their happiest days".[40] He had brought Emma into contact with as much of his past as he cared to show her; he had temporarily regained, even at a remove, his Dorset roots; and disillusion with her and the world that she came to stand for, had not yet fully set in, though the incident at Bournemouth had been a warning sign.

Yet from this time, Hardy shows evidence of the violence that his up-rooting from the past had done to his essential being. The settled sombreness of *The Return of the Native*, written at Sturminster, and the disorientated nature of all the actors in that story, show a man labour-ing under almost intolerable strain. It was this strain and fixed gloom that pursued him, like a haunted person, all the rest of his long life.

As for Emma, she was fixed too in the tragedy of two lives that, for no essential fault, were headed for personal disaster. The false glamour of their dramatic first meeting had concealed and disguised their deep-felt differences. Hardy was later to write poems regretting that he had ever uprooted her from the life and place where he found her. Even at this early time, though temporarily checked by the compromise of the Sturminster Newton idyll, the gulf was beginning to widen. Emma had begun to find that this obsessive, complicated, brooding mind could be unconsciously insensitive and accidentally cruel. She was nothing in herself unless she coincided with what was stirring in that tortuous process of his inner self. His vision of an epic of Napoleonic times, first conceived in 1874, and realized in *The Dynasts*, was a case in point. Hardy was pleased with her when she talked to the Waterloo veterans at Chelsea Hospital in June 1875;[41] he was angry with her when she became exhausted, exactly a year later, after he had tramped her all a long hot day over the battlefield itself.[42] His own obsessions, as much as her pathetic attempts to behave as she imagined a great writer's wife should, divided them. Yet she was no fool where her instincts were concerned. She suspected, if she did not fully know, the complications of his past. Her reactions to *Ethelberta* are noteworthy. "Too much about servants in it", she is alleged to have said;[43] and the inscribed copy her husband gave her remained uncut at her death.

# Old and Young

A WELL-ESTABLISHED family tradition illustrates how Hardy cut himself off from his Dorset relatives. In the summer of 1885, Hardy and Emma moved into their newly-built house, Max Gate, on the south-east borders of Dorchester; but they did not mix with his people. When they went visiting, it was to the gentry. In the early 1890s, Hardy and his wife were enthusiastic in the craze for bicycling. One of the few happy photographs of Hardy shows him with a brand-new bicycle, and he continued riding into his eighties. A very frequent ride was to Turnworth, whose church Hardy had architected, and whose vicar shared the Hardys' passion for the protection of animals.[1] Hardy read the lessons there, and it was remembered how, after a summer bike-ride of nearly twenty miles, his balding head would steam gently as he stood at the lectern.[2] Their route lay through Puddletown; and another memory records how the Hardys would bicycle stiffly through the main street, looking neither to right nor to left. Cottage doors were full of his close relatives, the Hands, the Antells, and visiting Sparkses; but Hardy neither gave nor acknowledged greetings as he pedalled resolutely on with Emma.

Although he was allied with her in rejecting his ancestry, there was no sign now of any common bond between them. He was therefore doubly isolated; he had given up one life, and found another to be an illusion. Even the fact that they went to church together was a mockery. His early experiences had settled him in the belief that any supreme power must be ignorant of or indifferent to any form of human life. Emma, on the other hand, "had various experiences . . . all showing that an Unseen Power of great benevolence directs my ways".[3] To Hardy's evident dismay, she founded this belief on the narrowest form of sectarian Protestant prejudice. Even on their honeymoon in France, her low-church fears of sacerdotalism were confirmed by the sight of "priests walking about whose age can be known by their harshness & closeness of expression . . . concealed concentrated wickedness . . . like liquid become hard substance".[4] Grappling with the inexplicable mystery and tragedy of life, which he had experienced to the full in his youth, Hardy found himself tied to a religious bigot. In the 1880s, as he saw her ignorant, girlish charms diminish into gross middle age and incongruous chatter,[5] he shut his eyes and ears to her, and explored philosophies that could help him bear the shattering, suppressed happenings of his own early history.

In the decade from 1878 to 1887, his major published work, from *The Return of the Native* to *The Woodlanders*, shows a settled attempt to put his characters in a philosophical frame. One critic[6] says: "It takes a philosophical tinge of universality, for which we should seek vainly in the early writings." Yet though he added to his youthful reading of Mill, Spencer, and Comte the impressive trio of Spinoza, Schopenhauer, and Von Hartmann, his human problems remained. The novels, though fully "Wessex" still in setting and anecdote, lack some of the human feeling of his earlier work. They are great exercises to demonstrate the thesis that the universe is totally indifferent to men and women. He did not allow into his work the actual incidents that had caused his settled gloom, "as if enveloped in a leaden cloud", as he once described it.[7] These events of his youth were still too painfully near. His mother's poverty-stricken origins and relatives, his own ambitions and loss of faith, his fascination by his three girl-cousins, his delusive marriage-impulse, his virtual renunciation of poetry, and, the height of tragedy, the disasters in sex, drink, and suicide of the man called "my friend" were still too close to be the subject of fiction. He hugged them to him, with all that side of life he concealed from the world, taciturn in clubs, society, and tea-parties.

This could not last for ever. After ten years of suppression, the themes that had shaped his life began to force their way into his notebooks. On 28 April 1888 he wrote,[8] as subject for a story,

> a young man—"who could not go to Oxford"—His struggles and ulti-
> mate failure. Suicide. . . . There is something . . . the world ought to be
> shown, and I am the one to show it to them—

His own class-conscious struggles, the wasted ambition of his cobbler uncle, John Antell, who had died in 1878, and, more deeply, the tragedy of Horace Moule, were all beginning to surface. Then on 30 September he recalled that a relative of his mother, Rebecca Swetman, used to speak proudly of the past glories of the Hardy family, who, she believed, owned land like his mother's ancestors, the Swetmans, in Woolcombe and Frome St. Quintin, which has a "Jude" brass.[9] In the week of 15 October, his mother recalled his paternal grandmother, Mary Head, telling stories of her girlhood and the time of the French Revolution.[10] On 19 February 1889, thinking perhaps of his three Sparks girl-cousins, with their differing ages but striking facial likenesses, he wrote[11]

> The story of a face which goes through three generations or more, would
> make a fine novel or poem of the passage of Time. The differences in
> personality to be ignored.

Everywhere the buried themes were stirring. Even the memory of his schoolboy passion for Louisa Harding sent him, early in 1889, to a music shop on the site of Oxford Circus Station, where an old man sang to him, at his request, the words of Sheridan's "How oft, Louisa", but could not find the music which had haunted Hardy's youth.[12] As for the central tragedy of his present life, a loveless marriage, a note of 9 July read, "Love lives on propinquity, but dies of contact".[13] Yet there were fresh dawnings of hope too. On Christmas Day 1890, when he was "thinking of resuming 'the viewless wings of poesy' . . . new horizons seemed to open, and worrying pettinesses to disappear".[14]

The theme of what poverty meant to women, its power to blight well-aspiring lives, like those of young girls, was the first to break through his defences with such force that he had to write about it. It was, after all, the deepest-laid memory. His mother's family history was still vivid to him, for he did not give up his visits to the Bockhampton cottage, especially as his father, old and rheumatic, was now growing feeble, before his death in 1892. The place itself was alive with the old stories of woman's tragedy, his mother's at Melbury Osmond, his grandmother's in Berkshire. Mary Head of Fawley had become a symbol of the harshness of providence to a young girl. Losing her father in the year she was born, her mother at six, she had probably lodged with her uncle, Henry Head, churchwarden of the nearby Chaddleworth. If so, at only eleven she was involved in yet another family tragedy; for Henry Head's wife and two sons all died in the same year, 1783.[15] These reiterated blows of fate on one of his own ancestors turned Hardy's mind to the peasant superstition of some sort of family curse, a malignant, doomed heredity. Poverty and predestined family failure are part—though only part—of the novel he began to write in autumn 1888, *Tess of the d'Urbervilles*.

As many people have remarked, Hardy spoke about Tess Durbeyfield as if she were a real person. In a letter[16] in 1891, he regretted that "I have not been able to put on paper all that she is, or was, to me". On the other hand, he indulged in a good deal of deliberate mystification about her. In private conversations he confessed that the only physical model was a Dorset girl he had once seen on a cart, and that there was no exact original;[17] but he told Arthur Compton-Rickett that he had "built up" Tess from three women, a Weymouth waitress, from whom he took Tess's physique and appearance, and her character from two Dorchester girls.[18] The Antell family said that Tess in her life, adventures, and final death was "practically what happened to a relative".[19] This remarkable statement has never been followed up; if it were to be, it might well lead to Hardy's cousins, the family of William Hand of Melbury Osmond, who certainly show at least one illegitimate birth and

considerable poverty.[20] It might also justify Hardy's confusing remark
to an interviewer in 1892 that "Tess had a real existence".[21]

Yet the poverty and predestined tragedy of Tess seems to come from
an earlier generation. The gang labour system, under which she suffers,
had been controlled by the Gangs Act of 1868, and by the time Hardy
wrote it was a thing of the past.[22] The steam threshing-machine, another
cause of her suffering, first took the place of horse-power as early as
1803. Hardy was more probably drawing on ancestral memories. Even
the weird tale, dredged up by Mary Hardy, about Farmer Head of
Chaddleworth, who left his wife after their wedding night, may have
contributed to Angel Clare's desertion of Tess after her bride-night
revelation of her past doings with d'Urberville. In spite of references in
the novel to "Victorian lucre" and the spectacular late nineteenth-
century growth of Bournemouth, there is a primitive timelessness about
the book. The end of Tess on the scaffold where she pays the penalty of
the law, without reprieve, echoes Hardy's adolescent experience of the
death of Martha Brown, and the harsher morality he had heard expressed in his youth.

It also must owe something to his abnormal interest in the hanging of
women—in a sense, the fictional Tess was doomed by her creator—
allied to the fact that, for all his temporary attractions to living women,
the most moving symbol to him was a woman in death. One of these
situations, with strange overtones, now occurred. In March 1890, during
a train journey, he began to write on the subject of Tryphena Sparks,[23]
whom he had not seen for many years, a poem beginning

> Not a line of her writing have I,
> Not a thread of her hair . . .

His memory, now searching the buried past, may have been prompted
by the fairly recent deaths of two of Tryphena's sisters, Emma in
1884 and Rebecca in 1885.[24] What he did not realize till later was that
Tryphena herself was dying when he wrote the lines. She was not
quite forty. He felt as if his three girl-cousins had somehow closed their
account with him. The fourth, Martha, was not indeed dead, but 8000
miles away in Queensland, looking after her own strong brood of children and her sister Emma's boys and girls. At all events, Hardy felt
somehow free to symbolize his attachment to three sisters in his next
work, *The Well-Beloved*. In a typical shift of fictional relationship, he
made the three girls in the book not sisters of widely-spaced ages, as in
real life, but three generations. His hero, Hardy himself thinly-dis-
guised in his search from one woman to another for ideal beauty, falls in
love at twenty-year intervals with three girls of the same family. There
is even a hint of self-mockery, when the third girl, finding the hero has

been the lover of her own grandmother and mother, innocently asks if he is old enough to have been her great-grandmother's lover too. Hardy drew a red herring across this autobiography by calling it a sketch of a temperament, letting it be known that he meant the artistic temperament of his sculptor hero: but it is a sketch of his own temperament in very realistic detail. Specially noteworthy are the portrayals of actual people in the fashionable society where Hardy now moved.[25] The actress Ellen Terry appears exactly as she appeared to Hardy in real life,[26] and so do many woman he knew. He treats his society acquaintances with the mixture of fascination and affected disdain that he felt for them, unable to stop staring at their décolletée beauty, and taking refuge from their attractions in a deliberate peasant rudeness and crude comment.[27] *The Well-Beloved*, in fact, is strikingly like *The Hand of Ethelberta*, a personal allegory carried to near-absurd lengths, and the same sort of puzzle was felt by the reviewers when it finally appeared, much later and heavily-revised, in volume form. They felt, obscurely, that there was something wrong with it. The wrongness was that it came uncomfortably near to self-revelation of some of the less attractive sides of Hardy's own character and physical make-up. In a letter replying to an unfavourable review in *The Academy*, Hardy stated that he had thought of the idea of the novel when young.[28] It would be more true to say that it was founded on his experiences when young, as *Ethelberta* had been, but wearing the heavy disguise that middle-age had taught him to adopt.

The serialization of *The Well-Beloved* in *The Illustrated London News* during 1892 does not seem to have aroused much attention. Yet the popular success of *Tess*, in spite of some violent attacks on its morality, made Hardy feel able to mount another assault on conventional society, and to release some of his oppressive, personal concealments. He was more than usually explicit about the literary origins of *Jude the Obscure*, though even more than usually reticent about some of its personal facets. He made notes for it in 1887 and onward, including the 1888 note, which has been quoted. As this would suggest, its first theme was that of a poor boy handicapped by social circumstances. This went back as far as *The Poor Man and the Lady*, and indeed much farther. The theme of suffering through poverty was so deeply associated with his Berkshire grandmother, Mary Head, that his hero was early called Jack Head, the actual name of a parish boy-relation of hers, who was, in real life as in the novel, a bird-scarer.[29] Even when he became Jude Fawley, his surname was the same as her birthplace. Jude the youth, dreaming of the spires of Oxford, haven of pure learning, is the self-taught Hardy, oblivious in his books to the coarse village life around him.[30] When Jude comes to Oxford as a young workman, another personal portrait takes over. This is John (known as "Jack") Antell, Hardy's self-taught cobbler uncle, who actually learnt enough Latin to open a "Latin school" in Puddletown, where he is even said to have taught the Squire's cricketing son. His fatal weakness for drink contributes to this picture of rural ambition and failure, which Hardy himself actually commemorated by composing an epitaph for his tombstone.

The second Mrs. Hardy, however, warned a correspondent that Jude was "only partly" based on John Antell, and herself later suggested the main model for the deeper shades of the character. This was, of course, the career of Horace Moule. The two sides of Jude, learning and intellect, contrasting with sex and drink, are Hardy's legacy from the tragic life and death of his great friend. Hardy saw the book as a series of such contrasts,[31] and Jude's correspond with the fatal battleground of Moule's temperament. In his previous published novel, Hardy had drawn Angel Clare's family, sometimes in unkind satire, from the Moules. Now, as if in expiation, he made his hero a fully sympathetic study of the terrible problems that had confronted and defeated his friend. His sensual attraction in the novel is Arabella, her name taken from the landlady of the Phoenix Inn, rendezvous for the Puddletown carrier's cart,[32] and her nature from Moule's Dorchester girl. His spiritual companion, herself ultimately just as fatal, is Sue Bridehead. The chief disaster in the book is when Jude's child by the former returns from Australia, where he has been brought up, and finally hangs both himself and Jude's children by Sue. The startling fact that Moule's own illegitimate child by the Dorchester girl was also brought up in Australia, and eventually hanged, is striking enough to make it clear that Hardy's hero owes much to Moule, besides his academic failures, his drink and depression, and virtual suicide. Such scenes as the drunken Jude reciting the Latin Creed to a scoffing pub audience are horribly reminiscent of what happened to Moule. The kind curate, who gives Jude fresh hope after this scene, may be taken from Moule's curate brother Frederick, who rescued him in such dilemmas. It would be a mistake to think of all the characters in this most carefully-constructed novel as personal portraits; but there is an even more probable identification of one of its most interesting characters, Phillotson, the middle-aged Berkshire schoolmaster who comes to teach in Dorset, and whose separation from Sue gets him into professional trouble. He may be based on the bachelor Mr. Holmes, schoolmaster of Athelhampton, under whom Tryphena Sparks had worked, a Berkshire man from a village near Fawley.[33] According to Tryphena, he too ran into some severe trouble in his fifties.[34]

Hardy's heroine, Sue Bridehead, was herself to be a schoolteacher, a symbol of class-emancipation in the 1860s, a suggestion that came, Hardy said, from "the death of a woman" in 1890—that is, the death of his former schoolteacher cousin Tryphena. In search of a realistic background for a rebel woman teacher, Hardy paid visits in 1891 first to Whitelands Training College at Putney,[35] then to Tryphena's old college at Stockwell,[36] and also to his own sisters' college at Salisbury. Jude and Sue were to be cousins, like himself and Tryphena, but, as another character remarks, they are more like brother and sister. It is worth noticing that he inscribed a copy of the completed book to his sister Mary,[37] and eventually set the scene of Sue's training in Mary's college, rather than at any of the others.

Sue's character, however, hung fire until the early summer of 1893, when it received a sudden new turn from Hardy's perpetual susceptibility to women. As if to illustrate his own allegory of *The Well-Beloved*, he became deeply attracted by Mrs. Florence Henniker, who seemed an 1890s reincarnation of the advanced woman on whom Sue was based. Together they went to the plays of Ibsen, cult-figure of emancipated thought. In the private language of their letters, Hardy became her Master Builder—he even took up church architecture again[38]—and she his Hilde Wangel, able to understand his "trollish" feelings.[39] Yet, as so often with Hardy, their relationship had what he called "the onesidedness"[40] of an illusion on his part. Far from being emancipated, she was not only conventionally married to a heavily-built military officer, but, to Hardy's horror, was an orthodox church-goer of High Church leanings. The scene in the novel where the innocent Jude, thinking Sue is wearing scent, discovers that it is the smell of incense from a church service she has just attended, almost certainly preserves some such moment of revelation. At all events, she became responsible for the final character of the heroine in Hardy's "hour-glass" construction of the novel. Sue begins freethinking and emancipated, but ends conventionally religious, while Jude passes through religion to utter unbelief, raging against marriage as an illustration of how "The letter killeth", the book's epigraph.

No one among Hardy's eventual readers was more shocked than his own wife. Though, according to her nephew,[41] it was the novel's general irreligion that alienated her, it was perhaps more the particular brand of religion adopted by the heroine that seemed such a personal outrage by her husband. To Emma, High Church was equivalent to the great enemy, Rome. It was this, as much as her husband's infatuation, that insured her well-attested disapproval of Mrs. Henniker.[42] She had even more cause for disapproval of Hardy's activities in ensuing years. Ever since he had felt 'the viewless wings of poesy' stirring again in 1890, Hardy began to write increasing numbers of poems, very often intensely personal. In 1898, 1901 and 1909, he published three volumes, *Wessex Poems*, *Poems of the Past and the Present*, and *Time's Laughingstocks*. To placate Emma, he tried in prefaces to pretend that none of these poems was personal, a transparent untruth; also scattered among them were many poems, also mainly personal, written in his youth. Exactly to whom most of these poems were addressed is still a matter of debate. It is not easy to detach poems which may refer to one of the Sparks sisters, or other early loves, from those more recently addressed to Florence Henniker or even to her namesake Florence Dugdale, whom she introduced to Hardy in 1904, to help with research for *The Dynasts*, and who ultimately became the second Mrs. Hardy. Some, dated in the early 1890s, may have been inspired plausibly either by Tryphena's death in 1890 or by Mrs. Henniker's advent in 1893. All, except one or two, had this in common; they were not about his wife.

Her protests were frequent and vigorous. Yet, if she had considered her husband's peculiar nature, she would have realized she had the last word over her rivals. She could die. When she did, in November 1912, his almost involuntary reaction to the death of a once-loved woman rose to a pitch it had never reached before. In the year following her death, he wrote a hundred poems to her. This astonishing feat by a seventy-two-year-old poet has often been remarked, praised and analysed. Even he himself seemed amazed at its vehemence, and tried to find reasons for it—"the mind goes back to the early times when each was much to the other—in her case and mine intensely much".[43] What was truly astonishing was the quality of the poems produced. Whenever the subject was Emma, whether in praise, regret, self-pity, self-reproach, or occasionally self-justification, his work takes on a new dimension of feeling, intensity, and emotional content. One cannot assess how much is due to the actual quality of the love these commemorate, but they seem to show, without doubt, that in retrospect his courtship of Emma was the great event of his early life, particularly in its exotic setting and circumstance. The unique gift of Hardy to associate place and person, the high point in his novels, is surpassed in this moving sequence of poems.

The outburst slackened after the first year of bereavement, and lessened after his remarriage in 1914 to Florence Dugdale. Other deaths produced their results to a minor degree. The death of his first, barely-known adolescent sweetheart, Louisa Harding, in 1913, brought its small clutch of wistful poems. A stronger impulse came from the death of his sister Mary in 1915. She had her poems too, in a deeper tone. His prose jottings also hint just how close their relationship had been. Even his mother, who had died in 1904, had not commanded such feeling. When he heard the verse he had long ago noted in his own prayer book read over Mary's grave, "I held my tongue and spake nothing: I kept silent, yea, even from good words", he commented, "That was my poor Mary exactly".[44] Ten years later, he wrote on her birthday, "She came into the world . . . And went out . . . And the world is just the same . . . not a ripple on the surface left".[45] It is not usually noticed that in the poem *Conjecture*, he brackets Mary with his two wives, as if he had been married to her too, and recalling the feeling between brother and sister in *Ethelberta*. One of his poems to her, *Molly Gone*, is as poignant as any other of the love-poems, especially in the typical broken rhythms of its final stanza:

> Where, then, is Molly, who's no more with me?
>     —As I stand on this lea,
> Thinking thus, there's a many-flamed star in the air
>     That tosses a sign
> That her glance is regarding its face from her home, so that there
>     Her eyes may have meetings with mine.

The same thought in one of his earliest poems, *The Imaginative Maiden*, confirms that there had been this lifelong sympathy between them, perhaps deeper in its way than any other love. Many poems suggested by her death, such as *Looking Across*, show him feeling more kinship with his dead family, and those he had known in youth, than those now around him. From childhood Mary had played Nekayah to his Rasselas.

Famous people came and went at Max Gate, including the then Prince of Wales; after a lunch of roast chicken, the bone the Prince had picked was appropriated by the gardener as a rustic trophy.[46] More and more, however, Hardy went back to the past and his youth for his real life. He rescued poems from his London years, he commemorated incidents from his youth in new poems, or in poems so personal that he had not dared publish them before. Many are mysterious colloquies with past women, so emotionally charged and yet so obliquely expressed that one can only guess at their meaning. The tragedy of Moule is crystallized, though not fully explained, in a poem that draws on details from their last meeting in Cambridge, *Standing by the Mantelpiece*. To the end, he was reliving his life in poetry. Outwardly, he was rich in honours and in material success. The child born in an isolated country cottage, the self-taught boy, died worth the modern equivalent of a million pounds. The process of cutting himself off from his family origins seemed complete; yet the poems, his inner life, tell a different story, a record of how the happenings of his young days were still as vivid and deeply-felt as when they had first occurred. Death brought Westminster Abbey, and his ashes in Poet's Corner. Yet even there, in the crowded, fashionable, and ill-organized service, so disliked by the surviving sister, Kate,[47] was a symbol of the stock they shared. In the reserved and ticketed seats, the daughter of a Dorset vicar, whose family were close friends of Hardy, found herself sitting next to an obvious tramp in ragged clothes. When she questioned him, he proved to know Hardy very well indeed.[48] In fact, he was probably a relative, one of the Hands of Melbury Osmond.[49] Kate Hardy herself already had the last word. While the ladies and gentlemen at Max Gate were making their important, national arrangements without consulting her, she had viewed the body, and gazed at the family face. She set it down in her diary:[50] "the same triumphant look on his face that all the others bore— but without the smile."

# Appendix:

# Hardy and Tryphena Sparks*

SINCE 1966, Hardy studies of all sorts have mentioned, in one way or another, a book published in that year under the title of *Providence and Mr. Hardy*. Some have dismissed it, some have accepted its claims, in part or on the whole. No one has quite been able to ignore it; for the thesis it sets out is biographically sensational. The young Thomas Hardy, according to this account, had a child by a very young girl, ostensibly his cousin, but really his niece. Apprised of this, he reproached himself (inaccurately) with the sin of incest. Guilt, atonement, and disillusion over this, it is said, lay at the bottom of all his work, and of his whole attitude to life. The story has been used in a sermon by a Bishop, in handbooks and companions to Hardy's works, in critical scholarly introductions, and has even found its way into a prize-winning modern novel. The theory has been canvassed with passionate intensity, for and against. It appeared in the colour supplement of a Sunday newspaper, and has passed, vaguely but persistently, into the popular conception of Hardy held by many general readers.

Yet perhaps the most extraordinary aspect of this whole bizarre affair is the nature of the book itself, and the fact that it ever could have been accepted, even at a superficial reading; for even to the ordinary non-specialist reader, the whole construction of the book must seem highly suspicious. It abounds in conditional sentences beginning "If . . ." and containing conditional verbs, such as "could have". *If* A was at a certain place at a certain time, she *could have* been seduced by B, and C *could have* been their child—and so on. It also deals with written documents in a quite arbitrary way. Those that fit the story are said to be true; those that do not are said to be forged or entered upon false information. All these conjectures are admitted, when they first appear, as conjectures only, but later in the book are treated as facts. Yet they obtained such a hold that in 1971 a quite serious critical work printed a photograph unequivocally captioned as being a portrait of the illegitimate son of Thomas Hardy and his girl-relative. [1]

The book, in fact, seems to have exercised some sort of hypnotic effect on many people's critical faculties. It is therefore important to see how it came into being, and to trace the different elements in it. In 1966, *Providence and Mr. Hardy* was published by Hutchinson, the authors' names being given as Lois Deacon and Terry Coleman. An explanation of the joint authorship is given in a preliminary "Author's Note" (though it does not say which author composed the note): "The original idea was Lois Deacon's, and she carried out, over several years, much the greater part of the necessary research. The

* This appendix is based on my previously printed article on this topic, by kind permission of Arthur Crook, formerly editor of *The Times Literary Supplement*.

writing is by Terry Coleman". This ignores the fact that the manuscript of much the same book had been submitted unsuccessfully to publishers "over several years" in Miss Deacon's name only. This version, however, was relatively incoherent in most of its arrangement and style. Certainly, the credit goes to Mr. Coleman for an extremely professional and skilful re-editing and re-writing of the whole and for the excellent provision and standardization of references.

Since Mr. Coleman modestly—perhaps too modestly—claims responsibility only for the actual writing, it is fair to study the ideas and research, to which he does not lay claim, as Miss Deacon's solely. These started, the note goes on to say, by a chance meeting in 1959 with someone who said, "my mother is a cousin [second cousin actually] of Thomas Hardy and her mother was once engaged to him". This was the original idea, which developed into the book published seven years later. The progress and expansion of all the ideas stemming from this statement can be divided fairly certainly into three main stages; in the survey that follows, however, one must recognize that these stages cannot be determined in a hard-and-fast way, and must sometimes have overlapped in time.

The first stage is fairly straightforward, and is an expansion of something already vaguely known. In 1940 Irene Cooper Willis, a friend of the second Mrs. Thomas Hardy, lawyer, executor, and trustee of Mrs. Hardy's estate, stated that when Hardy met his first wife, Emma Gifford, in 1870, he "broke off an understanding that there had been between him and a girl of his own countryside, and bestowed upon Emma the ring intended for the discarded maiden".[2] Twenty years later, Miss Cooper Willis confirmed this story, which, she said, she had had from the second Mrs. Hardy. As the result of her chance meeting, Miss Deacon in 1959 was introduced to Mrs. Eleanor Tryphena Bromell, then aged eighty. Mrs. Bromell was the daughter of Hardy's cousin Tryphena Sparks, who had married a man named Charles Gale. She confirmed that Tryphena Sparks was "the discarded maiden", with whom Hardy had once had an understanding. In conversations and letters she expanded the story, and in many ways gave it a new bearing. According to her, rather than an "understanding", there was an engagement of some years. Hardy did not merely "intend" the ring for Tryphena Sparks; he gave it to her. He still went on seeing her after he had met Emma Gifford in 1870, and it was Tryphena Sparks herself who sent him back the ring, after meeting her own future husband, Charles Gale, probably in 1873. Gale was said to have persuaded her to do this, and to marry him instead, on the grounds that she and Hardy were cousins. According to Mrs. Bromell, Hardy never saw Tryphena again; but when she died in 1890, after bearing Charles Gale four children, Hardy and his brother Henry visited her grave at Topsham in Devon, and placed a wreath on it. Her widowed husband refused to see Hardy on that occasion.

There seems little doubt that most of this story is true. It is difficult to say whether Mrs. Bromell ever actually spoke of a formal engagement between Tryphena Sparks and Thomas Hardy, but her own daughter did, and Mrs. Bromell did not demur when other people spoke of it in those terms. She herself was clear that Tryphena Sparks and Thomas Hardy had "walked out" for some time on the heath between their homes in Dorset, his at Higher

Bockhampton and hers at Puddletown. Miss Deacon did some further work on the rest of Tryphena's life, both before and after her marriage to Charles Gale, which took place on 15 December 1877, just over three years after Hardy's own marriage to Emma. In 1962 she published all this in a pamphlet.[3] This publication, despite a few aberrations, is reasonably accurate. Its only faults are a somewhat over-emphatic style—Hardy's association with Tryphena Sparks is called "an enduring and tragic love-story"—and an often arbitrary selection of dates. The "engagement" is dated precisely from late summer 1867 to early June 1872, though Mrs. Bromell never mentioned these times, and the latter date is contradicted by Miss Deacon herself in *Providence and Mr. Hardy*.[4] On the whole, however, the pamphlet is a useful small-scale work, and would have proved a valuable adjunct to any large-scale biography of Hardy. It is what may be called the first stage.

There were already signs, though, that Miss Deacon was not satisfied to leave it at that, and that her investigations had moved into a second stage, which was to elicit from Mrs. Bromell confirmation for ideas that had their sole origins in Miss Deacon's own mind. The chief of these was Miss Deacon's idea that Tryphena Sparks and Thomas Hardy had an illegitimate son. According to a friend, this was already a "surmise",[5] which she had confided to others, as early as September 1960, and probably much earlier. She had also selected, from loose photographs in the Gale family album, lent to her by Mrs. Bromell, the photograph of an unidentified boy; this selection seems to have been made quite at random. On 9 September 1960 she showed this photograph to Mrs. Bromell, who greeted it with the rather baffling remark, "Oh, that was a little boy who used to come and see Tryphena at Plymouth". Since Tryphena Sparks had moved from Plymouth, where she had been a schoolteacher, to Topsham when she married Charles Gale, her daughter (Mrs. Bromell) can never have seen the boy. The identification, even in such vague terms, must have been by hearsay only. In any case, it did not satisfy Miss Deacon's preconceived notion of an illegitimate son, and at various times during the next four years, she produced the same photograph, only to receive the same answer. It must be said that in spite of her ever-growing preconception, Miss Deacon did not act as an inquisitor, but always as a friend. She had also seen Mrs. Bromell's angry reaction in 1962 to another questioner, who had asked point-blank whether Hardy and Tryphena Sparks had had a child or not.[6]

In January 1964, however, Mrs. Bromell, then aged 85, was admitted to hospital, and died there just over a year later. Miss Deacon claims that for most of this year, Mrs. Bromell remained "in full command of her faculties, clear and lucid". According to official medical evidence, though, she suffered from cerebral atherosclerosis, primarily, with secondary epileptiform fits. Owing to this main condition of illness she was sometimes confused, and it was, of course, a condition that did not appear overnight, but was one of progressive deterioration. There are, in fact, signs of her being confused in answering questions as early as 1962. Although, again on the medical evidence, it is probable that her memory of the remote past could be reasonably accurate, it was noted that her condition did deteriorate still more during the latter part of her life in hospital.

By the middle of January 1965—actually only five or six weeks before her death—Mrs. Bromell was, as Miss Deacon herself admits, often confused and wandering in her thoughts. Up to this point she had spoken nothing of an illegitimate son of Hardy and Tryphena Sparks, and had always returned the same indeterminate answer about the portrait of the boy that Miss Deacon had selected. However, in three conversations on 17 January and on 7 and 10 February 1965, she spoke about this picture. She said it was "Hardy's boy" and that "he was a Sparks" and "he was a cousin". She gave his Christian name as Rantie or Randy, short for Randolph or Randal, and said he was also known as Henery. It may perhaps be some measure of her confused state of mind to remember that Hardy's wife, Emma Gifford, actually had a nephew with the unusual name of Randolph, and that Hardy himself had an uncle with the unusual name of Henery. Be that as it may, Mrs. Bromell went on to indicate that this boy was first of all brought up by Tryphena's sister, Rebecca, and then by Tryphena's brother Nathaniel, who lived in Bristol. Shown another random photograph of a youth, she said that this was the boy grown up, and that he had attended Tryphena's funeral. A fortnight after saying this, Mrs. Bromell died.

Mrs. Bromell died, it will be observed, without ever saying that Hardy and Tryphena Sparks had an illegitimate son. Once more, official medical authority states that it would be wise to treat unsupported statements made by her during the last few weeks of life with a degree of caution. Miss Deacon, however, regarded these last interviews as proof that her own preconception of an illegitimate son of Tryphena and Hardy was true. She had completed the second stage of her process, which was related to remarks made by Mrs. Bromell, regardless of the circumstances of health in which these remarks were made.

The third stage was to allow a number of other preconceptions, not connected in any way with Mrs. Bromell, nor with information given by her in her lifetime, to have free play. These included, among much else, arbitrary dates for the conception and birth of the alleged son, and a series of illegitimacies, unrecorded in any documents, to advance Miss Deacon's theory that Tryphena Sparks was not Hardy's cousin but really his niece.

This analysis of Miss Deacon's process into three stages will have made it clear that the major part of her story, the conception and birth of a child to Hardy by a young girl who was really his niece, was in what we have called her third stage, based entirely on her own imagination. It does not relate in any way to information given to her by Mrs. Bromell. This is important to note, since readers and scholars who have tried to deal with this question in the past decade have often tended to think it had some basis in something said by Mrs. Bromell. In view of this tendency, it must be emphasized that there is no evidence, either from Mrs. Bromell or from documents, for this third stage; or rather that it is based on a denial of all personal and documentary evidence—census returns, birth, marriage and death entries, and so on—that does not fit Miss Deacon's preconceived theories.

This general attitude towards evidence in her third stage can very easily be illustrated by one simple example. Miss Deacon attaches great importance to the conception of the alleged child in the late summer of 1867. "From weather records we know", she writes, "that 1867 was a year with a splendid Indian summer. . . . It was then in the late summer and long, hot autumn of 1867, that he [Hardy] and Tryphena . . . became lovers".[7] She associates this Indian summer with the line "Weeks and weeks we had loved beneath that blazing blue" of Hardy's poem *The Place on the Map*, and "the October month of wonderful afternoons" in *Tess of the d'Urbervilles*. Yet the plain truth is that such a summer in 1867 never existed. Far from consulting any weather records, as she claims, Miss Deacon cannot have looked at them. Nor, perhaps even more strangely, has any scholar. The weather at Weymouth, a few miles from Hardy's home, is given every day in *The Times*. 1867 was a wet year, with a rainfall above the average, and a bad summer. At Weymouth that August less than half the days had any blue sky at all, and there were only three days of continuous blue. Exactly the same was true of September. Finally, far from there being a long hot Indian summer, the October records show the reverse, as *The Times* duly noted. The month began by being very cold. The temperature on 4 October was only forty-one degrees. The record for the rest of the month reads:

> Overcast rain, cloudy, some blue sky rain, hail and cloud, rain and cloud, cloud some blue sky, overcast rain, overcast rain, fog and cloud, overcast, cloud, overcast and cloud, lightning thunder cloud, overcast cloud, overcast cloud, cloudy and rainy, rain and fog, fog and cloud, cloudy and overcast, cloudy some blue sky, cloudy some blue sky, cloudy blue then rain, cloudy and overcast, overcast mist and rain, overcast fog and mist.

Miss Deacon has invented the whole idea of a long, hot Indian summer in 1867. Indeed, she was unluckier than she could possibly have known. This year of 1867 ushered in a meteorological phenomenon, for which the highly-detailed *London Weather* by J. H. Brazell (Her Majesty's Stationery Office) has no explanation, though it records the facts. For the next forty years, including this year, there was an almost complete absence over the country of warm Octobers or Indian summers or whatever they may be called. The long hot summer of Hardy's wooing in 1867 exists only in Miss Deacon's imagination.

It may well be asked why Miss Deacon laid such emphasis on this particular (though, as it proves, non-existent) Indian summer; and the answer may be that, as is well known, both Hardy and his girl-cousin had watchful and powerful mothers. The alleged conception would have to take place out of doors. The point is, though, that the complete falsification of evidence, the statement that "from weather records we know", when, in fact, weather records cannot have been consulted, throws total doubt on all Miss Deacon's methods of "research" in this, the third stage of her investigations. Practically everything that can be checked in this third stage turns out to be guesswork, and when documents are cited, they often prove not to have been consulted. To take only one topic, Tryphena's education; she is said to have gone to College, to train as a teacher, in "autumn 1869", and College records are cited in evidence. In fact, the College records show that her date of entry was 28 January 1870. Her school as a child is described as "the school at Athelhampton . . . run by the *National Society for the Education of the Poor*", while a few lines later on the same page[8] it appears as "the Athelhampton school . . . run by the British and Foreign Bible Society". It is implied that educational records have been consulted; if they had, they would have shown that the second of these two contradictory statements is the true one. Finally, Tryphena is alleged to have been assisted to College by Mrs. Julia Augusta Martin, who had helped the very early stages of Hardy's own education. Mrs. Martin was a staunch Anglican, who had been hurt and angry that Hardy had eventually gone to a Nonconformist school. Tryphena's college was a Nonconformist foundation; it is therefore impossible that Mrs. Martin could assist her to such a place, where all the sponsoring bodies were composed of Nonconformists, as the records show. The so-called research into documents, claimed or implied by Miss Deacon, is pure invention.

What then about "Hardy's boy", elicited by Miss Deacon from Mrs. Bromell in the second stage of her investigations? It must be remembered again that official medical opinion states that, at the time of this particular questioning, it would be wise to treat unsupported statements made by Mrs. Bromell with a degree of caution. It is notable that the sole evidence for this boy's existence—for no birth, death, marriage, census, school, apprenticeship, or employment records have ever been found for him—depends largely on a statement made by Miss Deacon and a reply by Mrs. Bromell with no witnesses present.[9] Speaking of the home of Tryphena's brother Nathaniel in Bristol, where the boy was supposed to have been largely brought up, Miss Deacon said, "So that there were three boys there altogether", to which Mrs. Bromell is said to have replied, "Yes, two boys of his own and Hardy's boy as well". Does this have any supporting evidence, as medical opinion advises it should, before we accept its accuracy?

In point of fact, documents which are relevant to this question have appeared during the past few years. They consist of a section of Sparks family letters, to and from Bristol, dated at the precise time the "Hardy boy" is said to be living there. These are very full and unconstrained family letters, mentioning in one way or another every member of the family, and dealing with every kind of family matter, marriages, births, deaths, money troubles, illness, difficulties with in-laws, work, houses, emigration to Australia, the upbringing and education of children. In none is there the slightest mention of this boy being in the Bristol house; in fact, two boys only are always specifically mentioned, Nathaniel Sparks's sons, James and Nathaniel junior.

About 1883, Rebecca Sparks writes to Nathaniel Sparks's wife at Bristol.[10] She adds "Kiss my two good boys for me". There is no mention of the third boy (whom, incidentally, she is supposed to have brought up at an earlier stage). In October 1884, there is a letter,[11] to which one of the two Sparks boys has later added a note. He recalls that he and his brother played a practical joke on an interfering great-aunt, who tried to boss the Bristol home. He talks about "us two nippers", and says the joke—an attempt to blow up their great-aunt with gunpowder—was "not bad for two kids". There is no mention of any third nipper or kid in the household. Their mother, writing from Bristol in 1890,[12] speaks of bringing up two boys only, and having taught them both at home. Finally in 1896, in a very long and detailed letter to a nephew in Australia,[13] Nathaniel Sparks himself describes his Bristol household. He also mentions two boys only: "Jim is 19 years old now and Nat is 16 . . . both at the Art School." In short, one has either to imagine an extraordinary, concerted and elaborate conspiracy of silence by this very outspoken and voluble family, or to think these letters finally prove that the third child, "the Hardy boy", never existed. Far from supporting what is said to have been heard from a very ill and confused old lady on her death-bed, these letters contradict it.

The letters then disprove the second stage of Miss Deacon's story. Hardy's son is as much of a myth as the long, hot summer in which he is said to have been conceived. This is not to say that there is no truth in her first stage. With some reservations, as has been said, one can accept a great deal of her pamphlet published in 1962. Its chief fault, as has also been said, is the false emphasis that it places on Tryphena, the "enduring and tragic love-story". Hardy, as it now appears, knew and was attracted by a number of girls in his youth. Tryphena Sparks was one of a fairly long sequence, including her own older sisters, Rebecca and Martha. Hardy wrote many poems to many women in his lifetime; it would be unwise to identify any positively with Tryphena Sparks, except for the poems written in and about Weymouth in the year 1869–70, and the poem "Thoughts of Phena", written at the time of her death in 1890. She was certainly attractive, and Hardy was attracted by her. So was his cousin and hers, John Antell, who also wrote a moving little poem on her death. It would be wrong, in any case, to ascribe to any of these girls the whole nature and character of his later work, still less to see the special influence of Tryphena Sparks in numerous poems and novels. The making of a myth about Tryphena and Thomas Hardy, whether based on falsified evidence or unsupported evidence, has confused almost every critical account, biography, and handbook published in the past decade. It is in the hope of ending the confusion that this analysis has been made.

# Abbreviations Used in the Notes

Bailey: J. O. H. Bailey, *The Poetry of Thomas Hardy: A Handbook and Commentary*, Chapel Hill, 1970.

Beatty: C. J. P. Beatty (ed.), *The Architectural Notebook of Thomas Hardy*, Dorchester, 1966.

Beatty (thesis): C. J. P. Beatty, *The Part Played by Architecture in the Life and Work of Thomas Hardy, with Particular Reference to the Novels*. Unpublished dissertation, University of London (External), 1964.

DCC: *Dorset County Chronicle*.

DCL: Dorset County Library.

DCM: Dorset County Museum.

DCRO: Dorset County Record Office.

DEE: *Dorset Evening Echo*.

Halliday: F. E. Halliday, *Thomas Hardy: his life and work*, Bath, 1972.

LTH: F. E. Hardy, *Life of Thomas Hardy*, I vol., London, 1962.

MTH: *Materials for the Study of the Life, Times and Works of Thomas Hardy*, 72 monographs, St. Peter Port, Guernsey, Toucan Press. Various dates from 1962.

Millgate: M. Millgate, *Thomas Hardy: His career as a Novelist*, London, 1971.

Munby: A. J. Munby, MS. Diaries, The Library, Trinity College, Cambridge.

NTHL: F. E. Hardy, typescript " Notes of Thomas Hardy's life . . . (taken down in conversations etc.)". DCM.

ORFW: E. Hardy and F. B. Pinion (eds.), *One Rare Fair Woman: Thomas Hardy's Letters to Florence Henniker, 1893–1922*, London, 1972.

Pinion: F. B. Pinion, *A Hardy Companion*, London, 1968.

Purdy: R. L. Purdy, *Thomas Hardy: A Bibliographical Study*, Oxford, Repr., 1968.

Rutland: W. R. Rutland, *Thomas Hardy: A Study of His Writings and Their Background*, Oxford, 1938; repr. New York, 1962.

SREH: E. Hardy and R. Gittings (eds.), *Some Recollections by Emma Hardy with Some Relevant Poems by Thomas Hardy*, Oxford, 1961; repr. New York, 1973.

Sparks: Photostats of letters of the Sparks family, in the possession of Anna Winchcombe, at Hardy's Cottage (originals in the possession of Ian Kennedy, Queensland).

THN: E. Hardy (ed.), *Thomas Hardy's Notebooks*, London, 1955.

TLS: *Times Literary Supplement*.

Weber: C. J. Weber, *Hardy of Wessex: his Life and Literary Career*, 2nd ed., New York and London, 1965.

# Notes

## 1: YOUNG AND OLD, pp. 1–6

1. Cyril Clemens, 'My Chat with Thomas Hardy'. *Dalhousie Review*, April 1943.
2. R. L. Purdy, 'The Authorship of Hardy's Biography', TLS, 30 December 1960.
3. See, for example, F. R. Southerington, *Hardy's Vision of Man*, 250, for the totally fanciful suggestion that LTH, 214–215, is an elaborate and weird criticism by Hardy of his own father.
4. NTHL, DCM.
5. Some of these errors have been taken literally, with strange results. See Southerington, *Hardy's Vision of Man*, 248, who produces out of a simple mistype a theory that Hardy's mother had illegitimate children.
6. NTHL, 14.
7. Purdy, 266.
8. MTH, No. 6.
9. Weber, 42.
10. Note supplied by R. L. Purdy.
11. Sparks, No. 2, annotation.
12. Mary Hardy to Emma Hardy, 28 January 1881, DCM.
13. DCM.
14. Never R.A., as stated in *Providence and Mr. Hardy*, 196.
15. DCM.
16. MTH, No. 7.
17. Thomas Hardy to Arthur C. Benson, 8 May 1923. Maggs Bros. Catalogue, No. 664, 1938.
18. SREH, xiii.
19. ORFW, 54.
20. LTH, 255.
21. LTH, 253.
22. LTH, 378.

## 2: BOCKHAMPTON AND PUDDLETOWN, pp. 7–19

1. LTH, 215 and 8.
2. J. H. Antell, "Puddletown as Thomas Hardy knew it", DEE, 18 July 1973.
3. MS. accounts of will of Thomas Hardy (obit. 1837), DCM.
4. Census, Stinsford, 1841–71, DCL.
5. Probate of wills, Somerset House.
6. MTH, No. 53.
7. MTH, No. 44.
8. So described in most of the marriages of his children, Somerset House.
9. Elizabeth Hand to Mary Hand, 17 January 1842, Lock Collection, AI, DCL.
10. LTH, 8.
11. Melbury Osmond, Overseers of the Poor, Accounts, 1825–36, DCRO. The accounts for 1822–24 are missing, but the payment seems established.
12. Outdoor relief continued often after the Poor Law Act of 1834.
13. DCM. Hardy's idea that John Hardy had enough money to buy the land seems another instance of claiming a former importance. LTH, 8.
14. Census, Stinsford, 1841, DCL.
15. She was married in 1847 from the Bockhampton house.
16. Lock Collection, AI, DCL.
17. MTH, No. 22.

18. DCM.
19. Stinsford Parish registers, DCRO.
20. LTH, 13–15, 21–23.
21. NTHL, 6.
22. *Alumni Cantabrigiensis*. He later took Holy Orders.
23. THN, 65.
24. Lock Collection, A 10, DCL.
25. NTHL, 6–7.
26. THN, omitted in printed version.
27. LTH, 19.
28. THN, 127.
29. LTH, 15.
30. In DCM, with MS. note by Mary Hardy.
31. Evelyn Hardy, *Thomas Hardy*, 26–32, where Mrs. Martin's influence was first noted and discussed.
32. LTH, 16. Rutland, 25, 131, believes the books were given later, in 1850.
33. LTH, 18. Hardy says he was sent to the Dorchester school "after some postponements", which may refer to the Hertfordshire visit.
34. LTH, 19.
35. Churchwardens' accounts, Stinsford, DCRO.
36. Census, Stinsford, 1851, DCL.
37. NTHL, 8.
38. LTH, 102.
39. LTH, 6, 8, 18, 19.
40. Stinsford parish registers, DCRO. Hardy noted his baptism and his wife's without comment in a list of family information from the Stinsford registers, which he made in 1921 (omitted in the printed THN).
41. Renewal of lease to Thomas, James, and Thomas Hardy junior, DCM.
42. Modern Australian descendants of a John Hardy, claim relationship with Hardy. See *The Thomas Hardy Year Book*, 1971, 70–73.
43. Stinsford and Puddletown parish registers.
44. O. D. Harvey, *Puddletown*, 1968, reprinted 1971. The article "Arcadians in Dorset", *Daily Telegraph*, 30 April 1872, describing the new model village of Puddletown, is sometimes wrongly taken to describe the Puddletown that Hardy knew (as partly by Millgate, 100–102).
45. Puddletown, Population 1821, DCRO.
46. Puddletown, Church Rate Book, 1845–47, DCRO.
47. Preface to *Far From the Madding Crowd*, 1895 edition.
48. Lock Collection, A 1, DCL.
49. DCM.
50. Death certificate, Somerset House.
51. Census, Puddletown, 1851, DCL.
52. Florence Hardy to Alda, Lady Hoare, 30 July 1915, Stourhead Collection, Wiltshire County Archives.
53. Puddletown registers.
54. H. R. Haggard, *Rural England*, 1, 280.
55. *The Times*, 31 July 1846.
56. *The Times*, 4 February 1846.
57. LTH, 21.
58. H. W. Nevinson, *Thomas Hardy*, 13.
59. *Dorset County Chronicle*, bound volume for 1895, DCM.
60. MTH, No. 20.
61. DCM: omitted in the printed THN.
62. Literary Notebook III, f. 65, DCM.
63. Churchwardens' accounts, Stinsford, DCRO.
64. LTH, 420.
65. Mary Hardy to Thomas Hardy, 19 May 1864.
66. MTH, No. 20.
67. LTH, 248.

68. LTH, 15–16.
69. H. J. Moule to Thomas Hardy, 31 December 1883, DCM.
70. N. Flower, "Walks and Talks with Thomas Hardy", *Countryman*, xxxiv, 193.
71. Literary Notebook III, DCM.
72. LTH, 444.


3: DORCHESTER, pp. 20–30

1. Differences between the typescript notes and the *Early Life* (Mrs. Hardy's copy), DCM, obscure the exact time of year.
2. Halliday, 12.
3. LTH, 20.
4. C. J. Weber (ed.), *The Letters of Thomas Hardy*, 30.
5. Newman and Pevsner, *The Buildings of Dorset*, 350–351.
6. LTH, 21.
7. Newman and Pevsner, op. cit., 423 and 448.
8. LTH, 16 and 19.
9. Millgate, 38, for an excellent account of Hardy's self-education.
10. DCM.
11. MTH, No. 8.
12. DCC, 19 January 1928.
13. MTH, Nos. 22 and 44.
14. MTH, No. 22.
15. Not 1845, as said by Halliday, 11, nor were the riots caused by Newman's secession to Rome.
16. LTH, 21.
17. LTH, 126.
18. THN, 82–83.
19. DCRO.
20. Mary Carpenter, *Our Convicts*, I, 224.
21. On the rear fly-leaf of Alphonse Mariette's *Half-Hours of French Translation*, Colby College Library, Waterville, Maine.
22. MTH, No. 22.
23. DCC, 19 January 1928.
24. LTH, 22.
25. DCM.
26. NLTH, 9; LTH, 24.
27. DCM.
28. Unpublished letter, Thomas Hardy to James Murray, 9 July 1903.
29. LTH, 23.
30. Millgate, 38.
31. LTH, 25.
32. DCM.
33. LTH, 25.
34. Stinsford parish registers, DCRO; Census, Stinsford, 1851, DCL.
35. LTH, 206.
36. Stinsford parish registers, DCRO.
37. ibid.
38. Census, Stinsford, 1851, DCL.
39. LTH, 26 and 219.
40. MTH, No. 15.
41. MTH, No. 43.
42. LTH, 23.
43. MTH, No. 44.
44. *The Times*, 3 August 1846.
45. LTH, 23.
46. MS. Diary of Albert Brett of Puddletown, 26 December 1864. DCRO.

47. LTH, 32.
48. DCM. Bailey, 259, prints this dream in full.
49. Christopher Hassall, *Edward Marsh*, 18–23.
50. DCM; LTH, 25.
51. LTH, 27; NTHL, 10.

4: APPRENTICESHIP, pp. 31–43

1. Purdy, 325.
2. LTH, 27–29.
3. D. Jackman, *300 Years of Baptist Worship at Dorchester, 1645–1945.*
4. W. P. Wreden, *Books from the Library of Thomas Hardy*, Nos. 12 and 31.
5. LTH, 33.
6. Purdy, 291–292. The second Mrs. Hardy's idea that this *was* the Clock article is, however, unlikely. Even at the advanced old age, in which he wrote his reminiscences, Hardy surely would not confuse a clock at Dorchester with a pump at Wareham. Part of Hardy's Clock essay probably survives in his first published novel, *Desperate Remedies*, xix, 4.
7. Purdy, 293.
8. Newman and Pevsner, *The Buildings of Dorset*, 178.
9. LTH, 29; MTH, No. 25.
10. MTH, No. 25.
11. DCM, various drafts.
12. Thomas Hardy (Personal) Scrapbook, DCM.
13. Elliott Felkin, "Days with Thomas Hardy", *Encounter*, XVIII (April 1962).
14. LTH, 19.
15. Reprinted in *The Thomas Hardy Year Book 1970*, 84–93.
16. LTH, 28–29.
17. MTH, No. 27.
18. H. G. C. Moule, *Memories of a Vicarage*, 55–57.
19. R. W. M. Lewis, *The Family of Moule.*
20. Harold Orel (ed.), *Thomas Hardy's Personal Writings*, 66.
21. *Standard*, 23 September 1873.
22. TLS, letter from Mary A. Blyth, 13 March 1969.
23. H. C. G. Moule, *Memories of a Vicarage*, 35.
24. DCM.
25. Wreden, op. cit.
26. LTH, 33.
27. LTH, 87.
28. cf. *Before My Friend Arrived.*
29. Bailey, 458.
30. *The Saturday Review*, III, 239–240.
31. *Tempora Mutantur*, A Memorial of the Fordington Times Society, 19–21.
32. Thomas Hardy, "Thomas William Hooper Tolbort", DCC, 14 August 1883.
33. DCM.
34. LTH, 32.
35. LTH, 28.
36. LTH, 215.

5: RELIGION, pp. 44–54

1. LTH, 36.
2. DCM.
3. The 1841 Census was imperfect in many details.
4. G. Kitson Clark, *The Making of Victorian England*, 148.
5. ibid., 151.
6. LTH, 112.

7. Owen Chadwick, *The Victorian Church*, II, 171–174.
8. H. Taine, *Notes on England*, trans. E. Hyams, 118.
9. LTH, 50.
10. Millgate, 37–38.
11. LTH, 34.
12. Information, Pamela Stewart, Assistant Diocesan Archivist.
13. DCM.
14. Owen Chadwick, *The Victorian Church*, II, 76.
15. ibid., 77–78.
16. LTH, 33.
17. Owen Chadwick, *The Victorian Church*, II, 3.
18. ibid., II, 83.
19. *Saturday Review*, XI, 211–212, 2 March 1861.
20. DCM, for all three books.
21. LTH, 29.
22. LTH, 18.
23. DCM.
24. G. Battiscombe, *John Keble*, 104–105.
25. ibid. 69.
26. DCM.
27. LTH, 38.
28. Also the lesson for the evening before his own birthday; but not, as wrongly said, marked for this reason, since he dates it in April.
29. DCM. Oddly called "that vicar" in MTH, No. 32, with other errors.
30. LTH, 7, n. 1.
31. LTH, 22.
32. *Alumni Oxoniensis*.
33. LTH, 29.
34. LTH, 29–30.
35. DCM.
36. LTH, 31.
37. LTH, 390–391.
38. DCM.
39. Letters of H. M. Moule to Thomas Hardy, DCM.
40. C. W. Moule to Thomas Hardy, 11 May 1873, DCM.

## 6: LONDON, pp. 55–65

1. LTH, 443.
2. DCM.
3. Sparks, Nos. 15 and 23.
4. Parish registers, Hemington, Somerset; Beatty, 113.
5. Sparks, Nos. 17 and 18.
6. MTH, No. 40.
7. DCM. Wrongly dated June in MTH, No. 32, which has many such errors.
8. MTH, No. 11.
9. LTH, 36.
10. Prayer book fly-leaf, and MS. list of Hardy's dwelling-places, DCM. He moved for a few weeks to No. 9 in the middle of the following February, *The Christian Year*, annotation, DCM.
11. LTH, 35.
12. Census, Hampstead, sub-district No. 9, 1861.
13. R. Blomfield, *Memoirs of an Architect*, 35.
14. ibid., 36.
15. ibid., 35–36.
16. Frederick Dolman, "An Evening with Thomas Hardy", *Young Man*, VIII (March 1894).
17. Purdy, 296.
18. Census returns, Dorchester, 1851, DCL.

19. LTH, 34.
20. H. Taine, *Notes on England*, trans. Hyams, 37–38.
21. Munby, *Diary*.
22. LTH, 41.
23. Munby, *Diary*.
24. Henry Mayhew, *London Labour and the London Poor*, vol. iv, ed. P. Quennell.
25. Munby, *Diary*.
26. Munby, *Diary*.
27. *Rogue's Progress: An Autobiography of 'Lord Chief Baron' Nicholson* (rep. 1965), 327-329.
28. Munby, *Diary*, vol. 23, ff. 28–29.
29. Mayhew, op. cit., 99.
30. Munby, *Diary*, vol. 26, ff. 42–49 and 93–94.
31. Munby, *Diary*.
32. LTH, 45.
33. LTH, 43–44.
34. *The Oxford Companion to the Theatre.*
35. LTH, 35 and 38.
36. Munby, *Diary*.
37. DCM.
38. LTH, 38 and 42.
39. See p. 12.
40. F. P. B. Martin, *A Memoir on the Equinoctial Storms of March–April 1850*, 3.
41. ibid., 91.
42. ibid., 2.
43. ibid., 4.
44. Information, Royal Geographical Society; P.O. Directory, 1860.
45. LTH, 41; Census, Stinsford, 1851; Will of F. P. B. Martin, Somerset House.
46. LTH, 41.
47. See above, p. 12.
48. LTH, 256.
49. Will of F. P. B. Martin.
50. Personal information, John Hardy Antell.
51. Hardy to Mary Hardy, 19 August 1862. I owe this unprinted passage to a note from R. L. Purdy.
52. Munby, *Diary*, vol. 14, ff. 94.
53. Sparks, No. 2, annotation.
54. DCM.
55. NTH, 54–55.
56. Middle Temple records.
57. LTH, 38.
58. Beatty, 1.
59. Purdy, 293.
60. Halliday, 22.
61. He was still at Kilburn on 18 February. Prayer book annotation. DCM.
62. Prayer book, DCM.
63. Census returns, St. Stephen's, 1861.
64. R.I.B.A., Nominations for Fellowships, 1876, f. 38.
65. J. Kingsgate, "*Tess* and Thomas Hardy, New Facts about His Life in London". *Graphic*, cxii, 5 September 1925, 377.

7: SELF-HELP, pp. 66–75

1. Munby, *Diary*, vol. 23, ff. 141–142.
2. LTH, 37–38.
3. Beatty, 159–160.
4. DCM.
5. DCM.

6. Munby, *Diary*.
7. LTH, 37.
8. DCM.
9. Newman and Pevsner, *The Buildings of Dorset*, 131.
10. A. P. Webb, *A Bibliography of the Works of Thomas Hardy*, 41; Purdy, 159.
11. Beatty, 133.
12. Rutland, 35.
13. DCM.
14. Moule to Hardy, 2 March 1863; *Saturday Review*, 21 February and 7 March 1863.
15. Moule to Hardy, 2 July 1863, DCM.
16. DCM.
17. LTH, 48.
18. Literary Notebook I, DCM.
19. LTH, 345.
20. Moule to Hardy, 21 February 1864, DCM.
21. LTH, 40.
22. C. Holland, *Thomas Hardy*, 54, Rutland, 26, Beatty, 16; unconvincingly discussed in *The Thomas Hardy Year Book, 1972–1973*, 42–43.
23. LTH, 257. Beatty, 16, while accepting the Radcliffe Chapel legend, shows surprise at no evidence of a visit in Hardy's notebook.
24. Marlborough College Register.
25. Deacon and Coleman, *Providence and Mr. Hardy*, quotation from letter by H. G. C. Moule, 95.
26. D. A. Winstanley, *Later Victorian Cambridge*, 210 and 214.
27. Moule to Hardy (? June 1867), DCM.
28. See p. 37.
29. DCM.
30. LTH, 40.
31. MS. Diary of Arthur Brett, DCRO.
32. LTH, 56.
33. Mary Hardy to Thomas Hardy (MS. fragment), 19 May 1864, DCM.
34. *Descriptive Catalogue of the Grolier Club Centenary Exhibition of the Works of Thomas Hardy* (1940), No. 10.
35. DCM.
36. Moule to Hardy, 21 February 1864, DCM.
37. Goldwin Smith, *Does the Bible Sanction Slavery?*
38. Munby, *Diary*, vol. 24, ff. 85–96.
39. Christopher Hibbert, *Garibaldi and his Enemies*, 341.
40. ibid., 342.
41. Prayer book, MS. annotation, DCM.
42. MTH, No. 32, which states, on no evidence, that he was suffering from "nervous exhaustion".
43. Nairn and Pevsner, *The Buildings of England: Sussex*, 435.
44. Munby, *Diary*, vol. 23, ff. 40–43.
45. Beatty, 162.
46. ibid., 69.
47. D. Drew Cox, "The Poet and the Architect", *Agenda* (Spring–Summer, 1972), 57.

## 8 POETRY, pp. 76–87

1. DCM. Partly described by Evelyn Hardy, "Hardy and the Phrenologist", *John O'London's Weekly*, LXIII (26 February 1954).
2. Rutland, 111.
3. Information from the present tenant.
4. Orel, 168.
5. DCM, where poems of this type are ticked in the Index.
6. DCM.

7. By Weber, 52, who cites no evidence, and E. Hardy, 76, who wrongly dates this volume as being published in 1867.
8. LTH, 53.
9. Pinion, 215–217.
10. Rutland, 15, n. 1.
11. DCM.
12. Purdy, 297.
13. Pinion, 213.
14. Quoted Weber, 50, from "Barrie Reviews Hardy", *The Literary Digest* (2 February 1929), 22.
15. ORFW, 14.
16. Grolier, No. 4.
17. Partly described by Phyllis Bartlett, 'Hardy's Shelley', *Keats–Shelley Journal*, IV, (Winter 1955), who however confuses this volume with the two described by Barrie.
18. Rutland, 15.
19. Rutland, 13.
20. LTH, 49.
21. David Garnett (ed.), *Letters of T. E. Lawrence*, 193.
22. Pinion, 121–122.
23. Rutland, 71.
24. *Saturday Review*, xvi, 562–563, 24 October 1863.
25. LTH, 47.
26. One must, I think, accept Hardy's statement that his revision to his own early poems consisted only of "the mere change of a few words or the rewriting of a line or two", LTH, 47. The few available MSS. seem to bear this out.
27. DCM.
28. *Wessex Poems*, preface.
29. DCM. This marking and others in the Coleridge were first noted by E. Hardy, 75–76.
30. DCM.
31. Hardy, perhaps mischievously, gives her the christian name, Amelia, of one of his two spinster aunts (Amelia and Sarah Sparks) to whose cottage in Dorchester he went for his schoolboy lunches.
32. Originally, "laughter" for "gladness" made this even more obscure.
33. See Rutland, 266, who says it "suggests a club".
34. 1865 edition, DCM. It occurs in *The Hind and the Panther*.
35. Dated 1867 and "W.P.V." (by Hardy in the Wessex Edition). Hardy left this address in July of that year.
36. The MS. of *Wessex Poems*.

## 9: LOSS OF FAITH, pp. 88–99

1. Bailey, 611.
2. LTH, 50.
3. LTH, 330.
4. LTH, 264.
5. LTH, 51–52.
6. LTH, 50.
7. Prayer book, DCM.
8. *The Christian Year*, DCM.
9. LTH, 39 and 52.
10. DCM; LTH, 370.
11. Lock Collection, DCL.
12. Munby, *Diary*, 22 November 1865.
13. LTH, 272.
14. *At a Bridal*; the original of line 14, afterwards altered.
15. V. H. Collins, *Talks with Thomas Hardy . . . 1920–1922*, 23.
16. King's College, London, Evening Classes, Winter Session, 1865–6. King's College Archives.

17. Thomas Hardy to the Principal, King's College, 19 June 1926, King's College, London, Library.
18. Colby College Library, Waterville, Maine.
19. Purdy, 297.
20. *The Christian Year*, DCM; Beatty, 11–12.
21. LTH, 55.
22. Bailey, 199; Purdy, 143.
23. *Memoirs of Mark Pattison*, introduction by Jo Manton, xix.

## 10: FIRST NOVEL, pp. 100–110

1. Wreden, No. 19.
2. 9th Baron Digby of Sherborne to Mary Hardy, 27 May 1867; Lock Collection, B10, and Mary Hardy's sketch book, Lock Collection, H, DCL.
3. *The Times*, weather records for Weymouth, August–October 1867. The exceptionally fine hot summer, claimed by the authors of *Providence and Mr. Hardy*, and in numerous pamphlets by Lois Deacon, is a pure fiction, and not based on any records at all. See my "Thomas Hardy and Tryphena Sparks", TLS, 27 April 1973.
4. John Hardy Antell, "Puddletown as Thomas Hardy Knew It", DEE, 18 July 1973.
5. LTH, 56.
6. Actually current for some thirty years before, though not in Hardy's copy of J. R. M'Culloch, *Principles of Political Economy* (1825).
7. LTH, 59; Purdy, 275.
8. Best discussed by Rutland, 111–133.
9. As suggested by Evelyn Hardy, 88.
10. DCM.
11. LTH, 48.
12. 'Thomas Hardy and a Royal Occasion', *The Times*, 21 November 1963.
13. George Brereton Sharpe to Thomas Hardy, 21 January 1868, Lock Collection, B 1 and 2, DCL.
14. Sparks, No. 23.
15. LTH, 330.
16. DCM, where Hardy's copy is the 1867 edition.
17. LTH, 61.
18. NTH, 28, where it is mistranscribed.
19. LTH, 62.
20. LTH, 57–58.
21. S. Nowell-Smith (ed.), *Letters to Macmillan*, 129–130.
22. Charles Morgan, *The House of Macmillan*, 91.
23. LTH, 59.
24. Purdy, 275.
25. LTH, 61–63.
26. Purdy, 329.
27. See p. 72.
28. Education: Reports, Commissioners, 1868/9, xx. British Museum.
29. O. D. Harvey, *Puddletown (Thomas Hardy's Weatherbury)*, 27–28.
30. Puddletown School (Girls) Log-book, entries for April and August 1867.
31. F. G. Walcott, *The Origins of Culture and Anarchy*, 95–96.
32. Education: Reports, Commissioners, 1867, xxii.
33. As argued by F. R. Southerington, *Hardy's Vision of Man*, 261.
34. Education: Reports, Commissioners, 1868/9, xx.
35. Personal information, Miss Catherine Shepherd, Mrs. Hawkins's granddaughter.
36. Who only taught at "National" schools; see the announcement of Mary Hardy's death, *Dorset County Chronicle*.
37. Sparks, No. 2.
38. *Dorset County Chronicle*, 10 December 1868.
39. Plymouth Day Schools (Girls) Log-book, f. 292, Plymouth City Library.

40. Sparks, No. 2.
41. ibid., and census returns, Portesham, 1871, DCL.
42. Census returns, Portesham, 1871.
43. LTH, 57–58.
44. DCM.
45. Quoted Purdy, 242, with photograph of MS. on the opposite page.

## 11: TRYPHENA AND THE SPARKSES, pp. 111–125

1. See p. 90.
2. See particularly, *Providence and Mr. Hardy*.
3. Sparks, No. 9.
4. He is described as journeyman on his wife's death certificate.
5. Sparks, No. 10.
6. Death certificate, Somerset House.
7. Sparks, No. 18.
8. P.O. Directories.
9. Sparks, No. 2, annotation.
10. The poem *Unrealized* from *Time's Laughingstocks*.
11. Sparks, No. 2, annotation.
12. Sparks No. 1. Annotated much later as being to her brother James in London, it is clearly, from internal evidence, to Nathaniel in Somerset.
13. Entry Lists, College of Sarum St. Michael, Salisbury.
14. Certificates of Marriage and Birth, Somerset House.
15. Archives, College of Sarum St. Michael, Salisbury.
16. W. M. Payne, *Dial*, XXII, 16 May 1897.
17. Sparks, No. 2, annotation by Nathaniel Sparks junior; mistranscribed in *Dorset: A County Magazine*.
18. Earlier dates, as proposed in *Providence and Mr. Hardy*, are purely fictitious, and often produced by the falsification of documents. See my "Thomas Hardy and Tryphena Sparks", TLS, 28 April 1973.
19. Census returns, Stinsford, 1871.
20. Permissions for Faculties, Diocese of Salisbury, Diocesan Record Office, Salisbury.
21. Beatty (thesis), Appendix 1, 120.
22. Reproduced Beatty, 27.
23. Pinion, 369.
24. LTH, 65.
25. MS. table of places and dates, I. C. Willis's copy of LTH, DCM.
26. DCL.
27. With possibly the draft of a poem afterwards revised, *At a Seaside Town in 1869*, and *In the Vaulted Way* (dated in MS. 1870).
28. NTH, 33–34.
29. Manchester College, Oxford, MS.
30. Sparks, No. 2.
31. Irene Cooper Willis, MS., Colby College.
32. MTH, No. 3.
33. See p. 35.
34. *Dorset County Chronicle*, 28 October 1869.
35. ibid., March 1868.
36. Thomas J. Graham, *Modern Domestic Medicine*, 657–658 and 660.
37. Marriage certificate, Somerset House.
38. P.O. Directories, confirmed by birth certificates, 1870.
39. Sparks, No. 13.
40. DCM.
41. F. B. Pinion, *Notes and Queries*, November 1972, 430–431.
42. Census, Athelhampton 1871, DCL.
43. Reports of British and Foreign School Society, 1870 and 1871.
44. *Dorset County Chronicle*, 10 July 1866.

45. Report of the British and Foreign School Society, 1872, which tabulates the progress of students in the previous two years. The authors of *Providence and Mr. Hardy*, consulting the wrong report, give a totally inaccurate account of her entry.
46. Quoted in M. Sturt, *The Education of the People*.
47. Personal information, John Hardy Antell.
48. Archives, Stockwell College of Education.
49. LTH, 64.
50. DCM.
51. Chapter 1, verses 6, 7, and 18; chapter 2, verse 10.
52. LTH, 64.
53. Census, Stinsford, 1871. DCL.
54. Mary Hardy's sketch book, Lock Collection, H, DCL; and Archives, College of Sarum St. Michael, Salisbury.
55. LTH, 65.
56. LTH, 84.
57. Millgate, 381.
58. Personal information, Mary A. Blyth, Horace Moule's grand-niece.
59. Census, Fordington, 1871, DCL.
60. Literary Notebook IV, f. 31, DCM.
61. LTH, 64.
62. Beatty, 27.

## 12: EMMA AND THE GIFFORDS, pp. 126–37

1. Bishop's transcripts, St. Paul's parish, Bristol Archives Office.
2. SREH, 17. His late matriculation, aged 34 (*Alumni Oxoniensis*) may indicate failure in some previous profession.
3. Matthews Bristol Directories and Bristol 1812 Poll Book, Bristol Central Library.
4. SREH, 1, 14, 15, 18.
5. SREH, 22.
6. Probate of Wills, Somerset House.
7. SREH, 16–17.
8. Loose fragment of family memoirs by Emma Hardy, DCM.
9. Bristol Archives Office and Bristol Central Library.
10. *Felix Farley's Bristol Journal*, 7 April 1832, Bristol Central Library.
11. Bailey, 388, oddly confuses Emma herself with the spectre, applying the adjective "mirthless" in stanza 4 to her. Apart from the fact that this reading makes nonsense of the whole poem, the original word was "shadowless", which suggests a supernatural figure.
12. Irene Cooper Willis, MS. covering note to Selection of Letters to Emma Hardy, DCM.
13. "Some Notes on the Hardys", MS. by I. C. Willis, c. 1937, DCM.
14. DCM.
15. MS. Note to Selection of Letters to Emma Hardy, DCM.
16. Purdy, 11.
17. Emma Hardy's Diary, DCM.
18. Helen Catherine Holder to Emma Hardy, 28 November 1882, DCM.
19. Archives, Warneford Hospital.
20. Death certificate, Somerset House.
21. *Dictionary of National Biography*.
22. Probate of Wills, Somerset House.
23. *Felix Farley's Bristol Journal*, 1830, Bristol Central Library.
24. Gifford family papers.
25. I owe this suggestion to Dr. Ida Macalpine.
26. *The Times* index of bankrupts, 1860–80, does not show his name.
27. Death certificate, Somerset House.
28. MS. annotation, letter of Walter Gifford to Emma Hardy, DCM.
29. Hardy to Manager, Accident Dept., The London Assurance, draft, DCM.

30. Death certificate, Somerset House.
31. Lilian Gifford to Thomas Hardy, 27 November 1913, DCM.
32. Gifford family information.
33. ORFW, 155.
34. As said by Bailey, 387, who has not observed that Kate Gifford's letter of 25 November is simply a sympathetic reply to Hardy's of 23 November, repeating his words.
35. Archives, Warneford Hospital.
36. MS. Note to Selection of Letters to Emma Hardy, DCM.
37. Henry Gifford, "Thomas Hardy and Emma", *Essays and Studies 1966*.
38. ibid., 113. Letter conjecturally dated in 1911.
39. ibid., 115.
40. Letter from C. W. Moule to Emma Hardy, 1911, DCM.
41. SREH, 50, 51.
42. MTH, Nos. 5 and 17. She also wrote to the local press advocating bloomers, and sometimes wore a pair herself, MTH, No. 22.
43. Carl J. Weber, *Dearest Emmie*, 45.
44. MTH, No. 20.
45. A. Pretor to Emma Hardy, 1898, DCM.
46. Letter by Gordon Gifford, TLS, 1 January 1944.
47. ORFW, Preface 2.
48. ORFW, 29.
49. A. P. Watt to Emma Hardy, 10 January 1894, DCM.
50. Irene Cooper Willis, "Some Notes", DCM.
51. As thought by Millgate, 119.
52. SREH, 53.
53. *The Times*, weather reports, 1870.
54. SREH, 50.
55. Preface to new edition of *A Pair of Blue Eyes*, March 1895.
56. LTH, 74-75.
57. SREH, 50.
58. SREH, 7; Henry Gifford, op. cit., 114.
59. In his corrections to her own manuscript account, SREH, 52.
60. Census returns, Stinsford, 1871.
61. MS. curriculum vitae of E. H. Gifford in the possession of Henry Gifford.
62. SREH, 18-19.
63. Barbara Stephen, *Emily Davies and Girton College*, chapter viii.
64. SREH, 16, 20.

## 13: DESPERATE REMEDIES, pp. 138-48

1. LTH, 75.
2. Beatty, 27-29.
3. LTH, 75.
4. See p. 100.
5. S. M. Ellis, "Thomas Hardy: Some Personal Recollections", *Fortnightly Review*, N.S., cxxii (1928), 395.
6. W. L. Phelps, *Autobiography with Letters*, 391, 394.
7. Charles Morgan, *The House of Macmillan*, 93-94.
8. Phyllis Bartlett, "Hardy's Shelley", *Keats-Shelley Journal* IV (Winter 1955), 18.
9. Pinion, 165.
10. Beatty (thesis), Appendix 1. "Manston", the villain's surname, is a village nearby.
11. *Desperate Remedies*, 276-277, not 95-96, as said by Purdy, 98.
12. Charles Morgan, *The House of Macmillan*, 93-94.
13. Millgate, 32.
14. The cutting of an interview, in which this remark appears, is annotated by Hardy "(largely faked)". DCM.
15. Edmund Gosse, "Thomas Hardy's Lost Novel", *Sunday Times*, 22 January 1928.
16. Thomas Hardy, Obituary of Mary Hardy, DCC.

17. Purdy, 329.
18. LTH, 76.
19. LTH, 76.
20. Birth certificates, Somerset House.
21. NTH, 29.
22. LTH, 78.
23. Still less that Moule met her, as invented in *Providence and Mr. Hardy*.
24. About 9 August was the usual date. Archives, Stockwell College.
25. SREH, 56, n. 1.
26. LTH, 155–157.
27. *The Times*, 5 July and 4 August 1870.
28. Moule to Hardy, undated note, DCM.
29. Prayer book, DCM.
30. Wreden, No. 153.
31. DCM.
32. NTH, 31.
33. NTH, 32, where it is mistranscribed.
34. Bible, DCM. MTH, No. 32 quotes more than he actually marked.
35. NTH, 32, where it is mistranscribed.
36. LTH, 78.
37. LTH, 83.
38. Report of the British and Foreign School Society, 1872.
39. LTH, 83.
40. Purdy, 4–5. Hardy afterwards claimed (LTH, 83) that Tinsley had altered his terms for the worse; this seems untrue.
41. LTH, 84.
42. Sparks, No. 2.
43. Thomas Hardy to Miss Thomson, 22 February 1898(?). Christie's Sale Catalogue, 12 July 1972.
44. Bible, DCM, Isaiah, xiv, 16, wrongly transcribed verse 23 in MTH, No. 32.
45. NTH, 33.
46. LTH, 84.
47. Cyril Clemens, "My Chat with Thomas Hardy", *Dalhousie Review*, April 1943, 90.

## 14: UNDER THE GREENWOOD TREE, pp. 149–59

1. The reviewer had decided to use this pronoun as a matter of convenience.
2. LTH, 84.
3. Millgate, 36.
4. DCM.
5. LTH, 84.
6. SREH, 56, n. 1.
7. Beatty, 28–29.
8. LTH, 79.
9. LTH, 85.
10. Beatty, 21 and 33.
11. Beatty, 42, 56, 86.
12. Millgate, 45–48.
13. The paste-in of the MS. (DCM) seems to show this, rather than that he was intended first as a publican in *Under the Greenwood Tree*, as thought by Millgate, 53.
14. S. M. Ellis, "Thomas Hardy: Some Personal Recollections", *Fortnightly Review*, N.S., cxiii (1928), 397.
15. Triffy was her home name.
16. Morgan, op. cit., 95–97.
17. Weber, 65.
18. LTH, 59.
19. Purdy, 11.

20. LTH, 86.
21. Sparks, No. 2, annotation.
22. Her own daughter's evidence on this is full of contradiction; but its most coherent part is positive that Tryphena's eventual husband saw the ring. MTH, No. 3.
23. Personal information, John Hardy Antell.
24. Sparks, No. 15, annotation.
25. Purdy, 332.
26. Beatty, 2.
27. Moule to Hardy, 17 April 1872, DCM.
28. LTH, 88; Purdy, 332.
29. Purdy, 332.
30. Purdy, 332–333.
31. LTH, 89–90.
32. DCM, inscribed Thomas Hardy 1873.

## 15: A PAIR OF BLUE EYES, pp. 160–70

1. TLS, 13 March 1969, letter from Mary A. Blyth.
2. Administrations, Somerset House.
3. SREH, 57.
4. SREH, 16.
5. LTH, 91.
6. Not relations, as wrongly noted in SREH, 43, note 2.
7. DCM.
8. Florence Dugdale to Edward Clodd, 3 July 1913, Brotherton Library Collection, Leeds.
9. Bailey, 407–408.
10. V. H. Collins, *Talks with Thomas Hardy*, 26.
11. Bailey, 350, but who then, contradicting Hardy's own identification, thinks she was leaning on a nearby signpost, thus destroying the point of the whole poem.
12. Bailey, 351, believes this to be a reference "no doubt, to Emma's mental eccentricities", but this itself seems very doubtful.
13. MTH, No. 31.
14. Emma Hardy to Rebekah Owen, 24 April 1899, Colby College Library, quoted Bailey, 23.
15. NTH, 38.
16. NTH, 39.
17. Purdy, 333.
18. Bible, DCM.
19. Millgate, 75.
20. S. M. Ellis, op. cit.
21. MTH, 31–32.
22. Census, Stinsford, 1851, DCL, where the deafness is recorded.
23. Millgate, 62.
24. H. C. G. Moule, *Memories of a Vicarage*, 35.
25. Personal information, Mary A. Blyth.
26. Presumably copied by Hardy from one of his numerous volumes of general information; it is, in fact, a popular fallacy. See *Nouvelle Biographie Générale*, tome 39, Paris, 1862.
27. Millgate, 62.
28. LTH, 32.
29. LTH, 73.
30. Millgate, 67.
31. Moule to Hardy, May (?) 1873, DCM.
32. Hardy actually took the *height* from Beeny, but most of its other characteristics from Pentargan Cliff a little further south, as convincingly shown by Denys Kay-Robinson, *Hardy's Wessex Re-appraised*, 249–250.

## 16: FAR FROM THE MADDING CROWD, pp. 171–78

1. Purdy, 333.
2. ibid., 7.
3. ibid., 12.
4. ibid., 336–337.
5. LTH, 96.
6. Sparks No. 10 and annotation.
7. NTH, 39; not South Hill, as wrongly transcribed.
8. NTH, 42.
9. NTH, 40.
10. Accepted by Hardy's own family as the original of Bathsheba. See Kate Hardy's Diary, 24 July 1930, Lock Collection, H. 10, DCL.
11. Granvile D. Hill to Catherine Hawkins, 12 October 1865.
12. Catherine Hawkins to Miss Hill, 23 January 1866.
13. Sparks, No. 19, annotation.
14. Sparks, No. 18.
15. The death of William Keats, tranter, by which he dates it, had occurred two years earlier, in August 1870. MTH, No. 51.
16. J. I. M. Stewart, *Thomas Hardy*, 89–90.
17. NTH, 38.
18. NTH, 42.
19. John Hutton to Thomas Hardy, DCM.
20. As thought by Millgate.
21. John Hutton to Thomas Hardy, 29 April 1873, DCM.
22. Buttery Accounts, Queens' College, Cambridge University Library.
23. TLS, 27 January 1969 *et seq.*
24. DCM.
25. LTH, 93.
26. LTH, 93–94.
27. SREH, 60.
28. *Midnight on Beechen*, 187–, i.e. Beechen Cliff, just south of Bath.
29. Purdy, 16.

## 17: MOULE, pp. 179–86

1. *Cambridge Chronicle*, 27 September 1873.
2. DCM.
3. Not against the description of Hallam, as said by Evelyn Hardy, TLS, 29 January 1969.
4. By Bailey, 33, n. 8.
5. The two entries of "Moule" in Hardy's Bible (DCM) seem to refer to texts used by the Reverend Henry Moule.
6. NTH, omitted in printed text.
7. I owe all that follows on this topic to the unpublished notes of R. L. Purdy, taken down in 1933 in conversations with Florence Hardy at Max Gate.
8. See chapter 20.
9. DCM.
10. Bailey, 57.
11. Plymouth Day School's (Girls) Log-book, f. 294.
12. DCM.
13. Manuscript Room, Cambridge University Library.
14. As well argued by Millgate, 84–85, and 372, n. 15.
15. Information and note, R. L. Purdy.
16. See p. 15.
17. As put forward in *Providence and Mr. Hardy*, 192–193.

18. Bailey, 279, connects this with a boy, not consulting the MS.
19. MS., *Satires of Circumstance*, DCM.
20. See Appendix.

## 18: SUCCESS AND MARRIAGE, pp. 187–97

1. LTH, 100.
2. Not 1864, as said by Bailey, 282, who anyway confuses this with Stephen's resignation of his tutorship in 1862.
3. Noel Annan, *Leslie Stephen*, 66n.
4. LTH, 96.
5. NTH, 43, 44.
6. NTH, 44, where "fringe" is mistranscribed as "finger".
7. MTH, No. 20.
8. Cancelled draft pages, DCM.
9. Cancelled draft pages, DCM.
10. Purdy, 338.
11. Purdy, 15.
12. Purdy, 337; Millgate, 79–94, for a good account of Stephen's influence.
13. Millgate, 372, n. 11.
14. LTH, 99.
15. See p. 183.
16. C. J. Weber, 'Ainsworth and Thomas Hardy', *Review of English Studies*, XVII (April 1941), 193–200.
17. Hardy's copy of a book called *Manly Exercises* is inscribed "Thomas and Henry Hardy, Professors of Boxing", DCM.
18. Weber, 94.
19. LTH, 98.
20. NTH, 48.
21. SREH, 53.
22. The date is conjectural, but the London weather then corresponds with Hardy's description in F. W. Maitland, *Life and Letters of Leslie Stephen*.
23. F. W. Maitland, *Life and Letters of Leslie Stephen*, 273.
24. Viola Meynell (ed.), *The Best of Friends: Further Letters to Sydney Carlyle Cockerell*.
25. LTH, 98, 100.
26. LTH, 97.
27. Purdy, 337.
28. LTH, 99.
29. *The Opportunity: For H.P.*
30. Emma Hardy's Diary, DCM.
31. SREH, 60.
32. Thomas Hardy to Henry Hardy, 18 September 1874, DCM.
33. Emma Hardy's Diary, DCM, where the entry, though heavily crossed out, seems to be decipherable as this address.

## 19: ETHELBERTA, pp. 198–212

1. Emma Hardy's Diary, ff. 1–3, DCM.
2. ibid., f. 5, DCM.
3. ibid., ff. 20–21, DCM.
4. ibid., ff. 38–41, DCM.
5. ibid., f. 52, DCM.
6. ibid., f. 71, DCM.
7. *Saturday Review*, 16 January 1892.
8. Merryn Williams, *Thomas Hardy and Rural England*, 135.
9. Purdy, 339.
10. John Hutton to Hardy, 23 December 1874, DCM.

11. Purdy, 335.
12. Emma Hardy's Diary, attached to end-paper, DCM.
13. John Hutton to Hardy, 23 December 1874, DCM.
14. LTH, 101–102.
15. Kate Hardy's Diary, 12 January 1928, Lock Collection, N. 10, DCL.
16. Kate Hardy's Diary.
17. MTH, No. 20.
18. Purdy, 19.
19. LTH, 105–106.
20. LTH, 76.
21. He uses the expression twice. See Orel, 58 and 127.
22. Gordon S. Haight, *George Eliot*, 302.
23. LTH, 146. Hardy advocated "This as a matter of *policy*, without which no religion succeeds in making way".
24. Henry Gifford, "Thomas Hardy and Emma", *Essays and Studies 1966*, 113–114.
25. Baptisms, Melbury Osmond, DCRO.
26. LTH, 98.
27. Jo Manton, *Sister Dora*, 162, n. 31.
28. Sparks, No. 13.
29. Emma Hardy's Diary, ff. 6 and 9, DCM.
30. *The Times*, 22 March 1875.
31. Emma Hardy's Diary, ff. 89–92, DCM.
32. MS. version.
33. SREH, 90–91.
34. *Saturday Review*, 6 May 1876.
35. Sparks, No. 3.
36. Sparks, No. 23.
37. F. W. Maitland, *Life and Letters of Leslie Stephen*, 276.
38. LTH, 109.
39. Emma Hardy's Diary, DCM.
40. LTH, 111.
41. LTH, 106.
42. Emma Hardy's Diary, DCM.
43. C. J. Weber, *Hardy's Love Poems*, 43.

## 20: OLD AND YOUNG, pp. 213–22

1. ORFW, 57 and 82.
2. Guide to Turnworth Church.
3. SREH, 60–61.
4. Emma Hardy's Diary, DCM.
5. DCM.
6. Rutland, 85.
7. LTH, 176.
8. LTH, 207–208.
9. LTH, 214; information, Clare Gittings.
10. LTH, 215.
11. LTH, 217.
12. LTH, 219.
13. LTH, 220.
14. LTH, 230.
15. Chaddleworth parish registers, Berkshire County Archives.
16. Millgate, 267.
17. Personal information, Miss Mary Stickland. See also J. Henry Harper, *The House of Harper*.
18. A. Compton-Rickett, *I Look Back: Memories of Fifty Years*, 176–186.
19. MTH, No. 20.

20. Parish Records, Melbury Osmond, DCRO.
21. Millgate, 401, n. 11.
22. E. Royston Pike, *Human Documents of the Victorian Golden Age*, 217.
23. LTH, 224.
24. Sparks, Nos. 18, 19, 20.
25. Well described by Millgate, 299–303.
26. LTH, 232.
27. ORFW, 8, for an instance of such rudeness.
28. Millgate, 303.
29. Churchwardens' Accounts, Chaddleworth, Berkshire County Archives.
30. LTH.
31. LTH, 272–273.
32. Baptisms, All Saints, Dorchester, and P.O. Directory, Dorset, 1867, DCRO.
33. Census, Athelhampton, 1871, DCL.
34. Sparks, No. 4.
35. LTH, 235.
36. LTH, 236–237.
37. Purdy, 91.
38. In the restoration, August 1893–May 1894, of West Knighton Church, as first pointed out by Beatty, 30–34.
39. ORFW, 28.
40. ORFW, 5 and 23.
41. Letter by Gordon Gifford, TLS, 1 January 1944.
42. See chapter 12.
43. Hardy to Edward Clodd, 13 December 1912, British Museum, quoted Bailey, 25.
44. LTH, 371.
45. LTH, 430.
46. Personal information, Mrs. Dubben of Sydling.
47. Kate Hardy's Diary, Lock Collection, DCL.
48. Personal information, Miss Mary Stickland.
49. MTH, No. 34.
50. Kate Hardy's Diary, Lock Collection, DCL.

## APPENDIX: HARDY AND TRYPHENA SPARKS, pp. 223–29

1. F. R. Southerington, *Hardy's Vision of Man*, opposite page 136.
2. "Thomas Hardy", an unpublished signed typescript, Colby College Library.
3. MTH, No. 3.
4. *Providence and Mr. Hardy*, 22.
5. MTH, No. 71.
6. Southerington, op. cit., 262.
7. *Providence and Mr. Hardy*, 75 and 31.
8. ibid., 39.
9. ibid., 189.
10. Sparks, No. 16.
11. Sparks, No. 17.
12. Sparks, No. 20.
13. Sparks, No. 23.

# List of Sources

**A. MANUSCRIPT**

Antell, G. S. Family papers.
Antell, J. H. Family papers.
Berkshire County Record Office. Berkshire parish registers, etc.
Bristol Record Office. Parish registers, Bishops' transcripts, etc.
Cambridge University Library. Buttery accounts, Queens' College. Diaries of H. C. G. Moule.
College of Sarum St. Michael, Salisbury. Archives.
Dorset County Library. Lock Collection. Letters, etc.
Dorset County Museum. Hardy Collection. Letters, etc.
Dorset County Record Office. Dorset parish registers, etc.
Gifford, Henry. Gifford family papers.
Hardy's Cottage, Higher Bockhampton. Photostats of Sparks family letters.
Hawkins, the Misses. Letters of Catherine Hawkins.
Hemington, Somerset. Parish registers.
King's College, London. Archives.
Murray, K. M. E. Unpublished letters of Thomas Hardy to James Murray.
Plymouth (City of) Public Libraries. Log Books 1872–77, Plymouth Public Free School (for Girls), Cobourg Street, Plymouth.
Probate of Wills, Somerset House.
Public Record Office. Census Returns, 1841–71.
Puddletown School. Log Books.
Registers of Births, Marriages, Deaths. General Registry.
Royal Institute of British Architects. Archives.
Salisbury Diocesan Record Office. Faculties, Bishops' transcripts.
Stockwell College of Education. Archives.
Trinity College, Cambridge, Library. Diaries of A. J. Munby.
Warneford Hospital, Oxford. Case Books.

**B. TYPESCRIPT**

Beatty, C. J. P., "The Part Played by Architecture in the Life and Work of Thomas Hardy, with Particular Reference to the Novels". Unpublished dissertation, University of London (External), 1964.
Hardy, F. E., "Notes of Thomas Hardy's Life . . . (taken down in conversations, etc.)". Dorset County Museum. Hardy Collection.

**C. PUBLISHED**

*Alumni Cantabrigienses.*
*Alumni Oxoniensis.*
Annan, Noel, *Leslie Stephen*, London, 1951.
Anon., *Thomas Hardy from Behind*, Dorchester, 1965.
Antell, John H., "Puddletown as Thomas Hardy Knew It", *Dorset Evening Echo*, 18 July 1973.
Bailey, J. O., *The Poetry of Thomas Hardy: A Handbook and Commentary*, Chapel Hill, 1970.
Barnard, H. C., *A Short History of English Education, 1760–1944*, London, 1947.
Bartlett, Phyllis, "Hardy's Shelley", *Keats–Shelley Journal*, IV, 15–29.
Battiscombe, G., *John Keble*, London, 1963.
Beatty, C. J. P. (ed.), *The Architectural Notebook of Thomas Hardy*, Dorchester, 1966.
Bevington, M. M., *The Saturday Review. 1855–68*, Cambridge, 1941.
Blomfield, Sir Reginald, *Memoirs of an Architect*, London, 1932.
Bristol City Library, *Poll Books, Directories*, etc.

Brooks, Jean R., *Thomas Hardy: The Poetic Structure*, London, 1971.

Brown, Douglas, *Thomas Hardy*, London, 1961.

Chadwick, Owen, *The Victorian Church*, 2 vols., London, 1970.

Clark, G. S. R. Kitson, *The Making of Victorian England*, Oxford, 1960.

Clemens, Cyril, "My Chat with Thomas Hardy", *Dalhousie Review*, April 1943.

Colby Library Quarterly, *A Descriptive Catalogue . . . of the Works of Thomas Hardy*, Waterville, Maine, 1940.

Collins, V. H., *Talks with Thomas Hardy*, New York, 1928.

Compton-Rickett, A., *I Look Back: Memories of Fifty Years*, London, 1933.

Cox, D. Drew, "The Poet and Architect", *Agenda*, Spring–Summer 1972.

Cox, J. S. (gen. ed.), *Materials . . . for a Life of Thomas Hardy*, 72 vols. St. Peter Port, Guernsey, 1962–.

(ed.), *The Thomas Hardy Year Book*, 1970–.

Deacon, Lois and Coleman, Terry, *Providence and Mr. Hardy*, London, 1968.

Dolman, Frederick, "An Evening with Thomas Hardy", *Young Man*, VIII, March 1894, 74–79.

Ellis, S. M., "Some Personal Recollections of Thomas Hardy", *Fortnightly Review*, N.S. CXXIII, March 1928, 393–406.

Falk, Bernard, *The Naked Lady*, London, 1934.

Felkin, Elliott, "Days with Thomas Hardy: from a 1918–1919 diary", *Encounter*, XVIII, April 1962, 27–33.

Flower, Newman, *Just As It Happened*, New York, 1950.

"Walks and Talks with Thomas Hardy", *The Countryman*, XXXIV, Winter 1966, 193–195.

Haight, G. S., *George Eliot*, Oxford, 1968.

Gifford, Henry, "Thomas Hardy and Emma", *Essays and Studies*, N.S. XIX (1966), 106–121.

Gosse, Edmund, "Thomas Hardy's Lost Novel", *Sunday Times*, 22 January 1928.

Graham, Thomas J., *Modern Domestic Medicine*, 13th edn., London, 1864.

Guerard, Albert J., *Thomas Hardy, The Novels and Stories*. Oxford, 1959.

Haggard, H. Rider, *Rural England*, 2 vols., London, 1902.

Halliday, F. E., *Thomas Hardy: His Life and Work*, Bath, 1972.

Hardy, Evelyn, "Hardy and the Phrenologist", *John O' London's Weekly*, 26 February 1954.

"Some Unpublished Poems by Thomas Hardy", *London Magazine*, III (1956), 28–39.

*Thomas Hardy; A Critical Biography*. London, 1954.

"An Unpublished Poem by Thomas Hardy", *Times Literary Supplement*, 2 June 1966; and Robert Gittings (eds.), *Some Recollections by Emma Hardy*, Oxford, 1961; and F. B. Pinion (eds.), *One Rare Fair Woman: Letters of Thomas Hardy to Florence Henniker*, London, 1973.

Hardy, Florence E., *The Early Life of Thomas Hardy: 1840–1891*, London, 1928.

*The Later Years of Thomas Hardy: 1892–1928*, London, 1930.

*The Life of Thomas Hardy: 1840–1928*, London, 1962.

(*The Life* is a one-volume publication of *The Early Life* and *The Later Years*. All, except the last few years, was really written by Hardy himself.)

Hardy, Thomas, "Death of Miss Mary Hardy", *Dorset County Chronicle*, 2 December 1915.

Harvey, O. D., *Puddletown, the Weatherbury of " Far from the Madding Crowd"*, Dorchester, 1968.

Hawkins, Desmond, *Thomas Hardy*, London, 1950.

Hibbert, Christopher, *Garibaldi and his Enemies*, London, 1965.

Holland, Clive, "My Walks and Talks in Wessex with Thomas Hardy", *John O'London's Weekly*, 30 March 1951.

Howe, Irving, *Thomas Hardy*, London, 1967.

Hynes, Samuel, *The Pattern of Hardy's Poetry*, Chapel Hill, 1961.

Jackman, Douglas, *300 Years of Baptist Witness in Dorchester, 1645–1945*, Dorchester, 1945.

Jones, Bernard (ed.), *The Poems of William Barnes*, 2 vols., Fontwell, 1963.

Kay-Robinson, Denys, *Hardy's Wessex Re-Appraised*, Newton Abbot, 1972.

Kingsgate, J. " *Tess* and Thomas Hardy, New Facts about his Life in London", *Graphic*, CXII, 5 September 1925.

Lewis, R. W. M., *The Family of Moule of Melksham, Fordington, and Melbourne*, Privately printed (1938).

M'Culloch, J. R., *Principles of Political Economy*, Edinburgh, 1825.

Maitland, F. W., *The Life and Letters of Leslie Stephen*, London, 1906.

Manton, Jo, *Sister Dora: A Life of Dorothy Pattison*, London, 1971.

(ed.), *Memoirs of Mark Pattison*, Fontwell, 1969.

Martin, F. P. B., *A Memoir on the Equinoctial Storms, March–April 1850*. Privately printed, 1852.

Meynell, Viola (ed.), *Friends of a Lifetime: Letters to Sydney Cockerell*, London, 1940.

Miller, J. Hillis, *Thomas Hardy: Distance and Desire*. Cambridge, Mass. 1970.

Millgate, Michael, *Thomas Hardy, His Career as a Novelist*, Bodley Head, 1971.

Morgan, Charles, *The House of Macmillan*, London, 1943.

Morrell, Ray, *Thomas Hardy, The Will and the Way*, Kuala Lumpur, 1943.

Moule, H. C. G., *Memories of a Vicarage*, 1913.

Nevinson, H. W., *Thomas Hardy*, London, 1941.

Newman, J. and Pevsner, N., *The Buildings of Dorset*, London, 1972.

Orel, Harold (ed.), *Thomas Hardy's Personal Writings*, Kansas, 1966.

Phelps, W. L., *Autobiography and Letters*, Oxford, 1939.

Pike, E. Royston, *Human Documents of the Victorian Golden Age*, London, 1969.

Pinion, F. B., *A Hardy Companion*, London, 1968.

Purdy, R. L., *Thomas Hardy: A Bibliographical Study*, Oxford, 1954, rep. 1968.

"The authorship of Hardy's Biography", TLS, 30 December 1960.

*Reports of the British and Foreign School Society.*

Rutland, W. R., *Thomas Hardy: A Study of his Writings and Their Background*, London, 1938, New York, 1962.

Smith, Goldwin, *Does the Bible Sanction Slavery?* Oxford, 1863.

Smith, S. Nowell (ed.), *Letters to Macmillan*, London, 1967.

Smith, W. Sylvester, *The London Heretics, 1870–1914*, London, 1967.

Southerington, F. R., *Hardy's Vision of Man*, London, 1971.

Stephen, Barbara, *Emily Davies and Girton College*, London, 1937.

Stewart, J. I. M., *Thomas Hardy*, London, 1971.

Taine, H. trans. Hyams, E., *Notes on England*, London, 1957.

Walcott, Fred G., *The Origins of Culture and Anarchy*, London, 1970.

Webb, A. P., *A Bibliography of the Works of Thomas Hardy*, London, 1916.

Weber, Carl J., *Hardy of Wessex*, London, 1940; rev. and repr. 1965.

(ed.), *"Dearest Emmie"*, London, 1953.

(ed.), *Hardy at Colby*, Waterville, Maine, 1936; *Hardy and the Lady from Madison Square*, Waterville, Maine, 1952.

(ed.), *The Letters of Thomas Hardy*, Waterville, Maine, 1954.

Webster, H. C., *On a Darkling Plain: The Art and Thought of Thomas Hardy*, Chicago, 1947.

Williams, Merryn, *Thomas Hardy and Rural England*, London, 1972.

Winstanley, D. A., *Later Victorian Cambridge*, Cambridge, 1947.

Wreden, W. P., *Books from the Library of Thomas Hardy*, New York, 1938.

D. MAGAZINES, NEWSPAPERS, PERIODICALS

*Academy*
*Athenaeum*
*Cornhill Magazine*
*Daily News*
*Daily Telegraph*
*Dorset County Chronicle*
*Dorset Evening Echo*
*Englishwoman's Journal*
*Felix Farley's Bristol Journal*
*Frazer's Magazine*
*Gentleman's Magazine*

*Illustrated London News*
*London Review*
*Morning Post*
*Pall Mall Gazette*
*Saturday Review*
*Spectator*
*Standard*
*Sunday Times*
*The Times*
*Times Literary Supplement*

## ACKNOWLEDGEMENT OF QUOTATIONS

Extracts from the novels of Thomas Hardy and from his *Collected Poems*, and quotations from *The Life of Thomas Hardy* by Florence Hardy are reprinted by permission of the Trustees of the Hardy Estate, Macmillan, London and Basingstoke, and the Macmillan Company of Canada Limited.

# Index

# Thomas Hardy's
# Later Years

Thomas Hardy in old age, sketch by Augustus John

# Contents

# Illustrations

*Frontispiece*

Thomas Hardy in old age, sketch by Augustus John

*Following Page 84*

1. Two sketches from *The Illustrated Sporting and Dramatic News*, 7 January 1882

    John Hare playing in Pinero's *The Squire* at St. James's Theatre, and Hardy, J. Comyns Carr and George Lewis watching the performance

2. Scene from *Two Roses* with Helen Mathews, artist's impression by Harold Ludlow, January 1882

3. Hardy's four ladies of fashion in the 1890s, (a) Mary Jeune (hostess), (b) Rosamund Tomson (poet), (c) Florence Henniker (novelist), (d) Agnes Grove (journalist)

4. Hardy's brother, sisters, and best friend, (a) Henry Hardy, (b) Kate Hardy, (c) Mary Hardy, (d) Horace Moule

*Following Page 100*

5. Hardy with Emma at Max Gate, circa 1900

6. Hardy without Emma in London, circa 1900, from the painting "First Night at a Theatre" by Alfred Stevens

7. Hardy by Jacques-Emile Blanche, May 1906

8. Manuscript of Hardy's poem "Best Times", showing alterations to fit his version of events

*Following Page 148*

9. Hardy and Edward Clodd on the beach at Aldeburgh, circa 1909

10. Hardy and Florence Dugdale on the beach at Aldeburgh, circa 1909

Reproduced by permission of the Dorset County Museum, except for the frontispiece, 1 and 2, 3a, 3c, 3d, 4d, 7, 13, 15, which are by permission of James Gibson, Victoria and Albert Museum (Theatre Museum), Radio Times Hulton Picture Post Library, Macmillan, Desmond Hawkins, Miss K. M. E. Murray, Tate Gallery, Mrs. Gertrude Bugler, and Norman Atkins respectively.

To my wife

# Acknowledgements

THOMAS HARDY seems to have spent scarcely a single day when he did not have a pen in hand, whether to compose a novel or a story, draft or polish a poem, copy and comment on a passage from his reading, make notes in his commonplace book on every conceivable topic, undertake countless revisions for fresh editions of his work, and, all the time, to write tens of thousands of letters, personal, practical, or purely business. No one can claim to have read all that his meticulous classical script committed to paper. That I have been able to tackle even a portion of it has been due, in the first place, to the generous award of a Research Fellowship from the Leverhulme Trust Fund. The expenses of travel and transcription could not possibly have been faced without this grant.

Secondly, I could not have hoped to handle such material without a willing, skilful and informed helper. My research assistant has been my wife, Jo Manton, a biographer in her own right. Her accurate appreciation of sources and her historical acumen have led to many of the new and better insights into Hardy's life that this book may possess. Her enthusiasm has been unabated. It is a literal fact that this book would never have been finished without her help, which has extended to providing the first accurate translation from the French of the essay on Thomas Hardy in *Mes Modèles* by J.-E. Blanche.

I have been lucky in finding helpful specialist enthusiasts throughout. Among many, I should single out Jennifer Aylmer of the Theatre Museum, the Victoria and Albert Museum, Laurence Irving and his sister Lady Brunner, all for theatrical information; Graham Handley, Principal Lecturer in Education at the College of All Saints, Tottenham, for exhaustive enquiries in Enfield, and, in the same area, D. O. Pam, Local History and Museum Officer, London Borough of Enfield, P. A. Glennie, Headmaster of St. Andrew's C. of E. Primary School, Enfield, and J. D. Westaway, M.B.E., Correspondent to the School Managers. Finally, Michael Meredith, the Librarian, School Library, Eton College, gave me lively encouragement and generous access to his fine Hardy collection there.

Among libraries and archives, I have to thank primarily, as always, the staff of my local West Sussex County Reference Library at Chichester, who have solved my innumerable problems with charming efficiency. The same must be said of the staff of the Dorset County

Reference Library, the Dorset County Archivist and her staff, and, of course, the inimitable R. N. R. Peers, and the facilities which he provides so generously at the Dorset County Museum, with such considerable expense of his own often hard-pressed time. I must thank the librarians, and archivists, and staff of the Berkshire County Record Office, the Bodleian Library, the British Library Reading Room and Department of Manuscripts, the Brotherton Library of the University of Leeds, the General Registry, the Portsmouth City Library, the Public Record Office, the Warneford Hospital, and the Wiltshire County Record Office. Particular mention must be made of the Director and Staff of the Special Collections, Colby College Library, Waterville, Maine, for their prompt and efficient provision of material to keep pace with my work. Another special set of acknowledgements and thanks must go to the Trustees of the late E. A. Dugdale: in particular for permission to print large extracts from the letter of Emma Hardy to Mrs. Kenneth Grahame, and in general for their helpful acquiescence in my use of non-substantial quotation throughout the book from the letters of Thomas, Emma, and Florence Hardy.

I am most grateful to authorities already in the Hardy field: J. O. Bailey, Frank Giordano Jr., Evelyn Hardy and Desmond Hawkins (these last two authors of outstanding single-volume biographies of Hardy), Denys Kay-Robinson, John Laird, Michael Millgate, Harold Orel, Norman Page, F. B. Pinion, and R. L. Purdy, the authoritative bibliographer of Hardy, who will forgive some differences of interpretation in my general debt to his scholarship. Among all these, I must single out James Gibson, editor of the definitive *The Complete Poems of Thomas Hardy*. As with my first volume, he has not only given me the benefit of his extensive knowledge of Hardy texts, but has provided countless points of reference from his own collection of Hardiana, and has extended his many good offices to reading and commenting on the draft typescript of the present volume.

Help has notably come from interested individuals, whose names I can do no more than list, with apologies for any omissions: Gertrude S. Antell, John Antell, Norman Atkins, Melvyn Bragg, Daniel Farson, Dr. Roger Fiske, Violet Hilling, Dr. Richard Hunter, Mr. and Mrs. Jesty, Margaret E. Lane, Mrs. L. Largent, Mrs. Ann MacCaw, Mrs. K. Needham-Hurst, Lady Nihill, Kenneth Phelps, Elizabeth Potts, Professor Edward Sampson, Mrs. R. P. Voremberg, Terence de Vere White; with a special word of gratitude to Gertrude Bugler for giving me such full and accurate information, allowing me to see letters, and for reading and correcting those sections of my book in which she plays a part.

The following acknowledgements are made to the owners of these sets of letters: the Brotherton Library, the University of Leeds, for

letters from Florence Hardy to Edward Clodd; the Director, Special
Collections, Colby College, Waterville, Maine, for letters from Emma
Hardy to the Revd. Richard Bartelot and to Rebekah Owen and also
for letters from Florence Hardy to Paul Lemperly and to Rebekah
Owen; the Trustees of the Thomas Hardy Collection and the Curator of
the Dorset County Museum for various letters in the collection to and
from Thomas Hardy; the Provost and Fellows of Eton College for
letters from Florence Hardy to Siegfried Sassoon and to Louisa Yearsley
in the School Library, Eton College; Mr. H. P. R. Hoare and the
National Trust for a letter from Emma Hardy and letters from Florence
Hardy to Alda, Lady Hoare, in the Wiltshire County Record Office.
The sources of these sets of letters are not further indicated in the Notes.
My best thanks are due to Evelyn Hardy and F. B. Pinion for their
transcriptions from other named sources.

Copyright in illustrations belongs to the Thomas Hardy Collection,
Dorset County Museum, with the following exceptions: 1 and 2, the
Gabrielle Enthoven Collection, Theatre Museum, Victoria and Albert
Museum; 3a, the Radio Times Hulton Picture Post Library; 3c,
Macmillan; 3d, Desmond Hawkins; 4d, Miss K. M. E. Murray; 7, the
Tate Gallery; 13, Mrs. Gertrude Bugler; 15, Norman Atkins.

# Foreword

MY FIRST volume, *Young Thomas Hardy*, covered the first three-dozen years of Hardy's life, his origins in an obscure Dorset hamlet, his determined self-education, his vision of himself as a seer and prophet to his generation, his attempt to deny the rural past that had nurtured him, his hard-won achievement with his first successful novel, and a middle-class marriage. It also showed the damage these strenuous efforts had inflicted on an abnormally sensitive and secretive personality, always wistfully looking back across the gulf that success had created between his "simple self that was" and his carefully cultivated appearance as an English man of letters.

The remaining fifty years, summarized in a brief epilogue to the previous book, are the subject of the present volume, its sequel. To some degree, its story is an extension of these former events. Hardy remained a man torn between two worlds. His need to renew his Dorset roots brought him back to live and work near his birthplace. Yet the position he had reached in the world's eyes, and the heady effect of admirers—particularly women—dragged him only half-protesting into fashionable and aristocratic society, and the routines of the late Victorian and Edwardian London season. His obsession with the women of this world, especially with its amateurs of literature, added to the already formidable conflicts of his inner life. More obviously, it helped to bring about disaster in his first marriage to the erratic and not untalented Emma Gifford, the subject of so many ill-founded legends.

The strains of this double life marked him as a sad and worn man. His greatest inspiration came from his family and the dark rural history of his race. That story is intimately woven into the superb and dramatic artistry of his most mature novels. It permeates the poems he was to write in their hundreds up to the very end of his long life. Yet his unceasing search for love and understanding in a sophisticated world he never really managed to enter left him subject to continual disappointment and sometimes bitter revulsion.

In the last twenty years of his life, he seemed to have found an answer in a young woman who came from the same social background as himself, and had experienced much the same emergent and disillusioning struggles. Yet the accepted picture of an autumnal calm, enshrined in second marriage, proves as false as the other personal images he so sedulously projected. Stresses prevailed literally to his death-bed. What these were, and their intimate connection with his novels and poems, form the story this sequel attempts to tell.

# 1

# The Idyll

IN THE spring of 1876, Thomas and Emma Hardy, both then thirty-five years old, were living in furnished lodgings at Yeovil in Somerset. A year earlier, his fourth novel, *Far From the Madding Crowd*, had brought him the general acclaim and recognition his first three published works had lacked. Thomas Hardy's fifth novel, *The Hand of Ethelberta*, appeared on 5 April 1876. The reviews which emerged in that month, and early in the next, threw doubts on its quality. The *Athenaeum* found it carelessly written, the *Spectator* entertaining as a fable, but no more. The *Saturday Review* named it as frankly unworthy of the author of *Far From the Madding Crowd*, and George Saintsbury in *Academy*, though more favourable, noticed "a scrappiness which is the frequent drawback of novels written for periodicals".[1] Perhaps more ominously, for an author who had been married less than two years, Hardy's wife did not like it.

Emma's faith in their marriage, in spite of his peasant background and her middle-class family, had been justified by the triumphal progress of *Far From the Madding Crowd* in their first wedded year. Her unconcealed irritation that her only sister had been the first to marry was soothed when she found herself the wife of a successful novelist. It delighted her that the first long general review of her husband's work had come from Paris,[2] a city which held for her the happiest memories of their honeymoon. There are signs that she already saw Hardy as an international figure, like her beloved Balzac, and herself in the role of a great writer's intellectual helpmeet.

Biographers have always cast Emma Hardy as a thoroughly commonplace middle-class woman with no taste, whose attempts at literature were ridiculous. This was not how she appeared to herself, nor does it correspond with her modest but quite real achievements. She wrote in a vivid, well-observed, and even poetic style. The poor education given to middle-class Victorian girls may have left her shaky over spelling and grammar; but it had not damaged a lively turn of phrase and unusual imagery. Two magazine articles, "The Egyptian Pet" and "In Praise of Calais", show really excellent, sustained descriptive powers.[3] The latter is pictorial, in the manner of Hardy's favourite Bonington, with bright spots of significant colour picking out details of a bustling sea-port. Both won approval from literary friends, the first from Edmund Gosse,[4] the latter from Mrs. Watts-Dunton. Emma's four surviving travel diaries[5] are packed with equally delightful touches, both of character and colour. In the first year of their marriage, she had completed a story, *The Maid on the Shore*, whose Cornish setting at least bears comparison with Hardy's more mature *A Pair of Blue Eyes*. Critics have made an Aunt Sally of the deplorable poetry she tried to write in her sixties, and failed to realize the genuine talent latent in her prose. Finally, far from trying to adapt Hardy to a middle-class life, she was trying to live what she believed to be a bohemian existence with him, and to have a hand in his literary and creative life by her active partnership.

Under Hardy's direction, she had set herself to copy into a stout ruled notebook the extracts from books and newspapers he had made in previous years, and to bring them up to date with quotations from his recent reading. The raw material for a self-taught and self-improving novelist was laid out neatly in her still-schoolgirl hand, and by the beginning of April 1876, she had provided him with over 200 entries. The three largest categories were his historical reading in Macaulay, his weekly contemporary reading in the *Saturday Review*, and, apparently in the early months of 1876, laconic extracts from lives of the artists Raphael and Michelangelo. These, with a key word or two underlined, were just the kind of references Hardy loved to insert, somewhat self-consciously, into descriptive passages of his novels. Emma's labour was clearly designed to provide fodder for his future productions.[6] Whether, or not such self-improving interpretations were happy for the reader, they were a necessity for the writer.

The carping reviews of April brought a sudden urgency into the process. Hardy took over the notes himself,[7] and plunged into a bout of self-education. This was nothing new. At every turning point in his creative life, he had resorted to intensive study, in the belief that everything, poetry, prose, history, style, philosophy, was to be learnt by hard application and methodical treatment. There was concentration on the Greeks, including Plato and Aeschylus, but equally on such widely-spaced sources as the Greville Memoirs and J. G. Wood's *Insects at Home*.

By the end of May, with perhaps about 450 entries, old and new, copied, the process was broken for a fortnight by a short second honeymoon tour in Europe. It is not known whether this fulfilled some educational need in Hardy, or whether Emma felt it her due. It was probably paid for by the publication in the U.S.A. during that month of *The Hand of Ethelberta* in book form. At all events, the Hardys set off for Holland and the Rhine, their journey charted by Emma at the other end of the tiny notebook she had used as the diary of their original honeymoon in Rouen and Paris. On their way back, whether by chance or more likely by Hardy's deliberate design, they diverted through Belgium, and visited the field of Waterloo not many days before the anniversary of the battle on 18 June. Obsessed as always by this event, so much a part of his own folk and family history, Hardy spent the whole of a very long hot day dragging Emma all over the battlefield, until she felt faint and ill. He was also so obsessed by details, such as the exact location of the Duchess of Richmond's ball, that he could not restrain himself from investigating that too, and writing a letter to the papers about it. Emma's diary contains the pathetic little note—her first sign of any criticism of her single-minded and some-times intolerant husband—"Today I am still fatigued & Tom is cross about it."[8] A miserable passage back to Harwich, on a windy night with cattle aboard, can hardly have improved matters.[9]

The quarrel at Waterloo anticipated a strained situation when they re-turned home. The last entry in Emma's diary of their tour reads, "Going back to England where we have no home and no chosen county." A life of furnished lodgings was beginning to lose its glamour for her, in spite of the belief she was sharing it with an author who would redeem by some new classic work the comparative failure of his last book. It is possible that some members of her family shared her doubts. Hardy records "hints from relatives that he and his wife 'appeared to be wandering about like two tramps' ", although in fact they had simply returned to their old address at Yeovil in Somerset which, as Emma had said, was not "chosen county" for either. Yet the plethora of note-book entries suggests hours of solid work rather than an aimless exist-ence. The wounding phrase probably came from Emma's unsatis-factory but supercilious brothers, Walter and Willie Gifford. Living out of packing-cases was beginning to irk even Hardy. A diary entry on 25 June about "the irritating necessity of conforming to rules which them-selves have no virtue" was probably aimed at his brothers-in-law with their mystical regard for unfurnished rather than furnished rental. Yet he needed a more settled background for a deliberate campaign of self-improvement before he felt ripe for another major novel. Early in July, he and Emma went to Bristol, the Gifford family city, and bought £100 worth of furniture in two hours. On 3 July, they moved it into their first real home.

This was a small semi-detached house called Riverside Villa, looking over the willowy reaches of the Stour, in the little market-town of Sturminster Newton in north-east Dorset. The villa was rendered in dusky grey, and in the garden Hardy planted a monkey-puzzle, token of Victorian middle-class respectability. It was a friendly place, and in it Emma had her first taste of provincial Dorset society. Callers included the Dashwoods, members of the firm of local solicitors which had given the poet, William Barnes, his first job. Emma was able to pick up the neighbourhood's history and anecdotes, which she hoped to weave into novels, for she still regarded herself as a novelist too. It was a very real part of the Hardys' marriage that they had a shared appreciation of literature and especially of poetry. One of Hardy's many poems which look back on this time shows them reading together in their idyllic riverside setting, as the swallows swooped over the sunset water-meadows outside.

> A dwelling appears by a slow sweet stream
> Where two sit happy and half in the dark:
> They read, helped out by a frail-wicked gleam,
> Some rhythmic text . . .

Keats was one of the "rhythmic texts" they shared in this romantic mood. His poetry had been a continuing presence in the novel which Hardy always regarded as *their* story, *A Pair of Blue Eyes*.[10] Now another shared delight, Emma's singing to the piano in the dusk, may have brought back to his mind Keats's great love-narrative, *The Eve of St. Agnes*, for he copied into his notebook the line

> The music yearning like a god in pain . . .

and when he eventually came to write his next novel, he took the Song of the Indian Maiden, from Keats's *Endymion, as* its epigraph.

Yet the main purpose of their reading and copying was not to make an anthology of enjoyed literature. The hundreds of notes and quotations, with which they filled the pages of the notebook this idyllic summer and autumn, had a strictly practical purpose; they were to be ammunition in Hardy's new campaign to capture the heights of a really great novel.

Hardy's plan was not merely to copy extracts, but to select them as illustrations of some particular point of character, which could thus be reinforced and driven home in the pages of a narrative, providing a kind of home-made dictionary of learned and useful allusions. This involved selecting and heading each note with the characteristic to be illustrated, each carefully underlined, and then quoting from the source he was reading some pithy phrase or parallel allusion. For example, Note 345 reads:[11]

> Prominent mediocrity: conspicuous by the very intensity of his medi-ocrity—the late Bishop Sumner.

This illustration is annotated S.R., showing that Hardy had read it in his favourite *Saturday Review*. The allusion is exactly used to bolster a general comment on human nature in his next novel:

> Was Yeobright's mind well-proportioned? No. A well-proportioned mind is one which shows no particular bias . . . Its usual blessings are

happiness and mediocrity. It produces the poetry of Rogers, the paintings of West, the statecraft of North, the spiritual guidance of Sumner;

The interchangeable nature of such comments is shown by the fact that in later editions of *The Return of the Native*, Hardy substituted for Sumner's name that of his predecessor as Bishop of Winchester, Dr. Tomline. Such notes were simply used as fill-ups, to be slotted into a story wherever Hardy felt a strengthening allusion was needed. Two entries, numbers 611 and 613, based on Charles MacKay's *Memoirs of Extraordinary Popular Delusions and the Madness of Crowds*, an extremely popular work, whose first edition of 5000 copies had sold in three days, illustrate this purely practical novelistic purpose exactly. They read:

611 *Miraculous animation.* It is said that Albertus Magnus & Thos. Aquinas between them animated a brass statue, wh. chattered, & was their servant.

613 "Coup de Jarnac" a sly & unexpected blow so called from duel.

They then appear duly in *The Return of the Native* as

He seemed a mere automaton . . . He might have been the brass statue which Albertus Magnus is said to have animated just so far as to make it chatter and move, and be his servant.

. . . this species of *coup-de-Jarnac* from one he knew too well troubled the mind of Wildeve.

Only a few entries earlier, a note on the Pitt diamond, "carried in a hole cut in the heel of a shoe, for greater security", is repeated almost word for word in the novel, to reinforce the idea of Christian Cantle putting the guineas in his boots for safety. No less than seventy-five maxims or aphorisms from the Jesuit Balthasar Gracian, taken from an article in the *Fortnightly Review*,[12] are copied in Emma's hand, to be saved up by Hardy for extensive use a few years later in *A Laodicean*.

Apart however from a few entries which are possibly in Emma's hand, Hardy took care to copy himself the extracts from the largest single source in the whole notebook. This is the work of the founder of the system of Positive Philosophy, Auguste Comte, Hardy had read Comte intently in the years between 1870 and 1873, using mostly *A General View of Positivism*, translated by the English Positivist, J. H. Bridges, which he was given by his tragic friend and mentor, Horace Moule, some time before the latter's suicide in 1873. In 1875, he had discussed Positive Philosophy, encouraged by the man who succeeded Moule as his guiding intellectual influence, Leslie Stephen. Now, in 1876, he made a close study of one particular section of Comte's philosophic writing, *Social Dynamics, or the General Theory of Human*

*Progress*, from Comte's *System of Positive Polity*, just issued in a translation by another English Positivist, Edward Spencer Beesly. In the
summer and autumn of 1876, Hardy copied over 130 remarks, defini-
tions, and comments from Comte's *Social Dynamics*, a harvest which he
stored up for use in nearly all the novels he wrote for the next twenty
years. In the 1890s, *Tess of the d'Urbervilles* was hailed by English
Positivists as reading "like a Positivist allegory or sermon", while in
*Jude* Hardy actually provided a Positivist heroine, Sue.[13] This is not
to say that Hardy was ever a Positivist. He seems to have had doubts,
even during this time, especially about Comte's assumption of inevitable rational progress by mankind. However, he was sufficiently
immersed in the Comtian world to attempt a pen-and-ink illustration
of social progress as "a looped orbit", an idea which he had discussed
at length the previous summer with Leslie Stephen,[14] and to which he
returned several times in his own later writings.

Comte is not easy reading, and this all must have taken some highly
concentrated study, especially with the summer delights of the Stour
at his doorstep, and a boat always ready for excursions with Emma
among the reedy islands, with their rushes "standing like a palisade
against the bright sky". Yet Hardy not only mastered this philosophic
task, but found time for favourite passages from Carlyle's *French
Revolution*, which he seems to have read at various times in his life
both for the history and for its vivid phrases. This continued unbroken
until the end of October, when a change took place. On the last day of
this month, Tuesday the 31st, Emma's egregious brothers, Willie and
Walter, arrived for a two-day stay, leaving early on the morning of
the Thursday.[15] It was apparently the only time that any relatives of
either Hardy or Emma came to see how they were doing at Sturminster. The remark often attributed to them, that the Hardys were
living in a place so remote that a new species of bird on the lawn was
an event, is not perhaps true,[16] though it sounds like Walter Gifford's
captious style. What is more to the point, the brothers' stay marks a
complete change in Hardy's notebook habits. From this exact date, he
ceases to make extracts from full-length volumes, like Comte's *Social
Dynamics*. His notes now are taken almost entirely from articles in
magazines, the *Saturday Review*, *Fortnightly Review*, *Edinburgh Review*,
*Cornhill*, *Nineteenth Century*, *Blackwood's*, and even the *Daily News*,
which provided some lighter and more homely items such as one on
pigeons—"The best breed of homing pigeons is that known as Belgian
Voyageurs: will beat an express train." Even the highly provincial
*Dorset County Chronicle* was allowed its say among the more learned
notes with "*A Shorthorn Cow*—the highest price ever given was for the
'Duchess of Geneva'—7000 guineas."

Evidently the brothers' visit, or something said by them during it, had brought home to Hardy that he was not getting on with writing another book: now, as a result, his preparations did not allow time for more than periodical reading, sometimes much more trivial than during his lengthy period of pure learning. Now he must put his accumulation of information and philosophy to creative use. His relatives-in-law and even Emma herself may have reminded him that he had not even a contract for any money-earning book. He must have something to offer. A visit to London in December was probably for book purposes, though Hardy only mentions his attendance at a conference at St. James's Hall on the Eastern Question; there he heard Mr. Gladstone speak, and witnessed Anthony Trollope's refusal to sit down when the Duke of Westminster, in the chair, tried to stop him exceeding the time-limit for speakers.[17] A more important excursion, both for the book, and for his private life with Emma, was to Bockhampton, to spend Christmas with his parents.

Although Emma had been on expeditions with Hardy's sisters, during her stay the year before at Swanage, this seems to have been her first meeting with her mother-in-law. There is a complete silence by Hardy on this point, and to the end of his life he never commented on the relationship between the two women. Family tradition has it that Emma was not well received, and with Jemima Hardy's strong character and possessive attitude this seems likely enough. A woman who, in Hardy's childhood, had stood up to the powerful wife of the local landowner, Mrs. Martin, was not to be overawed by the daughter of a failed solicitor. Hardy himself only describes his father's anecdotes of village bands and Christmas entertainments. The real importance of the visit was that he once more renewed acquaintance with his greatest creative inspiration, the homestead and the Heath beyond it. Many critics, including Hardy himself, have expressed surprise that he lived at Sturminster, but made his homeland heath the setting of *The Return of the Native*. This is to ignore—as Hardy did for his own reasons—the tremendous impact this Christmas visit made. To take only one instance, the most powerful visual scene in the book, the gambling at night by the light of glow-worms, was derived from an anecdote about Hardy's grandfather, doubtless told him by his father on this occasion.[18] Nearly all critics of *The Return of the Native* have recognized that the major character in the story is the Heath itself. Hardy himself began the novel with a full-length chapter devoted to the Heath, its appearance, its history (with characteristic historical notes from the Domesday Book and Leland's *Itinerary*), and the relation of huge and "haggard Egdon" to the processes of human life. What nearly always surprises those who form a picture from the novel of this giant waste is how small it is in actual geographical fact, and how little it seems to contain, even in bad weather, of the brooding menace with which

Hardy invests it. The simple reason is that Hardy, returning to it this Christmas after an interval of very different experience, and in the company once more of his powerful mother, saw the place, in his novelist's imagination, as it had appeared to him as a child. The huge stature of Bhompton Heath, Duddle Heath, and Puddletown Heath, in the composite guise of the fictional Egdon Heath, is seen from the eye-level of a very small boy. It is not often noticed that *The Return of the Native* is the one novel by Hardy where a child plays a large part, and in which a completely convincing picture of a child is given. One has only to contrast Johnny Nunsuch in this novel with the weird, symbolic non-child Little Father Time in *Jude the Obscure*. Hardy's "sad little boy" and his adventures on Egdon are some of the most moving scenes of the novel, and the most important in the plot, from his unconscious part in the rendezvous of Eustacia and Wildeve on the evening of 5th November to his fateful meeting on the Heath with Mrs. Yeobright, and his gradual revelation to Clym Yeobright of her last hours.

There is little doubt that this realistic figure of a child, unique in all Hardy's work, embodies his own childhood experiences on and about the Heath. Later in life he confessed to Hermann Lea "the childish fears he had felt in crossing that lonely stretch of heathland by himself when it was dusk or even at times quite dark". He told Lea how "he had often run fast to escape his fears produced by the sudden movement of a pony or deer, or a form that loomed in the half-light before being recognizable as a mere bush".[19] Similarly, Johnny in the novel

> ran until he was out of breath . . . The thorn-bushes which arose in his path from time to time . . . whistled gloomily, and had a ghastly habit after dark of putting on the shapes of jumping madmen, sprawling giants, and hideous cripples.

In addition, the year and a day that the story occupies seems to fall some time during the decade 1840–50, that is, the exact years of Hardy's own childhood before he went to school in Dorchester; transportation to Australia, which was officially ended in 1850, is still invoked as a current fact by one of the characters in the novel. Hardy also uses other scenes, not connected with the boy Johnny, which appear to embody actual events known to have made a deep impression on his own childish mind. One is the "raffle" or competition decided by dice-throwing, where the childlike Christian Cantle wins an unwanted prize, just as the child Hardy had done. The Christmas Mummers scene, with its emotional prominence, and its strongly-felt sexual undercurrent, seems likely to be a transmuted memory of that Mummers' show at Puddletown, where the adolescent Hardy had made advances to his older cousin, Rebecca Sparks; for Rebecca's young brother, Jim

Sparks, appears in this scene of the novel, scarcely disguised, by
the alteration of one letter, as Jim Starks, a character not used
anywhere else in the book. He shows the nature of Rebecca's impulsive
and forthright brother by acting his part as the Valiant Soldier so
vigorously that he feigns death in the play by "coming down like a log
upon the stone floor with force enough to dislocate his shoulder". In
an exactly similar way their father, the carpenter James Sparks senior,
had appeared in Hardy's first published novel, *Desperate Remedies*, as
James Sparkman, a joiner.

These associations with his childhood, aided by renewed contact
with his mother's fund of folklore and legend, were what Hardy took
away to Sturminster from his Christmas visit to the Bockhampton
home; he seems to have started writing the novel immediately. Many
critics have suggested that the "return" of the hero is literally the
return of Hardy, and that Clym Yeobright should be identified in some
way as Hardy, while Mrs. Yeobright is a picture of Jemima Hardy. It
is claimed that Hardy himself said Mrs. Yeobright was based on his own
mother, though the witness for this, Sir Sydney Cockerell, is not always
reliable on other matters.[20] If this really were so, it seems strange that
Hardy himself placed Mrs. Yeobright as the least important of all the
main characters in the book, though here, admittedly, he was providing
hints for the illustrator of the serial version of the novel,[21] and not
necessarily passing judgement based on his own preferences. Yet, as
he wrote, a far more potent basis was provided by his deliberate notes
of the past summer. Nearly all the main themes which critics have
discovered in *The Return of the Native* have their origins in his notebook
entries. Clym Yeobright, that over-thoughtful man, who tries to apply
his philosophy of improvement by reason to rough Egdon, has come
back from Paris "acquainted with ethical systems popular at the time".
Within a year of the volume publication of the novel, he was recognized
by a reviewer as "in fact a humanitarian, touched with the asceticism
of a certain positivistic school". Though Hardy shows, much as his
mentor Leslie Stephen had done in his philosophical essays, how
Comte's positivist optimism is defeated by the nature of actual life,
Clym ends as he had begun, as an ethical teacher upon Egdon, taking
his texts from a much wider selection than the first book of Kings which
he quotes in the closing paragraphs. The battle which some have seen
between paganism and Christianity in the story, repeats many of the
ideas from Comte which Hardy had noted. "Fetichism"—defined in
note 641 from Comte as "universal adoration of matter"—is found by
many on Egdon; the precise word is used by Hardy to describe the
mood of the listener to the subtle sound of the dried heath-bells of the
past summer. The notes on Greek literature and tragedy bore fruit in
the strict classical unity of time, to a year and a day, the Oedipus

theme of Clym's partial blindness,[22] and the five-act structure, which many critics see in the five first books, marred only by the additional "Aftercourses" book to compensate the serial readers for so much unrelieved tragedy. Even such a minor source of notebook entries as J. G. Wood's *Insects at Home* played its part. From two notebook entries which Hardy had entitled *Beauty* and *The nearer the lovelier*, he extracted Wood's descriptions of the tiger-beetle, and applied them, almost word for word, to the impression created at various times by the beauty of Eustacia. Though he needed no book-source to tell him about the behaviour of ants on the Heath, Hardy also undoubtedly used Wood's comment that colonies of ants appear, year after year, at the same place, to strengthen Mrs. Yeobright's dying meditations as she lies on the Heath near one of these ant-processions.[23] There are many other minor transferences, such as the comparison of Egdon with "the ancient world of the carboniferous period", which Hardy had noted from a book-article in the *Saturday Review*, early in 1877, when he began to write the novel.[24]

For the urgent matter, directly he returned to Sturminster after Christmas, was to get his new-found impressions of boyhood down on paper, and provide something to tempt serial-publishers. Though he wrote quickly, drawing on the deep and well-stocked recess of early memory, it proved unexpectedly difficult to interest the magazines. Considering the brilliant popular success of *Far From the Madding Crowd* only three years before, this seems surprising. It may show that the disappointment felt by readers of *The Hand of Ethelberta* had been more serious for Hardy's reputation than has generally been reckoned. Feeling he could not try *Cornhill* again, since its editor, Leslie Stephen, had been doubtful about the propriety of the story for his readers, Hardy wrote to *Blackwood's Edinburgh Magazine* on 13 February 1877, offering them what he described as a pastoral story on the lines of *Far From the Madding Crowd*, hardly an accurate parallel, but one which, he hoped, would sell the novel for serial publication. *Blackwood's* were interested, but when he sent them the first fifteen chapters on 12 April, they rejected his offer within a fortnight.[25] This was a crisis. He was committed to writing with no assurance of money coming in. In these straits he made two moves. He suggested that Smith, Elder, who had published his last two novels in volume form, might like to reprint *A Pair of Blue Eyes*, in which the original publisher, Tinsley, had no further interest. Though negotiations broke down, the novel was in fact reprinted later that year, thanks to the interest of a fellow Dorset man, Charles Kegan Paul, literary adviser to the publishing house of S. King & Co., and founder, under his own name, of the firm that succeeded them.[26] He was to prove a needed standby. Hardy's second move was to submit the new story so far as it had gone to Stephen and the *Cornhill*, but the expected rejection soon came, and on 16 June Hardy offered the novel to yet another magazine, *Temple Bar*, with the same result. He was running through the recognized literary magazines which offered serialization, and it must have been with relief that he eventually placed the novel, sometime that autumn, with the magazine *Belgravia* for serial publication to begin in the January of 1878.[27] He also managed, on a visit to London, to sell the Americal serial rights to Henry Harper, who claimed to have picked the title from Hardy's list.[28]

By all signs, in spite of the delights of Sturminster, 1877 was a year of financial anxiety, ending as it did with yet one more attempt to raise money, a correspondence with Baron Tauchnitz about continental editions of Hardy's books.[29] Also, Hardy resorted this Christmas to selling a short story to a children's annual. As a further source of anxiety and expense, Hardy's father, now in his middle sixties, was suffering badly from rheumatism, and his son had to take him to Bath that autumn to undergo the cure. Serialization in *Belgravia* was accompanied, a month later in February 1878, by a serial publication in one of the magazines controlled by Harper, who was to be his principal American publisher, yet the strain of managing negotiations from such a remote place as Sturminster must have been considerable. There is no reason to doubt, therefore, that it was, as he himself says, on Hardy's own initiative that he and Emma went up to London early in February to look for a house, and signed a three-year agreement for one in the middle of the month. On 18 March their kindly neighbour Mrs. Dashwood gave them a bed while their furniture was being packed, and a few days later they moved into "The Larches", 1 Arundel Terrace, Trinity Road, Upper Tooting, close to Wandsworth Common, and the convenient transport of Wandworth Common Station. The Sturminster Newton idyll was over—"Our happiest time", as Hardy afterwards nostalgically noted.[30]

Many aspects of the stay had certainly been idyllic, the spring birdsong in the Blackmore Vale, the summer dancing on the green to celebrate Queen Victoria's fortieth Coronation anniversary, the lush cottage gardens where "the gooseberries that were ripening on the twigs at noon are in the tart an hour later". Yet it had been a year of professional setbacks and disappointments, and perhaps of personal ones too. One incident, soon after midsummer, disturbed Hardy. He and Emma found that their maid, Jane, whom they liked very much, had kept the bolts of the back door oiled, so that her young man could slip in silently, and frequently spend the night with her. When they discovered this, she crept out early next morning, and never came back, either to them or to her own cottage home. Six weeks later, on 13 August, Hardy made the pathetic and often-quoted note, "We hear that Jane, our late servant, is soon to have a baby. Yet never a sign of one is there for us." Exactly a month earlier, on 13 July, he had made another note, which may well be connected with this better-known one—"The sudden disappointment of a hope leaves a scar which the ultimate fulfilment of that hope never entirely removes."[31] For the Hardys, there was no ultimate fulfilment. Their marriage remained childless to the end. It is difficult and perhaps dangerous to come to any definite judgement about this. One can only say that it was this fact, as much as any, which made Hardy describe these Sturminster months in a much-later poem as

> A preface without any book,
> A trumpet uplipped, but no call;
> That seems it now.

Yet, like so much that Hardy wrote about his earlier years, this is not the final verdict. This poem, and many others of sad reminiscence, were conceived some forty years later, when he was full of remorse for his own imperceptions, for a happiness that was within his reach, but which he somehow did not grasp: of the good things at hand, which he was too self-absorbed to see. For Hardy, more than most creative artists, was deeply self-centred. He regarded himself as one of the chosen few who had a mission to his age; his obsessive markings in his Bible show a belief not in the message of that book—like so many Victorian thinkers, he lost his faith in the 1860s—but in himself as a kind of latter-day seer and prophet, an Isaiah or an Ezekiel. Human contact, especially domestic love once the initial excitement had worn off, meant little to him. Life was largely important as the material for his art. Morbid, brooding, an avid collector of oddity and irony, the term happiness is difficult ever to apply to him. Yet he was happy during what he called the Sturminster Newton idyll, even if his enjoyment showed itself in such form as his endless interest in sinister stories. He attended inquests, collected tales of gruesome country superstitions, accumulating them for use in *The Return of the Native*. He paid little attention to laying any sort of foundation for a real and mutually satisfying marriage. He was wedded to the overwhelming idea of himself as an author and seeker for truth. It was in furtherance of this search that he turned his back on this twenty-month idyll. Anne Thackeray, the novelist's daughter, had told him London was essential for authorship. For his career he would leave the native county to which he already owed so much. He was putting Clym Yeobright's experiment in reverse, and returning to London.

# 2

# The Theatre of Life

TRINITY ROAD is a long, straight avenue, running north to south from Wandsworth High Street to Tooting Bec Station. About two-thirds of the way along, on the east side, just beyond the last straggling outskirts of Wandsworth Common, is Arundel Terrace, which forms a short stretch of the main road. The terrace consists of eight three-storey yellow brick villas of a standard design—half-basement and area, bow-windowed first-floor front parlour. No. 1, into which the Hardys moved, was the northernmost corner house of the row; its situation, by any standards, was bleak. The entire north wall of the house was exposed, there was no south aspect whatsoever, and only a very small garden at the back. Wandsworth Common itself had been saved from builders and placed under public control in 1871; but it remained largely as it was described at that date, bare, muddy, and sloppy after a little rain, undrained, and almost devoid of any trees.[1] This did not, however, deter the builders in Trinity Road, and two large villas, afterwards a Girls' School, were going up opposite Arundel Terrace when the Hardys arrived in March 1878.[2]

Almost every biographer makes great play with Hardy's own words, written in old age, about this area and this house "at Tooting, where they seemed to feel that 'there had passed away a glory from the earth' ", to which he added, "And it was in this house that their troubles began." There is no need to imagine, however, a sudden and lasting disenchantment and marital disillusion directly Hardy and Emma set foot in Arundel Terrace. To do so is to ignore completely Hardy's next sentence—"This, however, is anticipating unduly." The difficulties of the next three years were at least partly due to the house itself. Whenever the wind was north-east there were bound to be "troubles". In the wet January of 1879, rain poured in through the exposed and badly-hung door.[3] In the cold January of 1881, snow drifted in thickly, covering the inside passages, and even forcing its way through the windows, so that Emma's cherished window-plants were as white as if they were growing out of doors.[4] Moreover, throughout their three-year lease, Hardy was clearly suffering from growing physical malaise, with lassitude and nervous fears, confirmed in autumn 1880 by a severe internal haemorrhage.

Yet these three years began as a time of real enjoyment. Hardy had renewed friendship with the elderly Alexander Macmillan, who had shown such sympathetic understanding over his first, unpublished novel. Macmillan, who now left much of the publishing business to his nephew Frederick, had lost his wife in 1871; he quickly remarried a younger woman, a school-friend of his children's governess, and of Italian extraction. They too had settled in South London. The two old Commons of Tooting Graveney and Tooting Bec had recently been acquired as open spaces for the public. Unlike Wandsworth Common they were charming and countrified, especially Tooting Graveney, with its small round pond and gypsy settlements. Splendid new houses, with very large tree-filled gardens, had sprung up on the north side,[5] and Macmillan bought one of these, which he rechristened Knapdale, after the home of his clan in Argyll.[6] This house, with its broad croquet lawns and beautiful view over the pond, was a constant port of call for the Hardys. Indeed, Hardy was guilty of innocent aggrandisement when he wrote of "their neighbours, the Macmillans" and "Knapdale, near our house". Macmillan's spacious detached mansion was at least a mile away from Hardy's little terrace-row, at the far end of Tooting Bec Road, then called Streatham Lane. This lane was the scene of Hardy's later, moving poem, *Beyond the Last Lamp*. The visit of some hours, which the poet pays, and during which two lovers continue sadly to pace the unlit lane, was clearly one which Hardy paid to the Macmillans; Hardy inscribed an autograph copy of the poem to Macmillan's son, George.[7]

Many of Hardy's fruitful London contacts were made or renewed at Knapdale. It was there that summer that he and Emma met Thomas Huxley, for whom Hardy already had a great admiration. The following summer, he was to meet again at Knapdale John Morley, whom he had not seen since the latter had advised him on his earliest attempt, *The Poor Man and the Lady*. Hardy, perhaps a little irked by the final débâcle of his first manuscript, represents Morley as talking in embarrassingly conventional platitudes—"Well, since we met, you have . . .", and so on. Emma enjoyed the successful garden-parties of the lively Mrs. Macmillan, and the friendship of her eldest step-daughter, Maggie. Further afield, in Kensington, they visited Hardy's Dorset admirer, Kegan Paul, himself now a publisher. Emma was also introduced to the household of yet another publisher, George Murray Smith, and Hardy justified his return to London by negotiating with Smith, on 20 September, the book publication of *The Return of the Native*. Besides these occasions where the Hardys visited together, there were many masculine gatherings when Hardy, in his own somewhat quaint phrase, "fell into line as a London man again". On 18 June he was elected a member of the Savile Club and visited the West End in hearty company. On 3 August, he and William Minto, critic and editor of the *Examiner*, who had proposed him for membership, were joined at the Club by Walter Herries Pollock, a dramatic collaborator. The evening ended in Henry Irving's dressing-room at the Lyceum, with Irving stripped to the waist, and all drinking champagne in tumblers.[8]

This was a very different life from the homely, quiet evenings with Emma at Sturminster Newton, the patient copying of hundreds of notes to fit Hardy for the task of becoming a great light in English literature. Though she loyally continued to take down nice things that other people said about her husband's work,[9] Emma was now left much alone. Hardy was out, dining at clubs, visiting the theatre, and, with a man friend, going to the Derby. Silent and shy, his small features disguised by a large, soft beard, he walked the streets observing men and women, especially the latter. He had a horror of attracting attention; sitting in a stage-box, he was seen hiding his face behind his hand.[10] At the same time, he listened and peered about him wherever he went, a confirmed eavesdropper and voyeur, recalling word-for-word conversations heard in John Steven's Holywell Street bookshop off the Strand, while himself appearing to be absorbed in a book.[11] Capitalizing on his return to London, he swiftly wrote and sold magazine stories. The most notable and longest was adapted and selected from his first rejected novel, *The Poor Man and the Lady*. Under the title, "An Indiscretion in the Life of an Heiress", it appeared in July in the *New Quarterly Magazine*, and in the U.S.A. in *Harper*'s. Over and above these immediate money-making tasks, there was the need to prepare a new novel. Hardy returned to the theme, learnt from his grandmother, of the war against Napoleon, and the rumoured threat to the Dorset coast in 1804-1805. He ransacked newpapers and books in the British Museum, copying into his notebook every detail of these invasion years. Army regulations, local Dorset news, the King's visit to Weymouth, military drill, and meticulous drawings of ladies' fashions and hair-styles, all were neatly chronicled in his small, classical script. Nor did he neglect eye-witness memory. On Sunday 27 October 1878, he met at Chelsea Hospital an old pensioner who had actually been in the terrible retreat of Sir John Moore to Corunna. If not the "grand drama of the wars with Napoleon" he had planned in 1877, this was going to be a miniature rehearsal in a realistic Dorset background, on his own cottage doorstep.

The need to make this new book a success was emphasized by a brutal shock. On 4 November, *The Return of the Native* was published in book form, embellished by a map of its Dorset setting, drawn in Hardy's own hand. On 23 November came the first review. It was in the *Athenaeum*, and it was as devastating as the first lethal review of Hardy's youth in the *Spectator*. The novel, over which Hardy had spent so many months of loving care and learned preparation at Sturminster Newton, was judged "a book distinctly inferior to anything of his which we have yet read". The old charges of immorality were raised; Eustacia and Wildeve "know no other law than the gratification of their own passion". Most wounding, his style was criticized, especially his handling of dialect. Hardy replied to this last charge with dignity and sense, in a letter which was printed the following week:[12]

> ... An author may be said to fairly convey the spirit of intelligent peasant talk if he retains the idiom, compass and characteristic expressions, although he may not encumber the page with obsolete pronunciations of the purely English words and with mispronunciations of those derived from Latin and Greek. In the printing of standard speech hardly any phonetic principle at all is observed: and if a writer attempts to exhibit on paper the precise accents of a rustic speaker he disturbs the proper balance of a true representation by unduly insisting upon the grotesque element; thus directing attention to a point of inferior interest, and diverting it from the speaker's meaning, which is by far the chief concern where the aim is to depict the men and their natures rather than their dialect forms.

His hurt feelings show through the measured prose. The popular idea of rustic speech was to stress "the grotesque". Yet the men Hardy wished to portray were those whose speech was, as he stresses, *"intelligent* peasant talk", not uncouth ignorant yokels. Nearer home than that, they were Hardy's own relatives, including his closest. Years later, Hardy's sister Mary, overhearing a Dorset man say, "Where's the coal-box to?", was reminded of the way their father spoke.[13]

Criticism, as usual, prostrated Hardy. In this week, between review and letter, he entered in his diary, *"November* 28. Woke before it was light. Felt that I had not enough staying power to hold my own in the world,"[14] a measure of the psychological shock he had just received. Although two days later, W. E. Henley in the *Academy* said the book "excites both interest and imagination, and takes a first place among the novels of the season", he also condemned most of the comic, rural dialogue as unnatural, while *The Times* on 5 December roundly remarked that Hardy's peculiarity of language was carried too far, though it grudgingly praised the descriptive scenes. Yet Hardy's other habitual reaction to attack was to fight back. The New Year saw him starting the new novel; it was, at any rate, sketched for Leslie Stephen's consideration by mid-February[15] 1879. With firm persistence, he retained its entirely Dorset setting, and its historical nature, even though Stephen himself demurred at his introducing actual historical characters; however, he admitted, "I like to have a bit of history in the background, so to speak", and cited Thackeray's skilful handling of the Waterloo scenes in *Vanity Fair*.[16]

Though precise dates are uncertain, the writing of the book, *The Trumpet Major*, went ahead fast in 1879. By mid-September half the book was finished, and the magazine *Good Words* had agreed to serialize it during 1880. Hardy's life all through the year 1879 was composed of three strands, which may be seen in the texture of the work itself. The first, of course, was his historical reading and study. More visits to the British Museum, more copying of exact period detail, including caricatures by Gillray, gave him the accurate flavour of the years 1804-1805. He even attended the funeral of Louis Napoleon at Chislehurst to study the features of Prince Napoleon, the Emperor's nephew. Secondly, he explored his own Dorset roots. Taking as excuse a New Year's Eve note from his father, saying his mother was ill and hoping to see him, he paid two visits of a fortnight each, one in the first half of February in icy cold and snow, and the other for the middle weeks of August, also unluckily in appalling wet. Yet the weather counted for little beside the memories and the cherished, familiar atmosphere he found there. His father, delighted to see him, told him innumerable tales of bygone days, with their usual gruesome quota of hangings and whippings, but also of exact details, such as the habits of the old Puddletown choir, and the location of the old Dorchester post office.[17] A story, probably told by his mother, spoke of a dumb woman in her original part of Dorset near the Somerset border, who suddenly uttered the rhyme

A cold winter, a forward spring,
A bloody summer, a dead King.

The French Revolution immediately followed. During his August visit, he also found staying with relatives his cousin, Jim Sparks, the Windsor carpenter, and discussed with him their common ancestors in faraway times.[18] Jim's builder employer in Windsor was himself also a Puddletown man, whose sister, true to his Dorset origins, Jim Sparks had married.[19]

These two strands, historical study and family reminiscence, are firmly woven into the construction of the novel, and give it remarkable unity and a steady sense of reality. Hardy was determined that the charges of unreality, brought against *The Return of the Native*, should not be repeated.[20] At the same time, there was a third factor, never noticed before. Without it, the characters would perhaps seem trivial: the girl who cannot make up her mind between suitors, familiar in so many Hardy novels, the stock elders, the comic chorus folk. What gives the work its solidity, in spite of its relatively small compass, is that these rest on universal figures from the traditional rituals of the theatre. The novel draws on Hardy's extreme, personal interest in the stage during the year 1879, when he was actually trying his hand at dramatic adaptation.

It is easy to see how the idea that he might adapt one of his own novels for the stage came into Hardy's mind just at this time. During the evening at the Lyceum on 3 August 1878, ending with the champ-agne party in Irving's dressing-room, Hardy had seen the actor perform in *Jingle*. This was a play adapted from *Pickwick Papers* by James Albery. Albery, like Hardy, had been trained as an architect. Like Hardy, he had deserted his profession, and after a number of unsuccess-ful plays, had at last found fame with *Two Roses;* this was the forerunner of much modern domestic comedy, in which Irving made his first notable mark in 1870 in the part of Digby Grant. If Albery could leave architecture for drama, Hardy, with the advantage of his own books to dramatize, might do so too. The obvious choice for stage-adaptation was *Far From the Madding Crowd*, both from its popularity as a novel, and its strong plot. It was an inspired time to begin dramatic work. Ellen Terry had joined Irving as his leading lady in 1878, and in 1879 she was playing Portia to his Shylock, both performances of great power and originality. Nor would Hardy lack advice on the difficult art of writing for the theatre. One of his companions in the *Jingle* evening had been Walter Herries Pollock, the play-adaptor, though Hardy claimed that his own first draft, which he called "*The Mistress of the Farm*—A pastoral drama", had been adapted "alone and unassisted".

The fate of this adaption was not vastly important, as it proved; yet Hardy's concentration in 1879 on theatrical matters held great import-ance for the novel he was also writing, *The Trumpet-Major*. Briefly, the pattern of the book, embracing nearly every major character, derives from the old Italian Comedy of Masks, whose debased form, the harle-quinade, was showing in nearly every Victorian theatre, burlesque, and ballet. To take character by character, Anne Garland, the heroine who dances tantalizingly between the brothers John and Bob Loveday, is the typical Columbine,[21] demure, coquettish, but susceptible enough to prefer in the end the flashy, spangled Harlequin. This, in the novel, is Bob Loveday, who has all the attributes of a stage harlequin, down to the merest detail. He dresses in startling finery, which he shows off in Chapter 30. When he wishes to make a special effort to win Anne, he deliberately "struts", as Hardy wrote, in his naval lieutenant's new uniform (Chapter 39). The scene where he escapes from the press-gang (Chapter 31) is very closely based on the theatrical rituals of the Italian comedy. It was traditional for Columbine and her lover to be hotly pursued by authority; it was known in stage terms as "The Chase". This happens in the novel when Anne and Bob are both pursued by the press-gang. Stronger even in tradition was the great "Leap" or "Jump" of Harlequin. One nineteenth-century harlequin made such a feature of this that the theatre where he performed was actually known as "the Jump".[22] Bob's huge jump out of the press-gang's hands into the apple-tree, his "figure flying like a raven's across the sky", is Harlequin's giant "Leap". Immediately after, he executes Harlequin's traditional trick-scenery routine, a sequence perfected by the great theatre family of Lupino, of diving through a set of trap-doors and collapsible stage-flats. Bob flies up on the hoist, through the trap-doors of the mill, with the skill of a stage-acrobat, "whirled up by the machinery", as if into the flies of a theatre.

There are even more striking resemblances in other characters. Old miser Derriman is the traditional Pantaloon, foolish-cunning, nervous, shrunk, wizened, at his death "little more than a light, empty husk". His odd fondness for Anne—"I believe the old gentleman is in love with you", says her mother—is the exact counterpart of Pantaloon's traditional feeling for Columbine. She was often his ward, just as Anne finds herself old Derriman's heiress. Next, in precise detail, is the Boasting Captain of the Italian masks—Shakespeare's Captains Pistol and Parolles—here represented by Festus Derriman. In the earliest draft of the novel, he was *Captain* Delaylynde, a Dorset family name which Hardy also used in his review of William Barnes' poems.[23] In every way Festus is the boasting soldier of the masks, cowardly when in danger, vainglorious when there is none, drunken, incompetent even in military matters (Chapter 7). There remains Anne's unsuccessful suitor, John Loveday, the trumpet-major himself. Here Hardy deserts the nineteenth-century English usage, common since Grimaldi, of the jovial Clown; he gives us, as many contemporary harlequin ballets did, the French creation of the sad, pensive, white-faced Pierrot. John's pallor is often remarked on; so is his thoughtfulness and simple-heartedness. "When he was a boy he was the simplest fellow alive," says his brother in Chapter 33. His tragic end, foreshadowed in the last sentence of the novel, is Pierrot's melancholy final exit. In fact, much of the novel is conceived theatrically in terms of entrances and exits, accompanied by stage-lighting effects. In Chapter 31, Bob is suddenly discovered by the light of the lantern when he enters "still radiant in the full dress he had worn with such effect at the Theatre Royal". John's exit on the last page is even more dramatic and stage-lit.

> The candle held by his father shed its waving light upon John's face and uniform as with a farewell smile he turned on the door-stone, backed by the black night;

His footsteps die away, off-stage, as the curtain falls on him for ever.

Was Hardy conscious of building his two other novelistic elements, those of historical event and Dorset local colour, upon this third structure of universal theatrical tradition? One can only say that his interest in the theatre at this time was personal in a very particular sense. In the novel, Festus, the boastful soldier, marries the comedy actress, Matilda—Captain marrying Soubrette, again in mask tradition. A real comedy actress was certainly in Hardy's mind at this time. In his diary for 4 December 1879, he entered this note.[24]

> Helen M—th—s's face. A profile not too Greek for an English fireside, yet Greek enough for an artist's eye: arch, saucy style of countenance, dark eyes, brows & hair, the last low on forehead.

The play-going Hardy had spotted an actress just beginning to make an impression on the London stage. This was Miss Helen Mathews. She did not attract "an artist's eye", in the theatrical journals of the time, until two years after she had attracted Hardy's; but the picture of her then playing a leading role is certainly "Greek enough", with its classical features.[25] She had also, by the time Hardy made his note, played some "saucy" roles, and won praise for her comedy. One of her characterizations was Lady Sneerwell in *The School for Scandal*, which she played on tour, and which pleased the critics when she gave it at the Olympic Theatre a year or so later.[26] As this suggests, Helen Mathews was no ingénue. She was now thirty years old, though Hardy, like his own Bob Loveday with Matilda, may have imagined her younger. She had already several years' theatrical experience in the provinces, with parts in contemporary plays by James Albery, and in Shakespeare with Emily Fowler's touring company.

Helen Mathews had, too, the brunette looks and the "arch" expression, which had always attracted Hardy, both in his own cousin, Tryphena Sparks, and in another actress of his earlier London days, Mrs. Scott-Siddons, whose Rosalind had set him off writing sonnets. Besides, it is clear from other entries in his diary that the eye of the impressionable Hardy was beginning to rove at this precise time, and to settle on chance-met young women. The train journey from Tooting gave him plenty of opportunities. On one such journey to Town, on 27 June 1879, he saw in the railway carriage, "a statuesque girl" with "absolutely perfect" features and a face "not unlike that of a nymph". On the homeward journey, by happy chance, he sat opposite "a contrasting girl of sly humour—the pupil of her eye being mostly under the eyelid".

The fact is, after five years of marriage, his thoughts were on the wing. Emma was nearly forty. Her heavy beauty had run to fat, her figure to dumpiness.[27] Her lameness and consequent lack of exercise in Town, where she missed the country horse-riding, contributed. The imaginative Hardy required nymphs and sylphs, of past memory or present discovery. It is likely Emma guessed. In August he took her on an appallingly wet holiday to Weymouth, the scene of this poem.

> She charged me with having said this and that
> To another woman long years before,
> In the very parlour where we sat,—

Sat on a night when the endless pour
Of rain on the roof and the road below
Bent the spring of the spirit more and more . . .

"Long years before" was the time of Hardy's Weymouth jaunts with Tryphena. Now, ten years later, Emma seems to have found him out.

Whatever difficulties may have begun to occur in private life, Hardy's novel, *The Trumpet-Major*, was a triumphant success with the critics. The historical setting, the realistic Dorset background, were both accepted as Hardy at his best. His careful study of the two water-mills at Sutton Poyntz, on the outskirts of Weymouth, had resulted in a convincing yet romantic setting for his story. Hardy himself was so involved in this that he actually designed the pictorial cover. The whole book shows his distinctive gift of making places and people at one. The mill itself is as much a leading personage in the story as the two families of Loveday and Garland. The substructure of theatre ritual gave a continuous dramatic interest to the plot. Though miniature in scale, it is thoroughly satisfying in achievement. It was serialized all through 1880 in *Good Words* with notable success, in spite of some minor bowdlerizing by Dr. Macleod, the Scottish clergyman editor. Its publication in volume form, in October of that year, was greeted with universal praise. The *Spectator*, relieved that Hardy did not attempt another high tragedy like *The Return*, found it "observant, truthful, humorous". The pontifical *Athenaeum* thought John Loveday the best character Hardy had yet drawn, and the *Westminster Review* "decidedly the best story which Mr. Hardy has yet written". Gosse, in a private letter, considered it to rank with the "cream" of Hardy's work. George Saintsbury congratulated him on abandoning the pretentious diction of previous books, and the *Saturday* praised the group scenes.

There was only one drawback to this success: but it was a daunting one. The book in volume form simply did not sell. Smith, Elder, had the same dismal response for it that *The Return of the Native* had received. Need for money forced Hardy to keep writing, though signs of distress and pressure had already begun to appear, even in *The Trumpet-Major*. Not only did he reproduce practically verbatim a chapter-opening from *Desperate Remedies*; in order to cut corners and meet serial demands, he had reproduced also almost word for word in Chapter 23 a humorous description of a militia drilling scene from one of his historical authorities, C. H. Gifford's *History of the Wars Occasioned by the French Revolution*. Unfortunately, it seems, he did not notice that Gifford himself had lifted the scene from an earlier fictional source.[29] His own silent plagiarism, when it was found out, caused him endless trouble and irritating controversy; here it is a witness to haste and stress. His remedy for small sales was now the American, Henry Harper. Harper's *Weekly* had published Hardy's two short stories in 1878, and Hardy gave him a smuggling tale, *The Distracted Preacher, in* spring 1870. Now he placed another with him, *Fellow-Townsmen*, which Harper serialized, immediately after it appeared in the English *New Quarterly*, in April/May 1880. Then Harper came forward with a new proposal. He was launching a European Edition of his *Weekly*; would Hardy provide a full-length serial? He offered excellent terms. It was a bait that Hardy could not refuse.

Yet, by a number of small but significant incidents, the illness, forewarned by his feeling of utter lassitude as long ago as November 1878, was beginning to gain on him. All through 1880, he suffered increasingly morbid and nervous fears. On 19 May, he felt oppressed by the horror of waking at three in the morning on the outskirts of crowded London, which he imagined as "a monster whose body had four million heads and eight million eyes". By 27 July, with nearly eight chapters of the new book written, the Hardys tried a holiday abroad. They toured Normandy, but the morbid horrors persisted. In Le Havre, he was terrified by a hotel room whose floor "was painted a bloody red . . . as if struggles had taken place there", and barricaded the door. At Honfleur, the figure of the Christ on a wayside Calvary "seemed to writhe and cry in the twilight".[30] A visit to Dorset after their return brought no respite, for Hardy was pushing on with the novel in haste to provide material for the illustrator, George Du Maurier. By 16 October he had practically finished the first book, but, during a stay in Cambridge, he felt "an indescribable physical weariness", coupled with weird fancies about the wax on the candles in King's Chapel, with their reminders of the last time he saw his friend Horace Moule before the latter's tragic suicide in 1873. Returning to London on 23 October, just before *The Trumpet-Major* came out, Hardy felt worse than ever, and on Sunday 28 October he sent for a doctor.

Dr. Henry Edward Beck, who lived exactly opposite in Trinity Road, had nothing but proximity to recommend him. It was forty years since he had acquired the minimum medical qualifications of L.S.A. and M.R.C.S. He came each day, diagnosed internal bleeding, but had no suggestions. Emma, in alarm, asked the Macmillans, who sent their own doctor, Arthur Shears, M.D.[31] He put Hardy, who was in considerable pain, firmly to bed and after a few days made the suggestion that Hardy, to minimize the haemorrhage, should lie with the foot of the bed raised, so that his feet were higher than his head. He had inflammation of the bladder, caused by calculus or stone, which might need a dangerous operation; in fact, this condition recurred for the rest of his life.[32] Stress, worry, fatigue, a very damp house, prolonged bathing in Normandy—which Hardy believed, in this instance, to have been the cause—and subsequent chill would all predispose him to it. In February 1880, he called in Sir Henry Thompson, the internationally famous surgeon, who practised exclusively in diseases of the bladder, and had operated on Napoleon III for stone. Thompson, who had been recommended by Kegan Paul,[33] evidently decided against operation, but advised continued rest.

Yet work must go on. He could not let Harper and the golden opportunity slip. He would dictate the novel to Emma, to whom he afterwards paid a tribute for working "bravely at both writing and nursing".[34] Yet, not unnaturally, the last five of the six books of *A Laodicean* show a terrible decline. The first book ended with a garden-party, based on one at the Macmillans, where the delicate relationships between hero and heroine are shown, combining the impact of a summer thunderstorm with the flickering emotions of the two. It recalls the great storm scene in *Far From the Madding Crowd*. From then onward, though, Hardy fell back on every sort of borrowed literary short-cut, to meet the numbers of the serial on time. Already, he had drawn heavily on the maxims of Balthasar Gracian the Jesuit, copied so faithfully into his notebook by Emma in their Sturminster days.[35] In describing old De Stancy, who uses these aphorisms, he also lifted about two hundred words from a sketch of a notable racing man in an article, "The Turf", from an old *Quarterly Review*.[36] Now, and as always under literary pressure, he drew on his boyhood reading of the tawdry historical romances of Harrison Ainsworth. Dare, the baby-faced villain of *A Laodicean*, is an Ainsworth villain like the evil Earl of Rochester in *Old St. Pauls*, who combines a spurious innocence with the blackest villainy.[37] Not only literature but topography was pressed into service, as the novel dragged to a close. Books five and six are a travelogue of the Hardys' journeys up the Rhine and to the Low Countries in 1876 and the recent visit to Normandy. Hardy's recent theatre experience is seen in the telegrams to and from the actress's agent (Book 3). Hardy afterwards told the American William Lyon Phelps that he feared he would die, and therefore perhaps put more of the facts of his own life into the book than anything he had then written.[38] Yet, unless one counts the lengthy travelogue, all the personal incidents from Hardy's early life, the dispute about infant baptism, the discussions on the architecture, had been written before he fell ill. There is obsessive use of coincidence, and what can only be called voyeuristic incidents, which are certainly typical of Hardy himself. Captain de Stancy, inflamed by unaccustomed drink, sees through a hole in a wall the heroine exercising in a pink gymnastic dress.

Though occasional London friends such as Edmund Gosse visited him, he was largely alone with Emma. His wife's devoted care through the appallingly cold winter of 1880–81 bore fruit; a letter to her from his sister Mary pays tribute, and incidentally shows how close the two women were at this time.[39] On 10 April 1881, Hardy went out of doors in a carriage, on 1 May he finished *A Laodicean* himself in pencil, and on 3 May was given a clean bill of health by Sir Henry Thompson. A few days later he walked out alone for the first time for six months on Wandsworth Common, and repeated happily to himself in the sunshine some lines from Gray's *Ode on the Pleasure Arising from Vicissitude*. He was well again; but the illness had convinced him of two things. One was that London was bad for his health; he may well have remembered his near-breakdown in 1867. The other was that, contrary to the advice he had believed, and which had caused him to come to London, living in or near a big city harmed his work. Perhaps the larger stage, crowded with characters, confused a mind formed in a solitary Dorset hamlet. The smaller provincial setting might, after all, profit him more. At all events, he and Emma decided to live again in Dorset, with visits of only a few months a year to London.

# 3

# Wimborne

"LANHERNE", The Avenue, Wimborne, where the Hardys moved on 25 June 1881, provided a setting, though in the town, which reminded them of their idyllic surroundings at Sturminster Newton. The road had a row of newly-planted lime trees, and, as Hardy wrote after a few days,

> Our garden has all sorts of old-fashioned flowers in full bloom: Canterbury bells, blue and white, and Sweet Williams of every variety, strawberries and cherries that are ripe, currants and gooseberries that are nearly ripe, peaches that are green, and apples that are decidedly immature.

Not only was there an orchard, a conservatory, and a vine on the wall, but they found the local society rewarding, and not at all unintelligent. There were musical evenings at the home of a County Court judge, Tindal Atkinson, and regular Shakespeare readings, in which the Hardys took part, though Dr. George Batterbury, who organized these, found Hardy very reticent.[1] Still, in such company and atmosphere, he began to feel himself again, both as a man and a writer.[2] Even the fact that *A Laodicean*, when published later in the year, was quickly remaindered, did not seem to disturb him unduly. Nor did the insult that *Harper's Magazine*, after having commissioned and serialized the work, attacked the book, when it appeared in volume form, in one of the most discouraging reviews that Hardy had ever received.[3] He may well have been compensated by a eulogistic survey of his works in the *British Quarterly Review*, a nonconformist paper which praised him to the skies.[4] By all signs, Hardy was at peace and in health again, and already exploring new plans for work.

The best evidence that Hardy found renewed health and enjoyment of life at Wimborne is that he composed a humorous poem, perhaps his first since *The Bride Night Fire*, printed half-a-dozen years before. He noticed that the churchyard of Wimborne Minster had been levelled, and all the tombstones redistributed. The architect Sir Arthur Blomfield, whom he had just met after fifteen years, reminded Hardy of the 1860s, when they had supervised the removal of hundreds of jumbled coffins from Old St. Pancras Churchyard, with strange results. "Do you remember," were Blomfield's first words, "how we found the man with two heads at St. Pancras?"[5] Hardy exploited this idea in a poem about

Wimborne Minster, *The Levelled Churchyard*, and invested it with an earthy humour suitable to its rural setting. Two of its verses read, in his manuscript,

> Where we are huddled none can trace,
> And if our names remain
> They pave some path or p—ing place
> Where we have never lain!
>
> There's not a modest maiden elf
> But dreads the final Trumpet,
> Lest half of her should rise herself,
> And half some local strumpet!

He clearly delighted in this fancy; for when much later he published the poem, the adjective "p—ing" for "pissing" was allowed to stand through several editions, and when finally changed to "porch or" in his *Collected Poems*, the alteration was made in an errata slip, which must have drawn even more attention to the word.

Even before launching into such light relief, Hardy had found inspiration for a new novel. By an astonishing chance this grew out of his recent illness. Hardy's final consultation had been with the specialist, Sir Henry Thompson. Handsome and slim, with dark penetrating eyes, Thompson was a man of myriad enthusiasms, quite outside medicine. Those who knew him well said that he hurled himself into each new subject, only to give it up after some years when he had exhausted its interest.[6] At the time Hardy met him in 1881, the ruling passion was astronomy. Thompson had made in his house at East Molesey a private observatory; he equipped it with the finest instruments, and employed a qualified assistant.[7] He was incapable of remaining quiet about whatever happened to be the reigning enthusiasm,[8] and the interview with Hardy at this time cannot have passed without a detailed description of his personal observatory. Hardy was primed for a novel set in an amateur observatory before he left for Wimborne: his first night in the new home confirmed it by the appearance of Tebbutt's Comet, which he and Emma saw from their little conservatory at "Lanherne".[9]

Hardy forged ahead with plans for his new astronomical novel. By another happy chance, on 23 July 1881, he, Emma, and his sister Kate, now a teacher at Sandford Orcas, just over the Somerset border, went from Wimborne on a wagonette drive past the estate of Charborough with its hilltop tower, a late Georgian folly, rebuilt in 1839 after being struck by lightning. Hardy seized on this for his hero's home-made observatory, though he later mixed it with features from other Dorset towers, notably the column near Milborne St. Andrew, which provided most of the setting as distinct from the architecture.[10] Moreover the old driver of the wagonette told them local stories of Miss

Drax, who once owned Charborough, and who had married a hand-some man much younger than herself.[11] From such hints came Viviette and Swithin, the heroine and hero of *Two on a Tower*, though Hardy invested them not only with age-difference but also with class-difference, on his old obsessive pattern of *The Poor Man and the Lady*.

Hardy was quick to use these ideas, in spite of spending the last week of August and the first fortnight of September touring Scotland, and the rest of September sitting under his garden-vine, correcting proofs of the volume-form *A Laodicean*.[12] At the beginning of October, *Atlantic Monthly* asked him for a serial. He clearly had the new story in preparation, since on 26 November he wrote to the Astronomer Royal for permission to see Greenwich Observatory, pretending to be asking "if it would be possible for him [Hardy] to adapt an old tower, built in a plantation in the West of England for other objects, to the requirements of a telescopic study of the stars by a young man very ardent in that pursuit". Evidently the shy Hardy had not sufficiently impressed Sir Henry Thompson, a connoisseur of conversation, to get an invitation to Molesey. However, this fictional ruse got him a pass to Greenwich, and proves that he had already fixed the details of tower and surround-ing landscape by that date; in December he was writing to William Cawthorne Unwin, the engineer, for information on lens-grinding and telescopes. He also consulted books on astronomy by Richard A. Proctor, founder of the recent scientific weekly, *Knowledge*.

This, and the speed at which Hardy was obviously working—he also completed two new short stories in these autumn months—show that he was finding no handicap in living once more in Dorset. Perhaps the three years just spent in London for literary purposes had been an unnecessary mistake. It has even been suggested that his difficulties as a writer in London—the hasty plagiarism in *The Trumpet-Major*, the lack of inspiration in *A Laodicean*—"may conceivably have derived, directly or indirectly, from the bad literary company he tended to keep" during those years.[13] There may be something in this, though the statement is a sweeping one. On analysis, Hardy's literary contacts in that period fall into two distinct groups. First, there were his encounters with Tennyson, Browning, Arnold, and Henry James, whose first major novels appeared in these years. Hardy recorded them in wry, thumbnail sketches—Tennyson's wife lying on the sofa "as if in a coffin", Matthew Arnold, with a young and inexperienced hostess, not letting the ladies retire after dinner, an action which must have inconvenienced them, but of whose results that high-minded thinker seemed happily unaware. Yet these, and his continued visits to the ancient literary widow of Barry Cornwall, were brief meetings. Hardy was too shy to follow them up, and, for instance, greatly regretted that, although invited, he never again went to see the Tennysons. A soirée musicale, to meet members of the 1878 International Literary Congress and of the Comédie Française, bewildered him.[14]

The second class of literary friends had been quite different. Perhaps the most reputable was Edmund Gosse; the rest were bookish, but without special spark, editors, translators, collaborators, part-time writers. W. H. Pollock and the heavily-bearded J. W. Comyns Carr were play-adaptors, Joseph Knight a dramatic critic, William Minto a minor novelist and editor of Scott. Frederick Locker was a minor poet, Charles Godfrey Leland, the craggy-faced American, a writer of light verse and translator of Heine, Sir Patrick Maccombaich Colquhoun was better known as an oarsman, secretary of Leander, than for his legal essays; Reginald Bosworth Smith, fellow Dorset man and Harrow schoolmaster, wrote books on North African history. Sir George Douglas, whose brother Frank was a neighbour of Hardy at Wimborne, tried to write romantic novels.

Perhaps the most congenial to Hardy was his exact contemporary, Edward Henry Palmer, the orientalist, a self-taught counterpart of the Dorchester boy Tolbort, whom Hardy had known in youth. While a poor clerk, Palmer had learnt languages from foreign waiters in London cafés. A Cambridge teacher of Hindustani had taken him up, as Horace Moule had Tolbort, and he became Fellow of a College and author of a book of Eastern travels. Sent on a secret mission to Egypt by Gladstone's government, Palmer, like Tolbort, died in his early forties, in his instance the victim of murder by Arabs. The moving spirit in the circle was Walter Besant, bearded like a sailor, jovial founder of the Rabelais Club, for writers who had shown "virility"—that is, sexual frankness— in their work, to which Hardy was flatteringly elected as an original member. Besant was the co-author with James Rice of robust historical romances, the Besant and Rice novels, natural successors to those of Hardy's youthful favourite, Harrison Ainsworth, though slightly more distinguished. With a finger in every pie, he helped in 1884 to start the Society of Authors, where, Hardy said, "he gloats over the villainies of publishers";[15] but he was hardly a great literary figure.

Nor had Hardy, in his three London years, encountered high society, though he had been introduced to Sir Percy Shelley, the poet's son, and the Russells had been present when he met Tennyson. By an irony, the middle-class Emma now became his passport into the circles which meant so much to him in his later London seasons.[16] Emma's uncle, Canon Edwin Hamilton Gifford, married as his second wife a daughter of Bishop Jeune of Peterborough. In summer 1881, just when the Hardys were settled at Wimborne, came the social step crucial to them. On 16 August, Francis Jeune, Canon Gifford's brother-in-law, married Susan Mary Elizabeth, the relatively young widow of Colonel the Hon. John Constantine Stanley. Stanley had been heir presumptive to his brother, the third Lord Stanley of Alderley, and his widow's remarriage in the Savoy Chapel was an excessively fashionable event, with royalty present. Emma was now connected, however remotely, with the highest society, including the powerful tribe of Stanley. Hardy soon became a favourite of the lively Mrs. Jeune, whose own background was aristocratic in its own right. It is ironical to think of Hardy, the son of a cook, beside this lady whose ancestors had owned half the Highlands "from sea to sea", and who complained of "the difficulty of getting a decent cook" for her lavish entertainment.[17] He at once noted a weird legend from her family history in Scotland,[18] and adopted for the name of his highborn heroine in *Two on a Tower*, Lady Constantine, the middle name of her first husband, John Constantine Stanley. He also adopted his nature for the unpleasant husband, Sir Blount Constantine; for "Johnnie" Stanley was as unreasonable and violent as the fictional Sir Blount.[19] Moreover, he took a chapter from her second husband's professional career. Francis Jeune had, as one of his first assignments in the law, the task of investigating the notorious Tichborne claimant. With a special commission, he actually visited Wagga Wagga in Australia, and came back with the impression—or so his wife afterwards asserted[20]—that the man who claimed to be the lost Sir Roger Tichborne, and who had been living in that town as a butcher, was an imposter named Arthur Orton. Jeune actually appeared *for* Orton, as a junior, and must have been relieved when his leader threw the case up. It has never been noticed before how echoes of the Tichborne case occur throughout one of the sub-plots of *Two on a Tower*. Sir Blount Constantine is reported in London when he should be hunting big game in Africa. Investigation by Hardy's young hero proves it to be a case of mistaken identity. Then again, the two reports at two different times of Sir Blount's death in Africa, on which the sub-plot hinges, at once suggest the actual death abroad of Sir Roger Tichborne, and the claimant's contention that he did not die. It may not be accidental that the Christian name of the credulous Lady Tichborne, Henriette, reminds one of Lady Constantine's name, Viviette, while her brother in the novel reappears from Rio, the last known habitation of the real Sir Roger. It is a fact, too, that Jeune used to regale guests, including Hardy, with details of the case.[21]

Hardy's portrayal of his passionate heroine, Viviette, owed less to real life than to a contemporary dramatic poem. In April 1882, when Hardy was writing the novel, Swinburne, whose work Hardy had adored in the 1860s, brought out his *Tristram of Lyonesse*. Hardy, deeply stirred by the setting where he himself had met and wooed Emma, read the new poem avidly. Physical descriptions of Hardy's heroine echo those of Iseult in the poem. He even quoted three lines of it in the novel, just before she yields to fatal passion.

He turn'd and saw the terror in her eyes,
That yearn'd upon him shining in such wise
As a star midway in the midnight fix'd.

Hardy also copied two passages from the Prologue into his notebooks,
and it is clear he saw in it a parallel to his own story. He had already
used the poetry of Tennyson for some of his own astronomical descriptions in the novel.[22] Here, in Swinburne's poem, he found the famous
women in love all through history, from Helen to Guinevere, compared
by Swinburne individually to various kinds of star. In Hardy's mind
the passionate nature of his heroine was at one with these great lovers
of history, and his prose when dealing with Viviette takes on the sensuous intensity of Swinburne's verse.

Aside from details of plot and sub-plots, the main design of *Two on a
Tower* was, in Hardy's own words, "to set the emotional history of two
infinitesimal lives against the stupendous background of the stellar
universe, and to impart to readers the sentiment that of these contrasting magnitudes the smaller might be the greater to them as men".[23]
This theme had been stated by Hardy fifteen years before, in two very
early sonnets, *At a Lunar Eclipse* and *In Vision I Roamed*.[24] The novel
shows how modern scientific discovery, by probing deeper into the
universe, seems to intensify purely human problems. In this, it continues
the process of *A Laodicean*, where innovations such as railway construction, the electric telegraph, technical improvement in architecture, and
even revolutionary bomb-making, form the material background to a
human love-story. The critics found in *Two on a Tower* not only the
usual traces of immorality they expected to deplore in a Hardy plot,
but also a satire on the Established Church. The editor of the *Atlantic
Monthly*, which serialized the work from May to December 1882, was
perturbed, and when it appeared, practically unrevised, in volume form
at the end of October, public and critics were offended too. Hardy's
own reply to the *St. James's Gazette* early in 1883, and his later defence,[25]
are surely disingenuous, or even possibly satirical in themselves. Hardy's
"studied insult to the Church", which critics found, was not confined
to his plot-device by which the pregnant heroine marries a Bishop
solely in order to pass off her illegitimate child as the seven months'
offspring of the Bishop himself. For all that Hardy might say, broad
satire of the established clergy runs right through the book, in which
the Bishop does not even make an appearance until over half-way. The
hero's father is a clergyman who marries beneath him, is snubbed by the
gentry, drops "a cuss or two", becomes a farmer, and falls dead, "it
being said . . . Master God was in tantrums wi'en for leaving his service".
When the hero and heroine get married—illegally, as the report of her
former husband's death is at that time false—the proceedings are

described farcically. The clergyman is a locum tenens, "apt to be rather wandering in his wits"; the clerk apologetically explains, "The best men goes into the brewing; or into the shipping now-a-days." When the parson actually appears, Hardy describes him as a "somewhat sorry clerical specimen", who has been found shambling about in the cemetery, under the impression it was a funeral and not a wedding. As for Mr. Torkingham, vicar of the heroine's own parish, he is largely a figure of fun, as his punning name suggests. His clerical accent produces a distressingly comic effect when he makes the church choir adopt it; when, "expecting a question on some local business", he finds Lady Constantine wishing to consult him on a point of conscience, he "altered his face to the higher branch of his profession". When he wishes to impress the Bishop at dinner, he prepares and delivers elaborate con-versation-pieces about the last Diocesan Synod, in which he quotes back at length the Bishop's own remarks on that occasion. As for the Bishop himself, he has, according to the heroine, "very pronounced views about his own position, and some other undesirable qualities." He "had personal weaknesses that were fatal to sympathy for more than a moment" and "a mind whose sensitive fear of danger to its own dignity hindered it from criticism elsewhere". He has "the air of a man too good for his destiny", and uses what he calls "the force of trained, logical reasoning" to persuade her that, as a husband, he is "Heaven's gift". Even the cautious Mr. Torkingham, after the Bishop's death, admits he had faults, "of which arrogance was not the least". Hardy was surely indulging in further satire, when in 1895 he claimed "that the Bishop is every inch a gentleman, and that the parish priest who figures in the narrative is one of the most estimable characters".[26]

Hardy, of course, had plenty of good precedent for satirizing the clergy, notably in his much-admired Trollope. Two things, however, seem new in *Two on a Tower*. One is the generalized satire on several types of clergy, which had never occurred before in a Hardy novel—indeed, clerical satire had hardly occurred at all. Only Mr. Swancourt in *A Pair of Blue Eyes* had been portrayed as a social snob throughout that novel. The other is the almost farcical tone of his description of the habits of these satirized clerics, a cause of offence. Yet Hardy had a particular professional motive for making this farcical treatment of the clergy such a part of his new novel. In 1879 he had adapted *Far From the Madding Crowd* as a stage play.[27] A re-adaptation then took place at the hands of J. W. Comyns Carr, who in the summer of 1880 submitted the play to the management of Hare and Kendal. It was accepted provisionally by Hare, but rejected on 11 November, to add to Hardy's depression as he lay ill in bed. Mrs. Kendal afterwards claimed that she never saw it and the rejection was Hare's. Either Hare or she, however, gave the plot to their rising young actor-dramatist Arthur Pinero, without telling him where it came from. Pinero wrote a romantic farce called *The Squire*, in which the leading lady's part was a woman farm-owner. The play was produced at the St. James's on 29 December 1881, and critics at once saw some likeness to *Far From the Madding Crowd*, especially when Hardy and Carr revealed that their play had been submitted to the same management over a year before. In the first week of January 1882, Hardy, up from Wimborne, took a box to see Pinero's play, together with Comyns Carr and the monocled lawyer George Lewis, having been advised by his Wimborne friend, Judge Tindal Atkinson, of a case "on all fours with yours".[28] No writ ensued, and indeed the plays had little in common, though Lewis said unofficially, according to Hardy, that similarity of situation might make a case.[29] There was, however, great newspaper controversy, annoying to Hardy. The *Illustrated Sporting and Dramatic News* suggested a solution

> which could really be best managed by immediately producing Messrs. Hardy and Comyns Carr's play. Surely a genial manager would, in the spirit of gentle rivalry, put the other in rehearsal.

This hint was taken. Comyns Carr drastically revised their play, and after a provincial try-out at Liverpool, which the Hardys attended, and in other towns, it opened at the Globe Theatre on 29 April 1882. However, it ran barely sixty performances in London, whereas Pinero's play had a triumph of 170 nights, followed by an immensely long and successful provincial tour.[30]

The great success of *The Squire* was galling to Hardy; but he doubt-less noticed, from his stage-box, that it depended largely on the part specially written into the play for John Hare himself. This was the character of a self-styled "mad parson", the Reverend Paul Dormer. It had, of course, nothing to do with *Far From the Madding Crowd*, and might not seem particularly funny to a modern audience. It certainly bore no relation to anything in the Hardy and Comyns Carr adaptation of the novel, but a farcical clergyman, with Hare's skilled playing, kept the St. James's audiences continuously amused. In search of a wider public than his recent books had achieved, Hardy tried the theme of comic clergy in the novel he was now writing. Unfortunately, he overdid the satire. It is another irony that when in 1888 the St. James's also pilloried clergy too savagely in *The Dean's Daughter*, that play received just the same sort of shocked notices as Hardy's novel, *Two on a Tower*.[31]

Hardy's visit to London in January 1882 imported yet another theatrical element into his novels and stories. He cannot have failed to go to the big current theatrical success, the very recent revival at the Lyceum of Albery's *Two Roses*, starring his favourite Helen Mathews.[32] She had been engaged, as her first appearance at the Lyceum, to play the part of Katryn in the curtain-raiser, Planché's old-fashioned comedictta, *The Captain of the Watch*. The "Two Roses" of the main play's title, Ida and Lottie, were to be played by two very popular actresses, Fanny Josephs and Winifred Emery. At the last moment, Miss Josephs was taken seriously ill. Helen Mathews had not played Ida before, but she had played Lottie with another company in the provinces, and so was familiar with the sister-part. In these difficult circumstances, she had a startling triumph in taking over the part of Ida; by contrast the pretty Miss Emery was said to be "inoffensive but colourless". In fact, Ida, though the smaller part, is by far the better-written, as clever Miss Mathews clearly had the wit to see. Her tall, dark, slender beauty also suited the stage-directions, which require exactly that. The reviews praised her animated style, her sympathetic voice, her "earnestness and intelligence" which was "deserving of the highest praise" and her "very natural and womanly feeling". Moreover, she scored a triumph in the curtain-raiser too, playing "with great spirit". A promising future was prophesied for her. Unhappily, for some reason, this did not materialize. A very few small parts were all that came her way in the next half-dozen years, and she died in January 1890 at the early age of forty: perhaps a tragedy of poor health.

This is not to say, of course, that Hardy ever met Helen Mathews, any more than he appears to have met Mrs. Scott-Siddons who had affected him so profoundly some years before. His appreciation of her beauty and intelligence was probably entirely from the stalls or the stage-box. The situation is described in his novel of the 1890s, *The Well-Beloved*, whose hero's temperament, by many signs, was exactly that of Hardy himself. In a chapter significantly entitled "Familiar Phenomena in the Distance", Hardy wrote of his hero's pursuit of his womanly transient ideal.

> For months he would find her on the stage of a theatre: then she would flit away, leaving the poor, empty carcase that had lodged her to mumm on as best it could without her—a sorry lay figure to his eyes, heaped with imperfections and sullied with commonplace. . . . Once she was a dancing-girl at the Royal Moorish Palace of Varieties, though during her whole continuance at that establishment he never once exchanged a word with her, nor did she first or last ever dream of his existence.

So though Hardy may have allowed himself, as was his habit, some wistful domestic daydreams, in which slender Miss Mathews took the place of his stout Emma—"a profile not too Greek for an English fireside"—it is unlikely he got any further than a "sweeping glance" from his opera-glass. His admiration, however, is indirectly connected with a grotesque incident later in this year of 1882. A trivial monthly publication, *London Society*, describing itself as "an illustrated

magazine of light and amusing literature for the hours of relaxation",
received a poem signed "Thomas Hardy", which was duly printed
above that signature in August. Entitled *Two Roses*, it played banally
with the comparison between a girl and a rose—

> Thou art a rose and so is she;
> Each blossoms in the bright today.

Challenged by Hardy, the editor lamely replied that there must be two
Thomas Hardys.[33] The poem had, in fact, been written, probably quite
cynically, by a rascally former colleague of Hardy's at Blomfield's
London office, who received and pocketed the cheque for it, and
forged Hardy's signature, familiar to him, as an endorsement.[34] Hardy's
indignation was immense, and justified. Not only were the verses bad,
but they were clearly based, as their title and treatment suggests, on
the play he had recently been watching with such a deep personal
interest, *Two Roses*. In the play, the two girls, acted by Miss Mathews
and Miss Emery, appear with bunches of roses, give their lovers the
roses, and are frequently compared with roses. For Hardy the hoax was
uncomfortably near a home-truth—and moreover a truth he could not
acknowledge to anyone, least of all to Emma.

All the same, contact with the theatre, especially if he had a personal
interest such as this, always had an influence on Hardy's work. His
theatrical enthusiasm can be seen in two short stories published early
in 1883. These are *The Three Strangers* and *The Romantic Adventures of
a Milkmaid*. The first of these, a grimly humorous little tale with almost perfect unity of setting and action, is so obviously dramatic, that
Hardy himself "used to think I w$^d$. arrange that little story for the
stage: and began doing it". He did not finish; but in 1893 James
Barrie wrote to ask Hardy for a one-act play, to be produced in London
with some others. Hardy took up the task again, adapting it as *The
Three Wayfarers*, described by *The Times* as "unquestionably the best
piece of the evening".[35] As for *The Romantic Adventures of a Milkmaid*,
this hastily-written piece is almost a pantomime, with innocent
Cinderella-like heroine, demon-king of a Baron offering a ball-dress, a
mysterious ball, a carriage and team of black horses, and a stagey
happy ending. Even his novel, *Two on a Tower*, published in volume
form late in October 1882, has a melodramatic ending—"Viviette was
dead. The Bishop was avenged." Though some critics have approved,
this comes perilously near the curtain lines of current melodramas such
as *East Lynne* or *Lady Audley's Secret*.

To balance the poor reviews of this novel, there appeared a long
survey praising Hardy's work. The writer of this anonymous article in
the *Westminster Review*[36] was in fact the young Havelock Ellis. Following his own preferences, this advocate of free love analysed all Hardy's

women, and summed up the novels in the words, "what one observes
about them first is that they are all love-stories". Ellis coined a vivid
general phrase for Hardy's women as "Undines of the earth", and
claimed that Hardy's attitude to all these "not too good" women was
"in a great degree, new". He praised Hardy as a poet in prose, compared
such writing favourably with the actual Dorset poetry of William
Barnes, and his descriptive passages with the verse of Emily Brontë.
After commending *The Return of the Native* as "above all, the life-
history of a woman in all its relations", Ellis made a surprising judgement on Hardy's more recent and future novels. He foresaw, he wrote,
that Hardy would develop along the lines of *Ethelberta*, *A Laodicean*,
and *Two on a Tower*, or, as he defined it, in delicate, ironic comedy.
Nothing could be farther from the course that Hardy's personal and
professional life was now to take. He was about to write a tragic novel
in which men played the chief part, a book in which the comic irony of
such previous novels, with their would-be upper-class setting, was so
lacking that a publisher's reader complained it had no gentry in it.[37]
Above all, he was about to move, for his own and the book's background, to his native Dorchester.

# 4

# Dorset Home

HARDY wrote an immediate and enthusiastic letter to Havelock Ellis, complimenting him on his charming style, and speaking of his own "unmethodical books".[1] This self-depreciation was not false modesty. Hardy had realized the light-weight quality of his last three novels, and was in the grip of one of his periodic wishes to improve his work, and to surpass himself as a writer. This, as usual, was allied with his desire, since youth, to be a prophet and a leader for his generation. Looking back on this time, a few years later, he set down these feelings:[2] "Ever since I began to write—certainly ever since I wrote *Two on a Tower* . . . I have felt that the doll of English fiction must be demolished, if England is to have a school of English fiction at all." The prophet was about to break the false idols of literary worship.

As usual, he went systematically to work. At Wimborne, only a few miles from the Hampshire border, he was living on the periphery of Dorset. For fulfilment as an artist, he needed the Dorset of his childhood; all through the two Wimborne years, there were signs that he wished to return to his natural centre. Even before going to Wimborne, he had told his brother that he was looking for a plot of building land in Dorchester. Early in 1882, he wrote to the Earl of Ilchester's agent about the possibility of a building site on Stinsford Hill, near his own family home. In the same year, he said Wimborne, with its mud and damp, was too low-lying for health, and he convinced himself that Dorchester would be healthier. Intellectually as well as physically, he wished to identify himself with the county town and the county. Also in 1882, he joined the Dorset Field Club, whose headquarters were in Dorchester.[3] In August 1881, when he had only been in Wimborne a few weeks, he was visited by H. J. Moule, the watercolourist, probably the earliest acquaintance of his youth among the Moule brothers. There was for a time a scheme, suggested by Emma, of a joint book on Dorset, text by Hardy, illustrations by Moule. It came to nothing, but in the last few months at Wimborne Hardy belatedly wrote, in response to an earlier request from *Longman's Magazine*, a long article on "The Dorsetshire Labourer".

The stage was therefore set for a return to the Dorchester district. In point of fact, Emma and Hardy had not spent a great deal of time at Wimborne, though they made some attempt to join in local gatherings, and even attended some first-aid lectures, where Hardy typically noted the odd effect of a dangling skeleton, beyond which, through the window, he could see small children dancing to an outdoor band.[4] They had toured Scotland in August and September 1881, visited London and Liverpool for Hardy's theatrical ventures in 1882, and taken a trip round neighbouring West of England counties later that year. Then, in autumn, Hardy and Emma left home to spend several weeks in a little Paris apartment of two bedrooms and a sitting-room on the Left Bank. This Bohemian expedition was the way Emma thought authors ought to live. She never lost this romantic picture of herself and Hardy as two carefree vagabonds, blown by the wind of artistic impulse. Seventeen years later, she explained with evident pride, "we are erratically-minded and *actioned*! rushing off when it occurs to be easy and nice, every way".[5] However sardonically Hardy viewed her breathless and ungrammatical programmes, he obviously enjoyed his part now, "studying the pictures in the Louvre and Luxembourg, practising housekeeping in the Parisian bourgeois manner, buying their own groceries and vegetables, dining at restaurants", though being Hardy he added, "and catching bad colds owing to the uncertain weather".[6]

The Hardys, it seems, in spite of early difficulties, and perhaps jealousies, still enjoyed married happiness on this light-hearted, informal holiday. One cannot live a picnic life except with a person one likes. Yet Hardy had not quite counted the risks to this happiness of taking Emma to live in Dorchester. His work blinded him to the obvious dangers. For one thing, Emma would be in the close and critical neighbourhood of his immediate family, for whom she had virtually given up her own relatives. Her only real contact was a favourite cousin, Edith Gifford of Launceston, who in 1882 had had an experience like some woman in a Hardy short story; finding her fiancé had made a local dressmaker pregnant, she broke off her engagement, and made the young man marry the girl.[7] Emma does not seem at this time to have visited her own parents, now living at Compton Gifford near Plymouth, and within comparatively easy reach. Nor does she seem to have gone to the funeral, which they attended, of her brother-in-law at the end of November 1882, though she still kept in touch with her widowed sister, who wrote in September 1883, on hearing of the move to Dorchester, "I suppose it will be a pretty cottage quite picturesque that you will choose for yourself."[8] Nothing could be farther from reality. Back in Hardy's home town, Emma had no choice. Thomas did the choosing. Not finding a house for sale in Dorchester, he rented, as a temporary measure, a gloomy, dark building in the narrow Shirehall Lane. "He have only one window and she do look into Gaol Lane" was the local description. For a permanent home, he decided to buy land

and build. By October he had negotiated with the Duchy of Cornwall, who owned the Fordington area of Dorchester, for a plot beside the Wareham road, near an old toll-gate. Hardy was his own architect, and his brother Henry, who had taken over from their rheumatic father, was the builder.

The work of design and building all through the winter months, naturally threw Hardy back into the centre of his family. Emma tried to adapt to the new environment. She got out her watercolours, and sketched the scenes of his boyhood, sometimes on the spot, sometimes from earlier paintings by their friend H. J. Moule;[9] but there are signs that she was never really taken into the family circle. Dr. F. B. Fisher, who now looked after Hardy's father and mother, remembered how, in the Bockhampton cottage, "the whole family [of Hardys], two sons and daughters, could tell stories, and did so during the long winter evenings round the big fireplace, criticizing one another's efforts very freely".[10] He does not suggest that Emma took part in these fireside evenings, when Hardy visited the others. Strong family tradition has it that she was not welcome in Jemima Hardy's household, and there is even stronger evidence in her own words. Some years later, Emma wrote an often-quoted letter[11] on the causes of estrangement between man and wife. One paragraph, which has never been quoted, is this:

> Interference from others is greatly to be feared—members of either family too often are the causes of estrangement—a woman does not object to be ruled by her husband, so much as she does by a relative at his back—a man seldom cares to control such matters, when in his power, & lets things glide, or throws his balance on the wrong side which is simply a terrible state of affairs, & may affect unfavourably himself in the end.

With her husband, the "relative at his back" can only have been his mother Jemima, who grew to dominate her family more and more with age. Of course, a more tactful and resourceful woman than Emma might have found ways to overcome this formidable handicap to their marriage. Up to this time, she seems to have had a very good relationship with Hardy's two sisters, Mary and Kate. In failing with Jemima, she cannot avoid some of the blame.

Hardy's return to the family seems to have been only to the immediate circle under his mother's wing, his father, brother, and two sisters. It hardly included the very numerous Hand, Sparks, and Antell cousins, whom Hardy virtually never mentions in his writing, except for one single reference by initials to one cousin, John Antell. Even when members die, he gives no word. Late in 1884, his cousin, Emma Sparks (Mrs. Cary), died within weeks of emigrating to Australia. She had recently been in his thoughts, for just before leaving

Wimborne he had written a story for boys, *Our Exploits at West Poley*, which he called "A Tale of the Mendips", and which described a caving adventure. She had lived in a little Somerset hamlet, full of Mendip miners, and her boys were the ages of those in the story. They were now looked after by Martha Mary Sparks (Mrs. Duffield), who had emigrated earlier to Queensland, and who had been one of Hardy's early loves. In 1885, Rebecca Sparks (Mrs. Pain) also died, at the Topsham home of the fourth sister Tryphena (Mrs. Gale). Rebecca had first attracted Hardy's adolescent attentions, and Tryphena had had some sort of engagement with him. Not a sign of this appears: but his diary is full of his immediate family. There are long descriptions of the plantation behind the Bockhampton cottage, "The Birds' Bedroom" as they called it in childhood, of strange local anecdotes by his mother and father. Even his unobtrusive but much-loved sister Mary provides remarks which he notes, while in August 1884 he goes off on a bachelor holiday with brother Henry to the Channel Isles.

The prophet had come home to his admiring family; but he had little honour in his county town. "Some people say he was a bit queer in the head," remembered one citizen, "But I think he was just strange like the stories he wrote."[12] He wandered about, half-unnoticed, among the scenes of his past loves, only to renounce them. In 1883, he wrote a poem with the chilling title, *He Abjures Love*. Even in its first stanza, he has the Biblical accent of the returned prophet.

> At last I put off love,
> For twice ten years
> The daysman of my thought,
> And hope, and doing;
> Being ashamed thereof,
> And faint of fears
> And desolations wrought
> In his pursuing.

The language is that of Hardy's heavily-marked Bible—the word "daysman" is actually underlined by him in the Book of Job—and the echoes of putting off the old man, putting away childish things, are pervasive. In the clinching final stanza, the prophet speaks, and yet admits a human doubt.

> —I speak as one who plumbs
> Life's dim profound,
> One who at length can sound
> Clear views and certain.
> But—after love what comes?
> A scene that lours,
> A few sad vacant hours,
> And then, the Curtain.

Next year, 1884, one of these loves forced herself into his mind's eye in
*A Countenance*, which began

> Her laugh was not in the middle of her face quite,
>     As a gay laugh springs,

and ended

> Alas, I knew not much of her,
> And lost all sight and touch of her!
>
> If otherwise, should I have minded
> The shy laugh not in the middle of her mouth quite,
> And would my kisses have died of drouth quite
> As love became unblinded?

Not only did Hardy turn away from the memories of his own former
loves. In his new serious purpose as a novelist, he turned away from all
former heroines. *The Mayor of Casterbridge*, which he started writing in
1884, has no woman who is like these "Undines of the earth", in Havelock Ellis's phrase, or who is "of the coming-on disposition", as Gosse
wrote a few years later. Such women had been the core of every previous novel; even the colourless heroine of his first published book,
*Desperate Remedies*, has her moments of caprice and coquetry. Now his
story demanded heroic and masculine stature. Its chief character,
Michael Henchard, is a tragic hero on Shakespearian scale. Some critics
have seen a likeness to King Lear; but Henchard's weakness, violence,
generous impulse, jealousies, mistakes, simplicities, superstitions, large
though often futile gestures, physical strength, and ultimate wish to
"extenuate nothing", are more like a Dorchester Othello.[13] The likeness to Cassio of Farfrae, his successful rival both professionally and in
love, is unmistakable. Hardy saw a performance of *Othello* by strolling
players during the first few months of writing the novel; and though
he records how the chief actor had to stop and rebuke a rustic audience,
he was perhaps more influenced than he realized.[14]

The leap forward in power, purpose, and construction is astonishing.
Even the Greek tragedy pattern of *The Return of the Native* is surpassed,
and there are several reasons for this. Hardy was not writing against
time; the novel was not due to be serialized in the *Graphic* until 1886.
Not only could he finish it well before serialization; he could, and did,
revise it substantially for publication in volume form. He was guiltily
conscious that he had not revised his last book, *Two on a Tower*; he had
gone instead on his Parisian holiday with Emma. Hardy thought he had
still failed to iron out the episodic serial shape of *The Mayor of Casterbridge*; but it remains the best plotted and the most dramatic of all his
novels.

Yet time to write, time to revise, cannot alone account for this advance. Hardy's artistic instinct had been right. He needed Dorchester. Rejecting a first notion of a novel about Roman Dorchester, prompted by the discovery that his building site was a Roman burial-ground, he set it in the town he knew as a child, round about 1850. Even then, it is not merely a historic picture. It evokes the spirit of a nineteenth-century county town at all times; Hardy combines both an older and a newer Dorchester. To start with, on 4 April, he was elected Justice of the Peace for the Borough of Dorchester.[15] Although "according to his own account he plays the part of Justice Silence with great assiduity", this not only brought him in touch with Dorchester affairs but may have contributed to the scene of the magistrates in the novel.[16] He also sought, for many incidents, the files of the *Dorset County Chronicle* for 1826-30. Wife-selling, living with a second "husband", the dinner at the King's Arms, Henchard's honourable conduct at his bankruptcy, his oath to abstain from drink, even his shaming of Abel Whittle, can all be found in these files.[17] Why did Hardy seek these events of the late 1820s? It was because they were the years of his mother's girlhood, and her own stories all come from this period. What he heard by the cottage fireside was supplemented by what he read in Dorchester, though not all the incidents he used had occurred in the town itself. Yet this picture of the generation past was itself supplemented by material from the immediate present. Dorchester was no longer the town of Hardy's childhood. From 1870, expansion and industry had appeared. When Hardy began to write *The Mayor of Casterbridge*, Eddison's Steam-Plough Works was well established in Dorchester. Francis Eddison was a Leeds man and the works were run by North-countrymen and Midlanders, whose ability, jobs, and pay were objects of local envy. Hardy simply shifted his fictional newcomer's origins a little north of the Border. Farfrae's northern skill and enterprise, even his new machinery, were intensely topical in the Dorchester of 1884-85. So was that accompaniment of industrial life, the cycle of boom and slump. Failures and bankruptcies abound in Dorchester of the 1880s; even Francis Eddison only saved his credit by ingeniously adapting his works from steam-ploughs to road-making machinery.[18] The ways of "foreigners" were resented. Hardy himself protested without sucess against the noise of Eddison's 5.45 a.m. factory hooter, while, later, Hardy's little pageboy, Fred Randall, was induced, probably by higher wages, to work for Eddison's as a water-cart boy.[19]

In the novel, this composite Dorchester is frequently seen through the eyes of one of Hardy's most remarkable characters, Elizabeth Jane, Henchard's supposed daughter. Her literary origins clearly derive from an unlikely source. In his last year at Wimborne, Hardy copied this passage[20] from J. H. Shorthouse's novel, *John Inglesant*:

From those high windows beyond the flower-pots young girls have looked out upon life, which their instincts told them was made for pleasure but which year after year convinced them was, somehow or other, given over to pain.

It is an almost exact picture of the girl who sees so many passing events of Hardy's "Casterbridge" from "high windows"—indeed, sometimes from windows in a house Hardy has called High Hall Place. Hardy ends the novel with her, in words that closely recall those of Shorthouse.

And in being forced to class herself among the fortunate she did not cease to wonder at the persistence of the unforeseen when the one to whom such unbroken tranquillity had been accorded in the adult stage was she whose youth had seemed to teach that happiness was but the occasional episode in a general drama of pain.

The self-effacing Elizabeth Jane is all the more moving for her personal origins. Hardy had returned to the one person who could move his sympathy almost as deeply as his mother. This was his sister Mary. She was now beside him in the streets of Dorchester itself; for just at this time, she moved from teaching in the village of Piddlehinton, and became head teacher at the "National" school in Bell Street, Dorchester, helped by her sister Kate, who took charge of children in the first class.[21] Mary's silent witness pervades the novel. Summing up Elizabeth Jane, Hardy wrote, "that she was not demonstratively thankful was no fault of hers". Years later, hearing the parson read over his sister's grave the verse, "I held my tongue and spake nothing: I kept silent, yea, even from good words," Hardy exclaimed, "That was my poor Mary, exactly."[22] Hardy's work at this stage displays a paradox. There is an enhanced tenderness, connected with close family relationships, yet an almost ruthless manipulation of the fortunes of men and women, as if he had cut his sympathies off from all but those nearest to him. Emma was not far out when she perceived that exclusive attention to his family could be a harmful influence.

Hardy's gloomy isolation was not decreased by the move on 29 June 1885 to Max Gate, the newly-built home called after Mack the toll-house keeper. The house was undistinguished and ill-designed, resembling any one of the turreted, nondescript suburban villas he and the local architect Crickmay had put up in the Greenhill area of Weymouth in the 1870s. It was cramped and inhospitable. The spare bedroom was at first only large enough for a bachelor visitor. Nor had brother Henry done his job too well as a builder. Within three years, a portion of the drawing-room ceiling fell down. Moreover, Hardy felt depressed in this way of life, which he called "cottage-like and lonely". In mid-November he recorded that for three days he suffered "a fit of depression, as if enveloped in a leaden cloud". This was followed by a two days' sick headache, and just over a month later he wrote, "the end of the old year 1885 finds me sadder than many previous New Year's Eves have done". He doubted the wisdom of building; but he had other doubts he could not put into words.[23] To add to his depression, he had a return of his bladder trouble. Though the family doctor, Fisher, claimed to cure him, it returned, at intervals, for the rest of his life.

It has been pointed out that the Hardys did not by any means spend all their time at Max Gate. Hardy spoke of "four or five months a year spent in London or elsewhere" and later claimed to be "half a Londoner". Yet according to the Hardys' fashionable friend, Mrs. Jeune, they were "very little in London".[24] It seems that their real centre was Dorchester. They usually came to London for "the season", that is, the three-and-a-half months from just after Easter until late July; but a sympathetic observer noted that, even after twenty years of this, Hardy and Emma were never at home in London society, appearing still as two dowdy and rather pathetic bourgeois provincials.[25] With the self-conscious deprecation of the country-dweller, Hardy wrote in 1886 of "us small people down here", and in London he was always quick to suspect a snub. At the following year's Royal Academy dinner he commented, "I spoke to a good many; was apparently unknown to a good many more I knew."[26] It was more than the two or three thousand Austrian pines he planted at Max Gate that isolated Hardy from his fellows.

One of the few to break through to him was Edmund Gosse. During the early 1880s, a slow friendship had grown between the two. Gosse had overcome in himself a restrictive childhood; now he began to overcome Hardy's reserve. In Hardy's last days at Wimborne, Gosse lured him up to London to stay a week-end at his own Paddington house— "Lord, how we would talk!"—and to join a literary and artistic party at the Savile on Monday 25 June 1883, to meet the American man of letters, William Dean Howells. Hardy's shyness made Howells feel, "I had only shaken hands with Hardy across his threshold", but it was a feat for Gosse to get him there at all.[27] Gosse, in turn, was the Hardys' first and probably for a long time only house-guest at Dorchester. He actually stayed with them during their first weeks in the town in 1883. He and Hardy visited William Barnes, now rector of Winterborne Came, attended one of his services there, and afterwards looked at his pictures in the rectory. Gosse was also the first to stay at Max Gate in 1886, when he was again able to see Barnes, just before the latter's death.

Gosse had other tastes in common with Hardy besides literature. His father and grandfather had lived in Poole and Blandford, and he himself knew East Dorset well as a boy. Another shared interest was a passion for cats. Gosse's London household was ruled at this time by a proud Persian tabby professional beauty called Atossa, the gift of

Walter Pater, whom she resembled in appearance and manner. She sat for her portrait to Laurence Alma-Tadema and was sculpted by Hamo Thornycroft, both mutual friends of Gosse and Hardy.[28] The cat in Hardy's Dorchester household in the 1880s had the very eccentric name of Kiddleywinkempoops-Trot. He (or she) was the forerunner of a long succession of cats, who inspired Hardy to poetry. One, Snow-dove, drew from Hardy one of his finest serious elegaic poems, *Last Words to a Dumb Friend*. All lie, named, under their respective head-stones in the garden at Max Gate. There were other elements of light distraction. Though the Hardys faced their tragedy of childlessness— Emma was now forty-five—they were not without a child in the house. Emma's tiresome brother Walter, though in a safe job as a Post Office official, had the habit of dumping his children on country relatives. Between 1885 and 1887, his daughter Lilian came several times. This little red-cheeked, round-faced creature, like a Dutch doll, charmed Hardy, and he drew a series of comic sketches for her. Over the next fifteen years she and her brother Gordon came to live for long periods, almost as adopted children.

Such diversions were welcome, for Hardy was now more continuously at work than ever before. In October 1884, while he was still in the midst of *The Mayor of Casterbridge*, John Morley asked for a new serial for *Macmillan's Magazine*. In the middle of March 1885, just before finishing *The Mayor of Casterbridge*, Hardy finally agreed.[29] A new full-scale work, begun immediately after such a highly-wrought performance, taxed Hardy's powers severely. He decided to use "the woodland story" he had put aside in 1875, when he wrote *The Hand of Ethelberta* instead. Even so, he was not sure whether its original design would do; but in mid-November 1885, he decided it would, and set himself to work from half-past ten in the morning till midnight. One instalment was actually finished in the taproom of a village inn.[30] It was a for-midable programme, even with Emma's considerable fair-copying and a ready-made plot.

*The Woodlanders*, in fact, naturally looks backs to his manner of a decade before, when the story was first conceived. It resembles out-wardly the plot of *Far From the Madding Crowd*, in its combination of faithful suitor, flashy rival, and a heroine who makes the fatal choice. With variations and minor excursions, this had been the basic Hardy plot in many other works. Yet here tragic realism is a new factor, already hinted in a much lighter work, *The Trumpet-Major*. There it had been the subject of a sardonic exchange between Hardy and Leslie Stephen. Stephen had said, "The heroine married the wrong man." Hardy replied that they mostly did. "Not in magazines," was Stephen's saturnine rejoinder. Now, although writing for a magazine, Hardy set out to demolish the "doll" of English fiction, which demanded a happy ending. There is no respite for his faithful suitor or his heroine. One dies, the other is left married to "the wrong man"; not even the new divorce laws can help her.

Many people have connected Hardy's increasing pessimism about marriage in his novels with the stresses of his own. One critic hints at finding, in the 1930s, evidence of an attachment between him and an unhappily-married local woman soon after his move back to Dorchester.[31] Stresses were certainly there; yet this theme of misalliance and mis-mating, always seen from the woman's point of view, sprang from his own deepest family history. The woman, who had made the first fatal mistake, was his mother's mother, Betsy Swetman; she married George Hand, and condemned herself to lifelong poverty and parish charity, at first eked out by taking in parish lodgers, later by the dole after her husband's death.[32] This was the burden of Hardy's own mother's fireside discourses, her unhappy beginnings as a charity child. It explains why he set *The Woodlanders* where he did, roughly in the rectangle of North Dorset bounded by Sherborne, Yeovil, Holywell, and Minterne. In 1912, on re-reading the novel in proof for the Wessex Edition, he remarked, "On taking up *The Woodlanders* and reading it after many years I think I like it, *as a story*, the best of all. Perhaps that is owing to the locality and scenery of the action, a part I am very fond of." Many critics, mistaking what Hardy said, believe that *The Wood-landers* comes closest to the terrain of his own childhood. It does not; *Far From the Madding Crowd* and, even more, *The Return of the Native* represent the places of young Hardy's playground. He was "very fond of" the locality of *The Woodlanders* because it was the place of his mother's childhood; doubtless, he liked it best "as a story" because it was of a piece with the stories she told. The cottage where her own widowed mother had brought up seven children including Jemima in shameful poverty was in the east quarter of the Melbury Osmond parish, in the direction of Hermitage and Minterne. Hardy was at special pains to point out, both by letter and postcard written to Gosse from abroad just after publication, that Great Hintock in *The Wood-landers* was largely based on Melbury Osmond, with Little Hintock as a hamlet two miles off.[33] The novel is lovingly constructed out of his mother's past, and some of its tragedy is that of his own mother and grandmother. Like *The Mayor of Casterbridge*, the inspiration had ele-ments of the remote past, a middle past, and an immediate present. Hardy's sister Mary had spent some time in 1867 on the deeply-afforested Digby estate at Minterne, where Hardy had visited her. One can again see her character of silent witness in Marty South, while Marty's father, old South, resembles, in one respect, their own father in the Bockhampton cottage at the time of writing. The bedridden John South is the last "life" of a lifehold possession. So was Thomas Hardy senior, now failing and crippled by rheumatism. The Bockhampton cottage was held on the usual three-life lease from 1835,[34] for the lives of Hardy's grandfather, Hardy's uncle James, and Hardy's father. The first two were dead, the grandfather long ago, uncle James in 1880. When Hardy's father died, the home would revert to the landlords, though they in fact, unlike the capricious Mrs. Charmond in the novel, allowed the family to stay on after the death of Thomas Hardy senior in 1892.

It is no accident that the novel opens unforgettably with the poverty of a woman; historians have singled out this district to illustrate the hard lot of working-women in nineteenth-century England. In this rectangle of coppice, woodland, and hedge, life was lived just above subsistence level. A single coppice meant security, its loss disaster. Giles Winterborne is a typical coppice-holder, and the subtle gradations of a society where so little meant so much is wonderfully caught in his relations with Melbury, the timber-merchant. Similarly, life for men could only be maintained by the subsidiary tasks of the women. Marty South's miserably-paid spar-making, mocked by the barber who tempts her to sell her hair to Mrs. Charmond, embodies the thousand minor employments of all forest women, in which Jemima and her sisters must have shared.[35] *The Woodlanders*, more than even *Far From the Madding Crowd*, shows a community linked together by desperately hard patterns of common work. When *Far From the Madding Crowd* appeared, *The Times* commented that all its characters were, in one sense or another, working-people. *The Woodlanders* shows a people even more unified in their labour, their reality contrasted with exotics like Mrs. Charmond and the doctor, Fitzpiers. For Hardy, perhaps to enhance the oddity of these extraneous characters, but more likely through haste or carelessness, throws realism to the winds with these two. In his first unpublished novel, he had conscientiously taken the advice of a doctor for medical details. Here, Fitzpiers stops his own bleeding from the capillaries of the scalp by making a self-applied tourniquet from a handkerchief and half pennies; this improbable treatment perhaps garbles one of Hardy's boyhood encyclopedias. Hardy's hero dies in comparative peace of some kind of delayed typhoid, which would realistically have been agonizing. The heroine kisses his dying lips, and the doctor gives her a preventative medicine, which she does not take, though when she does get typhoid, it unaccountably cures her. Finally, we are asked to believe that the doctor, a trained medical observer, cohabits with Mrs. Charmond for many months without realizing she wears false hair, until apprised by letter. Similarly, Mrs Charmond, who we are told with somewhat bated breath had been an actress, keeps an attic full of stage-properties and make-up, with which she disguises Fitzpiers so that no one in the area recognizes him.

Artificial treatment of the ruling classes had been a charge against Hardy since his earliest writing days. Yet, now that he aspired to the upper levels of society, Hardy may have believed he was treating them as realistically as the rest of the novel treated his woodlanders. When he went to visit his wife's aristocratic relative by marriage, in the later stages of writing the book, he

> Called on Mrs. Jeune. She was in a rich pinky-red gown, and looked handsome as we sat by the firelight *en tete-a-tete.*

Dr. Fitzpiers pays his calls on Mrs. Charmond, in the second half of the book. She is in "a deep purple dressing-gown", and, at a later stage, she has "a red-shaded lamp and candles burning . . . a large fire was burning in the grate . . . the rosy passionate lamplight".

This is far from saying, though, that in *The Woodlanders* Hardy merely brought his new-found realism to play on one of the poorest communities in Dorset—and therefore in all England—among his own mother's kin, and added to it his new appraisal of London society. For all its hard realism, *The Woodlanders* is also perhaps the most poetical and impressionistic of all his novels. A few years before, he had laid down his principles as the poet-prophet-novelist—"the seer", as he calls it.[36]

> *June* 3 [1882] As, in looking at a carpet, by following one colour a certain pattern is suggested, by following another colour, another; so in life the seer should watch that pattern among general things which his idiosyncracy moves him to observe, and describe that alone. This is, quite accurately, a going to Nature; yet the result is no mere photograph, but purely the product of the writer's own mind.

Now, a few weeks before finishing *The Woodlanders*, he wrote:[37]

> . . . I feel that Nature is played out as a Beauty, but not as a Mystery. I don't want to see landscapes, i.e., scenic paintings of them, because I don't want to see the original realities—as optical effects, that is. I want to see the deeper reality underlying the scenic, the expression of what are sometimes called abstract imaginings.
>
> The "simply natural" is interesting no longer. The much decried, mad, late-Turner rendering is now necessary to create my interest . . .

These principles are enacted in the novel. Its whole portrayal of Nature, especially when mingled with the human scene, is idiosyncratic and impressionistic. On one occasion even, a "late-Turner" painting reveals itself.[38]

> . . . the whole western sky was revealed. Between the broken clouds they could see far into the recesses of heaven, the eye journeying on under a species of golden arcades past fiery obstructions, fancied cairns, logan-stones, stalactites and stalagmites of topaz. Deeper than this

their gaze passed thin flakes of incandescence till it plunged into a bottomless medium of soft green fire.

Hardy's poetic and impressionistic descriptions of the woodlanders in relation to their woodland excel in this new technique. The trees have human attributes; the men and women, often, treelike ones. The young trees, in a famous passage, sigh humanly when they are planted, though indeed, Hardy had found this to be literally true while planting at Max Gate.[39] The death of a tree and the death of old South are interwined. Winterborne is presented as a spirit of the trees and of their fruits.

The effort of such a conception took its toll. Hardy ended with the exhausted comment:

> *February* 4 1887, 8.20 p.m. Finished *The Woodlanders*. Thought I should feel glad, but I do not particularly—though relieved.

The tremendous feat of writing two such novels with hardly a break in under three years could not have been achieved without some help from circumstances, For one thing, he was encouraged in the summer of 1886 by the flood of good reviews for *The Mayor of Casterbridge*. Nearly all agreed that Hardy had retrieved his sagging reputation as a novelist and moved into a new phase as an artist. Only the *Athenaeum* kept up its usual complaint about the unnatural use of rustic dialogue, while the *Saturday Review* concentrated, as Hardy complained to Gosse, on alleged "improbabilities", such as Farfrae's way of improving bad flour.[40] Otherwise, it was a complete triumph for his fresh, serious approach to novel-writing, and an incentive to press on with *The Woodlanders* to a climax, with Marty South's ultimate poetic soliloquy.

Some large-scale break in Hardy's life was now needed. At Max Gate he was intellectually more isolated than ever by the death of his old mentor, the poet William Barnes, on 7 October 1886. Hardy had sat and talked regularly with him in his illness and Emma was probably the last person, outside his family, to converse with him. Hardy busied himself with subscriptions for a memorial in the shape of a runic cross, suggested by the Bishop of Salisbury, but abandoned because some of the subscribers were Evangelical, and objected. The memorial eventually took the form of a lifelike statue by Roscoe Mullins. Hardy himself provided the best memorial, an article on Barnes in the *Athenaeum*, which caused Gosse to exclaim, "What a biographer was lost when Nature stamped novelist on your brow!" Barnes's death emphasized the need to leave Dorchester for a time, directly the novel was finished, and Emma felt it too. The cheerful Gosse might find, on his visits to Dorchester, that the bustle and life, the brightly-coloured uniforms from the barracks, the military bands, gave it "quite a foreign air",[41] but that was not how it appeared to Emma, who protested to the end of her days that her tastes were *"Continental"*,[42] and French, though, in strange contradiction, she suspected foreigners were all papists, and signed letters to the press "An Old-Fashioned English-woman".[43] Hardy had often longed to visit the scenes of his classical reading, the galleries and the architecture of his youthful study. On 14 March 1887, the day before *The Woodlanders* was published in volume form, he and Emma left for a spring holiday in Italy.

# 5

# The Original Tess

THE southern journey, their first experience of the Mediterranean, is witness that the Hardys still enjoyed some tastes in common. Long travel and uncertain hotels did not seem to damp a sense of freedom and pleasure in each other's company. Their actual relationship at this time drew conflicting accounts from two visitors to the newly-built Max Gate. In late summer 1885, Mrs. Robert Louis Stevenson called there with her husband on their way to Dartmoor. She described the Hardy ménage curiously and critically.

> A pale, gentle, frightened little man, that one felt an instinctive tenderness for, with a wife—ugly is no word for it!—who said "Whatever shall we do?" I had never heard a human being say it before.

One perhaps needs to set this often-quoted and ambiguous remark against an impression, by another American, of Mrs. Stevenson herself, written at about this time. Henry James's sharp-tongued invalid sister, in discussing "our own vulgar ones" from the western States, took Mrs. Stevenson as an example.[1]

> From her appearance Providence or Nature, which ever is responsible for her, designed her as an appendage to a hand organ, but I believe she is possessed of great wifely virtues . . . —but such egotism and so naked! giving one the strangest feeling of being in the presence of an unclothed being.

In the face of such powerful pot-calling-kettle statements, one can only remark that this was not to be the last time a dogmatic American lady weighed in with her verdict on the Hardys. A kinder and perhaps more balanced view comes from the English minor novelist F. Mabel Robinson, who stayed a week with the Hardys at this time. She later wrote:[2]

> Max Gate was then raw-new and I never thought it showed talent in the designer, but it was pleasant. . . . after dinner Emma lit a bright fire and he read aloud from the novel he was engaged on [*The Woodlanders*]. . . . Mrs. Hardy was inconsequent. Her thoughts hopped off like a bird on a bough, but never then or at any other time did the idea cross my mind that her mind (such as it was) was unhinged . . . as I saw her she was a perfectly normal woman without much brain power but who wanted to be a poet or novelist—I forget which. I found it hard that no one took her literary accomplishment seriously.

Certainly the Hardys must have seemed two "perfectly normal" British tourists, breaking their journey for a day or two at Aix-les-Bains. The South of France caught them out, as it does many travellers, and plunged them in snow, but the weather improved as they made their way south via Turin. One sign of happiness was that Hardy began to write poems, though his characteristic lines on seeing Genoa from the train through a tangle of clothes-lines were written "a long time after".[3] Leghorn gave him a poem on *Shelley's Skylark*, and, after a visit to Pisa with its architecture, and Florence, they reached Rome itself by the last day in March when he picked violets on Keats's grave.[4] As he himself teasingly wrote in his old age, "A visit to the graves of Shelley and Keats was also the inspiration of more verses—probably not written till later."[5] As for Rome itself, he felt "its measureless layers of history to lie upon him like a physical weight",[6] and even to be, as he confessed to Gosse,[7] "like a nightmare in my sleep". The physical dangers of Rome were successfully forestalled, on one occasion at least, by the energies of Emma.[8]

> . . . when Hardy was descending the Via di Aracoeli carrying a small old painting he had bought in a slum at the back of the Capitoline Hill, three men prepared to close on him as if to rob him . . . They could see that both his hands were occupied in holding the picture, but what they seemed not to be perceiving was that he was not alone, Mrs. Hardy being on the opposite side of the narrow way. She cried out to her husband to be aware, and with her usual courage rushed across at the back of the men, who disappeared as if by magic.

Though Emma confided to her own diary, "The attack by confederate thieves dreadful fright to me,"[9] three lazzarone were evidently no match for one "old-fashioned Englishwoman", who showed the same fearlessness when she found any of them ill-treating an animal, though one cabman disarmed her by thanks for taking an interest in his horse —"Italian suavity," she commented. It is interesting that the second Mrs Hardy removed from the printed *Life* several of Hardy's tributes to the courage and impulsiveness of her predecessor. Emma's enthusiasms, in fact, led to an attack of malaria, contracted, Hardy thought, by too long a stay in the romantic labyrinths of the mouldering Colosseum; the disease dogged her each spring for the next three or four years, but then subsided.

The Hardys spent Easter in a return visit to Florence, where, as before, their hostess was Lucy Baxter, the married daughter of the poet Barnes, who showed them the sights and took them to Fiesole, where the usual Italian child offering a Roman coin set him off on a poem about the Etruscan theatre. In spite of a gloomy note, also echoing the usual English travellers' surprise at the bitter Easter weather, particularly

in Rome—"all our Money gone in Coals and Gas"—and the fact that
such weather pursued them to Venice, Hardy found more pleasure there
than anywhere else in his Italian stay. He obviously disliked what he
thought the "humbug" of Ruskin about the architecture, distrusted
the semi-Oriental style, and clearly hated the mosaics, but clasped to
himself a typical source of comfort, when he found that the Campanile
sounded exactly the same bell-tone as the chimes of Piddlehinton and
Puddletown. Evening parties with friends of Browning and memories
of Byron completed Hardy's pleasure in the city itself. The whole tour
was rounded off by visits to places which fed Hardy's Napoleonic
obsession, never far from his mind when in Europe. The Cathedral at
Milan reminded him of the crowning of the Emperor, the Bridge of
Lodi not only of the battle, but, typically, of the song of that name
sung by his father.[10] Like many provincials, Hardy found reassurance in
some parochial reminders in foreign parts, a "gentle anchor", in Keats's
words, that drew him home.

Emma, on the other hand, for all her innate Englishness, was far
more adaptable to travel, and often childishly delighted by foreigners
for the simple reason that they were foreign.[11] "Italian gentlemen wear
black gloves," she noted. Whereas Hardy was "very vexed, dypeptic"
(her word), after one of those excellent French station buffet meals, she
adapted to continental food, and seldom felt as "weary" as he did. The
colour and sounds of Italy enchanted her. Genoa presented "a mass
of . . . red & blue & green & purple, the rest a soft harmonious mosaic
. . . I never saw such a superb city". Florence pleased her with its
"exquisite tone of bells", and the road to Rome had "fig trees pollard,
low like spread hand". There were irritating human elements, "a dirty
Italian man" in Santa Maria Novella, and a shoeblack in Rome so
importunate that she broke her umbrella "beating off" his attentions.
Her appreciation of Rome's wonders was deeply felt and spontaneous.
In the catacombs, "We seemed like magnified ants burrowing under
ground as we walked" in another era. Returned to Florence, the Arno
was a blue "with a dash of opal in it . . . a great contrast to the yellow
Tiber". Her appreciation of early paintings was often as primitive as
they themselves: the haloes in the Fra Angelicos struck her as being
"like straw hats", and she confided "old frescoes are horrid, entre
nous". Venice was a dream. "You are in a planet where things are
managed differently, or you are gone to the bottom of the sea & this is
a phantom city." The only real disappointments were the cats in the
Forum at Rome, in churches at Venice. "*No* lovely cats in Italy as in
France"—remembered from her honeymoon there—"all short-haired
ones."

By the time Hardy returned to London in the second week of April,
two letters were waiting which both, in their way, pointed to his future

as a novelist. Macmillan's serialization of *The Woodlanders* had attracted other magazines. On the day after it appeared in volume form, Tillotson and Son of Bolton, a newspaper syndicate, for which Hardy had already provided three short stories, wrote to suggest that Hardy should write another novel of the same length for them, and offered him £1000 for the serial rights. This was a gratifying result of the new technique Hardy felt he had successfully used in *The Woodlanders*. Yet, considering that the novel Tillotson's encouraged him to write turned out to be *Tess of the d'Urbervilles*, another letter inspired by the serialization of *The Woodlanders* was ominous. On 10 April, Macmillans had received a protest about the appearance of that story in their *Magazine*. Written from the Vicarage, Crewkerne, Somerset, it concluded:[12]

> A story which can hinge on conjugal infidelity, can describe coarse flirtations, and can end in pronouncing a married woman's avowed lover to be a "good man who did good things", is certainly not fit to be printed in a high-toned periodical and to be put into the hands of pure-minded English girls.

Warning had been given; Hardy might well have considered also that the proprietor of Tillotson's too had been a Sunday school worker, and that his magazine served the same type of public.[13]

As things turned out, during the coming half-dozen years Hardy needed some disinterested, practical advice in literary matters. Too often he is found in awkward situations, which he himself had manufactured, and with which he dealt by a mixture of blind indignation and grumbling. His chief literary adviser and regular correspondent at this time was Edmund Gosse. One cannot be sure, in spite of their long friendship and loyalty, that this association was wholly good for either. Both were abnormally sensitive to hostile criticism. Gosse, who, like many Victorians, concealed his homosexual inclinations under conventional marriage,[14] was almost embarrassing in his praise of his chosen friends; he was uniformly adulatory of all Hardy's work, of any sort. Easily moved, he often appears to be in tears, so he says, at quite run-of-the-mill poems by Hardy. His preference for the pastoral Hardy of *Under the Greenwood Tree*, from which Hardy had long been trying to escape, led Gosse to some fallible pronouncements on his friend's more mature work. In his reviews of *Jude*, he seems to suggest that the novel was not so attractive because it was set in North "Wessex", and not in the familiar area of true Dorset. Hardy, on his part, grossly overvalued Gosse as a poet, and even printed two quite trivial stanzas by Gosse in the middle of *The Woodlanders*. Each leapt to the other's rescue over any fancied slight. In the previous year, 1886, the American writer James Russell Lowell had been reported as describing Hardy as "small and unassuming in appearance—does not look like the genius of tradition". The touchy Hardy greeted this harmless remark with a wail of protest to Gosse that he had been "awfully belittled—corporeally".[15] Gosse rushed to write to friends in America his protest at "the sneer at Hardy's personal appearance", which he himself found "singularly cruel", and which had "very much wounded" his friend. Similarly, at this very same time when the axe-men among Victorian critics, Churton Collins—"Shirt and Collars" to the irreverent—attacked Gosse, quite rightly as it proved, for inaccuracy and sloppiness in his literary biographies, Gosse let out a howl of injured pride which Hardy hastened to soothe by long letters arguing that all critics were fools.

The fact was that each encouraged and sympathized with the other's neuroses. In August 1887, when the Hardys had returned to Max Gate after a London season spent at Campden Hill Road, the two men had a long exchange about their morbid fears and depressions. Hardy confessed to many nights when he had gone to bed never wishing to see daylight again. Victorian medicine tried to treat depressive illness as arising from stomach disorder; but Gosse and Hardy, though admitting some truth in this, knew better.[16] However, Hardy hoped, wrongly as it turned out, that the worst of these depressions were now things of the past. He made his usual New Year's Eve summary of the last year, on what was for him an almost excessively cheerful note: "The year has been a fairly friendly one to me." He instanced his successful Mediterranean expedition, from which he had returned "unharmed"—thanks to Emma's promptitude—"and much illuminated"—thanks to his own poetic imagination. He might have added that, while in London, he and Emma had seen the Jubilee procession from the Savile Club, then in Piccadilly, and that at Lady Carnarvon's he apparently cleared up the misunderstanding with Lowell, over in England for the occasion. What he did add was an impressive list of books and poems read or re-read. Its breadth and comprehensiveness shows that he was preparing himself for another step forward in his art.[17]

The main inspiration was, however, as always not in books but in people. In his last novel, *The Woodlanders*, he had looked deeply at his own family history on his mother's side, the mystery and tragedy of her own mother and the marriage at Melbury Osmond, whose overtones of mismating and class difference run throughout the book. Now, on frequent visits to the Bockhampton cottage, he heard Jemima talk of his other grandmother, her own mother-in-law, Mary Head.

From scattered hints and diary jottings over about a year from autumn 1887 to autumn 1888, it seems that two stories presented themselves as possible candidates to his mind for the new novel, whose contract he had signed with Tillotson on 29 June 1887, promising to deliver the manuscript by 30 June 1889. Both were deviously connected in some way with his own family history; they became eventually

*Tess of the d'Urbervilles* and *Jude the Obscure*. The idea of *Jude* seems to have been fractionally first in the field, to judge by the well-known note he made on 28 April 1888.[18]

> A short story of a young man—"who could not go to Oxford"—His struggles and ultimate failure. Suicide . . . There is something in this the world ought to be shown, and I am the one to show it to them—though I was not altogether hindered going, at least to Cambridge, and could have gone up easily at five-and-twenty.

Leaving aside the last remark, which was not altogether truthful, this was, as Hardy realized and noted in his old age, "the germ of *Jude the Obscure*". On the other hand, another note at the end of September shows him working on the background of *Tess*, and meditating on the fall in status of old Dorset families. His mother's anecdote, a year before, of a girl called Priddle, descended from the Paridelles, who clung to her far-off aristocratic origins by insisting on using her maiden name after marriage,[19] actually persuaded him to make her one of the dairymaids who companioned Tess in the novel. Another maternal anecdote, now remembered, of a parson's son working with "yarn-barton-wenches" gave him the idea of Parson Clare's son Angel working in the barton with the dairymaids.[20]

Hardy's father, as usual, weighed in with anecdotes about convicts, transportations, and hangings, to feed Hardy's mind with the dramas of a past age. They talked of how his grandmother remembered the exact details of what she was doing when she heard of the execution of Marie Antoinette, even down to the pattern of the gown she was ironing at the time: how she remembered William Keats, the tranter, their nearest neighbour in the cottage opposite, beating out time for dancing to the fiddle, so that they could hear it in their own cottage a hundred yards away. This paternal grandmother came back to his mind as the archetypal figure of his first seventeen years. Her home in Berkshire was well known to the whole family. When Mary Hardy had been a schoolmistress only a few miles away at Denchworth, all the Hardys, her father, Kate, Henry, Hardy himself, had visited there. Hardy, in 1864, visiting his sister, would find members of the Head family still farming that area. He knew it well, long before he was to explore it again as the setting for *Jude the Obscure*. He could have known, too, in his usual pottering about country churches, that a branch of the Turbervilles, remotely connected with the Dorset family of Bere Regis, had their arms quartered on monuments in that part of Berkshire.[21] Above all, the Fawley parish register told him that his own great-grandmother had an illegitimate son, who died in infancy.[22] Yet there was one even more vital influence for him.

Hardy's paternal grandmother, Mary Head, had been baptized on

30 October 1782 at Fawley. Her father had died earlier in the same year, and her mother died when Mary was five-and-a-half. She lived in Fawley, and perhaps also in its neighbouring parish of Chaddleworth, where there were Head relatives, until 1785, when her mother's father, William Hopson or Hobson, also died.[23] These first thirteen years were, Hardy said, so "poignant" that she would never return to Fawley. Hardy, however, was almost totally silent about her next fourteen years; for it was not until 19 December 1799 that she appeared in faraway Puddletown in Dorset, and married Hardy's grandfather, being herself already three months pregnant.[24] There is only one very brief reference in all Hardy's writing to these lost fourteen years. When in 1896 he visited Reading, he described it as "a town which had come into the life" of Mary Head, who, he added vaguely, "had lived here awhile".[25] Such phrases of studied vagueness in Hardy's careful auto-biography usually conceal some important personal knowledge. More-over, Reading, under the name of Aldbrickham, is consistently the setting for scenes and memories of disaster in *Jude the Obscure*.

The registers of the three Reading churches in these fourteen years, 1785 to 1799, produce only one entry for a Mary Head. It is sufficiently startling. Sometime in 1796, an illegitimate girl was born to Mary Head and John Reed. The child was baptized at St. Mary's, Reading, at the age of six or seven, in 1803, the entry recording also her year of birth.[26] She was christened Georgiana Reed, which suggests her mother had by then left the district, and that she was being brought up by the father; it may also suggest he was a person of standing.

Though this is the only church entry for a woman of this name in this period, there is a legal entry in the year 1797. On 3 February of that year, Mary Head was committed by a magistrate to the Bridewell or House of Correction at Reading, on the oath of Rosanna, wife of John Farmer of Winterborne, charged with having feloniously stolen a copper tea-kettle, the property of Mr. and Mrs. Farmer. She remained in the House of Correction for nearly three months, for it was not until the Quarter Sessions of 25 April that her case came up. When it did, the Farmers did not appear to give evidence, and the justices discharged her.[27]

She had by then spent nearly three months under the fear of death by hanging. The laws respecting larceny were in a confused state, but they were appallingly severe, and if the statutes had been strictly applied, executions would have occurred for a huge number of small thefts. A legal authority in 1771 had enunciated that "it is and hath been the law of England that in general all persons guilty of larceny above the value of 12 pence shall be hanged". Such severity often made witnesses, after the first accusation, loth to give evidence; this is probably what happened with the Farmers and Mary Head. If they had appeared, and convinced the Justices, Mary Head would almost certainly have been sentenced to death and probably hanged. In a case in that exact year, 1797, concerned with an article of similar value, a woman called Margaret Kennedy was sentenced to death for stealing a silver button, which she had attempted to conceal in her mouth.[28]

Winterborne, where the theft was alleged to have taken place, was part of the parish of Chieveley, the next parish to Chaddleworth and Fawley, where Hardy's grandmother was born. Mary Head in Reading House of Correction was listed as two years younger than Mary Head of Fawley, but an orphan with a chequered history might well not know her exact age. Hardy's poem about her speaks of her hearing shrieks "under the lash"; the judicial whipping of women in private was not abolished until 1820, and there were scenes of brutality in some Bridewells. The company was brutal too; Mary Head was incarcerated with Kitty Curtain, "a rogue and vagabond who refuses to give an account of herself" and Elizabeth Bloxham, "committed for a year as a lewd woman".[29]

These sole appearances of a Mary Head in Reading seem to dovetail in the story of Tess. A cousin of Hardy, John Antell, said positively, "Tess's life and adventures and final death are practically what happened to a relative of ours."[30] Hardy spoke of her as a real person. Mary Head, like Tess, had been seduced and had borne a child. She had not been executed, but had lived under the fear of execution for nearly three months. Hardy's grandmother had, like Tess, made a fresh start, just as Tess movingly does in Part Three of the book, "The Rally". With Tess, it takes place in another part of Dorset, remote from the district of her first disasters. With Hardy's grandmother, Mary Head, it took place because of some move from Berkshire, where her memories were so unbearable, to Dorset itself, and the area round Puddletown, where she married Hardy's grandfather. A very tenuous family legend that she had a "husband" already in Berkshire was all that remained of the past. There was one, and one only likely way that she might make the journey into this new life from a hundred miles away, and that was as a domestic servant in a landed family, with property in both counties. Two such families immediately come to mind. The Pitt family of Kingston Maurward House, Stinsford, for whom Hardy's grandfather actually worked, were closely connected with the Pitts of Stratfieldsaye, on the border of Hampshire and Berkshire, and very near to Reading. As a boy of twelve, Hardy's own father had been given a book of psalms by Lady Pitt.[31] Another possible employer is the Williams family, of Herringston, Dorset, very near Stinsford, which also had a branch in Berkshire. There is a curious and possible link here. Hardy told Edmund Blunden that he could have had a presentation to Christ's Hospital, but that the Governor, who would have sponsored him, died. When Hardy was just the age that such a presentation could have been made, a Governor, William Williams, of this family, did die.[32]

It is practically certain, then, that the story of Tess is a version of the true story of Hardy's much-loved grandmother. He did not use it at once. With the common background for both *Tess* and *Jude* equally in his mind, Hardy used some of the ideas for *Jude* in a powerful short story, *A Tragedy of Two Ambitions*, which he wrote and published in 1888. In this, two brothers "could not go to Oxford", because their drunken father squanders their mother's small inheritance. They manage to enter a theological college and be ordained, while they succeed in educating their attractive sister, who becomes engaged to a local landowner; but these successes are threatened by the reappearance of their father. After meeting and threatening them, while drunk, he falls into a culvert. They do not rescue him, and he drowns; but the brothers are haunted by guilt, and the story ends with forebodings of their own suicide. While this is obviously some rehearsal for *Jude*, it is also a rehearsal for aspects of *Tess*, which he was just beginning to write. The father is a foretaste of John Durbeyfield, whose drunken folly ends in tragedy for his children, Tess in particular. Another curious anticipation is that not only this story, but two others he wrote about this time, *Alicia's Diary* and *The Waiting Supper*, both depend for their dénouement on a man slipping from a plank and drowning in a stream. This is echoed, strangely and poetically, in *Tess*, when Angel Clare, sleep-walking, carries Tess across a narrow footbridge, and she has a momentary fear that he is going to drown her after her revelation, the previous night, of her seduction by Alec d'Urberville.

Hardy seems to have limbered up for the great effort of writing *Tess* by this succession of short stories. They included a macabre little sketch, *The Withered Arm*, which contains many of his own schoolboy obsessions: hanging and hangmen which form the melodramatic climax, a witch's curse, familiar to his fireside childhood, and even his own juvenile love-affair with the lady of the manor, Julia Augusta Martin, who had just written to him. The thrilling *frou-frou* of Mrs. Martin's silk dress, as she entered Stinsford church in those far-off days, is reproduced exactly in the fictional lady of the manor. Such stories brought in some money during the long haul of constructing yet another major novel. On 4 May 1888, Macmillans, having done well out of *The Woodlanders*, produced *The Withered Arm*, together with four previous short stories by Hardy, in a two-volume edition, which sold enough to warrant a single-volume reprint within a year.

Hardy now had the financial security, and comparative leisure, to explore the new depths he had uncovered while writing *The Woodlanders*. For that novel, he had tried to see "the deeper reality" beyond what

was merely visual, a technique akin to Turner's later paintings. This
search appears in many of his scattered notes at this time. "At a concert
at Prince's Hall I saw Souls outside Bodies", he wrote on 25 June
1887.[33] In the British Museum Reading Room on 9 March 1888, he
commented, "Souls are gliding about here in a sort of dream—screened
somewhat by their bodies, but imaginable behind them."[34] "I have",
he wrote three months later, "the habit of regarding the scene as if I
were a spectre not solid enough to influence my environment."[35] Early
in 1889, he feasted on the exhibition of Turner at the Academy. He
singled for special mention, among others, the painter's *Snowstorm*,
which has been brilliantly shown[36] to be the basis for the weird impressionistic passage about the Arctic birds in the Dorset uplands which he
eventually used in *Tess*. Hardy's lack of interest in prose techniques
was a later pose, when poetry had again become all to him; at this
stage he was clearly striving to surpass himself in the novel. Tess's
vision that "our souls can be made to go outside our bodies when we
are alive", which both puzzled Dairyman Crick and attracted Angel
Clare, derives directly from Hardy's determination to seek the spiritual
nature of the material world about him.

During early 1888 Hardy deliberately gathered material, from past
history or from present inspiration, as a way well known to all authors of
putting off the plunge into a large and exacting work. Among his tactical
expedients was a 6000-word article for the New York *Forum* on "The
Profitable Reading of Fiction". This collection of not very well expressed
platitudes about a writer and his public probably served its main purpose of postponing the evil hour. It was followed, during most of June
1888, by another long foreign trip with Emma, this time to Paris,
where they stayed in the Rue du Commandant Rivière, went to museums, archives, tombs, and famous buildings, but lightened the culture
with a day at Longchamps race-course for the Grand Prix de Paris.
Hardy noted with surprise that "the starter spoke to the jockeys
entirely in English, and most of the cursing and swearing was done in
English likewise, and done well". He had not realized that the starter
on this occasion was, in fact, an Englishman, Dick Fijus, and that the
French jockeys' swearing was meant to intimidate the foreigner in his
own terms.[37] July brought the London season, Kensington lodgings at
Upper Phillimore Place, opposite Walter Pater, but with constant
early-morning disturbance from market-carts on their way to Covent
Garden. Hardy, about to create his most attractive heroine, began to
make notes, even more obsessively than usual, about the feminine
beauties he encountered. On 3 July, he observed that Lady Portsmouth,
with whom he had stayed more than once in Devon, looked like "a
model countess, . . . her black brocaded silk fitting her well". On 8 July
he noted "red plumes and ribbons in two stylish girls' hats" in St. Mary

Abbots Church; next day he was attracted by Ada Rehan's performance in *The Taming of the Shrew*, in which she played at Daly's opposite her fellow-American, John Drew. Five days later, he met an unnamed and intriguingly Swinburnian type—"an Amazon, more, an Atalanta, most a Faustine. Smokes: handsome girl: cruel small mouth."³⁸

Some time in the autumn, however, Hardy got down to writing, and seems to have continued, without any obvious breaks apart from the 1889 London season, for a whole year. At all events, on 9 September 1889, he forwarded to Tillotson "a portion of the MS. . . . equal to about one half I think" of the novel, which at that stage was called "Too Late Beloved" or perhaps "Too Late, Beloved". From subsequent negotiations with other publishers, this seems to have taken the heroine through her seduction, her baby and its death, and into the section afterwards called "The Rally", where she goes as a dairymaid to Talbothays Farm, and meets Angel Clare. Though the seduced village maiden was not unknown in Victorian fiction, Tillotson's took fright at this as a fit subject for their magazine readers. Hardy must surely have anticipated this, for he allowed them to cancel their contract and return both set-up proofs and manuscript on 25 September. In old age, though, he suppressed all memory of his contract with Tillotson, and implied that Edward Arnold of *Murray's Magazine*, to whom he sent the MS on 5 October, was the first editor he had approached. Arnold, already cautious at Hardy's demand for £50 a month for the work, more than the magazine was in the habit of paying, consulted with Murray, and on 15 November rejected the story as "not . . . well adapted for publication in this magazine". He added to this vague phrase the remarkable statement, "I believe . . . it is quite possible and very desirable for women to grow up and pass through life without the knowledge of" matters which he termed "immoral situations" and their "tragedies". The warning from Crewkerne Vicarage about *The Woodlanders* had now been spelled out editorially. Nevertheless, Hardy immediately sent his MS, by now apparently nearly reaching the scene of Tess's wedding night, to Mowbray Morris, editor of *Macmillan's Magazine* itself, the very journal which had received the censure of his former novel. Rejection was inevitable, and only took ten days, during which Morris wrote a long letter, setting out his response to the story; he did not like the sensuous descriptions of Tess, nor the implication that she was ripe for seduction from the start.

He incidentally provided some idea of the original plot, which was very different from the finished novel. Briefly, it was a simple and ordinary story of a country working-girl's seduction by her employer's son, almost a commonplace of Victorian life. At this stage, the theme of villain and heroine sharing one apparent lineage, the whole ancestral d'Urberville background, simply did not exist. Her original surname was Woodrow, his Hawneferne; and incidentally, though his Christian name was always Alec, hers showed the mutations Love, Cis, Sue and Rose-Mary, before Tess. The whole atmosphere of inevitable and almost Darwinian replacement, so strong in the final *Tess*, the decay of old families and the theft of their titles by parvenus, painted upon some cosmic canvas, was completely absent. Instead, there was merely, as it must have appeared to Morris, and perhaps to any average reader, an account of the deflowering of a "succulent" innocent village maiden by "a handsome horsey dandy", as the original manuscript had read. Though Tess was aware "since her infancy" of the tradition of past noble blood, this had nothing to do with her fall to Hawneferne, since there was not the slightest resemblance even of names. Her original name of Woodrow was suggested by a true story,[39] on which Hardy drew later for Angel Clare's emigration to Brazil. This is the disastrous event of the 350 British who left Liverpool for Rio on 29 November 1872, one being a Dorset man named Woodrow. *Tess* was apparently at this stage unadorned by the spirit of those Greek tragedies with their suggestions of a malign fate, which formed a large part of Hardy's staple reading at this time.[40]

Hardy was therefore left, after a whole year's work, with a story which seemed unsaleable, in spite, or in certain quarters because, of his previous reputation as a novelist. It was a time of extreme professional crisis. It was also a time of personal crises in the lives of Hardy and his wife. Though Emma had had little contact with her own family since her marriage, apart from one visit to Plymouth in the year 1886, she received regular news, which, at this point, became a matter of horror. Her eldest brother, Richard Ireland Gifford, a bachelor, was a civil engineer in Cornwall. In January 1888, he began to show severe delusions and attempted suicide. He was difficult to feed, believed he was filthy, verminous, and unfit to live, and became beyond the control of his mother and of Emma's sister. After a year in the Cornwall County Asylum at Bodmin and in Bethlem Hospital, London, he was transferred on 15 March 1889 to the Warneford Hospital, Oxford.[41] He had always suffered from ill-health, which Emma, whose medical knowledge was sketchy, put down to a heart condition, angina pectoris.[42] In fact, he had a severe chronic kidney ailment, Bright's disease. Since the searching hospital enquiries showed no history of insanity in the Gifford family, and no sign of it in his four siblings, of whom Emma, of course, was one, it is likely that his mental disturbance would now be diagnosed as stemming from this poisoning of his system.[43]

At the time, however, and specially to one of Hardy's country-superstitious mind—he considered it dangerous even to be weighed—the idea of an hereditary taint in the Gifford family must have presented itself. Emma's "inconsequent" chatter, "without much brain power", as Mabel Robinson had noted, were to seem as sinister to Hardy as her father's previous alcoholic outbreaks, during which he is said to have chased Emma's mother out into the streets in her nightgown.[44] It was a seed of evil omen, sown in his own mind, to his later disquiet, though at this time it may have had the helpful effect of bringing the theme of family doom more powerfully to assist the deepening of the story of Tess, as she had now at last become in his unpublishable pages.

# 6

# Tess and Jude

AT THIS time of literary crisis, Hardy introduced a personal complication. Up to now, Emma had ignored the succession of shopgirls,
actresses, and society ladies, whom her husband had wistfully admired
from afar. She counted on the shared interests of their marriage, in country
life and folklore, in campaigns for the protection of animals, and, above
all, in the feeling that, in some sense, they had literary work in common.
He discussed this with her still, and fairly fully. She knew all the vicissitudes of the naming of Tess, in a way which suggests she read and
commented on all the early manuscript versions of the novel. She also
helped him to introduce an incident from her own unpublished, and
indeed not very publishable tale, *The Maid on the Shore*. When thinking,
as she must have done, about his barely-concealed appreciation of other
ladies, she could congratulate herself that he regarded her as his
helpmeet where literature was concerned, if only as a copyist and
captive audience. No other woman held that position.

Yet in 1889 and 1890, her position revealed its basic insecurity; for
from that date, and for the next decade, Hardy began to share his
literary confidences with a succession of ladies. To add to Emma's
chagrin, these were all ladies who not only had printed publications to
their credit, but who were recognized in London society. It is not at all
certain that Emma ever really made her often-quoted remark about the
London ladies who "spoilt" Thomas—"they are the poison, I am the
antidote".[1] Yet their advent now surely poisoned the deepest well from
which, she had felt, she and Thomas could still draw for their love, the
springs of literary creation.

This was all the more galling to her because she could and did produce,
at this time, work of a highly literate character. The tradition of her
virtual illiteracy, so universally stressed by Hardy's biographers, aided
by his second wife, is simply not true. Reading only her breathless and
erratic private letters, hearing only accounts of her inconsequent
conversational manner, all have ignored her serious pieces of writing.
On 5 September 1891, for instance, the *Daily Chronicle*, a most responsible paper, printed her letter[2] of over 1000 words—virtually an article
—on a serious topic, the education of the young. The letter is sustained
and extremely well expressed. It is advanced in its view of education as
the right and the salvation of all classes: "the houseless, bedless, ever-

63

comfortless poor should not exist in a *rightly-taught* nation". She saw education as beginning in the cradle, where "almost always the plastic minds and hearts are in ignorant hands". She drew a picture of poor children, starved of education, and pleaded for reform: "start another way altogether, get instructors of the Arnoldian stamp", who should be looked up to, not despised by society, especially the women. It is a well-reasoned, direct, enlightened, and admirable piece of writing. Yet Emma was despised by her husband, and other writing women preferred.

The first of these intruders can be detected just at this time. The beautiful Rosamund Ball had published an anonymous little book of verse entitled *Tares* in 1884, when she was only twenty-one. Shortly after, she married the artist Arthur Graham Tomson, and took the semi-pseudonym of "Graham R. Tomson". In June 1889, she inscribed a copy of her new collection, *The Bird Bride: A Volume of Ballads and Sonnets* to "Thomas Hardy, with the sincere admiration of G.R.T."[3] In the next few years she gave him two other books, written or edited by her, one an anthology concerned with one of their common interests, cats. There was also an exchange of letters, of which hers, embellished with a self-designed art-nouveau letter-head, still survive.[4] Nor were her attractions solely intellectual. She was "a tall, slight, brown-haired woman, with large grey eyes, that at times seemed to be a deep hazel".[5] In other words, she was of the slender brunette type that held such physical attraction for Hardy, noticeably akin to the actresses Mary Scott-Siddons and Helen Mathews. Her beauty was enhanced by "a striking individuality pervading her carriage, manner, and dress". The susceptible Hardy entered and preserved in his diary that, at a party at Mrs. Jeune's, he "Met Mrs. T[omson] and her great eyes in a corner of the rooms, as if washed up by the surging crowd."[6] He was sufficiently struck to obtain and keep her portrait, and to write an oddly-moving poem about it, *An Old Likeness (Recalling R.T.)*, about ten years after her death, which occurred in 1911. In it, he recalled

> Our early flows
> Of wit and laughter,
> And framing of rhymes
> At idle times.

The rhymes that Rosamund Tomson actually framed can hardly be said to be worth such recall. Empty little lyrics in artificial forms, the villanelles, rondeaux, ballades, made fashionable by Austin Dobson, were all that her poems display. They contain two undistinguished poems dedicated to Hardy himself; but her one possible direct inspiration to Hardy's own writing occurs in the title poem of the book she inscribed to him, *The Bird Bride*. This ballad, said to be on an Eskimo legend, could, at a stretch, be associated with Tess's strange vision of the weird Arctic birds, flown from the far north, where the ballad and its own birds originate. The lady was divorced by Tomson in 1896, married Henry Brereton Marriott-Watson, a prolific Antipodean popular novelist, produced other books of verse, but died comparatively young, deeply mourned by her second husband. To Hardy, she was a portent of his personal life during the coming decade of the 1890s. Some sort of shy flirtation, during which he wrote her wistful letters about seeing two lovers under one umbrella in the rain, or hesitated between two portraits of her, neither of which, he thought, did her justice, soon faded at the touch of reality. It has been assumed that she was the "enfranchised woman" who disgusted him "by exhibiting him as her admirer";[7] but this may equally have been another woman poet he knew about this time, Agnes Mary Francis Robinson, who wrote verse in much the same style, and appeared in the same anthology as Rosamund Tomson.

The next half-dozen years, from November 1889 to November 1895, were both packed with personal incident and the most prolific of Hardy's writing career. Something in his withdrawn and passive nature seemed to require the stimulus of other personalities to touch it into full creative life and output. The literary tally of these six years is remarkable. First, there was the virtual rewriting and reconstitution of *Tess*, far more extensive than his retrospective memory allowed,[8] and the production of that novel, his finest work, in serial and in volume form, both entailing large adjustment from one to another. Then came the writing and the publication in serial form of two other novels, *The Well-Beloved*, under the title of *The Pursuit of the Well-Beloved*, serialized in October, November, and December 1892, and *Jude the Obscure*, under the title of *Hearts Insurgent*, serialized from December 1894 to November 1895. This was by no means all. In 1891, he collected together and published the short stories called *A Group of Noble Dames*, and at this time wrote most of the stories collected in *Life's Little Ironies* (1893). In addition, two important essays on literature, "Candour in English Fiction" and "The Science of Fiction" were published in January 1890 and April 1891 respectively.[9] Then, on Christmas Day 1890, he woke feeling "the viewless wings of poesy" (in Keats's phrase) spread themselves, in a series of deeply-felt lyrics, which filled the next few years. These were not wholly given over to what he afterwards seemed to regard as the arid wastes of prose.

Hardy's personal life showed an equal complexity and variety. His "framing of rhymes", or at any rate literary correspondence, with Rosamund Tomson went on until at least late 1891. Such feverishly-begun but soon exhausted attractions to literary ladies show a consistent pattern. A new female personality, intense excitement, and hectic letter-writing, some stumbling-block, when reality contradicted the initial fantasy, and, to be just to Hardy, a milder but long-lasting friendship formed the usual sequence. His wilder hopes seldom lasted more than a few years, sometimes even months, before the ideal proved to be not what he had thought. A perpetual adolescent, even into his eighties, Hardy was out of love only shortly after he was in. "Love lives on propinquity but dies of contact", he had just remarked in the summer of 1889.[10] An average of about two or three years seems to be common, before a new idealization takes the place of a partly-disappointing one.

Death, on the other hand, proved a stimulant whose effects did not so easily wear off. The death of a woman remained the most powerful and lasting factor in his creative life. There were certainly three deaths of women in 1890 to rouse "the viewless wings of poesy" he felt beating again by the end of that year. The first fell only on the margin of his consciousness. In January 1890, Helen Mathews, the young actress he had so much admired in the early 1880s, died at Birmingham.[11] She had been acting in Henry Irving's Lyceum company, to which she had returned after a few years' absence, until very shortly before her death. Quite apart from his frequent play-going to the Lyceum—he saw Irving in *The Bells* only a few months later—Hardy met Irving a good deal socially at this time. He must have known of Miss Mathews's death, though he does not mention it in any diary notes which have survived.

A note about another woman's death,[12] at almost the same time and age, has survived, and has become a subject for speculation. This recorded the death on 11 May at Topsham of Mrs. Gale—Hardy's cousin Tryphena Sparks—to whom he had been so strongly attached in his late twenties and early thirties. According to his own account, he wrote the beginning of a poem to her without realizing, after years of complete separation from her life, that she was at the time on her death-bed. "A curious instance of sympathetic telepathy" he called this incident, which resulted in the finished poem, entitled in his manuscript *T—a, At news of her death*. Thirdly, and not usually noticed, came the death that summer of an older woman, his mother's sister, Aunt Mary Antell. She had looked after him in infancy, and virtually brought him up during the rather mysterious period when his own mother, by family hearsay, suffered an attack of "brain-fever".[13] Certainly his aunt's house in Puddletown had been a second home to him from a very early age; he was deeply attached to her, and to her wild, erratic, picturesque husband, the Puddletown cobbler, with his frustrated dreams and ambitions, who had died a dozen years before.

Finally, one cannot discount the death in this year of Hardy's father-in-law, that now-extinct volcano of a man, John Attersoll Gifford. Though he had long moved back from Cornwall to his more accessible native Devon, Hardy does not himself seem to have seen him. His former outbreaks of alcoholic violence were things of the past. Yet his death, and the recent news that his eldest son, Hardy's brother-in-law, was hopelessly insane, served to strengthen the idea of a family curse. The effect on Emma herself cannot be discounted either. Her father's funeral, which she attended, contributed to a latent violence which, as his favourite and spoilt child, she inherited from his temperament. Perhaps Hardy's fresh weakness for literary ladies wore her temper thin, or perhaps she began now to adopt the attitude of her contemptuous father. For she began from this time to keep a diary of bitter denigration of Hardy, of his ways, of his own family, which, according to later witness, she christened with the ominous title, "What I think of my Husband". John Gifford had written off Hardy as a "base churl"; his daughter now began to speak darkly and pejoratively of Hardy's "peasant origin". About now, she cut off relations with the women of his own family. Hardy had just bought a house in Wollaston Road, Dorchester, which his two schoolmistress sisters, Mary and Kate, shared conveniently for their teaching at the Girls' National School in Bell Street.[14] Jemima was companioned at the Bockhampton cottage by Mary Antell's daughter and namesake, whom Mary had implored Jemima to give a home. Emma may well have thought that Hardy was over-occupied with these domestic arrangements for his own family, and may have resented particularly his spending money to house his own sisters, and his special and obvious affection for the elder, Mary, his early inspiration.

All these recent deaths strongly influenced the novels Hardy produced in the next few years, the highly-reconstructed *Tess*, the deeply-conceived though in many ways imperfectly realized *Jude the Obscure*, and, sandwiched between them, the strange half-symbolic and wholly-personal "sketch of a temperament" remarkably like his own, *The Well-Beloved*. All three have their origins in a remote yet intimate past, of people, events, and family traits, which, it has been suggested,[15] he was trying to exorcise by writing them out of his system. Yet the novels transcend therapy. When we come to disregard all the circumstances of its initial rejections, its "dismemberment", its bowdlerized serial-form, and its final book publication in November 1891, *Tess of the d'Urbervilles* is his masterpiece, the fruit of over twenty years of a novelist's career, and of the chrysalis passion of a poet spreading new wings. Its heroine is perhaps the most memorable in all English literature. It has been argued she took a new, intimate reality from the death of Tryphena Sparks. Whatever the truth of the many explanations by Hardy that Tess "had a real existence"[16]—and they range, rather incongruously from a chance-seen girl driving a cart to the mixture of two Dorchester girls and a Weymouth waitress—he has used all his professional resources to convince us of her personal reality. Her basic story, of course, originates in his grandmother's tragedy; its portrayal belongs to his utmost art. On the mechanical note-taking side of an author's craft, he combed the files of the *Dorset County Chronicle* with more than usual care for incidents from the late 1820s to the late 1880s. The fatal horse-accident of an early chapter, the blood-stained ceiling of a later one, were all garnered in his own methodical way from these sources.[17] The puzzlement felt by critics at Hardy's obscure personal remarks about Tess, such as "I have not been able to put on paper all that she is, or was, to me", which certainly suggests a recent death, such as Tryphena's, should not distract attention from the fruition of his hard-won lifework as a prose-writer. To expand one casual true incident which Hardy witnessed, a drunken man boasting of a noble family vault, into the whole conception of ancestral decay, which runs throughout the novel, shows his power to grasp a huge general theme from a trivial particular. If, as has been suggested,[18] he owed much to the atmosphere of Zola's novels, several of which he had recently read, the poetry of his approach everywhere transcended them.

Similarly, the bare facts of his grandmother's story, deeply impressed on Hardy's adolescence, become a study of a woman's development through every stage of innocence to experience. Tess is unique in Hardy's work, since she literally seems to grow under our eyes. This is partly due to the poetic construction of her story. It is an epic in seven books, an Odyssey or an Aeneid, with Tess's journeys to each part of Hardy's Wessex forming a new emotional stage. The outward scenes are linked with Tess's inward development in a way which is more poetry than prose. This is achieved not by "poetic" fine writing, but by an artist's conception of the wholeness of life. Every scene is fitted to its human counterpart. The straggling valley of the early phases corresponds with the desultory though harmless life of Tess with her feckless family; the dark forest of the chase connives at her seduction. The lush, fruitful vale of the next phases is one with the slow full-bearing workings of recovery and love. The wonderful winter scenes in the barren uplands of Flintcombe Ash mirror the bleak horror of her desertion by Angel, and her bewildered, faithful efforts to maintain love in extreme adversity. Though physically they echo the actual experiences of Hardy's grandmother, who told him of walking on snow that reached the height of hedgerows, they are given the emotional force of a universal poem, as moving as the expulsion from Paradise in the last book of *Paradise Lost*. Indeed, with Alec reappearing as tempter here, it is not fanciful to compare Milton's epic with Hardy's. The new-rich, false Bournemouth becomes the scene of her shame's second surrender, which only murder can resolve; the price for this is paid among the stones of sacrifice at primitive Stonehenge. Every part is planned as a poem; within each part are separate poems, such as Angel's sleepwalk in the misty water-meads. Yet nothing is merely decorative. Every natural scene is calculated to underpin Hardy's concern, the growth of Tess's soul. The intensity of each image comes from the intense interest he feels for Tess as a person. However much the trials of his own family Tess, Mary Head, had coloured the imagination of his susceptible youth, his is the rarest of a novelist's creations, a character we accept without question as a revealed part of life, as real as if we knew her.

The effect on Hardy's popular reputation as a novelist was unprecedented, and surely comes from the complete reality of his main creation. From being the novelist of a discerning few, whose sales had barely satisfied various patient publishers, he became a best-seller. His last-minute designation of Tess as "a pure woman" was endlessly debated in circles which often had little notion of the whole novel. His men were held up for examination which often revealed more about the commentators than it did of the novelist's characters. John Addington Symonds, for example, found in Hardy "the right democratic spirit", which he himself had discovered in his "exile in the Alps" among handsome Swiss guides, and which enabled him to provide Edmund Gosse with photographs of Greek fisher boys to enliven Robert Browning's Abbey funeral on the last day of 1890. He became vehement about Angel Clare, "the loathsome male . . . I should have liked to kick . . . the fellow"—presumably for the "middle-class maudlin" sexual intolerance, which Symonds was still wistfully resenting as he neared the end of his own self-tormented life. Unlike some critics, he half-confessed a personal involvement. "My vehemence please take as a sign of the intense interest I took in the novel."[19]

*Tess* carried Hardy to fame, and, incidentally, fortune, thanks to the lucky coincidence of the U.S.A. Copyright Act, passed just a year earlier in December 1890. He now had prospects of vast, unpirated reward from the popular work which lay ready to hand. *Tess* also took him, finally and decisively, into the fashionable society he affected to despise, but really enjoyed. He might note, "But these women! If put into rough wrappers in a turnip field, where would their beauty be?" Yet such cynical speculation was sheer disguise; he admitted one of these beauties, Mrs. Hamo Thornycroft, as yet another physical model for Tess. He obviously revelled in fashionable dress, manners, aristocratic connections, distinguished company. He marked off each distinct social triumph like a schoolboy's tabulation of goal-scoring feats. He began to go to gatherings where royalty were guests, and met the future Queen Mary. A year before *Tess*, Lord Rowton, of the tramps' lodging-houses, had called him, not without sarcasm, Mrs. Jeune's "dosser". One lady carried away the impression of "a rough-looking man, dressed very unlike his fellows, with . . . a decided accent".[20] Now those who met the shy figure in Mary Jeune's drawing-room vied for his further acquaintance. Specially pleasing, among early landmarks, was an invitation from Sir Henry Thompson, whose patient he had been ten years before. At that time the famous society surgeon had barely noticed the still-struggling novelist. Now, "recalling I admit very slightly a personal acquaintance", he selected Hardy for one of his celebrated "Octaves", dinners of eight top people.[21] Hardy refrained from cynical comment on the delayed accolade. He was also elected a founder-member of the Omar Khayyam Club, started by the rationalist Edward Clodd in 1892, and took chief part in a notable dinner a few years later, when the Club went to Burford Bridge to honour the invalid Meredith.[22]

Fashionable interest and private appreciation for *Tess* was seconded by critical acclaim. Despite the author's occasional growls at critics' obtuseness, they were almost unanimous in praise. To quote one,[23] "the most difficult of all the tasks which a writer of fiction can attempt —the portraiture of a living woman" was generally acknowledged everywhere to have succeeded. A fellow-novelist, George Meredith, felt a falling-off in the later stages of Tess's story, but his opinion was not widely shared. Andrew Lang in *New Review* was the sole important dissentient, and he was at once countered by other critics. His doubts about the men in the novel, however, were echoed elsewhere. Angel was often judged the unrelieved prig that J. A. Symonds had found him; Alec was pilloried in *Punch* as luridly melodramatic. Yet altogether, 1891-92 provided a year of reviews flattering to any author, though Lang's criticism made Hardy momentarily think of resigning from the Savile Club, of which they were fellow-members, and making his West End base the Athenaeum, which had just elected him. Any adverse criticism was reserved for his uninspired collection of short stories, *A Group of Noble Dames*.

Success certainly inspired Hardy to a burst of fresh writing in 1891-92. He was under contract to Tillotson's to make up for the broken agreement over the original *Tess*, and to supply their syndicate with a shorter serial in a lighter vein, and so he embarked on *The Pursuit of the Well-Beloved*. Whether or not the death of Tryphena Sparks affected the characterization of Tess, it clearly called up memories which he took as the ground-plan of his newer and slighter novel. In his youth he had been attracted, to greater and lesser degrees, by his three girl-cousins, Rebecca, Martha, and Tryphena Sparks herself. In the large Sparks family, where the youngest, Tryphena, was actually twenty-one years younger than her eldest sister, Rebecca, these three girls had seemed almost like three generations. This, and their marked physical resemblance, led Hardy to construct a fantastic plot, in which his artist-hero falls in love with three generation of girls, when he himself is twenty, forty and sixty. Not only does this spring from Hardy's own past history, but the hero's temperament, the mainspring of the action is, perhaps, more self-centred than any other self-portrayal by Hardy. It is a study of a search for an ideal in a rapidly and constantly changing series of women. Actual women are hinted at throughout, actresses like Helen Mathews, literati like Rosamund Tomson, even half-remembered adolescent loves. His recent impressions of high society are packed into two more photographic and generally heavy-handed chapters. Here a good deal of exact identification has been worked out,[24] for instance a portrait of Ellen Terry, almost identical verbally with a diary note by Hardy on meeting her in society at this time.

This work, which Hardy never valued greatly, was written mainly in the year 1892. The same year saw the death of his father, whose sensible, reasonable nature Hardy compared with that of Hamlet's Horatio. It left his mother at the cottage, by courtesy of the landlord, since Thomas Hardy senior had been the third and final "life" of the lifeholding. His father's death gave Hardy further thought about the Grandmother at Fawley in Berkshire. The major theme, put aside for *Tess*, that of a young man "who could not go to Oxford", seemed ready to be written, in a setting akin to his own ancestry. *Tess*'s story, after all, had largely arisen from the tragic history of Mary Head. He visited Fawley in October 1892, and brooded on family history. "I can only see the dead here," he wrote, though no one knows quite what he found of those long-dead but to him living ghosts. The most recent dead spirit, that of his mason father, inspired him to sketch his hero, at first called by the name of an actual Berkshire relative, Jack Head, as a journeyman stonemason. This craft of the Dorset Hardy family was introduced into the Berkshire setting of the Head family. Later stages of the writing actually led Hardy to seek more exact detail by restoring a local church himself; he obtained from architectural work on a church near Max Gate, West Knighton, much of the physical background he always wanted for his characters.[25]

The novel, however, hung fire, perhaps because of the painful memories and discoveries it aroused, perhaps through lack of any creative inspiration in his over-clouded private life, with marriage tacitly worsening every day. Like the hero of his last serial, Hardy needed a fresh feminine excitement to set him forward. This came when on 19 May 1893, on a visit to the late Lord Houghton's son, viceroy of Ireland, he met one of Houghton's married daughters, Florence Henniker, "a charming, *intuitive* woman apparently".[26] Florence was acting as hostess for her widowed brother, in the weirdly-isolated colony of Dublin Castle, whose members went to church protected by armed police and detectives, one of whom had been blown to pieces under the walls the previous Christmas Day. From her earliest years she was accustomed to high society, cosmopolitan and literary, as befitted a daughter of Houghton, one of the best-known hosts in Europe. Swinburne had fallen at her feet, though not in a proposal but to observe her hair was getting darker. Her father had been the first biographer of Keats, and she, in spite of a country-house reputation for being "fast", followed a serious literary career, supplementing the income of her impoverished soldier-husband. Inheriting, like her handsome brother, the aristocratic features of their mother—their father's face, according to Disraeli, looked as if it had been cut out of an orange—Florence had looks, dash, style, and a moderate literary ability, with three tolerably successful novels already to her credit.[27] Tall, slim, and graceful, in her late twenties, she also had a slightly gamine sense of humour; her father, after all, had combined a Unitarian upbringing with a famous library of erotica. She wrote with fatal ease, and had dashed off her first society-novel during a summer holiday.[28]

The susceptible Hardy at once decided that this society woman-novelist with "apparently" liberal views was the "enfranchised" spirit of inspiration he needed. She was, he said, "Pre-eminently the child of the Shelleyean tradition"; for was she not daughter of a man who, as early as 1829, had publicly defended Shelley, at the time still an outcast in England?[29] She went to the plays of the advanced and daring Ibsen, in their translations by Hardy's friend Gosse and by Archer. Blinded by this, by her considerable charm and lack of family ties—she was childless—Hardy failed to see, for some weeks at least, that Florence's unconventionality did not preclude sincere religious belief, church attendance, and an entirely faithful marriage to a heavily-moustached and non-poetical military husband. A flurry of letters followed their return to England, interspersed with visits to the theatre (Ibsen, of course), and plans to educate her in the historical niceties of church architecture—"I want you to be able to walk into a church, and pronounce upon its date at a glance."[30] He was proprietorial, tender: "If you go to the ball . . . Don't fag yourself out . . . Promise you won't." In their private Ibsen-based language, he, architect son of a mason, was her Master Builder, she, the young inspirer, Hilda Wangel. Some unsurviving early letters were "trollish", that is, in the language of the same play, containing hints of sexual feeling.

The crash of these hopes, in this whirlwind progress, was bound to come sooner rather than later. On 16 July, only two months after their meeting, he was writing desperately but ominously, "as the mentor" of her hoped-for enfranchisement, "Depend upon it there are other valves for feeling than the ordinances of Mother Church."[31] Disillusion on this score came within another month. On 3 August he wrote her a

letter expressing to the full his "enfranchised" views, presumably on
love, marriage, and the relationship of men and women. On 8 August,
slipping away together, he from Emma at Max Gate, she from her out-
of-Town home at Southsea, they met at Eastleigh Junction for an
expedition to Winchester. Here, in the typically Victorian setting of a
railway carriage, she put paid to all his wilder hopes. He was crushed.
Never again would he write such a letter, though "I am always your
friend", as he told her in a slightly stunned communication nine days
later.[32] What he had hoped will never quite be known; perhaps he did
not know himself. An elopement? What his own Emma was to call
"Eastern ideas of matrimony", with some platonic extra-marital
relationship for both Hardy and Florence Henniker? Speculation must
fail in the face of conventional phrasing and the loss of letters such as
that of 3 August. Did she encourage him more than she intended? She
certainly sent him many portraits of herself, in fashionable décolletage,
and her own lush translation of Gautier's poem, *Affinity*. A daughter
of the notorious Lord Houghton too may have had a deceptively on-
coming manner. She succeeded in arousing passion, cooling it, and
establishing a more comfortable relationship. By 6 October he was
writing, "if we are not to be the *thorough* friends in future we have
hitherto been, life will have lost a very great attraction".[33] Passion
had dwindled to the milder temperature of collaboration in their joint
short-story, *The Spectre of the Real*, on whose probable reception he
ruefully and correctly prophesied, "all the wickedness . . . will be laid
on my unfortunate head, while all the tender and proper parts will be
attributed to you". This[34] might be a summing-up of his own six-month
illusion.

What these six months certainly gave was an impetus to his neglected
novel, *Jude*. "What name", he wrote to Florence Henniker on 22
October, "shall I give to the heroine of my coming long story?"[35] In
point of fact, he called her Susan Florence Mary Bridehead. The
Christian names were constructed by inserting the Florence of Mrs.
Henniker's between the two first names (Susan Mary) of their mutual
friend Mary Jeune, whose country house, Arlington Manor, was in
Jude's part of the county of Berkshire. For whatever Florence Henniker did or did not contribute to Sue Bridehead's nature, one must
consider Hardy's prefatory statement about the beginnings of the
novel.

> The scheme was jotted down in 1890, from notes made in 1887 and
> onwards, some of the circumstances being suggested by the death of
> a woman in the former year.

Three women, it has been seen, died in 1890. While the one intended
as supplying "some of the circumstances" was undoubtedly Hardy's

cousin Tryphena Sparks, since the protagonists, Sue and Jude, are cousins, the other two deaths also play a part. Helen Mathews, the actress, had made her London success in *Two Roses* as Ida, a part which has strange affinities with Sue—cool, independent, yet sudden in instinctive impulses. Mary Antell had been the wife of the man Hardy acknowledged to be partly the model for Jude, John Antell the Puddletown cobbler, with his self-taught Latin, Greek, and Hebrew, his little school, his changeable, violent black despondencies, his untoward surrenders to drink. Hardy had designed this man's tombstone, and composed an inscription which might have been an epitaph for his own fictional Jude.[36]

> In Memory of John Antell. He was a man of considerable local reputation as a self-made scholar, having acquired a varied knowledge of languages, literature and science by unaided study, & in the face of many untoward circumstances.

The death, in 1890, of the widow of this lonely, self-taught scholar must again have suggested "some of the circumstances" of the novel.

The external *circumstances* of the novel were suggested to Hardy by happenings in the early 1890s; the same is not necessarily true of the internal *characters*. This is specially so with Sue Bridehead. It is too neat an equation to say she began as Tryphena Sparks and developed as Florence Henniker, though she was, according to the second Mrs. Hardy, drawn from the latter.[37] It is only in circumstances, not in character, that this process took place. On her Tryphena side, Sue was a cousin, a pupil-teacher, and went to a training college. Among other minor circumstances, Tryphena actually signed a round robin asking the college staff for longer holidays, while Sue's fellow-students petition the staff about her with a similar document. Yet these are only, as Hardy truthfully wrote, the circumstances. There is evidence that the delicate, literary, fastidious, palely-sexed Sue was nothing like Tryphena in real life. Set beside the letters written by Sue in the book, bloodless, humourless, intellectual, the following section of a typical letter actually written by Tryphena Sparks to her brother Nat[38] tells a different story.

> . . . if only girls might propose—but alas! Well, there is a young schoolmaster of 34 or 35 has went and gone and done it in our place—married a young girl of 21—about a fortnight since—and hasn't he burnished himself up for the awful event with a new set of teeth—set bells ringing and people drunk—painted, papered and fitted his landlady's house with gas—sported Brussels carpets, walnut inlaid tables, chimney glasses of monstrous size and other things too much for my small brain to comprehend—(don't your sister wish she had baited her hook properly, that's all?)

Nothing could be less like Sue in character than this rumbustious young woman; Tryphena's letter might rather have been written by the novel's coarser symbol, Arabella Donn.

Similarly, the circumstances of Hardy's passage with Florence Henniker suggested some circumstances in the story of Sue and Jude. Sue, like Florence with Hardy, first appears to Jude as freethinking and enfranchised; she ends, in the hour-glass construction of the novel, as self-destructively wedded to Christian orthodoxy. Yet these are circumstances only. There is absolutely no hint that the character of Sue in the novel was drawn from the character of Florence Henniker as we know it, sophisticated, poised, calm, though at the same time imaginative and keenly humorous.

Once more, it is the *circumstances* of Hardy's passage with Florence Henniker which have been incorporated into the novel, not her character. Hardy was a thorough-going rationalist of a really rather old-fashioned sort, the kind of self-taught critical unbeliever of the mid-nineteenth-century stamp. G. K. Chesterton noted at this time that Hardy defended his views "with the innocence of a boys' debating club".[39]

His childhood religion, which he had abandoned with such pain in his middle twenties, had left him just as dogmatic about agnostic unbelief as he would have been about belief. To him, religious orthodoxy was something as horrifying as its agnostic opposite would have been to a conventional Christian. The one thing he could not stand about Florence, and which he satirized so obsessively and cruelly in Sue, was her belief. He could not keep his horror at this out of his letters to her, nor even, almost incredibly, out of the would-be eulogistic article he wrote about her for the *Illustrated London News* just a year after his disastrous disillusion with her on this score. Quite unnecessarily, he puts down her writing ambitions partly to her having shown in childhood "a quaint devotional fervour not unknown in imaginative children, taking the form of an enthusiasm for the writing of hymns".[40] Whether he consciously knew it or not, he was dismissing Florence's religion, which she herself was to declare, in a magazine interview, to be "very High Church", as something childish, which she had not grown out of. They are the terms in which Jude, in the horrendous last chapters of the book, raves against Sue's new-found orthodoxy, to him a betrayal almost to the point of obscenity.

Hardy wrote to Gosse, concerning Sue, that she was "a type of woman which has always had an attraction for me, but the difficulty of drawing the type has kept me from attempting it till now". He did not find her in Florence Henniker, whom he told bluntly, when his first illusions faded, that he "would have to trust to imagination". His admission that such a type "always had an attraction" may draw attention to his remote past. Hardy himself said that the novel was set in the 1860s, when he was in London.[41] The shadowy girl of his early London career, whom we only know by her initials, H.A., or the "H. Lond." of a note in his Bible may be the basis for this type and for Sue.[42] Again, we have little but circumstances to go on. "H. Lond." and Sue, for example, are both associated in Hardy's mind with the Epistle to the Thessalonians. Yet some huge emotional and spiritual shock, apparently associated with this girl, took place in Hardy in his middle twenties. Jude's continuous though changing sense of shock over the enigmatic character of Sue may be connected with this deep subliminal past. This must include Hardy's attachment to his own sister Mary, to whom he gave a copy of the novel. Sue and Jude, as a character remarks, are like brother and sister, and his sister's training college is chosen as Sue's. All through the 1890s, Mary and Kate shared the small house in Wollaston Avenue, Dorchester, where Hardy visited them frequently, and renewed sympathies he failed to find at Max Gate.

For one strand in the character of Jude, though Hardy at times hotly denied it, is the character and experiences of the young Hardy himself. Perhaps one should confine it to the boyhood and youth of Jude, but here it is almost photographic. The tenderness for wild things, especially birds, the schoolboy ambitions, the earnest self-education, hopes of the Church career, even the named books in his personal library, are all common to the fictional Jude and the real-life Hardy. Another strand, as also confirmed by the second Mrs. Hardy, is the real-life story of Hardy's uncle, John Antell, the self-taught. The third strand is the disastrous failure, defeated by drink and sex, of the man who was always to Hardy "my friend", Horace Moule. Moule's entanglement with a coarse girl like Arabella, the child he owned or was persuaded to own his, that child's shadowy history of going to Australia and being hanged, and Moule's eventual suicide, all add up to a set of circumstances unmistakably pointing to Moule as part-model. They also seem to point, more deeply, to his character as well. In the final, tragic flaw of an outwardly promising and noble character, Moule gave Hardy more than a hint of the heavy loading of life against happy fulfilment, which runs like a scar through the whole tissue of *Jude*.

The serialization of *Jude* under the title of *Hearts Insurgent*, with considerable bowdlerization for the magazine, *Harper's New Monthly*, did not arouse much critical notice except some which pointed out inconsistencies caused by the cuts. What it did arouse was a different kind of reading public. *Tess* had interested the fashionable, the conventionally-literate, the established. *Hearts Insurgent* spoke to the emerging, the new popularly-educated, the young, In the summer of 1895, its instalments were read avidly by the twenty-eight-year-old H. G. Wells. Just beginning his second marriage after a divorce, Wells had set up house at Woking, where he taught himself to bicycle by practising every day on the sandy tracks of open heathland, and suffered severe bruises in this novel sport. Seeing Jude's career as some parallel to his, he conceived a sort of Sue and Jude story of his own, carried out on a bicycle tour, the new symbol of emancipation, in a vein of light comedy, but with occasional serious social overtones. In Wells's *The Wheels of Chance*, Hoopdriver, the draper's assistant, and Jessica, the would-be emancipated girl, are Jude and Sue in another setting. Wells even provides a counterpart to Sue's mysterious Oxford graduate, who disillusioned her by wanting her to be not his companion but his mistress. When Jessica tries to take in hand Hoopdriver's education by encouraging him about self-educated working-class authors, she asks particularly if he has read *Hearts Insurgent*, by name; she desists (without mentioning Hardy's own name) when Hoopdriver confesses to reading only authors who "didn't seem to have much to do with me", the romantic novels of Walter Besant, Mrs. Braddon, Rider Haggard, Marie Corelli, and Ouida. To a representative of a really new literate class, Hardy now seemed "to have much to do with" life as Wells knew it to be.

It is perhaps ironic, then, that when the final instalments of *Hearts Insurgent* were appearing, Hardy plunged yet again into one more of his aristocratic literary infatuations. On 4 September 1895, he danced, as the guest of General Pitt-Rivers, with his married daughter Agnes Grove, at the Larmer Tree festivities, held at an ancient landmark of that name on the General's estate at Rushmore in Wiltshire. Through her mother, Agnes was of the progressive and liberal—though quarrelsome—family of Stanley, into which Mary Jeune had first married. Agnes herself had her share of vivid, imperious, sharp-tongued personality. She broke away early from her parents, whom she called "the Man" and "the minor one", and married the mild-mannered heir to a baronetcy, Walter Grove, who in later life referred to her philosophically as "my little pepper-pot". Dazzlingly beautiful in her extreme décolletage, flamboyant and vigorous, she was more robust, talented, and intellectual than Florence Henniker. She had a genuine journalistic gift, which she deployed with considerable success. Her articles which make up *The Social Fetich* (1907), dedicated to Hardy, anticipate, and indeed were probably copied by Nancy Mitford, in their witty demonstration of what was U and non-U in Edwardian times. Her attacks in these on the genteelisms of the middle-classes must have come uncomfortably near home to Hardy, and particularly to Emma, over whom she seems to have ridden rough-shod.[43] As a genuine unconventional aristocrat, she had a complete fascination for Hardy.

Hardy all too easily fell into a hopeful fantasy about Agnes Grove. He began to write innumerable letters, and tried to coach her still-inexperienced attempts at journalism. It was a familiar pattern with his literary ladies. Rosamund Tomson had felt encouraged by his interest to ask him for a contribution to her new artistic magazine;[44] Florence Henniker had obtained his collaboration in a short story, in addition to his adulatory though back-handed article in the August 1894 number of the *Illustrated London News*. Whatever the cost to his increasingly-strained marriage, Hardy must now have a literary lady— not his wife—whom he could mastermind, and who would appreciate him in return. It was a situation which clearly brought him satisfaction and happiness.

# 7

# Prose to Poetry

ON I NOVEMBER 1895, the day of the volume publication of *Jude the Obscure*, Hardy might well feel happy. *Tess* had weathered the storm raised by a few critics, and was a popular success, generally acknowledged as his finest book. The dramatized version, which he himself had just completed for a rising actor-manager, Johnston Forbes-Robertson, was eagerly awaited by a most distinguished leading-lady, Mrs. Patrick Campbell, who had scored such a success in 1893 as Mrs. Tanqueray. *Tess* had quickened public interest in all his previous novels. Since the beginning of the year, he had been revising these for collected publication in a uniform edition by Osgood, McIlvaine, to which *Jude* was added as the latest title. He had used his reputation over *Tess* to make some of the sexual expressions in these other novels more frank. For the first time, in this edition, the heroine of *The Woodlanders* was allowed to say to her rival, "O, my great God! He's had you." On the personal side, he now had two well-born ladies with literary ambitions under his tutelage. He was helping Florence Henniker with her forthcoming book of short stories, including their own collaboration *The Spectre of the Real*.[1] He was encouraging Agnes Grove to use her fine and decisive mind in topical journalism.[2] To both he at once sent copies of *Jude*. To Florence he wrote a little nervously, "not because I thought you narrow—but because I had rather bored you with him during the writing".[3] To Agnes he confidently wrote with her copy, "You are, I know, sufficiently broad of view to estimate without bias a tragedy of very unconventional lives."[4] Though he must have been uneasy at the effect of these talented ladies on Emma, he could congratulate himself that she seemed now able to compete as hostess with the best of them. That summer, the *Weekly Sun* had noticed her afternoon "at homes" at Ashley Gardens, where she had entertained, among others, Florence Henniker and Mrs. Patrick Campbell. Emma had been praised by the gossip-writer: "Mrs. Hardy is an excellent hostess. She sees that her guests are properly introduced and put completely at ease by a kind word or two. And she seems to know instinctively the people who desire to know each other."[5] Perhaps his literary fame would help to bring her satisfaction in her own social success.

The last two months in 1895 shattered what false calm he may have felt. Friends like Florence Henniker, who wrote at once to ask for a key to the great Oxford figures of the past mentioned in *Jude*, might be appreciative.[6] The critics could not have been more damning. The *Morning Post* could see no good in it, the *Pall Mall Gazette* found it full of "dirt, drivel, and damnation", and coined the sneer "Jude the Obscene". The *Athenaeum* dismissed it as the bad book of a great writer. Puritan America was particularly shocked. Jeannette Gilder, in the New York *World*, made her two notorious attacks, one entitled "Hardy the Degenerate". More deeply wounding, perhaps, than all this, and nearest home, were the doubts expressed by his usually adulatory supporter, Edmund Gosse. A week after publication, Gosse reviewed the book in the *St. James's Gazette*. He wrote of "a grimy story that Mr. Hardy has at last presented to his admirers". There were other cutting phrases. Hardy, though beginning a letter of 10 November by praising Gosse's article as "the most discriminating that has yet appeared", was very clearly hurt.[7] He had an even more unpleasant shock from Gosse in December, when he and Emma paid a flying visit to London, to see both Forbes-Robertson and Mrs. Patrick Campbell in *Romeo and Juliet*. At the common luncheon-table at the Savile Club, Gosse told Hardy publicly to his face that *Jude the Obscure* was the most indecent novel ever written.[8] For the first, and, as he afterwards said, the only time in his life, Hardy became really angry with his friend. Even a more "generous view", expressed by Gosse in a new magazine *Cosmopolis* at the New Year, did not easily make up for the shock. Considering how abnormally thin-skinned Hardy was, and how much this novel of all others meant to him, it is a tribute to both men that their friendship survived. Yet worse than the critics, worse even than temporary estrangement from Gosse, was the effect of the novel on Emma. Though this has almost always been exaggerated and distorted, it formed a serious break. Writing in April 1899, she exclaimed, "the last four or five [years] alas!"[9] Emma's jealousy and anger were connected with Hardy's slights, real or imaginary, to her intellect and beliefs. Her objection to the succession of lady authors was that her husband interested himself actively in their writing while paying little attention to her own far from pathetic attempts. So far this had not prevented her from trying to do what she could to help his own work. Now she was faced with a book in which she could not believe, and whose message, as she understood it, she detested. Her nephew, Gordon Gifford, later wrote, speaking of this exact time, a comment on Lord David Cecil's book on Hardy.[10]

> I was living with them at their house, and . . . I consider therefore that I should be in the best position as judge on this matter. The author [Cecil], in a footnote, adds that "Hardy was at odds with his wife at this time"—namely, the publication of "Jude the Obscure". With this I do not disagree, as my aunt, who was a very ardent Churchwoman

and believer in the virtues and qualities of women in general, strongly
objected to this book, and, I think, the outlook of some of the characters
depicted therein. I should, however, mention that this was the first of
the Hardy novels in which she had not assisted by her counsel, copious
notes for reference and mutual discussion.

The later part of this statement is true, and is proved by Emma's
familiarity with all the complicated stages of writing and rewriting
*Tess*, including her knowledge of the various changing names adopted
by Hardy for his heroine. She even took an interest in the *setting* of
*Jude*, as she had with all his novels, and as late as April 1895, on a visit
to Mary Jeune at Arlington Manor, she sketched the church at Chaddleworth, Berks.[11] It is likely, then, that Gordon Gifford's account of the
quarrel over *Jude* is true too; it is certainly more plausible than some
of the legends woven about Hardy and Emma at this time.

One of the most persistent of these legends is that Emma made a
special journey to Dr. Richard Garnett, keeper of printed books at the
British Museum, and asked him to suppress *Jude*, proposing herself to
burn the manuscript. The more one enquires into the origins of this
improbable story, the less likely is it to be true. It comes from Ford
Madox Ford, recognized as one of the great literary liars, with his
"tricky memory, his carelessness with details, his occasional outright
fantasies".[12] Even he does not claim it to be true. He was told, he says,
by "the young Garnetts" that Mrs. Hardy, who was "a Dean's daughter",
had come up from "a long white farmhouse with roses at the window"
to persuade their father. Ford then admits that what he calls "the
pother" about *Jude* "took place in circles remote from my own". When
he later visited Emma, he found that the young Garnetts "had projected an image" of a household where Emma burnt Hardy's manuscripts which was entirely false, even in its smallest details. Emma was
not "a Dean's daughter" but an Archdeacon's niece. Max Gate was far
from the "long white farmhouse" described by the Garnetts. The whole
story was, in Ford's words, "merely a Garnettian slant on the Hardy
household"; they had painted a picture of events which was "all
naturally nothing of the sort".[13] If even that arch-romancer Ford
Madox Ford was so sceptical, it is all the more astonishing that biographers have accepted the story.

At the same time, the break with Emma was severe. From now
onward, she suspected intellectual, society women not only for their
monopoly of her husband's literary interest, but if they could be judged
as "*Jude-ite*", a term of reproach coined by her.[14] She herself adopted
the popular outcry that the novel was in the manner of Zola, the stock
pornographic symbol of the English 1890s, his publisher and translator,
Vizetelly, having been fined and imprisoned in 1889. She did not, she
wrote, wish "T.H. to be hand-in-glove with Zola". In point of fact,

Hardy wrote disingenuously to Gosse that he was "read in Zola very little", and even tried to persuade Gosse that scenes in *Jude* were rather in the style of Fielding, a fellow Dorset author they mutually admired.[15] Hardy, of course, had read at least two of Vizetelly's Zola translations in the late 1880s. In 1891, he was asked by Vizetelly's son to sign an appeal against his father's imprisonment. To Emma, Hardy himself in *Jude* was both irreligious and immoral, and in both like Zola. Her powerful inherited Protestantism made her feel called to combat this tendency, in both Hardy and his friends. Her husband was an example of talents dangerously misused, in view of "the thickening clouds of evil advancing". A year or so later, she rebuked Hardy's freethinking friend Clodd for his *Pioneers of Evolution*.[16] One can guess, too, how the pleasure of her summer success as a London hostess was marred when she felt herself marked down as the wife of a notorious blasphemer and pornographer.

Hardy's busy outward life in 1896 seemed to ride out these storms. Early in January, Mrs. Pat Campbell arrived impressively at Max Gate, only to declare herself "heartbroken" a fortnight later at the slow negotiations over *Tess*. In London, early in February, Hardy took a walk with another thirty-year-old leading lady, Elizabeth Robins. She seems to have understood from him that the play was for her; once again, she expressed herself mortified when she heard next month that he had promised it to Mrs. Pat. In point of fact, Harpers of New York were after it for the beautiful and popular Mrs. Fiske, who was "wild to play it"; Hardy had wired his London publishers early in February to extract the script from the Jeunes' strong-box, where he was keeping it, and to send it overseas. On 28 February, Charles Frohman, the American impresario, offered terms—hence, probably, Hardy's prevarication with actresses in his own country, quite apart from his weakness for pleasing a pretty young woman. At the same time, he took care to have the terms vetted by his friend, the dramatist, Henry Arthur Jones. He was also involved in helping his two English lady literary protégées, Florence Henniker and Agnes Grove. On 9 March, he rescued from the magazine *Temple Bar* an unpublished story that Florence Henniker wanted for her collection, writing a special letter to the editor on her behalf.[17] Simultaneously, he was busy encouraging Agnes to capitalize on a remark she had made about the child in *Jude* by putting her thoughts into an article entitled "What should children be told?"; he offered to read her draft himself. April was spent polishing his "good little pupil's" article, sending it to the *New Review*, and writing to hurry up the editor.[18]

Such activities seem to have kept him happily occupied: and this was as well, since the attacks on *Jude* had now passed from the serious reviewers into the lunatic fringes of literature. In January 1896, the elderly Mrs. Oliphant, just at the end of a long life of penury and struggling journalism, seized on the novel as the pretext for a sensational article in *Blackwood's*, entitled "The Anti-Marriage League". She professed to regard the book as an attack on women and "an assault on the stronghold of marriage". In May, Arthur John Butler, the translator of Dante, wrote in the *National Review* on "Hardy as a Decadent", condemning Hardy's "night-cart" view of nature, and deploring in particular the pig-killing scene. In July, Thomas Gunn Selby, a former Wesleyan missionary to China, outdid nearly everyone in his Fernley Lecture at Liverpool—"Filth and defilement he faces with the calm, unshrinkable countenance of a Local Board labourer", picking up the idea of Hardy as concerned with "night-soil", and adding, "This gifted man has made his home in the slime-pits of Siddim." Not to be outdone by nonconformity, on 9 June, the Bishop of Wakefield announced he had thrown "such garbage" into his fire. Hardy, not appreciating the climate of Yorkshire, said he doubted if the Bishop had a fire to burn a thick novel in summer, adding wryly that, if so, he had done it in default of being able to burn the author; but he was hurt at the Bishop's alleged instructions to W. H. Smith not to stock the book. He also told young William Rothenstein that he hardly dared enter his new club, the Athenaeum;[19] seven months later, he wrote to the anticlerical Clodd about this "miserable second-class prelate".[20]

On top of these disturbances, Hardy was attacked that spring by the familial disease of rheumatism, which had crippled his father; he was subject to bouts of it for the rest of his life. When he and Emma came up to Pelham Gardens, a rented house, pain drove him south to try the air of Brighton in May, though he found more relief in retreating for a few days to Max Gate, in whose chalky situation he had great faith. Meantime, the attacks on *Jude* redoubled, but so did the ironic fame that the book acquired him. He refused to stand for the Rectorship of Glasgow University. More substantially, the sales of the book were enormous, 20,000 in three months. He was able to enjoy the London season, and plan extensive holidays. He found time to sit for Winifred Hope Thomson to complete the portrait she had begun the previous year. He and Emma attended once again the popular open-air concerts at the Imperial Institute. Meeting Agnes Grove at one of these, Hardy, inspired by memories of the Larmer Tree Gardens, took two or three turns with her to the strains of the Blue Danube Waltz "among the promenaders, who eyed them with a mild surmise as to whether they had been drinking".[21] It was not, perhaps, the most tactful behaviour towards Emma, who had been ill with shingles, a stress condition possibly caused by tension over *Jude*, and was just now suffering from one of her periodic attacks of lameness. However, he determined to take her on a more extended holiday than usual when the season ended. After briefly looking in at Dorchester early in August, where he found his mother well though aged—"her face looked smaller"—he and Emma set off for Worcestershire and Warwickshire. They returned south via Reading, where Hardy, still haunted by the family history that produced *Tess* and *Jude*, remembered his father's mother had lived. They then spent a fortnight at Dover before going abroad. Here he read *King Lear*, which he had begun at Stratford, and wrote against Arnold's *Dover Beach* "Sept. 1896—T.H./E.L.H." Some have seen this entry as a pathetic or remorseful comment on Arnold's lines

>Ah, love, let us be true
>To one another!

though, with Hardy's literalness of mind, it may simply record the parallel of the place where they found themselves.

Similarly, the month's holiday that followed in Flanders may have been both an attempt to relive their honeymoon tours of over twenty years before, and a further exploration of the epic scenery for a work about the Napoleonic Wars. There was one difference from their long-ago visit. Hardy perhaps remembered how exhausted Emma had become previously on the battlefield of Waterloo; she was twenty years older now, and more lame. Fortunately, the Hardys were in the forefront of the dominant craze of the 1890s, bicycling. Hardy himself had found in February "the loveliest 'Byke' for myself . . . 'The Rover Cob' ".[22] Emma had acquired for herself a splendid green-painted steed, named "The Grasshopper". Always more daring than her husband, and encouraged by the numerous lady bicyclists she saw boarding the Channel ferry, she took it abroad, where it became a constant source of adventure, disappearing again and again in train-transit but always emerging with triumphant cries of "V'la le veloze de Madame!" She was run into, hurt her shoulder, but continued defiantly in Ostend, Bruges, Dinant, Spa, and Liège. Only Brussels, which they visited twice en route, was too busy to bike in. Hardy explored the field of Waterloo alone. The memories of twenty years ago, the attempt to stay at the same hotel in Brussels, proved saddening. "I ask myself why I am here again and not underground", he confided in a letter to Florence Henniker, whom he emotionally addressed as "my dear little friend", adding, "if you should write put *Mr*", in case a response in the same vein should fall into Emma's hands.[23]

Emma and the Grasshopper returned to menace the steep streets of Dorchester, and Hardy went back to his study at Max Gate. Here, on 17 October, he made a note which marked what he called "the end of prose". In fact, it crystallized all that had been happening for the past year. The busy, social, literary, external events of his life were nothing

1 Two sketches from *The Illustrated Sporting and Dramatic News*, 7 January 1882

Hardy, J. Comyns Carr and George Lewis (*left*) watching John Hare (*right*) playing in Pinero's *The Squire* at St. James's Theatre; they are concerned about alleged plagiarism of Hardy's own play, based on *Far From the Madding Crowd*

2 Scene from *Two Roses* with Helen Mathews (*right*)
Artist's impression by Harold Ludlow, January 1882

(*a*) Mary Jeune (hostess)

(*b*) Rosamund Tomson (poet)

3 Hardy's four ladies of fashion in the 1890s

(*c*) Florence Henniker (novelist)

(*d*) Agnes Grove (journalist)

(a) Henry Hardy

(b) Kate Hardy

4 Hardy's brother, sisters, and best friend

(c) Mary Hardy

(d) Horace Moule

beside his inner, emotional existence. This was now to be expressed
completely in poems. In his note, he saw poetry too as a way of expressing intellectual beliefs freely. "If Galileo had said in verse that the
world moved, the Inquisition might have let him alone."[24] This decision, after what he called to Gosse twenty-five-and-a-half years of
prose, reckoned from his first novel publication of spring 1871, had
already been taken, and had helped to fulfil his secret emotional needs
ever since *Jude* had appeared. The new-found techniques of half-a-
dozen years, since he renewed "the viewless wings of poesy" in 1890,
resulted in three of his finest poems, written in the year from December
1895 to December 1896. These were *In Tenebris, The Dead Man Walking*,
and *Wessex Heights*. All three, totally different from each other in form
and method, fitted with new mastery the most urgent themes of his
inner life.

That three such fine poems were written in the year from December
1895 shows that Hardy's decision of mid-October 1896, to write poems
only, was neither arbitrary nor abrupt. The idea that it was taken in
pique or resentment at the critical reception of *Jude* is almost certainly
false, as Max Beerbohm pointed out.[25] One very simple explanation,
seldom given, is that poetry needed far less weight of words. As Hardy
grew older, novel-writing was becoming a physical burden. In summer
1895, revising *The Woodlanders*, he wanted to add a verse epigraph. Not
finding a quotation, he invented four lines himself to fit the book:

> Not boskiest bow'r,
> When hearts are ill affin'd,
> Hath tree of pow'r
> To shelter from the wind!

It is an extreme case; but if three volumes of prose could be summed up
in four lines of verse, Hardy may well now have decided for poetry.
Secondly, the highly personal themes of his secret youth were now
beginning to force themselves uncomfortably into his novels.[27] When he
attached them to a novelist's human characters, they became too
self-revealing. Poems could reveal more of the emotion, but less of the
biographical circumstances. Lastly, and again very simply, he had
alienated his help and amanuensis, Emma. From *Jude* onward, he could
no longer count on the faithful copying in her hand, which many of his
other novels had enjoyed. A new novel might now literally be beyond
his physical powers, especially as rheumatism began to affect his
fingers.

The first of this group of poems was written in late 1895 and early
1896, and was at first called *De Profundis*, and published under that
title in 1901. Oscar Wilde's posthumous autobiography of the same
name in 1905 probably caused Hardy later to alter his title to *In*

*Tenebris*. It consists of three parts, the first in notably short, and the next two in notably long lines. All bear the stamp of personal disillusion with the world and his own life, and the second has explicit reference to the reception of *Jude*, to whose author he imagines his fellows saying,

> Get him up and be gone as one shaped awry; he disturbs the order here.

This section also characterizes himself, in words which he was often to use later to refute charges of mere pessimism, as one

> Who holds that if way to a better there be, it exacts a full look at the worst.

All carry the message, if not of suicide, that he might as well be dead. The third embodies a series of highly personal and mysterious unrecorded incidents from his very early life as a child at Higher Bockhampton,

> Ere I had learnt that the world was a welter of futile doing:

he describes clearing the winter snow from the garden, with childish springtime hope, an incident in the evening on the Heath with his mother—"She who upheld me"—and a moment from his delicate childhood, "the smallest and feeblest of folk", by the cottage fireside, weak from some "baptism of pain". Now, he wishes he had died at one of those early moments, before adult disillusion had come.

The poem, *The Dead Man Walking*, written later in 1896, and in the clipped, laconic metre of the first section of *In Tenebris*, also recalls past and personal history. Its theme is how, though apparently alive, his soul has died gradually through the years of his life, since the time of optimistic "Troubadour-youth". Incident by incident, he has been "inched" on to living death. He was first "iced" by struggles and failures of ambition, "the goal of men". Then,

> When passed my friend, my kinsfolk,
> > Through the Last Door,
> And left me standing bleakly,
> > I died yet more.

The term "my friend", always used for Horace Moule, who committed suicide in 1873, leads on to the many "kinsfolk", who had died in the past decade, three of his Sparks girl cousins, his kindly Aunt Mary Antell, and finally his own father in 1892. Then, as a last and most recent blow,

> And when my Love's heart kindled
> > In hate of me,
> Wherefore I knew not, died I
> > One more degree.

Emma, since *Jude*, had abandoned sympathy with him; though his "Wherefore I knew not" may seem ingenuous, he was genuinely surprised at the violence of her rejection, implied by the word "hate".

The third and last great poem of 1896 was written in the December of that year, *Wessex Heights*. It is at once the most moving and the most enigmatic, and though it is grouped in feeling with the others, and even echoes an occasional phrase, some of its special aspects lie in what he was doing at the time of writing. In December 1896, he was particularly "hard-pressed in sending off a copy of *The Well-Beloved* to the printers". This was his volume-revision of the serial of 1892. He found this revision immensely difficult; he confessed to Gosse that he did not rewrite from beginning to end as he had intended, but only substantially altered the first part and the ending—though, it is true, both these gave very much a different bearing to the story.[29] This is again a reminder that he now lacked Emma's help in fair-copying; it also shows how weary he had become with prose generally. The story, partly conceived in youth as a poetic Shelleyan symbol, had become a burden of words, a dead weight.

Against this background, the long-lined quatrains of *Wessex Heights* were written. Apparently simple, even at times naïve, their tension and dramatic rhythm quiver with such intensity that one feels an intention far deeper than at first appears. The surface idea is one of extreme simplicity. Like his father, who used to take him to high places in Dorset to look through his telescope, Hardy seeks the hilltop viewpoints of his Wessex countryside—Ingpen Beacon, Wylls-Neck, Bulbarrow, Pilsdon—and feels at home and at peace there. He avoids the valleys, the "lowlands", the towns, where he cannot feel happy or at ease either with the inhabitants or his own past there.

Yet it seems clear that there is a strong current of emotion below this surface, which many critics have tried in various ways to explain. A factual start to some kind of explanation lies in two letters of the second Mrs. Hardy to Alda, Lady Hoare, written on 6 and 9 December 1914.[30] She wrote,

> When I read 'Wessex Heights' it wrung my heart. It made me miserable to think that he had ever suffered so much. It was written in '96, before I knew him, but the four people mentioned are actual women. One was dead & three living when it was written—now only one is living . . . 'Wessex Heights' will *always* wring my heart, for I know when it was written a little while after the publication of 'Jude', when he was so cruelly treated.

Though these letters reveal something, mainly that the distress of the poem is partly connected with the reception of *Jude*, in other ways they deepen the confusion, especially over the "four . . . actual women", and their respective lives and deaths when related to the year of composition, 1896, and the year Florence Hardy wrote, 1914.

For one thing, no critic has been able to agree which parts of the

poem are allusions to "actual women", so veiled are Hardy's references.
One of the oddest mistakes has been to take a reference in stanza two
to Hardy's favourite text from 1 Corinthians, chapter 13, "Her who
suffereth long and is kind"—that is, Charity—which he uses in several
other poems, as one of the women. It is, however, common sense to
assume that the "four women" would be self-evident, in reading the
poem, to Mrs. Hardy's correspondent, Lady Hoare. Otherwise, Florence
Hardy's explanation of the poem would be meaningless to her. This, and
Hardy's usual simplicity of construction, makes it certain that the four
women are not teasingly embedded in different parts of the poem, like
plums in a cake, but quite straightforwardly catalogued in these two
consecutive stanzas.

> There's a ghost at Yell'ham Bottom chiding loud at the fall of the night,
> There's a ghost in Froom-side Vale, thin-lipped and vague in a shroud
>     of white,
> There is one in the railway train whenever I do not want her there,[31]
> I see its profile against the pane, saying what I would not hear.
>
> As for one rare fair woman, I am now but a thought of hers,
> I enter her mind and another thought succeeds me that she prefers;
> Yet my love for her in its fulness she herself even did not know;
> Well, time cures hearts of tenderness, and now I can let her go.

Expanding what she had written about the four, Mrs. Hardy identified, to most people's satisfaction, the fourth "rare fair woman". Later
in her letter of 9 December 1914, she added

> *She* has always been a sincere & affectionate friend to him, staunch &
> unaltering—& I am glad to say she is my friend too.

This has been taken, almost certainly rightly, to mean Florence Henniker. At Mrs. Henniker's death in 1923, Mrs. Hardy wrote to another
woman friend that Mrs. Henniker had been "my dear friend for 13
[years]".[32] That is, they had been friends since 1910,[33] and therefore
were so in 1914. It is difficult to find another common friend of Hardy
and his second wife who fits these facts. Complete uncertainty, however,
still exists over the three "ghosts" from Hardy's past in the previous
stanza. Since Hardy, while writing the poem, was revising *The Well-
Beloved*, and since that novel was, at least in part, based on Hardy's
own youthful attraction towards his three girl-cousins, Rebecca,
Martha, and Tryphena Sparks, it would seem an easy solution if these
were the three. Yet Florence Hardy's formula of the dead and the
living will not allow this; for, by the time of *Wessex Heights*, not one but
two of the cousins, Rebecca and Tryphena, were dead. Possibly Florence,
as she confessed, did not always know the details of the times before she
met Hardy; for instance, she thought that Winifred Hope Thomson's

portrait of Hardy, painted at this period, 1895-96, had been painted in 1892.[34] Still, over a poem which moved her as much as *Wessex Heights*, she would surely have every reason to be accurate. It is only possible to say, then, that these three women, all associated with local places, are loves of Hardy's youth, just as the fourth, Mrs. Henniker, was that of his middle-age. A guess—but only a guess—is that the "ghost at Yell'ham Bottom" is Elizabeth Bishop, the beautiful red-haired daughter of the gamekeeper, who lived in the cottage at the bottom of Yellowham Hill, and who was celebrated by Hardy in the poem *To Lizbie Browne*. The "thin-lipped" ghost "in Froom-side Vale" might be Louisa Harding, another youthful love, who used to pass him without speaking. The "one in the railway train" could be Tryphena Sparks, who in 1870 chose to go and study in London, putting her career before their attachment, and thus "saying what I would not hear". Yet these, though fitting Florence's conditions, are pure conjecture.

In any case, the identification puzzle should not distract from the main meaning of the poem. Though these two stanzas have their own heartbeat, there is a pulse of urgency throughout the whole work which suggests great spiritual importance. The "lowlands", where Hardy seems "false to myself, my simple self that was,/And is not now", peopled with "phantoms" are a chilling symbol of real horror. One reasonable conjecture for this feeling is that these "lowlands" are associated with his works in prose, a lower level of writing, he now felt, than the "heights" of poetry, which he had assayed when very young— "my simple self that was"—and was attempting again now. This echoes his "Troubadour youth" of *The Dead Man Walking*. Probably this should not be pressed too exactly; but it gives meaning to the dark stanza which immediately precedes these other two:

> I cannot go to the Great grey Plain; there's a figure against the moon,
> Nobody sees it but I, and it makes my breast beat out of tune;
> I cannot go to the tall-spired town, being barred by the forms now passed
> For everybody but me, in whose long vision they stand there fast.

Here Florence Hardy's hint that the whole poem is concerned in some way with *Jude the Obscure* may help. In his note-gathering for that book, Hardy recorded, as we saw, a ghastly experience at Fawley, the scene of Jude's childhood, in what he calls a valley of melancholy— "though I am alive with the living, I can only see the dead here".[35] These "dead", who are the relatives of Hardy's mysterious grandmother, Mary Head, are connected, in the book, with a gibbet and a hanging. Was this the ancestral "figure against the moon" of "the Great grey Plain", seen only by Hardy himself? "The tall-spired town" is, of course, Salisbury, one of the other main scenes in *Jude*, where Hardy had had some traumatic experience—what, one does not quite know—in youth, when visiting his sister Mary there in 1860 at her training-college, so largely drawn on for the background to this part of the novel. The horror of these places seems to be associated in the poem with the horror felt in revulsion at the reception of his last prose work, and all that it had cost him spiritually.

The writing of *Wessex Heights*, at all events, seemed a release, and Hardy appeared to breathe more freely in the early months of 1897. News came from New York of the success of Mrs. Fiske in *Tess*, though the simultaneous reading of the script, to protect Hardy's copyright, at the St. James's Theatre on 2 March, cost Hardy twenty pounds and nervous dyspepsia.[36] Hardy's version had, in fact, been totally rewritten for New York by Lorimer Stoddard, who found it, as an English producer did later,[37] unplayably undramatic. In the middle of March 1897, the volume-form *The Well-Beloved* was published, and was at once highly praised by Gosse. Most other reviewers were puzzled, but generally respectful, and often relieved that it was not another *Jude*. Only the *World*, cashing in on the clamour about that novel, found this one immoral. "Of all forms of sex-mania in fiction we have no hesitation in pronouncing the most unpleasant to be the Wessex-mania of Mr. Thomas Hardy." Unluckily, Hardy showed over this one irresponsible and trivial comment the obsession, which had haunted him ever since his first printed book, that of letting one bad review outweigh all others. He wrote bitter protests to Gosse, to Mrs. Henniker, to everyone who would listen. Months later, he still refered to "that horrid *World*".[38] In fact, he protested too much for complete truth. It might have occurred to him that a hero who tried to marry three generations of girls might seem questionable, and invite personal comparison—he had just admitted privately to Gosse, after more rheumatism, that he himself was "getting old, like Pierston". Instead, he chose to regard the review as inspired by "personal malignity". Happily, his decision to let his secret and real life be expressed no more in novels, but in poetry, was gaining ground. On 4 February, he entered in his diary, "Title: 'Wessex Poems: with Sketches of their Scenes by the Author'." Two other entries, bracketing this one, show his poet's way of looking at things dominant. On 27 January he entered, "Today has length, breadth, thickness, colour, smell, voice. As soon as it becomes *yesterday* it is a thin layer among many layers, without substance, colour, or articulate sound." On 10 February, he wrote, "I cannot help noticing countenances and tempers in objects of scenery, e.g. trees, hills, houses."[39] The next two years were mostly spent in assembling and decorating his first printed volume of verse.

1897 was, of course, also Queen Victoria's Diamond Jubilee year. Emma and Hardy decided to spend it in an individual way, simply by not being present. Though compelled by habit to come to London for the start of "the season", they did not compete for a house or flat there, but stayed at Basingstoke, travelling up on day-trips by fast train. As usual, they went to the Imperial Institute, where Edward Strauss's Viennese band was playing that summer; in Hampshire, they visited the Roman city of Silchester, which Hardy found as sufficiently mournful as he had found Rome itself just ten years before. Then, in the middle of June, they left England for an empty Europe, everyone travelling the other way for the great occasion. On the actual day, 20 June, they were at Berne. At Interlaken, the rosy glow of the Jungfrau could be seen from Hardy's bedroom at three in the morning. With solemn humour, he read *The Times*'s account of the Jubilee "in the snowy presence of the maiden-monarch that dominated the whole place".[40] Looking at the peak, he conceived his impressive poem to the mountaineering literary man, Leslie Stephen, which was to be so much admired by the latter's daughter, Virginia Woolf. At Lausanne on 27 June, with an older literary association, he spent from eleven to midnight in Gibbon's old garden, where *The Decline and Fall* had been finished precisely 110 years before, a coincidence which also provided Hardy with a poem. A poetic note from Zermatt—"Could see where the Matterhorn was by the absence of stars within its outline"—gave him another sonnet, not unluckily as good as the original note. Over-fatigue made him ill at Geneva; Emma, "in excellent health and vigour", actually thought of hiring a bicycle. At all events, she found "the tomb of an ancestor" in the town.[41]

Returning to a post-Jubilee England, the Hardys toured cathedrals and great houses in the West country. At Salisbury, always an evocative place with memories of his sister Mary's sojourn there, Hardy was moved both by the reading by an old canon of a chapter from Jeremiah and by the beauty of the Close at night. The autumn was spent in a flurry of bicycling, accompanied for some days by Kipling, who was playing with the idea of making his home in Dorset. Winter, as usual now with Hardy, brought complaints of ill-health. In December he visited London but "retired ignominiously" with a three days' sick headache. In the first two months of 1898, he was involved by Gosse in an address to be presented by fellow-authors to George Meredith, on the occasion of his seventieth birthday on 28 February. Hardy approved strongly of Leslie Stephen's composition of this address. The summer season of 1898 found the Hardys, though less active, back in their London rhythm. They took a flat in Wynnstay Gardens, Kensington; but the bicycling craze brought them home to Dorset earlier than usual. Hardy was often joined on these tours by his brother Henry, whom he had introduced to the pleasures of the bicycle, and they visited their Sparks cousin in Bristol. In August, Hardy entertained Florence Henniker's military husband, who was on Southern Command manœuvres, and wrote to her, somewhat archly, of a "mysterious occupation" on which he himself was engaged. This was the sketching of his projected illustrations for the volume of *Wessex Poems*. He made the final decision to publish this, his first collected volume, in mid-September.[42] By mid-October, he was groaning over the numerous printing errors, and complaining that the news of his illustrative sketches had somehow got into the papers.[43] In mid-December, *Wessex Poems* was published. It was the first fully visible and public sign of his poetic resolve; it had consequences which he himself cannot have anticipated.

# 8

# War at Home and Abroad

"WELL", wrote Hardy to Edmund Gosse, "the poems were lying about, and I did not quite know what to do with them."[1] Since he had been planning for nearly two years to bring out a volume, the remark seems a little disingenuous. There was, in fact, a certain element of unease in his mind at the step he was taking, and for more than one reason. Would the public accept the well-known novelist as a poet? He fortified himself, as so often, by anticipatory abuse of his supposed critics. "Considering", he wrote, "that the Britisher resents a change of utterance, instrument, even of note, I do not expect a particularly gracious reception of them." Hardy's doubts, expressed in this way, do not themselves sound gracious; but there are signs that he was thinking not only of the critics, but of one Britisher in person. This was his own wife, whose reaction he tried to avert by a brief Preface. "The pieces", he claimed, "are in a large degree dramatic or personative in conception; and this even when they are not obviously so." What he meant by the second part of this cryptic sentence was that poems in which the poet, "I", speaks to or about women, should not be taken as his own personal feelings. This false claim was a naïve attempt to throw Emma off the scent for it was repeated in the two successive books of verse before her death, but never again after. Nor was Emma fooled. Plain for all to read was her husband's extreme susceptibility to women all through his life. Many of the twenty-odd love-poems, two-fifths of the total contents, were dated from the 1860s to the 1890s. Only one, *Ditty*, written during their courtship in 1870, was addressed to her. Hurt and indignant, she wrote at once to a friend and admirer. Alfred Pretor, a Cambridge don, Fellow of St. Catherine's, had earlier in the year actually dedicated his book of mild and animal-loving short stories "to Mrs. Thomas Hardy, who suggested and encouraged the publication of these tales", a gesture that, for all her encouragement of his novels, her own famous husband had signally failed to make. Pretor therefore seemed a fit confidant for her grievance about Thomas's implied insult to their love and marriage. The bachelor don, whose own schoolboy past included a sensational scandal at Harrow, did his best with the angry wife.[2] Hardy, he wrote, "has said again and again to me little casual things that are absolute proofs that all his reminiscences are little fancies evoked from the days of his youth and absolutely without bearing on the real happiness of his life." All the same, even the gentle Pretor could not help feeling disturbed. "I *do* wish T.H. wd. dedicate a book to you." Hardy showed no sign of doing so in the 1900s, and the faithful Pretor was forced to repeat his own gesture in 1905, when he again dedicated a book about his pet dog, Judy; "to my friend Mrs. Thomas Hardy, a true lover of animals, to whom I dedicated Judy's first memoirs, I dedicate the last".

It is clear that Emma's indignation with her husband had been coming to the boil all through the 1890s. According to the second Mrs. Hardy, Emma round about 1891 began to confide to her diary "bitter denunciations" of Hardy, "full of venom, hatred and abuse".[3] According to another though less reliable witness, she actually gave these the heading "What I think of my Husband".[4] The literal truth will never be known, since Hardy, horrified by reading the manuscript in the months after Emma's death, eventually burned it. Yet a summary of her feelings during this decade has survived in a letter written by Emma in August 1899.[5] This was addressed to the sister of Winifred Hope Thomson, who had recently painted Hardy's portrait. In 1899, Elspeth Thomson married the writer Kenneth Grahame. It was a late marriage, and Grahame, set in the bachelor ways he presented with such loving sympathy in the all-male establishment of furry animals in *The Wind in the Willows*, was something of a domestic disaster. His wife, in some perplexity, and perhaps acting on hints, wrote for advice to Emma Hardy. Emma's reply was barbed by the knowledge that Hardy had been indulging in one of his minor literary flirtations with Mrs. Grahame just before her marriage. On 20 May 1897, he had been shown her verses by Justin McCarthy, and liked them so much for their "tender humour—slyness, if I may say so"[6] that he had kept them by him. In February 1898, he praised a valentine she had sent him.[7] Emma therefore had the double satisfaction of showing the younger wife she was not to be trifled with, and of trumpeting the wrongs she felt she had suffered from her own husband during the past decade. Her opening, in all the circumstances, was itself sufficiently remarkable.

> It is really too "early days" with you to be benefitted by one who has just come to the twenty-fifth year of matrimony: (I knew T.H. in 1870 (April) married Sep[r]. 1874). You are *both* at present in a Benedict state (Women can be anything in these days.)

Having established her long-standing authority as a wife, Emma then launched on the experience of nearly twenty-five years.

> Do I know your choice, perhaps I have met him, perhaps not. However it is impossible to give "directions for use"—besides characters change so greatly with time, and circumstances. I can scarcely think that love proper and enduring is in the nature of men—as a rule—perhaps there

is no woman "whom custom will not stale". There is ever a desire to give but little in return for our devotion, & affection—theirs being akin to children's—a sort of easy affectionate*ness*—& at fifty, a man's feelings too often take a new course altogether. Eastern ideas of matrimony secretly pervade his thoughts, & he wearies of the most perfect & suitable wife chosen in his earlier life. Of course he gets over it usually somehow, or hides it, or is lucky!

Since Hardy had notably failed to hide or get over his "Eastern ideas" about other women, one wonders if Emma reckoned he had been "lucky", and what form the luck had taken. She then proceeded to the attack on the influence of her husband's relatives, which was noticed earlier,[8] and in which her deep-laid resentment at all she had suffered from the possessive Jemima Hardy found full expression. She continued with her own rules of conduct.

Keeping separate a good deal is a wise plan in crises—and being both free—and expecting little neither gratitude, nor attention, love, nor *justice*, nor anything you may set your heart on—Love interest— adoration, & all that kind of thing is usually a failure complete—some one comes by & upsets your pail of milk in the end—If he belongs to the public in any way, years of devotion count for nothing—Influence can seldom be retained as years go by, & *hundreds* of wives go through a phase of disillusion—it is really a pity to have any ideals in the first place.

"This is gruesome, horrid, you will say", Emma continued, with the alarming fancy that Kenneth Grahame might be actually "looking over the bride's shoulder as bridegrooms often do". However, after somewhat obscurely advocating stoicism—"The Spartan style was wise doubtless" —she concluded with a grudging concession to exceptional happy marriages, by adding, "Yet I must qualify all this by saying that occasionally marriage undoubtedly is the happy state, (With Christians always if *both* are) which it was intended to be." The forceful underlining of *both* shows the nub of the main difference between Emma and Hardy after *Jude the Obscure*. She then gathered up her forces for a final onslaught on him.

There must of necessity be great purity in the mind of the *man*, joined with magnanimity, & *justice*, and where, or *rather* how often are these qualities to be found combined? Similarity of taste is not to be depended upon, though it goes some way, but rivalry, fear, jealousy, steps in. Often a love-match has failed completely over & over again—Christian philosophy is the only oil certain to work the complication. I see that continually.

Emma ended her bizarre and pathetic diatribe with characteristic congratulations—"though I rather congratulate a man in these cases" —and an invitation to "drop into our roadside cottage". Her eccentric grammar and phrasing cannot obscure the real bitterness and hurt she had suffered in the 1890s at the sequence of talented women, Rosamund Tomson, Florence Henniker, Agnes Grove, who had "come by and upset her pail of milk" with the "similarity of taste" she had once believed unique to herself and her husband. Any hope of a shared belief in orthodox Christianity had been killed by the writing and publication of *Jude*. The final betrayal, as Emma must have seen it, was the publication of *Wessex Poems*, ranging from her husband's "little fancies" of the 1860s before he had known her, through dated poems from the early 1890s, such as *Thoughts of Phena*, on the death in 1890 of one of these earlier loves, Tryphena Sparks, and still more hurtfully through poems written a few years later and clearly addressed in the most deeply-felt terms to Florence Henniker. Illogical and ill-educated as the letter shows Emma to be, it is sincere in its portrayal of "What I think of my Husband", and a succinct summary of "that awful diary" which her death thirteen years later left as her legacy to Hardy. A similar letter of about the same date to Clement Shorter[9] sums up her openly-expressed disillusion with Hardy—"he is like no other man—nor himself as he *was*". A final, terrible blow was his poem, *The Ivy Wife*, in which Emma saw, all too clearly, Hardy's own bitter reaction to herself.[10]

Both husband and wife were adult enough to make, each in characteristic fashion, gestures of reconciliation, at this time. Just a month before *Wessex Poems* appeared, Hardy, seemingly conscious that Emma was so poorly represented in its pages, started to write a poem recalling their earlier, happier love. Its title alone would remind Emma of those days, since the lines were an attempt to fit words to Mozart's well-known Symphony in E Flat, the minuet and trio movement. The refrain of each stanza, as it emerged, is an invocation of their past happiness and his magical wooing in Cornwall.

> Show me again the time
> When in the Junetide's prime
> We flew by meads and mountains northerly!—
> Yea, to such freshness, fairness, fulness, fineness, freeness,
> Love lures life on.

> Show me again the day
> When from the sandy bay
> We looked together upon the pestered sea!—
> Yea, to such surging, swaying, sighing, swelling, shrinking,
> Love lures life on.

Possibly technical difficulties put him off, to leave the poem for completion many years later. According to a distinguished musicologist, the stanza form suggests but does not finally fit either minuet or trio of

Mozart's composition.[11] Yet the association with Emma and the past is evident and poignant. Hardy was remembering the themes in the popular piano duet version played by Emma and her sister long ago. Now Emma was estranged, and the sister, the widowed Catherine Holder, dying in a nursing-home at Lee-on-Solent in Hampshire, far from Cornwall.

Emma too made her attempt to revive in her husband a happier past. On his birthday, 2 June 1899, while staying for the London season at a flat in Wynnstay Gardens, near the one they had rented in the previous year, she gave and inscribed to him a Bible. She may have thought that there was even now some chance *"both"* could share the Evangelical Christian worship that meant so much to her, or at any rate the church attendance which was Hardy's lasting legacy from his "churchy" upbringing. Hardy actually spent his birthday listening to the beautiful Duchess of Manchester reciting Gray's *Elegy* by the poet's grave. Yet he appreciated Emma's gift enough to copy into it the date of the last time they had gone to church together, at Salisbury Cathedral in the summer of 1897. He had been so moved then by the old canon's reading of Jeremiah that he now put the initials of himself and Emma against the text.

Yet none of this lasted. The poem, revised and completed, was not published until after Emma's death, and the Bible contains to this day hardly any other markings.[12] The flicker of middle-aged reconciliation went out almost before it began. Its brief life was recorded by Hardy in another poem, which movingly summarizes this abortive effort by both to revive their first, inspired meeting, "thirty years after". He gave it the title *A Second Attempt*. It ends "Twice-over cannot be!"

Yet the picture could not all be gloom, nor gloom all the time, a fact of nearly everyone's married life which Hardy's biographers have too often forgotten. Looking back, at Hardy's death, Sir George Douglas, who knew both well, thought that Emma and Thomas were as well assorted as most of the happily married couples that one comes across in life, and that each had sacrificed something to the other.[13] They had, moreover, even at this time of crisis, interests in common to paper the cracks of a strained partnership. One was their mutual passion for the defence of animals. Emma shared hers with Alfred Pretor, Hardy his with Florence Henniker, which may partly have reconciled Emma to other aspects of the lady. Emma and Hardy themselves were allies in the cause, and also members of the London Anti-Vivisection Society, whose secretary, Sidney Trist, visited Max Gate in September 1898. Emma doubtless approved of Hardy's letter to the journalist, W. T. Stead, who asked him for an opinion on movements for peace, to be printed in a new periodical in the first half of 1899. Hardy wrote that "As a preliminary, all civilized nations might at least show their humanity by covenanting that no horses be employed in battle except for transport", a message to be horribly ignored in the South African War later that year.[14] Hardy equally must have approved of Emma's forthright letter to the *Daily Chronicle* of 8 September in the same year, lambasting the English excursionists who on 3 September had gone to a bull-fight in Boulogne, and "thus trailed our national reputation in the dirt".[15] When the American professor W. L. Phelps came to tea at Max Gate in summer 1900, primed with enquiries about Hardy's novels, and desiring to exchange opinions about the relations of poetry and prose in Hardy's work, he found himself to his evident amazement surrounded by an army of cats. "Are all these your own cats?" he exclaimed. "Oh, dear, no," replied Hardy. "Some of them are, and some are cats who come regularly to have tea, and some are still other cats, not invited by us, but who seem to find out about this time of day that tea will be going."[16] After this pronouncement by the great literary man, it must have been even more inexplicable to Phelps that Hardy was "evidently pained" by the idea that his poetry was less good than his prose, and wished to be regarded as an English poet who had written some stories in prose. The eccentricity of the English is a constant theme in the writings of many of Hardy's American admirers, and his preference for poetry and cats, and even his poems *about* cats, seemed to these transatlantic ladies and gentlemen "too funny".[17] In fact, man's injustice to his fellow-creatures, with the conviction that he could now powerfully express his deepest sympathies about this, and other topics, in verse of increasing effect, were from now onward among the ruling forces in Hardy's life. The first was a passion he could still share with Emma; the second, the passion for poetry, and his vision of himself as primarily a poet, was one she totally failed to grasp, though it was in the end to immortalize her.

At the same time, Emma, as we have already seen, was most certainly not the ninny that many biographers of Hardy have assumed. She studied and deeply appreciated the latest Ibsen, *John Gabriel Borkman*, in Archer's translation, finding it "pathetically powerful and true".[18] She read Tolstoi's *Resurrection* (though she could not spell its title) in a French translation.[19] She tried to cope with a certain amount of "modern" poetry, though perplexed by Yeats, and preferring the easier O'Shaughnessy.[20] Her blind eye in the way of literary appreciation was now reserved for her husband's work, and for what she took to be its message. A not unkindly visitor, Bertha Newcombe, described her in the year 1900 to Mrs. Gosse.[21]

> I felt a great sympathy & pity for "Emma" this time. It is pathetic to see her struggling against her woes. She asserts herself as much as possible and is a great bore, but at the same time is so kind and good-hearted, and one cannot help realising what she must have been to her

husband . . . [She told me] that she had a fresh complexion and was nick-named "the peony". Now imagine, to this full-blown young girl, coming an ill-grown, under-sized young architect . . . I don't wonder she resents being slighted by everyone, now that her ugly duckling has grown into such a charming swan. It is so silly of her though isn't it not to rejoice in the privilege of being wife to so great a man?

Emma, anticipating later attitudes, did not see this "privilege". She commented, "I often wonder if women's rule of the world would not have produced a better world than it is".[22] Yet she felt no urge to do anything publicly about this, "getting shyer as I get older".[23]

All through January 1899, Hardy read the reviews of his first so-long-delayed book of verse, and brooded on the function and nature of a poet. "No man's poetry can be truly judged till its last line is written. What is the last line? The death of the poet."[24] Some of Hardy's "last lines", if he had known, would have amazed even him. For the present, he went into his characteristic growling cavern of determination to be misunderstood. On 25 January he wrote, "A principle of conduct: acquiescence but recognition"; a few days later, stung by a casual review, "Pessimism. Was there ever any great poetry which was not 'pessimistic'?";[25] on 30 January, to Florence Henniker, "The reviews have . . . had their say about the poems—a poor say."[26] She evidently rallied him briskly on his unreasonableness, and in another letter a fortnight later he retracted his strictures on the book's reception. In this fortnight, the first half of February, he wrote a new cluster of poems, proof that the venture into public had encouraged his verse, and not damped it.

In this little group, *I have Lived With Shades* (2 February), *The To-Be-Forgotten* (probably 9 February), and *On a Fine Morning*, the first-named and first-written was the most considerable. In form and tone, it resembles the first of Hardy's *In Tenebris* group; all were destined, together with the *In Tenebris* poems, for his next book of verse. *I Have Lived With Shades*, because of its direct simplicity, has tempted some rather metaphysical speculation.[27] The "Shades", however, are surely and straightforwardly his memories of actual dead people—ancestors, friends, relatives from family history. After showing him visions of the past and what is to be, they show him a picture "Of man, So common-place. He moves me not at all." The man is, of course, his unrecognized self, whom to contemplate realistically would cause Hardy "Deep pain". The message of morbidity, repeated in *The To-Be-Forgotten*, and only half-allayed in *On a Fine Morning*, might have set his future verse into a mould of monotonous introspection, but for a historical accident, lucky for the poet though shattering for the nation, which occurred later in the same year.

This was the outbreak, early in October, of the South African War against the Boers of the Transvaal. Ironically, this sordid struggle gave Hardy the poet an objective interest and a theme which resulted in a dozen poems, many of considerable stature. It also gave him another much-needed link of sympathy with Emma, to match their shared concern for the animals in war. Both were what came to be known as "Pro-Boer". Many English "liberals" were, though in point of fact the Boers were almost totally illiberal. The common "liberal" view was put by Emma in her usual vivid if breathless way. Well before the war started, she wrote, "The battles will be on a huge scale that's certain—& a terrible ending it will all have. But the Boers fight for homes & liberties—we fight for the Transvaal Funds, diamonds & gold!"[28] She did not see, any more than Agnes Grove, the Stanley ladies, and other typical English "liberals", that the Boers were also fighting for Hottentot slave labour and their own command of the huge Rand profits, hitherto pillaged by foreign outlanders. Emma's "terrible ending", whether she foresaw it or not, included the introduction by Kitchener of the shame of our century, the concentration camp. As a minor compensation, the poor physical condition of young British recruits resulted in the first School Meals Service; but "this is a man's world", as Emma wrote. "It is in fact a terrible failure as to peace & joy."[29]

Hardy's practical concern was not with such issues, but with the personal, human, and purely local domestic effects of the war. In spite of his own "dreadful langour" after a bad summer—he was convinced a bout of influenza had permanently affected his eyes—and feeling "weak as a cat", he bicycled fifty miles and back to see the embarkations from Southampton, with Dorset lads in the troopships. He missed the departure on 9 November of the troopship carrying Florence Henniker's husband, though some of the Major's character may have gone into the laconic Horatian form of a poem Hardy had already written, *The Colonel's Soliloquy*. His feeling for Florence's anxiety may be traced in several poems about the suffering wives of soldiers. *The Going of the Battery* was, Hardy told her, "almost an exact report of the scene & expressions I overheard".[30] *A Wife in London* was first written, as the manuscript shows, in the first person, with the woman speaking.

The most remarkable, though so far unremarked, feature of these War Poems, is that many are partly in the style of other poets. It is as if Hardy were flexing his muscles at this chance of exercise in his chosen art. Notably, they are in the styles of poets who had engaged his attention, in reflection or by actual contact, earlier in this year of 1899. On 6 March, he had written his celebrated meditations to Gosse about the mystery of Robert Browning.[31] On 18 June, he met A. E. Housman. On 20 June, he visited Swinburne at Putney.[32] It can hardly be fortuitous that three (and three of the best) of the War Poems Hardy wrote late in the same year are strongly in the respective manners of

5　Hardy with Emma at Max Gate, circa 1900

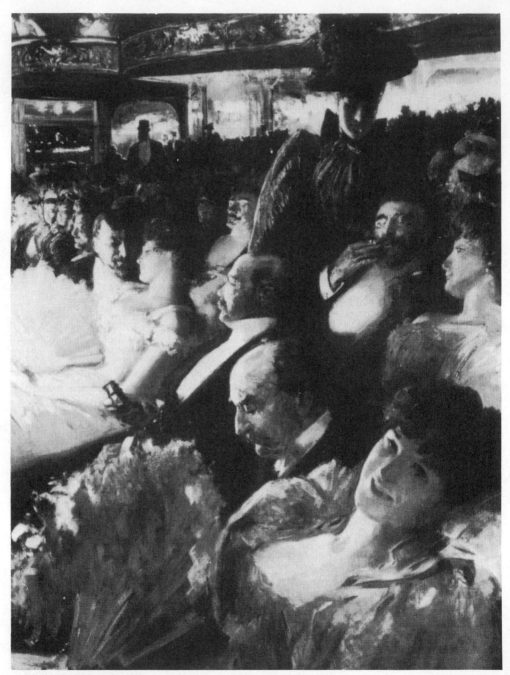

6   Hardy without Emma in London, circa 1900
From the painting "First Night at a Theatre" by Alfred Stevens. Joseph Conrad
(smoking) is also portrayed, giving an approximate date

7   Hardy by Jacques-Emile Blanche, May 1906

Best Times. ~~Never Again~~.

We went a day's excursion to the stream,
And climbed the bank, & looked at the rippled gleam,
    And I did not know
     That life would show,
However it might bloom, no finer glow.

    —

I walked in the Sunday sunshine by the road
That wound towards the gate of your abode,
    And I did not think
     That life would shrink
To nothing ere it shed a rosier pink

    —

Unlooked for I arrived on a rainy night,
And you hailed me at the door by the swaying light,
    And I quite forgot
     That life might not
Again be touching that ecstatic height.

And that calm evening when you climbed the stair,
    gaiety prolonged and rare;
After a b~~anquet room too~~ ~~~~
    No thought soever
     That you might never
Walk down again, struck me as I stood there.

    —⟳

Rewritten from an old draft.

8  Manuscript of Hardy's poem "Best Times", showing alterations to fit his version of events

these three poets. The Browningesque effort, *The Going of the Battery*, has almost a touch of pastiche or unconscious parody, particularly in its last stanza.

> —Yet, voices haunting us, daunting us, taunting us,
> Hint in the night-time when life beats are low
> Other and graver things . . . Hold we to braver things,
> Wait we, in trust, what Time's fulness shall show.

Yet even more astonishing, since it uses, masters, and revivifies its model, is *Drummer Hodge*, first printed under a title that underlines still further its A. E. Housman pattern, *The Dead Drummer*. Housman's *A Shropshire Lad* had appeared three years earlier, and its classical monodies for adorable, scarlet-clad soldier lads and strong youthful rustic heroes were therefore well known to Hardy. His own *Dead Drummer* could have appeared in Housman's sequence. Yet Hardy somehow outdoes the acidulous but passionate bachelor don in human sympathy, even when he is most like him in thought and technique.

> Yet portion of that unknown plain
> Will Hodge for ever be;
> His homely Northern breast and brain
> Grow to some Southern tree,
> And strange-eyed constellations reign
> His stars eternally.

Hardy's poem remained the finest war-time expression of how "the poetry is in the pity" until Wilfred Owen's own First World War poem *Futility*, which resembles it in personal feeling, with the added accent of a personal experience.

As for Swinburne, Hardy, though reduced almost to a delirium of admiration as a young man in the 1860s, had never before written in his manner. Now he used it openly in the most considerable poem of the whole sequence, *The Souls of the Slain*. In its deliberate use of universal alliteration, its six-line stanza form with a long fifth line followed by an ultra-short sixth, it has the exact accent of Swinburnian works such as *Hertha*, *The Deserted Garden*, or those choruses from *Atalanta in Calydon*, on which Hardy had feasted in his twenties. It is, too, in its own right, a very fine and accomplished poem, individual to Hardy. Its vast, imaginative panorama was emphasized, in its first printing in the *Cornhill* of April 1900, by a note:

The spot indicated in the following poem is the Bill of Portland, which stands, roughly, on a line drawn from South Africa to the middle of the United Kingdom; in other words, the flight of a bird along a 'great circle' of the earth, cutting through South Africa and the British Isles, might land him at Portland Bill . . .

The flocking spirits of slain soldiers "homing", like migrant birds, on the Bill, the ironies of their return, the world-span against which their lives are measured, anticipate the final form in which Hardy was soon to cast his epic *The Dynasts*. Though the ending is technically most Swinburnian, it is typical of Hardy, in that the poet himself remains, when all is over, the solitary figure in the huge, natural Dorset landscape—

> And the spirits of those who were homing
> Passed on, rushingly,
> Like the Pentecost wind;
> And the whirr of their wayfaring thinned
> And surceased on the sky, and but left in the gloaming
> Sea-mutterings and me.

The Biblical reference leads to Hardy's own lifelong vision of himself as the seer or prophet of his generation: "like some terrible old prophet crying in the wilderness", as one admirer wrote to him half-a-dozen years later.[33]

Not everyone appreciated Hardy's cries in the wilderness of a nation deeply at odds about its own warring role. A seemingly innocent poem, *A Christmas Ghost Story*, was attacked in the *Daily Chronicle* on Christmas Day, of all times, for its pacifism. Hardy gave as good as he got in reply;[34] it must be remembered that, at the New Year, British garrisons in Ladysmith, Mafeking, and Kimberley, were all besieged, there were many casualties, and feeling was high. Even after Lord Roberts's successful spring campaign, Hardy reported to Emma, while on a visit to Town, "Hardly any London season. No balls, no money: people in mourning."[35] Jubilation only returned in summer 1900, with the flight of Kruger, the annexation of the Transvaal, and British possession of the real issue at stake, the Rand mines.

In spite of his conviction that "This Imperial idea is, I fear, leading us into strange waters",[36] Hardy probably shared the public impression that the war was over that warm summer of 1900 when he wrote "to make it warmer there is news of the entry into Pretoria",[37] and he greeted the returning troopships gleefully with his *Song of the Soldiers' Wives*. He and the British public were wrong, since the most deadly campaign, punitive on the British side, guerilla on the part of the Boers, was just about to start. He, on the other hand, had to turn his attention back from public to private stresses. One of Emma's answers to his immersion in poetry, and his published poems about other women, was to write and publish poetry herself. On 14 April 1900, twelve days after Hardy's magnificent *The Souls of the Slain* was printed in the *Cornhill*, Emma's lyric *Spring Song* appeated in *The Sphere* with a comment by the embarrassed editor, Clement Shorter.

We all know that Mr. Thomas Hardy began his literary career writing poetry. It is interesting to know that his wife has also written poems. Mrs. Hardy sends me the following verses, which I am happy, as one of the most enthusiastic admirers of her husband's books, to print . . .

Anyone less armoured by indignation than Emma would have felt the implication of the last sentence. Instead, she made Shorter, all through the 1900s, a repository for her injured feelings about Hardy, who, she once wrote with sarcasm, was determined to keep her out of his affairs "lest the dimmest ray should alight upon me of his supreme glory".[38]

Another stress for Hardy came from Emma's nephew and niece, Gordon and Lilian Gifford. Now in their early twenties, and virtually adopted children to the childless Hardys, they were an added burden, for which he felt responsible. Lilian, though of uncertain temperament, was a useful, cheerful companion for her aunt; but her love of parties, company, and gossip was time-consuming to the routine of Max Gate.[39] Gordon was a professional responsibility. Largely and perhaps irregularly educated in Dorchester, followed by a stay in Paris to learn French, he was now apparently unemployed; it seemed to Hardy that he might find a niche for him in his own first profession of architect. In May 1899, Hardy had called on Gordon's egregious father, Walter Gifford, in Maida Vale to discuss this,[40] and in January 1900 he established the young man in the office of his own old London employers, Blomfields. Hardy showed an active interest, taking Gordon to the Kensington Art Library to get out books, and behaving generally as if the youth were himself in the 1860s. Yet, in spite of good reports, punctiliously relayed to Emma, there are hints that the arrangement did not altogether work. There cannot have been anything seriously wrong, since Gordon achieved a reasonably successful career as an L.C.C. architect, but he was a cause for concern at this time. Another, which had already come up, was the possibility that Gordon's unmanageable younger brother, Randolph, might also come to Max Gate, but even his own father vetoed this.[41]

Gifford family troubles, however, persisted. Emma's widowed sister, Helen Catherine, was dying in Lee-on-Solent, near Portsmouth. Emma, who in September had enjoyed several cycle tours with Hardy, spent most of October away from home nursing the dying woman, while Lilian kept house for Hardy, and shared his bike-riding. Emma returned on 9 November, "rather broken down", but was away again a fortnight later. During this second absence, Max Gate was invaded by Hardy's most egocentric and thick-skinned admirer, Miss Rebekah Owen, who had arrived with her own sister from the house they had acquired in the Lake District. She monopolized Hardy, gossiped with Lilian about her aunt's shortcomings, retailed spiteful Dorchester

criticism of Emma, and altogether behaved in an insufferably proprietorial way. When Emma returned unexpectedly, probably because
she wished to arrange for power of attorney to deal with her sister's
affairs, Rebekah Owen found it "so rude in Mrs. T.H." that she herself
was not invited to Max Gate as much as she had expected, in spite of
the fact that Emma had actually found time, in her troubles, to write
a friendly note. Emma had been nursing for two months a woman in
an advanced stage of premature senility, yet this was ignored by the
American lady, who lamented that she herself was being kept from her
literary idol; she regarded Emma's comings and goings between Dorset
and Hampshire as the whims of an unreasonable and jealous wife. Miss
Owen's monstrous complacency was to have still more sinister manifestations later; firm dealing by the second Mrs. Hardy eventually put
a stop to it. Emma and the power of attorney arrived back at Lee-on-
Solent only just in time for her sister's death on 6 December, and she
stayed for the funeral on 10 December. Hardy wrote to her kindly,
telling her how they had pulled the blinds down at Max Gate, how
Lilian had ordered mourning, and advising her to "'take it stiddy', as
they say here"—and indeed still do say in Dorset.[42] If Hardy cannot
quite be absolved from the sin of not keeping his lady admirers in order,
it must be remembered that his habitual lack of confidence gave him
some real need for flattery, even of the most brash kind.

1900 had been a punishing year for Hardy; he wrote its epitaph in
one of his finest poems, *By the Century's Death-Bed*, now universally
known and anthologized as *The Darkling Thrush*. 1901 was a happier,
and, incidentally, healthier time. By June he was organizing a second
book of verse, which at that stage he intended to call *Poems of Feeling,
Dream and Deed*. The War sequence had given him the idea of a book
in several defined sections. He resuscitated as *Poems of Pilgrimage* the
dozen-odd poems he had written on his two last holidays abroad with
Emma, in 1887 and again in 1897. Most characteristically, he included
a poem about refusing an invitation to the United States. In fact, he
never in his life visited America and so, perhaps instinctively, avoided
those women's literary organizations, peopled by their Miss Owens.
About sixty poems came under the general heading of "Miscellaneous".
There was a powerful section of grey philosophy, both recently and
earlier written. There were, by contrast, and also from past and present,
a number of love poems, more fuel for Emma, since they were all to
"miscellaneous" loves, the gamekeeper's daughter, Elizabeth Bishop
of young days, and other girls, jostling poems to be associated with
Florence Henniker, all, as Emma said, "Written *to please* . . . others! or
himself—but not ME, far otherwise".[43] Earlier and funnier poems were
included, slightly bowdlerized to fit volume form, *The Ruined Maid* and
*The Levelled Churchyard*. There were poems connected with novels,

*Tess* and *The Well-Beloved*, a little bunch of translations, designated "Imitations Etc.", and finer, recent poems of the dying century—the *In Tenebris* group, *I Have Lived With Shades* and *The Darkling Thrush*. The whole collection, now appropriately called *Poems of the Past and of the Present*, came out in mid-November. In spite of Hardy's usual gloomy prognostications to Gosse—"Alas for that volume"—it was an instant success. The first edition of 500 was quickly sold, and by 3 December he was preparing a second edition. He was established, as he had wished, as a recognized poet, and not merely a novelist turned poet. No longer would a new poem in a magazine be announced as "by Mr. Thomas Hardy, the distinguished novelist".[44] Now was the time for putting into practice the huge poetic idea, whose various schemes had engaged his last thirty years: the Napoleonic, philosophic epic, *The Dynasts*.

# 9

# Dynasts and Destinies

THE SPIRITS IRONIC, who provide some of the catchier moments in *The Dynasts*, with sprightly lyric stanzas such as W. S. Gilbert might have written in *The Sorcerer* or *The Pirates of Penzance*, complete with musical comedy rhymes like "baby" and "maybe", can be held to have presided over Hardy's initial penning of that long-contemplated work. He began writing it in 1902. Only a year or so earlier, by a coincidence of ultra-Hardy irony, his insane brother-in-law, Richard Ireland Gifford, long-term inmate in the Warneford Asylum, entered into a huge poetic epic on practically the same subject, "a poem describing the battle of Waterloo for which he is industriously collecting geographical, climatological and other interesting local facts". Further, according to the hospital case-book,[1] he "has great faith in the success which will attend the publication . . . and is arranging for his discharge in order to attend to the details . . ." The delusion of poetic ability, which this brother shared with Emma, and the subject in which he chose to display it, which he shared with Hardy, provide the weirdest possible backdrop to Hardy's own extraordinary production, on which he lavished his next five years.

Why did he choose this moment to embark upon it? One reason was the feeling, common to all men in their sixties, that time may be running out. Again and again, and particularly in his intimate letters to Edmund Gosse, Hardy stresses how he has pushed on with his great task in case he should not be allowed time to finish it; "flying years compelled me to send out the whole, red-hot".[2] To Henry Newbolt, on 16 January 1909, he admitted "periodic frights lest I should never live to finish". Nor was this the nervous hypochondria of a man in his mid-sixties. Influenza, rheumatism, eye-trouble, sick headache, and intermittent returns of his bladder complaint all seem real enough, though perhaps over-obsessively chronicled. Many eye-witnesses observed that Hardy, in these years, literally looked like death. In 1903, H. W. Nevinson recorded his appearance:[3]

Face a peculiar grey-white like an invalid's or one soon to die; with many scattered red marks under the skin, and much wrinkled—sad wrinkles, thoughtful and pathetic, but none of power or rage or active courage. Eyes bluish grey and growing a little white with age, eyebrows and moustache half light brown, half grey. Head nearly bald on top but fringed with thin and soft light hair . . . Figure spare and straight; hands very white and soft and loose-skinned.

In 1906, the painter Jacques-Emile Blanche similarly observed[4]

. . . the hand he extended to me, a gouty hand: white, puffy and limp, with its fingers rigid and awkward like those of Prince Hamlet in the picture by Delacroix . . . The harsh light of mid-day in a sky bleached with heat tinted the scalp, the hollow cheeks, the drooping moustaches . . . with a corpse-like green.

Arthritis, then as now, could be a killer, and Hardy's arthritic hands are common to both accounts. H. G. Wells, who had hailed the closing passages of *Jude* as "the voice of the educated proletarian, speaking more distinctly than it has ever spoken before in English literature", exclaimed, on first seeing Hardy, "What? Not that grey little man!"[5] Ethel Smyth's friend, Henry Brewster, records a similar shock on meeting Hardy.[6] When in 1904 A. C. Benson tried to entertain Henry James and Hardy, he noted how deafness prevented either from hearing what the other was saying.[7]

There were other, more positive, reasons for Hardy to hurry forward with his great work. One was, of course, his commitment to poetry, and his resolve never to be entrapped into the writing of novels again. Then, the excitement of the South African War threw him back to that other and greater war, which had been the background to his grandparents' early lives at his own birthplace, and in which his own grandfather had played a local part. His poems at this time touched on the lives of that generation next but one to his. His other grandmother, his mother's mother, is almost certainly the subject of two poems he wrote in 1901. *Autumn in King's Hintock Park* and *Her Late Husband* (*King's Hintock, 182–* ) tell the story of her poverty and of her husband's death in the 1820s at her village of Melbury Osmond (Hardy's "King's Hintock"). *Bereft*, also 1901, may too record her experience, with its sad, haunting folk-song refrain.

Essentially, however, his mind dwelt most on his Bockhampton grandmother, his father's mother, and the subject of his first known poem. Now, on 20 May 1902, he made her the subject of one more tender and moving poem, recalling her at the family fireside during the first seventeen years of his own life. The poem, published in America under the simple title, *Remembrance*, and headed in England by the inscription of pure personal meaning, *One We Knew* (*M.H. 1772–1857*), harked back to her memories of the early days of the nineteenth century, and even the last decade of the eighteenth.

> She told of that far-back day when they learnt astounded
> Of the death of the King of France:

Of the Terror; and than of Bonaparte's unbounded
  Ambition and arrogance.

Of how his threats woke warlike preparations
  Along the Southern strand,
And how each night brought tremors and trepidations
  Lest morning should see him land.

This was where Hardy's mind now was. It is no accident that here, and
at this time in history, he started to write his epic. Indeed, he may even
have written this poem on the same day as the first words of *The
Dynasts*, whose very first scene, once its supernatural machinery is
disposed of, is set on "A Ridge in Wessex" only a few miles from
Hardy's birthplace, and in the year of Napoleon's threatened invasion.
At all events, by the second half of 1902, the huge poem, in all its coils,
was slowly unfolding itself.

Hardy had just proved to his own satisfaction his complete mastery
of the form in which he had first planned to write his epic poem. This
was the ballad form; in one of his earliest relevant jottings, as long ago
as May 1875, Hardy had conceived of his Napoleonic panorama in the
following terms.

Mem: A Ballad of the Hundred Days. Then another of Moscow. Others
of earlier campaigns—forming altogether an Iliad of Europe from 1789
to 1815.

Something of this still remains in the occasional ballad links from
scene to scene in the finished *The Dynasts*. It is no accident that in
April 1902, just before starting, Hardy wrote his finest ballad, or even,
as he himself thought it, his most successful poem. It was written after
a long, thirsty bicycle trip across the Polden hills in Somerset and on to
Glastonbury. The scenery, which offers a splendid view of the county
to north and south, reminded Hardy of a tragic story from his youth,
probably told him by his mother, and dating, like so many of her
reminiscences, from her own youth in the 1820s. This was the recital
of jealousy, murder, and hanging: *A Trampwoman's Tradegy*. It
concerned an actual trampwoman, Mary Ann Taylor, and her lurid and
true story, "though", as he wrote to Gosse, "she has been dust for half
a century". Hardy's confidence that he could write a totally successful
dramatic poem in ballad form brimmed over into the "Iliad" he was
now attempting, though the most obvious feature of *The Dynasts* is the
multiplicity of verse-forms it employs, no less than thirty in all.[8]

The complicated nature of this master-plan was to occupy five exact
years of Hardy's writing life, if we assume he began to draft Part I in
June 1902, and finished the draft, though not the completed version of
Part III, at the end of May 1907. It is, as he himself announced, "an
epic drama . . . in three parts, nineteen acts, and one hundred & thirty

scenes". Later statisticians have found 1470 lines of prose, 7931 of blank verse, and 1152 of rhymed verse, making 10,553 lines in all; but this is to exclude the stage-directions and "dumb-shows"—descriptions of gigantic mimes—which must add several thousand more lines of prose. With such complexity, one can only try to look at the work's different elements; and this, in fact, is suggested by Hardy's own notes through the thirty years when the design was forming. We have seen his first plan in 1875 for an amalgam of long and narrative ballads. In June 1877 he planned "a grand drama, based on the wars with Napoleon, or some one campaign (but not as Shakespeare's historical dramas)"[9]. When *The Trumpet-Major* was published on 23 October 1880, Hardy felt it only "touched the fringe of a vast international tragedy",[10] though by 27 March 1881, he was back to the idea of "A Homeric Ballad, in which Napoleon is a sort of Achilles".[11] On 16 February 1882, a philosophic scheme begins to appear in a note, "Write a history of human automatism, or impulsion",[12] which, Hardy says, he later adopted as a framework for *The Dynasts*. This was developed on 4 March 1886 into a scheme which ruled all his work from *The Woodlanders* onward, and which forms an essential part of the eventual *The Dynasts*:[13]

> The human race to be shown as one great network or tissue which quivers in every part when one point is shaken, like a spider's web if touched. Abstract realisms to be in the form of Spirits, Spectral figures etc.
>
> The Realities to be the true realities of life, hitherto called abstractions. The old material realities to be placed behind the former, as shadowy accessories.

In November 1887, he shaped and abandoned another outline scheme, "in which Napoleon was represented as haunted by an Evil Genius or Familiar, whose existence he has to confess to his wives".[14] This seemed, rightly, too petty, and on 21 September 1889, he confessed,[15] "For carrying out that idea of Napoleon, the Empress, Pitt, Fox, etc., I feel continually that I require a larger canvas . . . A spectral tone must be adopted . . . Royal ghosts. . . . Title: 'A Drama of Kings'." On 26 April 1890, this larger canvas had developed into the idea to "View the Prime Cause of Invariable Antecedent as 'It' and recount its doings."[16] On 26 June 1892,[17] he "considered methods for the Napoleon drama. Forces; emotions, tendencies. The characters do not act under the influence of reason." In autumn 1896, on his attempted second honeymoon with Emma in Flanders, he wrote in his notebook:[18]

Europe in Throes.
Three Parts. Five Acts each.
*Characters*. Burke, Pitt, Napoleon, George III, Wellington . . .
and many others.

These various elements in its gradual assembly can be assessed separately in the finished work. The first is the element of dramatic writing and particularly of dramatic dialogue. This is almost entirely absent in any normal sense. Hardy never had any ear for effective stage dialogue. His first attempt, the dramatization of *Far From the Madding Crowd*, had had to be very heavily play-doctored by Comyns Carr before it could be put on the stage.[19] Though his one-acter, *The Three Wayfarers*, performed in 1893, was adjudged better than its companions in a quintuple bill, it was soon withdrawn, and Hardy himself revised the dialogue heavily for later amateur performance. His own version of *Tess* had to be almost entirely rewritten by Lorimer Stoddard for its 1897 New York production, and similarly treated by A. E. Filmer for the London production of 1925. Filmer indeed described the script he received from Hardy as "a theatrical impossibility". "That is not *speech*," was his reaction to Hardy's dialogue.[20]

Such criticism applies to nearly all the dialogue in *The Dynasts*. It is "not *speech*". Hardy never got over the dramatist's first pitfall, that of making people tell other people things of which they are perfectly well aware. Many key events are reported to characters who must have known about them already. There are scenes of patent absurdity. Spies discuss out loud, at great length, and frequently in public, minute details of secret information they have just gathered. It is often said that Hardy's prose scenes between Wessex locals are Shakespearian, like similar scenes in his novels; yet unlike Shakespeare, they contain no Dogberry or First Gravedigger, not even a Joseph Poorgrass. The jokes are as laboured as the dialogue, and can be seen coming many speeches ahead. To do Hardy justice he eventually tacitly withdrew his claim, in defence of Part I, that "the methods of a book and the methods of a play . . . are fundamentally similar", and admitted that what he had written was "a spectacular poem . . . more or less resembling a stage-play, though not one".[21]

How then, does *The Dynasts* stand the test as "a spectacular poem"? Since, as the statistics have shown, three-quarters of it is in blank verse, it stands or falls, as poetry, by his handling of this medium. Once more, it must be regretted, Hardy shows little of the skill he had already achieved in lyric utterance. One of the first and best critics of Part I, John Buchan, noted, "his verse throughout is full of the gravest technical faults. He has a habit of falling into that unpleasing form of blank verse where every line is a complete sentence."[22] This end-stopping does, indeed, give a terrible monotony, and must have something to do with Hardy's method of constructing speeches throughout the complete work. As his manuscript often shows, a speech would first be written in prose. It was then literally chopped into blank verse, with dashes to make up the metre and spin out the line, which were then filled in and the whole line finally revised into a regular iambic pentameter.[23] For example, Napoleon's speech in the first scene of Part III began as prose:

Soldiers! war has begun again. The last ended at Friedland at Tilsit .... At Tilsit Russia swore an eternal allegiance with France war against England. Today she violates her oaths:

This became four lines of imperfect blank verse, as follows:

Soldiers! wild war is to the fore again.
The — — — alliance Russia swore
At Tilsit for the English realm's undoing
Is violate beyond refurbishing

Hardy's final revision and printed version reads:

Soldiers, wild war is on the board again;
The lifetime-long alliance Russia swore
At Tilsit, for the English realm's undoing,
Is violate beyond refurbishment,

It is noticeable that the flat-footed "lifetime-long" is revealed, by this process, as simply a space-filler, to make up the requisite number of feet in the whole line. This is hardly the way great blank verse is written.

In this, however, Hardy may be viewed as the victim of his age, one of the most uninspired in English dramatic verse. Henry Irving's Lyceum seasons, to which Hardy was a constant play-goer, interspersed Shakespeare with fustian drama of the most stale and undistinguished blank verse. As Shaw wrote in anguish to Ellen Terry, Irving seemed unable to see any difference between the best and the worst writing. Nor was he alone among contemporary actor-managers. In 1901, a verse play called *Herod*, with Frank Benson, was produced by Beerbohm Tree, and in 1902 *Paolo and Francesca*, with the young Henry Ainley, was produced by Sir George Alexander. Both were by Stephen Phillips, whose turgid blank verse and pretentious drama became the target for Max Beerbohm in his *Savonarola Brown*. Yet the critics hailed him as a superlative dramatic poet, finer than anyone since the Elizabethan age. Professor Churton Collins, the *bête noire* of Edmund Gosse and Hardy, actually put Phillips in the same class as Sophocles. The taste of the age, which seems to have been his own taste as a play-goer, must bear some responsibility for the blankness of Hardy's blank verse in *The Dynasts*, though this is surprising in view of the rhythmic originality he always showed as a lyric poet.

One wonders if, as far as poetry was concerned, his own original instinct about telling the story as a succession of long narrative ballads was not a more happy one. It is the lyric links and choruses that one remembers from *The Dynasts*. The Trafalgar chorus, the song of the cavalry men at Weymouth, the woman's song, "My love's gone a-fighting", and, most of all, the lyric of the Spirits before Waterloo, are in a class of their own. They are among Hardy's finest writing. He himself thought the last-named was an example of his own most original work, with its entirely characteristic evocation of the small creatures in the field where the battle is to be fought.

> . . . Yea, the coneys are scared by the thud of hoofs,
> And their white scuts flash at their vanishing heels,
> And swallows abandon the hamlet-roofs.
>
> The mole's tunnelled chambers are crushed by wheels,
> The lark's eggs scattered, their owners fled,
> And the hedgehog's household the sapper unseals.
>
> The snail draws in at the terrible tread,
> But in vain; he is crushed by the felloe-rim;
> The worm asks what can be overhead,
>
> And wriggles deep from a scene so grim,
> And guesses him safe; for he does not know
> What a foul red rain will be soaking him.
>
> Beaten about by the heel and toe
> Are butterflies, sick of the day's long rheum,
> To die of a worse than the weather-foe.
>
> Trodden and bruised to a miry tomb
> Are ears that have greened but will never be gold,
> And flowers in the bud that will never bloom.
>
> So the season's intent, ere its fruit unfold,
> Is frustrate, and mangled, and made succumb,
> Like a youth of promise struck stark and cold.

Yet though the prosody may not impress, the scope and scale of the work, which we have seen becoming more and more ambitious in Hardy's mind, certainly does. Just as he was, in some sense, the victim of the taste of his age in actual verse, so he may have benefited from the public taste in Edwardian times for the spectacular and the grandiose. It was a public which loved display, from the opulence of the chorus line at Daly's and the Gaiety Theatre to the elaborate oratorios and the richly-orchestrated works of Edward Elgar, rewarded by his knighthood in 1904. In the theatre, the productions of Tree were lavish and crowded; Max Beerbohm's sly parody of Stephen Phillips has the stage-direction "Enter Guelphs and Ghibellines fighting". Hardy's work, however impossible to stage, had the advantage of being able to impress by sheer size. This accounts for the favourable reception of the completed work, after the first doubts and carpings at Part I were overcome by the even more broadly conceived Parts II and III. By taking all Europe for a setting, he forced admiration at the hugeness of his canvas alone. This accounts for the unreserved praise of such essential Edwardians as Arthur Quiller-Couch, who called *The Dynasts* "the grandest poetic structure planned and raised in England in our time", and the signed tribute of younger writers in 1921 "for all that you have written . . . but most of all, perhaps for *The Dynasts*". The Great War seemed to set a seal on his epic; it even made feasible Granville-Barker's stage abridgement in 1914.

Hardy achieved this sense of space and size, and of relevance to great issues, by employing, as is well known, an Overworld, Here the Spirits, who themselves are automata in the mind of the sleeping "It" or Immanent Will, discuss the affairs of men, who are themselves, without knowing, mere puppets in the universal view of the Spirits. These Spirits, whether of Irony or Pity, Rumour and many others, fulfil what Hardy had found awkward in his later novels, the function of a commentator on events. The Spirit of the Years, for example, in a well-known passage, can speak of

> A local cult called Christianity . . .
> Beyond whose span, uninfluenced, unconcerned,
> The systems of the sun go sweeping on . . .

This is Hardy speaking through a convenient spirit, or rather paraphrasing, for his own purpose, a passage from Mrs. Humphrey Ward's novel, *Robert Elsmere*, to which he has given his own satiric and agnostic twist.[24] These Spirits, helpless as they are to affect the Will's unknowing predestined paths, in which they resemble Hardy's just-published poem, *The Subalterns*, have themselves some minor and impish free-will. They sometimes come to earth in plausible disguise, and try their effect on mankind. They whisper doubts to Napoleon, false information to English politicians. The Spirit of Rumour even has, in Part I, a long discussion about Austerlitz and Trafalgar with a Parisian street-walker, who decides not to sleep with such a "creepy man". This kind of impersonative intervention is the reminder of Hardy's original plan to write "an Iliad"; for in the *Iliad*—and, indeed, though less often, in the *Odyssey*—gods and goddesses appear in the guise of known heroes and warriors, and even take part in the fighting for their own favoured champions.

The epic scope, then, is on the scale of Homer's two great examples, and of other epics, down to Camoens's *Lusiads*, where Vasco de Gama's voyage to India is aided or hindered by favouring or unfavourable deities. *The Dynasts* does, in fact, resemble *The Lusiads*, in that it tells a more or less accurate historical story, but incorporates divine machinery. Though critics admired this sheer size and scope, the philosophy implied received a cautious reception at first, while later academic critics have generally concentrated on the philosophic ideas, to the virtual exclusion of other elements in the work. An impressive roll-call of philosophers, English, French, and German, has been assembled as influences on Hardy's final philosophic pattern. Writing to a critic who in 1911 treated the work as an illustration of the philosophy of Schopenhauer, Hardy claimed, "My pages show harmony of view with Darwin, Huxley, Spencer, Comte, Hume, Mill, and others, all of whom I used to read more than Schopenhauer." Yet this disclaimer is similar to his statement, over the later novels, that he had read very little Zola, and in both the motive is the same. He did not wish to acknowledge an easy tag-label, under which lazy critics or reviewers could summarize or dismiss his original work. Yet the list, to which he could well have added Fourier, illustrations of whose philosophy he copied into his earliest notebooks, does far from justice to the breadth of his philosophic reading, and its effect on *The Dynasts*. There is, it has been shown, a great deal of Schopenhauer, whom he read and noted industriously in the late 1880s and 1890s, and still more of Von Hartmann, in particular, and of Haeckel, though the latter's philosophy has been seen not so much as an influence but as a reinforcement of what were already Hardy's own views.[25] Hardy's preoccupation in *The Dynasts* with the idea of an immanent unconscious Will was, however, highly eclectic; he may have taken much from both his early reading of English deterministic philosophers and his later reading of the Germans. Yet the result is his own, and is repeated in miniature throughout the poems of this period, such as *The Subalterns*, first printed in November 1901, where, as we have seen, Climate, Sickness, and Death, personified as forces which have a considerable effect on mankind's doings, are made to say that they themselves are helpless servants of a huge Unconsciousness, a thought which gives the poet an ironic comfort.

> We smiled upon each other then,
> And life to me had less
> Of that fell look it wore ere when
> They owned their passiveness.

The advantages of this Overworld or universal viewpoint are best seen in Hardy's numerous and lengthy "stage"-directions or "dumb-shows". Here is the real heart of the epic, and it often appears in phrases far more poetic than the poetry, far more dramatic than the drama. Without spoken words, and by sheer descriptive power, these parts of *The Dynasts* conjure up an unforgettable scene or plant an undying impression. They are often like a stage design painted on a gigantic, world-wide canvas. On the eve of Waterloo, for instance,

From all parts of Europe long and sinister black files are crawling

hitherward in serpentine lines, like slowworms through grass. They
are the advancing armies of the allies.

Grotesque and haunting incidents enhance the action. When the Madrid
mob sacks the rooms of the Minister, Godoy,

> In the rout a musical box is swept off a table, and starts playing a
> serenade as it falls to the floor . . . The mob desists dubiously and goes
> out; the musical box upon the floor plays on, the taper burns to its
> socket, and the room becomes wrapt in the shades of night.

Macabre touches of realism, such as this, also pinpoint the burning
of Moscow.

> The blaze gains the Kremlin, and licks its walls, but does not kindle
> it. Explosions and hissings are constantly audible, amid which can be
> fancied cries and yells of people caught in the combustion. Large
> pieces of canvas aflare sail away on the gale like balloons. Cocks crow,
> thinking it sunrise, ere they are burnt to death.

It is an Overworld view of Europe which opens and closes the whole
spectacle. From the Fore Scene at the beginning of Part I, we see

> The nether sky opens, and Europe is disclosed as a prone and emaciated
> figure, the Alps shaping like a backbone, and the branching mountain-
> chains like ribs, the peninsular plateau of Spain forming a head. Broad
> and lengthy lowlands stretch from the north of France across Russia
> like a grey-green garment hemmed by the Ural mountains and the
> glistening Arctic Ocean.
>     The point of view then sinks downward through space, and draws
> near to the surface of the perturbed countries, where the peoples, dis-
> tressed by events which they did not cause, are seen writhing, crawling,
> heaving, and vibrating in their various cities and nationalities.

After Napoleon's final defeat, we return to where we started:

> Europe has now sunk netherward to its far-off position as in the Fore
> Scene, and it is beheld again as a prone and emaciated figure of which
> the Alps form the vertebrae, and the branching mountain-chains the
> ribs, the Spanish Peninsula shaping the head of the écorché. The low-
> lands look like a grey-green garment half-thrown off, and the sea
> around like a disturbed bed on which the figure lies.

Such images, poetic, natural, yet deeply disturbing, do not have any
counterpart in our literature, except perhaps for Shelley's *Prometheus
Unbound* and a minor work of little value, Robert Buchanan's *The Drama
of Kings*, both of which may have influenced Hardy to some slight
degree. They seem occasionally echoed in Wilfred Owen's First World
War poems, such as *The Show*, though Owen read little Hardy except
*Under the Greenwood Tree*, and dismissed Hardy's poetry, in the arrogant
and arbitrary way he treated most contemporary verse ("who on earth

are . . . de la Mare etc?''), with the words "Quite potatoey".[26] If he had only known it, his own poignant vision of war had been anticipated a decade earlier by the older poet. In our time, World War Two audiences appreciated the B.B.C.'s radio version of *The Dynasts*, which largely relied on these prose directions by Hardy, arranged as narration.

In the five years of vast concentration, from summer 1902 to summer 1907, it is a wonder that Hardy had time for any personal life. Indeed, he does not seem to have had much. At any rate, his diaries were largely empty of incident, though the outward mechanics of his life, bicycle rides and the yearly London trips for "the season" still went on. Mostly he seems to have been occupied with the effort to keep at bay the spectre that he might die before *The Dynasts* could be completed, as if he saw himself like one of his own soldiers leaving the ballroom at Brussels for the battlefields of Waterloo to the summons of the drums, and in the spectral conduct of "That figure—of a pale drum-major kind" pirouetting before each one, the figure of Death itself. He confessed as much, more than once, to his closest friend, Gosse. Those who observed him noticed not only the extreme marks of apparent ill-health, which we have seen, but the impression of almost total exhaustion which he conveyed. Jacques-Emile Blanche, who painted Hardy's portrait in 1906, wrote not only of Hardy's deathly appearance but of his evident distress of body in the exceptionally hot summer; his straw hat "trickled with sweat; he looked so frail, so pale", that Blanche got his family to revive the poet, in the studio, with fresh iced lemon drinks. Blanche, however, also noted the activity of Hardy's mind, and his concentration, not understood by Blanche at the time, on the theme whose third part he was just beginning, Part II of *The Dynasts* having just been published.

> Without my realising it, his questions on the survival of the Napoleonic legend in France related to some work he was pursuing, which was no less than his tragic poem, *The Dynasts*. This frail old man was brooding over a work which would come to light in a renewed and creative youth . . .

Blanche, incidentally, noticed, with more sympathy than many later observers,[27] the pathetic attempts of Emma Hardy to renew her youth, though

> . . . little remained of that full high-coloured vigorous bloom, described by those who saw her when she was still young . . . Yet although shrunken and shrivelled by age, she posed as a beauty, keeping the fixed smile of bygone days, as if trapped for ever in a photograph.

Though Blanche did not know it, Emma too had had her premonitions of death during these years. In that very summer, only a few weeks earlier, while at Max Gate, she had a sudden fainting fit, and it is

probable that she was already suffering acute pain, at times, from the
impacted gall-stones, which were the primary cause of her death. She
also had her moments of mental anguish from the continued dominance of Agnes Grove over her husband, also noticed by Blanche
whose portrait of Hardy had to be submitted to Lady Grove as well as
to his wife.[28] It was apparently to assert her own right of judgement
that Emma exclaimed to Blanche the often-quoted remark, "Don't
make him look miserable!" The further remark, frequently though
wrongly attributed to her, "a real gentleman never does", is in fact a
garbled version[29] of Blanche's own personal sly and Gallic comment
"ce qui eût été si peu d'un gentleman", which expresses the French-
man's whimsical shrug at fashionable English manners. Emma's own
comment was certainly reasonable; Hardy in the portrait, still more in
Blanche's revealing preliminary sketch, looks not so much miserable as
utterly crushed. It is possible, even with his loyalty to her, that he now
found the attentions of Agnes Grove somewhat overpowering. Her
Stanley dominance was beginning to be too much even for her own
long-suffering husband Sir Walter Grove. Her comment[30] on the
expressions of would-be genteel people—"They will always commence,
when they ought to begin"—is itself almost a criticism of Hardy's own
style. Blanche's description includes an impression of Agnes ruling and
directing the guests at the Hardys' own tea-party in their furnished
London lodgings in the flat rented to them by Lady Thompson at Hyde
Park Gardens, while Emma sat fuming among the literary company, to
which she felt she had more right than Agnes. Nor can it have helped
that Hardy was still overseeing Agnes Grove's journalistic and other
literary work, to the covert amusement of editors. Emma, with no
assistance from her husband, had to be content with the columns of the
*Dorset County Chronicle* for her innocuous verses.

Husband and wife indeed seem to have kept up a modicum of unity,
partly owing to Emma's principle, enunciated in her letter to Mrs.
Kenneth Grahame, of "Keeping separate a good deal". In November
1903, Emma took a month's holiday in Calais with her niece Lilian
Gifford, leaving Hardy at Max Gate to cope with the cats, Markie,
Snowdove, Pixie, and Comfy.[31] Hardy, in his turn, was very frequently
at the British Museum, doing the immense historical research for *The
Dynasts*; he went on his own in 1905 to receive an honorary doctorate
from the University of Aberdeen, the first of the academic honours
which so much delighted him. Yet he cannot have been happy that the
previous New Year's Eve had found him "quite alone on a bridge".[32]

For both Emma and Hardy, these years brought intimations of
mortality. For them, 1904 was a year of deaths. The first was the death
of Hardy's old friend, mentor, and best, creative editor, Leslie Stephen.
Hardy had not seen much of him recently, but in the days when *Far*

*From the Madding Crowd* and *The Hand of Ethelberta* were appearing in Stephen's *Cornhill*, they had been very close in personal and intellectual sympathy. Stephen had always seemed to Hardy like one of his own doomed heroes. "I have always felt that a tragic atmosphere encircled L.S.'s history— & was suggested in some indescribable way by his presence."[33] To him, the great mountaineer as well as editor, Hardy had written his poem about the Schreckhorn, "gaunt and difficult, like himself". He included the poem in his considerable contribution, about half a chapter, to F. W. Maitland's *Life and Letters of Leslie Stephen*, which came out in 1906. Stephen died in the last week of February 1904. In the next few weeks, Hardy lost another close friend, of forty-seven years' standing. This was a surviving brother of Hardy's deepest friend, Horace Moule. Henry Moule had himself become an intimate friend; in the previous summer he had occupied Max Gate while the Hardys were in London. Hardy wrote an affectionate little memoir of him,[34] also printed in 1906.

Hardy's major loss in this year came early in April. For some years his mother at the Bockhampton cottage had been gently failing, though keeping almost to the last a bright-eyed independence, typical of her early days. In May 1901, when a literary and journalist club called the Whitefriars had visited Hardy at Max Gate, Jemima Hardy had found that the ladies and gentlemen, with their fine London clothes, were to pass in open carriages along the Puddletown–Dorchester road, only a quarter of a mile from her cottage. She got Hardy's sisters, Mary and Kate, to put her wheel-chair by the roadside, from which she waved her handkerchief at the well-dressed concourse. Now, on 1 April 1904, aged ninety, she failed for the first time to recognize her famous son. Two days later she died. His usual reticence concealed under formal tributes what she, the real guiding star of his early life, had meant to him. Only one cry of anguish, in a letter to near relatives, gives a hint.[35]

His more direct and formal expression of grief, in a poem probably written at her death-bed, ends with a philosophy that echoes much of the message of *The Dynasts*.

> And yet we feel that something savours well;
> We note a numb relief withheld before;
> Our well-beloved is prisoner in the cell
>     Of Time no more.
>
> We see by littles now the deft achievement
> Whereby she has escaped the Wrongers all,
> In view of which our momentary bereavement
>     Outshapes but small.

"The Wrongers" are not so much, perhaps, those of the Overworld of spirits, as the physical pains and disabilities Jemima had suffered in recent years, deafness and the rheumatism which confined her to a wheel-chair. Remembering how, in 1890, at the age of seventy-seven, his mother had walked in slippery winter weather from Bockhampton to Max Gate, and made nothing of it, Hardy felt a sad relief at her final escape. It meant, too, a rearrangement in family affairs that brought him even more back into contact with his boyhood home at the cottage. So that Mary ("Polly") Antell, Jemima's niece, should not be alone there, Mary and Kate let furnished the house Hardy had bought them in Wollaston Road, Dorchester, and moved back to the homestead. With Kate's bustling good humour, still more his beloved Mary's quiet, unobtrusive cheerfulness, the fireside, though bereaved, took on the character of their childhood, especially when brother Henry, the builder, called in with his bluff and hearty presence. Hardy gained in family feeling, much though he lost by his mother's mourned-for death.

Emma too had her griefs and deaths in this year. In October, her brother Walter, whose two elder children she had virtually adopted, died in London. Next month he was followed by her eldest brother Richard, who died in the Warneford Asylum. The supercilious Willy Gifford had died two years before. Emma was the surviving sibling. Though she had seen little enough of her brothers, she felt a sense of isolation. There was a new and slightly ominous symptom of this. The Gifford family had been brought up by their mother and grandmother in a narrow religious fundamentalism. The insane Richard, for some years before he rivalled Hardy in his own Waterloo epic, had spent his time in hospital writing and rewriting a great religious epic in verse, which he sometimes read to other patients in the recreation room.[36] Soon after his death, Emma's own occasional verses show a change. From inept but perfectly coherent poems about garden flowers, trees, and landscapes, she turned to a new strain of somewhat brooding religiosity and dark apocalyptic vision. One such poem, *Ten Moons*, was published in 1907 in the *Dorset County Chronicle*.

> In misery swirled
>   Is this one-moon whirled,
> But there's no sorrow or darkness there
>   In that mighty Planet where
> There is no night.
>   Ten moons ever revolving
> All matter its long years resolving
>   To sweetness and light.

This new note, in her otherwise not unusual Protestant theme, sounded increasingly in following years, and was observed by her husband. Not that this yet affected Emma's outward social life or withdrew her from topical affairs. She still took part in the London season, kept up her animal-loving societies and subscriptions, in spite of the death of her friend Pretor in 1907. One topic where she and Hardy agreed was women's suffrage, which he had favoured "for a long time"; and on 6 February of that year, she had shown her interest by marching with other "advanced" women in a suffrage procession from Hyde Park to the Strand, known as "The Mud March" because of the heavy rain.[37] On her home ground at Max Gate she continued her regular garden-parties, and on 1 September 1905 had organized a tea-party on the lawn for no less than 200 members of the Institute of Journalists.[38]

Hardy too had a perennial method for resisting the encroachment of physical weakness, old age, and death. He was, exactly like his hero in *The Well-Beloved*, on perpetual look-out for beauty, particularly the young beauty of women of about twenty-five, successors to his earliest loves, to actresses such as Mary Scott-Siddons and Helen Mathews, and to his more recent and more aristocratic loves, Rosamund Tomson, the Honorable Mrs. Florence Henniker, and Lady Grove.

In his late fifties, he had mapped the emotional course of the rest of his life in the poem with which he appropriately concluded his collection, *Wessex Poems*.

> I look into my glass,
> And view my wasting skin,
> And say, 'Would God it came to pass
> My heart had shrunk as thin!'
>
> For then, I, undistrest
> By hearts grown cold to me,
> Could lonely wait my endless rest
> With equanimity.
>
> But Time, to make me grieve,
> Part steals, lets part abide;
> And shakes this fragile frame at eve
> With throbbings of noontide.

Such "throbbings" occurred, as we know, at fairly frequent intervals. Summer 1907, with *The Dynasts* finished in draft, and Hardy revising Part III at the British Museum, saw the most important, though not the final, manifestation. He met a young woman of twenty-eight, Florence Emily Dugdale. She was always said to have been a "young friend" of Florence Henniker, and introduced by the latter to Hardy in 1904; yet Florence's own letters give the lie to this legend. They prove she did not know Mrs. Henniker till 1910, nor did Mrs. Henniker ask if she could call her "Florence" until 1914.[39] The myth may have arisen because Mrs. Henniker had as a friend the aristocratic Sir William Dugdale of Merevale Hall, Warwickshire,[40] descendant and namesake of the famous seventeenth-century Garter King-of-Arms. Florence Emily Dugdale, however, had far different attractions for

Hardy. She was brown-haired, slim, intelligent, of Dorset origin; above all she shared almost exactly his own social background and working-class family history. At last, at sixty-seven, he had found a natural companion and mate.

# 10

# Florence and the Dugdales

FLORENCE EMILY DUGDALE was the grand-daughter of a Dorset blacksmith, William Dugdale.[1] Her grandmother, Emily Hibbs, was the daughter of a labourer and carter at Langton Matravers, Dorset.[2] Seeking anxiously some more distinguished ancestry for the young woman who became his second wife, Hardy annexed as her great-grandfather another William Dugdale, whose memorial he copied (inexactly) from Hutchins's *History of Dorset*, and who was Mayor of Wareham in 1838 and 1844. Unluckily Florence's real great-grandfather was Elias Dugdale, a carpenter, undistinguished in the borough annals, though both were probably descended from Daniel Dugdale, who had been a Wareham alderman in 1728.

Florence's father, Edward Dugdale, one of four brothers, was born in the crowded working-class back-streets of St. Paul's parish, Portsea, Hampshire. There seems to have been considerable sea traffic between Wareham and the greater port of Portsmouth; the parish showed a little colony of Dorset families at the time of Edward's birth.[3] Portsmouth provided Edward Dugdale with vivid and unusual childhood experiences. He saw the shipping come and go in the busy port, became a fine swimmer, and is known to have saved people from drowning on three occasions before he left the town in his late teens. He entered St. John's College, Battersea, in 1871, and qualified as a certificated elementary teacher. In 1873, he settled in the north London suburb of Enfield, and at once became head of the "National" or church school, St. Andrew's, a post he was to hold for the rest of his working life.[4]

On her mother's side, Florence was of an Enfield family settled in Brighton. Her mother, Emma Taylor, who married Edward Dugdale there on 1 August 1876, was the daughter of a butcher, James Tuckney Taylor.[5] The business of pork butcher was carried on by at least three generations of Taylors in Brighton. The women of the family let respectable furnished apartments near the sea-front at 47 Marine Parade, the address from which Florence's mother was married. When Florence met Hardy, and for many years after, the furnished apartments were kept by her great-aunt, Ann Maria Taylor, and her aunt, Alicia Taylor. One of the men in the butchery business, Charles Taylor, also let apartments at another address.[6]

Florence was born on 12 January 1879, the second of Edward Dugdale's family of five daughters. Their father, according to a former pupil at the school,[7] was strict but just; he was a pillar of the local Conservative, Temperance, and Philanthropic Societies, a well-set-up man, who looked younger than his age.[8] By the 1900s, the Dugdales lived at 5 River Front, Enfield, having seen that town grow from "a green and pleasant little place", in Edward's words, to a suburban sprawl, whose considerable working-class population swelled the numbers of the school. The small hamlets, townships, and clusters of cottages round old Enfield were over-run and fused together by red brick, the market-town atmosphere almost lost in the industrial suburb surrounding the Royal Small Arms factory.

According to a former maid-of-all-work, the Dugdale family was an extremely happy and united one.[9] The mother had a weak heart, and the five girls were brought up to be self-reliant. Three, including Florence, became school-teachers, one a nurse, and the youngest trained at a domestic science college. All five went to the St. Andrew's, Enfield, elementary school for girls, where the education was free. For their secondary education, they all proceeded to the St. Andrew's Upper Grade School, where their father paid ninepence a week for them[10]—a history not unlike Hardy's experiences in Dorchester, first with free education, then at a school for which his father paid a small fee. Florence probably then had four years, from the age of fifteen, as a pupil-teacher, but she never went to college. She began work as an uncertificated teacher in her father's school at the age of exactly nineteen. She taught from January 1898 to April 1908, and did not take her certificate until September 1906, when she received special credit in English Literature, Composition, and the Principles of Education.[11]

Theirs was the standard minimal secondary education for the time, but the girls seem to have entered into it with responsibility and earnestness, fitting for a school-teacher father and a home where there can have been very little money to spare. All, including Florence, were expected to earn a living as soon as possible. There was not much question of choice. Though she taught notably well, Florence was not happy. The classes in the boys' school were between forty and fifty; eight teachers, most of them unqualified, coped with an average attendance of 350 boys.[12] The noise, the frequent need to shout, were exhausting. Moreover, Florence was what her father called "a Radical"; she hated the subservience expected from a church school-teacher. When the vicar called, she must not sit down; she must attend church services where the vicar's wife might object to her hat. Any complaint could not be communicated direct to the school managers; she had to wait for the visiting Inspector in order to state her case. Even after the Education Act of 1902, a teacher could still be dismissed by the managers "on grounds connected with the giving of religious instruction", without consent from the local authority. It is no wonder that she grew up acutely, often morbidly, conscious of social distinctions after a teaching experience that began in the last years of the reign of Queen Victoria.

This social background, handicapping and often frustrating, applied, of course, equally to her sisters; but in addition, Florence had a hard time physically. The school logbooks record her frequent absences through illness, feverish colds, chills, and influenza. These began to take a more serious form over the years. The reason for three months' leave of absence in April 1908, from which she never returned to teaching, is given as chronic pharyngitis.[13] Bad experience with adenoids and tonsils probably led to a lifelong horror of operations and to the depressions from which she suffered. A former pupil remembers her very quiet voice,[14] also probably due to these illnesses. In spite of the to-and-fro of a family of sisters, there is a solitary strain in Florence, which contrasts with the others, and one may guess it developed in lonely times of illness. She seems to have been not so much a Radical as a Romantic, slightly the odd one out, Her family affections, however, were extremely strong, and she kept in very close touch with all her sisters. Of these, the eldest, Ethel, married in the early 1900s, and the youngest, Margaret, during the First World War. The two unmarried sisters, Constance the teacher and Eva the nurse, were deeply loved. In spite of occasional tiffs between these two,[15] and Constance's later jealousies of her married sisters,[16] all were prompt and generous to help one another.

Florence was the only one of the sisters, however, to show an inclination towards self-expression, prompted by her somewhat lonely and introspective temperament. The secret path she chose was literature, though at first in the most humble way, which can be traced in the files of the local paper.[17] In 1901, at the age of twenty-two, she is recorded as giving a talk on "The Idylls of the King" to the Enfield Literary Union at the Bycullah Athenaeum. Later in life, when she persuaded London acquaintances to speak at an Enfield literary society, they left unflattering pictures of its provincial dreariness; but she obviously found inspiration, as many girls struggling with an unpromising and limited background have done. One can find this sympathetically treated in the great topical novel of such struggles in the 1900s, H. G. Wells's *Ann Veronica*, where Ann comes from just such a suburban setting as Florence. She spread her literary wings from this beginning in the only way open to her, the children's pages of the local paper. Her first initial-signed contribution, a little story called "A Summer Lane", appeared in its columns on 31 July 1903. Other contributions followed, and encouraged her to apply to publishers of children's books in the next few years, where, though her efforts were not very distinguished, she at last began to get a hearing.

Pathetic as some of these efforts were, Florence never lost this vision of herself as a creative writer. One of the happiest moments of her later life was when she heard of a boy still reading one of the small children's books she had written as a young woman, and felt her work was wanted. This enthusiasm brought some of the most rewarding experiences of her narrow and dull life. When she began this minor journalistic work, she found that the expenses of having her manuscripts professionally typed swallowed up her meagre earnings. Her belief in herself, however, impressed a well-to-do friend, and he generously gave her a typewriter.[18] She taught herself to type, for, as Hardy wrote in the summer of 1909, "she learns anything",[19] and it was with her own typescripts that she first contributed to the *Tales for the Children* series of readers, a set of little 100-odd-page books, in which she was responsible for No. 10, *Old Time Tales* in 1907, followed by No. 20, *Country Life*. In 1907, she also managed a book of about 150 pages, *Tim's Sister*, for the Christian Knowledge Society, evidently putting aside her radical rejection of organized religion for the sake of getting the small volume published. All through her later life, she spoke of her pleasure in writing, her ambition to write in other forms. Belief in her creative gift, however undistinguished her actual work, buoyed her up in times of sadness.

Such was the young woman whom Hardy met, somewhere and somehow in London in the summer of the year 1907, when he himself was completing what he had felt to be a race against death, and had emerged thinking that there was no more left in life for him. For Hardy, Florence Dugdale held every possible attraction. She was of his own social class, but like him had risen in the world through careful self-education. She was, as he had once been, an apprentice writer, contributing to the local press, and, very recently, composing elementary school books for Chambers and Collins, including some adaptation of stories as supplementary readers.[20] She was the exact physical type to which he always eagerly returned, a slight, willowy, intense brunette, the counterpart of the actresses, Mary Scott-Siddons and Helen Mathews, and of the poetess, Rosamund Tomson. To crown all, like Pierston's last love in *The Well-Beloved*, she was forty years younger than he. There were of course, other attractions, not solely physical. She was, as he had been in his youth, radical in her outlook, shocking her conservative father, who was born of cautious peasant stock. Here again, she brought youth back to Hardy. Perhaps her highest single attraction was that she had, as she confessed, absolutely no religious belief, doubted if there were a God, or, if there were, whether there could be a beneficent one.[21] This view, moreover, was not merely a gesture of youthful rebellion against orthodoxy. It was learnt from a genuinely tragic experience of life, as full of the malignancy of Providence as anything which had caused Hardy's own dark philosophy. Already her past had prepared her for their coming-together.

What did Florence feel about the very distinguished elderly literary gentleman, who wandered eagerly and wistfully eyeing girls in London, where he was at this time, he confessed, "distracted" on the tops of omnibuses "by young women in fluffy blouses"?[22] What did she think when he took her to Liverpool Street Station, kissed her at the barrier, and watched her own "spot of muslin fluff"[23] recede down the platform to catch the crowded Enfield train? If he was moved enough to describe this in a poem, *On the Departure Platform*, what were her own feelings? One fact in her history has never emerged before, and needs now to be considered. Hardy was not the first elderly and distinguished gentleman to play an intimate part in her life. Florence was already the friend of another married man, nearly thirty-five years older than herself, handsome, dark-haired, the possessor of unlimited charm and a knighthood, but also of a secret and central personal tragedy.

Sir William Thornley Stoker[24] was one of the five sons of Abraham Stoker, for fifty years Chief Secretary at Dublin Castle. He was a brilliant member of a highly versatile and distinguished family. One of his brothers, "Bram" Stoker, for many years Irving's manager and right-hand man at the Lyceum and elsewhere, was the author of *Dracula*. Thornley Stoker was a famous surgeon, and one of the leading lights in Dublin society. He was respected by colleagues, loved by medical students at the Richmond Hospital, Dublin, and venerated by the poor law patients for whom he did so much. A man of wide culture and a Governor of the Dublin National Gallery, he built up a fine private art collection in his beautiful residence, Ely House, Dublin. Childless, he was known for his generosity in the causes of young people; he established a school of Nursing in the Richmond Hospital, which was a model of its kind for the training of young nurses.[25] His tragedy—Florence's too—was that Ely House contained a mad wife, who occasionally had been known to escape her attendants.

Such was Florence Dugdale's "dear kind friend in Dublin", about whom she always wrote in terms of the deepest affection.[26] It was Sir Thornley who gave her the typewriter, an expensive present in those days, and continued to show her kindly favours. One does not know how they met, nor when she came to stay at Ely House. To her romantic mind, nourished on books, he may well have been Lancelot to her Elaine, in the idyll she considered the finest poem in the language. Hardy, too, fulfilled a bookish ideal. He inscribed gifts of books to her, in June 1907 his own *Wessex Poems*, in July a copy of *The Rubaiyat of Omar Khayyam*, which came to have a special meaning for them, though Emma had found the sentiments in that poem "pernicious".[27]

Above all, he made instant and strenuous efforts to forward her literary ambitions. The pains he had taken for Mrs. Henniker or for Agnes Grove were nothing to his new endeavours on Florence's behalf. Regardless or innocent of the chance that his letters might be compared or exchanged in the smoking-rooms of London literary clubs, Hardy wrote to nearly every editor or publisher with whom he had any previous connection. On 8 July he wrote a long personal letter to the head of his own publishers, Frederick Macmillan, setting out Florence Dugdale's previous history and her abilities.[28] She had teaching experience, and could do anything they might offer on their educational side, both editorial and contributory. Stretching the point that she had offered to help him check and revise the draft of *The Dynasts* Part III, he wrote that she had helped him with work at the British Museum. She could do shorthand and typing (not altogether skilfully, as later typescripts show) and could make herself useful in any way. Soliciting a personal interview for her, he added that she came from an old Dorset family, well known to himself. The remark, meant to convey a background of gentility or even of landed property, was a smokescreen, in which the blacksmith grandfather, the farm-labourers and carters of her Dorset forebears were conveniently obscured. Whether Florence herself consciously aided and abetted this and similar deceptions, or whether she genuinely had been brought up to know little of this side of her family, is uncertain. She knew she had a Dorset grandfather, but never mentioned his occupation; while, shortly after her marriage, she remarked, "There are Dugdales at Wareham, but, as far as I know, not the least relation to me."[29]

At all events, on the very next day, with well-judged alterations, Hardy wrote practically the same letter to Archibald Marshall, literary editor of the *Daily Mail*.[30] Marshall was a Cambridge graduate of some taste and ability, which included acting, playwriting, song-writing, and, ultimately, novel-writing. He maintained a high standard for the literary page of the *Mail*, where he had recently published Hardy's King's Hintock Park poem about the old woman sweeping up leaves. Attracted by the lyric, Marshall himself had composed a setting for it, and his daughter remembers singing it about the house as a small girl.[31] In May 1907 he had asked Hardy for another contribution. Hardy, away from his papers in Max Gate, and embroiled in revising Part III of *The Dynasts* in London, had asked for time. Now he himself wrote to Marshall, still with no contribution, but using the bait of a future poem to ask an immediate favour. This was, of course, on behalf of Miss Florence Dugdale. Would Marshall consider her work for his columns, or, indeed, use his influence for her in any other suitable department of the *Mail*? Her qualities were listed in the same way as in the previous day's Macmillan letter, with the emphasis on literature rather than on education, the shorthand and typing being added, apparently as an afterthought, in a postscript. Marshall seems to have seen her, and impressed her as "quite a well-bred sort of man",[32] but there is no evidence he found her employment.

There were probably other letters to other editors and publishers in August. In September, Hardy wrote to the editor of the *Cornhill*, Reginald Smith, with whose family and publications he was closely connected. This time it was a most glowing recommendation and eulogy of a short story signed "F. E. Dugdale". Smith was quick and worldly-wise in his response.[33] Yes, he would publish the story, though he wished he might print with it Hardy's letter of praise; that, surely, would attract the interest of readers. Could he know more about Miss Dugdale—he supposed he was right in believing "F. E. Dugdale" to be a lady? He also added a sly postscript to congratulate Hardy on the way he was helping the work of Agnes Grove, whose book, *The Social Fetich*, published this year, was dedicated to him. The insinuation behind Smith's last remark was clear. Agnes Grove's work showed internal evidence of Hardy's hand in its forms of expression and creative editing. Surely, Smith implied, he could detect Hardy's style in parts of Miss Dugdale's story too.

The story, which Smith eventually printed in the *Cornhill* of June 1908, was indeed a remarkable production, not the least for its title, *The Apotheosis of the Minx*, which so confused a later editor of a checklist of Hardy's correspondence[34] in the Dorset County Museum that he catalogued it as "The Apotheosis of the Min*d*". The basic construction and philosophy of the story is typical of Hardy himself. Robert Engle, an innocent, idealistic young schoolmaster, a devotee of Shelley, falls in love with a tawdry, common girl he meets at his landlady's. They arrange a date, and go for a walk together in the country, so reminiscent of Jude and Arabella that this incident, the best in the story, might have come straight out of the earlier pages of *Jude the Obscure*. He is shy; she is disgusted at his lack of "go". Besides, she has her eye on a flashy young grocer. She rounds on Robert for his lack of sexual enterprise; yet, unlike Arabella, she does not tempt him out of it, but chooses to marry the grocer. Robert is stunned and dismisses her as unworthy of his own Shelleyan ideals. Later, he hears she has died in childbed, and meets her widower, who tells him, too late, that the girl had really loved the schoolmaster. The latter begins to idealize her once more, though he cannot rid himself of a repugnance because she had belonged to another. Later still, he meets the grocer again. He is about to be married for a second time. The schoolmaster feels this has released him to idealize the first wife fully. In his memory, he deifies her ideal attributes, associating her with his love of Keats and Shelley. The commonplace, unworthy girl has become a perpetual object of worship for the remainder of the schoolmaster's life. In irony, parodox, mistiming of circumstances, places, and persons, in its Shelleyan idealism, and the author's implied cynical conclusion, the pattern of the story is everywhere typical of Hardy.

How much can one trace Hardy's hand, which Reginald Smith of the *Cornhill* evidently thought he could detect, in the actual writing? The opening paragraphs are obviously taken by Florence from life and from her father's and her own experience, a restless, bored classroom of inattentive boys, to whom the magic incantation of Shelley's *Skylark* means nothing. Robert Engle and his dreary North London school, from which he and the girl go on the traditional country walk of Green Lanes, seems an accurate and individual enough description of Florence's father and his suburban setting, described by a writer,[35] who visited the Dugdales about this time, as depressing and uninspiring. Florence herself hated the North London suburbs, and had some gift for catching an atmosphere. It is rather in small phrases and expressions, which seem to be additional afterthoughts, that one hears an echo of Hardy in his mode of slightly pedantic clumsiness, on which all critics of his prose had commented. A good guide to this type of emendation by Hardy exists in his alterations, some years later, to a manuscript by his first wife. Emma, at her death in 1912, left a charming, spontaneous account of her youthful days up to her marriage, entitled "Some Recollections". Hardy quoted and edited this, not always for the best, in his own autobiography. Emma's vivid description of Hardy's round-about journey to Cornwall, "a sort of cross jump-journey, like a chess-Knight's move", was brought flatly to earth by Hardy's additional explanatory words, pencilled in his hand, "by the route necessitated". Similarly, one suspects, such phrases in Florence's story as "the grocer's assistant aforesaid" must be Hardy's; for the disconcertingly lawyer-like "aforesaid" in this is found everywhere in Hardy's prose, even in his later and more skilled work. On a less prosaic note, Florence's "heavenly singer" in the story is not unreminiscent of Hardy's own descriptions of Shelley—"high singer" and "matchless singer"— though all are equally clichés.[36]

Florence regarded herself as a serious writer, though her small children's books for Chambers and Collins were more or less hackwork, miserably paid. On the basis of *The Apotheosis of the Minx*, though, there is little evidence of much talent, and it seems unlikely that without Hardy's eulogistic covering letter it would have been printed in a leading magazine, which, at this precise time, was publishing the early work of Virginia Stephen (Virginia Woolf). There is no evidence that Florence had any other story accepted, except for one printed early in 1911, under the most curious circumstances.[37] This one successful excursion into serious literature was launched on Hardy's recommendation.

Some small volumes of what are really fictionalized nature studies for children, and some natural history "descriptions", with embarrassing little verses for children, comprised much of her future output. She learnt, however, to write a good, lively, and expressive letter, not without a certain sardonic humour. Her style is strongly in contrast with that of Emma's ungrammatical, illogical, and sometimes ill-spelled screeds, with their occasional touches of maverick imaginative quality. Many perhaps, though, will agree with Beatrix Potter (Mrs. Healis), who preferred Emma's artless style to Florence's "more 'show-off' epistles".[38] Certainly, Emma's printed articles, such as "In Praise of Calais" and "The Egyptian Pet", show more talent than Florence's.

The problem of this new awakening relationship for Hardy was, of course, how to introduce it acceptably into his life with Emma. For the time being, he simply did not dare to try the hazardous experiment. In spite of her alarming forewarning the previous summer of increasing pain and exhaustion from gall-stones, allied with feelings of depression, and distinct weakness of eyesight, Emma was in this year of 1907 at the top of her form as the scourge of husbands. June 1907, two or three weeks before Hardy had written his July letters of appeal on Florence's behalf, brought an incident concerning Emma which has often been retold, though not always with complete accuracy. This was the occasion of Edward VII's garden-party on the 22nd of the month at Windsor Castle. When the trains from Paddington arrived at Windsor station, a number of royal landaus were waiting to pick up the guests for the castle. The carriages proved to be too few for the visitors from the train in which the Hardys had travelled down with Blanche, the painter. Mrs. Hardy was wearing a long green floating "Victorian" veil, a reminder that, as Blanche noticed, she habitually dressed, in her late sixties, in girlish fashions of a bygone age. She and some other ladies settled themselves in the landau, but a lady from Blanche's household at first refused the one spare seat next to Emma, suggesting that the elderly and frail-looking Hardy should sit next to his wife. It is not certain, from Blanche's eye-witness account, that Emma actually made her opprobrious and often-quoted retort to this suggestion—"the walk will do him good"—but the upshot, at all events, was that the poet and the painter followed on foot, while Emma's green veil floated from the royal carriage ahead like a banner: and, as Blanche slyly commented, "such must have been the usual form, the customary rhythm of home life in this illustrious household".[39]

As it happens, there is another eye-witness account of the Hardy's home life, in the following summer of 1908, a little more sympathetic to Emma, and perhaps a little nearer the impression made by Hardy at this time on an observant stranger. In June 1908, Hardy sat again for his portrait, this time to Sir Hubert von Herkomer, who had illustrated some of the serial of *Tess*. Herkomer, was elderly, academic, ponderous, pedestrian, Germanic (he was born in Bavaria), a typical Victorian "subject" painter, well known for his "The Last Muster". This painting, showing a group of Army veterans in Chelsea Hospital, naturally recommended him to Hardy's taste. The portrait was duly despatched to Max Gate, and became the show-piece of Emma's at-homes and garden-parties later that summer. Winifred Fortescue, an intelligent young débutante, described one of these occasions. "Bitterly disappointed", as most people were, by the mean architecture and prosaic setting of Max Gate, the first thing she noticed was a tragi-comic reminder of Emma's attempts to create the setting of a great writer. The hall-porch held a small plaster reproduction of the Capitoline Venus, probably a relic of their visit to Rome twenty years before. From the little wooden bracket on which it stood was suspended a placard addressed in Emma's hand to the housemaid; in rickety capitals it warned, "When dusting, please *blow* but do not touch." Once inside, every guest had to be led by Emma to see what she described with "panting pride" as "the Herkomer of Mr. Hardy". Winifred Fortescue found her pathetic but likeable; she did not form such a favourable view of "her formidable husband".

> To me he made the rather sinister impression of an ancient moulting eagle, with his piercing, restless dark eyes and lean naked neck rising in folds above a low collar, and his bald peering head moving ceaselessly from side to side . . .

She echoes the unfavourable physical shock most admirers had experienced for the last twenty or thirty years on first meeting Hardy. She adds one extra point, perhaps significant at this time: his evident and suspiciously restless sense of unease.[40] The new attachment, outside his marriage, was one more reason for embarrassment in the presence of his wife, quite apart from those she was all too capable of creating on her own account.

Once again, however, it is rather Hardy's biographers than anything really observed about the marriage that has created the legend of an open, public warfare between Emma and Thomas. Among many examples, the biographers have invented an entirely fictitious scene, in which Dame Rebecca West—no less—was present, and heard Emma say to Hardy, "Thomas Hardy, try to remember you married a lady." Since, as Dame Rebecca has pointed out,[41] she herself never at any time met Emma, this story, elaborated to the legend that Emma "often reminded Hardy that he had 'married a lady' ",[42] is not only apocryphal but impossible. It has its origin in something that happened in the 1920s, about ten years after Emma died. An elderly member of a Dorset family, who had known Emma and Thomas, said, in Dame Rebecca's hearing, that the remark was made very naturally

. . . in a matrimonial flurry . . . Hardy and his wife had been going to some local function and he had appeared before her dressed inappropriately at the hour when they should have been leaving the house.

One can even conjecture what this "inappropriate" dress, which caused such an understandable reaction, may have been. In 1900, Hardy bought a pair of trousers, which became "his study trousers", and to which he was inordinately attached. Twenty years later, he was found mending them with string and a packing needle,[43] though even the servants at Max Gate commented unfavourably on them, and defying his second wife to burn them. These trousers are the likely cause of this particular legend of public discord between Hardy and Emma, and the incident a commonplace in most married lives.

Whatever his personal manœuvres, Hardy the writer was fully at work. The main matter on hand was an edition of William Barnes, about which he had been approached by the Clarendon Press early in 1907. His response[44] was enthusiastic and prompt to accept. Of Barnes, he wrote:

Hitherto he has been badly handled by most of those who have given specimens of his work—from the point of view of the few of us still left who know the dialect as Barnes knew it, which the rising generation of rustics do not, on account of the schools whose tendency is to kill it off rapidly.

In spite of his prejudice against popular education, the self-taught Hardy himself got down to work in a way that proved him a better and more practical scholar than the distinguished men who hired him for the task, including Sir Walter Raleigh; they, indeed, made elementary errors of taste and judgement, and the monumental blunder, unforgivable in an academic publishing firm, of not finding out which works of Barnes were still in copyright. Hardy wrote nearly two dozen letters to the Press in 1907 and 1908 after he had finally laid aside *The Dynasts*.[45] He comes very well out of the correspondence, hard-working, meticulous as an editor, patient about copyright difficulties, but above all intensely loyal to Barnes's poetry and the selection itself.

He offered to make the selection, edit the texts, and provide a necessary glossary, either free of charge, or for a nominal fee at the publisher's discretion. He worked, on this agreement, for a year, before the Clarendon Press discovered that Kegan Paul's copyright on Barnes's later improved editions had still two years to run. Rather than reprint earlier, inferior drafts and printings, Hardy offered all his own textual work free of charge to Kegan Paul in return for the copyright, though the offer seems to have been rejected. Hardy was therefore forced to compromise, using out-of-copyright versions and poems.

It is striking that in all the long, tedious negotiations Hardy does not complain of the quite unnecessary trouble, to which he himself has been put, but only of the injustice to Barnes as a poet, and consequent loss to the book itself. He was even generous about the money involved, and courteous under provocation and incompetence by the high-handed Press. He valued this work more than most, and he inscribed an advance copy to Florence Dugdale with evident affection for both the book and for her.

Hardy's literary career was therefore as full as his emotional life, and the two were intertwined. He was collecting a fresh book of verse, now that Barnes and the monumental *Dynasts* were both safely off his hands, and his new love-attachment made him exhume love-poems to other women, even those of his remotest past, under the comprehensive sub-title of "More Love Lyrics". Among these special two-dozen poems, were many youthful love-lyrics from the 1860s. These included two sonnets to his early theatre infatuation, the dark, slender actress, Mrs. Mary Scott-Siddons. Others can be associated with Weymouth and the brunette Tryphena Sparks. Discreetly sandwiched between them, undated, was *On the Departure Platform*, describing an encounter with his new dark-haired, deep-eyed young lady, Florence Dugdale. In deference to Emma, the whole volume was preceded by what was now his stock disclaimer. He wrote,

> the sense of disconnection, particularly in respect of those lyrics penned in the first person, will be immaterial when it is borne in mind that they are to be regarded, in the main, as dramatic monologues by different characters.

One wonders if he really supposed this would placate Emma. The "different characters" are so patently Hardy himself; the love section ends deliberately with his very personal 1883 lyric *He Abjures Love*. From the manuscript, it appears he had several last-minute thoughts about where to insert the poem silently reserved for Miss Dugdale, *On the Departure Platform*. Far from abjuring love, Hardy was now, in his late sixties, as firmly as ever in love's toils. Florence Dugdale and her distinctive feature, her "large, luminous eyes",[46] begin to dominate his life and work. On her part, she promoted the book by lecturing on him to her local literary society, comparing his lyrics to those of Heine.

The general tone of *Time's Laughingstocks*, published on 3 December 1909, contrasts with his previous collection, *Poems of the Past and of the Present*, almost exactly eight years earlier. That had, on the whole, been weighted heavily on the side of philosophic, sceptical, and quasi-religious poems. The poems in *Time's Laughingstocks*, with the exception of one short sequence, a rural *Set of Country Songs*, are connected with people close to Hardy and the intimate relationships of his life. There are poems concerned with both his grandmothers, Betsy Hand and

Mary Head, the latter immortalized in the superb evocation of her home in the Bockhampton cottage, laconically entitled *One We Knew* (*M.H 1772–1857*) and ending, with beautiful reminiscence,

> With cap-framed face and long gaze into the embers—
> We seated around her knees—
> She would dwell on such dead themes, not as one who remembers,
> But rather as one who sees.

> She seemed one left behind of a band gone distant
> So far that no tongue could hail:
> Past things retold were to her as things existent,
> Things present but as a tale.

Several poems seem to have more than a shadowy connection with his other grandmother. She is the old woman "Raking up leaves" in the verses *Autumn in King's Hinton Park* at Melbury Osmond, where she made the improvident marriage which earned her an old age of penury. She is the widow of *Bereft* and *She Hears the Storm*. Hardy's own mother and father are idealized in *A Church Romance*. Its line about their meeting, "Thus their hearts' bond began, in due time signed", begs the questionable fact that their bond of marriage was certainly not signed until it was considerably overdue, when the baby Hardy was already four months on the way. Interspersed with poems to his galaxy of brunette beauties, Hardy included two poems about his previous Florence of the 1890s, Florence Henniker, one, *The Division*, dated 1893, and the other, a little less surely about her, called *The End of the Episode*. All in all, this volume is far more concerned with touchingly portrayed human relationships than his last, though the gritting grimace at the sour taste of life can be felt in 1909 as it had been in 1901.

This is not to neglect one or two charming comic Dorset dialect verse-sketches, like *The Curate's Kindness* and *Rose-Ann*, little masterpieces of sly rural humour, probably derived from his recent editing of William Barnes. The more ambitious narratives, however, are of unrelieved and tragic irony. They include two ballad-form tales in verse, to both of which Hardy applied the term "tragedy": *A Trampwoman's Tragedy* and *A Sunday Morning Tragedy*. The long rolling ballad-like lines of *The Rash Bride* and the more conventional short ballad-stanzas, *The Vampirine Fair*, fall into the same group. Finally, and in a late position, designed to attract attention, Hardy tried an exercise in narrative blank verse, *Panthera*, using a legend designed— successfully—to shock the orthodox Christian reader, based on the second-century story that Christ himself was the illegitimate son of a Roman soldier.

*A Trampwoman's Tragedy* was, Hardy thought, his most successful poem: to the end, he had a prejudice in favour of the ballad-form, with refrain and repetition. The refrain of another, shorter poem, *Bereft*, has a distinct folk-song echo.

> Leave the door unbarred,
> The clock unwound.
> Make my lone bed hard—
> Would 't were underground!

This is the accent, form, and rhythm of the ballad *Lord Randal*. In *A Sunday Morning Tragedy*, written in January 1904, Hardy reprinted a ballad-form poem, which marked the extreme of his attempts, in prose and poetry, to write "adult" literature. It was a poem about unsuccessful, rural abortion. Hardy had even planned to make a short play of it, called *Birthwort*, since it hinged on a herbal abortifacient, provided by "a subtle man". The poem had first been printed in the *English Review* of December 1907, its first number. The story that the *Review* was actually founded in order to publish this poem of Hardy's, which several other magazines had refused, seems to be one more of the exuberant fancies of its editor, the notorious Ford Madox Ford. Ford, also the inventor of the story about Emma, Richard Garnett, and her attempted suppression of *Jude the Obscure*, persuaded the future that he had made this dramatic literary gesture on behalf of Hardy's controversial poem. In fact, as his own biographer hints,[47] he had already solicited Hardy and several leading writers for contributions to give his new magazine a rousing send-off. Hardy submitted the poem himself, and Ford was glad to accept it, only later casting himself in the flamboyant role of Hardy's broadminded benefactor. The poem, Wordsworthian and direct, had no need of help; it is a picture of real rural life such as, Hardy had earlier told William Rothenstein, the public "would not stand". To that extent, the magazine provided a forum, and Hardy was to use its pages again for verses of an explicit sexual character.

The reviews of this volume, and of the fully-completed *Dynasts*, were more than respectful. Hardy was now acclaimed as a poet as he had been a novelist, his stature assured as the senior figure in contemporary English literature. He began to be sought for, and to make, oracular judgements, some of which sound dubious to modern ears. He was consistently modest about his own work, and when Gosse in March 1908 voted the whole *Dynasts* "one of the most original and beautiful productions of the modern age",[48] Hardy expressed regret that he had not improved it far more by rewriting. On other writers, though, however eminent, he could be obstinately pontifical. On Shakespeare, he wrote to a correspondent,[49] "I do not think that Shakespeare appertains particularly to the theatrical world nowadays, if ever he did . . . I would hazard the guess that he will someday cease altogether to be acted." On a lighter and more domestic note, when asked by the Dorset regiment for a marching tune, he sent them an old one of his grandfather's, called "The Dorchester Hornpipe", which he himself had fiddled at dances as a boy.[50] Official occasions, to which he was deferentially invited, included the John Milton tercentenary celebrations at Cambridge, which he attended in July 1908. Approaching his seventieth year, he was bidding fair to steer a latter-day settled course as a Grand Old Man of English Letters, beginning to relish his stature, and to dismiss as "cheeky" an invitation to the Whitefriars journalistic club,[51] whose members he had entertained at Max Gate a few years earlier. Only his jealously secretive emotional life indicated another side of him, those "throbbings of noon-tide" which were shaking him still, and were to shake him yet further, into the most startling old age of any English poet.

# 11

# Florence and Emma and Thomas

WHAT Florence now drew from Hardy was a tenderness he did not always display to people. Tenderness of the quality he had shown towards his fictional women—Tess, Fanny Robin, Marty South—now appeared rarely in his life. In poetry, it belonged not to human beings, but the small wild creatures—worm, lark, mole, rabbit—in the wonderful Waterloo chorus of Part III of *The Dynasts*. Towards his fellow-men, as we have seen, he was now frequently curt and arbitrary. In letters to his wife, such as those written to her late in autumn 1908, he wrote of being concerned about her welfare, but with no very apparent conviction or feeling. With Florence it was different. Her youth, her difficulties, her ill-health specially, touched springs of sympathy, anxiety, understanding. Real thought for her health seems even to have cured his crushing hypochondria about his own at least for a time. In 1909, he made Edward Clodd his first close acquaintance to know of Florence's existence, and actually to meet her. The free-thinking advanced Clodd perhaps seemed most naturally suitable; Hardy did not reveal Florence's existence to the more conventional Gosse for another five years. He wrote to Clodd about "my young friend" or "my young friend and assistant", in a vein of entire tenderness. She was so delicate, so susceptible to illness; she must be made to wrap up well against the damp night air. "Please make her wrap up", he wrote to Clodd, "as she is so very delicate." Sea air was good for her; she must have holidays at the seaside, and Hardy would take her on them. So it was that they went together to Aldeburgh in August 1909, and again probably later that year, Ventnor in March 1910, Aldeburgh again in October 1911 and in May 1912.[1]

When Hardy wrote his autobiography, a few years later, he either did not mention these visits, or, more often, when he did, invariably concealed the fact that Florence had been with him. Sometimes the concealment took a highly devious form. On this first visit to Aldeburgh, in summer 1909, he wrote in his autobiography that he had had to put off his trip to Clodd owing to an attack of influenza, but recovered sufficiently later in the summer to go. His letters to Edward Clodd at Aldeburgh, however, reveal that this was far from the case. Hardy did not have influenza at all. It was Florence who had recurring trouble with her throat, which the visit was intended to cure—"it will be an excellent restorative", Hardy wrote about her to Clodd. The stay with Clodd was postponed twice because of her renewed illness, and only took place in August, when she was well again.[2] Hardy, not mentioning her name at all, has accounted for the postponed visit by pretending that he, not she, was too ill to travel to Suffolk,[3] and, of course, equally, pretending that he went alone to Clodd.

Hardy was caught in a web of concealment in more ways than one. One of its more complicated enmeshings, in this same summer of 1909, surrounded the performance at Covent Garden, on 14 July, of the opera of *Tess of the d'Urbervilles* by Baron D'Erlanger. Hardy wanted to take Florence to the first night; but the question was whether Emma would want to come up for it from Dorchester, where she was spending a semi-invalid existence for the second summer in succession. On 9 July, Hardy wrote to Emma, stressing the fatigues and difficulties of London, and mentioning that she could come to a later performance. Emma, decided, however, to come to this one. At short notice, Clodd enrolled himself as the understanding friend. He would be Florence's partner to Covent Garden, having first—something Hardy himself had forgotten —taken her out for a light dinner—"this bright idea of yours she highly appreciates",[4] Hardy wrote. Hardy would visit them, if he could, in the intervals, and at curtain-fall Clodd would put her into a cab for her London aunt's, while Hardy took Emma back to the hotel. So it was that both Florence and Emma heard "a Dorset dairymaid singing her woes in choice Italian", as Hardy described to Gosse the performance of Destinn.[5]

All this sounds like the exercise in real life of a novelist's craft, yet it is too much to accuse Hardy of completely deliberate plotting. Half the time, he may scarcely have known what he was doing, or what its remoter consequences might be. Many of his statements, even to the trusted Clodd, have an ambiguity which could either be studied, or the result of sheer bewilderment. Writing from Max Gate on 1 May, he spoke to Clodd of "my domestic circumstances which, between ourselves, make it embarrassing for me to return hospitalities received".[6] This may hint at some domestic human tangle, or it may simply recall the lambasting that Clodd had received from Emma a dozen years before over his open irreligion;[7] for, in fact, many other people continued to be invited to Max Gate about this time. The general impression is that Hardy, during these years, was like his own Napoleon in *The Dynasts*, swept along helpless by forces beyond control, however much he might appear to be master in outward life.

Yet some step must be taken to avoid the to-and-fro, the manœuvres, the reliance on the secrecy and goodwill of friends, which had taken place in summer 1909 over the opera seats. Somehow Emma and Florence must get to know each other; ideally, Florence should be introduced so that she could come and go freely at Max Gate. This was the problem Hardy now set himself to achieve. It cannot have been easy; but, according to a passage in Hardy's autobiography, by at least summer 1910, Florence had become an accepted visitor at Max Gate, and a partner in its strange atmosphere.[8]

The Max Gate household in 1909 consisted of Emma, Thomas, a visiting gardener called Trevis,[9] and three living-in maids, Jane, Daisy, and Florence Griffin.[10] The last-named was slightly better-educated than the others, and was entrusted with small tasks, such as paying the gardener, forwarding letters, and looking after the cats when the Hardys were in London.[11] On these occasions, she was sometimes aided by Henry Hardy, who came over from Bockhampton, and who, as a builder, did any house repairs for the Hardys. He was, in fact, now beginning to build his own house, Talbothays, on the land at West Stafford he had inherited from his father.

In what manner and when was Florence introduced into what she called "The Max Gate ménage"? Hardy said she had met Emma at a club in London, a minor resort for artistic ladies, very often of little achievement, but with ambitions to write and to meet writers. This was the Lyceum Club at 128 Piccadilly, fairly near Emma's more fashionable club, the Alexandra, and very close indeed to Hardy's club, the Savile. One does not quite know if Hardy himself engineered this meeting, but the probability is that he did. It is definitely confirmed by Florence's literary executor and trustee, Irene Cooper Willis, who wrote that Florence said she was "1st at Max Gate taken there by Emma who had picked her up at the Lyceum Club and taken a fancy to her".[12] Thus was successfully launched the fiction, sedulously maintained in later years, that Florence was really *Emma's* friend. It was true only in so far as Emma was the means of bringing Florence into the Hardys' home. It ignores the fact that Hardy had met Florence, and had been seeing her in London and elsewhere, ever since summer 1907, apparently without Emma's knowledge, a space of between two or three years in all. Her first visit to Max Gate seems to have been in 1909 or 1910; for writing soon after her death, W. R. Rutland, who had spoken with both Florence and Irene Cooper Willis, stated, "Mrs. Hardy had brought to Max Gate a young woman ... Florence Emily Dugdale, one of five sisters, [who] was then about thirty."[13] This places her advent roughly in 1909–10.

The situation was complex for Florence. Emma Hardy too, of course, provided personal complexities in abundance. One false impression, however, needs to be corrected. This is that, in what were to prove the last few years of her life, Emma withdrew to an attic in eccentric reclusion. This picture of a Miss Havisham-like existence arises from a misunderstanding of something probably said by Florence to Irene

Cooper Willis. The truth is far different. As long ago as the year 1898, Emma had determined to rival the aristocratic "women in London" of whom she was so jealously contemptuous, by having a set of boudoir apartments of her own, copying the fashion of these emancipated ladies who had often entertained her husband *tête à tête* in such intimate surroundings. Early in 1899, she wrote of "my little apartment where not a sound—even the dinner bell—scarcely reaches me". Two months later, she described this arrangement in ecstatic terms. "I sleep in an *Attic*—or two! My boudoir is my sweet refuge and solace—not a sound scarcely penetrates hither. I see the sun and stars and moon rise and the birds come to my bird-table." She wrote with evident enjoyment, though poor spelling, of her "eerie",[14] where she could have her private possessions and her small library, since, she complained, her husband never now allowed her to come into his, or to borrow his books. In 1908, she improved the set of apartments by having a dormer window put in, to widen her view of the beauties of the world from this vantage. The picture handed down of a half-mad creature huddled in a dusty attic could not be farther from the truth, though there was certainly pathos in Emma's bid for an independent life, when resentful disillusion with her distinguished husband set in during the 1890s.

At the same time, from her fainting fit in the summer of 1906, Emma's physical rather than her mental health began to fail. Jacques-Emile Blanche noticed, later that summer, that she seemed bewildered and out-of-place in London society, and allowed, though resentfully, the drawing-room tea-party of her London apartments to be dominated by Lady Grove. From 1900, she had suffered from nervousness in London, and what she called "shyness"; she found it difficult to cross roads in the heavy traffic, and domestic arrangements were too much for her now. In December of this year, 1906, after influenza, she wrote of the difficulties of old age and illness, and her lack of resilience in "getting over the after-weakness".[15] By November 1907[16] her eyes were troubling her—"my ill-disposed eyesight"—and on 20 May 1908 she admitted "strength and sight are fast failing". Sadly, she felt she had "no really *sweet* attentive relatives" to rely upon; "a useful companion", tried in spring 1908, did not satisfy her.[17] Yet her long, well-expressed letter to the *Nation* on the subject of women's suffrage shows she was still enterprising, and though she felt she could not that summer manage the usual seasonal stay in London, she was sufficiently well and capable to go, by herself, that autumn to "France, the country I love most after our own"; she spent several weeks alone in Calais.[18] It was quite a feat for a poor-sighted, shy, elderly English lady of close on sixty-eight, and also quite a shrewd move, since by doing it she left Hardy to deal with the discomforts of builders in the house for the new dormer window. Moreover, she managed on her return to write an article on Calais, which was printed in the *Dorset County Chronicle*; it, too, is a really well-written piece of vivid, descriptive prose.[19]

Yet there were some disquieting developments, not altogether physical. Emma's habitual rampant Protestantism—Hardy had to forward Protestant papers to her in France—was taking an odd turn towards apocalyptic mysticism, such as her 1907 poem *Ten Moons*, which has been quoted.[20] Her horror of Roman Catholics became acute, and she castigated them roundly. She took to distributing "beautiful little booklets . . . of pure Protestantism"; at her bank in Dorchester, the Devon and Cornwall, she pressed these upon an embarrassed junior bank-clerk, who happened to be a Catholic.[21] Then, too, her language about her husband began to show lack of control. Ten years before, for instance, her long letter to Mrs. Kenneth Grahame about the trials and woes of married life, though forceful, was rationally expressed and in many ways true. Now, in 1908, such statements became extreme and idiosyncratic. "My eminent partner", she wrote, "will have a softening of the brain if he goes on as he does and the rest of the world does."[22]

What in fact was happening to Hardy, under these strange and novel circumstances, was a kind of rejuvenation. It was not merely the old story of an elderly man meeting a young woman. For six years, during the writing of *The Dynasts*, he had been "a dead man walking". He had literally expected to die. He had looked, as everyone remarked, like death. George Meredith, whom he visited in 1905, had been depressed by Hardy's "twilight view of life"—just as, to be fair, Hardy had been depressed by Meredith's perennial cheerfulness. Now life had shown a glimmer, and he gratefully responded. When she first met him, Florence said, "his mind was luminous". Some of its new light was certainly borrowed from her, from the sun of her young and devoted admiration.

Hardy, for his part, rewarded Florence with poems to her, which, though few, were of an intensity he had not shown for years. One of these commemorated her advent at Max Gate, and, incidentally, helps to date her arrival there. It was not included in the *Time's Laughing-stocks* collection of 1909, but was first printed in the *Spectator* of 13 August 1910, when it appears to be a freshly-written piece. On that occasion, it did not, of course, have the inscription "To F.E.D.", for it speaks openly of Hardy's overwhelming emotion on seeing her move about the house which had otherwise become such a prison for himself and Emma, like a spirit of new freedom and renewed hope from his ingrown despair.

> Come again to the place
> Where your presence was as a leaf that skims
> Down a drouthy way whose ascent bedims
> The bloom on the farer's face.

> Come again, with the feet
> That were light on the green as a thistledown ball,
> And those mute ministrations to one and to all
> Beyond a man's saying sweet.

Florence's "large luminous living eyes" seemed to him to weigh

> Scarce consciously,
> The eternal question of what Life was,
> And why we were there, and by whose strange laws
> That which mattered most could not be.

Indeed, this year, 1910, during which both Emma and Hardy were seventy, was a crucial time at Max Gate. For one thing, Florence was now there very frequently; by the later months of the year she wrote, "I go there now so often", the implication again being that this was a recent development. On the other hand, Emma, increasingly ill, and in severe pain, was attempting to stage a comeback into society. In mid-April she went up with her husband to London, to try and arrange a flat for "the season". Illness drove her back to Dorchester.

Fortunately for the convenience of meeting Hardy, while he was thus alone in London, Florence this spring secured a small, central flat of her own, in a block near Baker Street. The owner, a friend of hers, had gone abroad and lent her the flat, where she and Hardy were able to see each other without attracting undue public attention. Privately, she was now able to begin introducing him for the first time to her own family. Her elder sister Ethel, who had trained as a teacher at St. Katherine's, Tottenham, from 1897 to 1899, was now married, with a little boy of six. Florence invited her and this nephew to meet the distinguished author at the Baker Street flat. Hardy was relaxed and cheerful, in contrast with his demeanour at Max Gate. Indeed, Florence's sister, Mrs. Richardson, always found him friendly and affectionate. On this occasion, he took her small boy on his knee, and asked him, kindly if conventionally, what he wanted to be when he grew up. The boy, who had just been to Kew watching the gardeners among the bulbs, startled his mother and amused Hardy by answering, "A gardener". So began a situation in which the Dugdale family, one by one, became aware of Hardy's interest in Florence. They accepted in general the idea that she was his "secretary", and even that she was engaged in "research" for him in London, though by this date, his work, which consisted entirely of correcting proofs and writing poems, did not need anything that could be called research.[23]

Meanwhile, at Max Gate without him, Emma poured out her woes in a letter to a new animal-loving friend, Alda, Lady Hoare, of Stourhead in Wiltshire, an advocate of slaughter-house reform. She took the opportunity to ensconce herself in Hardy's study, from which she was now normally banished—"not as formerly"—and to complain of the difficulties of being an author's wife.[24] However, she joined him next month in London, at the flat at 4 Blomfield Court, Maida Vale. The day after she moved in with some of the Max Gate servants, the death of Edward VII placarded the streets.[25] Hardy found fresh encouragement that a new young actress, Lillah McCarthy, wanted to revive the idea of his *Tess* play; but a greater excitement was at hand. On 2 July, Asquith wrote privately to say that the new King wanted to confer on Hardy the Order of Merit.[26]

Two years before, Asquith had offered a knighthood, which Hardy refused. Dorchester gossip, when this leaked out, reckoned this refusal a shame for "dear old Mrs. Hardy", who would have surely loved to be Lady Hardy. Even now, she could not share this triumph. The presentation was fixed for 19 July: but Emma, who had already found the Season too much for her, felt so ill that she went home a week before. With "Miss Dugdale", as he wrote to Emma, to type his acknowledgements of congratulations, Hardy was left alone to receive the honour, and in his own opinion, "failed in the customary formalities".[27] He shared these with another reserved and irritable genius, Sir Edward Elgar. In their complex natures and distrust of the world, the two men were alike, from very much the same cause. Elgar never forgot he had been known locally as the errand boy from his father's Worcester shop; Hardy never forgot his cottage home and charity-child mother. The two struck up an acquaintanceship, which led to desultory correspondence about a possible collaboration; but nothing came of the chance contact of two prickly natures. This was unfortunate since, on the more attractive, creative side, Elgar's music had so much in common with Hardy's poetry—sadness, nostalgia, and deep emotion. What inadequacy Hardy felt at Marlborough House was more than compensated later in the year when Dorchester conferred its freedom on him, and he delivered what was, for him, a remarkably long speech of thanks, in the presence of the borough notables, Emma, Florence, and the poet Henry Newbolt.

His position was now so assured, after the public recognition of the O.M., that he was inundated with literary suggestions and requests. He became, among other things, a mark for forceful approach. Sydney Cockerell, the tireless and shameless director of the Fitzwilliam Museum, Cambridge, wrote outrageously to say that though he had not read any of Hardy's work, he would like some of his MSS for the Museum. Such was Cockerell's powerful and insinuating personality that he not only obtained the manuscripts of *Jude the Obscure* and *Time's Laughingstocks*, but extracted from Hardy permission to distribute his other MSS to various museums, and ultimately got himself the post of Hardy's literary executor, with the right to destroy or preserve as he pleased. Hardy, often curiously innocent, seemed glad to trust a decisive person, who would take the mountainous load of past paper off his hands; and for the rest of his life Cockerell, it was observed, "reckoned himself, Hardy's 'manager' as it were".[28]

"The 'Max Gate ménage'", wrote Florence late in 1910,[29] "always does wear the aspect of comedy to me. Mrs Hardy is good to me . . . I am *intensely* sorry for her, sorry indeed for both." Sometimes the comedy could only be described as black. The summer and autumn of 1910 had seen the arrest, trial, and execution of Dr. Crippen, who murdered his bullying wife, and went off with his secretary, Miss Le Neve. One morning in November, when newspapers were full of photographs of the little murderer with the drooping moustaches, Emma approached Florence "in deadly seriousness" with an idea. Had not Florence noticed how extremely like Crippen Hardy was in personal appearance? It was by no means an unfair observation; but when Emma continued to speculate whether her own body would not be found buried in the Max Gate cellar, Florence left hastily "or she would be asking if I didn't think I resembled Miss Le Neve".[30]

Florence retailed this, and other stories of Emma's eccentricity, to Edward Clodd, who had become yet another of her elderly admirers— he was exactly the same age as Hardy. She phrased her comments in an amused and half-sympathetic way, and in fact, in later conversations with Irene Cooper Willis, she said her early impressions were that Hardy was somewhat unfair to his wife. There was not at this time any of the darker suggestions she came to make continually that Emma was "mad".[31] Nor did she, at this time, ever suggest that Emma came, as Florence put it, "from tainted stock".[32] These seem to have grown through the years, for two reasons. One was to protect Hardy from thinking that Emma had any justification for jealousy against him, by suggesting that these suspicions by Emma were "delusions". The second was her natural reaction to meeting, yet again, by what seemed a gratuitous irony, a situation in which the man she loved had a wife he could not display in public. With Sir Thornley Stoker, the wife was sufficiently *non compos* to be hidden away in the confines of Ely House in Dublin. Just when Florence was laughing at Emma's Crippen fancies, Lady Stoker died; but, worn by the stress of his many years of attempting to conceal her, Stoker himself was beginning to succumb to a fatal disease. Florence might well feel her path was haunted by madwomen, though she had been fond of Lady Stoker, and still liked Emma. In point of fact, Emma would not need to be at all eccentric to make inferences about Hardy's "secretary". In the study at Max Gate, from which Emma was totally excluded, "my secretary", as Hardy called Florence, described how she herself "ramped around", and flippantly criticized phrases in Hardy's poem about "the study cat", Kitsy, which he had just buried.[33] Yet Emma "instead of cooling towards me . . . grows more and more affectionate".

Florence had happy experiences with Mary, Kate, and Henry Hardy, to whom she was introduced this autumn at the Bockhampton cottage, which enchanted her. Returning home for a few days she sent them all postcards of Enfield, apologizing for its dreariness compared with their beautiful surroundings.[34] Hardy now took the step, in December 1910, of introducing her to Florence Henniker as a secretary-help.

The two women, from such different backgrounds, struck up an instant friendship, and Florence was at Mrs. Henniker's house for weeks on end. Mrs. Henniker almost at once wrote a short story about "a modern, emancipated young woman of cities"—Florence—who was, in Hardy's words now, "by far the most interesting type of femininity the world provides for men's eyes".[35]

The "most interesting type of femininity" did not appear at Max Gate so frequently in 1911. Instead, Hardy was more often found with her in London, in spite of his fear of the climate. He came up in midwinter, and the end of January 1911, and, as Florence wrote, halfsatirically, he "has a sore throat because I make him talk in the London streets and then the germs attack him".[36] Most of 1911 was for the Max Gate trio predominantly a year of literary productions, often of a curious and roundabout kind. Hardy's own primary task was a straightforward one. Macmillan & Co., had become his publishers in 1902, on the expiry of his agreements with Osgood, McIlvain & Co., and Harper & Brothers, reprinting from the former's plates. Now Frederick Macmillan wished to produce, the following year, in 1912, a new and definitive edition of verse and novels, the Wessex Edition. Hardy's first task was to write a "General Preface to the Novels and Poems", which he completed in October 1911 and which he worked over heavily in the revise proof.[37] It contains his most positive claim to the kinship of his novels to Greek tragedy, even comparing "Wessex" in actual physical size with Attica. As for poetry—"the more individual part of my literary fruitage"—he claimed it was less "circumscribed" than his prose. As if to emphasize this claim, in April 1911 he had printed in the *Fortnightly Review* twelve of the fifteen mordant little short stories in verse he had written the previous year, *Satires of Circumstance*. These were founded on notes made twenty years before, "and then found were more fit for verse than prose".[38]

Other literary doings were less straightforward. In October 1911, Hodder and Stoughton published a book of animal pictures in colour by the young artist E. J. Detmold, intended for children and called *The Book of Baby Beasts*. The pictures had "Descriptions by Florence E. Dugdale", in verse and prose. One poem, *The Calf*, though unsigned, was entirely by Hardy,[39] and is characteristic of him. Another, much neater and more rhythmic than Florence's inept verses, is *The Kitten*. He did more, however, this year than write verses for his "young friend". His January visit to London had been to see the editor of the *Cornhill*; for in the February number there appeared a 3000-word factual story, *Blue Jimmy: The Horse Stealer*, signed F. E. Dugdale. There is no doubt that every word of this story is Hardy's. In style, it is unlike her previous *Cornhill* story, *The Apotheosis of the Minx*, though that itself had shown Hardy's hand in plot and minor detail. It is still more unlike a short article for the *Evening Standard* Florence had recently written on Hardy's seventieth birthday.[40] It is in every way like Hardy in style, and the proof copy is corrected and expanded entirely in Hardy's own hand.[41]

It was Hardy's fate always to be involved with literary ladies; but he had never before passed off his own original work publicly as theirs. One must wonder what Florence felt about such manœuvres. Was her literary ambition greater than her literary pride? Had they made some compact that he would now do everything to launch her? Long after, she wrote in a diary[42] that she remembered Christmas Day 1910 most especially; it may have marked some new stage in their relationship. Certainly the efforts he made for Florence in 1911 were more than he ever made for his wife. Emma had to strike out unaided on her own account. In the previous year, she had disinterred her early story, *The Maid on the Shore*, and asked Florence to type it. Faced with the necessity of saying something about it, Florence did her best[43]—"I do quite *honestly* admire the story. There is a certain charm . . ." Perhaps encouraged, Emma in the quiet isolation of her attic boudoir filled the pages of an exercise book with what she called "Some Recollections". This was an account of her childhood, youth, and family life before her marriage to Hardy, and by the time she had finished, on 4 January 1911, it ran to 15,000 words. It has, without any doubt at all, "a certain charm"; moreover, there is no doubt it is all her own work. Even with the breathless punctuation, spelling, and grammar, it has distinct flashes of real poetic observation and expression; though it had to wait exactly fifty years for publication, it can be read with delight, perhaps most of all for its evocations of the wild North Cornish coast where she had first met Hardy. Nor was this Emma's only bid for literary fame. In December 1911, she persuaded the local publisher-printer, Longman's of Dorchester, to produce her collection of the poems which she had written since 1900. The tiny pamphlet of fifteen poems, enigmatically entitled *Alleys*, concluded with her latest, a rousing antiphon shared by India and Great Britain, *God Save Our Emperor King*.[44] At the same time, she could write a cheerful letter to a relative, making light of the encroachments of age on her and Thomas—"We have both got old, but feel young still."[45]

Yet in spite of such defiant gestures, all was far from well with Emma. Late in 1911, she engaged a fourteen-year-old school-leaver from Piddlehinton to be her personal help.[46] This girl, Dolly Gale, was to carry breakfast and lunch up to Emma's boudoir on the third floor, brush her hair, and be available for help, day or night. She soon found that Emma was in almost constant pain; one of Dolly Gale's chief duties was to massage Emma's back. Gall-stones, or hepatic colic, is characterized by sudden, acute spasms of pain, which radiate over the abdomen and into the back. These may persist for days on end, and a contemporary textbook description of the pain is "agonizing", so extreme that morphia or chloroform were often prescribed.[47] Successful surgery was technically just possible by 1912, but Emma (and Hardy) had a horror of "the Knife". It may seem incredible that Hardy never now, nor at any time, admitted that his wife was in such agony, in the same house. It is true, they only met at dinner, and then did not speak; but now, every Sunday, Trevis the gardener had to push her to St. George's church, Fordington, in a newly-bought bath-chair, which was parked during the service in the Vicarage garden.[48] This was her regular "journey of one day a week" mentioned by Hardy in a later poem. Hardy was, of course, often away from home; on more than one occasion, to "run down" to Aldeburgh "with my young friend", whom he now called "Dear F.D."[49] When at home, he was immured in the study with the immense "drudgery of 20 vols. of proofs" for the Wessex Edition.

The "comedy" Florence had observed at Max Gate was becoming grim tragedy. There were breaks in the darkness. On 24 April, Hardy wrote one of the finest poems he ever composed for a public occasion, his lines on the *Titanic* disaster, *The Convergence of the Twain*, included in a programme of performances for the Disaster Fund in May. On his birthday, 2 June, Newbolt and W. B. Yeats came to Max Gate to present Hardy with the Gold Medal of the Royal Society of Literature; on a sunny day in mid-July, Emma managed to give a garden-party, and nine days later, she took the girls of the parish sewing-guild on an outing to Osmington Mills beach, planning the expedition with entire competence in making all the arrangements for the children. They even took Lilian Gifford, who was with them on a short stay, to a performance at Weymouth of the new comedy, *Bunty Pulls the Strings*. Winter began to close in like a doom upon the household. On a dark day in November, both Hardy and his wife wrote a poem. Hers was pathetic and brief.

> Oh! would I were a dancing child,
> Oh! would I were again
> Dancing in the grass of Spring
> Dancing in the rain

> Leaping with the birds on wing
> Singing with the birds that sing.[50]

Did this now non-speaking couple somehow communicate? For Hardy's poem, far longer and ultimately one of his finest, is permeated with bird-imagery too. *The Bird-Catcher's Boy*, written now, was heavily revised by Hardy a dozen years later for his collection, *Human Shows, Far Phantasies*. These revisions were purely technical and poetic. The poem was originally written in alternate rhyming and non-rhyming lines: Hardy's skilful feat was to make all the lines rhyme, and this revision greatly improved the poem. Yet its story was identical in both versions. The boy, son of a dealer in caged wild birds, protests at his father's inhuman trade. The father orders him roughly to bed. As he climbs the stairs, he runs his fingers along the wires of the bird-cages. That night, he runs away. His father and mother, heart-broken and remorseful, leave the door always unlocked. One night, they again hear his fingers on the cage-wires. They rush to his room. It is still empty. The same night, the body of a ship's boy is washed ashore on the Dorset coast.

Does this haunting poem symbolize Emma's nightly footfall to her attic boudoir after her silent dinners with Hardy? Did he, the husband, unconsciously project his indifference to her feelings, and anticipate his remorse, in the father's roughness? Everybody noticed Emma's almost magical powers with the birds she observed so tenderly from her attic windows. When she called, every kind of bird came fluttering to her, flocking about her, as if she could speak their language, companioning her in their own.[51] This strange, tragic poem is perhaps an allegory of Emma's life and death. It certainly mirrors what Hardy may have felt as he heard her dragging, pain-ridden climb up the stairs each night at Max Gate, when he describes the boy in the poem: how

> . . . without a word
> Bedwise he fares;
> Groping his way is heard
> Seek the dark stairs
>
> Through the long passage, where
> Hang the caged choirs:
> Harp-like his fingers there
> Sweep on the wires . . . .
>
> Hopping there long anon
> Still the birds hung
> Like those in Babylon
> Captive they sung.

9 Hardy and Edward Clodd on the beach at Aldeburgh, circa 1909

10  Hardy and Florence Dugdale on the beach at Aldeburgh, circa 1909

11    Emma on the beach at Worthing with Florence standing behind, circa 1911

12   Florence Dugdale sketched at Max Gate by William Strang, 26 September 1910

13   Gertrude Bugler as Eustacia Vye in *The Return of the Native*, 1920

14   Hardy, Florence, and "Wessex" in Dorchester, 29 October 1924, three weeks after Florence's return from her operation

15  Cast of the Hardy Players in *Tess of the D'Urbervilles* at Weymouth, 11 December 1924 (*seated left to right*) Gertrude Bugler, Hardy, the Mayor of Weymouth, Florence, the Mayoress of Weymouth

*Note. Biographical details imagined from details in the novels, & gathered from newspapers, are mostly wrong.*

# CHAPITRE I

# BIOGRAPHIE

Le nom de Thomas Hardy s'est irrévocablement attaché à une seule contrée de l'Angleterre, à cette partie du sud-ouest qui s'étend de la Tamise jusqu'à la mer, du Devonshire à l'ouest jusqu'au Hampshire à l'est, et qui composait jadis le royaume saxon du Wessex. S'imaginer, cependant, avec certains critiques, que son œuvre est seulement le roman de son pays, ce serait par trop la restreindre ; son œuvre, comme celle de tout romancier digne du nom, est une représentation artistique de la vie en général. Le génie de M. Hardy le pousse même vers les plus grands thèmes dramatiques. Émule moderne des tragiques grecs et des dramaturges anglais de l'époque élisabethenne, il cherche à présenter les vieux problèmes "enrichis de vérités nouvelles." [1] Mais les types qui doivent vivre ces problèmes, comme la scène où ils doivent jouer leur rôle, il les trouve dans la région qu'il connaît le mieux ; là, il est chez lui, il sait interpréter le visage de la nature et l'âme des hommes ; là, il juge sans erreur et, avec les matériaux qu'il recueille, sait nous construire tout un monde en raccourci.

Aussi, pour celui qui a lu les romans de M. Hardy, penser à lui, c'est penser d'abord au Dorsetshire, aux arides étendues de bruyère, aux petites vallées où broutent des troupeaux de vaches, et aux riches vergers où les pommiers laissent

---

[1] Voir *New Review*, Avril 1890 : "*Candour in English Fiction.*"

# 12

# A Satire of Circumstance

EVENTS now moved with horrible swiftness. On 23 November, Emma felt seriously unwell. On the next day, her birthday, she was deeply depressed. On 25 November, there came an event as macabre as any of Hardy's own short stories, or indeed any one of the *Satires of Circumstance* poems he had recently printed. Unannounced, Rebekah Owen, Hardy's egregious elderly American admirer, arrived with her sister from the Lake District. Since they had come from so far, Emma dragged herself downstairs to give the ladies tea. She was obviously very ill, weeping, and in great pain, fearing an operation, and speaking of her dread of "the Knife". Anyone with less of a rhinoceros hide than Miss Owen would have gone away. She refused to budge, intent on seeing her idol, Hardy, ensconced all this time in his study with the Wessex Edition. She seemed to regard Emma's acute physical distress as evidence of mental disturbance, and demanded to see Hardy. When Emma demurred, Miss Owen herself told the maid, Florence Griffin, to go and fetch Hardy. He came, was charming to his flatterers, apparently oblivious to his wife's sufferings, which she cannot possibly have concealed. When the Americans at last left, she went to bed where she stayed all the following day. In the evening of 26 November Hardy went to a dress rehearsal of a stage version of *The Trumpet-Major*. which the Hardy Players were about to present in Dorchester.

The morning after, Emma's little personal maid, Dolly Gale, went to her mistress's boudoir at 8 o'clock. She found her moaning, in great pain, terribly ill and drawn, asking to see Hardy. Dolly Gale rushed to his study with the news. Whether from shock, or from habitual indifference. Hardy stared coldly at the girl, and remarking, "Your collar is crooked", paused to straighten his papers, before going. When he saw how ill Emma was, he was at last shaken. "Em, Em, don't you know me!" he cried. She was too far gone to answer him; her heart, overstrained by months of pain, was failing, and in five minutes she was dead. The little maid stood at the end of the bed, and saw Emma die with Thomas bending over her. It was the first time she had seen death.

This could not be said of Hardy; and the question remains how he could possibly have ignored Emma's sufferings over so long a period. To everyone, he pretended that her death was sudden and unexpected. He softened every aspect of it in the autobiography he wrote a few years

149

later, and excused himself. Even at the time he wrote to Mrs. Henniker, "Emma's death was absolutely unexpected by me, the doctor, and everybody . . . I have reproached myself for not having guessed there might be some internal mischief at work." Yet Dr. Gowring, who had just succeeded Dr. Fisher, signed the death-certificate, without a post-mortem or any apparent hesitation, giving the primary cause of death as impacted gall-stones. Dolly Gale had seen her sufferings for a year. To Rebekah Owen, Emma had spoken of "the Knife", implying that an operation had at least been discussed. The terrible conclusion is that Hardy shut his own eyes to his wife's state, and tried to shut the eyes of others after her death.

One of his very first actions was to send a telegram to Florence Dugdale, who was on her way to attend the performance of *The Trumpet-Major*, from whose stage in Dorchester Emma's death was announced that evening. Within a month she was installed at Max Gate. Dorchester buzzed with gossip. At first the locals thought Hardy would marry his housekeeper-maid, Florence Griffin, but some trial of strength soon took place between the two Florences, and Miss Griffin left. From mid-December to mid-January Emma's niece Lilian made an abortive stay, during which she told Florence that Hardy would never have been a great writer without her aunt. Florence also got rid of her, "Mrs. Hardy in little", as she wrote to Clodd,[1] though not for long. This miniature Emma was to return and subject Florence to the sort of social snubbing, to which she was most sensitive—"I am—so she implies—quite a low sort of person."[2] Florence herself, in fact, fled for a little relief to Enfield, where she had persuaded Edward Clodd to come down and give a lecture to her local literary society. While she was briefly away from Max Gate, she received letters from Hardy, couched in unmistakable terms. "If I once get you here again", he wrote, "won't I clutch you tight."[3] Of course, this need not mean they were sleeping together, though the maids at Max Gate had no doubt they were.[4] Even more to the point, Hardy had determined, whether or not he slept with her in life, to sleep with her in death. He had taken her on his favourite pilgrimage to Stinsford churchyard, where Emma now lay beside his father and mother. There he would eventually lie himself, and wrote Florence, "a corner, I am told, will be reserved for me".[5] He had, in his mind, already married her in the place most real to him, the grave. Dorchester, of course, had already bedded them, in every sense. Before she arrived, there had been rumours of a mistress in London. Now the tongues were wagging. Florence reported Hardy's warning that[6] "if I am seen walking about in Dorchester with him, or even if it is known I am staying at Max Gate, they will comment unpleasantly".

It was indeed a baptism of fire for the young woman. On the day of Emma's death, she afterwards wrote, she passed from youth "to dreary middle-age". This was an exaggeration; but what cannot be exaggerated is her pitying horror at Hardy's attitude to his late wife. She confessed to Irene Cooper Willis that his instant veneration of the dead woman was a deep shock to her. Though she could say in March, "I have never before realized the depth of his affection and unselfishness as I have done these last three months", his behaviour amazed her.[7] He had found, as well as Emma's "Some Recollections", the twenty years of diary-entries, which were supposedly called "What I think of my Husband"; yet he put down Emma's abuse as "sheer hallucination",[8] and his virtual worship of her memory went on "side by side with the reading of those diabolical diaries", so Florence incredulously wrote.[9] Indeed, he clutched at any sign of Emma's "hallucinations", encouraged by Florence, to save himself from admitting that the diaries represented Emma's real feelings. He had some corroborative evidence for this comforting theory. Shortly before her death, Emma had followed her pamphlet of poems by printing with Longman's of Dorchester an apocalyptic prose vision called *Spaces*, which she had first submitted to Charles Moule, now President of Corpus Christi College. The tactful Cambridge don had advised against publication, on the grounds that the world was not yet ready for Emma's message.[10] However, she ignored his advice, and this remarkable document had appeared over her name. Though Hardy, by January 1913, was actually finding justification, in retrospect, for Emma's extreme evangelical views, and causing these to "weigh heavily on my shoulders", as Florence wrote despondently to Clodd,[11] *Spaces* was too much for him to stomach. It is probably the cause of his writing to both Mrs. Henniker and to Emma's cousin about Emma's recent "delusions".[12] It has certainly all the marks of mild religious mania. Such mental states often attach themselves to whatever is the latest scientific invention. In the 1920s, people with a degree of religious dottiness thought they were receiving divine or demonic messages through wireless waves, just as in the nineteenth century they had similar obsessions about domestic gas.[13] Emma's imagery shows a fixation on the fairly recent phenomenon of electric light. In her description of the Day of Judgement

> Peoples of the world everywhere will prostrate themselves, the electric lights of the world will shine forth again, not *lit* by mortal hands which will have failed to set them aglow . . . They will gleam and burn fiercely with an awful intensity toward their final burning up of the earth . . .

There are other passages, even more extravagant. We may not, however, be as ready as Hardy to put this down to deep-seated hallucination. The jaundice, which frequently supervenes in cases of acute gall-stone trouble, can cause severe delusion, while the standard treatment by morphia might well result in opium dreams, of which poor Emma's "vision" is a not unusual example. Moreover, the contemporary novels by Marie Corelli, of whose work Emma was a reader, though not a whole-hearted admirer,[14] provide almost exact parallels, in style, punctuation, and rhythm: for example,

> Not long now shall we wait for the Divine Pronouncement of the End. Hints of it are in the air—signs and portents of it are about us in our almost terrific discoveries of the invisible forces of Light and Sound.[15]

However oddly expressed Emma's religious visions may seem, one must set against any suggestion of her insanity the businesslike, rational, and practical letters she wrote to the Vicar of Fordington, only a few months before her death, about religious and parish matters.

The swiftest and most striking effect of Emma's death upon Hardy was the sequence of poems he immediately began to write about her. These poems, beginning in December 1912, and actually numbering over fifty in the next two years, have been exhaustively examined by critics. Some of the most austere commentators have judged a few of them to be among the best, or perhaps the only, front-rank poems that Hardy ever wrote.[16] In them, his personal voice is most clear, the emotion most intimately welded to an amazing variety of forms. They seem a totally intimate confession; he himself called them "an expiation"; for most, though not all, are expressions of deep remorse. Yet their full meaning has never been examined, since the circumstances of his last years with Emma have never been fully understood or appreciated. Indeed, on the face of it the remorse, the need for expiation, might well seem a little far-fetched. Hardy's almost necrophiliac habit of loving the dead woman better than the living might seem exaggerated. Yet his guilt was indeed more frightful and more deep than he dared describe in these poems. All he confesses to is a neglect and indifference, of which many husbands could reproach themselves. He has hardly spoken to her, taken little interest in her doings or wishes, has failed to give her holidays in her favourite places, neglected his old loving habits. All this is most movingly expressed at the end of what is perhaps the earliest and best in this series of poems, *The Going*.

> Why, then, latterly did we not speak,
> Did we not think of those days long dead,
> And ere your vanishing strive to seek
> That time's renewal? We might have said
>    'In this bright spring weather
>    We'll visit together
> Those places that once we visited.'
>
>    Well, well! All's past amend,
>    Unchangeable. It must go.
> I seem but a dead man held on end

> To sink down soon . . . O you could not know
>     That such swift fleeing
>     No soul foreseeing—
> Not even I—would undo me so.

In these stanzas, he reproaches himself for their silent dinner-meetings, for having let love fade, for not taking Emma back to her beloved Devon—though, indeed, a cancelled passage in his autobiography shows they had recently planned an expedition to the West Country.[17] Yet this catalogue of relatively small omissions of sympathy and understanding hardly seems to justify the depth of guilt in the final stanza. For of course the whole truth is not revealed in this apparently all-revealing poem, and its fellows. His full guilt was too horrible to face. He had seen her suffer for months the utmost physical agony, had deliberately turned his eyes away, and pretended not to notice; he even feigned surprise, and underlined with continual guilty insistence the suddenness and unexpectedness of her death, "such swift fleeing". He must now have realized that he had only been able to do this by devoting, for the past five years, all his best care, tenderness, and consideration to another, much younger woman. All this explains the profound remorse which gives these remarkable poems their secret, unspoken intensity and painful inward passion.

They were surely supremely painful also to Florence Dugdale. She was caught up in a situation of guilty connivance. Her extreme sensitivity over gossip about herself and Hardy was noticed by everyone and lasted to the end of her life; she thought biographers "hoped to find something to make into a scandal".[18] His obsession with the dead Emma did not yet check his solicitous concern for Florence. In fact, it was now extended openly to other members of her family. On 4 January 1913, he printed in *The Sphere* the early version of the poem *The Bird-Catcher's Boy*. It had a decorative border designed and signed "C. T. Dugdale"—that is, Constance Taylor Dugdale, Florence's younger sister, art teacher and afterwards headmistress of Enfield Girls School.[19] Yet the spate of poems about Emma was a blow to Florence. She had herself received only a handful of poems in the past five years, the early *On the Departure Platform*, the poem about her at Max Gate, *After the Visit*, and the highly-charged *Had You Wept*, but not much more. These certainly spoke movingly of what seemed their hopeless love. *After the Visit* originally had ended by questioning

> what sad strange laws
> Made us crave that which could not be!

—that is, the fulfilment of their love while Emma was still alive. Now that Emma was gone, Florence found these wistful, delicate tributes to herself swamped by a succession of passionate poems to the dead woman. Within a month, in December 1912, Hardy had written at least half-a-dozen, *The Going, Your Last Drive, I found her out there, The Prospect, The Voice,* and *The Last Performance.* In January and February, his tone to the dead Emma became even more tender. Though still fingering over in fascinated horror her "diabolical diaries", he was now also reading Emma's artless and evocative "Some Recollections" of her life up to their marriage, including their romantic courtship. On the last day of January, he wrote the poem, *Rain on a Grave,* recalling her love of daisies, mentioned in these recollections. He recalled in *The Change* incidents of their first meeting in Cornwall, and continued the poem to include Emma's arrival in London for their marriage. By the end of February, he had decided to go and visit the places of her upbringing and of their falling-in-love, Plymouth and North Cornwall, a decision embodied in the poem, *A Dream or No.* He wished to be at St. Juliot by 7 March, the exact day he had first met Emma there.

He did not propose to take Florence, nor could she have stood it. His companion was brother Henry, who had been a tower of strength ever since Emma's death; it was even he, not Thomas, who had informed the Registrar of Deaths. Florence was left behind in gloomy cold Max Gate, its walls discoloured with great patches of damp.[20] Isolated and dark, behind its forest of Austrian pines, the house provided a nerve-racking experience for her. She slept with a loaded revolver in her bedroom, and thoughts of Hardy's obsessed expedition for company. Luckily, she had support from his sisters. Mary, as usual, was sympathetic though reticent. Kate, brisk and bluff, blew away the cobwebs of Thomas's pilgrimage. On his stay in Emma's birthplace at Plymouth, she remarked to Florence, "so long as he doesn't pick up another Gifford there, no harm will be done".[21] To his family, who had just moved from the cottage to Talbothays, Henry's new-built house at nearby West Stafford, Hardy had been moaning that "The girl he married died 20 years ago"—that is, at the time of their deep estrangement in the early 1890s. Kate (and the Hardys), who had no cause to love Emma, maintained to Florence "*that* girl never existed". Though Florence herself added, in fairness, "but she did exist to him no doubt", she was heartened, sitting in dark Max Gate with Emma's glaring portrait for sole company, by the forthright attacks of the family on her dead and now all-powerful rival.[22] She permitted herself some sarcasms about Emma and the Gifford family, and was cheered by Kate saying that Hardy "now has his youthful happy laugh".

Meanwhile, Hardy was in Plymouth and St. Juliot, following the track of Emma's "Some Recollections", and inspired as he had never been before. Poems poured from him, at Plymouth *Places* and *The West-of-Wessex Girl,* in Cornwall *After a Journey, Beeny Cliff, At Castle Boterel, The Phantom Horsewoman, St. Launce's Revisited, Looking at a*

*Picture on an Anniversary, Under the Waterfall.* Many use phrases, incidents, scenes, taken directly from Emma's own written recollections, which he must have carried with him, so close are the likenesses.[23] All tell very much the same tale.

> Summer gave us sweets, but autumn wrought division?
> Things were not lastly as firstly well
>     With us twain, you tell.
> But all's closed now, despite Time's derision . . .

He was creating a myth of their life, and writing out of himself the nagging guilt of reality.

Florence, having to live with the reality, naturally could not stand much more at Max Gate, in spite of the sympathy of the sisters, and, on his return with Hardy, that of Henry, whom she always loved—"true, strong and generous in every thought and deed—Giles Winterborne in the flesh".[24] To relieve her, Hardy took her in April to Mrs. Henniker, who had a house at Southwold in Suffolk. Florence had spent much of the previous year working for Mrs. Henniker on a memorial volume for her husband, the General, who had died on 6 February 1912, and to whose memory Hardy had contributed a poem. Florence felt herself fully at home with the older woman. She and Edward Clodd were among the few who were allowed to know of her existence and her connection with Hardy. "I told her every detail of my life and she entered into it as a sister."[25] After months of gloom, she enjoyed the bustle, the coming and going of distinguished guests at Mrs. Henniker's, who like her father before her, was a prolific entertainer. The sea air revived her.

A revival for Hardy himself at this time, after the ordeals of remorse and retrospective composition, was the offer of a high academic honour. In the middle of April, he was asked to accept the award of an honorary Litt.D. by the University of Cambridge, and on 25 April this was followed by an invitation to become an Honorary Fellow of Magdalene College. The degree, which he went to take at Cambridge early in June, particularly delighted him. He lunched with A. C. Benson, Vice Chancellor elect and Master of Magdalene. To senior members of the university, the self-taught Hardy seemed an intriguing mixture of an old countryman and a pass degree man, with his notebook interest in architecture and literary associations, In his autobiography, a few years later, Hardy claimed that he could have taken a pass degree in the 1860s, but was deterred "mainly owing to his discovery that he could not conscientiously carry out his idea of taking Orders".[26] An unpublished letter of 1866 to his sister Mary, however, gives the reason as being the long time which would have been wasted in complying with the University regulations,[27] studied in a handbook lent him by Horace Moule.

Cambridge in June was full of memories of Horace Moule, the tragic friend whom Hardy had seen for the last time there exactly forty years earlier, a few months before Moule cut his throat in his room in Queens'. The strongest reminder of this man who meant so much to Hardy came, however, from an unexpected source. On 12 June, Hardy's sister Mary, habitually so self-effacing that she would never uncover the slightest hint of emotion, wrote him a letter about the honorary doctorate. It began in what was, for her, a startling manner.[28]

> This is to congratulate you on the honour Cambridge has now conferred on you. It seems as if it came from that dear soul, whose dust, for so many years has been lying in Fordington Churchyard. I came unexpectedly upon an old letter of his yesterday . . .

Hardy himself had described Moule's grave in Fordington churchyard in a poem of deep-felt emotion, *Before My Friend Arrived*, but, with Mary, usually so silent that she would never dream of speaking about any personal matter, the words about Moule are a revelation of the deepest feeling. They strongly suggest—as does the fact that she had kept a letter of his for over forty years—that this withdrawn girl, the model for the hero's sister in *The Hand of Ethelberta* and for Elizabeth-Jane in *The Mayor of Casterbridge*, had been in love with Moule, without perhaps his even being aware of it. If so—and her words make it highly likely—his ruined life and fearful death were her tragedy as well as Hardy's, and had heightened her brother's sense of the universal irony of events.

The final twist to Moule's real-life disaster was that he had been persuaded he was the father of a bastard boy, born to a girl in the lowest quarter of his father's parish of Fordington. This was known to Florence, who could only have learnt it from Hardy. Within a month or so of his sister's reminder about Moule, Hardy wrote a powerful poem which seems based on this story. *The Place on the Map* was printed in the September 1913 number of the *English Review*. This was the magazine which had published Hardy's poem about village abortion, *A Sunday Morning Tragedy*, and which Hardy felt was enlightened enough for narrative poems on frankly sexual topics. The poem is subtitled "A Poor Schoolmaster's Story", and is told in the first person by the schoolmaster.[29] In the schoolroom, he looks at a map showing "a jutting height/Coloured purple, with a margin of blue sea". It is a headland where in "latter summer", he and a girl had walked (or in the manuscript "rode") after having loved there for "weeks and weeks" of "beaming blue, which had lost the art of raining". She tells him she will have a baby—"the thing we found we had to face before the next year's prime". This, which

in realms of reason would have joyed our double soul

Wore a torrid tragic light
Under superstition's hideous control.

Hardy had recently been writing a whole series of poems, in some of which he actually made the speaker of the poem not himself but Emma —for example, *Under the Waterfall*, *Lost Love*, and *The Haunter*. Now, faced with a reminder of an intense relationship forty or fifty years back, he makes Moule speak in this poem. By a climatic freak, the "latter summer" with "weeks and weeks" of unbroken blue sky late in the season can be dated. For some unexplained reason, the year 1865 was the last time for nearly fifty years that there had been such an abnormal late dry season, remarked on by Hardy in the poem, "hot and dry, Ay, even the waves seemed drying". In September 1865, the rainfall at Weymouth was nil. *The Times* commented on the "extraordinary weather", during which "the sun shone with unmitigated splendour" with temperatures often in the eighties. "The Place" of the poem seems certainly to have been Portland Bill. In Hardy's manuscript, he arranged for it to be followed by *Where the Picnic Was*, which has been plausibly shown[30] to be at a spot on the Ridgeway, overlooking Portland, and in 1914 and again in 1919, he printed the two in conjunction in this way. In 1865, Horace Moule was a schoolmaster; one of seven brothers in a clergy family, ill-paid for his literary journalism, and spending his money on drunken bouts, he was always poor. The bastard child was the crowning blow of his ill-fated life. There seems little doubt that Hardy, painfully recalled to memories of Moule this summer, gave his story in this poem.

Moule also came into Hardy's mind when, in August, he put together "a dozen minor novels", short stories which had never been reprinted, in a volume called *A Changed Man*; for the title story was largely based on the part played in the Dorchester cholera epidemic by Moule's father, which had made him the hero of Fordington. Further, when Hardy in November returned to Cambridge to be installed as Fellow of Magdalene, he revisited the President of Corpus, Charlie Moule, who had actually been in the next room when Horace Moule cut his throat. In the story of *The Changed Man*, the story-telling onlooker, Hardy himself, composes a little uncharacteristic poem about swift and impulsive marriage leading to apparent happiness, though there is a studied ambiguity about the poem, an ingenious exercise in triolet form, called *At a Hasty Wedding*. The question of his own remarriage was now coming up.

What were the thoughts of Thomas and Florence on this subject, at this time? He was still obsessed by Emma and the careless cruelty he had shown her. "I wounded one . . . and now know well I wounded her." Yet criticism, fostered by Florence, Henry, and Kate, was creeping in.

"But, ah, she does not know that she wounded me." The poem, *She Charged Me*, is a chilling indictment of Emma's bullying manner. Besides, the death in September of his childhood sweetheart, Louisa Harding, made him realize that all dead women shared a mysterious attraction for him, though Emma was still "the elect one". The brooding shadow of Emma's ghost between him and Florence was beginning to disperse. For Florence, he still felt some of the tenderness he had shown a few years before. She wrote[31] of his "tender protective affection for me—as a father for a child—a feeling quite apart from passion". She rated it, rather sadly, as something other than love. "He wanted a housekeeper who could be a companion and read to him—etc.—so I came in."[32] Colouring every feeling was the great theme of all his poetry now, that he would anyway die soon. On his seventy-third birthday, he wrote *Exeunt Omnes*, ending

> Folk all fade. And whither
> As I wait alone where the fair was?
> Into the clammy and numbing night-fog
> Whence they entered hither.
> Soon one more goes thither!

Florence's emotions were more complex. She had spent a searing year at Max Gate, where "Life under the conditions that have prevailed for the last twelve months" could no longer be endured by her.[33] Loneliness and humiliation had been her lot. To mitigate the first, she now introduced as companion for herself a dog, a fashionable Caesar terrier, the notorious "Wessex"; but there were more intractable elements in the second. Her year's stay there with Hardy had, in the language of the day, totally compromised her. Modern woman as she was—and also she was now nearly thirty-five—she could not still the storm of tongues in Dorchester, nor most probably the pressures of her own family. At her age, and with this history, no one else would now marry her. Her periodic bad health, too, was a terrible liability. Emotionally, her life had already suffered considerable tragedy. Two years before, on 1 June 1912, she had lost Sir Thornley Stoker.[34] Florence's elderly benefactor had been widowed in November 1910,[35] and in the same year he found himself obliged to retire from his post and governorship at the Richmond Hospital in Dublin. At the age of sixty-five, this energetic and busy surgeon had begun to show signs of arterio-sclerosis and cardiac weakness. He sold his unique collection of antique art, the English and Irish silver, the bronzes and oriental porcelains, which had made Ely House a place of pilgrimage for connoisseurs. A year later, failing still more, he instructed his executors to sell his exquisite old furniture, to add to the personal legacies he intended to leave. When he passed away quietly and gradually in the summer of 1912, Florence was one of the chief beneficiaries under his will. She received £2000, twice as much as his brother Bram, and about one-sixth of the residue of the estate.[36] Typically generous, Florence used some of the income from investing Sir Thornley's legacy in a way that he would have approved, in generosity to her own family. She paid with it the fees for her youngest sister Marjorie to go for three years to a domestic science college. One does not know if, after his wife's death, she had hoped to marry Sir Thornley. Bram Stoker's relatives, irritated at the legacy, were convinced she was Sir Thornley's mistress under the guise of employment at Ely House. It is equally likely that she genuinely had been at some time the junior of Lady Stoker's two attendants, the senior being an Irish nurse called Betty Webb, who benefited even more from the will. Miss Webb's character and reputation are known to have been above reproach. Though fond of Sir Thornley, Florence may have been misjudged.

What, then, caused this romantic young woman, who had been so much attached to one of the most attractive figures of the day, to consider marriage with Hardy, who, for all his fame, could not compete in personal charm and generosity of temperament? It was, one must remember, the heyday of the idea, now healthily almost defunct, that a wife should devote herself to serving a great artist or writer, and to protecting him from the encroachments of the outside world, as if he were some delicate or awkward child. Florence agreed with the self-centred Sydney Cockerell's definition of marriage as providing for a woman "the right to express . . . devotion". She felt towards Hardy "as a mother toward a child with whom things have somehow gone wrong".[38] He confessed to her that "he thought he had never grown up".[39] In this relationship, she could renew Jemima Hardy's role, and at the same time, herself receive the protection of a man at least nominally older in years. For a woman so intellectually alert, there was also an element of ambition. She hoped that the coming year, 1914, would see him receive the Nobel Prize for Literature.[40]

Like many deeply-considered and deeply-felt projects, action was precipitated by casual circumstances. The catalyst was Emma's niece, Lilian. Arriving for Christmas and the New Year, treating Hardy as her "daddy-uncle", she tried to take over her dead aunt's place, and manage Max Gate permanently. To Florence, after the past year of "domestic jars & all sorts of complications",[41] this was the last straw. Florence had made a "compact" with Hardy to care for him, eventually as his wife; but "if it is settled that she [Lilian] stays, I return to my own home, and remain there".[42] Henry and Kate Hardy backed her in refusing to tolerate such a "ménage à trois". Lilian went; but Florence now was convinced "that I should have some position of authority at Max Gate".[43] So the decision was taken.

On 10 February 1914, Florence's father, headmaster of St. Andrew's elementary school, Enfield, entered in his logbook,[44] "The Head Master was absent from duty until 10.45 a.m. owing to the marriage of his daughter with Mr. Thos Hardy O.M., D.C.L. etc., the eminent novelist." The ceremony at Enfield Parish Church took place at eight in the morning "in keeping with the retiring disposition of the well-known author". Apart from her father, who gave her away, the only people present were Florence's youngest sister Marjorie and Henry Hardy. After a wedding breakfast with Mrs. Dugdale at 5 River Front, Mr. Dugdale quietly resumed his school duties, while Florence and Hardy took an early train on their way back to Dorchester. An hour after they had left Enfield, twenty-six reporters knocked at Mr. Dugdale's front door.[45] Hardy's caution had been justified.

Congratulations of friends flowed in. The few who knew of Florence's existence were delighted. To some of them, it seemed that Florence "was so exactly one of your women that it seemed as though you had made her",[46] as, in a sense, he had. The many who did not know of her, such as Edmund Gosse, responded to the news with puzzled warmth, asking for introductions to the new unknown. To them, Hardy's descriptions of Florence ranged from "my long-time secretary" to "a literary woman but not a blue-stocking at all".[47] His official announcement, repeated by the Press, was that Florence had been for many years a close friend of his first wife. He emphasized this in his third-person autobiography, written a few years later. Thus Florence Hardy was, from the first, compelled to be party to a deceit. Only after his death did she rebel over this. She crossed out some sentences in the autobiography (to be printed as her biography of her late husband), and the event stands to this day baldly in the laconic sentence, "In February of the year following [1914] the subject of this memoir married the present writer."

For the time, "there is sunshine within Max Gate", Florence wrote.[48] Hardy, more conservatively, hoped that "the union of two rather melancholy temperaments may result in cheerfulness".[49] Florence at once made her presence felt. "We are having a bedroom enlarged, so that, if T.H. feels equal to it, we may have two or three people together, to amuse one another."[50] She saw herself as a hostess, like her friend Mrs. Henniker, Max Gate full of distinguished literary guests. While the workmen were at it, she and Hardy went off to Cambridge. It was her first public and acknowledged appearance with him, and she revelled in the company, the Cockerells, Quiller-Couch, the Mac-Taggarts, and many others, including Charles Moule, now Hardy's most longstanding friend. Yet there were new-found responsibilities. Henry Hardy had a slight stroke in March, and in May Florence had to take his place as Hardy's companion in yet another expedition to the Gifford tombs at Plymouth. "The whole process was melancholy", she wrote, and wished Henry could be there instead of her. In June, a living Gifford took up the irritating reminder. Emma's nephew Gordon, an L.C.C. architect, invited himself to Max Gate. To Florence's indignation, he informed her that Emma had said he should inherit the house on Hardy's death.[51] There were other problems in marriage. Just before Emma died, Florence had produced another set of "descriptions" for the artist Detmold, entitled *The Book of Baby Birds*, once more with unacknowledged verse-contributions by Hardy. Shortly after her marriage, the publisher asked her to do a similar illustrated book about dogs, prompted by the photograph of her and "Wessex", which had appeared in the press. For Hardy's sake, she refused; but she was perturbed. "Ought I—in fairness to my husband—to give up my scribbling? . . . I have a feeling, deep within me, that my husband rather dislikes my being a scribbling woman. Personally", she added, pathetically, "I *love* writing."[52] Happily for her she managed to quiet her conscience towards him, and *The Book of Baby Pets*, with Detmold's pictures, appeared during the following year.

On 4 August, such personal problems were temporarily blotted out by the huge tragedy of Europe. Hardy and she were "both almost paralysed with horror", Hardy regarded it as mankind's final rejection of all hope and sanity. In a month after the outbreak of war, he seemed to age ten years.[53] The horror obsessed him; in addition, he was convinced the Germans would land on the Dorset coast. He could not bear Florence to leave him for a single night. He would not have ended *The Dynasts* on its final brief note of hope had he ever foreseen this. In desperate gloom, he shut himself in his study, revising and working over a new collection of poems. In the twilight days just before war, he had already written his personal epilogue[54] to the volume.

> Whatever the message his to tell,
> Two thoughtful women loved him well.
> Stand and say that amid the dim:
> It will be praise enough for him.

*Satires of Circumstance* appeared on 17 November. Its title, taken from the group of story-poems printed in the *Fortnightly Review* for April 1911, and new expanded, was his publisher's choice, not Hardy's.[55] He himself had expressed grave doubts about reprinting this sardonic section, since it contrasted so sharply with the new-found tenderness of his more recent poems. "The scales had not fallen from my eyes when I wrote them, and when I reprinted them they had."[56] The Emma poems too caused him doubts. Were they too intimate to publish? He questioned Benson at Magdalene in November 1913, and Gosse as late as 28 June 1914. He knew, though, that they contained some of the finest poetry he had so far written. This finally decided him.

Yet the book as a whole by no means depends on the section "Poems of 1912–13", with its Virgilian motto *Veteris vestigia flammae*—"ashes of an old flame". For one thing, it contains many other poems to and about Emma. It also has poems of great power from Hardy's past work, some previously printed, *Beyond the Last Lamp, The Convergence of the Twain, The Place on the Map, Channel Firing, The Schreckhorn*, others appearing for the first time, *Wessex Heights* and *A Thunderstorm in Town*. The actual *Satires of Circumstance* sequence, does, in fact, as Hardy had feared, clash with many of these other poems, most especially in quality. Some reviewers suggested rightly that they would have made better short stories, as Hardy had originally conceived them.

The quality of most of the rest is remarkable, and in many ways new. It is not only that deep feeling has given Hardy a deeper style of utterance; it is also a matter of technical mastery. One feature is his echo and use of folk-tune for dramatic effect. In *Beyond the Last Lamp*, the monotonous movement of two lovers in the rainy evening is given a haunting dance-like quality by the refrain in mid-stanza "Walking slowly, walking sadly" and its variants. It was a folk-dance memory he was to use later in *Voices from Things Growing in a Churchyard*, where it became "All day cheerily, All night eerily." The lilting rhythm of *The Voice*, which opens, "Woman much missed, how you call to me, call to me", is suddenly and totally broken, as if by a fiddler double-stopping to indicate the approaching finish of the dance, by the last four lines:

> Thus I; faltering forward,
> Leaves around me falling,
> Wind oozing thin through the thorn from norward,
> And the woman calling.

Again and again, Hardy almost lulls one with rhythm, to effect a sudden and dramatic musical break, such as this.

Another remarkable point is the realistic conversational quality. In no less than three very different poems, a piece of scene-setting leads to the story-teller's interjection "Well", followed by a climax. In *The Going*

> Well, well! All's past amend,
> Unchangeable. It must go

*The Convergence of the Twain*

> Well, while was fashioning
> This creature of cleaving wing,

and in *Wessex Heights*

> Yet my love for her in its fulness she herself even did not know;
> Well, time cures hearts of tenderness, and now I can let her go.

This conversational style, allied often with the utmost metrical and rhythmic ingenuity, is one reason why Hardy commends himself so much as a model to poets in the second half of our century.

The *Satires of Circumstance* volume, one suspects, is the most read and most quoted book of Hardy's poems today. It did not seem particularly notable in its own day. Most of the reviewers were puzzled or at best lukewarm. They seem to have preferred the recent short-story collection, *A Changed Man*, and found most of these poems merely painful and gloomy. This feeling, by what is perhaps the greatest satire of circumstance, was one shared by Hardy's wife, Florence herself.

# 13

# Deaths and Visions

HARDY'S book of poems gave Florence great pain. She had put off a full reading in order to rush up to London to Harley Granville-Barker's patriotic adaptation of scenes from *The Dynasts* on 25 November. In spite of having been given an uneatable dinner at Max Gate[1]—Florence always had trouble with her cooks—Granville Barker had done a neat job of stage craftsmanship, and produced a piece in key with the highly emotional feeling of the times. Hardy cynically commented that "the good Barker's abridgement" made the original author seem "as orthodox as a churchwarden"; but it was a huge success, and did much to ensure that, throughout the 1914–18 War, *The Dynasts* became a tract for the times.[2] Henry Ainley spoke the special epilogue, and then led the entire audience at the Kingsway Theatre in speaking in unison the words of God Save the King. Florence was deeply moved (Hardy himself was absent with a cold), and was proud to receive praise from such people as H. G. Wells and John Masefield.[3] Now as she sat poring over her husband's poems, her changeable temperament swung to the other extreme. She seemed to herself an utter failure for her husband to produce "such a *sad, sad* book". She was full of self-blame. Yet her feelings were more complicated. After all, she had accepted apparently with pleasure a much more gloomy collection of poems five years before, *Time's Laughingstocks*, which Edmund Gosse had found to be "poignantly sad". The fact was that *Satires of Circumstance* contained about thirty poems connected with Emma, and only a tenth of that number to herself. This was why she felt she should have been "a different sort of woman".[4] The "crucifixion" that Emma herself had felt in 1898 over Hardy's published poems to so many other women was now repeated in Florence's bitter experience over this book. The poem in which she was bracketed with Emma was not improved, in her eyes, by the two being called "bright-souled" rather than "thoughtful".

Hardy had, as he had told her, never outgrown adolescence. He had, like an adolescent, not the slightest inkling of the pain he was causing. With age, too, his more generous earlier sympathies were hardening. Scrooge-like, he thought that as a social reformer Dickens was "a humbug", only writing for popularity. He privately dismissed the Georgian poets as "The Tibbalds' Row school of rhymeless youngsters". When British and German soldiers fraternized in No Man's Land at

Christmas 1914, Hardy strongly disapproved, and even praised a German lieutenant who stopped his men "hobnobbing".[5] He found "the attitude of Labour" over compulsory conscription "a very ugly one". He said that the mistake of the English over Ireland lay in not "crushing utterly" the 1916 rebellion.[6] Life with him was also hardening Florence. She castigated women who "use him to their own advancement", forgetful that she herself had passed off work written by him as her own. A course of philosophy he gave himself early in the New Year, G. E. Moore and Bergson, did not make him any the more approachable on a human scale, though he admired the latter for his poetical, intuitive, and human side. Florence's physical weaknesses, which once seemed to hold such tender attraction for Hardy, now only exposed her to his intractable temperament. In March she suffered a whole month of sciatica; he would not take her (as he had taken his father) to Bath for a cure because he was absorbed in writing, while he made it clear that if she went alone he would be miserable.[7] In May, her health forced just such a separation. Recurrent nose and throat infections demanded a nasal operation. Hardy strangely dismissed it as "a slight external operation".[8] It was certainly not "external" or "slight"; it put Florence in a London nursing-home for several days, during which he did not visit her, followed by convalescence in Welbeck Street with Mary Jeune.

While Florence was absent, a Hardy family conference took place at Max Gate. It was a peasant discussion about money. Hardy was probably the richest author in England, but he liked to pretend the war might ruin him. "I suppose if the worst came to the worst we would be given a pension", he told Florence. She had asked for a settlement on their marriage, "but it seemed to annoy my husband, so I desisted".[9] He gave her instead a housekeeping allowance so small that she had to rob her own dress allowance, something she hated. Brother Henry and sister Kate, however, were not impressed by Thomas's protestations of poverty. They knew there was money, and were determined it should not go to Florence. It must be left to "a Hardy born". They picked on a remote cousin, descended from Hardy's uncle James, the jobbing mason at Higher Bockhampton.[10] Hardy was not persuaded; but the astounding fact remains that the wealthy author made absolutely no attempt to pay his wife's London surgeon, the nursing-home fees, nor anything to do with her operation. This came out of Florence's own private income and savings, £70 in all, the whole of her annual income from Sir Thornley's legacy, nearly £1000 in modern terms.[11] Six years before, no trouble had been too much for him to protect her health. He had worried continually about her wrapping up at night, had arranged innumerable visits to the seaside, had shown her constant tenderness. There was only one conclusion she could draw. Self-absorbed to a degree she had never anticipated, Hardy clearly no longer loved her in

any real sense. His attitude was like the half-hearted obligatory gestures of consideration he had previously shown towards Emma. He
talked vaguely of taking Florence "to the western coast when she had
got over it, to pick up". In practice, all she got was one night in an
Exeter hotel after a day's long, hot, tiring, and dusty drive along the
Devon coast.[12] Hermann Lea, who now lived in the Bockhampton
cottage, drove them on one or two small local picnic outings but "T.
says he has had enough motoring for the present"[13]—he had to pay
Lea for the petrol.

Though Florence was still painstakingly loyal to him, from this time
onward a note of complaint and criticism enters into much that she
writes about Hardy. In particular, after years of restraint and trying
to be fair, she unloosed her tongue about Emma and the Giffords. She
repeated with relish a story Mary Jeune had told her. Years earlier
Mary had invited Archdeacon Gifford to one of her distinguished
dinner parties, so large that the hostess did not really know everyone
who was there. She asked the Archdeacon to take Mrs. Thomas Hardy
down to dinner, and stirred by subconscious memory had said, "I think
she is a relative of yours." He replied, "Mrs. Thomas Hardy is my niece,
and she is the most horrible woman in the world." Florence commented how "keen and understanding" Mary Jeune was,[14] and added
some ironical news about Emma's nephew, Gordon Gifford. The self-
styled "heir" to Max Gate had blotted his copybook for good by getting
married to a waitress in a teashop. "T. seems very quiet about it."
Wickedly, Florence saw this as a chance to get rid of the oppressive
Gifford property at Max Gate. Why not give Gordon the overpowering
clock, the gloomy furniture, the Gifford family portraits left in the
house by Emma? "I could spare them well enough," she remarked
and hinted so to Hardy. Hardy replied shortly to her teasing that he
himself had paid good money for them to Emma's family, and they
were now his.[15] Florence's sarcasm did not stop there. In summer 1915,
after a year of war, hopes of a quick settlement were over. The long
slog of trench warfare would require huge armies. Voluntary recruiting
would not be enough. Conscription was in the air, though unpopular;
some politicians were suggesting it should be confined to single men.
Florence said that Gordon was marrying his "tea-shop girl" only to
avoid being called up, and her shrewd conjecture was confirmed when
Gordon's sister naïvely let the cat out of the bag. At all events, she
ensured that he was never asked to Max Gate again; yet her open resentment of the Gifford family continued. She maintained that if her
own name were Gifford, Hardy would have provided her with holidays,
more money, new furniture, stays with her mother's relatives in
Brighton, invitations for her own friends and relatives to Max Gate.[16]
The only way to get him to take her anywhere, she wrote, would be if

she promised to go and "hunt up Giffords—and I really cannot stand more of that".[17]

The name Gifford, in fact, was a safety valve for Florence. Resentment directed at her husband would have left her plunged into remorse at criticizing one so old and so distinguished. Yet one criticism, though unspoken to him, was fundamental, and she was quick to define it. "His liking for people seems quite apart from any sense of obligation to them."[18] He would accept hospitality, help, advice, kindnesses from his friends, but feel absolutely no necessity to do anything for them in return. Florence, with her spontaneous if erratic generosity, was pained and embarrassed for them both, but particularly on her own account, since people, she found, suspected she was the cause. As she said, her own instinct would be "to make this a second home for the people I like, and who have been good to me".[19] Instead, she found her  husband determined to be increasingly "a recluse", though she might have been warned, since from the moment of her marriage "it was impressed upon me that I must *keep off* people".[20] She had hardly reckoned this would include the affectionate friends of both Hardy and herself.

More happily, there was one subject on which her generous instincts and his inclinations could work together. This was the topic of "the heir" to Max Gate, who would inherit the house and a large number of Hardy's family possessions, and also be "a strong arm" to Hardy in his last years, like an adopted son.[21] They had discussed this ever since they were married, and made plans. This fact, incidentally, disposes of the idea, sometimes debated, that they hoped for any child of their own marriage; and obviously, such an idea[22] had equally never entered into the calculations of either Gordon Gifford or of Hardy's own immediate family. Florence acted tactfully. Realizing that Hardy, like his own relatives, would not tolerate anyone who was not "a Hardy born", she pressed the claims of someone whom Hardy already knew and liked, and who had the right qualification. Frank William George was, on the face of it, only a remote cousin; but he had an impressive array of Hardys in his ancestry. His great-grandfather, John, was a young brother of Hardy's grandfather, Thomas; his grandfather was William Jenkins Hardy, and his mother was Angelina Hardy. All these male Hardys were Puddletown bricklayers and masons, like Hardy's own direct ancestors.[23] Angelina Hardy had married, in 1878, William George, who kept the Royal Oak Inn at Bere Regis. Their son, Frank William George, was born at Bere on 5 December 1880, and was therefore nearly two years younger than Florence. He grew up tall and extremely good-looking. What was more, he managed to enter one of the gentlemanly professions, so all-important to Hardy. He was a barrister and a member of Gray's Inn. He was called to the Bar on 17 November

1913, shortly after Hardy had enlisted his old legal friend, Sir Frederick Pollock, on his behalf. This put him apart from all Hardy's other relatives. Florence had met one of the sons of Nat Sparks, Hardy's carpenter cousin at Bristol. Both Nat's sons, James and Nathaniel junior, were artists of considerable achievement, but to Florence the Sparks cousin she met was "a perfect young cad . . . the sort of man one would not care to have as chauffeur". Her attitudes in such matters were, unfortunately, increasingly those of Hardy, who left out of his family tree everyone who did not have gentlemanly pretensions, or professional qualifications. Frank George seemed to both of them the ideal selection, "the only decent relation". It is fair to say that their dislike of the other relatives was returned in kind by the Sparks cousin, who referred pointedly to Hardy as "*Mr*. Thomas".[24]

The choice of heir was dogged by the Hardyesque irony and fatality that affected all his most cherished concerns. On 22 August 1915, Frank George, who had joined the 5th Dorsetshire Regiment as a second-lieutenant, was killed at Gallipoli. Within only a few more months, disaster again assailed Hardy. His beloved sister Mary, his second self, had suffered lately from her chest. A year before, Dr. Gowring had diagnosed this as asthma.[25] It was a wrong diagnosis, but Gowring, a competent physician, did not deserve the scorn poured on him by Hardy and Florence afterwards.[26] In the early stages, it is often difficult to distinguish asthma, marked by inability to expand the lungs, from its opposite, emphysema, or inability to contract them. Mary died of this on 24 November,[27] her last days painfully distressing as she struggled for breath. Even more distressing, in another way, were the scenes before her funeral. Mary, reticent to the last, failed to make a will, and it was known she had a modest fortune, which Thomas would have to administer.[28] The Hardys were suspicious. To Florence, the shy withdrawn woman had been a "dearest sister". Would Thomas let Florence have some money? How would the estate be shared? Tempers were uncontrolled. To Florence's horror, the cheerful, friendly Henry shouted at his famous brother, Kate was sulky and difficult, and quarrels continued on the day of the funeral itself. Even worse for Florence was the old country custom of continually going into the death-chamber to kiss the corpse. Morbidly conscious of infection, from her own nose and throat troubles, Florence was sickened by this peasant crudity. For the first time, she began to realize some of the difficulties Emma had encountered.[29]

For Hardy, however, his sister's death was a profound and momentous experience. Nearest to him in age, temperament, and tastes, she had been his closest companion all through his life. He regarded their relationship as a spiritual marriage. In the poem *Conjecture*, he spoke of her literally as a third wife.

> If there were in my Kalendar
> No Emma, Florence, Mary,
> What would be my existence now—
> A hermit's? Wanderer's weary?—

Her innocent pride in him had been his greatest inspiration from their earliest days. It was maintained in their old age. In March 1912, she wrote[30] to a relative about the Latin inscription chosen by Hardy for the family memorial at Stinsford,

> I would rather it had been an English inscription and no Latin, and I daresay you would also, but you know how fond Tom is of books and languages and I think he could not feel satisfied unless there was some show of learning in this.

On her scanty holidays, she wrote careful postcards to him about places connected with books and authors.[31] That he and she had, as now seems likely, both loved the same man, Horace Moule, was a double bond. The dead woman seemed present everywhere with him, even at her own funeral service. "As Mr. Cowley read the words of the psalm . . . they reminded me of her nature, particularly when she was young: 'I held my tongue and spoke nothing: I kept silence, yea, even from good words.' That was my poor Mary exactly." Even after ten years, he wrote of her with deep feeling, "She came into the world . . . and went out . . . and the world is just the same . . . not a ripple on the surface left."[32] He was immediately moved to recreate her in poems, just as he still recalled Emma. He wrote of their happy youth, climbing trees together.

> My fellow-climber rises dim
> From her chilly grave—
> Just as she was, her foot near mine on the bending limb,
> Laughing, her young brown hand awave.

He even recalled, in new poems, the ideas of poems he had written to Mary fifty years before. In *The Musing Maiden* (1866) he had imagined her in Dorset, himself in London, both looking at the moon, so that

> Up there our eyesights touch at will

*Molly Gone* (1916), one of his most beautiful poems, carried the identical thought.

> Thinking thus, there's a many-flamed star in the air
> That tosses a sign.
> That her glance is regarding its face from her home so that there
> Her eyes may have meetings with mine.

Many poems to Mary, written in this effort to revive their past, have been mistaken for poems to Emma. "You were the sort that men forget" is obviously Mary—Emma, for good or ill, was hardly the sort one would forget—and *The Man with a Past*, written shortly after Mary's death, seems a picture of brother and sister.

> Innocent was she,
> Innocent was I,
> Too simple we!

This mysterious poem of menace speaks of three blows "which she dumbly endured". Again, "dumbly" is hardly a credible picture of the voluble Emma, remembered by Hugh Walpole as talking incessantly; but it is a faithful one of Mary.

Mary's death at the end of 1915 signalled a fundamental change in Hardy's life. Not only was he thrown back on the past as he had been at Emma's death three years before; the past now almost wholly absorbed him. His "recluse" element took possession from the beginning of 1916. He retired to his study and shut out the present. It was a self-protective retirement. For one thing, it was becoming impossible for him to think about the progress of the war. "He says he keeps from brooding over present affairs by concentrating his mind on the poems he is writing."[33] Present affairs, in the years 1916–17, were indeed practically unthinkable. The huge slaughter of the Somme in one year, and of Passchendaele in the other, made the war seem mankind's final madness. As a culmination of the general tragedy, Hardy heard on Christmas Eve 1917 that one of his most sympathetic friends, Alda, Lady Hoare, had lost her only son, the heir of Stourhead.[34] Hardy might well live only for the past and for poetry. With some minor exceptions this was the pattern of the dozen years of life that now remained to him. The young poets and writers who shortly began to visit him, Robert Graves, Walter de la Mare, Virginia Woolf, Siegfried Sassoon, recorded their common impressions of the benevolent, ancient, and smiling English Man of Letters, who came down for his tea and twinkled mildly at them. Only Sassoon commented that the real Hardy was not there with them, in a poem of rare insight, called *Max Gate*.

> Old Mr. Hardy, upright in his chair,
> Courteous to visiting acquaintances chatted
> With unaloof alertness while he patted
> The sheepdog whose society he preferred.
> He wore an air of never having heard
> That there was much that needed putting right.
> Hardy, the Wessex wizard, wasn't there.
> Good care was taken to keep him out of sight . . .

Up in Hardy's study, it was a different matter. Not only was his world peopled by his parents, Emma, Mary, Horace Moule, and hosts of others from the past; Hardy was evolving, in poem after poem, a new personal poetic mythology. He rejected, apart from a few sad instances of nostalgia, the Biblical mythology of his youthful verse. He rejected his hard-won classical mythology. He rejected any easy Wordsworthian pantheistic myth-making. His own mythology, private to the outside world, was built upon the lives, events, and associations of those he had known deeply and closely. With a set of personal symbols, he freed his poetry for supreme expression. The key to some of these symbols is lost; many are crystal-clear. The month of March stands for adventure and new life, instead of the poetically-conventional April, because in March he had first met Emma. September stands for fulfilled happiness, since then he married her. November symbolizes disaster and death, being the death-month of both Emma and now Mary. The words "My friend" nearly always symbolize wisdom unable to save or guide itself, though able to guide others, drawn from Horace Moule. The love of his mother's peasant fireside represents a wealth of superstition, which is somehow nearer the truth than either rational thought or religion, as in his poem, *The Oxen*, written shortly after Mary's death, and based on a country legend from their mother, telling how at twelve on Christmas Eve, the oxen knelt in their stalls, and how, in his words,

> So fair a fancy few would weave
> In these years! Yet, I feel,
> If someone said on Christmas Eve,
> "Come; see the oxen kneel

> "In the lonely barton by yonder coomb
> Our childhood used to know,"
> I should go with him in the gloom,
> Hoping it might be so.

With a mythology totally explicable to himself, though not always to others, Hardy could write with a freedom greater than ever before. Often Nature provides symbols, which are connected with places and persons in his life. Sometimes these may be identified, more often not. A sunny stream represents happiness, though often happiness of an impermanent kind, because Hardy's "two years idyll" with Emma was spent overlooking the millstream at Sturminster Newton. We cannot tell the origin of its opposite symbol for unhappiness, a pond on a heath, often reflecting moonlight, always an image of coldness and parting. The flight of a heron from trees beside the pond always means some final loss. We do not need to know or guess what experience with what girl gave Hardy this heartfelt symbol. It is enshrined in his mythology as an image of uttermost despair and deprivation.

The two years, 1916 and 1917, saw Hardy creating poems of intense meaning and feeling through this highly personal mythology. Shut up in his study, he evolved a tender and tragic world from the past. For

Florence, who had to live below in the present, these two years were a terrible experience. In December 1917, she wrote of them, "I have had home worries, of a kind sufficient to break down any woman's nerve, I think", and in the same month, after a rare visit to the theatre to see Barrie's *Dear Brutus*, she did break down and wept uncontrollably.[35] By "home worries',' she meant both her responsibilities at Max Gate, and those connected with the Dugdale family. The first incident was a tragi-comedy of guilty conscience by the Max Gate pair. In January 1916, both still dazed by influenza, Thomas and Florence heard with horror, accompanied by self-centred indignation, that Edward Clodd was going to publish his reminiscences. There was panic at Max Gate, as they thought of their stays together at Aldeburgh before marriage, well before Emma's death. They had considered Clodd "perfectly safe". Now it transpired, "he has been keeping a record of all conversations etc." Florence impulsively wrote one of her furious letters to Clodd, threatening that Thomas would expose him in the Press.[36] What she meant by these threats is not clear, but her letter is unfortunately only the first of a number of examples of her wild fluctuations of personal feeling. Siegfried Sassoon wrote, "She had very little judgment about people, was easily prejudiced."[37] The most striking example is the see-saw of her feelings in this same year, 1916, about Sydney Cockerell. She began by judging Cockerell "a wonderfully fine man".[38] During the year he was a regular visitor, and by October Florence found "a hateful expression" on his face.[39] Yet by 14 December, she wrote, "I want to retract anything I may have said . . . All badness must have been in myself."[40] In this case her fluctuations correspond with the contradictions of Cockerell's own tortuous character, and he himself ungenerously was to dismiss Florence as "an inferior woman with a suburban mind". Yet these rash judgements were more unfortunate when Florence applied them to many other friends, servants, and even relations. On the downswing of a temporary mood, she would not only attack in letters, but would write, in letters to a third party, the most harmful and unjust opinions and stories. Examining Florence's large series of letters to Rebekah Owen, which started in 1913, Beatrix Potter (Mrs. Healis) burnt many of the most indiscreet letters, including "several that seemed positively libellous".[41] Such letters afterwards caused her intense shame, and her correspondence is punctuated with sudden implorings to destroy letters, and even more, to return and forgive letters in which she has attacked the friends or acquaintances to whom she has taken a sudden, unreasoning dislike. Her letter to Clodd naturally blighted one of Hardy's longest and most sympathetic friendships. Clodd, who had largely educated himself, like Hardy, with evening reading, including classes at Birkbeck College, was a real ally, as Thomas and Florence had found. The break not only deprived Hardy

of profitable financial advice, which Clodd, a banker, dispensed over
his investments. It alienated and disillusioned his friend and exact
contemporary, and although Clodd patched the quarrel up in the 1920s,
when both were eighty, things were never the same. Clodd, who had a
reputation for generosity and loyalty, outlived Hardy by some two
years and wrote that he "was a great author: he was not a great man;
there was no largeness of soul".[42] The whole exercise was ridiculously
unnecessary; when Florence read Clodd's *Memories* later that year,
she found it "so *dull*", and in it, in fact, Clodd explicitly rejected the
idea of "prying" into private lives. However, it intensified the Max
Gate suspicions of the outside world. Much of 1916 was taken up with
Florence's alternate admiration and horror over Sydney Cockerell.
Her wide-eyed reverence for one who had personally known both
"Tolstoi and Ouida" makes pathetic reading; yet she was shrewd
enough to feel there was something wrong or even sinister about this
assiduous and rather unpleasant name-dropper. Besides—another
horror—he too "takes notes of conversations here".[43]

Everywhere at Max Gate was the shadow of Emma. "I may not
alter the shape of a garden bed, or cut down or move the smallest bush,
any more than I may alter the position of an article of furniture."[44]
Sarcastically quoting Milton, she wrote of Thomas's "late espoused
saint",[45] and spoke of his wish to visit Plymouth, "to gaze, once again,
I suppose, at the house where SHE was born."[46] She herself was frequently ill. In spite of operation, the nose infection seemed ready to
spread to the ear, and threaten mastoid. She had two series of expensive
inoculations, and the surgeon Yearsley advised a long holiday.[47]
Florence's ironic prophecy came true. The only way for her to have a
holiday was to agree to go with Thomas "to hunt up Giffords", alive
and dead. In September 1916, they went to see Emma's cousins, the
Giffords of Launceston, whom Hardy had never known, and then on
to St. Juliot to see the memorial to Emma he had designed and paid to
be put up there. As Florence wrote, it was an effort of self-control on
her part. "One has to go through a sort of mental hoodwinking and
blind one's self to the past."[48] Not that the present, at bathless Max
Gate, was very desirable for an often-ill woman. "I have to bath in a
puddle—a quart or three pints of hot water in a smallish hip bath."[49]

Dugdale family affairs were a constant strain. Her strong, self-
reliant father, who added to his life-saving tally by successfully
rescuing two children from drowning, had a complete, though fortunately not permanent, nervous collapse. Her mother was always
delicate, her sister Eva, a nurse, had difficulties with her jobs. Her
youngest sister Marjorie, whom Florence had seen through college on a
three-year domestic science course, became engaged and married a
young airman with no money. Florence for once defied her husband,

and had the penniless bridal pair to spend their honeymoon at Max Gate. Kate Hardy, who had no illusions about her famous brother, applauded Florence for this. "Bravo F!!!!!", she wrote in her diary with multiple exclamation marks.

By the end of 1916, Florence herself wrote, "Sometimes I feel *eighty*", older than her husband, who seemed well and cheerful, "in spite of his gloomy poems". These, of course, so far as they concerned Emma, were still a thorn in the flesh to Florence. At the end of 1916, "strangers must imagine that his only wish is to die & be in the grave with the only woman who ever gave him any happiness".[50] At the end of 1917, "the idea of the general reader will be that T.H.'s second marriage is a most disastrous one and that his sole wish is to find refuge in the grave with her with whom alone he found happiness". For on 30 November 1917, "the general reader" was given a chance to see what Hardy had achieved in this concentrated, solitary life of poetry over the past few years. On that date, *Moments of Vision* was published, his largest collection, and in many instances his finest. He had already tested the public demand, just over a year before, with a carefully-chosen *Selected Poems*, in which nine of his latest were included. The enthusiastic response demanded a second impression within a month. In this selection, he had also made a belated gesture to Florence. Three out of the first four reprinted poems were poems addressed to her; he also signed a presentation copy for her married, older sister.[51]

The *Moments of Vision* collection of 1917 differs in many important ways from all Hardy's previous or subsequent collections. It dates from one recent period of composition; a mere handful of poems gives evidence of earlier work. Instead of a rag-bag effect, as in all other volumes, there is an impressive unity. If Hardy felt need of justification for his self-imposed, self-centred "recluse" life, it is here. The work is different in outlook from poems written before the war. The confident self-righteousness of the fourteen *Poems of War and Patriotism* had been badly shaken by a visit in 1916 to a Dorchester prison-camp. There is a new, human tone. Briefly, where before Hardy had always blamed man's troubled affairs on a First Cause or Immanent Will, often in poems of turgid, versified philosophy, he now saw Man himself as a creature of weakness and unreason, and even included his own failings in this criticism. His philosophic correspondence with Galsworthy, in the spring of 1916,[52] shows Hardy far less dogmatic and confident as a prophet, seer, and reasoner—"a miserable reasoner", he confesses. *Moments of Vision* is wholly on a human scale, the scale, too, of Hardy's own personal mythology. In no other volume has he followed so closely Sir Philip Sidney's advice, "Look in thy heart and write." Though Hardy said of these poems "they mortify the human sense of self-importance", their concern for human failing celebrates true humanity.

As in *Satires of Circumstance*, there were about thirty poems connected with Emma, but these show a new aspect of memory. Several poems are directly inspired by Emma's own words in her manuscript of early "recollections" which Hardy was now re-reading, the disturbing "diabolical diary" having been at last consigned to the flames. Some of his finest poems draw on Emma's phrases. *During Wind and Rain* describes her two childhood houses at Plymouth in detail; even its title and theme echo the storm on the day she left Plymouth, as if it washed away her happy past. *The Interloper* begins with her descriptions of the Cornish coast, *The Five Students*, with its refrain of "dark she, fair she", echoes exactly Emma's words about herself and her sister, "she dark, I fair", though her sister is not included in the "students" of the poem. The poem, *Near Lanivet, 1872*, describes an actual incident in their courtship. Poems about a still older past are concerned with his sister Mary, and set in the Bockhampton cottage. An admiration for "a *very* good-looking girl", young Mrs. Hanbury of Kingston Maurward, noted by Florence was wistfully responsible for a pathetic poem about the great house, entitled *In her precincts*, to which Hardy himself added the words "Mrs. H..bury".[53]

Another source of inspiration from the past is the rhythm of folk-tune refrains from Hardy's own childhood. An unusually high proportion of poems have this folk-song pattern. The "Ah, no; the years, oh!" of *During Wind and Rain* is the best known; a poem to his sister Mary, written at the same time, *Logs on the Hearth*, had the refrain, "That time, oh!", which was removed in later printings. Other poems have a folk-song story-pattern, the scheme, for instance, of the traditional song, *Ten Green Bottles*, in which each verse subtracts one. Such are *The Five Students*, where the students diminish stanza by stanza, or *Looking Across*, where the Hardy family one by one—father, mother, daughter-in-law, daughter—go "across" to live in Stinsford Churchyard, leaving Hardy alone "looking". The events of his life with Emma are charted in simple, folk-tale succession: the persistent image of sun on a stream always takes its place as their brief, early happiness. In *The Five Students* similarly, the death of the "dark and fair he, dark and fair she" are chronological, though the "students" never, in fact, met in any place but in Hardy's mind. They are probably Horace Moule (died 1873), Tryphena Sparks (1890), Moule's brother Henry (1904), and Emma (1912). A cancelled last stanza identifies "the course" that all (Hardy being the fifth) followed. It is Love, "Heaven's central star", in the stanza's Shelleyan phrase. Like so many in *Moments of Vision*, this poem is a celebration of the ideal of Love.

So Hardy, neglecting the present-day world around him, delved into the deep past for evidences of love. He was perhaps only dimly conscious of neglecting those nearest to him now, especially the much-tried Florence, with her almost overwhelming problems. Perhaps some of the tenderness drawn from the past did at last spill over into the present, and to her. Though he had been able to ignore his first wife's physical suffering, something of his second wife's mental suffering seems belatedly to have struck him. When he received the first copy of *Moments of Vision* from the printers late in November, he inscribed it "this first copy of the first edition, to the first of women Florence Hardy".[54] It was some compensation for the pain she inevitably received from many of the poems within. Moreover, earlier in this same year 1917, he and she had concocted a scheme which would at least bring them into closer touch, and allow her, even though in a most curious way, some literary work at last.

# 14

# Late and Early

*Moments of Vision* was a critical success. The Georgian poets Hardy had privately disparaged were generous in praises.[1] At the age of seventy-seven-and-a-half, the great achievement of *Moments of Vision* seemed to Hardy his final word in verse. He had indicated this by ending the collection with the famous, personal poem about his own death, *Afterwards*. He had now, he wrote to Gosse in a letter[2] whose arithmetic seems difficult to confirm, spent fractionally more of his life in producing verse than in producing prose. This constituted a fitting resting place for his reputation. In *Afterwards*, too, he most significantly reversed a process of his youth. In the 1860s, finding no magazine would accept his poems, he "prosed" them into early novels: a passage in *Desperate Remedies* paraphrases completely a youthful sonnet. *Afterwards* begins by turning two passages from a novel into poetry.

> When the Present has latched its postern behind my tremulous stay,
>     And the May month flaps its glad green leaves like wings,
> Delicate-filmed as new-spun silk, will the neighbours say,
>     "He was a man who used to notice such things"?
>
> If it be in the dusk when, like an eyelid's soundless blink,
>     The dewfall-hawk comes crossing the shades to alight
> Upon the wind-warped upland thorn, a gazer may think,
>     "To him this must have been a familiar sight."

In the novel *The Return of the Native*, there are "new leaves, delicate as butterflies' wings"—there is a similar passage in *The Woodlanders*—and on "the isolated and stunted thorns . . . a night-hawk revealed his presence . . . flapping his wings . . . alighting". The images of the novel have been cannibalized for the poem. Hardy was making what seemed to him his final statement that he was, and always had been, essentially a poet.

Yet what of himself as a man? What would, in literal fact, "the neighbours say" about him? What picture would the world get? To one so morbidly self-conscious and secretive, this question was supremely important. Should he write an autobiography as many of his friends suggested? "My reminiscences; no, never!" he exclaimed in a letter[3] to Sir George Douglas in December 1915: but the supposed threat of

Clodd's reminiscences just a month later made him think again. He could hardly go on prohibiting all his friends to write about him. Besides, Clodd's published *Memories* showed Hardy the dangers of attempting to enforce such suppression. It seemed suspicious to any intelligent reader, who knew the long friendship, similar tastes and background of the two men, that Clodd wrote separate sections on several less close friends, such as Sir Henry Thompson, yet none on Hardy, although the book was dotted with anecdotes revealing him as a principal guest at Clodd's Aldeburgh home for many years. From as early as 1894, a couplet of a fellow-guest, Grant Allen, was quoted,[4] describing a Whitsun week spent at Aldeburgh.

> How late we tarried, slow and tardy,
> Yet loth to lose one tale from Hardy!

Hardy, to the end of his days, never quite realized that omission and silence aroused more suspicions than they allayed; but *Memories* must have made him think again about the wisdom of further prohibitions.

If he wrote an autobiography, it would have to disguise more than his comparatively recent indiscretions with Florence. The process would stretch back to the beginnings of his life, and even beyond. From quite early in his years of fame, he had sedulously built up a fictitious history of his past life and ancestry. He had abandoned as unbecoming to a great author his own family's humble origins and struggles. He never breathed to anyone, for instance, that his mother was one of seven children brought up on parish charity; that close relatives, like his uncle John Hardy, were labourers; that several were disreputable or drunk; that his mother, and both his grandmothers, had been pregnant well before their marriages; and that the women in his family, with few exceptions, were domestic servants. He had shoals of living cousins, one of whom, Augustus Hardy, who had just died, was a prison warder at Portland Gaol. He wrote to them on business only, if at all. With who knows what damage to his own integrity and personality, he had cut himself off from his native roots. Yet he still lived a life where this past might uncomfortably break in. Though he was genuinely fond, for instance, of his brother and surviving sister, Henry and Kate, and saw them frequently, it is clear from the latter's diary that these two, simple-mannered and speaking broad Dorset, were hustled out of the way if they happened to coincide at Max Gate with their brother's more distinguished callers.[5] He himself was morbidly conscious that his own education had been nothing like that of these visitors. He had spent a year or so at a "National" village school, some few more at a Nonconformist school of the British and Foreign Bible Society in Dorchester. When the master of this school set up a small fee-paying school of his own in the town, Thomas's parents had paid the guinea a term for him to continue there;[6] but at sixteen he had left to be articled to a local architect. A great deal of Thomas's considerable learning had been self-acquired and self-taught, though aided and to some extent inspired by the ill-fated son of the Dorchester clergy family, his older friend Horace Moule. Two terms of elementary French in his twenties, when he was an architectural assistant in Town, and went to evening classes at King's College, London, completed the tally of his formal education. In a sense, the Order of Merit at seventy, and the Cambridge doctorate and college fellowship at seventy-three, had come too late, either to restore his personal confidence over this lack, or to lift the obsession about it that had been gathering over the years.

It is easy to condemn Hardy for snobbery, both intellectual and social. He was certainly more culpable here than his first wife, who has always been blamed for such tendencies; it was, after all, he not she who inserted into his entry in *Who's Who* the information, unique in that publication, that his wife was the niece of an archdeacon. Yet the simple label of snobbery misses the deep wound in his nature, which caused his extraordinary manœuvres of concealment. The rigid class divisions of Victorian society were nowhere in the British Isles so fixed as in Dorset. In Scotland, for instance, where self-education was recognized and indeed honoured, Hardy's close contemporary, Sir James Murray, could proceed from obscurity to social acclaim and the learned achievement of the *Oxford English Dictionary*. Hardy felt his own achievement continually threatened by the past, from which he had broken with such pains, and particularly by any fancied hint of contempt at his educational and social origins. The tragedy was that any such contempt was largely self-created by his own suspicious imagination.

What then was to be done, to sum up his life in prose as, he felt, his last book, with the last poem in it, had done in poetry? How should he produce what would seem an authoritative version, which would not be subject to contradictions nor risk the appearance of bias? One natural solution suggested itself. He was, after all, now married to a self-styled "scribbling woman", and one, unlike poor Emma, whose spelling, grammar, and arrangement of sentences were generally above reproach. Yet difficulties at once presented themselves. Florence's unaided style and experience might not be up to the work. Her half-dozen or so short tales for children and her brief natural history "descriptions" gave no guarantee of capability for an adult work of such scope. True, she had kept her hand in, after marriage, by reviewing novels; but this ephemeral, mechanical work gave no sign of anything but routine competence.

However, sometime in 1917, they made a start; Hardy would give

Florence factual notes, which she would write up and expand. She began to type what she called "Notes of Thomas Hardy's Life . . . (taken down in conversations etc.)".[7] These fragmentary typescript notes soon proved unsatisfactory. For one thing, Florence was a self-taught and not particularly accurate typist. When rushed or bothered, she could produce distinct errors, even mis-typing the titles of poems.[8] Several obvious mistakes creep into even the opening pages of these notes, and some over-eager modern scholarship has produced biographical conjectures out of what are simple mis-types. One of these mistakes, in fact, shows when these notes were being taken down. Page 14 of the typescript reaches the point, in the middle of April 1862, when Hardy first seeks work as an architectural assistant in London. At this juncture, it is clear that Florence was distracted from the typescript. She was having more than usual difficulty over servants in mid-1917. At a tactless remark of hers, the cook had "bristled up and said 'Please, m'm, I think I'd better leave'."[9] When she returned from domestic discord to continue her notes about Hardy in April 1862, she headed the next section, "Last week in April 1917". This method was clearly not going to work. The typescript in fact peters out half-a-dozen pages later.

A new and very natural idea now succeeded this abortive beginning. It would be more efficient than the haphazard taking-down and writing-up of notes, and would satisfy Hardy's imperative need to furnish the world with a flattering portrait of his life. It arose from two stories which had appeared some years before over Florence's maiden name in the pages of the *Cornhill*, the highlights for her of serious literature. Yet neither was really her work. The first, *The Apotheosis of the Minx*, shows signs, in plot, construction, and actual words, of Hardy's hand; the second, *Blue Jimmy*, was entirely written by him, and passed off as hers. No one had apparently recognized the deception. It was natural for the two to believe that if Hardy wrote his own autobiography, in the third person throughout, it could be passed off, after his death, as a biography written by Florence.

Once again, one must wonder how she could acquiesce in such a literary deception. One answer is that the idea coincided with a revival of her ambitions to be known as a writer. In the summer of 1917 a new personal attachment gave a fresh impetus, in the midst of "home worries", to her natural zest for life. She found a friend who lightened the burden. In London again for inoculations under the supervision of Macleod Yearsley, Florence was taken home to meet his wife. Louisa Yearsley, herself the daughter of a physician, was lively, interesting, and sympathetic. She divined how nervous and uncertain Florence was, how repressed by the régime at Max Gate, and she drew her out and made much of her. Florence responded to Louisa, younger than herself, with the warmth and gratitude of one who has been starved. With habitual self-criticism, she at first felt she had chattered absurdly. Louisa reassured her, seeing how terrified Florence was, even of her kindly surgeon husband. "I am afraid of all these things," Florence confessed.[10] Louisa, to shake her out of the gloom of Max Gate, invited her often to their cheerful London house. "What pleasure it was to be in such a happy and delightful home," wrote Florence, unconsciously comparing the two households.[11] Louisa took her to London stores, for Florence to dream among furniture and clothes. "Max Gate furniture looks very mid-Victorian and ugly after the wonderful things we saw at Heals," Florence sighed.[12] Louisa directed Florence's unaccustomed dress-shopping; at Jaeger's, "I should have chosen an absurd golf-coat had you not been there to advise."[13] Above all, persuading her to leave Hardy for a night or so, in the care of Kate from Talbothays, the Yearsleys took her to London theatres and cinemas. "Going to a play two days in succession was a wonderful occurrence for me," wrote Florence, ruefully adding, "not likely to happen again for many years."[14] These experiences made her feel a person again; the vision of herself as a writer flamed up freshly in this new breath of pleasure. "I want to plunge anew into a literary career. I want to write a play." Yet the vision of Hardy and dog "Wessex" waiting for her on Dorchester station-platform stilled such hopes. "Of course I never shall."[15]

Florence was therefore ripe for this curious literary imposture, however strangely and dishonestly it would bring her name before an eventual public. To another friend she wrote, mysteriously, "I have a tremendous job in hand—literary."[16] The stage-management of a system, to conceal the true process of authorship, was worked out with Hardy's usual minute care and secrecy. Diaries and notebooks were used, excerpts selected to be introduced into the text and originals destroyed, with almost no exception. Letters were sorted into some kind of order, mostly by Florence, and many of these also ultimately destroyed. Hardy wrote, page by page, and this was typed by Florence. When each section of typescript was completed, his original manuscript, like the diaries, notebooks, and letters, on which it was based, was destroyed too. Alterations and additions to Florence's typescript were made by Hardy, and sometimes by Florence, in a typographical hand, possibly as an attempt at disguise.[17] Naturally, Hardy wrote throughout, and described all his doings in the third person, sometimes with deliberate vagueness, particularly when associating poems and other works with actual events and persons, as if Florence had been uncertain of the true facts. Whether even Florence was allowed to see every source is doubtful. Hardy's life up to the age of thirty is specially sparse in its quotation of letters, only a very few to his sister Mary being admitted. The originals, kept by Kate, show that even these had passages omitted. Florence was spared having to read and copy love-letters to and from Hardy and Emma during their wooing. At some tempestuous time during Hardy's first marriage, Emma not only burnt Hardy's love-letters to her, but had demanded back her letters to him, and burnt them too.[18] When Florence reached this period in his life, Hardy produced for her an edited version of sections of Emma's "Some Recollections". Luckily Emma's manuscript did not share the fate of others, and it can be seen today, with Hardy's own somewhat officious and often clumsy attempts to improve Emma's spelling, grammar, and punctuation, together with his instructions to Florence how to dovetail the pages together.

Not unnaturally, the work produced by such curious means, over the next decade, is itself a curiosity. For one thing, the extracts from Hardy's notebooks, diaries, and letters, printed as they stand, were written anything up to fifty-five years earlier. They therefore often have the freshness, interest, excitement, and thought of a comparatively young man. The linking narrative, however, is naturally that of a very old man. Moreover, it is that of a man who had not written prose for over twenty years, since the publication of his last novel. It is stiff, awkward, without trace of fire and enthusiasm, a pedestrian jog from one fact to another, often with extraordinary and clumsy circumlocutions. Among many examples, when Hardy wishes to say that he and Emma avoided the Diamond Jubilee of 1897 by choosing to go abroad, he writes,

> All the world, including the people of fashion habitually abroad, was in London or arriving there, and the charm of a lonely Continent impressed the twain much.

When such circumlocutions become most extravagant, one suspects, often rightly, that some embarrassing fact is being concealed. Above all, such a style in itself defeats the fiction that the book is written by Florence. Its allusions and idioms are all of a generation far older than her own.

The extreme contrast between the pedestrian narrative and the vivid diary and notebook entries has at any rate the effect of making the latter memorable. Remarks on poetry, painting, philosophy, nature, folklore, shine out like lumps of quartz embedded in commonplace clay. Among them runs one distinct vein which is highly individual to Hardy. Like Keats, but without his exuberant gusto, Hardy had an appetite for the grotesque, verging on the morbid. One of the few critics who has really studied this autobiography,[19] says it affords "an astonishing anthology or necrology of mortuary occasions". Hardy is shown, in Devon, "a bridge over which bastards were thrown and drowned": he recalls lovingly famous murders and hangings, and the exploits of hangmen. Grotesque country tales are recalled. A village girl bore a bastard to a squinting man, and trained the baby to squint likewise by hanging a bobbin between its eyes. This fondness for grotesque was noted by Hardy himself. He cannot go to Paris on holiday but "As was the case with Hardy almost always, a strange bizarre effect was noticed by him at the Moulin Rouge."[20] In church, he speculates on "the bizarre world of thoughts" in the minds of the congregation. Skeletons, coffins, portents, and apparitions crop up everywhere. This is to say, Hardy remains a traditional, complete countryman. The autobiography has all the virtues and vices of village gossip, admirable in human interest, but avid to chronicle disaster. It is the epitome of what Emma called "his peasant origins".

Hardy also loved to chronicle obsessively the doings of the great and famous in high society, and his own success in entering that society. He wrote long lists of fellow-guests at dinners, country houses, and dances. Even Florence found this excessive, though she copied them; in the brief months between his death and the book's publication, she curtailed many such catalogues. With Hardy, it was more than a countryman's need to gossip about the great, notorious, or beautiful. He wished to make claims for his own family. Hence arose his obsession, like that of his own John Durbeyfield in *Tess*, that the Hardys had once been important, but had come down in the world. The extraordinary effect of this was that it led him to belittle, in these pages of the autobiography, his own attractive father. Thomas Hardy senior was one of six children (four never mentioned by Hardy), whose share of cash to start a career was just over £14 each.[21] In fifty-five years, he increased this to £850, plus the considerable goodwill of a thriving business, and some valuable real estate. Yet Hardy, in order to pretend to past glories for the Hardy family, represents his father as an amiable idler, who "had not the tradesman's soul",[22] neglected his business and lost money. It is the most astonishing result of what may be called Hardy's own d'Urberville complex.

So Hardy and Florence became in several ways the prisoners of this deception they had deliberately started. The long-drawn process proved a strain on both participants. Hardy found that to read the mass of personal letters from the past thirty or forty years, before destroying them, was a searing experience. "They raise ghosts", he wrote to Sir George Douglas in May 1919, and again, in a similar vein, the following autumn. Until now, his memory had been able to select past themes for poems: now the past forced itself upon him. Yet there were, for Hardy, compensations. In the wads of paper, there were sketches and drafts of early poems themselves, which he had forgotten. These often seemed worth rescuing and revising. From now onward, many of his published poems have a note "from an old copy" or "Rewritten from an old draft". Besides, however painful, memories kept alive the poetry in him. To his surprise, he found himself, after saying farewell in 1917, actually accumulating enough verse, new and old, for a fresh book. This, appropriately called *Late Lyrics and Earlier*, gradually began to grow.

Its growth was sometimes strangely subject to the needs and demands of the course set by Hardy's mind in the autobiography. What if an experience, recorded truly in a poem, conflicted with the half-truth or concealment he had adopted in his prose account? There is a startling example of how Hardy now had to tailor even a poem to fit the story of the autobiography. As he progressed to the fateful year 1912, his version of his life laid more and more stress on how unforeseen Emma's death in that year had been: how up to the last days, he had no inkling. Yet he found a draft of a poem, written under the shock of her death, where the final stanza began in a way that showed Emma far from well in her last days.

> And that calm evening when you climbed the stair,
> After a languid rising from your chair,

Her last pain-ridden climb, night after night, up the Max Gate stairs could not be admitted by the husband, who had now produced his prose version of a wife relatively pain-free and healthy to the last. Dictated by the story he had now told in the autobiography, he completely altered the lines.

> And that calm eve when you walked up the stair,
> After a gaiety prolonged and rare,

The fact that Emma was half-weeping with pain during that last evening, on which she tried to entertain her guests, had at all costs to be denied. Even "climbed", suggesting difficulty, had to go, and the independent "walked up" substituted; while the entirely fictional "gaiety prolonged and rare" was introduced to exonerate the guilty Hardy from his neglect, so that the poem could conclude

> No thought soever
> That you might never
> Walk down again, struck me as I stood there.

Florence became even more a close prisoner and sufferer under the task she had undertaken. Reminders of Emma were everywhere. From a notebook of 1896, she found Hardy had taken Emma more than once to Brighton. Florence was morbidly sensitive on this point, since Hardy consistently refused to take her to Brighton to see her own relations— "and not poor relations, either".[23] There were worse and more wounding shocks. Her life was becoming a series of frustrating ironies, as if she were some character in Chekhov, whose stories she had just discovered, "the best thing in literature I have come across lately".[24] In Hardy's diaries, she read and copied his lament that, in their late thirties, he and Emma had no child. Florence was now in her own late thirties; she had no hope of a child herself. In May 1918, her friend, Louisa Yearsley, had a baby son. In November, Florence's own sister Marjorie had one also. Florence's thoughts were resigned and sombre. "There is nothing like having a child I am convinced. It gives purpose and dignity to life; it should make middle-age and old-age beautiful and contented."[25] Such beauty and content were not for her, while there were even more ominous reminders of her own coming middle-age. In 1919, Lilian Gifford, a year younger than Florence, had a severe menopausal breakdown. Though she ultimately recovered, it confined her for over a year in a London asylum, where Florence had to visit her for Hardy.[26] The strain of copy-typing his book, in intervals of house-keeping, was increased by his ever-increasing correspondence. On his eightieth birthday in 1920, there were 200 telegrams of congratulation for Florence to answer. She burst out to St. John Ervine in 1921 that during the last seven years she had only been away from Max Gate for one clear week, and that, in 1915, spent in a nursing-home. "I begin to feel the strain mentally."[27] It was an understatement.

There were, of course, compensations and light relief. In the excitement of writing to a rich Middle-West book-collector, with a well-appointed house in Ohio, Florence determined, early in 1919, to get something done about the main inconvenience of Max Gate. This was the water, pumped from a well, heated in saucepans and kettles over the kitchen fire, and poured into hip-baths—"no bathroom even. I expect this is the only house of this size in Dorchester without."[28] She got to work on Hardy, and, though moving slowly, by October he was consulting brother Henry about hot water systems.[29] In August 1920, "a bathroom with a glorious big bath and lots of very hot water" delighted Florence, who added, "I tremble to think what T.H. will say when he has to pay the bill."[30] He had been partly persuaded by hopes of a Nobel Prize that year. The *Daily Mail* had advocated his claims in an article entitled "Our Greatest", and Florence, who had just bought bacon from Selfridge's through the Yearsleys, commented, "If he does get the Nobel Prize . . . we shall be able to have bacon from Selfridge's for breakfast every day."[31] Though the award to Knut Hamsun disappointed their hopes, there were other tributes pleasing to Hardy. The praises on his eightieth birthday were universal and included a special deputation from the Society of Authors, though Hardy probably enjoyed best "a really most elegant speech of congratulation" by the postman.[32] The year before, he received a tribute, organized by Siegfried Sassoon, of a volume of holograph poems by nearly fifty living poets. The year after, 1921, he received a birthday address from 106 younger writers, together with a first edition of the 1820 volume of

Keats, whom he himself celebrated shortly afterwards in two haunting poems.

In 1919, his publishers arranged for his *Collected Poems* in two volumes and in 1919–20 for a *de luxe* printing of all his works, poetry and prose, the Mellstock Edition, on paper watermarked with Hardy's initials.[33] In 1920, Oxford gave him an honorary D.Lit., and the O.U.D.S. performed *The Dynasts* on the same occasion, while he and Florence were there.

Florence consoled herself for her husband's difficult temperament by realizing that it was remarkable for him still to be writing at the age of nearly eighty.[34] She paid tribute to his qualities by having her baby nephew named Thomas after Hardy, "whom I hope he may resemble in as many ways as possible".[35] Everyone was impressed by him. At seventy-five, in 1915, Galsworthy found him "a nice alert old fellow".[36] At nearly eighty, in 1920, the undergraduate manager of O.U.D.S., Charles Morgan, saw him as "sprightly, alert, birdlike".[37] Only along two lines did he show the effects of age, or any sign of senile obsession. The first, common enough in the old, and part of his native temperament, was excessive closeness over money. His refusal, in 1915, to pay Florence's surgeon, was only a start. In 1917, her London inoculations cost her £100, though "If I were a Gifford of course all this would be paid for me."[38] In 1918, this trait developed into a resentful suspicion that other people might make money out of his works. Hearing that dealers and collectors were profiting from signed copies, he refused to autograph books, even for close friends. He actually prepared for the unfortunate Florence a formal letter of refusal to autograph books except for charities, whom he would alone wish to benefit, "and he has alas, nothing to spare in cash". Sending such a statement for her rich husband at once put Florence into difficulty, especially as he was not even consistent. He autographed many books for Paul Lemperly, the wealthy American collector, in return for presents of sugar, candies, chocolate, and sugar wafers for his own sweet tooth, skilfully begged by Florence.[39]

Hardy's other out-of-hand obsession was his impatience over literary criticism. Visiting him at Max Gate, just after going down from Oxford, Charles Morgan was embarrassed at his complaints about contemporary critics. "I could not understand what general reason he had to complain of them."[40] About the same time, Florence found him talking to himself, "and I heard a few sentences about critics—of what nature you may guess".[41] He was now so childishly touchy that she had the unenviable task of preventing his seeing even the mildest printed criticism. "As it was in the [London] Mercury I naturally thought it would be at least a just estimate," she lamented when one such article slipped through her net.[42] E. M. Forster at this time considered Hardy "very vain" to take magazine criticism so badly. Hardy was particularly enraged when criticism was mixed with attempted biography. Once more, as his concocted autobiography progressed, he was the prisoner of his own invented life-story, and had to stick to it at all costs, even at the cost of truth. Florence began to catch her husband's vituperative style. When Llewellyn Powys, returned from five years in Africa, wrote a quite innocent account of a conversation with Hardy, Florence commented,[43] "We were told he was a lion hunter from Central Africa, and he proved to be a lion hunter of another type"; she sent an angry letter to the unfortunate Powys.

This, in the summer of 1922, coincided with the most violent outburst of Hardy's obsession. Fifteen years before, a young scholar, F. A. Hedgcock, who was preparing a thesis in French for the University of Paris, wrote for information to help with his study, *Thomas Hardy, Penseur et Artiste*. He asked questions which, though expressed with diffidence, were innocently tactless. "Is it possible to enquire what your studies at King's College comprised?" was natural enough, for a French thesis; but an honest answer would have revealed the elementary nature of Hardy's French classes there. After three years, Hedgcock obtained an interview through Gosse, assuring Hardy, "I shall bring none of the aggressiveness of the interviewer";[44] and indeed he found Hardy very uncommunicative on personal matters. His published thesis arrived in 1911; Hardy pencilled in it, "Biographical details . . . mostly wrong", and forgot this apparently minor work in a foreign language.

On 22 June 1922, however, a somewhat casual letter arrived at Max Gate from Vere Collins, a director of the Oxford University Press, on holiday in Skye. Collins proposed the Press should issue an English version of Hedgcock's book, which Collins himself would translate. Hardy at once sent a telegram disapproving of "publication in English as it stands", and a series of letters, five in three weeks, followed. Hardy heavily annotated Hedgcock's early biographical chapters. He enlarged, to fit his own version, the Bockhampton birthplace, "seven-roomed . . . and rambling . . . with a paddock and till lately stablings"; he exaggerated his own education, "Greek & Latin", he denied that the Dorset dialect was "spoken in his mother's house". He was furious at the quite unmistakable likeness in early novels between his architect-heroes and himself—"impertinent and unmannerly in its personalities". Hedgcock was told, through Florence, at Hardy's dictation, that a translation could not appear unless all personal details "be omitted except those authenticated by Mr. Hardy". He replied, with dignity, that "far from seeking to pry into private matters", his book was a serious philosophic study, an example of "criticism à la Taine, into which ancestry, environment, all enter as determining factors". He withdrew, but stipulated, reasonably, that all Hardy's notes about his "inaccuracies" should be destroyed as damaging to his own professional reputation.[45]

Instantly, a similar incident occurred. Professor Samuel Chew, of Bryn Mawr, had visited the Hardys in 1921, and in 1922 they received his monograph on Hardy. In September he asked for comments for revision, and received more than he bargained for, pages of typescript notes from Florence, on the exact lines of Hardy's annotations to Hedgcock. The Bockhampton cottage had now grown even larger, "House and premises . . . with two gardens, horse-paddock, sand and gravel pits . . . and outbuildings." The Hardys became a "landed" family. Any resemblance between Hardy and his heroes is false. "Jude was a working man, not at all in Hardy's position . . . there is not one word of autobiography." Hardy was deeply stung by one commonplace criticism, his inability to portray Society. "Eveline 5th Countess of Portsmouth obtained an introduction to the author because this novel [*The Hand of Ethelberta*] was the *only* one she had lately met with which 'showed society people as they really were'." Poor Chew was made to pay for his innocent request.[46] "Is this banal fact worth stating?" was the mildest of Hardy's comments on what the author doubtless considered a complimentary book.

Some of this may be explained, though hardly excused, by the fact that a few months earlier, in January and February, 1922, Hardy had a recurrence of his chronic inflammation of the bladder. At his age it was serious, and two doctors and Florence's sister, the nurse, Eva Dugdale, were called in. Hardy, even more in character, spent his time in bed writing a long introduction to the new book of poems he had just sent to the publishers. It was in the main yet another swingeing attack on critics. "Some of his friends"— probably Gosse and Cockerell, whom he consulted—"regretted this preface, thinking it betrayed an over-sensitiveness to criticism." Hardy brazened it out by claiming that, as a poet, he had a right to be sensitive.[47]

The deepest root of these obsessions lay in the fear that his poetry would not be appreciated as much as his novels. Florence commented later that year, "He thinks it impossible for any book to be good that treats only of his novels";[48] the well-meaning Chew was told that his sympathetic treatment of the poems "would bear lengthening" to do justice to what "the best critics acknowledge" as Hardy's finest work. Rejoicing in his self-made miracle that he was still writing poems in his eighties, he determined that the world should recognize it. For all the often-told story of his enclosing a stamped addressed envelope with poetry for magazines, he was the opposite of modest about his verse. He had much justification. Though *Late Lyrics and Earlier* is not as satisfying a volume as *Moments of Vision*, it is an astonishing collection for a man in his eighties, and shows all sides of him. As usual, the narrative poems are least happy. There were about half-a-dozen of these, mostly about fictional women, all somewhat oddities. The longest, so much in the style of Browning as to risk parody, is about a woman organist, dismissed for her immoral life, who commits suicide in the organ loft; another is about the ghost of a prostitute, who died in the Lock Hospital for Venereal Diseases, while a third was a Gothic fantasy, written fifteen years before, about a widow haunted by the memorial brass in which she vowed not to wed again. In contrast with these laboured efforts, the lyrics, old and new, are among Hardy's best. The Bockhampton cottage was now so full of memories, that he found it painful to visit, especially after having to break into it with Barrie one day in May 1921.[49] Yet it provided him with a perfect lyric of a place where wild life always stood at the lonely threshold, peering in, *The Fallow Deer at the Lonely House.*

> One without looks in tonight
>     Through the curtain-chink
> From the sheet of glistening white;
> One without looks in tonight
>     As we sit and think
>     By the fender-brink
>
> We do not discern those eyes
>     Watching in the snow;
> Lit by lamps of rosy dyes
> We do not discern those eyes
>     Wondering, aglow,
>     Fourfooted, tiptoe.

The lyric background to the birthplace, the rhythms of folk-songs from his mother and father, pervade this collection. One West Country folk tune, which he had already used for a poem in the early months of the war,[50] provided the basis for two more poems here, *Meditations on a Holiday* and *The Colour*. The same folk-rhythm that had been heard in *Beyond the Last Lamp* was heard again in *Voices from Things Growing in a Churchyard*; the poem itself was an offshoot of "his favourite walk" to the Stinsford family graves, where Florence found it "so depressing to go and look at the tomb under which I shall probably lie some day— very soon I think".[51] Her own trials were, of course, augmented by the usual large quota of poems concerned with Emma, about thirty in all. There was some comfort that these did not idealize the first marriage so whole-heartedly; its early years were now poignantly summarized as

> A preface without any book,
> A trumpet uplipped, but no call;

Florence was allowed one of his rare tributes to herself in a moving and beautiful lyric, ending

> . . . For one did care,
> And, spiriting into my house, to, fro
> Like wind on the stair,
> Cares still, heeds all, and will, even though
> I may despair.

Hardy, for all the tortuous deceptions of his outward life, was seldom anything but honest in poetry. Stress of poetic utterance forced the truth from him. As he approached the final pages of the book, he faced the problem of which poem to put last. In *Moments of Vision*, the poem *Afterwards* was intended to be his personal summary of a long life. Now that life had prolonged itself for five more unexpected years, what self-portrait should he now give? Mean or even uncharitable as many of his recent actions were, he had not lost the penetrating power of self-knowledge, or self-criticism. He could realize in poetry what he would not admit in life. In a mood only approached by W. B. Yeats, in his own old age, Hardy faced himself and his betrayals. He used an image centred on the cottage fireside, now more real to him than any other scene. He recalled his mother's saying, as the green and wet wood sighed and muttered in the flames, that it was his own voice talking to him. The primitive fancy, together with that other childhood echo, the resounding texts from the New Testament, mingled into a message of humility that spanned his experience, as he comprehended it in the title of the poem, *Surview*.

> A cry from the green-grained sticks of the fire
>     Made me gaze where it seemed to be:
> 'Twas my own voice talking therefrom to me
> On how I had walked when my sun was higher—
>     My heart in its arrogancy.
>
> *"You held not to whatsoever was true,"*
>     Said my own voice talking to me:
> *"Whatsoever was just you were slack to see;*
> *Kept not things lovely and pure in view,"*
>     Said my own voice talking to me.
>
> *"You slighted her that endureth all,"*
>     Said my own voice talking to me;
> *"Vaunteth not, trusteth hopefully;*
> *That suffereth long and is kind withal,"*
>     Said my own voice talking to me.
>
> *"You taught not that which you set about,"*
>     Said my own voice talking to me;
> *"That the greatest of things is charity . . ."*
> —And the sticks burnt low, and the fire went out,
>     And my voice ceased talking to me.

# 15

# A Human Show

FOR a man well into his eighties, Hardy continued to show remarkable activity and freshness of mind and body. There were, of course, his twin obsessions, money and the imbecility of critics, which could still rouse him to malevolent grumbles. There was also, and again naturally, an elderly conviction that the country was going to the dogs. With post-war freedoms, and bright young manifestations in the arts and in society, the 1920s was a great decade for gloomy and moralistic prophets of doom. Dean Inge's *Outspoken Essays*, that cleric's profitable ventures into popular journalism, were favoured reading with Hardy, and, indeed, with Florence also.[1] Hardy himself could contribute suitable warnings of disaster. "England and Europe", he wrote to Galsworthy in 1921, "do not look particularly attractive in their political aspects."[2] He added the conviction, historically unjustified though heard in various guises during this century, that books would decay, and the only form of writing would be "for football and boxing journals", and for the cinema. He spoke of a new "dark age".

In spite of such pessimistic judgements, Hardy was in fact as much involved in the demands of literature as he had been in the busiest periods of his life. He corrected with keen attention the proofs of his *Collected Poems* and of the Mellstock edition of his works. Proof-correction with him meant meticulous revision, and he did not spare himself. "He allows nothing to interfere with his morning's work," wrote Florence,[3] rather ruefully, since all the extraneous chores of an author, such as answering letters, and dealing with requests and permissions, now fell on her. The task was sometimes less than amusing. She found herself faced by communications such as that of the exasperated correspondent, who wrote, "Dear Sir, I am wondering why the devil you don't answer letters!"[4]

Nor was Hardy's literary work by any means solely revision. In spite of eye trouble, his only physical defect, and one to which the dim oil-lamps at Max Gate must have added, he was actually in his eighty-fourth year producing new work. This proved, of all things, to be a play. *The Famous Tragedy of the Queen of Cornwall* is both a literary and dramatic curiosity, and, on its own terms, a very considerable achievement. The Tristram and Iseult story had, of course, an immense attraction for Hardy since his own Cornish wooing fifty years before, renewed by his revisitings there with the reluctant Florence. Indeed his dedication of the printed version shows how, when obsessed, he could be unconsciously cruel. The play is inscribed to Emma, her sister, her brother-in-law, and Florence, "those with whom I formerly spent many hours at the scene of the tradition, who have now all passed away save one". He seemed oblivious that the "many hours" spent by the survivor, Florence, had meant her acquiescence in what she considered a lie about the past, while he eulogized "an Iseult of my own", Emma. Apart from such considerations, there was an ironic compression in the writing; much of this stemmed from the construction of the play. Hardy decided to maintain the unities of time and place as, he remembered, he had done with *The Return of the Native*. His one hour of events, from Tristram's return to the death of the lovers, was composed in strict Greek tragedy form, with Chorus. Wishing "to avoid turning the rude personages of, say, the fifth century, into respectable Victorians, as was done by Tennyson, Swinburne, Arnold etc.",[5] Hardy used a style of verse which was classically laconic, but whose convoluted brevity was more in the manner of Browning, "intricate oddity", as one critic remarked.[6] It was certainly too difficult for the local players, who were entrusted with first performance in Dorchester in November 1923, and in London early next year. Yet the dramatic power, even in awkward phrases, was unmistakable. Florence, whatever her feelings over the dedication, judged the play itself, *"really* good".[7] Granville-Barker flirted with the idea of a professional production, while Rutland Boughton found the brief text ideal for the libretto of an opera, which he composed, and which was successfully performed at the Glastonbury Music Festival.

The creative vitality of Hardy's life was due in large measure to his lifelong self-discipline in reading and note-taking. This had continued steadily since he first started in the 1860s. In the 1890s when he began to turn from prose to poetry, his main reading naturally took the same direction. There was always a steady interest in philosophy, and extracts from Schopenhauer, Haeckel, and Von Hartmann are prominent; but the emphasis gradually changes to poetry and to theories of how to write poems. He copied many paragraphs, at various times, from a periodical called *Literature*, and from the *Quarterly Review* on "English Prosody". The last, in July 1911, is notable in that half his extract is copied for him in Florence's hand, showing that over a year before Emma's death, she had taken Emma's place as notebook amanuensis. Appreciation of modern poetry, in his notebooks, was disappointingly small. He was still suspicious of the "Georgians", and seems not to have heard of the Imagists. It is true that he copied two long extracts from "Prufrock"; but he got these at second-hand from a publication by S. P. B. Mais called *From Shelley to O. Henry*, and annotated them merely as an example of the work of "T. S. Eliot—a poet of the vers libre school".[8]

He was, however, keenly alive to all forms of twentieth-century thought. In January 1920, he extracted from the *Quarterly Review* A. S. Eddington's article on Einstein, and on 21 June 1921, Florence wrote that he "ponders over Einstein's Theory of Relativity in the night".[9] He referred to Einstein in poems and other notebooks, and was clearly fascinated by the implications of the idea of relativity. Though, as always, politics found little place in his life and thought, he extracted from *The Times* long reviews of books on scientific humanism, and notably one about Spengler's *The Decline of the West*.

His intellectual life seemed to burn brighter as his body grew feebler. Not that his physical energies showed much of the flagging one would expect from a man of his age. Only a few months after his severe illness of February 1922, the summer found him bicycling, at the age of eighty-two, over to Talbothays to see Kate and Henry. Nor did he, as he got older, shy off from social occasions as much as he had done in the war years. London society, of course, was now too much, but his London ladies, such as Florence Henniker and Agnes Grove, were welcome guests still. He had even more noteworthy callers. On 20 July 1923, Hardy achieved one of the highest of those social distinctions so dear to him. Edward, Prince of Wales, drove through the streets of Dorchester with him, and afterwards lunched at Max Gate. True, there were Hardyesque ironies even in this event. The Prince was late coming downstairs for lunch, and Florence, hovering anxiously, heard a violent quarrel between him and the equerry. The Max Gate staff was inadequate for their needs, and the gardener, having opened the gate, nipped round to the back door, and did double duty serving the meal. "The eldest son of the sovereign has never before, I think, paid such a compliment to literature," Florence proudly meditated;[10] but Max Beerbohm's amusing parody of the occasion probably comes nearer the truth. Nor was it without strain. Kate Hardy found Tom and Florence "very highly strung" after it.[11]

For Florence generally, life was very much a mingled yarn of dark and light threads. Intellectually, she was gaining confidence through increasing responsibility, however exhausting this might be. The floods of letters to be answered, from his eightieth birthday onward, might be "a nightmare", "an avalanche". The mechanical tasks of the auto-biography were hers too. By 1919, she had only brought her arrangement and sorting of Hardy's correspondence up to 1900—"nineteen years more to do". Yet her work was now more than secretarial, and involved a considerable amount of trust. It also gave her experience in handling literary matters, which her past history of little books for children had hardly provided. One literary venture, with which she was entrusted, was the printing in pamphlet form of small separate works by Hardy, mostly poems. This originated oddly in competition with Clement Shorter, the editor of *The Sphere*, who had at one time given her employment. Shorter between 1914 and 1916 had printed half-a-dozen such pamphlets himself in a series called "A Bookman's Hobby". These printings were irksome to Hardy, and Cockerell advised that Hardy or his wife should prevent them by producing their own. Florence was allowed this welcome task, and from 1916 to Hardy's death, several appeared at irregular intervals under her supervision; though details were also overseen by Cockerell himself, it gave her more of a stake in Hardy's work than she had hitherto been allowed.[12]

Intellectually, she also began to gain confidence from welcome literary visitors. Max Gate was not so isolated as she was apt to complain in moments of depression—"I feel rather covered with blue mould."[13] Sassoon, de la Mare, E. M. Forster, Galsworthy, T. E. Lawrence were favoured guests, Barrie a frequent one. She entertained Charlotte Mew, and felt great fondness for her, and admiration for her work—"She has genius, I think".[14] It was a far cry from the children's stories in the *Enfield Gazette*, for Florence to be in such literary company. Her judgements became clearer, though too often tinged with personal feeling. She distrusted Edward Clodd's account of Meredith, largely because she knew Clodd had the key to some of her own secrets. Yet stimulating company made her grow as a person. She took her place locally, though always remembering how Hardy had criticized Emma for running after local people, and agreeing with him. "The local clergy are the greatest sinners. They want to make T.H. a spectacle."[15] There was even a visit from a bishop—"It does get a bit stifling at times". In February 1924, she became a Borough Magistrate,[16] a position Hardy himself had held to the end of the war, yet repudiated the idea of having too close Dorset connections. "I do not think I could ever bring myself to live at a place called Puddletown",[17] where numerous Hardy relations still lived. She openly preferred the local aristocracy, like the Ilchesters, and felt herself of their world.

Nor were her preoccupations exclusively intellectual and literary. Thanks mainly to kind friends, like the Yearsleys, she made periodic, though brief escapes from the Max Gate atmosphere to more frivolous pursuits. A few months before the crushing duties of her husband's eightieth birthday, she spent her last two hours of one such visit to London having alterations made to "a quite delightful little evening gown—a very full skirt of petunia coloured charmeuse . . . the bodice entirely of gold lace". Even over this pleasure hung the shadow of missing the train back to Dorchester, with Hardy waiting. Another pleasure was the installation at Max Gate of a telephone, so that,

Hardy grumbled, she could talk to her friends in London, though he himself regarded the instrument with obstinate suspicion.

On the other hand, Florence had a heavy load of nervous and physical problems, quite apart from the nightmare of managing a house totally unfitted for domestic comfort. On the physical side, Hardy's life and her own were becoming like some terrible fairy tale. He threw off illnesses, even the serious one of February 1922, and seemed to become in some ways more spry and active as his years mounted, while she continually worsened in health, as if his incredible life was feeding on the failing vitality of hers. In 1920, in spite of the many inoculations two years before, Florence was, she wrote to Louisa Yearsley,[18] "feeling all anyhow", and was *"afraid"* she would have to see the surgeon again. On 29 October 1922, the local doctor, Gowring, advised the removal of a gland from Florence's neck.[19] At the beginning of the following year, Florence had her neck X-rayed. One trouble was Hardy's peasant unwillingness to allow surgery. On 7 June 1923, he himself wrote to Macleod Yearsley asking whether the gland in Florence's neck really needed an operation.[20] He ended typically, "I rather wish it could be dispensed with altogether, if you think no further harm would arise beyond the slight disfigurement it causes, which we do not mind." One wonders whether "we" really included Florence. Photographs round about this time showed her strained expression. The thistledown lightness Hardy once praised had changed to a watchful, anxious look. In spite of physical stress, she could still manage a joke. On one of her rare visits to London, late in 1923, she wrote, "I stayed the night at Barrie's flat, and whether it was the effect of my presence there . . . he was taken to a nursing home the next day."[21] Nine months later, Florence herself was in a London nursing-home. Though Yearsley had at first agreed with Hardy not to touch the gland, the operation for its removal now appeared urgent. She entered the Fitzroy House Nursing Home on 29 September 1924, and the operation took place the next day.

Florence returned from her ten days in the Fitzroy House Nursing Home, in a hired car, driven by Henry Hardy and the Dorchester garage hand, Voss.[22] Weak, nervous, and run-down, so much aged that, though only forty-five, she looked almost an old woman, she soon found herself facing one of the worst trials in her whole life. Whether or not this was largely a figment of weakness and illness, allied with her own uncertain temperament, it is necessary to go back, at this point, over the past seventeen years.

In 1908, the year Part III of *The Dynasts* was published, the Dorchester Debating, Literary and Dramatic Society was addressed by one of its members on Napoleon's threatened invasion of England. Another member, A. H. Evans, had the idea that a dramatized scene from

Hardy's *The Trumpet-Major* would help to illustrate the lecture. From this arose the project that the Society, instead of Shakespeare, Goldsmith or Sheridan, should perform a full dramatic adaptation of Hardy's novel. Evans, father of the famous actor Maurice Evans, made an episodic version of scenes, stressing the comedy. He persuaded Hardy to agree to this, to write additional dialogue himself, and actually to suggest and sanction a happy ending, instead of the dark final curtain of the book. Otherwise, fidelity to detail was fanatical. Genuine old pikes and firelocks were used, uniforms copied from those still existing in family attics. On 18 November, the play attracted not only a local audience but many London critics to the improvised theatre in Dorchester Corn Exchange. So began an annual custom of presenting a Hardy play at about that date, to which was added a London performance each December at the Cripplegate Institute and elsewhere to an audience of the Society of Dorset Men in London. These ritual performances were taken over by a Dorchester builder, T. H. Tilley, and continued, to a limited extent, through the war, during which the Wessex scenes from *The Dynasts* and some love-scenes from *Far From the Madding Crowd* were given. Hardy showed a great interest in all rehearsals, and in 1910 for *The Mellstock Quire*, a version of *Under the Greenwood Tree*, he supplied old carols; at one rehearsal, though seventy, he nimbly stepped forward to demonstrate one of the old country-dances.[23]

In 1913, the chosen play was an adaptation of *The Woodlanders*. Hardy, this time, insisted on the tragic ending of the novel, with Marty South's poignant speech at Giles's grave. The words were spoken by a seventeen-year-old girl, Gertrude Bugler, daughter of a South Street, Dorchester, confectioner. Her performance moved even the London critics, and on 20 November, her picture in costume appeared in the *Daily Mail*.[24] She was a natural actress, slender, with expressive eyes and very dark hair. When the plays were fully revived in 1920, she was an obvious choice for Eustacia Vye in *The Return of the Native*, which she performed brilliantly, particularly in the scene where Eustacia joins the Christmas Mummers. The happy idea was conceived that the Players should perform the mumming play at Max Gate. When they did, Gertrude Bugler charmed not only Hardy but also Florence, who wrote, "She is a beautiful creature, only 24, and really nice and refined." At the same time, there was a puzzle. "She tells everyone she is taking my advice *not* to go on the stage and I am puzzled as to *when* I did give that advice." She concluded that the advice must have been Hardy's, and joked about Hardy's partiality for Miss Bugler, whom she herself greatly liked.[25] Florence had, as a matter of fact, already discussed the idea of a stage career with Gertrude Bugler, but offered no advice.

No play was produced in 1921. The play for 1922 was *A Desperate Remedy*, a version, with slightly altered title, of Hardy's first published novel. Gertrude Bugler was cast; but in 1921, she had married a farming cousin, also named Bugler, and by May 1922 she was pregnant. She told the society's secretary she must resign the part. Hardy was disappointed, and a message reached her that he would like her to call at Max Gate for one of his books, which he had inscribed for her. Early in June, she called, and was received by Florence with a total absence of her former friendliness. She returned, puzzled, to Beaminster, where she now lived, to be followed on 13 June by a letter of violent complaint from Florence, rebuking her for her call. "It is simply 'not done' in our station of life for any lady to call on a gentleman . . . I am regarded and treated as hostess."[26] One wonders that Florence's two grandfathers, one in his butcher's shop, the other in his smithy, did not cross her mind as she wrote of "our station in life"; but she had by now adopted Hardy's own facility for adjusting the past to fit the present. Mrs. Bugler, so far as she could understand the drift of Florence's letter, wrote back with spirit and common sense; and there the matter rested. Unhappily, Mrs. Bugler's child died at birth about the time of the November play performance.

These stage productions had stimulated Hardy's desire, never far below the surface, though he often denied it, to write in dramatic form. A talented amateur actress was also a stimulus, and *The Queen of Cornwall* was created, with the leading part intended for Mrs. Bugler. The players assembled at Max Gate to read through the difficult verse-speeches. Mrs. Bugler was a fine verse-speaker, among her other accomplishments, but once more she was not to play the part. Another baby, happily to be safely delivered, was found to be on the way, and again she had to resign. She managed, however, a long and friendly talk with Florence, and affairs seemed to be on the old footing.

It was an ambition among some of the Hardy Players, as they had come to be called, to stage *Tess of the d'Urbervilles*, though there was a certain nervousness about how Dorchester would take a work still thought to be immoral. However, in 1924, Hardy resurrected for them his own dramatic version, made in the 1890s, and never performed on any stage, since Stoddard had rewritten it so drastically for production in New York. Hardy's original version was being rehearsed by the Players when Florence returned from her operation early in October. Gertrude Bugler was to play Tess, in spite of the responsibility of a very young child at home. Quite apart from the recent operation, Florence had many things on her mind. In June, she had written to the sympathetic Louisa Yearsley,[27] "I do wish you were nearer so that we could discuss all sort of things that one cannot write about." As well as these unmentioned problems, Florence added that the difficulty of housekeeping, unrealized by Hardy, "is almost enough to drive anyone into an asylum".[28]

The first night of *Tess* took place on 26 November. Hardy did not attend, being terrified of strangers at first nights, one of whom had actually "*asked him questions*, a thing he hates".[29] At the dress rehearsal and other performances, however, he was wildly excited, and, as one eye-witness noticed, more often in the wings than in the auditorium. The four nights and a matinee in Dorchester were followed by two performances at the Pavilion Theatre, Weymouth. The Mayor of Weymouth gave a dinner to the company, and Gertrude Bugler sat at Hardy's right hand. Florence was noticeably irritable and nervous during these days. Early in December, Mrs. Bugler, back in Beaminster, received an extraordinary letter from Florence, strained and angry, but impossible to understand; nor could her husband interpret it when she handed it to him. Almost immediately, on 9 December, there followed a telegram and another letter. This letter was in a style familiar to many people who had received violent epistles from Florence. Her first letter, Florence now wrote, had been written when she was "completely unstrung and utterly miserable". She mentioned her operation, only two months ago. She hoped that Mrs. Bugler had burnt the letter. In fact, Mrs. Bugler kept it, but returned it after Hardy's death. Its exact contents have escaped Mrs. Bugler's memory.

There was quiet for a month; but Gertrude Bugler's superb performance with its "reserve, pathos, and charm" had won appreciation in other places than Dorchester. On 8 January 1925, Frederick Harrison, who managed the Haymarket in London, wrote to ask if Gertrude Bugler would play Tess with a professional cast at his theatre. The scheme was to stage in April or May a series of matinees, while John Barrymore was appearing in a six weeks' season as Hamlet. If the matinees caught on, *Tess* would go into evening performance, after Barrymore returned to America. Hardy had written a new prologue-scene at Harrison's suggestion, and fresh lines for a later scene. Mrs. Bugler went to Max Gate to discuss these with Harrison and Hardy. Salary and rehearsal-times were agreed upon.[30] Florence was helpful and kind, suggesting where Mrs. Bugler might stay in London, and reassuring her that other actresses with husband and child had managed their careers successfully.

Mrs. Bugler returned to Beaminster, and began to learn her new lines; but one day, in the second half of January, came another telegram from Florence, followed almost immediately by Florence herself, announcing that she was there without Hardy's knowledge. She had come to implore Mrs. Bugler to give up the idea of playing in London. Hardy was in an excited state; he would want to go to London, and might damage his health. Florence herself spoke wildly of a poem written by Hardy about an elopement, which she had burnt. Mrs. Bugler found this an alarming interview. She did not at once agree, though Florence followed up with a letter written on 25 January, saying that it would be "a tragedy to go to London". Early in February, Mrs. Bugler wrote to both Harrison and Hardy, renouncing the part. A happier, though long delayed sequel, came in the year after Hardy's death. The two women met again as friends, and Florence invited Mrs. Bugler to play in a revival, which Philip Ridgeway was staging at the Duke of York's. She played with great success, with her name in lights as "Thomas Hardy's Own Tess". One of the company paid her the tribute of praising her performance "with that huge part surrounded by a lot of hard-baked professionals".[31]

Mrs. Bugler remembered Hardy as a man of the generation of her own grandfather—he had died in 1918—who had been kind to her, and who had said, as he walked with her down the Max Gate drive, after the meeting there with Frederick Harrison, "if anyone asks you if you knew Thomas Hardy, say, 'Yes, he was my friend'." That afternoon, on 12 January 1925, the assiduous Sydney Cockerell was also present. Nearly forty years later in February 1964, long after Florence's death, Mrs. Bugler received a rough draft of the chapter by Cockerell's biographer entitled "Thomas and Florence Hardy". Florence had been right when she wrote, as far back as October 1916, that Cockerell "takes notes of conversations here". Cockerell recorded in his diary for 10, 11, and 12 January that there was "a cloud" over Max Gate, and gave Florence's words. She had said Hardy was absorbed in Mrs. Bugler. He was off-hand with Florence, spoke roughly to her, showed her she was in the way, and forgot her birthday (the 12th)—as, incidentally, Florence always said he had done with Emma's. Florence had felt in the night she would go mad, and wondered if it were her time of life; she was now forty-five. As late as the following August, she returned, on a walk with Cockerell, to the topic of what Cockerell called Hardy's "infatuation" with Mrs. Bugler. Hearing of all this for the first time, Mrs. Bugler wrote a calm and sensible letter, much as she had done after Florence's first outburst in 1922, and it is printed in Cockerell's biography.[32]

It is virtually impossible to make any final judgement on what these occurrences meant, but there are a few certain points. Florence certainly hinted to Gertrude Bugler that Hardy was easily carried away when talking to a young woman, though it is not sure what incidents in his past she had in mind. Mrs. Bugler believed, as was suggested by Hardy's inscriptions in books to her, that he saw in her the heroines of some of his most deeply-felt novels come to life through her performances. It is also certain that only a few days after Mrs. Bugler renounced the part, in February 1925, Florence sent a violent and hurtful letter to the elderly Rebekah Owen. Almost immediately, on 16 February, she followed with another letter to Miss Owen of contrition and appeal. "Please burn it, and forgive and forget." She added, "I have had a rather bad nervous illness and am still feeling unwell."[33] People noticed that at this time she had a nervous tic, a habit of pursing or twisting her mouth when talking, particularly at the beginning of a conversation.[34]

Also, within the next few weeks, Florence took a more than usually angry and unbalanced part over yet another book which aroused Hardy's indignation. A young American graduate, Ernest Brennecke, junior, of Columbia University, had brought out in 1924 a short critical study, *Thomas Hardy's Universe*. This was intended as only the first part of his doctoral dissertation, and early in 1925 he produced a biographical part, *The Life of Thomas Hardy*, virtually the first independent attempt at biography. He had visited Max Gate, and been given lunch. Unluckily, Brennecke, as many more distinguished overseas enquirers were to do, had made a muddle of his notes when writing them up, and his mistakes, trival in themselves, roused Florence's extreme wrath. To her disproportionate anger, he had described the Max Gate lunch wrongly. "We loathe plum tart and custard," wrote Florence, and surmised he had confused this with some hotel meal in Dorchester. He had committed the solecism of showing the non-smoking Hardy with a cigarette between his lips. Worst of all, he had reproduced the "most revolting" photograph of Florence in motoring costume, taken at Oxford in 1920, which she had been lamenting to her friends ever since. Her tone was vindictive to a degree, verging on paranoia. "I disliked the man when I first saw him, and he must have realised this, which accounts for the way in which he writes of me."[35] Not that Hardy was far behind, sending a cable of protest to Brennecke's New York publishers, repudiating the book through Macmillan, and threatening an injunction for breach of copyright.[36] Such anger over an innocuous book, with its foolish but harmless statements, was excessive; but Brennecke had fallen over the perpetual stumbling-block in mentioning Hardy's lack of formal education.

One luckier American visitor, who got away with a whole skin this summer, was a nephew of Mark Twain, Cyril Clemens. He indeed claimed later that Hardy confided to him the process by which he and Florence were constructing the concealed autobiography, now very nearly up to date. Though he probably embroidered and expanded this from other sources, such as J. M. Barrie's reminiscences, there is no cause to doubt him, as other overseas visitors later in the field have done. The same information also slipped out to an English writer, Lascelles Abercrombie, who in his *Encyclopedia Britannica* bibliography of Hardy in 1929, mentioned a "Memoir" or autobiography in Hardy's Works, and got castigated by other bibliographers for his pains.

For, amazingly, considering Hardy's age, Florence's trials, and all other distractions, the work of collecting, examining, editing, and shaping the past still went on. So did its greatest by-product, the finding and reviving of old poems, the reliving of old themes to provide new poetry. Some memories lay too deep. The death in April 1923 of Mrs. Henniker "after a friendship of 30 years", produced only a laconic note in the autobiography,[37] and no poems. Yet steadily the poems, revised, restored, and newly written, grew to a book of the same size as *Late Lyrics and Earlier*, and by summer 1925 it was ready for the press, under its first title of *Poems Imaginative and Incidental*, soon changed to *Human Shows, Far Phantasies* as being, Hardy wrote, "not quite so commonplace". In spite of the change of title, the collection still verges on the commonplace when compared with some of Hardy's others. Many of the early rescued and revised poems, *Retty's Phases*, for instance, seem trivial, and only interesting when, as in this instance, there is an original manuscript—as early as 1868—to show that Hardy's shaping hand, even in old age, had not lost its skill. The technical improvements to *The Birdcatcher's Boy*, now first collected here, have been mentioned. Yet, in spite of one long narrative poem, and one in dramatic or at least dialogue form, the impression left by the book is thin. As usual, memories of past loves and affections have the most quality. Emma, Louisa Harding, Rosamund Tomson, Tryphena Sparks (possibly), and Horace Moule (notably) stir Hardy's lines to lyric intensities. Florence has no part; but a poem dated on the day in 1924 when she left the London nursing-home after her operation, *Nobody Comes*, shows the bleak loneliness at Max Gate, with Hardy waiting for the car to draw up there. His anxieties and disappointments emerge more movingly than in any direct love-poem. It is also a poem as "modern" as anything by the younger generation.

> Tree-leaves labour up and down,
>     And through them the fainting light
>     Succumbs to the crawl of night.
> Outside in the road the telegraph wire
>     To the town from the darkening land
> Intones to travellers like a spectral lyre
>     Swept by a spectral hand.
>
> A car comes up, with lamps full-glare,
>     That flash upon a tree:
>     It has nothing to do with me,
> And whangs along in a world of its own,
>     Leaving a blacker air;

> And mute by the gate I stand again alone,
> And nobody pulls up there.

Hardy could not say there was any public lack of appreciation of him as a poet over this book. An edition of 5000 copies, published on 20 November, was practically sold out the day before publication.[38] The book went on selling and was well noticed. One critic, Edward Shanks, commended Hardy's technical dexterity by naming him "the most fertile inventor of stanza-forms in all English literature".[39] The gist of its reception was that Hardy, far from being an outmoded poet, was perhaps more truly of the twentieth century than many of its younger poets. He was now recognized as the spiritual parent of the whole generation of modern poets.

# 16

# Winter's Last Word

WRITING in the *Nation and Athenaeum*, early in December 1925, Leonard Woolf saw Hardy as one of the spiritual parents of the modern generation of poets. For all his eighty-five years, his "queer, original personality" seemed as individual and modern as anything they were trying to express. Young writers, as essentially different as Woolf's wife, Virginia, Robert Graves, Siegfried Sassoon, and J. C. Squire, were all ready to recognize and to learn from him. Partly, too, in a mellower old age than had once seemed likely, he seemed equally ready to learn from them. He had seen signs of genius in Charlotte Mew, and acknowledged them by catching an echo of her "queer original" voice. The feeling and diction of his own *Nobody Comes* has strong resemblance to some lines in the moving final stanza of her finest poem, *The Quiet House*.

> Tonight I heard a bell again—
> Outside it was the same mist of fine rain,
> The lamps just lighted down the long, dim street,
> No one for me . . .

He accepted new experience with youthful if cautious enthusiasm. Though he took Florence's advice and did not venture to London for the professional production of his dramatization of *Tess*, he was eager about it. Kate Hardy found her brother "highly-strung" about the outcome.[1] Thanks to an enterprising new manager, Philip Ridgeway, and a brilliant young actress, Gwen Ffrangcon-Davies, it was a success. After its 100th performance on 25 November 1925, attended by Florence on his behalf, a plot was hatched. On 6 December, the company arrived at Max Gate to give a drawing-room performance of the play. Hardy was delighted, chatted happily with the young actors and actresses, and charmed them all with his innocent appreciation of their work. He was surprised to find himself liking "a job I quite disbelieve in—a dramatised novel".[2]

*Tess* was performed in the cramped Max Gate drawing-room, with the London cast sitting literally at Hardy's feet. In these last years, many young poets and writers came to the house to sit metaphorically in the same position. One of the foremost was Siegfried Sassoon. This tall, handsome yet strangley uneasy member of an exotic, oriental family, who had somehow become more English than the English, was capable both of feeling and inspiring extravagant affection. Wilfred Owen addressed him as "Keats + Christ + Elijah + my Colonel + my father-confessor + Amenophis IV in profile."[3] For Hardy, according to Florence, he was his "adored Siegfried Sassoon", and it is clear he attracted her too. On his part, Sassoon could see no wrong in Hardy, though he was secretly and somewhat meanly critical of Florence, who admittedly reported his charms in terms of almost schoolgirl gush. When Sassoon toured the United States in 1920, reading his own poetry, he would pause in his hesitant and embarrassed recital to substitute a favourite poem by Hardy.[4] Edmund Blunden flitted in and out of Max Gate, with his perennial topics of the past war, Christ's Hospital, cricket, and Keats; he won from Hardy the valued though hardly correct opinion that he had an air of Keats himself. De la Mare was another constant and approved guest, while T. E. Lawrence, now settled in Dorset as Private Shaw, "utterly captivated" Hardy[5] by a life and personality that had been so unlike Hardy's own. All of them, in their turn, were fascinated by Hardy. To them he seemed a living link with an incredible past of English letters, a Victorian who had achieved his reputation before the Queen died, now creating work that was as much of the twentieth century as their own. He was one with the monolithic past, when there were giants in literature, Tennyson, Browning, Swinburne, Dickens. In a world of the 1920s, whose growth seemed to have been cut away by the great scythe of the war, he was a symbol of continuity.

Some young writers used their visits frankly as copy for their impressions of the great man. Robert Graves, who claimed to have "kept a record" of his talk with Hardy, managed to get the highest possible score of mistakes into a few pages.[6] He caused Florence pain by writing that Hardy criticized Gosse for imitating Hardy's "old friend Henry James" drinking soup. Since Gosse, not James, was the "old friend", and it was Florence, not Hardy, who had given—to her everlasting regret—an account of the soup-drinking imitation,[7] there is little need to believe the rest of Graves's "record". Virginia Woolf also gave a Bloomsbury-eye view of the Max Gate ménage, new style, and commented how much Florence talked about and addressed the dog.[8] Since meeting Virginia Woolf could be a nerve-racking experience, Florence was understandably taking refuge. She had been brave enough at the uncanny advent of T. F. Powys. On his notoriously weird approach, Hardy jumped in the air in alarm, but Florence calmly carried off the situation.[9] One importunate admirer and visitor was John Middleton Murry. He spun such a tale—though indeed a true one—of his financial difficulties, with a second wife, like his first, dying of tuberculosis, that Hardy obtained, through Gosse, £250 for him,[10] from the Prime Minister, Stanley Baldwin. Florence, too, pitied the handsome Murry's predicaments and godmothered one of his children.

The respect, not to say veneration, in which Hardy was held by these young writers, was a constant pleasure to Florence. In spite of continued disappointments over the Nobel Prize, she felt this was immortality, and a justification of her faith in his universal greatness. It brought her into contact with people of her own age, or even younger. She could feel, however small her own literary efforts, some sort of kinship. Max Gate was more populous than during the lonely, early years of her marriage; she could now, because he was less solitary, poke fun at Hardy's indifference to company, and report dialogues such as this.[11]

F.H. It's twelve days since you spoke to anyone outside the house.
T.H. (triumphantly) I have spoken to someone.
F.H. (surprised) Who was it?
T.H. The man who drove the manure cart.
F.H. (much impressed) What did you say?
T.H. 'Good morning'.

Yet Hardy in company could sometimes be a liability and anxiety for Florence. With extreme age, his mind and his tongue reverted to some of the less seemly obsessional topics of his youth. One was the hanging and public execution of women, originating when he was sixteen from the Dorchester execution of Martha Brown, sublimated in middle-age into the execution of Tess, but always morbidly present. In 1919, with Lady Ilchester and daughter, he recounted the terrible details, told him by an ancestor, of the burning of Mary Channing, the murderess—"I tried in vain to stop him, for the daughter turned quite white—she is only fifteen."[12] In 1925, after a visit to Lady Pinney, "he was bustled into the car"[13] by Florence, to stop him talking about Martha, while, when the Galsworthys visited him in 1927, he insisted on discussing a sensational murder which he remembered his parents talking about when he was a boy.[14]

Generally, however, the picture was one of twinkling benevolence, or the dignified, ageless ancient of the Augustus John portrait in 1923, and Florence could breathe freely. He learned at last to accept honours and tributes gracefully. On 15 July 1925, a deputation from Bristol University arrived by appointment at Max Gate, to confer the degree of Hon. D.Litt, from that young academic body, joining the honours bestowed on him by the older universities, Cambridge, Oxford, Aberdeen, and St. Andrew's. It was suggested about this time that there should be a Thomas Hardy Chair of Literature at a future University of Wessex, a project which has never materialized. Hardy even overcame his dislike of displaying himself in public. When John Drinkwater's stage adaptation of *The Mayor of Casterbridge* was performed at

Weymouth, on 20 September 1926, Hardy accepted the invitation to attend, and received an ovation in the packed theatre. On 21 July 1927, he consented to lay the foundation stone of the new Dorchester Grammar School, and managed a vigorous speech in the teeth of a strong wind. Characteristically, he half-suggested a relationship between his namesake, the Elizabethan local philanthropist, and himself, though he must have been aware there was no evidence for its existence. Ironically, he partly owed the reputation he had now acquired in his home town to the Prince of Wales's visit in 1923. After he was seen driving with the Prince, and tales began to circulate about the royal lunch at Max Gate, the majority of Dorchester's citizens realized that he was a famous man. Indeed, on the day itself, the final hopeful chorus from *The Dynasts* was sung in the Prince's honour by the choir of Holy Trinity, Dorchester, in a setting by their organist, Edgar A. Lane.[15]

By sheer endurance and longevity, he had established a position for himself everywhere, a living miracle. There was the further miracle of his continuing poetry. Lyrics still poured from him, some of them as moving and accomplished as anything he had written in all his long life. As always, the death of a woman he had loved in the past provided the most potent inspiration. On 7 December 1926, Agnes Grove died. Two-and-a-half years before, after receiving birthday greetings from her, he sent her a note saying he often thought of her, and of their dancing together in 1895 at the Larmer Tree festivities. Like her compatriot at that far-off time in Hardy's affections, Florence Henniker, Agnes had fallen on evil days. For ladies of their class, depending on dividends, the war was a crippling blow. Florence Henniker's will showed her unable to make the generous bequests she wished: Agnes, before her death, was confined by comparative poverty to her country home. A journey into Shaftesbury to buy cheap meat in the market had to be made in a rickety motor-cycle and side-car[16], a sad comedown for one of the dashing Stanleys.

Hardy, deeply affected by the loss of this impetuous, domineering, but warm-hearted companion of his difficult middle-age, wrote her into history in his briefly-titled poem *Concerning Agnes*. The dancing, the summer setting, their holding hands, all "That old Romance" were contrasted with the woman now dead, as he imagined her, "white, straight, features marble-keen". The final stanza was classically noble, like some threnody of those Athenian poets to whom he felt his work akin.

> There she may rest like some vague goddess, shaped
> As out of snow;
> Say Aphrodite sleeping; or bedraped
> Like Kalupso;
> Or Amphitrite stretched on the Mid-sea swell,
> Or one of the Nine grown stiff from thought. I cannot tell!

Not all Hardy's memorial verses were of such quality, or inspired by a subject which could equally pluck at a reader's heart. Less than three weeks later, Hardy suffered another loss, though not a human one. The notorious dog, Wessex, whom Florence had brought to Max Gate in 1913, died. The childless Hardy was a doting master. He excited the dog to frenzied naughtiness with tit-bits of cheese-rind. At Christmas, he made Wessex ill with goose and plum-pudding. The indulged dog was a menace to all guests, dominating the lunch table. According to Cynthia Asquith, it "contested" every forkful on the way to her mouth. With less respect than Florence for the local aristocracy, it insisted on eating dinner with the Ilchesters when the Hardys visited Melbury House. Distinguished guests were savaged and even bitten. The respectable trousers of both John Galsworthy and the surgeon, Sir Frederick Treves, were reduced to tatters. The dog was yet another of Florence's constant anxieties. Her dread that something would happen at Max Gate, during one of her infrequent absences, was caused as much by Wessex as by the elderly Hardy. She was afraid that the dog might bite someone so badly that the police would destroy it before she could return to plead for reprieve. The sight of a policeman standing at the front door of Max Gate, on some quite innocuous errand, brought the instant reaction, "Oh, not Wessie again!" She and Hardy justified the dog in all its anti-social actions. Servants seemed stupidly alarmed; Florence felt they should realize that Wessex only "flew at" them, and did not mean to bite. She was genuinely indignant when a postman, not realizing such fine distinctions, kicked out a couple of Wessex's teeth in self-defence. Only T. E. Lawrence of Arabia, perhaps by some esoteric desert magic, managed to remain unscathed. Yet there is a pathetic insight into the emptiness of Florence's life at Max Gate in her lament over the dog's death. "He was only a dog, and not a good dog always but *thousands* (actually thousands) of afternoons and evenings I would have been alone but for him."[17] Wessex was laid to rest in the pets' cemetery to the left of the front door, with the graves of numerous cats, and with Moss, the old, quiet dog of long ago, who had gained no such dubious notoriety.

The dog Wessex also claimed like Agnes Grove a memorial poem, *Dead 'Wessex' the Dog to the Household*, though hardly one of the same quality. Yet the standard of the new collection accumulating in Hardy's study was astounding. *Winter Words*, though not his finest volume, represents almost every manner of Hardy's verse, lyric, narrative, reflective, humorous, love-poems, nature-poems, epigrams, dialogue, and philosophic pieces. Nothing like it had been produced by a man of his age since Goethe. All his themes are represented. If any one dominates, it is tragic love.

> Love is a terrible thing; sweet for a space,
> And then all mourning, mourning.

Deep-laid family history raises its perennial ghosts, in haunting folk-melody.

> Three picture-drawn people stepped out of their frames—
> The blast how it blew!
> And the white-shrouded candles flapped smoke-headed flames
> —Three picture-drawn people came down from their frames
> And dumbly in lippings they told me their names . . .

Hardy does not tell us, though these "Family Portraits" are surely of the generation of the real Tess, and belong, as he says, to "my blood's tendance". Another candlelit portrait is named, as the man speaks.

> This candle-wax is shaping to a shroud
> To-night. (They call it that, as you may know)—
> By touching it the claimant is avowed,
> And hence I press it with my finger—so.
>
> Tonight . . .

The initials H.M.M.—Horace Moseley Moule—introduce the speaker. Though many of the conjectures about the "story" of *Standing by the Mantelpiece* are as mysterious as the poem itself,[18] perhaps the most simple and the most likely has been overlooked. Horace Moule cut his throat in his bedroom at Queens' College, Cambridge. In the outer keeping-room was his brother, Charles Moule, also a close friend of Hardy, part-original of Angel Clare. The brothers, according to Charles's evidence at the inquest, had argued all afternoon about some distressing, unknown matter. It would be like the literal method of Hardy's habitual composition to make Horace address his own brother in this enigmatic poem, the subject of their discussion still an unsolved mystery—

> And let the candle-wax thus mould a shape
> Whose meaning now, if hid before, you know,
> And how by touch one present claims its drape,
> And that it's I who press my finger—so.

It was not the first time Hardy had written a poem in the person of his own youth's tragic mentor.[19]

Yet, in astonishing variety, Hardy's protean verse is comic too. *Liddell and Scott*, a tongue-in-cheek account of the great lexicon, is in Hardy's best style of learned humour. One of its most sprightly Browning-like couplets was actually added in the last few months of Hardy's life, rhyming the name of Donnegan, an earlier lexicographer, with "con again". Love, of course, especially lost love, is the most persistent theme. Emma, Louisa Harding, Tryphena Sparks (perhaps), Agnes

Grove, are joined by several unidentified loves, such as the girl rescued from a poem dated 1884, ten years after Hardy's first marriage. The most striking, the girl of *The Mound*, is surely the one on whom Sue in *Jude* is based, for the poem is parallel to Sue's confession, in Jude's lodging, of her past life.

> . . . saying she'd not be bound
> For life to one man, young, ripe-yeared, or old,
> Left me—an innocent simpleton to her viewing;
> For, though my accompt of years outscored her own,
> Hers had more hotly flown.

The revisions to the manuscript show that this poem was at first even more direct and personal; Hardy drew a simple self-portrait.

> I was an innocent simpleton to her viewing.

His account of the girl's previous sexual experience had "feverishly flown" and "fervidly flown" before settling for the less explicit "hotly flown". Identification, as with so many of Hardy's love-poems, is both unnecessary and impossible; but it seems we are here in the presence of that mysterious "H.A.", the advanced girl of the innocent Hardy's first London days in the 1860s, from whose encounters he returned shattered to his native Dorset, with a store of emotional experience to last him literally a whole lifetime as a poet.

A lifetime of poetry was what *Winter Words* was meant to summarize. Hardy wrote for it an introduction, which started with a bold but true claim.

> So far as I am aware I happen to be the only English poet who has brought out a new volume of his verse on his . . . . . . birthday.

Landor, the only other English poet with a comparable length of life, produced no new volume in his last twenty-five years. Unfortunately, Hardy's ruling obsession about the critics occupied more than half of a short statement which one would hope to have the dignity and maturity of much of the poetry itself. Hardy was to do even worse than this, and produce a mean-minded attack on critics while actually lying on his death-bed. Nor unfortunately, could the adjective "eighty-eighth", which Hardy had probably intended, be inserted in the blank and dotted space; for 2 June 1928 was a date which Hardy never lived to see.

Thursday 24 November 1927 was the twelfth anniversary of the death of Mary Hardy; Sunday 27 November was the fifteenth anniversary of the death of Emma. Florence had a superstitious feeling that the double occasion portended some fate for Hardy. Hardy was equally prone to superstition, especially over anniversaries. For two or three days, he wore "a very shabby little black hat he must have had for twenty years"[20] and carried Emma's black walking-stick. "Very pathetic," commented Florence, "all the more when one remembers what their married life was like."[21] He was still revising poems for *Winter Words*, and on that Sunday, he wrote a new and good poem, *An Unkindly May*, with its typical later-Hardy couplet.

'Nature, you're not commendable to-day!'
I think. 'Better to-morrow!' she seems to say.

As so often, Nature was wrong, and Hardy right, at least about his own immediate future. On 11 December, he took to his bed. He felt immensely tired, though alert enough mentally to talk theology with Florence, both agreeing that "there was not a single grain of evidence that the gospel story is true". His physical weakness alarmed Florence. Though she asserted to herself, "this may be the beginning of the end, but I do not think so", she sent for Eva Dugdale, who had nursed Hardy through the kidney attack of 1922. Dr. Gowring, when asked what was wrong, now merely said, "old age". On Christmas Day, Hardy said he would never have a drawing-room tea-party again. His mind was still intensely clear, and seeing likenesses between the present and the remote past. He observed that the youthful aesthete, Stephen Tennant, was the only other man he had ever met who walked like Swinburne,[22] an instance of his century-bridging which so fascinated the young.

Among ominous arrivals during the New Year was Sydney Cockerell. The Cambridge reputation of the Director of the Fitzwilliam Museum was that when he appeared at a distinguished bedside, no doctor's skill could save the patient. Barrie also came down for a night. Outside the weather was bitterly cold with deep snow-drifts. Hardy had occasional rallies in the first ten days of the year and a specialist, called in from Bournemouth, said that his arteries were those of a man of sixty.[23] On 10 January, he insisted on signing a cheque subscribing to the Pension Fund of the Society of Authors, which still preserves it. In the evening he asked Florence to read him the whole of Browning's *Rabbi Ben Ezra*. The next morning, his mind had reverted to his earliest cottage days at Bockhampton, in the little mudwall home, of which he had written a loving description only a few months before.[24] He asked the parlour-maid, Nellie Titterington, to prepare him the sort of breakfast his mother gave him long ago. This was kettle-broth— parsley, onions, and bread boiled up in water—and a rasher of bacon, cooked in front of him in the flame of his bedroom fire. Thus, as the aristocracy of literature began to whisper about Westminster Abbey, Hardy enacted the part of the rough carpenter in *The Hand of Ethelberta*, who instructs the Marquis's brother how to grill his rasher on the bars. Eva Dugdale, Florence, and Nellie Titterington took turns in watching him. As it grew dusk, he asked Florence to read him a verse from

*The Rubaiyat of Omar Khayyam.* It was the first book, outside his own work, that he had given her as a love-token in the summer of 1907. She read to him.

> Oh, Thou, who Man of baser earth didst make,
> And ev'n with Paradise devise the snake:
> For all the Sin wherewith the Face of Man
> Is blackened—Man's forgiveness give—and take!

He motioned her to read no more. It was his last gesture towards the Prime Mover. Just before nine in the evening, Nellie Titterington heard him call out to Florence's sister, "Eva, Eva, what is this?" The doctor was fetched and joined Florence at the bedside, but Hardy, though conscious almost to the end, spoke no more.

It was over. The delicate child, who one day, with his abnormally quick ears, overheard his own parents say that they did not expect him to live, had lasted more than eighty-seven years, and left an achievement of work that challenged any other English writer. They dressed him in his scarlet doctoral robes, in state at Max Gate, a symbol of success; yet sister Kate, coming to view the body, saw only the likeness to his own local kin—"the same triumphant look on his face that all the others bore—but without the smile".[25] For the tokens of the hard-won struggle from obscurity to status were to continue even after his body was at last cold.

Even before, when his brain for the first time had begun to cloud, an incident had demonstrated his strange division of nature. Beckoning to Florence, in the stillness of his last days, he had dictated two virulent, inept, and unworthy satirical jingles on two most hated critics, George Moore and G. K. Chesterton. Such were the great author's very last literary works, justifying the genial Clodd's reluctant verdict, "There was no largeness of soul". The events of the next few days—to say nothing of the next decade—somehow typify the tragi-comic contrast between mean and noble that had haunted his living days. More especially, they ranged his humble beginning against his exalted ending in conflicts that would have been laughable if they had not more often been matters for weeping. Hence the "bitter humiliations", which Florence, two months later, confessed that these days brought her,[26] and which she never forgot to the end of her own life.

The immediate cause was her co-executor and trustee. As a relative at another family funeral complained, "Cockerell took charge and ordered everybody about."[27] Ignoring the wishes of Hardy, Florence, Kate, and Henry, whom he dismissed as "a rough kind of man with no literary leanings",[28] Cockerell rang up Barrie asking him to fix a Westminster Abbey funeral with the Dean; Barrie wrote by return to say all was arranged.[29] Yet Florence knew Hardy had specifically willed he should lie at Stinsford "out there" with his parents, his sister, and Emma. To Kate, the decision was "a staggering blow".[30] Florence was caught between two fires, "the nation" (as interpreted by Cockerell) and the village. In distress, she consulted the Vicar, with whom Hardy had grimly joked about his burial. He suggested a gruesome though historic compromise. Let Hardy's heart be buried at Stinsford, his ashes in the Abbey. Florence allowed herself to be persuaded, only to find that to Kate this was "another staggering blow", disgusting for Hardy's intimate friends, such as Clodd, who found it "repellent". The whole operation caused local cynicism mixed with ribaldry. "Almighty, 'e'll say; ''Ere be 'eart, but where be rest of 'e?' " Irony persisted in every detail. At the solemn early-morning moment, when the heart-casket was brought out of Max Gate to the waiting hearse, the siren from Eddison's steam-roller factory, against which Hardy had vainly protested, hooted derision at his death. In London, the Abbey service, hastily organized by Hardy's publishers, was a chaos of wrong invitations and uninvited gate-crashers, "a sick horror" for years to Florence.[31] The Dean of Westminster, too, had been assailed by complaints, one from "the head of a great religious body" throwing doubt on Hardy's Christianity, morals, and general suitability for the Abbey. He even privately consulted the Vicar of Fordington, whose aid Emma had enlisted twenty years before "to try & make Tom more religious."[32]

Worse was to come. Florence was too dazed to understand much of what was said in Barrie's flat after the ceremony; but shortly, she found Cockerell claiming that she had consented to a memorial in Dorset to match the huge seventy-foot stone column on Blackdown commemorating the other Hardy, Nelson's captain. A bare six weeks after Hardy's death, she and his other trustee were at open war. By July, sick of the whole business, she tried to resign her own trusteeship, but was dissuaded by Sir Daniel Macmillan.[33] Henry Hardy added a family note to the quarrel by offering to build a tower at his own expense, provided "he could have it done by himself and according to his own ideas".[34] Meanwhile, the one thing on which she and Cockerell agreed was that much of Hardy's remote past should be destroyed. Funeral pyres of burnt letters, especially those from the early part of his life, darkened the garden at Max Gate. Year by year, the ironies deepened. In November 1930, local subscription provided for a stained-glass memorial window in Stinsford Church. Florence was naturally asked to unveil it, and would have accepted; but earlier that year, William Heinemann had published Somerset Maugham's *Cakes and Ale*. The germ of the story, in Maugham's words, lay in a great novelist marrying as second wife "his secretary, who guards him and makes him into a figure". The publisher's advertisement spoke of this character as "exploiting" her husband's fame "before and after death". To Florence, always guiltily sensitive, this seemed "A barely-veiled attack on me".[35] Maugham disingenuously denied his book was based on the Hardys, and, indeed, his Rosie, the first wife, was the very opposite of Emma; but there were certainly strong hints of Florence in the second Mrs. Driffield. These were enough, anyway, for Florence's feeling that "to unveil the window might give colour to that accusation". Similar untoward events marred other attempts at memorial. A. E. Newton, the American book collector, put up a ten-foot granite column opposite the Bockhampton cottage, and enraged Cockerell. Kate objected to a site in Dorchester because it had been a public lavatory. Eventually, in September 1931, Eric Kennington's small-headed statue was unveiled at the top of High West Street by Sir James Barrie, with a whimsical speech.

Hardy had died on the very eve of Florence's forty-ninth birthday. The ten years of Florence's survival were almost totally sad. New furniture, a car, a visit to Italy—all things she had longed for—did not lift the gloom. The year of her husband's death saw the death of his cousin Theresa, who, Florence was horrified to find, died in poverty, and of his brother Henry, Florence's one true local ally—"The kindest soul imaginable" . . . "a great loss to me".[36] The first volume of her so-called *Life* of Hardy was produced with suspicious speed on 2 November of that year. Florence had only time to remove firmly nearly every complimentary reference to Emma, to her courage, her decision, her encouragement, her successful London lunch-parties, above all, any suggestion that she and Florence had been friends.[37] The book, in all its oddity, with an inaccurate index reprinted to this day, had a disappointing press, as Florence gloomily reported; yet it was followed in 1930 by its sequel, *The Later Years*, equally unsatisfactory, for obvious reasons only known to Florence and to some friends such as Barrie. More satisfying were her work as J.P., and in the Mill Road Building Association scheme to clear the slums of "Mixen Lane".[38] Her personal life, lacking its centre, had unhappy aberrations. She wrote some violent and terrible letters, notably to H. M. Tomlinson and to other people who, she thought, belittled life at Max Gate in the last years.[39] Her repentance, after such outbursts, was pathetic. She was more than half in love with Sassoon, and her letter on his marriage[40] in 1933 is tragically humble. "I have made many mistakes in the past and no doubt have forfeited your friendship." Relations with the overbearing Cockerell were increasingly stormy, and after he attacked her in the *Times Literary Supplement*, "to the amazement of even his own friends",[41] she took the sole trusteeship, with the assistance of Irene Cooper Willis. By then, in the spring of 1937, she was herself a dying woman; many of the utterances she is said to have made to eager researchers may owe their provable inaccuracy to her alleviants for pain. The enemy she had dreaded in her many operations on ear, nose, and throat, attacked her elsewhere. She died on 17 October 1937 of cancer of the rectum.[42]

Max Gate, and some of the Hardy wealth, though not, of course, his copyrights, "my most prized possession", as Florence called them,[43] devolved on Kate. She also became the last repository of the Hardy family secrets. Returning to Talbothays from the opening, on 10 May 1939, of the reconstruction of Hardy's study in the Dorset County Museum, Kate threw down her bonnet on the sofa, laughed heartily, and referring to the complimentary speakers, exclaimed, "If they only knew!"[44] The last "Hardy born", she too was about to take his secrets to the grave. On 7 August 1939, her diary recorded[45] bravely, "Another break down . . . Brain seems spent but I've got to carry on." In 1940 she marked the hundredth anniversary of his birth by her own death. It was a coincidence Hardy himself would have appreciated.

# Abbreviations Used in the Notes

Bailey: J. O. Bailey, *The Poetry of Thomas Hardy: A Handbook and Commentary*, Chapel Hill, 1970.

Beatty: C. J. P. Beatty (ed.), *The Architectural Notebook of Thomas Hardy*, Dorchester, 1966.

Björk: Lennart A. Björk (ed.), *The Literary Notes of Thomas Hardy*, 2 vols., Gothenburg Studies in English, No. 29, Gothenburg, Sweden, 1974.

*"Dearest Emmie"*: C. J. Weber (ed.), *'Dearest Emmie', Thomas Hardy's Letters to his First Wife*, London, 1963.

DCC: *Dorset County Chronicle.*

DCL: Dorset County Library.

DCM: Dorset County Museum.

DCRO: Dorset County Record Office.

Gerber and Davis: Helmut E. Gerber and W. Eugene Davis (eds.), *Thomas Hardy: An Annotated Bibliography of Writings about Him*, Northern Illinois, 1973.

Hawkins: Desmond Hawkins, *Hardy, Novelist and Poet*, Newton Abbot, 1976.

LTH: F. E. Hardy, *Life of Thomas Hardy*, 1 vol., London, 1962.

MTH: *Materials for the Study of the Life, Times and Works of Thomas Hardy*, 72 monographs, St. Peter Port, Guernsey. Various dates from 1962.

Millgate: M. Millgate, *Thomas Hardy: His Career as a Novelist*, London, 1971.

ORFW: E. Hardy and F. B. Pinion (eds.), *One Rare Fair Woman: Thomas Hardy's Letters to Florence Henniker, 1893–1922*, London, 1972.

Orel: Harold Orel (ed.), *Thomas Hardy's Personal Writings*, London, 1967.

Purdy: R. L. Purdy, *Thomas Hardy, A Bibliographical Study*, Oxford, repr. 1968.

Rutland: W. R. Rutland, *Thomas Hardy: A Study of His Writings and Their Background*, repr. New York, 1962.

SREH: E. Hardy and R. Gittings (eds.), *Some Recollections by Emma Hardy ...*, Oxford, 1961; repr. New York, 1973.

THN: E. Hardy (ed.), *Thomas Hardy's Notebooks*, London, 1955.

TLS: *Times Literary Supplement.*

YTH: Robert Gittings, *Young Thomas Hardy*, London, 1975.

# Notes

## 1: THE IDYLL, pp. 1–12

1. Gerber and Davis, 26–27.
2. ibid., 23–24.
3. Both in DCM.
4. Gosse to Emma Hardy, 9 May 1907, DCM.
5. In DCM.
6. Björk, 208–243.
7. ibid., xxxv, though some later notes are in Emma's hand.
8. Emma Hardy, *Diary*, DCM.
9. LTH, 110–111.
10. David B. Green, " 'The Eve of St. Agnes' and *A Pair of Blue Eyes*", *Notes & Queries*, N.S. IV (1957), 153.
11. Björk, 36.
12. ibid., 95–103.
13. YTH, 94–95.
14. YTH, 204.
15. Emma Hardy's Diary, DCM.
16. I. C. Willis, notebook, DCM.
17. LTH, 112–113.
18. D. F. Barber (ed.), *Concerning Thomas Hardy*, 126.
19. MTH, No. 25.
20. As, for example, the reasons for the tragedy of Horace Moule.
21. Millgate, 140 et seq., for good discussion of the novel.
22. Though Hardy had intended to use this in his earliest and unpublished novel, *The Poor Man and the Lady*, YTH, 102.
23. Björk, 253.
24. ibid., 322.
25. Millgate, 124, and National Library of Scotland.
26. Millgate, 118.
27. Purdy, 27.
28. J. Henry Harper, *I Remember*, 166, quoted C. J. Weber, *Hardy of Wessex*, 108.
29. LTH, 118.
30. LTH, 118–120.
31. LTH, 115–116.

## 2: THE THEATRE OF LIFE, pp. 13–24

1. Harold P. Clunn, *The Face of London*, 495.
2. The year is incised on the houses.
3. See the poem, *A January Night*, 1879.
4. LTH, 147.
5. Harold P. Clunn, *The Face of London*, 487.
6. Charles Morgan, *The House of Macmillan*, 66.
7. *The Thomas Hardy Year Book 1972–1973.*
8. LTH, 121–122.
9. F. Mabel Robinson to Irene Cooper Willis, 17 December 1939, DCM.
10. See illustration, No. 1.
11. LTH, 124–125.
12. *Athenaeum*, No. 2666, 30 November 1878. Reprinted in Orel.
13. Mary Hardy to Mary Antell, 8 October 1908, postcard, Eton School Library.
14. LTH, 124.

15. Purdy, 34.
16. Millgate, 160, shows parallels between *The Trumpet-Major* and *Vanity Fair*.
17. LTH, 125–126, 129; THN, 52.
18. LTH, 126; THN, 53.
19. Personal information, Benjamin Bishop.
20. See, for example, *The Times* for 5 December 1878.
21. Though, as a purely human influence, Hardy partly had the veteran Anne Procter in mind. Hardy to Sir George Forrest, 21 March 1925, Sotheby's Sale Catalogue, 9 July 1968.
22. Harold Scott, *The Early Doors*, 35, n. 1.
23. Orel, 95.
24. THN, 54; but so mistranscribed as to be meaningless.
25. See illustration, No. 2.
26. *The Era*, 4 July 1881.
27. G. Atherton, *Adventures of a Novelist*, 263.
28. LTH, 129. Hardy's prose notes and the poem are similar in description.
29. C. J. Weber, *Hardy of Wessex*, 116–122, gives the best summary of these events.
30. LTH, 137–139; Purdy, 38–39.
31. P.O. London Directory, London Suburbs (South), 1880.
32. Hardy to Gosse, 14 February 1922.
33. Kegan Paul to Hardy, 24 February 1881, DCM.
34. LTH, 146.
35. Björk, 327–329.
36. C. J. Weber, *Hardy of Wessex*, 126.
37. YTH, 139–140.
38. Millgate, 165.
39. Mary Hardy to Emma Hardy, 28 January 1881, DCM.

### 3: WIMBORNE, pp. 25–35

1. Clive Holland, *Thomas Hardy, O.M.*, 99.
2. LTH, 151–152.
3. C. J. Weber, *Hardy of Wessex*, 127.
4. *Thomas Hardy: The Critical Heritage*, 89.
5. LTH, 44–45.
6. St. Helier, *Memories of Fifty years*, 195.
7. *The Lancet*, 1904, i, 1163–1167; *British Medical Journal*, 1904, i, 991–993.
8. St. Helier, op.cit., 196.
9. LTH, 149.
10. Denys Kay-Robinson, *Hardy's Wessex Re-appraised*, 97–99.
11. THN, 61–62.
12. LTH, 150–151.
13. Millgate, 148.
14. LTH, 134, 136, and 126.
15. Thomas Hardy to Emma Hardy, 13 April 1891, DCM.
16. J. M. Barrie to Florence Hardy, 3 February 1928, quoted Millgate, 203.
17. St. Helier, *Memories of Fifty Years*, 2 and 188.
18. THN, 57.
19. B. and P. Russell (eds.), *The Amberley Papers* I, 24, 87, 349.
20. St. Helier, *Memories of Fifty Years*, 295–296.
21. LTH, 251.
22. Millgate, 187–188.
23. Preface to new edition, July 1895.
24. Rutland, 194–195.
25. Orel, 242 and 17.
26. See J. C. Maxwell, "Mrs. Grundy and 'Two on a Tower' ", *Thomas Hardy Year Book 1971*, 45–46 on Hardy's "impish sense of humour".
27. See above, p. 18.

28. Tindal Atkinson to Hardy, 31 December 1881, DCM.
29. D. F. Barber (ed.), *Concerning Thomas Hardy*, 141.
30. Purdy, 28–30, gives the best account, though it obscures the shortness of Hardy's *London* run.
31. Barry Duncan, *The St. James's Theatre*, 207–208.
32. Most of what follows is contained in various sources in the Theatre Museum, Victoria and Albert Museum.
33. DCM.
34. Purdy, 296, who does not, however, see the contemporary bearing of the verse.
35. ibid., 78–80.
36. *Thomas Hardy: The Critical Heritage*, 118–132.
37. LTH, 180.

## 4: DORSET HOME, pp. 35–49

1. Gerber and Davis, No. 1902.
2. ibid., No. 2318.
3. Millgate, 200 and 204.
4. LTH, 157.
5. C. J. Weber, *Hardy and the Lady from Madison Square*, 130.
6. LTH, 155.
7. THN, 62–63.
8. DCM.
9. DCM.
10. MTH, No. 22.
11. Bodleian Library, MS. Eng. Misc., d. 530, f. 93.
12. Camille Honig, "In Search of Thomas Hardy", *New Statesman*, 10 June 1944.
13. As suggested, but not developed, by Millgate, 233.
14. LTH, 167.
15. DCRO.
16. Edward Sampson, "Thomas Hardy—Justice of the Peace" (unpublished).
17. Millgate, 237–248.
18. Barbara Kerr, *Bound to the Soil: A Social History of Dorset*, Chapter X, "Dorchester: The Sovereign Seekers".
19. Personal information, Mrs. L. Largent.
20. Björk, 151.
21. *Kelly's Directory*, Dorchester, 1885; Kate Hardy's Teachers' Certificate, DCL.
22. LTH, 371.
23. LTH, 176.
24. St. Helier, *Memories of Fifty Years*, 240.
25. J.-E. Blanche, *Mes Modèles* (trans. Jo Manton).
26. LTH, 199.
27. Millgate, 198–199.
28. Philip Gosse, *A Naturalist Goes to War*, 78 (Penguin edition).
29. Letters to Hardy from Morley and Alexander Macmillan, DCM, contradict Hardy's own memory (LTH, 168), which is followed by Purdy, 56.
30. S. L. Bensusan, quoted Blunden, *Thomas Hardy*, 173.
31. W. R. Rutland, *Thomas Hardy*, 87.
32. Accounts, Overseers of the Poor, Melbury Osmond, DCRO.
33. Hardy to Gosse, 3 and 5 April, 1887.
34. DCM.
35. Barbara Kerr, *Bound to the Soil: A Social History of Dorset*, Chapter VII "Thornford: The Clay and Coppice People".
36. LTH, 153.
37. LTH, 185.
38. As pointed out by Evelyn Hardy, "Thomas Hardy and Turner", *London Magazine*, June/July 1975.
39. William Rothenstein, *Men and Memories*, 302.

40. Hardy to Gosse, 24 December 1886.
41. E. Charteris, *Life of Edmund Gosse*, 157.
42. Henry Gifford, "Thomas Hardy and Emma", *Essays and Studies* (1966), 113.
43. C. J. Weber, *Hardy and the Lady from Madison Square*, 131.


5: THE ORIGINAL TESS, pp. 50–62

1. L. Edel (ed.), *The Diary of Alice James*, 93.
2. F. Mabel Robinson to Irene Cooper Willis, 17 December 1939, DCM.
3. LTH, 187.
4. Hardy to Gosse, 3 April 1887.
5. LTH, 189.
6. LTH, 188.
7. Hardy to Gosse, 3 April 1887.
8. Typescript of *Life* (Mrs. Hardy's copy), DCM. Cancelled passage.
9. Emma Hardy's Italian Diary, 1887, DCM.
10. LTH, 190–196.
11. Emma Hardy's Italian Diary, 1887, DCM.
12. Simon Nowell-Smith (ed.), *Letters to Macmillan*, 130–131.
13. Purdy, 72.
14. Gosse to J. A. Symonds, 24 February 1890, University of Bristol, quoted Phyllis Grosskurth, *John Addington Symonds*, 280–281.
15. Hardy to Gosse, 11 November 1886.
16. Gosse to Hardy, 28 August 1887, DCM.
17. LTH, 200, 201, 203.
18. LTH, 207–208.
19. LTH, 202.
20. LTH, 153. Other facets of this unnamed character anticipate Alec d'Urberville.
21. *Victoria County History*, Berkshire, Fawley and Chaddleworth, P.O. Directory.
22. Fawley parish registers.
23. ibid.
24. Puddletown parish registers.
25. LTH, 282.
26. Register of baptisms, St. Mary's, Reading.
27. Calendar of prisoners in the County Bridewell, QSR/253, Berkshire County Record Office; Court Order Book, ibid.
28. L. Radzinowitz, *A History of English Criminal Law and its Administration from 1750*, 144, n. 23, 578, 670, 703, Appendix II.
29. QSR/253, Berkshire County Record Office.
30. MTH, No. 20.
31. DCM.
32. Christ's Hospital Records, Guildhall.
33. LTH, 201.
34. LTH, 207.
35. LTH, 210.
36. By Evelyn Hardy, "Thomas Hardy and Turner", *London Magazine* June/July 1975, 23–25.
37. Personal information, Norman Atkins.
38. LTH, 209–212.
39. I owe my knowledge of this story to Professor Norman Page. It was fully reported in *The Times*.
40. J. T. Laird, *The Shaping of "Tess of the d'Urbervilles"*, which gives an admirably full account of the various forms *Tess* took.
41. Warneford Hospital, Case Book VI. Class No. WV/7/vi.
42. SREH, 28.
43. Personal comment, Dr. Richard Hunter.
44. Florence Hardy to Rebekah Owen, 24 October 1915.

## 6: TESS AND JUDE, pp. 63–78

1. T. P. O'Connor, reporting, perhaps not trustworthily, a remark to his wife. Repr. MTH, No. 54.
2. Emma Hardy to the Editor, *Daily Chronicle*, 5 September 1891, DCM.
3. Maggs Sale Catalogue, 1938, No. 664, item 197.
4. DCM.
5. Quoted Millgate, 302.
6. LTH, 224.
7. ORFW, 15, 82.
8. J. T. Laird, *The Shaping of "Tess of the d'Urbervilles"*, 5.
9. Millgate, 263, offers an excellent summary of some of these activities.
10. LTH, 220.
11. Theatre Museum, Victoria and Albert Museum.
12. LTH, 224.
13. Information, John Antell.
14. Kelly's P.O. Directory, 1890, 1895, 1900. Hardy also bought 51 High West Street.
15. By Melvyn Bragg. See below, p. 85.
16. YTH, 215–216; Millgate, 401, n. 11. See also above, Chapter 5, p. 57.
17. See Millgate, 265, for many similar examples.
18. Björk, 11, 404, 405.
19. J. A. Symonds to Hardy, 9 April 1889 and 7 January 1892, DCM.
20. Katherine Adams to Sydney Cockerell, 4 August 1920, *The Best of friends*, 24–25.
21. Sir Henry Thompson to Hardy, 22 October 1890, DCM.
22. Edward Clodd, *Memories*, 161–162.
23. *Speaker* (London) IV, 26 December 1891.
24. Millgate, 300–302.
25. Beatty, 33.
26. LTH, 254.
27. J. Pope-Hennessey, *Lord Crewe*, 3–5, 14–15, 19, 38, 40.
28. Raymond Blathwayt, "The Hon. Mrs. Arthur Henniker", *The Woman at Home*, 1895.
29. ORFW, 14–15.
30. ORFW, 3.
31. ORFW, 15.
32. ORFW, 20.
33. ORFW, 29.
34. ORFW, 33.
35. ORFW, 31.
36. YTH, illustration 14b.
37. Purdy, 345.
38. Anna Winchcombe, "Four Letters from Tryphena", *Dorset*.
39. G. K. Chesterton, *Autobiography*, 277.
40. (Unsigned) *Illustrated London News*, 18 August 1894, p. 195.
41. LTH, 433.
42. YTH, Chapter 9.
43. J.-E. Blanche, *Mes Modèles*, 84 (trans. Jo Manton).
44. Rosamund Tomson to Hardy, [1889], DCM.

## 7: PROSE TO POETRY, pp. 79–92

1. ORFW, 46.
2. Hawkins, 147.
3. ORFW, 47.
4. Hawkins, 147.
5. *Weekly Sun*, repr. in DCC, 20 June 1895.
6. ORFW, 48.
7. Millgate, 325.

8. Hardy to Gosse, 14 July 1909.
9. Emma Hardy to Rebekah Owen, 24 April 1899.
10. TLS, 1 January 1940.
11. DCM.
12. Richard M. Ludwig (ed.), *Letters of Ford Madox Ford* viii.
13. Ford Madox Ford *Mightier Than the Sword*, 128–130. Copied and adapted, without discrimination or acknowledgement, three years later by Carl J. Weber in his *Hardy of Wessex* (1st ed., 1940) which began the legend.
14. Emma Hardy to Rebekah Owen, 17 February 1897.
15. Hardy to Gosse.
16. Emma Hardy to Edward Clodd, 29 March 1897, Brotherton Library.
17. Hardy to the Editor, *Temple Bar*, 9 March 1896, Eton School Library.
18. D. Hawkins, "Concerning Agnes", *Encounter*, February 1977.
19. William Rothenstein, *Men and Memories*, I, 303.
20. Hardy to Edward Clodd, 17 January 1907, Ashley 5723, f. 2, British Library.
21. LTH, 281.
22. *"Dearest Emmie"*, 37.
23. ORFW, 53–54.
24. LTH, 285.
25. Quoted Blunden, *Thomas Hardy*, 112.
26. ORFW, 44.
27. As suggested by Melvyn Bragg in his Royal Society of Literature lecture, May 1975.
28. ORFW, 58.
29. J. Hillis Miller (ed.) provides useful details of both versions (New Wessex edition).
30. Stourhead Collection, Wiltshire County Archives.
31. MS. version; altered in printed version to end "it near".
32. Florence Hardy to Louise Yearsley, 18 April 1923.
33. Not 1904, as all biographies repeat; but see below, Chapter 9.
34. Florence Hardy to Winifred Thomson, 29 August 1928, Bodleian MS. Eng. Misc., d. 534, f. 132.
35. LTH, 250–251.
36. *"Dearest Emmie"*, 39–40.
37. A. E. Filmer, quoted Blunden, *Thomas Hardy*, 170–171.
38. ORFW, 66.
39. LTH, 285.
40. LTH, 293.
41. ORFW, 65–66; LTH, 295.
42. ORFW, 71.
43. ORFW, 72.


## 8: WAR AT HOME AND ABROAD, pp. 93–105

1. Hardy to Gosse, 27 December 1898.
2. Alfred Pretor to Emma Hardy, December 1898, DCM. See also Phyllis Grosskurth, *John Addington Symonds*, 33, 35–36.
3. Quoted Bailey, 21.
4. Newman Flower, *Just As It Happened*, 96.
5. Bodleian MS. Eng. Misc., d. 530, ff. 93–96.
6. ibid., 89.
7. Quoted YTH, 148.
8. See above, p. 38.
9. No. 775, Sotheby's Sale Catalogue, 9 July 1968.
10. Emma Hardy to Rebekah Owen, 27 December 1899.
11. Dr. Roger Fiske, personal communication.
12. DCM.
13. Gerber and Davis, No. 1229.
14. LTH, 303.
15. *Daily Chronicle*, 8 September 1899.

16. Quoted Blunden, *Thomas Hardy*, 106 and 109.
17. Carl J. Weber, *Hardy and the Lady from Madison Square*, 134.
18. Emma Hardy to Rebekah Owen, 19 February 1897.
19. Emma Hardy to Rebekah Owen, May 1900.
20. Emma Hardy to Rebekah Owen, 24 April 1899.
21. Bertha Newcome to Mrs. Gosse, 8 March, Brotherton Library.
22. Emma Hardy to Rebekah Owen, 24 April 1899.
23. Emma Hardy to Rebekah Owen, 27 December 1899.
24. LTH, 302.
25. THN, 68.
26. ORFW, 76.
27. See Bailey, 191–192.
28. Emma Hardy to Rebekah Owen, 27 February 1899, quoted Bailey, 114.
29. Emma Hardy to Rebekah Owen, 31 December 1900.
30. ORFW, 88.
31. Hardy to Gosse, 6 March 1899.
32. LTH, 304.
33. LTH, 328.
34. Orel, 201–203.
35. "*Dearest Emmie*", 43.
36. ORFW, 89.
37. Quoted Carl J. Weber, *Hardy and the Lady from Madison Square*, 132.
38. No. 775, Sotheby's Sale Catalogue, 9 July 1968.
39. "*Dearest Emmie*", 41.
40. ibid.
41. Walter Gifford to Emma, 7 September 1898, DCM.
42. "*Dearest Emmie*", 43–45, though confused by the editor, C. J. Weber's assumptions, such as the idea that Emma's sister was still living in Cornwall, which she had left years before.
43. Emma Hardy to Rebekah Owen, 4 March 1902.
44. "Wives in the Sere", *The Tatler*, 31 July 1901.

## 9: DYNASTS AND DESTINIES, pp. 106–121

1. Warneford Hospital, Case Book VII, W.V./7/vii, 1 March 1900.
2. Hardy to Gosse, 31 January 1904, 28 February 1906, 5 March 1908.
3. H. W. Nevinson, *Changes and Chances*, 307–308, quoted Blunden, *Thomas Hardy*, 110.
4. J.-E. Blanche, *Mes Modèles*, 82 (trans. Jo Manton).
5. Gerber and Davis, Nos. 305, 1427, 1731.
6. E. Smyth, *As Time Went On*, 205.
7. A. C. Benson, *The Diary of Arthur Christopher Benson*, 81–82.
8. Elizabeth Cathcart Hickson, *The Versification of Thomas Hardy*.
9. LTH, 114.
10. LTH, 145 and Preface to *The Dynasts*.
11. LTH, 148.
12. LTH, 152.
13. LTH, 177.
14. LTH, 203.
15. LTH, 221.
16. LTH, 225.
17. LTH, 247.
18. LTH, 284.
19. See above, p. 32.
20. A. E. Filmer to Edmund Blunden, quoted Blunden, *Thomas Hardy*, 170–171.
21. Orel, 145.
22. *Thomas Hardy: The Critical Heritage*, 344.
23. Walter F. Wright, *The Shaping of "The Dynasts"*, 304–305.
24. ibid., 37.

25. ibid., 38–53 & 53 n.
26. *Wilfred Owen: Collected Letters*, ed. Owen and Bell, 355, 487, 547–8.
27. J.-E. Blanche, *Mes Modèles*, 81, 83, 84, 87–88 (trans. Jo Manton).
28. ibid., 83.
29. In *Portraits of a Lifetime*, a so-called translation of *Mes Modèles* by Walter Clement, 179.
30. Agnes Grove, *The Social Fetich*, 14.
31. *"Dearest Emmie"*, 54–62.
32. Hardy to Gosse, 3 January 1905.
33. Bodleian, MS. Eng. Misc., d. 177, ff. 314–317.
34. Orel, 66–72.
35. Personal information, John Antell.
36. Warneford Hospital, Case Book VI, W.V./7/vi, 1897–1899.
37. LTH, 333; Roger Fulford, *Votes for Women*, 137; Thomas Hardy to Millicent Fawcett, 30 November 1906, Fawcett Library. Emma "marched" in a carriage.
38. LTH, 326.
39. Florence Hardy to Louise Yearsley, 10 April 1923, and Mrs. Henniker to Hardy, 20 March 1914, DCM.
40. ORFW, 19 and note 62.

## 10: FLORENCE AND THE DUGDALES, pp. 122–136

1. Birth certificate, Edward Dugdale, General Registry.
2. Langton Matravers, parish records, DCRO.
3. Census, 1851, Portsmouth.
4. Logbook, St. Andrew's School, Enfield.
5. General Registry.
6. Kelly's Directories, 1899, 1903, 1907, 1909, 1915, 1918, 1922.
7. Obituary of Edward Dugdale, *Enfield Gazette*, 5 June 1936.
8. MTH, No. 2.
9. MTH, No. 14.
10. Letter from a contemporary, Violet Hilling.
11. St. Andrew's (Boys) School logbooks.
12. St. Andrew's School logbooks and P.O. Directories.
13. St. Andrew's School logbooks.
14. Personal information, J. E. Westaway.
15. Kate Hardy's postcard collection.
16. Florence Hardy to Rebekah Owen, 24 June 1917.
17. *Meyer's Observer and Local and General Advertiser*, Enfield.
18. Florence Hardy to Rebekah Owen, 1 March 1916.
19. Hardy to Edward Clodd, 22 July 1909, Ashley 5723, f. 6, British Library.
20. Macmillan archive, British Library.
21. Various letters to Rebekah Owen.
22. Hardy to Elspeth Grahame, 31 August 1907, Bodleian Misc. MSS.
23. See poem *On the Departure Platform*.
24. Florence Dugdale to Edward Clodd, 11 November 1910, reveals his name.
25. Obituary, *Lancet*, 8 June 1912, *Who Was Who*.
26. Florence Hardy to Rebekah Owen, 3 and 17 December 1915.
27. Emma Hardy to Rebekah Owen, 27 December 1899.
28. Hardy to Macmillan, 8 July 1907, Macmillan archive, British Library.
29. Florence Hardy to Rebekah Owen, 26 October 1916.
30. Hardy to Archibald Marshall, 9 July 1907.
31. Personal information.
32. Florence Hardy to Rebekah Owen, 22 November 1915.
33. Reginald Smith to Hardy, 22 September 1907, DCM.
34. C. J. Weber and C. C. Weber (eds.), *Thomas Hardy's Correspondence*.
35. Netta Syrett, *The Sheltering Tree*, 194.
36. Cf. Hardy's poems *Her Initials* and *At the Pyramid of Cestius*.

37. See below, p. 146.
38. MS. notes by Mrs. Healis, Colby College Library.
39. J.-E. Blanche, *Mes Modèles*, 85 (trans. Jo Manton).
40. Winifred Fortescue, *There's Rosemary . . . There's Rue*, 110.
41. In a letter to the author.
42. Bailey, 22.
43. V. Meynell (ed.), *Friends of a Lifetime*, 304.
44. Hardy to Clarendon Press, 19 January 1907, Bodleian Eng. lett. E i.
45. Hardy to Clarendon Press, 1907–1908, Bodleian Eng. lett. E i.
46. See the poems *Had You Wept* and *After the Visit* (to F.E.D.).
47. "Perhaps apocryphal though "symbolically true"
48. Gosse to Hardy, 4 March 1908.
49. Quoted LTH, 341.
50. LTH, 336.
51. Hardy to Edward Clodd, 29 October 1909, Ashley 5723, f. 9, British Library.

## 11: FLORENCE AND EMMA AND THOMAS, pp. 137–148

1. Hardy to Edward Clodd, 22 and 28 July, 30 August, 3 November 1909; LTH, 349, Kate Hardy's postcard collection; Hardy to Edward Clodd, October 1911, May 1912.
2. Hardy to Edward Clodd, Ashley 5768 f. 44, 5723 f. 6, 5768 f. 45, A3350 p. 132, f. 67, British Library.
3. LTH, 346, 347.
4. Hardy to Edware Clodd, 13 July 1909, Ashley 5723, f. 4, British Library.
5. Hardy to Edmund Gosse, 14 July 1909.
6. Hardy to Edward Clodd, 1 May 1909, Ashley 5768, f. 43.
7. See above, p. 82.
8. Typescript of *The Later Years* (Mrs. Hardy's copy), DCM.
9. Wrongly named "Trevett" in MTH, No. 65.
10. Wrongly named "Griffiths", ibid.
11. *"Dearest Emmie"*, 68, wrongly assumes her to be Florence Dugdale.
12. I. C. Willis to Evelyn Hardy, 1961. I am greatly indebted to Evelyn Hardy for this information.
13. W. R. Rutland, *Thomas Hardy* (O.M. Series), 110.
14. Emma Hardy to Rebekah Owen, 14 February and 24 April 1899; 26 December 1906.
15. Emma Hardy to Rebekah Owen, 26 December 1906.
16. Emma Hardy to Rebekah Owen, 7 November 1907.
17. Emma Hardy to Rebekah Owen, 13 May 1908.
18. *"Dearest Emmie"*, 72–82.
19. Mrs. Watts Dunton to Emma Hardy, January 1909, Miriam Lutcher Stark Library, University of Texas, and DCC.
20. See above, p. 119.
21. Personal information, Norman Atkins.
22. Emma Hardy to Rebekah Owen, 20 May 1908.
23. Ethel M. Richardson, "Recollections of Thomas Hardy, O.M. (1910–1928)", *St. Katherine's College Magazine* (1961), 26.
24. Emma Hardy to Alda, Lady Hoare, 20 April 1910.
25. LTH, 350.
26. DCM.
27. LTH, 350.
28. W. F. Oakeshot, *The Times Saturday Review*, 19 February 1977.
29. Florence Dugdale to Edward Clodd, 11 November 1910.
30. ibid.
31. DCM.
32. V. H. Collins to C. J. Weber, 13 September 1943.
33. Florence Dugdale to Edward Clodd, 9 November 1910.
34. Kate Hardy's postcard collection, Eton School Library.
35. ORFW, 147.

36. Florence Dugdale to Edward Clodd, 2 February 1911.
37. Purdy, 285–286.
38. ORFW, 146.
39. According to Florence's sisters. Purdy, 314.
40. Hardy to Edward Clodd, 17 June 1910, Brotherton Library.
41. Purdy, 314.
42. DCM.
43. Florence Dugdale to Emma Hardy, 22 August 1910, DCM.
44. Reprinted MTH, No. 29.
45. Henry Gifford, "Thomas Hardy and Emma", *Essays and Studies*, N.S. XIX (1966), 114.
46. "I was Emma Lavinia's personal maid", *Hardy Year Book* No. 4.
47. A. M. Ashdown, *A Complete System of Nursing* (1917), 195–196.
48. Emma Hardy to the Rev. R. G. Bartelot, Colby College Library.
49. ORFW, 153.
50. Beinecke Library, Yale University.
51. D. F. Barber (ed.), *Concerning Thomas Hardy*, 77.


12: A SATIRE OF CIRCUMSTANCE, pp. 149–163

1. Florence Dugdale to Edward Clodd, 16 January 1913.
2. Florence Dugdale to Edward Clodd, 21 August 1913.
3. Florence Dugdale to Edward Clodd, 30 January 1913.
4. "I Was Emma Lavinia's personal maid". *Thomas Hardy Year Book*, No. 4.
5. Florence Dugdale to Edward Clodd, 7 March 1913.
6. Florence Dugdale to Edward Clodd, 30 January 1913.
7. Florence Hardy to Edward Clodd, 7 March 1913.
8. Florence Hardy to Edward Clodd, 30 January 1913.
9. Florence Hardy to Edward Clodd, 7 March 1913.
10. Charles Moule to Emma Hardy, DCM.
11. Florence Hardy to Edward Clodd, 30 January 1913.
12. ORFW, 154.
13. Richard Hunter, *Psychiatry for the Poor*, 191.
14. Emma Hardy to Rebekah Owen, 19 February 1897.
15. *The Master Christian* (1900), 89.
16. F. R. Leavis, "Hardy the Poet", *The Southern Review*, Summer 1940.
17. DCM.
18. Florence Hardy to Howard Bliss, 9 March 1936, Princeton University Library.
19. Mistranscribed "T. C. Dugdale" in Purdy, 246.
20. Florence Dugdale to Edward Clodd, 11 March 1913.
21. ibid.
22. ibid.
23. See SREH, *passim*.
24. Florence Hardy to Rebekah Owen, 20 March 1914.
25. Florence Hardy to Louisa Yearsley, 10 April 1923.
26. LTH.
27. DCM, H. 1975. 316.22.
28. Mary Hardy to Thomas Hardy, June 1913, DCM.
29. All quotations are from the *English Review* version.
30. By Bailey, 307–308.
31. Florence Hardy to Alda, Lady Hoare, 9 April 1914.
32. Florence Hardy to Alda, Lady Hoare, 22 July 1914.
33. Florence Hardy to Rebekah Owen, 9 February 1914.
34. Florence Hardy to Rebekah Owen, 15 December 1915.
35. Florence Dugdale to Edward Clodd, 11 November 1911.
36. P.C.C. Wills, Somerset House. Obituary, *British Medical Journal*, June 1912.
37. Personal information.
38. Florence Hardy to Alda, Lady Hoare, 9 December 1914.

39. Florence Hardy to Alda, Lady Hoare, 7 April 1914.
40. Florence Dugdale to Rebekah Owen, 31 December 1913.
41. Florence Hardy to Rebekah Owen, 10 February 1914.
42. Florence Dugdale to Edward Clodd, 1 January 1914.
43. Florence Hardy to Rebekah Owen, 9 February 1914.
44. St. Andrew's School logbook.
45. Hardy to Alda, Lady Hoare, 13 February 1914.
46. F. Mabel Robinson to Hardy, 12 February 1914, DCM.
47. Hardy to Alda, Lady Hoare, 13 February 1914.
48. Florence Hardy to Rebekah Owen, 13 February 1914.
49. Hardy to Frederic Harrison, 17 February 1914, Miriam Lutcher Stark Library, University of Texas.
50. Florence Hardy to Alda, Lady Hoare, 5 April 1914.
51. Florence Hardy to Rebekah Owen, 1 June 1914.
52. Florence Hardy to Alda, Lady Hoare, 22 and 26 July 1914.
53. Florence Hardy to Rebekah Owen, 5 September 1914.
54. From "A Poet".
55. Purdy, 172.
56. Hardy to Gosse, 16 April 1918.

## 13: DEATHS AND VISIONS, pp. 164-176

1. Florence Hardy to Rebekah Owen, 17 October 1914.
2. Anne [Thackeray] Ritchie to Hardy, 24 July [1917].
3. Florence Hardy to Alda, Lady Hoare, 29 November 1914.
4. Florence Hardy to Alda, Lady Hoare, 6 December 1914.
5. Florence Hardy to Alda, Lady Hoare, 27 January 1915.
6. Florence Hardy to Alda, Lady Hoare, 7 January 1922.
7. Florence Hardy to Alda, Lady Hoare, 23 March 1915.
8. Hardy to Alfred Pope, 28 May 1915, quoted in *Concerning Thomas Hardy*, 144.
9. Florence Hardy to Rebekah Owen, 30 December 1915.
10. Florence Hardy to Rebekah Owen, 1 October 1915.
11. ibid.
12. Florence Hardy to Rebekah Owen, 23 June 1915.
13. ibid.
14. Florence Hardy to Rebekah Owen, 17 July 1915.
15. Florence Hardy to Rebekah Owen, 23 June 1915.
16. Florence Hardy to Rebekah Owen, 4 March 1917.
17. Florence Hardy to Rebekah Owen, 5 May 1915.
18. Florence Hardy to Rebekah Owen, 17 July 1915.
19. ibid.
20. Florence Hardy to Rebekah Owen, 22 September 1916.
21. Florence Hardy to Alda, Lady Hoare, 24 August 1915.
22. Hardy later said "he would have welcomed a child" in 1914, but there is no evidence he "hoped" for one. The provision for one in his 1922 will is a legal formality; in 1923 the idea "fills him with horror". Add. MSS. 58498, British Library.
23. Puddletown registers, General Registry.
24. Kate Hardy's postcard collection, Eton School Library.
25. Florence Hardy to Rebekah Owen, 1 December 1914.
26. Florence Hardy to Alda, Lady Hoare, 6 February 1916.
27. Death certificate, General Registry.
28. Admons. P.C.C., Somerset House.
29. Florence Hardy to Rebekah Owen, 30 December 1915.
30. Mary Hardy to Augustus Hardy, March 1912, in the possession of James Gibson.
31. Kate Hardy's postcard collection, Eton School Library.
32. LTH, 371 and 430.
33. Florence Hardy to Alda, Lady Hoare, 20 May 1917.
34. Florence Hardy to Alda, Lady Hoare, 26 December 1917.

35. Florence Hardy to Rebekah Owen, 13 December 1916.
36. Florence Hardy to Rebekah Owen, 18 January 1916.
37. Sassoon to Sydney Cockerell, 14 October 1940.
38. Florence Hardy to Rebekah Owen, January 1916.
39. Florence Hardy to Rebekah Owen, 22 October 1916.
40. Florence Hardy to Rebekah Owen, 14 December 1916.
41. Mrs. Healis, MS. notes on Florence's letters, Colby College Library.
42. Edward Clodd to J. H. Bulloch, 14 January 1928, Miriam Lutcher Stark Library, University of Texas.
43. Florence Hardy to Rebekah Owen, 26 October 1916.
44. Florence Hardy to Rebekah Owen, 15 May 1916.
45. Florence Hardy to Rebekah Owen, 5 June 1916.
46. Florence Hardy to Rebekah Owen, 4 March 1917.
47. Florence Hardy to Rebekah Owen, 5 May 1916.
48. Florence Hardy to Alda, Lady Hoare, 5 September 1916.
49. Florence Hardy to Rebekah Owen, 5 June 1916.
50. Florence Hardy to Rebekah Owen, 3 December 1916.
51. Purdy, 187.
52. H. V. Marrot (ed.), *The Life and Letters of John Galsworthy*, 750–753.
53. Florence Hardy to Alda, Lady Hoare, 6 August 1915; List of titles, Hardy's copy of *Collected Poems* (1923), DCM.
54. Purdy, 208.

## 14: LATE AND EARLY, pp. 177–190

1. Notably J. C. Squire and Edward Shanks.
2. Hardy to Gosse, 18 February 1918, Ashley MS. A. 858, British Library.
3. Hardy to Sir George Douglas, 12 December 1915, Royal Library of Scotland.
4. E. Clodd, *Memories*, 34.
5. Kate Hardy's Diary, DCL.
6. Receipt, Lock Collection, DCL.
7. DCM.
8. Bodleian, 28001, d. 533.
9. Florence Hardy to Louisa Yearsley, 10 June 1917.
10. Florence Hardy to Louisa Yearsley, May 1917.
11. Florence Hardy to Louisa Yearsley, 17 June 1917.
12. ibid.
13. Florence Hardy to Louisa Yearsley, August 1917.
14. ibid.
15. Florence Hardy to Louisa Yearsley, 17 June 1917.
16. Florence Hardy to Rebekah Owen, 28 August 1917.
17. Purdy, 266.
18. Florence Hardy to Howard Bliss, 10 January 1931, Princeton University Library.
19. J. I. M. Stewart, *Thomas Hardy*, Chapter 1.
20. LTH, 229.
21. Lock Collection, DCL.
22. LTH, 21.
23. Florence Hardy to Rebekah Owen, 24 June 1917.
24. Florence Hardy to Rebekah Owen, 28 August 1917.
25. Florence Hardy to Louisa Yearsley, July 1918.
26. Florence Hardy to Louisa Yearsley, August 1919.
27. Florence Hardy to St. John Ervine, 8 August 1921, Miriam Lutcher Stark Library, University of Texas.
28. Florence Hardy to Paul Lemperly, 19 March 1919, Colby College Library.
29. Kate Hardy's Diary.
30. Florence Hardy to Rebekah Owen, 4 August 1920. Hardy still used a hip-bath.
31. Florence Hardy to Louisa Yearsley, 7 July 1920.
32. Florence Hardy to Louisa Yearsley, 1 June 1920.

33. Purdy, 287–288.
34. Florence Hardy to Louisa Yearsley, 16 May 1920.
35. ibid., 10 November 1918.
36. H. M. Marrot (ed.), *Life and Letters of John Galsworthy*, 416.
37. LTH, 400.
38. Florence Hardy to Rebekah Owen, 8 July 1917.
39. Florence Hardy to Paul Lemperly, 28 October 1918.
40. LTH, 402.
41. Florence Hardy to Siegfried Sassoon, 9 February 1922.
42. ibid.
43. Florence Hardy to Paul Lemperly, 13 May 1922.
44. August 1910, DCM.
45. DCM, for the whole correspondence and Hardy's notes.
46. DCM.
47. LTH, 415.
48. Florence Hardy to Paul Lemperly, 5 December 1922.
49. D. Mackail, *The Story of J. M. Barrie*, 555.
50. "A Jingle on the Times", December 1914.
51. Florence Hardy to Louisa Yearsley, 27 February 1920.

## 15: A HUMAN SHOW, pp. 191–202

1. V. Meynell (ed.), *Friends of a Lifetime*, 306.
2. H. V. Marrot (ed.), *Life and Letters of John Galsworthy*, 507.
3. Florence Hardy to Louisa Yearsley, 16 May 1920.
4. Florence Hardy to Rebekah Owen, 15 October 1920.
5. LTH, 422–423.
6. L. Abercrombie, "Mr Hardy's Play", *Nation and Athenaeum*, XXXIV, 29 December 1923.
7. Florence Hardy to Louisa Yearsley, 21 December 1923.
8. Literary Notebook 11, DCM.
9. Florence Hardy to Alda, Lady Hoare, 21 June 1921.
10. Florence Hardy to Paul Lemperly, 2 August 1923.
11. Kate Hardy's Diary.
12. Purdy, 349–350.
13. Florence Hardy to Louisa Yearsley, undated, c. 1923.
14. V. Meynell (ed.), *Friends of a Lifetime*, 300.
15. Florence Hardy to Louisa Yearsley, 19 June 1921.
16. Kate Hardy's Diary, DCL.
17. Florence Hardy to Louisa Yearsley, 17 September 1922.
18. ibid., 30 September 1920.
19. Florence Hardy to Rebekah Owen, 29 October 1922.
20. Hardy to Macleod Yearsley, 7 June 1923.
21. Florence Hardy to Louisa Yearsley, 21 December 1923.
22. Kate Hardy's Diary.
23. MTH, No. 17.
24. Kate Hardy's Diary.
25. Florence Hardy to Louisa Yearsley, 30 December 1920.
26. Florence Hardy to Gertrude Bugler, 13 June 1922, in the possession of Mrs. Bugler.
27. Florence Hardy to Louisa Yearsley, 20 June 1924.
28. ibid.
29. Florence Hardy to Rebekah Owen, 24 November 1924.
30. Personal information, Gertrude Bugler.
31. MTH, No. 1.
32. Wilfred Blunt, *Cockerell*, 214–216.
33. Florence Hardy to Rebekah Owen, 16 February 1925.
34. MTH, No. 2.
35. Florence Hardy to Paul Lemperly, 25 March 1925.

36. Purdy, 265.
37. LTH, 419.
38. Purdy, 247.
39. "Two Innovators", *Saturday Review*, CXL, 19 December 1925.


16: WINTER'S LAST WORD, pp. 203-214

1. Kate Hardy's Diary.
2. V. Meynell (ed.), *Friends of a Lifetime*, 293.
3. Harold Owen and John Bell (eds.), *Letters of Wilfred Owen*, 505.
4. S. Jackson, *The Sassoons*, 179.
5. Florence Hardy to Louisa Yearsley, n.d., c. 1925.
6. R. Graves, *Goodbye to All That*, 268-272.
7. Florence Hardy to Siegfried Sassoon, 17 December 1924.
8. Virginia Woolf, *A Writer's Diary*, 89-94.
9. C. Tolchard (ed.), *Letters to Clifford Tolchard from John Cowper Powys*, 29.
10. Gosse to Hardy, 9 November 1927.
11. V. Meynell (ed.), *Friends of a Lifetime*, 309-310.
12. ibid., 301.
13. MTH, no. 25.
14. LTH, 440.
15. E. Margaret Lane, *Edgar A. Lane, Musician*, 17.
16. Desmond Hawkins, "Concerning Agnes", *Encounter*, February 1977.
17. V. Meynell (ed.), *Friends of a Lifetime*, 314.
18. Purdy, 257, says, "It is a woman addressed", but gives no authority.
19. See above, pp. 156-7.
20. Florence Hardy's Diary, DCM.
21. ibid.
22. ibid.
23. Florence Hardy to Siegfried Sassoon, 4 January 1928.
24. Orel, 233-235
25. Kate Hardy's Diary.
26. Florence Hardy to Siegfried Sassoon, 13 March 1928.
27. W. Blunt, *Cockerell*, 184.
28. ibid., 218.
29. V. Meynell (ed.), *Friends of a Lifetime*, 315.
30. Kate Hardy's Diary, 315.
31. Florence Hardy to R. A. Scott-James, 9 May 1930, Miriam Lutcher Stark Library, University of Texas.
32. Dean of Westminster to the Rev. R. G. Bartelot, 17 January 1928.
33. W. Blunt, *Cockerell*, 219.
34. ibid., 220.
35. Florence Hardy to Colonel Weber, churchwarden of Stinsford, 11 November 1930, DCRO.
36. Florence Hardy to Paul Lemperly, 28 December 1928.
37. DCM.
38. Mrs. Thomas Hardy, obituary, *Enfield Gazette*.
39. Florence Hardy to Siegried Sassoon, 24 February and 13 March 1928.
40. ibid., 8 November 1933.
41. Florence Hardy to Paul Lemperly, 7 March 1937.
42. General Registry, deaths.
43. Florence Hardy to Paul Lemperly, 7 April 1935.
44. Information, John Antell.
45. Kate Hardy's Diary.

# List of Sources

A. MANUSCRIPT

Berkshire County Record Office. Berkshire parish records, Quarter Sessions, etc.
Bodleian Library. Letters of Emma Hardy and Thomas Hardy to Mrs. Kenneth Grahame.
British Library. Letters of Thomas Hardy to Edward Clodd and Edmund Gosse.
Macmillan Archive. Stopes Archive.
Brotherton Library. Letters of Florence Hardy to Edward Clodd. Letters of Thomas
Hardy to Clodd and Gosse.
Bugler, Gertrude. Letters, etc.
Colby College, Waterville, Maine. Special Collections. Letters. Emma Hardy to the
Revd. Richard Bartelot and to Rebekah Owen. Letters of Florence Hardy to
Paul Lemperly and Rebekah Owen.
Dorset County Library. Lock Collection. Kate Hardy's Diary.
Dorset County Museum. Hardy Collection. Letters, etc.
Dorset County Record Office. Dorset Parish registers, etc.
School Library, Eton College. Letters. Florence Hardy to Siegfried Sassoon and Louisa
Yearsley. Letter of Thomas Hardy to Macleod Yearsley.
Portsmouth City Library. Census. St. Paul's parish.
Probate of Wills, Public Record Office and Somerset House.
Potts, Mrs. Elizabeth. Letter. Thomas Hardy to Archibald Marshall.
Registers of Births, Marriages, and Deaths. General Registry.
St. Andrew's School (Boys), Enfield. Log Books.
Voremberg, Mrs. R. P. MSS. of the Revd. Richard Bartelot.
Warneford Hospital. Case Books.
Wiltshire County Record Office. Letters. Emma Hardy to Alda, Lady Hoare. Florence
Hardy to Alda, Lady Hoare.


B. TYPESCRIPT

Hardy, F. E., "Notes of Thomas Hardy's Life . . . (taken down in conversations, etc.)".
Dorset County Museum.
Sampson, Edward, "Thomas Hardy—Justice of the Peace".


C. PUBLISHED

Atherton, G., *Adventures of a Novelist*, New York, 1932.
Bailey, J. O., *The Poetry of Thomas Hardy: A Handbook and Commentary*, Chapel Hill,
1970.
Barber, D. F. (ed.), *Concerning Thomas Hardy*, London, 1968.
Beatty, C. J. P. (ed.), *The Architectural Notebook of Thomas Hardy*, Dorchester, 1966.
Björk, Lennart A. (ed.), *The Literary Notes of Thomas Hardy*, 2 vols., Gothenburg,
1974.
Blanche, J.-E., *Mes Modèles*, Paris, 1928.
Blunt, Wilfred, *Cockerell*, London, 1964.
Brooks, Jean R., *Thomas Hardy: The Poetic Structure*, London, 1971.
Brown, Douglas, *Thomas Hardy*, London, 1961.
Chadwick, Owen, *The Victorian Church*, 2 vols., London, 1970.
Clark, G. S. R. Kitson, *The Making of Victorian England*, Oxford. 1960.
Clemens, Cyril, "My Chat with Thomas Hardy", *Dalhousie Review*, April 1943.
Clodd, E., *Memories*, London, 1916.
Colby Library Quarterly, *A Descriptive Catalogue . . . of the Works of Thomas Hardy*,
Waterville, Maine, 1940.
Collins, V. H., *Talks with Thomas Hardy*, New York, 1928.
Compton-Rickett, A., *I Look Back: Memories of Fifty Years*, London, 1933.

Cox, J. S. (gen. ed.), *Materials . . . for a Life of Thomas Hardy*, 72 vols., St. Peter Port, Guernsey, 1962–.

(ed.), *The Thomas Hardy Year Book*, 1970–.

Deacon, Lois and Coleman, Terry, *Providence and Mr. Hardy*, London, 1966.

Dolman, Frederick, "An Evening with Thomas Hardy", *Young Man*, VIII, March 1894, 74–9.

Ellis, S. M., "Some Personal Recollections of Thomas Hardy", *Fortnightly Review*, N. S. CXXIII, March 1928, 393–406.

Felkin, Elliott, "Days with Thomas Hardy: from a 1918–1919 diary", *Encounter*, XVIII, April 1962, 27–33.

Flower, Newman, *Just As It Happened*, New York, 1950.

"Walks and Talks with Thomas Hardy", *The Countryman*, XXXIV, Winter 1966, 193–5.

Ford, F. Madox, *Mightier than the Sword*, London, 1938.

Gerber, H. E. and Davis, W. E. (eds.), *Thomas Hardy: An Annotated Bibliography of Writings about Him*, Northern Illinois, 1973.

Gifford, Henry, "Thomas Hardy and Emma", *Essays and Studies*, N. S. XIX (1966), 106–121.

Grosskurth, P., *John Addington Symonds*, London, 1964.

Grove, Agnes, *The Social Fetich*, London, 1907.

Guerard, Albert J., *Thomas Hardy, The Novels and Stories*, Oxford, 1959.

Haggard, H. Rider, *Rural England*, 2 vols., London, 1902.

Halliday, F. E., *Thomas Hardy: His Life and Work*, Bath, 1972.

Hardy, Evelyn, "Hardy and the Phrenologist", *John O'London's Weekly*, 26 February 1954.

"Some Unpublished Poems by Thomas Hardy", *London Magazine*, III (1956), 28–39.

*Thomas Hardy: A Critical Biography*, London, 1954.

"An Unpublished Poem by Thomas Hardy", *Times Literary Supplement*, 2 June 1966; and Robert Gittings (eds.), *Some Recollections by Emma Hardy*, Oxford, 1961; and F. B. Pinion (eds.), *One Rare Fair Woman: Letters of Thomas Hardy to Florence Henniker*, London, 1973.

Hardy, Florence E., *The Early Life of Thomas Hardy: 1840–1891*, London, 1928.

*The Later Years of Thomas Hardy: 1892–1928*, London, 1930.

*The Life of Thomas Hardy: 1840–1928*, London, 1962. (*The Life* is a one-volume publication of *The Early Life* and *The Later Years*. All, except the last few years, was really written by Hardy himself.)

Hardy, Thomas, "Death of Miss Mary Hardy", *Dorset County Chronicle*, 2 December 1915.

Hawkins, Desmond, *Thomas Hardy*, Newton Abbot, 1976.

Hickson, E. Cathcart, *The Versification of Thomas Hardy*, Pennsylvania, 1931.

Holland, Clive, "My Walks and Talks in Wessex with Thomas Hardy", *John O'London's Weekly*, 30 March 1951.

Howe, Irving, *Thomas Hardy*, London, 1967.

Hunter, R. and Macalpine, I., *Psychiatry for the Poor*, London, 1974.

Hynes, Samuel, *The Pattern of Hardy's Poetry*, Chapel Hill, 1961.

Jones, Bernard (ed.), *The Poems of William Barnes*, 2 vols., Fontwell, 1963.

Kay-Robinson, Denys, *Hardy's Wessex Re-Appraised*, Newton Abbot, 1972.

Kerr, Barbara, *Bound to the Soil: A Social History of Dorset*, repr. Wakefield, 1975.

Kingsgate, J., "*Tess* and Thomas Hardy, New Facts about his Life in London", *Graphic*, CXII, 5 September 1925.

Lane, E. Margaret, *Edgar Lane, Musician*, Dorchester, 1976.

Lewis, R. W. M., *The Family of Moule of Melksham, Fordington, and Melbourne*, privately printed (1938).

Maitland, F. W., *The Life and Letters of Leslie Stephen*, London, 1906.

Marrot, H. V. (ed.), *Life and Letters of John Galsworthy*, London, 1935.

Meynell, Viola (ed.), *Friends of a Lifetime: Letters to Sydney Cockerell*, London, 1940.

Miller, J. Hillis, *Thomas Hardy: Distance and Desire*, Cambridge, Mass., 1970.

Millgate, Michael, *Thomas Hardy, His Career as a Novelist*, Bodley Head, 1971.

Morgan, Charles, *The House of Macmillan*, London, 1943.
Morrell, Ray, *Thomas Hardy, The Will and the Way*, Kuala Lumpur, 1943.
Moule, H. C. G., *Memories of a Vicarage*, 1913.
Nevinson, H. W., *Thomas Hardy*, London, 1941.
Newman, J. and Pevsner, N., *The Buildings of Dorset*, London, 1972.
Orel, Harold (ed.), *Thomas Hardy's Personal Writings*, Kansas, 1966.
Owen, H. and Bell, J., *Letters of Wilfred Owen*, Oxford, 1967.
Phelps, W. L., *Autobiography and Letters*, Oxford, 1939.
Pike, E. Royston, *Human Documents of the Victorian Golden Age*, London, 1969.
Pinion, F. B., *A Hardy Companion*, London, 1968.
Purdy, R. L., *Thomas Hardy: A Bibliographical Study*, Oxford, 1954, repr. 1968.
  "The authorship of Hardy's Biography", TLS, 30 December 1960.
*Reports of the British and Foreign School Society.*
Rutland, W. R., *Thomas Hardy: A Study of his Writings and their Background*, Oxford,
  1938, New York, 1962.
  *Thomas Hardy*, London, 1938.
St. Helier, *Memories of 50 Years*, London, 1909.
Scott, Harold, *The Early Doors*, London, 1946.
Smith, S. Nowell (ed.), *Letters to Macmillan*, London, 1967.
Smith, W. Sylvester, *The London Heretics, 1870–1914*, London, 1967.
Southerington, F. R., *Hardy's Vision of Man*, London, 1971.
Stewart, J. I. M., *Thomas Hardy*, London, 1971.
Webb, A. P., *A Bibliography of the Works of Thomas Hardy*, London, 1916.
Weber, Carl J., *Hardy of Wessex*, London, 1940; rev. and repr. 1965.
  (ed.), *"Dearest Emmie"*, London, 1953.
  (ed.), *Hardy at Colby*, Waterville, Maine, 1936; *Hardy and the Lady from Madison
  Square*, Waterville, Maine, 1952.
  (ed.), *The Letters of Thomas Hardy*, Waterville, Maine, 1954.
Webster, H. C., *On a Darkling Plain: The Art and Thought of Thomas Hardy*, Chicago,
  1947.
Williams, Merryn, *Thomas Hardy and Rural England*, London, 1972.
Wreden, W. P., *Books from the Library of Thomas Hardy*, New York, 1938.
Wright, W. F., *The Shaping of "The Dynasts"*. Nebraska, 1967.

D. MAGAZINES, NEWSPAPERS, PERIODICALS
*Academy*
*Athenaeum*
*Cornhill Magazine*
*Daily News*
*Daily Telegraph*
*Dorset County Chronicle*
*Dorset Evening Echo*
*Encounter*
*Enfield Gazette*
*Gentleman's Magazine*
*Illustrated London News*
*Saturday Review*
*Spectator*
*The Sphere*
*Times Literary Supplement*

## ACKNOWLEDGEMENT OF QUOTATIONS

Extracts from the novels of Thomas Hardy and from *The Complete Poems of Thomas Hardy*, The New Wessex Edition, edited by James Gibson, 1976, and *The Dynasts*, and quotations from *The Life of Thomas Hardy* by Florence Hardy are reprinted by permission of the Trustees of the Estate of the late Miss E. A. Dugdale; Macmillan, London and Basingstoke; and the Macmillan Company of Canada Limited.

# Index